The Gemstone File
A Memoir

By
Stephanie Caruana

Order this book online at www.trafford.com
or email orders@trafford.com

Most Trafford titles are also available at major online book retailers.

© Copyright 2007 Stephanie Caruana.

All rights reserved. No part of this publication may be reproduced, stored in a retrieval system, or transmitted, in any form or by any means, electronic, mechanical, photocopying, recording, or otherwise, without the written prior permission of the author.

Print information available on the last page.

ISBN: 978-1-4120-6137-7 (sc)

Because of the dynamic nature of the Internet, any web addresses or links contained in this book may have changed since publication and may no longer be valid. The views expressed in this work are solely those of the author and do not necessarily reflect the views of the publisher, and the publisher hereby disclaims any responsibility for them.

Any people depicted in stock imagery provided by Getty Images are models, and
such images are being used for illustrative purposes only.
Certain stock imagery © Getty Images.

Trafford rev. 02/20/2019

Trafford
PUBLISHING www.trafford.com

North America & international
toll-free: 1 888 232 4444 (USA & Canada)
fax: 812 355 4082

The Gemstone File
A Memoir

by Stephanie Caruana

For the first time ever in print, includes 250 pages from the mysterious Gemstone File of Bruce Roberts

~

Onassis, Howard Hughes, JFK, Nixon and the CIA/Mafia/Big Business Take-Over of the United States in 1963

~

20th Century History for Grown-ups

TRAFFORD PUBLISHING

BRUCE ROBERTS AND CARMEN MIRANDA

Long before the *Gemstone File*, Bruce Roberts pins an artificial gemstone decoration onto Carmen Miranda's headdress, in this photo from a newspaper supplement, *American Weekly*. (October 12, 1952) unearthed by Gerald Carroll.

The accompanying text reads: "Bruce Roberts, former actor turned jewelry designer, can be thankful that Carmen Miranda got tired of her famous basket-of-fruit hat and sought something new. Her quest resulted in a new Miranda "look" and a market for Roberts in costume jewelry that is more costume than jewelry. When Carmen approached Roberts and outlined her dilemma, he realized one thing: Any accoutrements would have to withstand her lively antics. So he strung his semi-precious stones—synthetic pearls, rubies, sapphires, topazes, on nylon parachute thread guaranteed to hold up under 360 pounds of weight."

DEDICATED TO THE MEMORY OF
Bruce Porter Roberts
Florynce R. Kennedy
Sherman Skolnick
AND TO
Kenn Thomas
Gerald A. Carroll
Sherwood Ross
friends, writers, countrymen

Contents

PROLOGUE BY BRUCE ROBERTS	9
PREFACE BY KENN THOMAS	10
FOREWORD BY GERALD A. CARROLL	12
INTRODUCTION	14
PART I—*SKELETON KEY*	**22**
1. Inside The Pergola: Brading and a Smoking Gun at Dealey Plaza?	22
2. March—May 1974: Inside the Hearst Kidnapping	27
3 *Playgirl* Magazine: Is Howard Hughes Dead and Buried Off a Greek Island?	44
4 June 1974-July 1975: Bruce Roberts and Me	55
5 A Skeleton Key to the Gemstone File	61
The Murder of John Fitzgerald Kennedy	*67*
Murder at Chappaquiddick	*77*
Clifford Irving's "Hoax" biography, and Howard Hughes' Death	*81*
PART II—BRUCE ROBERTS' GEMSTONE FILE	101
6 August 10, 1970: To Ralph Nader	101
7 August 12 1971: To Recipients of First "Nader" letter; Chappaquiddick	105
8 October 7, 1971: To Nader: Death of Nader's "Consumers' Party"	116
9 November 26, 1971: To Nader: Mustapha Bey's Diary on Onassis	125
December 2, 1971: To This Group	*147*
10 December 8, 1971: To Nader: From Cradle to Grave with the Mafia	149
11 February 10, 1972: To Nader: My Father's Illness	151
12 A Chronology	155
13 Clifford Irving's "Hughes Autobiography" Hoax	159
14 February 19, 1972: To Nader: Bouncing Onassis Through the Tropics	174
15 March 12, 1972: To Whom It May Concern: My Father's Murder	181
16 The $6 Billion Heroin Bust, September 15, 1971	192
17 March 20-April 9, 1972: Letters to Mother	195
18 Dickie's Moscow Trip; News Round-up	211
19 George Wallace's Gut Shot	218
20 Cardinal Tisserant's Papers	224
21 June 1972: Good Housekeeping: "We Ate Mary Jo's Liver" [A Satire]	228
22 Mafia Democratic Convention in Mafia Miami	239
23 July 10, 1972: Charles Garry and the Murders of Black Panthers Hampton & Clark	248
24 The Bullet Holes of Dallas: John Connally and Dr. "Red" Duke	258
"Magic Bullet" Theory Exploded	*266*
25 Saving Daniel Ellsberg	271
27 August 3, 1972: My father's birthday	292
28 V.P. Convention: Unanimous for Shriver	298
29 August 16,1972: My Father's Murder	307
30 Watergate 5 at the Drift Inn	311
PART III—WHERE I CAME IN	**320**
31 October 1974-Spring 1975: A Cross for Mary Jo	320
32 January 15, 1975: Letter to Anwar Sadat of Egypt	326
33 February 10, 1975: Letter to President Tito of Yugoslavia	330
PART IV AFTERMATH	**333**
34 Leaving California (July 1975)	333

35 LIVE INTERVIEW WITH BRUCE ROBERTS: CITY OF SAN FRANCISCO, SEPTEMBER 9, 1975	335
"Beyond the Gemstone File": First Book Based on the Skeleton Key, 1976	*339*
36 1977-78: "DIALOGUE CONSPIRACY" OR WHY I AM NOT A "BRUSSELL SPROUT"	341
37 1978: GEMSTONE AND *HUSTLER:* LARRY FLYNT SEEKS TRUTH ON JFK; GETS SHOT	352
38 1988: THE OPAL FILE (A/K/A KIWI GEMSTONE FILE)	360
39 1992: INTERVIEW BY JIM KEITH	382
40 1993: INTERVIEW BY KENN THOMAS	393
41 1994: PROJECT SEEK: GERALD A. CARROLL DOES GEMSTONE	396
42 1994: SHERMAN SKOLNICK SOUNDS OFF!	403
43 1999: INSIDE THE GEMSTONE FILE: JAMES BOND AND GEMSTONE	416
44 WHICH CAME FIRST? ROBERTS' GEMSTONE FILE, OR LIDDY'S GEMSTONE PLAN?	422
45 2005: ROMANCE AND THE GIANT BURMESE RUBY	444
46 A VERY BRIEF BIOGRAPHY OF BRUCE ROBERTS	447
EPILOGUE BY SHERWOOD ROSS: PRAY FOR ME, FATHER	449
BIBLIOGRAPHY	450
APPENDIX A: ANTONIO IGLESIAS'S FOIA CIA/FBI-FILE	454
INDEX	455

PROLOGUE by Bruce Roberts

Jefferson said: "Political power belongs to the people. If tyranny corrupts, then the public should be informed. They should be educated so that they can control their own destiny."

Rochefort said: "Presidents fear one thing: An historian, who writes with knowledge of events; who writes of current history—and traces it back. This man has the power to change the inscriptions on tombstones, and shape the course of the history he writes about."

Write the following quote—my own words:

Aristotle (not Onassis) said: "Give me a pivot and a long lever and I will lift the world."

That's a simple experiment. A written history became the lever.

An historian (not Aristotle) has placed a weight of writings on the long end of that lever. The pivot arrived at Chappaquiddick.

Daily, the lever of history lengthens. And this writer pushes the weight further out. And adds a chapter. And then he listens for the creaks. And then he writes chapters on these. And adds that.

And assistants push the weight further out.

That's an interesting experiment.

Jefferson said, "Educate 'em."

Have you learned anything yet?

PREFACE by Kenn Thomas

Stephanie Caruana comes once again to the body of para-political exposition known as the Gemstone File, and this is a momentous and long overdue occasion. In the mid 1970s, her *Skeleton Key to the Gemstone File* became the only link between interested readers—truth seekers not content with the whitewash of public events appearing in the daily news—and the insights of Bruce Roberts, author of the Gemstone letters.

Caruana first recognized the value of this material when she encountered it in Mae Brussell's files. She later encapsulated it for broader consumption in her *Skeleton Key*, which she began to circulate in May 1975. In the days before the Internet, this multigenerational, photocopied *samizdat* outline became the word-of-mouth reality that belied the corporate news and official government pronouncements.

In form alone, Caruana became a great champion of getting out that other point of view. In content, she preserved and publicized Roberts' plight and how it illuminated the corrupt circumstances of American political life in the late 1960s to 1975, and on into today.

After 1975, Caruana lost touch with the largest known cache of original Roberts letters, as did everyone after Mae Brussell's death, and her *Skeleton Key* was for many years the only way to access the Gemstone information.

Bruce Roberts' letters resurfaced recently, and with the assistance of the venerable Tom Davis Books in Aptos, California, Stephanie Caruana obtained copies.

Since her original encounter with them, she had gone on to many other things, notably work on *Spearshaker Review*, a journal dedicated to ferreting out the secret truth behind the authorship of the Shakespeare plays.

The *Skeleton Key to the Gemstone File* also picked up a history of its own. It retained its *samizdat* form for nearly twenty years, from 1975 to 1992, until my late writing partner Jim Keith included it in his volume of commentary on Gemstone entitled *The Gemstone File* (IllumiNet). I met Stephanie Caruana shortly thereafter at a conference in Atlanta, where she sat on a Gemstone panel and tried mightily to guide the discussion on to Gemstone and not in the myriad directions where the panel ultimately drifted—not too much unlike Keith's Gemstone book, in fact. Since then, close to a half-dozen other books on Gemstone have been published, interpreting, re-interpreting and misinterpreting the unseen Roberts' letters to one degree or another.

The last one, a volume I edited called *Inside the Gemstone File* (Adventures Unlimited Press, 1999), collected commentary on Gemstone from over the years and for the first time published one page of one of the handwritten Roberts letters, which Caruana had sent me. My effort made no claims about advancing anyone's understanding of Bruce Roberts; it merely collected in one spot what had already been written. I also put the *Skeleton Key* together with the *Kiwi Gemstone* and the COM-12 documents as a demonstration of the *samizdat* process and the continuity of information that sometimes surfaces from disparate sources. This current volume of Bruce Roberts' letters and Stephanie Caruana's articles and analysis makes a more significant contribution than all the previous books on the subject.

Based on the *Skeleton Key*, Roberts has been called "crazy", even by writers with an intense interest in the Gemstone File; and the Gemstone thesis has been dismissed by some as simply "the mother of all conspiracy rants." That same "crazy" label has been applied to Mae Brussell, as well as to John Judge, Jim Garrison, Danny Casolaro, and any number of other people who have become deeply engaged in para-political criticism. The Gemstone letters are indeed an exhaustive venting of the conspiracy complexity in Bruce Roberts' life, but that's obviously not "crazy." What else can one do in an unresponsive and unjust world? The only real dementia found in the Gemstone letters reflects the depravity of the world's power mongers—Onassis, Hughes, Nixon, Kennedy, etc.—that

Roberts became entangled with through no fault of his own.

It has been Stephanie Caruana's role to make that venting manageable, first through *the Skeleton Key* and now, with this volume, to take readers deeper into Roberts' reality.

In the winter of 2000, and again in 2004, with the painfully obvious theft of the White House by extra-electoral and corrupt procedures, perhaps her job may become less difficult. During the election season, many have tried in vain to understand how democracy has slipped so far from the hands of the voters. I would suggest that this newly surfaced collection of Roberts' letters might contribute to that understanding. Rather than blaming the voting machines, or the obvious widespread fraud, Roberts' letters show nakedly the power grabbers themselves, removed from the very idea that any kind of democratic process is at work.

In particular, Roberts casts a light on Ralph Nader, regarded by many as the progressive reformer and spoiler of the 2000 election. Roberts reviews Nader's 1970 acceptance of a small settlement with General Motors in a lawsuit that could have decimated the irresponsible automaker. Nader evidenced the same pattern in the campaign of 2000, unsuccessfully seeking short-term gain in the form of federal funds for his presidential campaign while ignoring the campaign's broader impact. Nader's myopia, his work as a corporate safety consultant and his questionable investments demonstrate how far gone even the alternative candidates for president have become.

In the end, predictable election rigging prevailed in both 2000 and 2004, and the Conspiracy was put before American citizens in a more in-your-face way than ever before. Surely Bruce Roberts looks less "crazy" to more people now. It is a good moment, as economic disaster looms while corruption reigns, for Stephanie Caruana to re-examine the Gemstone File and expand on its original insights.

Kenn Thomas is a prolific author, editor and publisher. He is co-author of the most recent book on Gemstone: *Inside the Gemstone File* **(1999). Check out his many Steam Shovel Press offerings on his website (www.steamshovelpress.com).**

FOREWORD by Gerald A. Carroll

There is an old expression: Some people can't see the forest for the trees. Anyone exposed to the urban legend and folklore of the Gemstone file, and daily life, is witness to millions of trees with no hope of ever seeing a single solitary forest. It is too big of a story to be contained in any one volume, person or culture.

Yet here it is. Stephanie Caruana has pulled it off. Just sit back, read and let it soak in slowly, because it cannot be ingested quickly. It won't take a week. Maybe a month. A year. Many years. Even the rest of your life. The entire story will challenge everything you have ever learned about anything humanity experienced through the 20th century.

In the 1960's and '70's when Bruce Roberts' information-laden "gemstones, with history" were careening around the planet, younger readers were first captivated by the bold assertion that Greek shipping billionaire Aristotle Onassis was directly involved in much of the skullduggery of the middle portion of the 1900's. Howard Hughes. The Kennedys. Nixon and Watergate. Big-time drug-dealing. Behind-the-scenes power plays. It added up to an epic accusation worthy of countless semi-fictitious spin-off novels, Hollywood screenplays, Oliver Stone movies and a host of television series, subplots, radio talk-show grist; you name it.

But hold on there. Anyone with an ounce of intelligence can see a Da Vinci Code-like sense to it all as time continues to roll on into a remarkably prophetic future (our present), a future Bruce Roberts knew was going to occur. As this book comes out, Roberts' prophecies have matured in a more gruesome form than anything imaginable. Artificially engineered disease? AIDS exploded only a few years after Roberts died of what he thought was a CIA-planted cancer in his chest. America as the ultimate pariah state? Roberts' analysis was but a preview of the craziness of today. Moving on, we have the ultimate military quagmire, Iraq, at our doorsteps three decades after Roberts preached at length about dubious dealings with Islamic dictators and Arab oil sheiks.

September 11, 2001? Reading Roberts' relentless narrative of Hughes-JFK-RFK-MLK-Nixon-Watergate sets the stage for just such a nightmare. And Roberts' pounding away at Chappaquiddick, the Vatican and the tidal wave of oil-produced corruption provides a solid basis point for the mess we are now in.

And what of Ralph Nader? Stephanie Caruana wisely mentioned Nader's name but once in her original global *Skeleton Key to the Gemstone File*. Just his name, nothing more, no context. But as she digs into Roberts' letters and unleashes their full content in this volume, a staggering historical statement is made. Nader, as it turned out, was the ultimate horror, the ultimate Trojan horse, in the late 20th century, and even into the 21st.

Also, the original 23-page Key, with its current annotations and additions, has morphed to triple size, and is stunning. It is reminiscent of a biblical scholar, for example, unearthing and decoding the Dead Sea scrolls

Face facts. Nader sunk our ship and Roberts knew it was going to happen. Nader handed over the White House and the world to George W. Bush and the catbird "radical neo-conservative" Republicans, by stealing enough of a sliver of the far-left American vote to push Florida over the edge in 2000, destroying Al Gore and the scalded Democrats. Nader gave the modern occupiers of the Onassis-Gemstone legacy—Bush and the Arab oil republics—a dream victory. It was something out of a novel. Maybe a Bruce Roberts novel had he lived long enough to produce one.

As Dickens might have said of today: It is the worst of times. It is the best of times. On the "worst" side, we seem to be living in the world of George Orwell's *1984*: surrounded by Newspeak (War is Peace; Freedom is slavery, etc.,) and in the middle of an image of brutal international fascism: A boot, smashing into a human face, forever and ever.

On the "best" side, armloads of great stuff (books, independent media—cable TV, the Internet, etc.) are coming out about Bush, the shocking fraud of 9/11, and the world in general. The real "news" is spreading much more quickly than news about what was in Gemstone did, in the late 1970's. And I'd like to think that Gemstone plus its commentaries have helped make it easier for aware people to understand what is happening than they did 30 years ago.

Fortunately for us, there still exist the carriers of light, the prophets of our age who keep fighting, keep informing, to preserve truth and the real story of our lives and culture.

And a window has been opened for the revelation of one man's vision, Bruce Roberts' vision, of why a world went wrong and the reasons behind our present suffering and angst.

It *is The Gemstone File: A Memoir.* Read with caution, watch your back, and give Stephanie Caruana the floor.

Gerald A. Carroll is a journalist, and author of *Project Seek: Kennedy, Onassis and the Gemstone Thesis* **(1994).**

INTRODUCTION

Rochefort said: "Presidents fear one thing: An historian, who writes with knowledge of events; who writes of current history—and traces it back. This man has the power to change the inscriptions on tombstones, and shape the course of the history he writes about." Bruce Roberts liked that quote; it may have been one of his favorites. If you think about it, it is a tall order. Who dreams of changing current history through his writing? And yet he set about it, like a scientist. In fact, he dedicated his life to doing just that. His "history" was written from day to day, in the form of letters, or papers. And he never stopped living, investigating, writing, and "pushing the weight further out," long enough to rearrange and organize it into book form.

But he may have accomplished his aim, or at least some of it. At the very least, his writing reflects a point of view that is uniquely his own, quite different from any other account of the time he wrote about. For many, even in the brief, truncated version presented in *the Skeleton Key*, it has aroused fascinated curiosity.

He left behind huge stacks of unedited writing, none of which have been published before this.

He gave away, or sold to interested buyers, copies of various parts of his work, which he referred to at one time in 1971 as "about the thickness of four telephone books." Many of these copies have been destroyed or lost. Others may still exist in carefully guarded archives, here and around the world.

When I knew him, he was frequently broke; his copying bills at San Francisco's xerox machines were enormous. Several times I had the distinct honor of buying him a beer at one of his favorite San Francisco bars.

And yet—in his letter to President Anwar Sadat, of Egypt, in 1975, he refers to "a solid performance record."

What record? The man died broke, apparently, and unknown to the public. Biographical facts about his life are hard to come by. A complete stack of his writing—which he began as early as 1968, and which I estimate may have been about six telephone books thick by the time of his death in 1976—is not known to exist anywhere. But it is equally possible that a friend or relative has the complete file stashed away somewhere.

Bruce Roberts was a bold and fearless man, who spoke and wrote his mind with disregard to his own personal safety. Or maybe he just decided that his freedom of speech and thought were more precious to him than his own personal safety. Whatever his reasoning, he was also a scientist, and a careful man in many ways. For instance, he had a safe deposit box or boxes in which he kept his most valuable possessions. As well as precious and synthetic gemstones, these included the collectible coins he inherited from his father, LaVerne Dayle Roberts, and I am sure, a huge stack of his original letters and papers. Someone inherited the contents of that safety deposit box. In addition, he liberally papered the neighborhood of San Francisco with copies of various of his writings. Though many people may have burned or otherwise destroyed them, through fear, or for whatever reason, I believe others may have kept them carefully stashed away. If so, I wish they would contact me, since I think it is time Bruce Roberts and his writings came in from the cold.

People have asked me how Roberts could have had access to so much secret information about the events he described. It appears that some of his relatives worked in intelligence areas. He himself may have worked for the OSS (precursor of the CIA) during World War II.

He had significant family connections with inside information. Bruce's brother, Dayle, was

married at one time to Marina Iglesias, sister of Antonio Iglesias. Antonio Iglesias was one of the CIA-Cuban mob involved in the Bay of Pigs Operation. Roberts told me Iglesias was also present at the JFK assassination, with a camera, taking photos in and around the pergola adjacent to the "grassy knoll" in Dealey Plaza. Excerpts from Iglesias's FBI (FOIA) files appear in Appendix A. Some of the photos were of Eugene Brading; one showed him stuffing his rifle under his coat after shooting at JFK from the shelter of this pergola I have included one photo here showing Brading at Dealey Plaza in his distinctive X-marked leather sombrero. This photo first turned up in Peter Noyes' book, *Legacy of Doubt* (Pinnacle Books, October, 1973.) The source of the photo is not indicated.

Roberts also referred to his CIA-connected uncle, C. J. Kimball, and a Kimball cousin who was apparently busy destabilizing Nigeria for the CIA at the time the family black sheep, Bruce, was writing his Gemstone papers.

For all of his obscurity Bruce seems to have pushed history around, deliberately, and quite a bit, during his lifetime. He claims that his writing, and the evidence that he collected to support it, were used by Richard Nixon to gain the Presidency, and later forced him to resign it. Roberts also claims that he used his writing to change the national composition of the United Nations, and to drive various U.S. Intelligence groups crazy.

From studying his writing, I conclude that what he said and wrote may have been a truthful account. However, even if it is exaggerated, or even tragically limited because it is from his own point of view, perhaps too self-centered, and does not take into account enough other factors to be called "history", it is still the most astonishing story I have ever read, far beyond the most daring derring-do of fictional spies and adventure heroes. But I will add that research efforts by others, recent publications and historical developments have confirmed many if not all of Roberts' statements.

The pale fractional 23-to-30-odd page shadow (in several versions) of his story that I wrote in a hurry and distributed free, urgently and out of what I deemed to be a necessity, early in March through July 1975, which I called "*A Skeleton Key to the Gemstone File,*" was too brief and fragile to hold Roberts' entire story of the huge network of top-level conspiracy that surrounds us and robs us of our freedom every day. Looking at a battered, lop-eared "original" copy that has survived all these years, I am amazed at both its longevity and its brashness. It certain doesn't look strong enough to make it on its own. But like the Flying Dutchman, it has drifted, rudderless, around the world many times over, inspiring fear, ridicule, belief, disbelief—but also research, to prove or disprove its claims.

On the way, it has engendered millions of copies, many in formats and languages that I know nothing about. And at least six books, several movies, and countless TV episodes. The Gemstone File, itself unseen, has become a popular catchword for all the secrets of deliberate high-level government involvement in "population control", worldwide wars, "secret" military actions, incredible financial rip-offs by the military supply systems, drug trafficking on a world scale, tax free money laundering, media control and suppression, electoral fraud, and the general human devastation that we live with every day. Books and movies use the term freely and it is understood.

Not bad for 23 pages! I'm proud of it. It has served its purpose well.

On the negative side, its unchaperoned, uncopyrighted state has led to its being "claimed" and distorted by several "*Skeleton Key*" wanna-be writers, co-opted for causes which it was never meant to serve, condemned as hogwash by some reputable folks who appear to miss the point completely, and sliced, diced and served up in formats and satires which are nearly unrecognizable. I regret this, but I had no control over it.

Today, thirty-five years later, the *Skeleton Key* is still available on the Internet in a variety of languages, in thousands of copies and references, most of which were not posted by me. It has been reprinted innumerable times, in "unauthorized" and frequently "anonymous" versions, in various

newspapers and magazines including *Penthouse* and *Hustler*, "others whose names I know not" and most of all, in the "conspiracy" magazines and web sites around the world. Frequently with a disclaimer: "We don't believe a word of this, but here it is anyway. You decide."

Though it has been called an incredible notorious rant (and other less complimentary things), it has outlived many other "theories" and a loud, persistent chorus of nay-sayers. In fact, it is sometimes termed the "granddaddy of all conspiracy theories." Though why the phrase used is "conspiracy theory," I can't imagine. As Kenn Thomas puts it on his Steam Shovel Press website: "All Conspiracy; No Theory." A generation of Americans has grown up with it. Its statements, though shocking to many when it was first released, are now almost commonplace, at least among those who are interested and informed on such subjects.

To me, a "conspiracy theory" is an attempted explanation of a number of isolated facts, cooked up by someone who is attempting to shape a coherent story from these isolated facts. But Bruce Roberts' Gemstone file is not a conspiracy theory; it is a personal history, written on a day to day level, as he experienced it. As a "history," if it is valid, the story will connect with other contemporary accounts and evidence. And the Gemstone File does connect as history, in this way.

The world has changed around the *Skeleton Key*. Most people now recognize and understand that we live in a society dominated by the Mafia, by whatever name you choose to call it: High Society, the moneyed elite, the military-industrial complex, the Company, the Organization, the Outfit, the CIA, the Good Guys, the Wise Guys, Big Business, International Corporations, the New World Order, etc. Thirty years ago, many people preferred to pretend that the Mafia didn't exist as a real force. Today, it is promoted as popular entertainment on TV shows such as The Sopranos and Vegas, and various "Mafia Princesses" parading their culture of brutal violence for us, on TV stations busy nonstop in brainwashing us to think this is how life is, ought to be, and will be forever.

Bruce Roberts, who hated it with a passion, referred to it as "MMORDIS" which stood for "Moldering Mass Of Rotten Dribbling Infectious Shit." But then, he always did have a way with a phrase.

During all this time since the *Key's* first appearance, readers have clamored to see the original Bruce Roberts letters—for many reasons. First, they wanted assurance that there really was such a person. Second, they wanted to know whether the *Key* was an accurate reflection of the original. Third, they were interested in learning more about the events and the people described.

Unfortunately, I was not in a position to do much about that. I had only a small sampling of (copies of) the original letters. The contents of the original *Key* were based almost entirely on notes I took, from late 1974 to June, 1975, from two of Roberts' long letters that were in the possession of a foreign consulate in San Francisco, where I read them. These notes were amplified by personal contacts and conversations I had with Bruce at that time, plus memories of earlier Roberts letters that I had read in Mae Brussell's home six months earlier, plus a few more Gemstone letters I got directly from him in late 1974.

The first release of the Key, dated April, 1975, actually started going out in late March. On March 22, Bruce Roberts called me from a hospital in San Francisco and told me that X-rays showed a "tumor the size of a grapefruit" in his chest; his doctors assumed it was cancer and were treating it that way. But he did not believe it was cancer. The full story appears later in the book. I will say here that I believed the CIA and their associates were trying to kill him, and that his father had died under strange circumstances while in a hospital two years earlier. I felt the only thing I could do about it was to release my notes immediately, in a succinct and dramatic form, to get the basic story out, hoping that it would give the CIA something different to think about and that maybe they wouldn't kill him. At that time, my notes existed only in a loose-leaf three-hole notebook, with the events described arranged in chronological order. I began typing the notes, and it turned out to be 23 pages long. I called it *A Skeleton Key to the Gemstone File*, made a batch of Xerox copies, and mailed them out to major media and some friends. At the end of this summary was the instruction, or plea,

that readers could make as many copies as they wished, and pass them out to people. And they did; and they did!

So—imperfect as it was—the *Skeleton Key* was launched on its long journey.

I never anticipated that the *Key* would be the only representation of Roberts' work to emerge over the intervening years.

Mae Brussell, a well-known conspiracy researcher living in Carmel Valley, CA, suppressed her 360-page cache of Roberts' letters and papers, dated 1970-1972, for many years, until her death in 1988—and even after her death. Worse yet, she deliberately lied about the nature of his writing, in two radio broadcasts in 1976-77, and in letters and conversations with others. I was unaware of these broadcasts for a number of years, since I was living in the Miami area during that time, and quite out of touch with political matters and the California crowd. When I became aware of Mae's lies, I was unable to refute them because I did not have copies of the portion of the file in her possession. Since then, I have obtained copies of most of the material Mae had, and have been able to compare Mae's comments with the original material.

After Mae's death, the three copies she left were kept hidden by three chosen confidantes who suppressed them. And for many years, I did not know who they were.

Several years ago, I was able to acquire a copy (although various sections, totaling about 60 pages, had been yanked from the copy I received.) Still, it was a substantial haul. I set out to prepare this book, adding these earlier files to the information I had from 1974-5. About 250 edited pages from Bruce Roberts' original Gemstone letters are presented here for the first time in printed form..

To answer early critics of the original *Skeleton Key*, who stated correctly that no documentation had been provided with the "sensational" statements made, other writers have been inspired enough to seek such documentation, and to publish it. Two of the best for documentation are *Project Seek: Onassis, Kennedy and the Gemstone Thesis* by Gerald A. Carroll, and *The Gemstone File: Sixty Years of Corruption and Manipulation Within World Government, Detailing the Events Surrounding the Assassination of JFK*, by "Richard Alan" (a pen name). Each of these very different books weighs in with about 400 pages of solid information. I suggest that people interested in the Gemstone File locate one or both of these for back-up information. I believe it is a rare occurrence for a 23-page "rant" to inspire 800 pages of documentation. This observation applies in spades to those writers and "conspiracy researchers" who have dismissed the *Skeleton Key* as fantasy or disinformation. Some have chosen to ignore this documentary support and keep repeating the old refrain. I wonder why.

From 1968, when Bruce Roberts began to circulate his writings about the Mafia's role in, and rule of, the United States, until his death in 1976 at the age of 56, he seems to have written steadily. He was a keen observer with a photographic memory. He wrote by hand with a ball-point pen, usually on cheap yellow lined legal pads, 8-1/2"x14", ignoring the margins and filling each page from top to bottom. (But he did make some exceptions, when writing to heads of state. From what I can tell from the copies, he switched to 8-1/2"x11" white lined paper. More dignified, I guess.)

He would write at home, or sitting at a quiet table in the Library. He never rewrote anything, and only rarely corrected a word of what he had written. It was all "first draft." It takes another writer, I expect, to appreciate what that means: intense clarity of mind, a sure grasp of the material, and a brilliant creative power that reaches for, and finds, just the right words and phrases to send forth a stream of sentences that are powerful, vivid and unique in style.

The "down side" was two-fold. Since he was writing in incremental units, and the writing was going out to different individuals and groups of people, in succession, he had to recap the general thread or outline over and over. This made the information presented repetitious to some extent, although each letter or paper discussed additional current events as they related to the past "history," or extended the details in unpredictable directions.

Another difficulty was that he was frequently VERY angry while he was writing. At times,

bursts of profanity marred the otherwise fluent procedure of his prose.

I elected to deal with both of these problems in time-honored editorial mode: I CUT like mad. (But I kept every word that extended the story.) I believe the result is extremely readable, and tells a powerful story as it unfolded.

Roberts was able to reel his complex, detailed story off from memory, varying only occasionally in minor details, each time focusing on a different aspect, or taking off from a current TV, newspaper or magazine story or interview that carried the story forward in time.

The first time I met him, in September of 1974, he told me the tale of our U.S. Mafia history from August, 1972 to the then-present, in about an hour and a half, without stopping. He was standing in the doorway of his apartment in the Sunset District of San Francisco wearing a white terry-cloth bathrobe. He was in his fifties; tall and blue-eyed; his close-cropped dark gray hair was still wet from the shower. He looked like a retired Marine drill sergeant who kept himself in shape. Still standing in the hallway, he told me a tale of horror, filled with murders, bribery, and criminal betrayals of a nation's trust by its political leaders. He apologized for not letting me into his apartment, saying that a friend was inside copying some material. He was telling me all this history because I had asked him to.

I had spent the spring and summer of 1974 bouncing back and forth from Berkeley to the Carmel Valley, then to Big Sur and Carmel. It had been a fascinating and productive summer. For part of the time, I lived in the tiny spare bedroom of Mae Brussell's house in Carmel Valley. Mae was a well-known "conspiracy researcher", who had written the first articles to appear with real information about the Watergate "burglars", which had been published in Paul Krassner's *The Realist*. Her filing cabinets were irresistible, and she knew a lot.

Mae and I collaborated on an article about the Patty Hearst kidnapping, Donald DeFreeze, known as "Cinque ", and the Symbionese Liberation Army (a.k.a. "S.L.A."), which was published in the *Berkeley Barb*, a small local newspaper.[1] A week after it was published, Cinque and the rest of the CIA-inspired, created and managed "Symbionese Liberation Army" of freed prisoners and hapless stooges (all six of them) were barbecued, stapled and mutilated by a Los Angeles SWAT Team.

This well-planned slaughter happened in broad daylight, with a TV crew conveniently on hand, for the edification of the Nation, with Patty Hearst (supposedly) posted at a nearby window by her CIA handlers to watch the action. The message, for the Rest of Us, was clear enough: "See what happens when you mess with a CIA-staged 'national terrorist media event'?"

Yes; it was clear enough. And yet, for some reason, Mae and I bumbled on, instead of taking up safer pursuits like knitting, gardening, or trying to save the few surviving sea otters who bobbed cheerfully in the long kelp beds just offshore chewing on sea urchins and abalone.

I wrote an interview with Mae for *Playgirl* magazine's "About Women" section.

We didn't know it, but we were about to bumble into the hottest, most secret, and most dangerous story of the 70's, and we had no idea what we were getting into. (At least, I didn't.) This was the story of the 1957 kidnap and takeover of Howard Hughes, by Aristotle Onassis. The article was published in December 1974, in *Playgirl,* under the title: "Is Howard Hughes Dead and Buried off a Greek Island?"[2] We didn't know how important the story was, but the CIA/Mob/Big Money boys did. Marin Milam, the Editor of *Playgirl*, told me she had been in Times Square, New York City, when the first copies were delivered to the newsstand.

"I have never seen so many men in black overcoats running up to buy *Playgirl* in all my life," she said.

The articles on Patty Hearst and the SLA, and Howard Hughes and Onassis are included

---

[1] See Chapter 1 for this article.
[2] See Chapter 3 for this article.

here, together with an account of why they are important for this story.

***

In April 1975, a small group of Native Americans and others had gathered somewhere in New Mexico for a "Third World Conference," which had been abruptly canceled without notice. But someone had brought along a single copy of the *Skeleton Key*. So, with no meeting space available, they drove out into the desert night, parked their cars in a circle, and read their copy in the glow of the headlights, passing the pages around the circle, one by one. Then they drove for an hour across the desert to the nearest copying machine. One, young, handsome, serious, determined, with a pony tail, came to see me later in San Francisco. He showed up at my door without notice, just as I had showed up on Bruce Roberts' doorstep a few months earlier. He told me about their desert reading session, and asked for 10 fresh copies, since their single copy had been re-copied so many times as to be almost illegible.

He told me that his group had friends in every Bureau of Indian Affairs office in the country, that every office had a printer, and that copies would be made and circulated from every BIA Office in the country. I gave him 10 copies of the newest "edition," dated May 1, and I believe this is the "edition" which has received the greatest circulation.

The *Skeleton Key* has been praised, denounced, purloined, imitated, and satirized; it has been turned into comic strips, and so on. But it has never gone away.

At least six books that I know of have been written that were based directly on it. This will be the seventh—but the first to include any of the original Gemstone File material itself. In addition, it has been the sometimes undeclared subject and source of innumerable novels, TV shows, and movies.

During the course of wholesale anonymous copying and recopying of Xerox copies, my name and address on Prosper Street in San Francisco disappeared and reappeared in its original place at the top corner of the "original" copies. I distributed at least 3 "issues," with minor variations, ranging in length from 22 to 35 pages, and variously dated in April, May and June of 1975. Typos, omissions, additions, misinterpretations and distortions, some of them deliberate, have crept into many of the published and unpublished versions. For this reason, I have included an updated and corrected *Skeleton Key* here. It will serve as a useful guide to the events described by Bruce Roberts. I suggest that readers unfamiliar with the Gemstone thesis read the *Skeleton Key* first, before tackling the Gemstone File itself.

There was no way the CIA, or anyone else, could prevent the inexorable duplication and march of those little *Skeleton Keys* around the globe. Whenever I need a laugh, I think of the "Sorcerer's Apprentice" scene in the movie *Fantasia*, where Mickey Mouse steals the Magician's cap and wand and puts a spell on an old broom, which comes to life, splits in half and begins carrying buckets of water for him. The rapidly multiplying brooms and buckets soon fill the screen.

The newly corrected, expanded and updated *Skeleton Key* provides a useful simplified time line, with comments, of the events and personalities described in the original writing of Bruce Roberts.

I think that Roberts will eventually emerge as the best historian of our troubled times. I can hear the objections:

This is history written in the vernacular; street speech. How dare I call it "history"? But you, the reader, will judge for yourself. And you may agree that the *Gemstone File* is better than many histories, in that it at least attempts to be honest about important events that have shaped our lives and our future, and that of the entire planet.

This is Bruce Roberts' own personal story, based on his own experiences and discoveries. As such, it is unique. He was an educated, literate man, who read books and newspapers and watched television, like the rest of us. And he refers to these sources from time to time. But he also did a lot of

"research" using unfamiliar sources that were never published, as well as his own experiences in the streets, bars, hotel lobbies and offices of San Francisco and the woods, mountains and casinos of Lake Tahoe.

Many researchers have attempted to analyze his "sources", and have drawn a variety of conclusions. For some, Roberts' statements that can not be verified from published sources "prove" that his story is unsubstantiated. On the other hand, if they discover a book or source that contains some bit of the information he provides, they claim that he is only repeating information available to anyone, and that this too lessens his credibility. I wish to remind readers that no one else has developed a coherent version of the traumatic events that shaped our history from the mid-fifties to the mid-seventies. Once the basic story is understood, as well as its implications, it provides us with background information by means of which we can better understand current developments.

This book contains edited transcripts of all of the Roberts source material that I have. Repetitious material has been omitted. None of the Roberts material has ever been published before. I believe it will be as startling and informative to the reader as the *Skeleton Key* has been over the years. And I hope it will provide a better understanding of our past history, which sheds a harsh but steady light on our present reality.

After all, why shouldn't our history be written in the style of James Joyce's *Finnegan's Wake*? Fragmented, shimmering, like a faceted gemstone that you can turn from one side to another, each time seeing more depths and connections than you ever thought possible? And why shouldn't there be a *Skeleton Key* to guide you in your explorations, like a thread through the labyrinth of an enormous deep red ruby? With James Joyce, all you ever got was a guided tour of Joyce's brain—interesting, but inconclusive; and, in the long run, perhaps, so what?

For the perhaps thirty million Americans who spend their lives actively involved in this ruthless worldwide oligarchy, ripping off the rest of us through deliberately created scams, wars, stock market crashes, bribes, CIA assassinations of world leaders, planned "democratic revolutions" setting up dictatorships, mass and individual murders, training and releasing brain-washed and manipulated killers, media cover-ups, planned and manipulated "shortages," Congressional and Presidential and Supreme Court "legislation" that amounts to criminal attacks on our liberties and on the national income, and the rest of the mess, much of this will not be news. They will collect their dividend checks, or handsome salaries, and smile. These thirty million make up the 10% of the population who possess/control 90% of the country's wealth; leaving 10% to be divided among the remaining 90% of the population. Hey…any more questions about why most of us are so broke?

I am thinking of one such "friend" from Virginia who took to calling me during the preparation of this book. He preferred, as many do, to pooh-pooh these matters as "crackpot conspiracy theories." When I pointed out some undeniable realities to him, he shifted his ground abruptly and began talking about a $20,000 check he had just received. He seemed to be suggesting that I would be better off, at least financially, if I would just shut up and get on the gravy train with the rest of the "Mob."

But this book is for everyone else—the 270,000,000 victims, in this country, and the billions elsewhere in the world. The conflict between our stated national ideals and the reality of our national actions and our own lives has led to a perpetual world-wide Civil War which has split our families, devalued, destroyed and impoverished many of our people, and causes grave concern about our nation's and the world's future.

I write this shortly after the second inauguration of "Republican" George W. Bush, son of ex-CIA Chief, ex-President George Bush and Barbara Walker Bush. Grandson of Prescott Bush, one of the major American financiers of Hitler. (Look him up on the Internet if you don't believe it. Try Google.com, and search terms "Prescott Bush Nazi financier." This ought to get you 40 or 50 relevant articles.) Then ask yourself how likely it would be that the office of President of the United States should fall into the clutches of someone so eminently unqualified for the office as George Dubya, if it

had not been for his descent from Prescott Bush, who perhaps should have been tried as a war criminal after World War II. Then ask yourself what is the likelihood of this crucial relationship being mentioned in a "traditional" History, and I think you might agree that the percentage of mentions is far less than that of the frequency of a fingernail paring on one finger of one hand. The public awareness of the "Banana Republic" reality of our present government is acute. Widespread election fraud, amounting to theft, was present in the 2000 election, and augmented and refined in 2004 by Diebold Corporation's "voting machines", designed for easier and more precise and reliable election stealing.

On the other side of the political aisle, "Democrat" John Kerry's 2004 campaign ended not with a bang but with a whimper, as he refused to fight against the Bush machine. We are left wondering whether the United States' election process will ever regain a modicum of trust and confidence among its citizens.

Such is the state of the Union, no matter what they are saying in Washington or on your TV.

Knowledge is power, it is said. *Gemstone* plus *Key* plus some mental effort may give many people a better understanding of our lives and the way we live now, than they have ever had.

And besides, it's one of the few relevant histories of our time that I know about.

Part I—*Skeleton Key*

1. Inside The Pergola: Brading and a Smoking Gun at Dealey Plaza?

When Bruce Roberts described John F. Kennedy's assassination to me in 1974, he said that Eugene Brading had shot at Kennedy from "the pergola at Dealey Plaza." He added that Johnny Roselli and Jimmy Fratianno had shot simultaneously, and that their volley had placed JFK in the center of a triangulated hail of bullets. No evidence has emerged that I know of that places either Roselli or Fratianno in Dealey Plaza that day, but Eugene Brading's presence is known. He was photographed in Dealey Plaza, then walked up to the Texas School Book Depository to "make a phone call." There, he was arrested, under the name of "Eugene Braden," and quickly release by the Dallas Police. (He is also the only known Mafia member known to have been present at both the JFK and the RFK assassinations.) Since that time, I have been looking for any evidence that places Brading, or a gunman, in the pergola itself at the time of the shooting. While preparing this book, I bought a number of books that might be helpful. They included Robert J. Groden's book, *The Killing of a President: The Complete Photographic Record of the JFK Assassination, the Conspiracy, and the Cover-Up* (1992). The book contains "650 photographs, maps, drawings, and documents...." Many of the photographs were taken just before, at, or immediately after the assassination. Looking through the book, I was struck by a color photograph which appears on page 47. Groden identified this picture as a frame from a film shot that day, from Bell Film (made by J. M. "Mark" Bell). Groden's caption reads: "The immediate response of several motorcycle police officers was to jump from their bikes and rush up the Knoll." The camera was aimed straight at the left-hand doorway of the pergola. In Groden's book, the photo was 2" high x 3" wide. A cropped portion of this picture appears on the cover of this book.

The doorway of the pergola, and the frame, were about 3/4" square on the page. The inside of the pergola was in deep shadow which looked black. Yet as I peered at it, I got the impression that there was a man standing inside—a deep black silhouette, against near-black. I scanned the photo into my computer, then enlarged and cropped it so that the area around the pergola doorway appeared full-page. Then I enhanced the contrast. The black of the background inside the pergola dissolved into midnight blue, but the black silhouette in the foreground stayed black. When I printed the page on glossy photo paper, the black silhouette was still there, but I noticed something else: a pinkish-white streak rising from the right side of the silhouette, like three small round puffs of smoke. The result is pictured on Page 25.

It seems to me that this streak is smoke, or heated air, rising from a gun barrel.

I am not a photography expert in any sense. I used an Epson Perfection 2480 Photo Scanner, and printed my enlargement on an Epson Stylus Photo R320. I am sure that others with more photographic sophistication and more professional equipment will be able to do better than this, but this is what I have found so far. . Perhaps someone more capable than I will do so for a future edition, if there is one. Groden's photograph has many points of interest. Shots have been fired, and the people in the picture are moving—or not. In the lower left corner of the photo, a spectator named Jean Hill is just beginning to run up to the Grassy Knoll after someone thought to be an assassin.. Someone in light-colored clothing appears to be walking away from the pergola doorway. According to Jack White[3], a well-known and expert researcher specializing in color photography relating to the JFK assassination, this is Beverly Sitzman, Abraham Zapruder's assistant. A policeman—possibly Bobby Hargis, mentioned by Groden—is directly in front of the pergola, in the street, running toward what is called the Grassy Knoll. A couple in the foreground—identified as

---

[3] See White's masterful photo section in Fetzer's book, *Murder in Dealey Plaza*.

the "Newman family"—has dropped to the ground on the lawn, attempting to shield their children with their bodies in case there is more gunfire.

On the righthand edge of the photo is the figure of a man in what appears to be a dark suit, white shirt and tie, standing motionless in front of the arc-shaped pergola building, at approximately the center of the building. I don't know who he is supposed to be. He may be one of the men mentioned in various witnesses' accounts whose role appeared to be to warn people away from several areas, identifying themselves as Secret Service, perhaps carrying forged I.D. as described by Chauncey Holt in *Murder in Dealey Plaza*, p. 14-15.

The light coming in through the windows at the back of the pergola doorway is partially blocked by a dark shape that might be a head. This shape disappears in photos of the area taken a little later.

Another frame from the same Bell film source appears in Groden's book on page 50. The camera has panned to the left, following the disappearing motorcade bearing JFK's body. This one gives a longer view of Elm Street, and the left-hand doorway of the pergola building. It shows a man walking away from this doorway, toward the center of the building. He is walking toward the man who appears on the righthand side of the photo.

Another interesting photo appears on page 20 of *The Day JFK Died*.[4] It shows the other end of the semicircular pergola. Here we get a different view of the Newman family. Two photographers are running after the departing presidential motorcade; one is photographing the Newmans, and the fourth is looking after the motorcade.

Meanwhile, in the righthand doorway of the pergola building stand two young men in a casual pose, apparently motionless. Almost everyone else is running, ducking, or photographing. These two have just watched the slaughter of a President, but they look as though nothing has happened. To me, they look "posted" there, possibly to discourage passersby from walking or seeing into the pergola.

Jack White, one of the very best researchers of the JFK photo evidence, disagrees with my interpretation of these photos. In e-mail correspondence dated 06/16/06, he states:

"This Bell frame allegedly shows [Beverly] Sitzman after she and Zapruder got down from the pedestal...quite a while after the shooting. So it could not show a gunman inside the pergola, since it is considerably later than the shots.... The [Bell] photo on page 50 of TKOAP is several minutes after the shooting. No gunman would stand around that long... There is a person in the doorway. [But] this is minutes after the shooting and is unlikely to be a shooter. That would be an illogical location for a shooter anyway. The person may be Charles Hester, who went into the pergola well after the shooting. Shooters would be in hidden positions, not standing in plain sight... I have examined the Bell frames showing the person and there is not enough information to "analyze." It is just a dark figure in silhouette, and it is too long afterward...

"I had examined all the people within the pergola in various images, and had found nothing of interest, or anyone identifiable. Trying to identify somebody there I have long ago considered is not possible, and would just be speculation. I have seen nothing to change that opinion. The two kids at the other end of the pergola were teenagers. The identities of all these people have been determined by researchers."

I respectfully disagree with Jack White's interpretation of these photos. He has spent decades working with the photos available from the JFK assassination. Based on the accumulated evidence, his photo section on the frame-by-frame phonying of the Abraham Zapruder, "The Great Zapruder Film Hoax", in Fetzer's book, is a marvelous achievement. But if his own theorizing, as in how long an assassin would hang around the site, prevents him from considering the possibility that this, too, was part of the careful plan, then we part company.

---

[4] A book of photographs published in 1993 by the *Dallas Morning News*.

Jim Marrs, in his excellent book, *Crossfire*, includes a mention by a witness of another possible source of the gunfire:

"At the time of the shooting, even persons at the Depository believed the shots came from elsewhere.

"Steven F. Wilson was vice president of a school textbook-publishing company and had an office on the third floor of the Depository. Wilson told the FBI he watched the motorcade go by from a closed third-floor window but lost sight of the President when he "became obscured by some trees which are on Elm Street."

"He further stated: "In a matter of ten seconds or less…I heard three shots… There was a greater space of time between the second and third shots than between the first and second. The three shots were fired within a matter of less than five seconds. The shots sounded to me like rifle shots. At that time, it seemed like the shots came from the west end of the building or from the colonnade located on Elm Street across from the west end of the building. The shots really did not sound like they came from above me."—Marrs, p.44.

Page 26 is a recreation of the first page of Bruce Roberts' satire, "We Ate Mary Jo's Liver," which is a "Gemstone" fantasy told from Joan Kennedy's point of view

A transcription appears as Chapter 26.

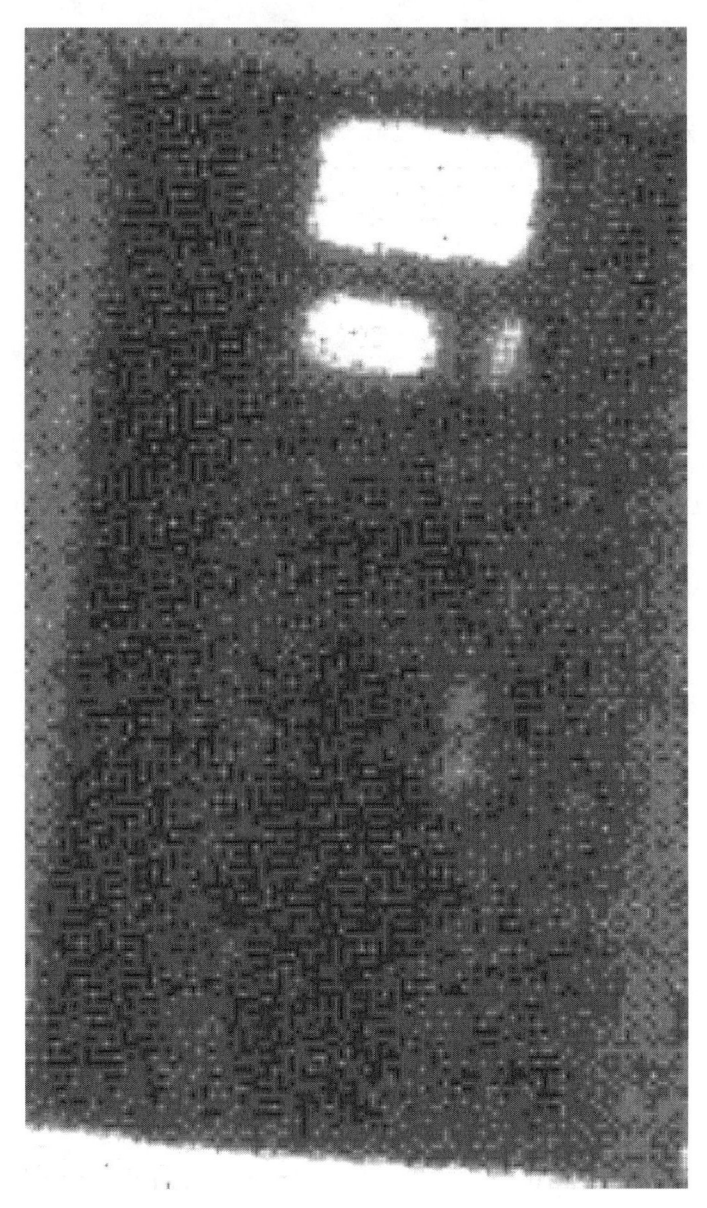

Is this another smoking gun at Dealey Plaza?

JUNE 1972 ● 60¢
Good Housekeeping
Joan Kennedy talks frankly about herself and Ted–
a revealing and exclusive profile
Excerpts from
Bruce Roberts'
Gemstone File
WE ATE MARY
JO'S LIVER

2. March—May 1974: Inside the Hearst Kidnapping

I had been living in Los Angeles for several years, and was a contributing editor at *Playgirl* magazine. Regular writing assignments from *Playgirl* and interesting friends and contacts in the San Francisco Bay area encouraged me to relocate to Berkeley in 1973. And that's where I was living on February 4, 1974, when Patty Hearst's strange kidnapping sent shock waves through the Berkeley community and riveted national media attention on the puzzling events which followed. There were long, pompous headline-grabbing "communiques" from the mysterious self-proclaimed "Symbionese Liberation Army" and its revolutionary black leader, "Cinque." These culminated in elaborately staged and publicized phony "food give-aways" by Hearst in the rather embarrassed community of Oakland.

Within weeks, sweet wealthy white girl U.C. Berkeley student Patty Hearst had inexplicably metamorphosed into gun-toting revolutionary "Tanya," who obligingly posed for pictures with a rifle while participating in a bank robbery with her "brothers and sisters in the struggle." It was enough to turn any wealthy capitalist pig parent's hair white. What in hell was going on?

Was this "reality", or the playing out of a carefully planned political charade? And if so, for what unfathomable end?

Eventually my friends tired of hearing me ask questions that no one seemed able to answer. One of them, the news director of a radio station, told me, "Ask Mae Brussell. If anyone knows what's going on, it will be Mae."

She told me that Mae had a weekly half-hour radio broadcast coming out of KLRB-FM in Carmel, which was syndicated to a network of non-profit radio stations throughout the country. It was called "Dialogue Conspiracy."

A few days later I drove to Carmel, armed with Mae's phone number. I called her at her home in Carmel Valley, told her I was a journalist writing for *Playgirl*, and asked whether I could come and talk to her about Patty Hearst. She promised me ten minutes; it turned into three hours.

I offered to work with her as a "writing slave" on an article about Patty Hearst and the SLA, and she agreed. A few days later, I moved temporarily into her small guest bedroom, sat down with her, and turned on my tape recorder. The next day I began transcribing, organizing and editing. The resulting article, reprinted below, was published shortly after in the *Berkeley Barb*. [Cut slightly because of space limitations.]

INSIDE THE HEARST KIDNAPPING
(*Berkeley Barb*, May 1974 - No. 18)

(Copyright © 1974 by Stephanie Caruana and Mae Brussell)

DONALD DeFREEZE WAS FIRST BLACK PATSY IN SECRET GOVERNMENT PLAN TO TAKE OVER U.S.

Mae Brussell is a researcher who has spent ten years studying political assassinations and conspiracies in the United States. On July 11, 1972, she wrote the first and so far the only article to give a reasonable explanation for the break-in and arrest at the Watergate—three weeks after the event. The article, "Why Was Martha Mitchell Kidnapped?" and a long companion piece, "The Senate Select Committee is Part of the Cover-Up," were published in Paul Krassner's *The Realist*.

Stephanie Caruana is a Contributing Editor at Playgirl. Her published articles include interviews with poet Maya Angelou and civil rights leader Florynce Kennedy.

CARUANA: Can you please explain what is going on? Who or what is the Symbionese Liberation

Army, and why did they kidnap Patricia Hearst?

BRUSSELL: The script from the very beginning was to have the nice rich white princess kidnapped by the mean black prison "escapees;" to drag out the scenario until the whole nation was involved with Patty's fate; and then to sacrifice her. Donald DeFreeze and Thero Wheeler would be the patsies. DeFreeze would be the main patsy: the first black Lee Harvey Oswald. He would wind up dead, or in jail, silenced, like Sirhan Sirhan, Jack Ruby, Lee Harvey Oswald, James Earl Ray, Arthur Bremer, and many others. The intelligence agencies behind the plot didn't plan that Patty Hearst, DeFreeze and Wheeler would survive to tell their story. The whole plot for the paramilitary take-over of the United States might come out in the open if the truth were revealed about this kidnapping.

But if the plan to assassinate Patty Hearst is carried out, the military intelligence agencies will be stuck with something around their necks that could be just as difficult to cover up as the truth about the Kennedy assassination. Evidence of a high-level conspiracy will crop up again and again, and many more people will be murdered. Since the Watergate story began to emerge, people have become more sophisticated, and more suspicious. They know they have been lied to by people on the highest level of our government.

The Hearst kidnapping is a domestic conspiracy. It has to be understood in its historical context.

The past ten years have seen the murder of a President, a Senator, Congressmen, civil rights leaders, and hundreds of other victims of what I believe are related conspiracies.

The next ten years will be bloody and fearful for all minorities in the United States. It appears that there will be a concerted effort on the part of the Defense Intelligence Agency to continue the policies of the Nazis they brought into this country following World War II. Genocide will be made possible by the same techniques used in Germany.

Two large airports will be utilized to move large masses of people. In addition to the Dallas-Ft. Worth airport, a new airport is planned in San Diego, next to the Mexican border. These airports have been designed with extra-thick runways, to accommodate giant 747 planes. The planes themselves, which have proved "impractical for civilian use," have just been purchased by the military, and are being remodeled for mass transport. Two large new prisons, costing over $186 million, are proposed for California. One will be located in San Diego, next to the "new airport." The proposed prisons in Vacaville and San Diego will specialize in "mental problems," turning inmates into zombies.[5]

Twelve and a half million acres of California desert land, stretching from the Mexican border near San Diego to the Sierra Nevada, have been secretly closed off to all vehicles. "Fear of dune buggies" was the cover story. There should be regular examination of this territory for new fences and structures of any kind.

A new $105-million hospital, the most expensive in the world, is being planned for Travis Air Force Base in California. It is located on 82 private acres, inaccessible to most people. It will include a revolutionary "one-room treatment center." Colonel Oliver C. Hood admitted that this "one-stop treatment, laboratory, drug dispensing examining room may be controversial

---

[5] Mae was right about the prisons. "High-security" prisons now dot the landscape; many are privately owned and operated. In fact, prisons are one of the few "growth industries" in the United States. The U.S. of Imprisonment now has the highest percentage of prison population in the world: 1 out of every 136 people in the United States is now in prison. A disproportionate number are minorities; a disproportionate number are in prison for "illegal use of drugs," even though drug use was largely introduced, and has been supported, and managed for profit by "organized crime" with the aid of elements of the U.S. Intelligence groups. That's one way of insuring that "undesirables" won't be able to vote.

and not universally accepted at this time." It might turn out to be an exterminating room instead.

The point should be made clear. Given enough violence, murders, and kidnappings in the U.S.A., the new hospitals, prisons, and airports will be used for mass genocide. There is nothing going on in our economy to assure housing, jobs, or education for minorities. Congress is impounding funds, cutting off school bussing, and denying legal aid for the poor. President Nixon is moving to reduce welfare funds drastically, at a time when job opportunities for minorities are scarce. All steps towards equal opportunity and racial progress are being halted.

Preceding the Hearst kidnapping in February, there was a series of carefully staged "senseless, motiveless" killings. They were blamed upon "cults." Persons who survived the murderous attacks described their assailants as "zombies." It was termed "Operation Zebra": meaning black versus white.

A series of so-called "Fillmore fires" took place before the killings. They were named after Fillmore Street in San Francisco—a street in a black part of town. CIA arsonists have been known to do such things as burn churches and set fire to buildings in order to blame "hippies." The association of minorities with murder and arson was achieved.

We are experiencing the importation of the dreaded "Operation Phoenix" program into the United States. William E. Colby, Director of the CIA, will conduct domestic paramilitary operations to demonstrate the apparent necessity for martial law. Through various created and manipulated acts of violence, the only "solution" to "chaos, anarchy, and senseless violent acts" will be a police state.

Colby's CIA specialty, the "Phoenix Operation" in Southeast Asia, was known for its torture, political assassinations, mass murders (20,000 to 40,000 civilians), tiger cages, rigged elections, and slanted intelligence.

The fact that this person was approved for appointment as Director of the CIA by a Senate vote of 83-13 indicates that the Senate both agrees with, and rewards, an agent of theirs for these acts against mankind.

It is no coincidence that the same Senate turned down a vote, after 25 years of stalling, on an agreement that would outlaw genocide as late as March, 1974.

A government that funds, promotes, recognizes, and allows war criminals to direct its domestic affairs reveals a total disrespect for our lives. This monster and its vicious machinery will now turn upon us at home.

The Hearst kidnapping is part of the Phoenix program inside the United States.

CARUANA: Is the Hearst kidnapping related to other political assassinations and conspiracies?

BRUSSELL: Yes. It is the most important domestic military action since the murder of President John Kennedy.

CARUANA: How are they related?

BRUSSELL: The killing of John Kennedy marked the overthrow of a government elected by the majority. It was also the signal for the beginning of a domestic "war" against minorities, students, and prisoners, and for the escalation of the war in Southeast Asia. The Hearst kidnapping is the beginning of the reign of terror on our streets. It is part of a deliberate campaign of terror. It will be used to justify larger private police forces, more repression, and larger prisons. There will be carefully orchestrated increased public distrust of blacks, Maoists, prisoners, lesbians, gays, hippies, radicals, communes, and genuine protesters, who will be described as terrorist guerrillas.

CARUANA: What about the spate of kidnappings that have suddenly occurred since the Hearst

kidnapping? Are they related?

BRUSSELL: The kidnapping of Reg Murphy, editor of the *Atlanta Constitution*, was supposed to be synchronized with the Hearst kidnapping. There is other evidence that the two events were planned by the same officials.

John Patterson, the American diplomat who was allegedly kidnapped in Mexico, was seen at a service station less then ten minutes after he drove away from the Consulate and "vanished." His car was chained to a camper truck, being towed away. Witnesses said he appeared "calm and not guarded," and Mexican authorities doubted the kidnap report.

Eunice Kronholm, the banker's wife from Minneapolis, came home laughing after her instant departure from a shopping center. Her husband paid $200,000 "ransom" to a group of three men who were not even charged with kidnapping.

There has been a series of faked "mini-kidnappings," similar to the rash of military-trained airplane hijackings a few years ago, which have led to the stationing of armed police guards and X-ray machines at every airport. Just because the media terms an event a "kidnapping" does not necessarily make it a kidnapping at all.

CARUANA: Are you saying that these are acts committed by provocateurs to create a climate of fear?

BRUSSELL: Of course. All the recent kidnappings were planned, funded and carried out by the same intelligence agencies. Once the people are terrorized, you can force a police state on them. *The San Francisco Chronicle* recently ran an article with the headline, "A Constant Watch on Radicals Urged." The article talks about a report made to a California Senate Subcommittee, based on the recommendations of a 63-page manual. Where did this manual come from? They don't even know who or what the SLA is yet, but the manual is already there, and the report is ready within five weeks of the Hearst kidnapping. They recommend increased security for homes and offices, a constant watch on "radicals" such as blacks, chicanos, and labor organizations, and a neighborhood spy on every block. This is Nazi Germany.

CARUANA: Attorney General William Saxbe suggested that the Hearst kidnapping could be part of a world-wide conspiracy. He cited various manuals and textbooks circulating among terrorist and revolutionary groups that have been examined by the FBI.

BRUSSELL: The structure for the book I am writing, *Murderville, U.S.A.*, is taken from a U.S. Armed Forces manual, printed in South Carolina, called Unconventional Warfare Operating Procedures. The U.S. military are being trained in counter-intelligence and domestic warfare. The parallels between our DIA and CIA operations are proof that military agents and provocateurs could cause economic chaos, social unrest, and domestic fear in the United States, using the identical methods that we have used overseas. There is a closer relationship between our National Security Council and its intelligence operations and Nazi military intelligence than there is between so-called "terrorist books" and the kidnappings taking place.

CARUANA: Three weeks before the Hearst kidnapping, Joseph Remiro and Russell Little were arrested and later charged with the murder of Oakland's Superintendent of schools, Dr. Marcus Foster. The SLA claimed the "credit" for this murder, and later for the Hearst kidnapping. What is the relationship between these events?

BRUSSELL: The purpose of the Foster murder was to establish the existence of the SLA. In October, 1973, the American Nazi Party was passing out leaflets in the San Leandro shopping center, outside Oakland, that stated, "There might be shotgun blasts into the guts of Mix Master principals and superintendents." Dr. Foster was black, and his co-worker and close friend, Mr. Blackburn, is white. A well-respected black educator was eliminated, and the murder was

associated with black radicals to spread terror among the community.

Two different kinds of bullets were used for the shootings, which allowed the white educator to live. But the black man never had a chance; the bullets that murdered him were tipped with cyanide.

The result was that when Patricia Hearst was kidnapped, it appeared that America's first political kidnapping was an act performed by already-existing militant forces.

Alioto's Zebras

CARUANA: There seems to have been a number of unexplained murders and senseless acts of violence in the San Francisco area recently. Do you think they are related to the Hearst kidnapping?

BRUSSELL: San Francisco Mayor Joseph Alioto hinted in a news conference on April 5 that he "suspects a possible relationship between the Patricia Hearst kidnapping and the city's recent wave of random slayings." And he said: "We'll have something to say about that matter next week, depending on the resolution of the Hearst case."

As long as Patricia Hearst, DeFreeze and Wheeler are alive, there is no way to link the SLA to the Bay Area murders, because they were not involved in any of them. But if the political patsies are killed, the law enforcement agents will associate a huge secret "army" and "cult" of blacks with all the murders.

Attorney General Evelle Younger, closely connected to the Los Angeles Police Department and the national and prison conspiracies that have existed for the past few years, has been strangely silent about the Hearst case. He announced that he would have "plenty to say" when it is all over. In order to whip up a synchronized smear of radicals, Younger and Alioto, along with Attorney General Saxbe in Washington, will link up all CIA intelligence operations involving terrorists, and blame them on an international radical conspiracy.

While the *Report of the Warren Commission* was being written, there was a problem about denying Jack Ruby's involvement in a conspiracy, and whether or not they could pass him off as a "lone killer." Commission member Burt Griffin wrote to Howard Willens on this matter, on August 4, 1964. He said, "The preface and conclusion state that the Commission has found no evidence that anyone assisted Jack Ruby in the shooting of Oswald. We have not conducted an investigation which would effectively exhaust the possibility that someone did assist Ruby even if the assistance was unwitting. Inasmuch as Ruby is still alive and will continue to dicker concerning his fate, [our emphasis] I think it is a mistake for the Commission to make any statement which would indicate that its investigation in that regard has been exhaustive."

The Mayor, the Attorney General, the F.B.I. and the police departments must keep mum and delay their propaganda until the killings are over. Nothing can be smeared more easily than a dead body.

Remiro & Little

CARUANA: The way Remiro and Little were captured seemed strange to me. They were driving around and around in a van at two o'clock in the morning, until a policeman came along and stopped them. They told him they were looking for the home of Mr. and Mrs. DeVoto.

BRUSSELL: They had SLA literature inside the van. Russell Little drove away in the van, and was captured by the police. Little had false identification papers indicating that his name was Robert Scalise. Joseph Remiro ran off and made it to his house, a few blocks away. The house had been rented by Remiro, under still another alias: George DeVoto. According to one newspaper

account, Remiro conferred with several other people in the house for several hours about what to do. One of the people in the house may have been Donald DeFreeze. The police were in the area, looking for Remiro, but they did not come to the "DeVoto" house.

The group inside the "safe house" agreed to "sacrifice" Remiro. He left the house to meet the police in the area. At the time, he wore a gun which was alleged to be the same gun used to kill Dr. Foster. The question is, since Remiro went to meet the police, why would he wear the murder weapon?

CARUANA: Do you think they were out to get busted?

BRUSSELL: It might be. Having two self-confessed "soldiers" in jail gave the nonexistent SLA a little more reality. It also linked the fictitious SLA to the prisons.

After Remiro and Little were arrested, they were put directly into San Quentin, a prison, without being tried or convicted. This is unheard-of. Nobody goes into a prison that way. Normally, accused prisoners are held in a jail. Then they are brought to trial.

One of the motives behind the Hearst conspiracy was to involve radical prisoners, and to suggest that those men, although behind bars, had some influence on the violence in the streets. The original script may have read that supposedly vicious black prisoners would avenge Foster's death by killing Remiro and Little while they were housed on death row. But prisoners sometimes show more compassion toward their comrades, black and white, than prison guards and intelligence agencies want to believe. They all got along, and helped each other.

The government underestimates the intelligence of prisoners, hippies, and minority group members. When Remiro and Little found themselves in San Quentin, they realized what was going on. They were chained up at night; they were dragged past the gas chamber on a special "tour," and were carried off by three carloads of FBI men for two hours to a "secret meeting place" without their lawyers present. Instead of being killed, Remiro and Little began to get an education. They ended up in the cells of some very educated and intelligent men, up on Death Row, who understood what was happening and who could sit and rap with them.

A very aware prisoner who was kept in one of the isolation cells at San Quentin wrote to me: "My keepers put two people back here with me. The Foster mess, you dig? Anyway, they are some beautiful people, and there was no reason at all for the establishment to take them out of the Adjustment Center and put them up here, in the quiet [isolation] cells, of all places. The officials don't like it, really, because all of us get along so good with each other. But you know how that goes."

When Remiro and Little realized that they had become patsies, they tried to get a message across to DeFreeze: "Release Patty Hearst." Remiro and Little may have realized that the whole SLA idea—the murder and the kidnapping—had been staged under the direction of intelligence agents.

Lee Harvey Oswald recognized that he was being framed immediately after his arrest. He lived only long enough to say, "I am a patsy," and "I didn't kill anybody." Remiro and Little wanted to prevent the climax of the plot from taking place: the murder of Patty Hearst. They got the message through, in spite of official obstacles.

How the CIA Invented the SLA

CARUANA: Are you saying there is no such thing as the SLA?

BRUSSELL: The SLA "army" was a fabrication of the CIA to make a small group of people believe they had the support of "radicals", and could become heroes. This entire production was staged to create the impression that all clandestine intelligence operations, in India, the Philippines, Ethiopia, South America, Africa, Mexico etc., are the work of one united "radical" front, instead

of the work of well-paid secret agencies of our own government.

Some kidnappings actually do take place for political reasons. This has not yet happened inside the U.S.A.

The Hearst kidnapping can be recognized for what it is by the methods it uses; they are all part of every past CIA operation. There is a tendency to simplify the culprits, such as trying to blame the CIA alone for the Watergate affair, or other political assassinations and conspiracies. The fact is that the Pentagon, all branches of the armed forces, and the combined intelligence agencies work together in these plots. Extermination, murder, mutilation, electrode implants, and torture are a continuation of policies begun in Nazi Germany and imported into the United States during and after World War II.

America is basically a racist country. It is obvious that we do not intend to utilize one of our greatest resources, our minority groups, within the system. Because the CIA is responsible for their links with known Nazis, I blame them for the "zombie killings" and the California murders, as well as other mass murders across the nation.

Victor Marchetti, who left the CIA after sixteen years, is exposing some of their clandestine operations. He warned that "the CIA is targeting groups in this country that they feel are subversive." The specialty of Mr. Colby's CIA has been to create chaos and social upheaval.

CARUANA: What are the links of the CIA, and the "fictitious SLA," to the prison system?

BRUSSELL: I have been studying political assassinations and conspiracies for ten years. I have an intimate acquaintance with all of these agencies: their personnel, funding, history, dummy front organizations and methods of operation. For the past several years, I have broadened my research into the prison system. It is necessary to understand the use of prisons and prisoners to conceal political murders. The name "Hitler" is synonymous with prisons, because without a sophisticated prison system, Fascism would be no different from a democracy.

CARUANA: But what would be the purpose of creating the SLA?

BRUSSELL: The fear of the ruling class is that underdeveloped nations and third-world people have begun to demand that attention be paid to their basic needs, such as food, health and education. And the population explosion means that more people must be "provided for" by the small handful that makes up the ruling class. To maintain power and what some people consider a "fair" degree of profit from their investments, whether in oil, minerals, industry or agriculture, the elimination of large masses of people would mean they would have fewer people to deal with.

The average person would not permit or condone genocide, gas chambers or mass extermination unless he felt personally threatened. Terror is purposely spread in the communities by pitting blacks against blacks, blacks against whites, Chicanos against blacks and whites, and prisoners against the communities on the outside. Decreasing the population by drastic measures, instigated through fear, begins to seem feasible and even desirable.

The Man Who Cried 'I Am', a novel by John Williams, includes what is supposed to be a National Security Council document on the systematic planned genocide of all blacks in America. Black leaders today fear, and with good reason, that the "King Alfred Plan" is not fiction.

The Senate Select Committee and other Congressional investigations have remained silent about James McCord's position in relation to the military departments that would be utilized for a police state. Captain Richard L. Franz, Naval Reserve, said McCord was a member of the Office of Emergency Preparedness. This special division met monthly to develop a list of radicals and contingency plans for censorship of news and U.S. mail in the "event of war." That did not rule out civil war.

CARUANA: The romantic and obviously artificial style of the SLA "manifestoes" talked about uniting all kinds of people: Blacks, Indians, Chicanos and so on. Do you think this was done to associate all these groups with kidnappings and murders, in order to justify their extermination later on?

BRUSSELL: Yes; and the media will continue to spread these messages of fear until we expose these early para-military operations for what they are.

CARUANA: To spread terror, make people distrust each other, and deliberately create the conditions for a police state…it is difficult to believe that such planning and execution can be going on. This type of activity is so far outside the sphere of most people's lives and desires as to be almost unthinkable.

Planned Genocide

BRUSSELL: Just read your morning paper, and see what is taking place in India, Ethiopia, Africa, Southeast Asia, and South America. Ethiopia is exporting food, while one million Ethiopians are starving. If the Ethiopians are eliminating huge masses of their population, we could do the same thing. One article in this morning's paper stated that the "famine in Ethiopia is bringing prosperity."

With scarcities of food, water and energy, riots and murders begin to take place that seem to call for punishment of the most "violent" kind. The evidence of planned genocide is there, right in front of us.

CARUANA: It is true that what seem to be artificially created scarcities of gasoline and food staples such as meat and grain have forced prices up to a point where it is becoming more and more difficult for people to feed themselves and their families. "Famine" is a word that couldn't be used in polite society to refer to conditions in democratic, prosperous, freedom-loving America; but it is easy to see how these present conditions could be pushed slightly further, to the point where it would become impossible for large masses of people to obtain enough food. But we seem to be straying from the subject of the Hearst kidnapping.

BRUSSELL: Keep in mind that the Hearst script is only the beginning. Wait and see what follows. The SLA demanded that there be food give-aways by Hearst in Oakland. Why Oakland, specifically? It has a largely black population. The "poor" were lined up for food distribution. The bags of food were thrown at them from trucks. A suggestion was made by Governor Reagan that they should be fed "botulism." The stage is set here for looking at hungry people and insulting them for their lack of "appreciation"…and their acceptance of bags of cabbages disguised as steaks.

CARUANA: Did the FBI know where Patricia Hearst was all along?

BRUSSELL: The FBI has been behind every "domestic conspiracy" for the past thirty years. The intelligence agencies provided the safe houses, the agents, the weapons, and the funding.

The fictitious SLA "army" numbers 25 people at most. And it is not an "army" at all. Their salaries, their cars, their copy machines and their cyanide bullets are paid for by the same secret military agencies that funded Oswald, Sirhan, Bremer, James Earl Ray, and other "conspirators", or relatively naïve participants in government-planned "conspiracies." It takes several launderings of cash before it reaches the hands of many agents. Some are in the army; others are teachers, and others work voluntarily, not knowing they are part of a larger plot.

The Media Cooperate

CARUANA: What was the role of the media in the Hearst kidnapping?

BRUSSELL: From a "public relations" point of view, it was a beautiful scheme to abduct the

daughter of the famous Hearst family, known for their newspaper chain. Because she was a member of this family, her kidnapping is immediate front-page news all over the country. It costs $30,000 to buy one minute of advertising, but they get all the minute-by-minute prime time publicity for their U.S.-funded domestic terrorism campaigns free.

Ben Maidenburg, of Akron, Ohio, is the publisher of a newspaper. On March 6, 1974, a group calling itself the American Revolutionary Army made an extortion threat to WJW-TV and WAJR-TV in Cleveland, threatening to kidnap Maidenburg and his son, and demanding that $2 million be given to "feed the poor." It is exactly the scenario of the SLA "plot" in Oakland, and it came from the same government intelligence operations planning desk that created the SLA, and for the same reasons.

Lawrence Kwong made an assassination attempt against Jim Dunbar, a well-known radio personality in San Francisco. Kwong held a weapon up to a glass window at KGO, while Dunbar was on the air. The alarming statement that a killer was at the window went out over the radio. Then Kwong went inside the building, and killed an employee named Ben Munsen. Following that, he ran down the street and committed suicide. There is good reason to believe that Kwong was surgically programmed, drugged, and/or hypnotized to commit this violence. Secrecy regarding his purchase of the weapon, his previous hospital care, his trip to Hawaii, and his autopsy strongly suggest a conspiracy. The "official" investigation was hushed up, and left more room for doubts than questions answered.

The pattern has been set. The media is geared to expect more kidnappings and wild "cult" murders. They can now kidnap any person at all, not media-related, and receive instant coverage. People are now being kidnapped at random, to spread terror even further. The message is that no one is safe, rich or poor, princess or pauper.

CARUANA: Another result of a wave of kidnappings might be that people would get used to the idea that other people can suddenly vanish. People who are considered hostile or dangerous to the system could be picked off at will, and it would be explained as "just another kidnapping."

BRUSSELL: This serves as an alternative to some of the recent elaborate plane crashes, involving the deaths of hundreds of innocent people, which have been arranged to disguise the murder of one or more people aboard who were the real targets. There seems to be official secrecy as to how Mrs. Howard Hunt's plane was downed. Was it in order to end, or at least control, demands for blackmail money made to the White House?

CARUANA: The mass media seems to come up with glib, quick answers to all these puzzling events. Key figures are rubbed out while surrounded by thousands of people and "security guards," and the media quickly goes into the "Lone Assassin Chorus." Watergate was instantly declared by the press to be a "third-rate burglary;" crucial potential witnesses like Murray Chotiner and William Knowland die mysteriously, and their deaths are immediately proclaimed suicides or accidents.

BRUSSELL: The usual pattern is for the media to reveal about half of the story. The other half—such as evidence that conspiracies exist—is carefully covered up. Only enough is "revealed" to program the public, convince them they are being told what is going on, confuse them, and throw them off the track.

An important ingredient in the military kidnapping operation was the SLA's insistence that Patricia's life depended on publication by the media of so-called "radical" tracts. The newspapers and radio were filled with insults and threats to the "fascist ruling class," the "corporate insect that preys on the people." They listed the financial holdings of Randolph Hearst, an act which would make any corporate burglar jump right through the roof.

CARUANA: The millionaires are getting scared. They are hiring private police to act as personal bodyguards. I understand that the Wackenhut Corporation, a large private police force with headquarters in Florida, headed by a "retired" FBI agent, reports that business is booming, and they are having a hard time keeping up with the demand for their services. The average working person probably wishes he could afford to hire a bodyguard too, but will probably be glad to settle for "free" police protection.

BRUSSELL: The Shah of Iran was mentioned in one of the early SLA communiques. The purpose was to link the oil rulers to U.S. and international terrorist groups. With former CIA chief Richard Helms now stationed in Iran, many provocateur actions in the Middle East and Europe will be associated with the SLA in San Francisco. Listing the investments and the worth of Hearst's possessions has made other greedy feudal lords even more anxious to keep the knowledge of the extent of their fortunes from the public. International police will continue to discredit the poor through planned acts of violence, while multiplying the weapons which guard fortunes and investments.

The DeFreeze Story

CARUANA: Where does Donald DeFreeze fit into the Hearst conspiracy?

BRUSSELL: De Freeze was selected to be a patsy several years ago by the Los Angeles Police Department. He had a long police record of arrests: for stealing 200 guns, for shooting a policeman, and for allegedly making bombs. But he never seemed to get put in jail for these crimes. The L.A.P.D. had enough on him to keep him in jail for the rest of his life, if they wanted to. I refer to such men, who have criminal records but are let out on parole, and who are completely at the mercy of the police department, as "yo-yos," because they are kept on a string and can be pulled back into jail at any time.

Somebody in law enforcement finally decided it was time to "use" Donald DeFreeze. He was suddenly convicted on various charges in 1969, and sent to Vacaville prison on a 6-to-14-year sentence.

DeFreeze received extensive psychological testing. He comes from a broken home, has been on the street since he was thirteen, and is divorced. He is highly intelligent; he understands law and represented himself in court. The L.A.P.D. reports describe him as "a man who lacks an identity."

The criminal conspiracy section of the L.A.P.D., described by Louis Tackwood in his book, *The Glass House Tapes*, sent DeFreeze to the California Medical Facility, at Vacaville prison, which is famous for its behavior modification programs.

Since DeFreeze had been certified by the L.A.P.D. as a man who "had no identity of his own," the behavior modification people at Vacaville decided to give him one. They profiled him after Ruchell Magee, a student of law, a black man who is serving time at San Quentin prison. DeFreeze took the name of "Cinque," a black slave leader, which was also Magee's chosen name for himself.

CARUANA: How would you go about giving a black man a new identity in the California prison system in 1969?

BRUSSELL: A "Black Cultural Association" (BCA) was formally "recognized" by prison officials at Vacaville in 1969. "Tutors" from the community were allowed to come into the program. Various newspaper articles state that the purpose of the "tutors" was "to help inmates with academic subjects, and to introduce new subjects dealing with black culture, such as black and African history." The "tutors" were to help black inmates "understand themselves" and prepare for outside relationships when they were released.

DeFreeze, sent to Vacaville on a 6-to-14-year sentence, and an important member of the new Black Cultural Association, was hardly thinking about, or eligible for, parole. After his conviction on charges of stealing weapons and shooting a policeman, there is no possible way that DeFreeze would be encouraged or permitted to get revolutionary training while in the regular California prison system in the normal course of events.

In those days, Chief Warden Nelson at San Quentin, was saying, "No one can shake hands with a man who has his fist clenched over his head." And Raymond Procunier, Director of the California State Department of Corrections, proudly announced, "If we find a group out there preaching revolution, and we think it's dangerous, we lock them up."

Why would the California prison system, hell-bent on eliminating all radicals and creating conspiracies to separate and segregate potential leaders, sponsor tutors teaching Maoist doctrine and revolutionary ideas to a new recruit—and in Vacaville, of all places? And why bend DeFreeze's and Wheeler's ears with talk about Dr. Marcus Foster, the evil black school superintendent in Oakland, when DeFreeze and Wheeler were not even eligible for parole for many years? Since 1961, J. Edgar Hoover had been sending memos to all the top FBI leaders around the country, ordering them to disrupt any potential racial movements, and to prevent the emergence of a black Messiah who would be able to unite his people.

CARUANA: What kind of tutors would be instructing prisoners in radical politics?

BRUSSELL: White racists; what other kind? Who are Remiro and Little? Who is Colston Westbrook, the black man who headed the Black Cultural Association at Vacaville? DeFreeze, also known as "Cinque," described Westbrook, his teacher, as "a member of the CIA intelligence, and part of the deadly Phoenix program in Vietnam." The similarities between the terrorization going on in Asia and what is now happening in the San Francisco Bay area are too striking to take this charge lightly. William E. Colby, now Chief of CIA operations in the United States, formerly headed the Phoenix program in Vietnam. We can expect the planned terrorization of the U.S. population to escalate rapidly.

Westbrook was mistrusted by even the straight press when he gave them an interview. He served seven years in the military: three in the Army, and four in the Air Force, including four years in Korea. He told the *Daily Californian* that in 1965, he went to the American Embassy in Tokyo to "try to get some veteran's benefits," and was offered "ten grand to go to Vietnam." He spent five years in Vietnam and Cambodia, "doing all sorts of things." When one reporter asked him exactly what he did in Vietnam, he said, "I was working on contracts for an architectural firm."

The Watergate exposures documented how Miami architects were offered huge amounts of money, all from the CIA, coming from the White House, to supply crucial plans of rooms and air conditioning vents in the rooms where the 1972 Convention nominations would take place. Governments can be overthrown and regimes can be toppled if palace entrances are known and sealed off. There are other advantages, from a military point of view, of knowing architectural entrances and exits; i.e., Robert Kennedy's fatal walk through the kitchen pantry at the Ambassador Hotel in Los Angeles.

Westbrook said he had a "personal line of communication with the Premier of Cambodia." DeFreeze and Wheeler, black prisoners, must have been proud of their elite instructor, who visited them every week, twice a week, for two years.

The Daily Californian reported: "Newsmen present were puzzled by Westbrook. Some thought it was just an ego trip. Others went away with all sorts of uncomfortable suspicions."

Florida's former governor, Claude Kirk, ran a campaign a few years ago from Miami, which

included threats to "break the University of California." The day after Ronald Reagan and Claude Kirk were elected Governors of the two states, they met for lunch in Los Angeles. On the following day, Clark Kerr, President of the then-outstanding University of California, was fired, with absolutely no notice, and no severance pay.

Kirk was also the first Governor in the United States to hire a private police force—the same Wackenhut group whose contracts have increased following the Hearst kidnapping. A spokesman for the group said that thirty-eight requests for information about protection had been received in a 24-hour period.

George Wackenhut, head of the Corporation, put it so well: "The days of the open, relaxed American way of life are over."

CARUANA: Is that what the Patricia Hearst kidnapping is all about?

BRUSSELL: Exactly. There was a mass migration of at least eight out-of-state people to Berkeley. Willie Wolfe came from Pennsylvania in 1971, but was not known to have any interest in blacks before he went west. Russell Little and Robyn Steiner migrated to Berkeley in the fall of 1972, from Florida. Emily and Bill Harris and Angela and Gary Atwood all came from Indiana, in the fall of 1972. California prisons were suddenly exploding with racial violence and imported provocateurs. Why were out-of-state agents brought in to stir up more trouble? What social and political background did these people have to qualify them to enter the California prisons?

All these white "migratory birds" became involved in helping DeFreeze get his "black education." After the kidnapping of Patricia Hearst, they split, and have not been seen since. Incredible, and impossible—and identical to all the previous conspiracies I have studied. They suddenly cropped up in the California prisons; they all lived near each other; and after their assignment was over, they simply melted back into the woodwork, going on to other cities, other jobs, other schools. The media said they "vanished."

This reminds me of another white "do-gooder" who was involved in the untimely and tragic death of prisoner George Jackson at San Quentin. Stephen Bingham provided the excuse for what was to be a big shoot-out, following his visit with Jackson. Bingham was last seen, after leaving San Quentin, visiting with his uncle, Woodridge Bingham, who served in the U.S. Navy, with Naval Intelligence, and the O.S.S. (Office of Strategic Services), the forerunner of the CIA, from 1943-1945. Were there military connections behind the long imprisonment of the victims of this conspiracy?

While in prison, Donald DeFreeze was told he could become a hero to the poor, oppressed minorities. He was surrounded by military intelligence.

CARUANA: Are mind control, psychosurgery, or hypnotism used in political assassinations and conspiracies?

BRUSSELL: The extent and scope of these methods of ordering behavior and erasing memory, following these acts of murder, has to be exposed. You can erase the memory of a murder from a person's mind through hypnosis. You can also implant the conviction that a man has committed a murder, when in fact, he has not.

This happened in the assassination of Robert F. Kennedy, where it was suggested to Sirhan Sirhan, by his psychiatrist, how he had killed Robert Kennedy.

It is vital that we scrutinize what sort of "treatment" is going on in our hospitals and prisons. If the "King Alfred Plan" is to be put into effect, it requires secrecy. Including the prison system in the race-war kidnapping script provides an excuse to keep "outside visitors" out of the prison system. The official excuse will be that they are causing violence inside the prison, or that violence from inside the prison is "spilling out on the streets." Through the planned use of

selected provocateurs, the Department of Corrections can now screen prisoners' mail, visitors, media interviews, and accessibility to medical records.

CARUANA: DeFreeze and Wheeler both escaped from California prisons within a short time of each other. That seemed a little peculiar to me. Do you find any similarities between the prison escapes of DeFreeze, Wheeler, and James Earl Ray?

A Staged Escape

BRUSSELL: After two years of heavy programming, DeFreeze's mentors at Vacaville apparently decided that he was ready for the next step in the script: his "escape." DeFreeze was transferred from Vacaville to Soledad Prison, near Salinas, California in December, 1972. Four months later, in March, 1973, DeFreeze "escaped" from Soledad. But using the word "escape" is misleading; the facts are that DeFreeze was placed in a situation at Soledad where all he had to do was to walk away from the prison.

DeFreeze's "escape" from Soledad parallels James Earl Ray's "escape" from the Missouri penitentiary. Eighteen months later, Ray became the alleged assassin of Martin Luther King. Ray was a patsy too. Now Ray seems to want to tell the truth about the assassination of Martin Luther King. One of the things he said in a recent press conference was, "Ask them how I got out of jail."

A prisoner in Soledad Prison wrote to me, "While Donald DeFreeze was here, I had a few conversations with him. I have always questioned his departure as being a simple walk-away. I didn't come in contact with him personally until his last couple of weeks here. There weren't many who would associate with him. He tried to give the impression of being super-cool, and he came across as cold. When I met him, he was working in the maintenance shop. I asked him if he was happy on his job, because if not, I might be able to find him something else. He replied that within a few days he was going to be assigned to work in the boiler room at the South Facility.

"On his first night on the job at the South Facility he was dropped off at midnight, and given a few instructions. His job was automatic; it only required an overseer. Then he was left to himself, and when an officer returned an hour later to check on him, he was gone."

CARUANA: First night on the job!

BRUSSELL: He went right over the fence, and a change of clothing was provided for him by a still anonymous friend. I might add that most of the residents around Soledad are families of prison guards. They are not noted for giving changes of clothing to black convicts who come to their doors between midnight and 1:00 a.m. A car picked him up outside of the prison and gave him a lift to the Bay area. Another convenience: Amanda de Normanville, who reportedly had visited DeFreeze at Vacaville, "was suspected of giving him refuge after he escaped from Soledad."

Now let's say that an intelligent man escapes from prison. Ordinarily, he would assume that the authorities would be looking for him. He would certainly not associate with people who had been known to visit him in prison. He would try to avoid contact with these people. Russell Little and Robyn Steiner had corresponded with the Department of Corrections about DeFreeze.

But DeFreeze did just the opposite of what you might expect. He phoned his pals in the Berkeley-Oakland area immediately. They housed him. He associated with his "tutors" from Vacaville, who had various part-time jobs in the Berkeley area. All of them were "underemployed" in terms of their educational background. Two of them worked in adjacent food stalls near the U.C. Berkeley campus, yet supposedly they did not know each other.

After DeFreeze's escape, the police made no attempt to contact any of the people he had spent

so much time with while he was at Vacaville. To me this indicates police collusion.

DeFreeze escaped from Soledad in March, 1973. Patty Hearst was kidnapped one year later. During the year in between, DeFreeze tried to join Los Venceremos, offering himself as a "hit man." Venceremos turned him down. They did not trust him; and they were not into killing and violence. The radical groups in the Bay area wanted nothing to do with DeFreeze.

CARUANA: I can't understand where DeFreeze's head was at this time. Did he know he was acting as a government agent? Had he accepted the role of Spy, in order to get out of jail? If so, then he couldn't really believe he was going to be a hero; he would know the whole operation was staged to hurt black people. He must have been aware that his jail break had been planned and engineered for him.

BRUSSELL: DeFreeze was probably given a large hero pitch—probably something to the effect that the abduction of Patricia Hearst would rally the radical groups and cause them to become socially involved once more. Violence by provocateurs had broken up all political movements following the Kent State killings and the bombing of Cambodia.

He accepted the favors given to him by the L.A.P.D. and the Department of Corrections. I am sure "Cinque" thought there was a large army of sympathetic people outside who would back him up.

The L.A.P.D. had fore-knowledge of the Marin County Courthouse shoot-out, where Judge Haley was killed and others were wounded—and I don't mean fore-knowledge of the psychic variety. Jonathan Jackson, the patsy, had been promised a back-up, and another truck to assist him to free the captive prisoners. But when the action started, nobody was there to help him, and Jonathan Jackson was slain. So-called "friends" can leave their patsies in the lurch, as in the case of Lee Harvey Oswald. It would appear that Jackson and other escapees and hostages were all patsies in what was essentially an attempt to convict Angela Davis of murder for having procured the guns used by Jackson.

Eight months after the killing of Oswald, Jack Ruby begged Chief Justice Earl Warren, Representative Gerald Ford, and CIA attorney Leon Jaworski to give him a chance to tell about what really happened in Dallas. Ruby realized that he had been double-crossed, and warned that if he were not heeded, "a whole new form of government would take place." He said, "Because of the act I committed, there will be massive killings and violence." But Ruby was never given the chance to tell his story; he died shortly after this interview.

DeFreeze knew how to get out of prison, where to go, and how to live for almost a year without being arrested. He was provided with homes, food, weapons, transportation, and companions. At the Berkeley Library he and his buddies copied drawings of a seven-headed cobra, used in SLA literature, which had also been used as a symbol by black CIA agent Ron Karenga and the L.A.P.D. (**Note:** This scenario appears in the 1969 novel, *The Spook Who Sat By the Door*, by Sam Greenlee. In the novel Dan Freedman, the first black CIA agent, defects to organize a secret guerrilla army, known as the Cobras.)

Russell Little, a close associate of DeFreeze and well-known to the Department of Corrections, both at Vacaville and Soledad, was arrested on charges of killing Dr. Marcus Foster on January 11, 1974. The law enforcement officials had three weeks in which to link suspect Little to prison escapee DeFreeze.

The proof of a giant conspiracy is that no police went to search for Little's or DeFreeze's other mutual contacts in the weeks before the Hearst kidnapping. The "instructors" had talked frequently about Dr. Marcus Foster while "instructing inside the prisons." Yet nobody looked into the various Bay area dwellings where their companions were getting ready for "America's

first political kidnapping."

These military agents presented themselves to DeFreeze as romantic Robin Hoods. When the heat was on, they split.

After two months of public anxiety regarding Patty Hearst, a photograph and tape were sent out to further outrage middle America. This lovely girl, who only two months before had been happily selecting her china in anticipation of a traditional wedding, was publicly calling her father a "liar," holding a machine gun, promising to fight alongside of her "brothers and sisters" in the SLA, and denouncing her fiance and family.

Tension was building in the San Francisco Bay area. Was Patty really a member of the SLA? Had she been forced to renounce her background? Was she making love to DeFreeze? How far would the establishment go in allowing such a display of arrogance? And how dumb can the American people be?

Patty's Fate

The media, the Hearst family, and the public are being fed the propaganda that the terrorists may have brainwashed Patty Hearst. Nobody considers the fact that the CIA and the intelligence establishment could brainwash Patty, as they have the many other people, or victims, used in their conspiracies.

We are going to see a great number of articles in the future from so-called experts and public officials. They will warn about more violence, more kidnappings, and more terrorists.

Mass media, the armed forces, and intelligence agencies will saturate our lives with fascist scare tactics and "predictions" that have been pre-planned to come true.

Whether Patty Hearst will be allowed to live, or whether she is murdered, is no longer important in the general game plan. The scare tactics, armed forces in the streets, prolonged anger against her abduction, and fear for the future safety of others, is moving along well.

CARUANA: The majority of citizens believe radicals have been responsible for these acts of violence. Is there any way we can halt this devastating process?

BRUSSELL: It is the American fantasy that our President was not assassinated by a planned conspiracy in Dallas. Only "lone assassins" are capable of this act. It is the same fantasy that conspiracies don't kill our own citizens, including the daughter of one of the team. What links the future murders to past murders is a chain of evidence that becomes easier to identify with every criminal act.

All that is required to halt this madness is enough aroused citizens to examine the evidence of government complicity and conspiracy in this case.

***

NOTE: *"February, 1974: Mafia Hearst's daughter Patty was "kidnapped" by Hal Lipset's SLA—in a fake terrorist action."-Skeleton Key. I agree with author Gerald Carroll, who in his excellent book: Project Seek: Onassis, Kennedy and the Gemstone Thesis, expounded upon this sentence as: "Hal Lipset has simply denied any connection with the so-called Symbionese Liberation Army (SLA), which we feel staged a series of events—including the Patricia Hearst "kidnapping"—designed to take media pressure off the red-hot, ongoing Watergate revelations. The time frame for the Hearst kidnapping brings it within the midst of the Watergate turmoil, and only after Patricia Hearst was reunited with her family did the media spotlight again turn to Nixon, who resigned soon thereafter...."-Project Seek, p.273-4.*

Gerry's book is simply the best book yet available on the Gemstone Skeleton Key. Here, he points out that the whole Hearst kidnapping was designed to distract public attention from the important political events going on simultaneously—namely, Watergate and the dissolution of Nixon's Presidency.

We see the same pattern again and again. The "major news sources", both TV and Newspapers, have evolved to serve only as "amusement," providing "bread and circuses" instead of news. They leap with unanimous calculated enthusiasm on one or another dreadful event or murder, and bombard us to the point of euthanasia by bored surfeit, while sweeping the "real news" into a cobwebbed corner.

Frequently the "horrible event of choice" chosen for such distraction from important events is performed by a "free-lancer," i.e., a murderous member of the public who is only doing his own thing, like Scott Peterson or O.J. Simpson. But there are apparently a few prepared scenarios ready to be popped on the public when the time is right (that is, when a MAJOR DISTRACTION from significant news is deemed necessary, or when a major attack on our "relaxed" way of life is about to get under way. Example: 9/11, which obviously could have been prevented, if it wasn't in fact pre-planned and staged, and wired, with the help of a well-known controlled demolition company in addition to the hijacked planes. This tragic disaster has led to our acceptance of a continued "war" on any chosen target, preferably one with lots of oil and not too many defenses; the Patriot act, a massive assault on our freedom; armed guards and the massive destruction of our right to travel by air without search and seizure on any, or no excuse, etc., etc.). The Hearst kidnap scenario appears to be one of these planned scenarios.. The "planning" must have included the public murders at the end, which puts it into a special category of cold-blooded murder designed to terrorize the public. There is no way that Donald DeFreeze would have been allowed to survive to tell his version of what happened, and why.

Although Mae was a dedicated researcher and worked like a dog on obtaining and filing information, it seems to me that she had her limits as to interpretation. As she stated in this article, she believed that Patty Hearst may have been "doomed to die," and was not Media Mogul Hearst's "contribution" to this media event. I agreed with Mae at the time we prepared this article. but since then I have come to suspect that Patty was never in serious danger. Her CIA handlers were apparently always on hand to supervise and control the situation. One question that I have is whether a truly alarmed millionaire dad like Hearst would have staged a media food give-away for the TV cameras and the public, but risked the rage of Patty's captors and the Oakland recipients of the cabbage-head "largesse" as he did. A growing suspicion that Mae's interpretations were not the whole story is why I chose to move out from under her wing and follow the lead she gave me to Bruce Roberts. Her later lies about and suppression of her portion of the Gemstone File seem to me to support this impression.

During the week that followed the publication of this article in the Berkeley Barb, the "Symbionese Liberation Army" was apparently hastily moved from the Bay area to a "safe house" in Los Angeles. The timing suggests that this may have been done after a top-level decision to "liquidate" the operation. The LAPD had just initiated its now-famous "SWAT Team" operation, for domestic liquidation of Americans. This would be their first "wet" operation. Apparently, after a couple of months of living unmolested in a Berkeley apartment, the SLA suddenly got an urge to move from the San Francisco Bay area to the Los Angeles area. So they piled into their handy government-issue van and drove to Los Angeles. There they found a "safe house" available to them, with no immediate problems with the police, or the SWAT Team. When all was ready, the "raid" occurred. The press was notified in advance, so news cameras were all lined up and ready to go. The media event was a prequel to Waco, another public slaughter of American citizens, this one including innocent children.

It is quite possible that the "SLA" sacrificial group were either drugged or poisoned shortly before the deadly SWAT Team assault, via a large fried chicken take-out order that wended its way unmolested through the thick screen of police and "intelligence" watchers around the "safe house." The fried chicken order passed through the circle of guns and fire bombs without any moves from the SWAT Team. After the "chicken" order arrived, there was a long pause. Finally, one more figure emerged from the house and departed, also unmolested. It's not a far reach to consider the possibility that this last "survivor" had arranged the bodies, unconscious or perhaps already dead, before departing from the house just before the slaughter began. Patty Hearst had been taken out of the house by two of her CIA "handlers" to a place of safety, and Cinque and the rest of the SLA patsies were then shot and burned to a crisp by the Los Angeles Police Department "SWAT Team." That may be why the dead bodies were lined up in "battle formation" when the flames died down, but

there was no defensive fire from the safe house before or during the attack. No one escaped; no one moved. No one fired a shot from the house; the fireworks were all incoming, with the SLA "Army" perhaps unconscious or dead, for the final tableau.

As it happened, I watched the final assault, live, in the middle of the day, on a TV set in a laundromat window in Berkeley which I happened to be passing. The news media had been alerted beforehand, so TV cameras were on hand to film the entire thing. That's planning for you!!!! It's hard to avoid the suspicion that our article nipped the "SLA" saga in the bud, and that the people who had planned and carried out the "kidnapping" and dramatic use of Patty Hearst in this hideous scenario decided to cut the drama short and thus end any investigation into the reality behind the "terrorist" plot. A year later, in March 1975, my original Gemstone Skeleton Key described the whole Patty Hearst/SLA affair in one pithy sentence: February, 1974: Mafia Hearst's daughter Patty "kidnapped" by Hal Lipset's SLA—in a fake terrorist action."

3 *Playgirl* Magazine:
Is Howard Hughes Dead and Buried Off a Greek Island?

At this time, I was writing a monthly column for *Playgirl* called "About Women." I suggested to Editor-in-Chief Marin Milam that Mae Brussell might be an interesting subject for the next column. She agreed, and I wrote the article. It appeared in the August 1974 issue. [I have omitted it due to lack of space.]

Marin was pleased with the column and interested in Mae Brussell. She was intrigued by what I told her of Mae's roomful of filing cabinets, filled to overflowing with carefully sorted and filed copies of news articles, books and other papers on a wide variety of political events going back to the JFK assassination in 1963. She felt, as I did, that this was a potential mine of information for articles or books. And since I had been providing major articles for the magazine for over a year, she felt confident of my ability to write articles that were well-written and interesting.

Mae was intrigued by the prospect of substantially increasing the size of her readership. Her earliest and best-known articles, on Watergate, had appeared in Paul Krassner's *Realist*, shortly after the break-in in May, 1972. Because of her voluminous files, she was able to put together background information on all of the people arrested in what was being called in the "establishment" media a "third-rate burglary." And because Paul Krassner was willing to publish Mae's articles, in effect, she had "scooped" the whole country. The major media obediently followed the networks' "third-rate burglary" story. They were so busy covering up the reality of Watergate, that they were glacially slow to follow.

The Realist was well-known as an *avant garde* satirical "underground" magazine with a relatively small but fairly sophisticated audience. But *Playgirl* had zoomed within the space of a year to a circulation of over 2,000,000.

I was excited at the prospect of moving into the area of politically oriented writing. I had already written a number of research-based articles. For each of these, I had a tendency to do enough research to write a book. I greatly appreciated the depth and thoroughness of Mae's well-stuffed file folders, accumulated over a 10-year period *SLA slaughter house.*, since JFK's assassination in 1963. In return for access to those files, I was quite willing to split writing credits and payment with Mae. However, it was clearly understood by all of us that I would do the actual writing.

All that remained was to settle on a topic.

I was staying temporarily in Mae's tiny guest room, in her secluded house in Carmel Valley, about a hundred miles south of San Francisco. I got on the phone with Marin in Los Angeles, and we began to kick around various ideas for articles.

Marin said, "Ask Mae whether she knows anything about Howard Hughes."

It was an interesting topic. At the time, which was mid-1974, the media often speculated on Hughes, his where-abouts, the state of his health and that of his vast business enterprises, and the strange goings-on among his "friends" and employees—most of whom, supposedly, had never seen him. Was his beard really as long as Methuselah's, and if so, how was he managing his gambling empire in Los Angeles, as well as his airlines and defense contracts?

Mae replied immediately: "Howard Hughes is dead. Onassis kidnapped him. Hughes was buried at sea three years ago, off Onassis's island, Skorpios."

I stared at her in amazement.

She said, "Onassis grabbed him in 1957, and he died in 1971."

I turned back to the phone and repeated this astonishing statement to Marin.

Marin was excited. This would indeed be a hot story—IF Mae had the information to back it up, and IF I could complete the article in time. On this premise she committed to the article, and to making it the lead article for the December, 1974 issue.

I had already written a number of excellent articles for *Playgirl* before this, and Marin had by this time no doubt that I would be able to write a successful article. On my part, I had no doubt that Mae had some definite proof, or at least, some strong indications that the bizarre scenario she had outlined was true. I wish to add that Mae and I were indeed a "team", at least for this article, but the team members had very different functions. Mae's function was to supply the research materials; my function was to do the writing and organizing.

We set to work at once. It was a rush job, with little time before the deadline. Mae pulled out a thick file folder of magazine and newspaper clippings on Howard Hughes, and another thick file folder on Onassis, together with other clippings, and handed them to me.

I started reading and taking notes. But after several days of intensely searching through the files, I saw no evidence of Mae's statement that Onassis had kidnapped Howard Hughes, and the rest of it. Finally I said, "Mae, I don't see it. I see articles about Hughes and about Onassis, but I don't see any cross between them. So where are you getting this idea from?"

I explained to Mae that while her files on each man contained many interesting details, if she didn't have anything more definite that tied them together in the relationship she had suggested, I couldn't write the article. I wasn't willing to write it if I didn't have something substantial to say. I was distressed, because it would leave Marin without her major article. I would have disappointed her, and myself, as well as wasting all the time and effort I had already put in on reading the filed articles.

Many people have remarked on Mae's rambling, disjointed and frequently incoherent style, evident in many of her radio broadcasts and also in some of her articles which were not carefully edited. I knew this style wouldn't fly at *Playgirl*. Mae was clearly disappointed. She had just watched me produce two excellent, salable articles: one, an interview with her, for *Playgirl*; the other, the "Cinque-Patty Hearst-SLA-CIA" piece published in the *Berkeley Barb*. (*Rolling Stone* had turned it down, saying they were too scared to publish it. ☹) She saw herself reaching a relatively large national audience for the first time; all she had to do was give me the right research materials and then shut up and leave me alone. And she saw it all going away, because I couldn't, and wouldn't, pretend to have a story if I didn't really have one.

At this point, Mae very reluctantly told me about a (nameless) file she had. She said, "Well, I have these other letters from a man named Bruce Roberts who lives in San Francisco. He gave me these letters back in 1972. I read them, and I thought he might be just a crazy person. I didn't know anything about him, and I had no corroboration or evidence for the things he wrote. But since then I have received some confirmation of his statements from a couple of other sources. So I tend to put more credence in it than I did originally."

The second source she had was a Canadian tabloid called *Midnight*, which had a story about an unknown man, big, confined to a wheelchair, the back of whose head was covered with scars over a terrible injury, who never moved or spoke, but who had lived in the "hospital" on Onassis's Island of Skorpios, or Tenos, another small Greek Island which also belonged to Onassis but was not publicized like Skorpios. According to the people quoted in this article, the mystery man had lived in this very private "hospital" for a number of years, and then had disappeared in 1971. The article had some photographs, and speculated on whether the silent crippled man had been JFK himself. There was also another article speculating about a mysterious "burial at sea" off Skorpios. It featured a photo of Teddy Kennedy, Jackie Onassis, and an unidentified man wearing a clerical collar, all sitting in a small boat and looking forlorn. Quotes from these articles are contained in the

Onassis-Hughes article I ultimately wrote, which follows.[6] These two tabloid articles were slender reeds to hang a *Playgirl* article on. They were better than nothing, but I told her I needed more than that.

Mae obviously felt a strong reluctance to show me the mysterious file of letters. She only did so because she understood that I was not going to write the article unless I had something more to go on—another source for this strange idea, which would have to be believable to me. She gave me bizarre instructions as to how I should read the file. She ordered me to skim each page visually, but not to stop to read or comprehend anything unless there was a mention of Onassis or Hughes. In other words, she ordered me to put mental blinkers on while I read the file. She also gave me strict orders not to make copies of any of this material. (She had a copy machine in her filing room, and I could have made copies behind her back, when she was out doing her regular errands. But I did not copy a single page.) And she said I was not to read this file during the day, but to continue reading and taking notes from the materials in her other files. I was only to read this last file at night, after a full day's work on the article. I agreed to everything, and I followed her instructions as best I could.

After all these preliminary instructions, she pulled out a legal-sized file folder. It was stuffed with 360 legal-sized Xerox copies of handwritten, hand-numbered pages, held together by a thick rubber band. The originals had apparently been written on yellow legal-sized pads, from margin to margin and top to bottom. Each page had two page numbers on it. One was a small number at the top righthand corner, and was obviously the original sequence number written on each page of the original letter or paper. The second, larger number could appear on various parts of the page, and was a sequencing number for the whole series of pages that Mae had, which totaled 360.

And here I will restate what I have said whenever I have been asked. I will put it in caps this time, hoping that whoever wants to know what I have to say, and does not wish to indulge in fantasies about what Mae had, and why the "whole file," or "the originals" (!!!) can't be found in Mae's archives, etc., etc., will understand that I have no reason whatsoever to lie about it, and I never have:

MAE BRUSSELL'S PORTION OF THE GEMSTONE FILE CONTAINED XEROX COPIES OF LETTERS AND PAPERS WRITTEN BY BRUCE ROBERTS. THE FIRST ONE, A LETTER ADDRESSED TO RALPH NADER, WAS DATED IN 1970. THE OTHERS WERE DATED FROM AUGUST 1971 THROUGH SEPTEMBER 1972. NOT A SINGLE PAGE WAS AN "ORIGINAL." THEY WERE ALL XEROX COPIES. AND AS FAR AS I KNOW, THAT IS ALL SHE EVER HAD.

At midnight, tucked into my small bed in Mae's tiny guest room, exhausted after a long hard day of reading and writing, I started to read this new material. The first page was chock full of murders, poison, and profanity. My immediate reaction was: Hey, this guy must be a paranoid schizophrenic. I've been told all my life about them.

Thinking about my strong negative reaction, I realized that I had been brainwashed to automatically reject anyone who talked as he did. I had to pull back and take a look at my reactions. I decided that I would read the material with an open mind. It was shocking, but fascinating. I read all that night, and well into the second night. There was more information in that file about our current and past history than I had ever encountered. But Mae was right in one sense: if I had allowed myself to think about anything other than Onassis and Hughes at that time, I would never have been able to write the article I had to write.

From what I could see, the basic story held together—from first to last page. There were no contradictions that I saw. If Bruce Roberts was a paranoid schizophrenic and these were his fantasies, then he was an extraordinarily gifted one—writing such a long, complicated account of public events over a two-year period, and even interweaving current events into these "fantasies" as

---

[6] Mae showed me the two tabloid articles, which had the photos I described, and I referred to them in the article I wrote for *Playgirl*. But I did not make copies of them, or any of the other material I used as source material for the article. I had no inkling at the time of how the story, or my relationship with Mae, would develop in the future.—sc)

though they belonged there! Of course, there was always the possibility that he was right; and that these stories were accounts of reality, but told from a different perception from the one usually presented to us.

We have all been taught to dismiss statements like Roberts' as insane—perhaps because the oligarchs and spooks who tyrannize over us would prefer that we automatically disbelieve anyone who tells us unwelcome bits of information that might wake us up from our fatal trance.

The article that follows drew its information from a wide variety of sources, chosen from Mae's thick file folders on Hughes and Onassis. But the connecting thread that determined which information was selected—the sense of the whole that informs it—came from Bruce Roberts' letters.

***

Is Howard Hughes Dead and Buried Off a Greek Island?

(*Playgirl*, December 1974)

Copyright (c) 1974 by Stephanie Caruana and Mae Brussell

A noted theorist on conspiracies, a contributing editor, and an informer named Tiger Eye bring us an unlikely tale. Or is it?

"howard Hughes is dead," said Tiger Eye. "He died on Skorpios, Onassis's island, on April 16, 1971. His coffin was lowered into the sea the next day, off the coast. Lots of people know, they just don't talk about it. It's called the Golden Silence—Omerta."

Reference: a front-page article in *Midnight*, a Canadian tabloid, dated October 18, 1971, showing two photographs. In one, a feeble-looking man is seated in a wheelchair, his head covered with what appears to be a bandage or surgical cap. He is attended by two men and a woman, who, according to *Midnight*, "bears a startling resemblance to Jackie Kennedy Onassis." In the second snapshot, the two men are helping the paralyzed figure walk, while the woman looks on.

"I took the pictures from the cruise ship Oriana, on which my wife and I were enjoying a 10-day holiday," explained George Duncastle. "We passed close to Skorpios, and the guide on board called our attention to the island."

On August 30, 1971, *Midnight* had published an article with "eyewitness reports" about a mysterious, crippled old man on the Island of Skorpios. *Midnight* speculated, unbelievably, that the man was John F. Kennedy, who supposedly did not die in Dallas in 1963. As a result of this article, according to *Midnight*, a number of people came forward with additional information.

Koula Markopolis, a Greek national and a registered nurse, told *Midnight* that she had been on Aristotle Onassis's personal payroll for two and a half months, from November, 1968, until January, 1969.

"I was hired because I have a good knowledge of English," she said. "Mr. Onassis told me that the patient I would be taking care of was an Englishman. The job was on the Island of Skorpios. I was paid a very high salary to go there. I was told that people who talk about Mr. Onassis's personal business do not work for him long. There were three other nurses and two doctors at Mr. Onassis's private hospital on Skorpios, but there was only one patient. I thought at the time that he was about 50, but he could have been older or younger."

[Hughes would have been 63 in 1968].

"We had to feed him, bathe him, and clean up after him. Sometimes he seemed to listen to us talk, but there was seldom any sign that he understood. Mostly he stared. He was quite tall, probably well over six feet tall before he was injured."

[Hughes was 6'3"]

"He weighed practically nothing, just skin and bones, no muscles. He was helpless, like a baby. His body was wasted away."

The Greek nurse said her patient was called Mr. Smith. Miss Markopolis describes his injury:

"It was one of the worst I've ever seen. The entire back of his head was a scarred mess, as though he had been operated on several times. There was a metal plate under the skin to protect the brain where the bone was broken away.

"I was told that part of his brain had been removed years ago. From the condition of the man I could only assume that it was true. He really had no reason to be alive. He must have had a tremendous will and a strong constitution before he was injured."

Miss Markopolis left the employ of Aristotle Onassis in January, 1969.

"Mr. Onassis gave me a large bonus and said he knew I would protect the privacy of 'my poor friend,' as he put it," she continued. "There was a paralyzed and brain-damaged man on Skorpios. He was being taken care of like a prince by Mr. Onassis."

Was Onassis's mysterious patient Howard Hughes? If so, who was back in the States minding the machinations of a multi-billion-dollar empire? Or could it be that a "control center" existed somewhere else?

Midnight quotes a tour guide on the Greek ship Hellas:

"I saw the man in the wheelchair many times during the past three years. Our ship always moved close to Skorpios to let tourists have a look at Onassis's island. The man in the wheelchair was outside the building sitting in the sun on nearly every good day. It was this past spring [1971] that I last saw him. He is no longer there."

A Burial at Sea

According to *Midnight*, American Army Major David Cordrey said he saw the same man:

"Major Cordrey witnessed on April 18 of this year [1971], a burial service in the Ionian Sea. 'Two high-powered speedboats came out from Skorpios and started clearing the boats away from the waters around a rocky point at one end of the island,' said the major. "Later in the day, several people gathered on the rocky point. I was curious and watched through my binoculars. One was a priest. One was Jackie Onassis, and one was Ted Kennedy. They and the others went through a ceremony over a coffin, and then watched while it was lowered into the sea."

This article included a photograph of Jackie Onassis and Teddy Kennedy, and an unidentified man, sitting forlornly in a small boat off a wild rocky shore.[7]

Tiger Eye said that Howard Hughes had been helpless and out of the country since 1957.

Could a shift from the natural desire of a powerful man for privacy, to a calculated effort by others to conceal the fact that he was no longer running the Hughes empire be distinguished?

Much of the basic information about Howard Hughes' pre-1957 existence was published in *Howard: The Amazing Mr. Hughes*, by Noah Dietrich, Hughes's righthand man—from 1925 to March 12, 1957.

The background of the man who, in 1925, inherited the Hughes Tool Company, is well known. During the '30's, Hughes, the famous aviator, broke the record for an around-the-world flight and was greeted by a ticker-tape parade in New York City. He designed airplanes and angled unsuccessfully for government contracts. He adored women, made movies, and had his picture taken with a stream of beautiful actresses and protegees. In 1942, he hired John Meyer, a press agent, to curry favor with politicians, generals, and the like. (John Meyer is now press aide to Aristotle Onassis; one of his responsibilities is watching over Jackie.)

"During the late 1940s and through the 1950s Howard's political contributions ran between

$100,000 and $400,000 per year," says Dietrich in his book. Among the recipients were "councilmen and supervisors, tax assessors, sheriffs, DA's governors, Congressmen, Senators, judges, Vice Presidents and Presidents."

Johnny Meyer seasoned the bait with glamorous women. And it worked. In 1943, Hughes Aircraft was awarded its first large government contract—for $70 million.

Hughes's "reclusiveness" seems to date from a plane crash on July 7, 1946, when he was critically injured. Reports of his injuries vary. Dietrich mentions nine broken ribs, bad burns on the left hand, and left lung collapsed and filled with blood. Other accounts include severe facial burns, a skull fracture, and a crushed cheekbone that had to be removed. Hughes was left with facial scars and could no longer make normal use of his left hand. Apparently, he also suffered a hearing impairment, and he became increasingly deaf.

After his recovery, Hughes grew a mustache to help cover his scars. He became obsessed with the need to protect himself and spent nearly all his time in seclusion. He surrounded himself with a large body-guard consisting of ex-FBI men like Robert Maheu, ex-cops, and Mormons, who he thought might be more trustworthy than others. Tales of his eccentricities were never-ending. Hughes and Dietrich did most of their business over the phone.

Early in 1957, one of Hughes's Houston lawyers suggested that Dietrich have a guardian appointed for Hughes, because the lawyer believed he was out of his mind. Dietrich refused. Two weeks later, Dr. Verne Mason, Hughes's personal physician and by this time, Director of the Hughes Medical Foundation, made the same suggestion: "Declare Howard Hughes incompetent." Again, says Dietrich, he refused.

On March 12, 1957, Dietrich states, he quit, over the phone, in a conversation with "Hughes," who was supposedly then in residence at his very private bungalow at the Beverly Hills Hotel.

Marriage, Howard Hughes Style

According to many accounts, Howard Hughes "married" actress Jean Peters the very next day—March 13, 1957. They had dated on and off for a number of years. But Hughes had also squired a long string of beautiful, famous actresses, and had shown no inclination to settle down with any one of them.

Stanton O'Keefe, in his book, *The Real Howard Hughes Story*, describes the marriage ceremony:

> It was a classic example of Hughes' penchant for secrecy. It took place in Tonopah, Nevada. Senator Howard Cannon, who was then the city attorney of Las Vegas and a personal friend of Hughes, took care of all the legal arrangements—including the trick maneuver that protected the validity of the marriage contract while allowing the couple to register under assumed names.

The wedding was "announced" in Louella Parsons's column. Reporters combed Nevada, but were unable to find any trace of the marriage. One of them finally remarked, "The nearest I can come to it is that they were married by a Parson named Louella."

For several years after their "marriage," Hughes and Jean Peters were supposed to be living in a Bel Air mansion, but the owner of the house never saw the "husband." The couple was not seen once in public together in over thirteen years of marriage, and there is no record of their ever having been photographed with each other.

After "Hughes" moved to Las Vegas late in 1966, their "marital life" consisted, or so it seemed, of devoted Jean Peters flying out from an empty house in Bel Air to visit "Howard" in Las Vegas for half an hour or so, every couple of weeks. After thirteen years of this strange "marriage," Jean Peters filed for a divorce. It came through in June 1971—just two months after Tiger Eye claimed that Howard Hughes had been buried at sea off of Onassis's island, Skorpios. Jean allegedly got $2 million out of the deal.

Was this entire 13-year "marriage" only an elaborate hoax used to explain why Hughes stopped chasing movie actresses in 1957?

If Hughes was buried at sea in April, 1971, was his "divorce" in June a ploy to quell persistent rumors that he was dead, or dying? Dead men don't get divorces. Or do they?

Jean Peters isn't talking.

Doubles

When Noah Dietrich faded from the scene in 1957, other men in the Hughes organization moved up—among them, ex-FBI man Robert Maheu and Chester Davis.

A San Francisco paper quotes Maheu:

> In 1957 (Hughes) went to Montreal. Then he traveled to the Bahamas, where he stayed for six or seven weeks on the fifth floor of the Emerald Beach Hotel in Nassau before returning to Los Angeles.

But Maheu admitted that he himself had only seen "Hughes" twice, and briefly—in 1954 and 1966—during the sixteen years he worked for the Hughes organization. Someone came back from Nassau to Los Angeles. Was it Hughes, or a Hughes double?

There are many photos of Howard Hughes circa 1947, a year after the plane crash which almost killed him. The face is slightly twisted; the mustache is a bit too long; and the smile is almost gone.

According to a story in the *San Jose Mercury*, January 24, 1972, Brucks Randell, a bit actor, was hired by a Hughes employee, Gerald Chouinard, to pose as Howard Hughes's double in 1957 and 1958, to "draw newsmen and others off the recluse's trail."

"I did this on my own incentive because I was afraid to ask Hughes's permission," Chouinard said. "We fooled the press. We fooled everybody. We never had to say, 'This is Howard Hughes' anywhere we went. We never mentioned that name to anyone. We let people draw their own conclusions."

Has anyone seen Brucks Randell recently—the only (as far as we know) publicly identified Hughes double—and during the critical years of 1957 and 1958?

Early in 1958, Frank McCullough of Time sought to interview Hughes. McCullough made a list of about fifty questions and passed them along to a Hughes aide. Two days later, the phone rang, and a flat, nasal voice at the other end identified himself as Howard Hughes.

"Hughes" began calling McCullough at all hours of the night, and engaged in long monologues, answering one or another of McCullough's fifty questions. When McCullough insisted on a personal meeting, "Hughes" sent a car and driver to take him to an unfinished runway at Los Angeles International Airport.

McCullough writes:

> A lanky six-footer came ambling out of the dark, asked my name and stood there. I stuck out my hand and said, "Good to meet you personally, Howard."
>
> The figure beat a hasty retreat, clutching his right hand to his chest. "Oh," he explained, "I can't shake hands. I was just sitting in my car eating a hot dog, and I got mustard on my hand. What's more, I was shaving and I cut my hand..." (Hughes is dreadfully afraid of picking up germs through human contact.)

Was "Hughes" also afraid of leaving unnecessary fingerprints lying around?

"Hughes" took McCullough for a ride in a 707, with a co-pilot and Jean Peters. McCullough reports that "Hughes," the crack aviator, was a lousy pilot. When "Hughes" landed the plane it "hit hard, bounced about five times, and rolled to a screeching halt just before the fence."

That was the first—and last—time "Howard and Jean" ever made a dual appearance.

Was the lousy pilot really Howard Hughes, or his double, Brucks Randell? And who would

have the motive to stage such an elaborate hoax?

The "Hughes" mythology since 1957 is littered with references to various doubles.

Robert Maheu, describing the "military maneuvers" used to transport "Hughes" from Boston to Las Vegas, in November 1966, says that a man "posing as Hughes" got onto one railway train, while "the real Hughes" sneaked into another train.

At the other end of the line, Maheu informs us, a "false Hughes" was carried "surreptitiously" through the lobby of the Desert Inn on a stretcher while "the real Hughes" strode unnoticed through the lobby with the rest of the mob.

According to Omar Garrison's book, *Howard Hughes in Las Vegas*:

> A favorite game among many Las Vegas residents…is 'watching for Hughes.' He has been reported—in various disguises—in restaurants, bars, casinos…at airports, and (in jest) walking across Lake Mead… Most of these sightings have been of a Hughes look-alike who, until 1968 [our italics], was employed by the invisible man as a decoy.
>
> The Hughes stand-in was discharged for undisclosed reasons… Thereafter, he disappeared into a private home in Van Nuys, California, and has not been seen in public since.

How do you "disappear" into a private home? And where does the back door take you?

A Farewell to Vegas

"Hughes" supposedly departed from the penthouse at the Desert Inn, Las Vegas, on Thanksgiving Eve, 1970. The timing is important. Rumors were rife that Hughes was ill or dying; demands were being made that he appear in person to reorganize his Las Vegas empire. Things were getting hot.

Was it really Howard Hughes who departed from Las Vegas? Or was it, once more, the Hughes double?

Then someone surfaced in the Bahamas. "Hughes" was quickly passed through Customs under the watchful eye of the U.S. Consul without ever making an appearance.

> *Kleenex Boxes*
> *Without Topses*
> *Were the Shoes*
> *Of Howard Hughes*

After December, 1970, some descriptions of the rare "Hughes" sightings became increasingly bizarre.

Was the real Hughes seriously ailing somewhere? Were careful preparations being made to see that even his death did not interfere with the smooth operation of the Hughes empire? And by whom?

From the many conflicting descriptions of "Hughes(?)" sightings in 1971 and 1972, there may even have been two Hughes doubles floating around the world for a time.

One was described as a tall, scrawny, sickly, bearded semi-cripple, weighing less than one hundred pounds, with six-inch-long fingernails and scraggly white hair down to the middle of his back, who occasionally wore Kleenex boxes on his feet to avoid contact with the ground.

The other "Hughes" was a vigorous, well-groomed executive, who wore a neat Van Dyke beard, kept his gray hair cut to the normal length, shook hands freely, was said to chat with visitors, and gave interviews every now and then—but only to people like the President of Nicaragua, or else over the phone.

Bob Rehak, the skipper of a luxury yacht who said he brought "Hughes" from the Bahamas to Florida in February 1972, gave a newspaper interview describing his "Hughes" this way:

> He had this stringy beard, real thin, and it came halfway to his waist. His hair was real fine, too,

down over his shoulders. . . During those twenty-two hours, he used up six to eight boxes of tissues, wiping his chin, wiping his face, his hands, his spoon, nearly everything he touched.

Rehak said his passenger constantly wrote notes on a yellow legal pad:

> It was a funny thing; after he got through writing something on a pad or using a box of Kleenex, his men would tear it up in little bits and throw it overboard.

Tiger Eye insists that Hughes died in 1971. Yet the masquerade continued. Why?

Little Green Reasons

To quote Clifford Irving: "There are about two billion little reasons—all of them green."

Dietrich reports Howard Hughes's first "major" purchase of an election. It involved the contribution of $60,000 to a successful senatorial campaign in 1952. From there, Hughes moved on to bigger things.

A few weeks after the election in November 1956, Hughes negotiated a $205,000 "non-repayable loan" to new Vice President Richard M. Nixon's brother, Donald. (See *The Nixon-Hughes "Loan"; the "Loan" No One Repaid*, by Nicholas North-Broome.) The loan was said to be for the purpose of bailing out Donald's failing restaurant, Nixon's, in Whittier, California. The *specialite de la maison* was the "Nixonburger."

"Security" for the loan was a vacant lot, assessed for tax purposes at $13,000. The lot belonged to Nixon's mother. The restaurant went bankrupt a few months later. No one knows what happened to the $205,000. "Hughes" got the $13,000 vacant lot.

Some observers have intimated that Hughes's loan to Donald Nixon, in effect, "bought" Vice President Nixon for Hughes. Shortly thereafter, the troubles of Hughes's airline, TWA:, were over; an antitrust suit against Hughes Tool was quietly shelved; and various investigations of other Hughes operations ground to a halt.

But perhaps the nicest thing that happened to the Hughes empire is described by Noah Dietrich:

> "Something curious happened one month after the loan was made [in February 1957]. The Internal Revenue Service made a reversal and ruled that the Howard Hughes Medical Foundation was entitled to tax-exempt status. The request for tax exemption had twice been refused by the IRS and the Treasury Department. But early in 1957, Howard was able to win that status for his foundation, which owned all the stock in Hughes Aircraft." [Dietrich, p.285.]

Result: All the proceeds from Hughes Aircraft, estimated as at least half a million dollars a year, are swallowed up by the Hughes Medical Foundation, with headquarters in Miami, Florida. The sole trustee of the Foundation is Howard Hughes. As a privately-owned, tax-exempt foundation, the Howard Hughes Medical Foundation is not required to render any account of how much money it receives, and how it is spent, except to the IRS.

Was an open-ended money funnel set up, into which millions—or even billions—of tax-free dollars could disappear? Wouldn't the man who controlled such a money funnel be in a position to control U.S. elections—and thus, the United States—through tax-free "contributions"?

And what about the Hughes Las Vegas casinos which, oddly, lose money while the other casinos rake it in?

Does the "lost" money find its way somehow into the "Hughes" tax-free Hughes Medical Foundation? And if so, where does it go from there?

Hughes has been reported to have tried to "buy" the Bahamas. Or was it Nicaragua?

What about "buying" Biafra, reputed to be sitting on a pool of oil, and subjecting it to some "top secret medical research"—conducted by a "top-secret" Hughes communications and weather satellite?

Hank Greenspun, editor of the *Las Vegas Sun*, explained that the unsuccessful attempt to break into his files in the summer of 1972 was because his files contained "Hughes's game plans for the election of Presidents, Senators, and Governors...."

If the price of a Vice President is a quarter of a million dollars, what would a President cost?

Is Howard Hughes Really a Computer?

An article in the *Los Angeles Times*, January 28, 1971, described a computer which had been programmed to "write" the signature of Howard Hughes—with a photo of the computer "signing" a piece of paper. Handwriting experts argued that the computer's signature was an obvious fake. "But," they added, "the digitizer-computer-plotter system could be used with greater sophistication to produce handwriting good enough to fool a handwriting expert."

In 1968 a Hughes aide ordered a computer record prepared: "a chronological synopsis of every news story or book which had ever been published about Hughes, plus private material supplied by the Hughes Tool Company."

The result was an inch-and-a-half-thick cross-referenced biography of Howard R. Hughes. "Only a few copies of the print-out were ever made. They were distributed only to top Hughes executives."

Had the metamorphosis from man to machine begun?

In January 1972, the Associated Press reports, in an effort to "prove" once and for all that Hughes, 1972 was alive and well somewhere, seven hand-picked (by the Hughes organization) reporters sat in a conference room, speaking with "a voice emanating from a small box.... All agreed the voice was indeed that of Hughes. Two voiceprint experts concurred."

But other still small voices remark that voice machines can be constructed to alter voices to match almost any desired voiceprint.

The reporters agreed that the man they spoke to had to be Hughes, because of his detailed answers to some of the questions. But other observers found the answers inadequate. Even computers don't win them all.

Sophisticated new photographic techniques can easily detect differences between one person's physiognomy and another's. Is this why, around 1968, the Hughes organization was reported to be quietly buying up every old newsreel with Hughes in it that they could find?

In 1972, the Hughes empire, disguised this time as Rosemont Enterprises, successfully suppressed the publication of Clifford Irving's "biography" of Hughes. But it simultaneously "allowed" other material to slip through to the public, in the form of excerpts from a forthcoming Hughes "autobiography," *My Life and Opinions*, "edited" by Robert P. Eaton. Eaton claimed his book was based on two manuscripts given to him by Hughes in 1970, after a thirteen-year, "almost clandestine" friendship dating back to 1957. But Tiger Eye tells us Hughes had been out of the country and helpless all that time. (P.S.: The "forthcoming" book never came forth.)

The excerpts were published in the *Ladies' Home Journal*, in February 1972—the same month that skipper Bob Rehak conveyed his weird-looking "Howard Hughes" to Miami, while his men tore up every bit of anything he wrote and threw it overboard.

The excerpts contained this remark by "Hughes":

"It is possible to keep a man's death hidden for several years through use of computerized voice tapes which can continue to communicate and even answer questions completely in character by means of the telephone."

Hughes on Ice

Eaton disclosed Hughes's desire to have his body deep-frozen after death, to be revived later when medical science developed the proper techniques.

Here is "Hughes" speaking, via Eaton in *Ladies' Home Journal*:

"If instructions were left that the estate was to remain the continued responsibility of the deceased, the computer would instruct those charged with its management by relaying instructions as though the deceased were still alive."

Why was the Eaton book proposed? What purpose was it meant to serve? Could it have been to establish Hughes as a man whose dearest wish is to run his empire even from the grave if necessary? In accordance with an elaborate will, every effort would then be made by Howard Hughes's estate to keep the Hughes estate intact until its rightful owner could rise again from his icy tomb, like a second Christ, thanks to the theoretical miracles of scientific rejuvenation, and take the reins himself. Or was it to establish Hughes as a cryogenics "nut"? Then his "frozen remains" would remain securely sealed up in a capsule, safe from any possibly embarrassing examinations to determine whether they were really Hughes's or those of a double.

The capsule might even contain other items: a "voice box"; a cross-referenced biographical computer print-out; several thousand assorted, verified "fingerprints"; some old newsreels, and a magnetic tape that knows how to write Howard R. Hughes a million times without making a single mistake.

Today, a $250 million ship, the 618-foot "Hughes" Glomar Explorer, is writing Howard Hughes's name across the bottom of the ocean. Like a giant phonograph needle, the Hughes rig circles the ocean floor, sucking up 5,000 tons of minerals a day. Hughes communications satellites encircle the globe, with the potential of reaching into every TV set in the world. In Las Vegas, Hughes's casinos rake in the chips.

Howard Hughes has recently been indicted in two criminal cases—and is still a major recipient of multimillion-dollar government defense contracts, paid for out of our tax dollars.

Hughes has allegedly influenced every major election, contributing liberally to both Democrats and Republicans, up to the Presidential level, since 1956.

Hughes's name has been linked with the Watergate conspiracy, at the highest level of our government.

Hughes oil-well drill bits suck the oil from thousands of wells, world wide. Hughes airplanes ferry us back and forth, and Hughes police helicopters keep us in line.

For the public, the questions remain.

Is Howard Hughes dead?

Are the gnarled remains of the legendary billionaire resting in a coffin at the bottom of the Aegean Sea? Is Howard Hughes a computer?

Has Aristotle Onassis, like a great green octopus, got hold of yet another empire?

***

4 June 1974-July 1975: Bruce Roberts and Me

While I was staying at Mae's house, her family life continued on its normal course. Mae had two daughters living at home: Barbara, a teen-ager, and a younger girl named Cayenne. Mae did the cooking, and we all ate breakfast together at a big round table in her sunny, plant-filled kitchen. Breakfast conversation was relaxed and pleasant; we didn't get into grim subjects. But I gradually learned about a third sister, Bonnie, who had died in 1971 in a tragic automobile accident. Barbara and Bonnie Brussell, with two other teen-aged girl friends, had been driving along a quiet country road in Carmel when their car was side-swiped or driven off the road by another vehicle. Bonnie died in the accident; Barbara was injured, and still walked with a slight limp. Another girl died, and the fourth girl was also injured. It must have been a nightmarish scene.

After breakfast, Mae would tackle the daily mail, while I went to work on the Patty Hearst article, and later, on the *Playgirl* article about "Hughes" and Onassis. Eight major newspapers and a stack of magazines would arrive each day in the mail. And every morning, Mae spent several hours reading through this material, underlining important points, clipping articles, making copies on her copying machine if necessary, and filing the copies in appropriate folders.

Later on, when Mae decided to let me read Bruce Roberts' letters in connection with the *Playgirl* article, she told me more about when and why he had given her the file. It had to do with the accident in which her daughter Bonnie had been killed. She told me that when it happened, she had talked about it on her "Dialogue: Conspiracy" radio broadcast. And she had mentioned the name of a witness to the accident who had come forth sympathetically after it occurred: Genovese. Bruce Roberts contacted her after this broadcast, and told her he had some information to give her about the man who had been so sympathetic. The file he gave her had letters and papers dated from 1970 through the summer of 1972, and these are the series originating from Mae's file which, in edited form, appear in Chapters 10 through 36. Bonnie Brussell is mentioned several times in this file. Bruce also gave Mae some earlier pages of this series, probably to give her some context and demonstrate that he knew a lot of things, and because this also might help Mae.

Mae's account of her meeting with Bruce Roberts in San Francisco in 1972 appears in chapter 43. When I asked her what Bruce was like, she told me he was "Caspar Milquetoast." I was surprised. The impression I had gotten from reading the file had been that Roberts was that of a more fierce individual—perhaps a cross between John Wayne and Clint Eastwood. She explained that he had invited her to his home in San Francisco. When she went there, she learned that he was living with his mother—a sweet little old Irish lady who served them tea, wearing white gloves. Mae reasoned that any man in his 50's, living with his mother, had to be Caspar Milquetoast. I accordingly deflated my expectations to...well...Woody Allen? I would soon be on my way to meeting him myself.

There was a 4-month lead time between my submission of the "Onassis is Hughes" article to *Playgirl* and its publication. In the meantime, my situation had changed.

In June 1974, I had just completed the article for *Playgirl* when Mae announced that I would have to move out of her spare bedroom because someone else would be moving in. I later heard that the man who moved in had been a prisoner in the California prison system.

I assumed, wrongly as it turns out, that he had been a prisoner at Soledad Prison, with whom Mae had been corresponding after the SLA murder of Dr. Marcus Foster and the brief reign of "Cinque" and the SLA during Patty Hearst's captivity. This man had briefly known Donald DeFreeze, who had been "reinvented" as the Symbionese Liberation Army's General, "Cinque." And he had spoken to him the day before DeFreeze's arranged "walk-away" escape from Soledad. He was still there when the SLA was wiped out by the LAPD Swat Team. (Some interesting quotes

from this prison correspondence appear in the *Berkeley Barb* article. See Chapter 2).

Mae added that she hoped to be able to continue our writing collaboration soon, and that a friend of hers had a trailer in nearby Big Sur which I could rent for the rest of the summer. In that way, we could continue our work together later on.

A summer in Big Sur didn't sound too bad! I moved into the trailer with the tools of my trade: typewriter, tape recorder, and a few books—whatever fit into the back seat of my VW Beetle.

For my next article, I approached Marin Milam at *Playgirl* on the subject of Teddy Kennedy, Mary Jo Kopechne, and Chappaquiddick. This was another astonishing story, the outlines of which I had gotten from my quick scan of Roberts' letters while at Mae's. Marin was interested, and agreed.

This time I did not plan to "co-author" the article with Mae. I would do my own research to dig out whatever details I could find.

I began by telephoning John Farrar, the Chappaquiddick diver who dove down to the car submerged by the bridge over Poucha Pond, and discovered Mary Jo's body, stretched upward to breath in the last air bubble, in rigor mortis, just as Roberts had described the scene. Farrar gave me a wonderful interview over the phone. He has always been honest and open in his description of what he saw. I did other research, wrote the article and sent it in to *Playgirl*. They told me the lawyers were going over it.

I spent the rest of the summer waiting for Mae to resume our work. While waiting, I enjoyed the special ambiance of Big Sur, particularly nightly excursions to the bubbling hot springs and baths at the Esalen Institute, in cliff-side caves open to the night sky with the mists rolling in from the sea. It was a magical place—the perfect place to forget about national politics, assassinations, and all that jazz.

A couple of months later, I awoke with a start to realize that summer was definitely over, and with it my summer trailer rental.

Mae showed no signs of wishing to resume our work together. She seemed preoccupied with her new situation, whatever it was. (More details are included in Chapter 43.)

I said farewell, put my typewriter and suitcase into my car, and drove north along the beautiful coastline to San Francisco. There I moved into the parlor floor of a gorgeous pre-earthquake Victorian house on Prosper Street.

Those familiar with the geographical peculiarities of San Francisco are aware that it is exposed on the west to the chilly fog and rolling in from the Pacific. But inland, steep hills and valleys create mini-climates with characteristic weather patterns. Prosper Street was in the Castro Street area, also known as the "Banana Belt" because it was generally warm and sunny.

Bruce Roberts' address, written with his phone number at the top of the letters I had read at Mae's, was located in the cold, rainy Sunset district. It was the only information I had copied from Mae's file.

During the drive north, I decided to go directly to Bruce Roberts' address and try to meet with him. Mae had assured me that Roberts had given her permission to use his letters in any way she saw fit. But I thought the forthcoming article would be a good excuse, at least: as a journalistic courtesy, I would tell him that Mae and I had written an article based largely on his letters, which would be published in the December issue of *Playgirl*. I had gotten the impression from Mae that she was on friendly terms with Roberts. I thought he would welcome a visit from an admiring reader, and I half-expected an invitation to tea with this splendid writer, a politically-oriented Woody Allen type, and his mother.

He had written in the File that his phone was tapped, and I didn't want to announce my arrival, or the forthcoming article, to whoever might be listening in.

So I drove directly to his address, and parked right in front of his house. This turned out to

be a large, impersonal-looking brick building. It was the middle of a sunny afternoon, and there was no one visible on the street. It was quite a different scene from the Banana Belt, where there always seemed to be a few friendly hippies lounging about. I went to the building entrance, and pressed the button marked "Roberts." No answer.

Okay, Bruce Roberts wasn't home. I decided to leave him a note with my phone number. I was sitting in the front seat of my Volkswagen, writing the note, when a tall, burly-looking middle-aged man in khaki shorts and a T-shirt came jogging up the street. As he passed the car, he looked intently at me, and I looked at him. I decided he couldn't be Bruce Roberts; he just didn't look at all like Caspar Milquetoast, or Woody Allen. He looked like a retired Marine drill sergeant who kept himself in shape. He went into the right building, however.

When I finished my note, I went back into the building to leave it somewhere where it could be found. I tried the buzzer again, and this time I got a response. So I went upstairs, and this time, he was standing in the doorway of his apartment, wearing a white terry-cloth bathrobe. Close up, he was tall and blue-eyed; his close-cropped dark gray hair was still wet from the shower.

He told me a tale of horror, filled with murders, bribery, and criminal betrayals of a nation's trust. The reason he was telling me all this was because I had asked him to.

***

I wrote three versions of the *Skeleton Key to the Gemstone File*, dated in April, May, and June, of 1975. (And a later one, in New York City, which had some illustrations in it.) But people took their copies and changed, added, deleted, and rewrote them. One copy, of uncertain origin, was given to Larry Flynt of *Hustler* magazine (not by me) and published by him ("sanitized") in 1979. This version has gotten wide circulation. The various versions do not coincide completely. In some cases, people making copies from Xeroxed and re-Xeroxed originals inevitably misread the dim originals, and typos crept in. As an example, one embarrassing misreading turns up in Gerald Carroll's book, *Project Seek—Onassis, Kennedy and the Gemstone Thesis*[8] in the *Skeleton Key* entry for November 1, 1963, as:

"Jackie stayed on board the Christina, and descended the gangplank a few days later on Onassis' arm, in Turkey, to impress the Turkish boy, Mustapha."

In the original versions, this read: "The Turkish Bey, Mustapha." And there is a big difference.

Another: In the original versions, the JFK assassination team member arrested in Chicago is identified in the original versions as "Tom Vallee." Various misreadings and misspellings in the recopied versions have included "Malley", Walley," etc. "Tom Vallee" has meaning, because Sherman Skolnick also names Thomas Vallee as one of the Chicago assassination team. (see Chapter 48.)

Another: Bruce Roberts told me verbally about Eugene Brading shooting at JFK from the pergola at Dealey Plaza. At the time, I was unfamiliar with the architecture and layout at Dealey Plaza. He was saying "pergola;" I was hearing "pagoda," and that was how it appeared in a couple of early versions of the *Skeleton Key*. Eventually I realized he meant "pergola," not "pagoda," but then there were more problems: WHICH pergola? Which end? Photographs from Dealey Plaza offered some clues, but no definite conclusion. That is, until I saw the photograph of the pergola doorway in Groden's book.

The present version has been rewritten, to include additional information or interpretations from the Brussell section of the Gemstone File, which I purchased from Tom Davis in the year 2000. Tom Davis was one of three people to whom Mae had entrusted copies of the manuscript which she had so determinedly suppressed during her lifetime. This material was written by Bruce Roberts

---

[8] This is one of the best books done so far on the *Gemstone File*. See Bibliography for details.—sc

between August 1971 through September 23, 1972.

(This was the thick sheaf of xerox copies of letters that I read at Mae Brussell's in the summer of 1974, as background material for the *Playgirl* article on Onassis and Howard Hughes. An edited transcript of this material makes up Chapters 10 through 42 here.)

I have added some information gleaned from this source and other sources to the original *Skeleton Key*, as well as some personal details of Bruce Roberts' life that I did not wish to include in the original Keys because I felt they would be an invasion of his privacy, and might cause inconvenience, harassment and/or danger to his family members. I have also included some more recent interpretations of events. This version is therefore considerably longer than the previous versions. In a few cases, I have included information not present in the Gemstone File, and not originating from conversations I had with Bruce Roberts. I have put these additions in brackets, and have tried to provide footnotes regarding their sources.

Numerous older versions of the *Skeleton Key*, some correct and some not, and some co-opted and rewritten to reflect the coopter's own ideas, still abound on the Internet. In many cases my name does not appear. The original editions had my name, address and phone number in San Francisco on the top corner of the first page, but it was a simple matter to remove or lose or replace this information. (This was back in the days before personal computers, when we still wrote things on typewriters!) In one case, a man (Jim Moore) claimed the Gemstone File *Skeleton Key* as his own work, apparently tried to get money from Larry Flynt for it, and is still lying about it like a bad-tempered cricket on the Internet, thirty-five years later!!! So it goes…. If there is a hell and if there is a place in it for liars, I hope he roasts in it some day. If not…well, what's the difference?

(The following pages contain some of the Cartoon version of the Gemstone File published in International Times, UK, in 1977-8. Hey! I don't get no respect! ☺!)

Stephanie Caruana

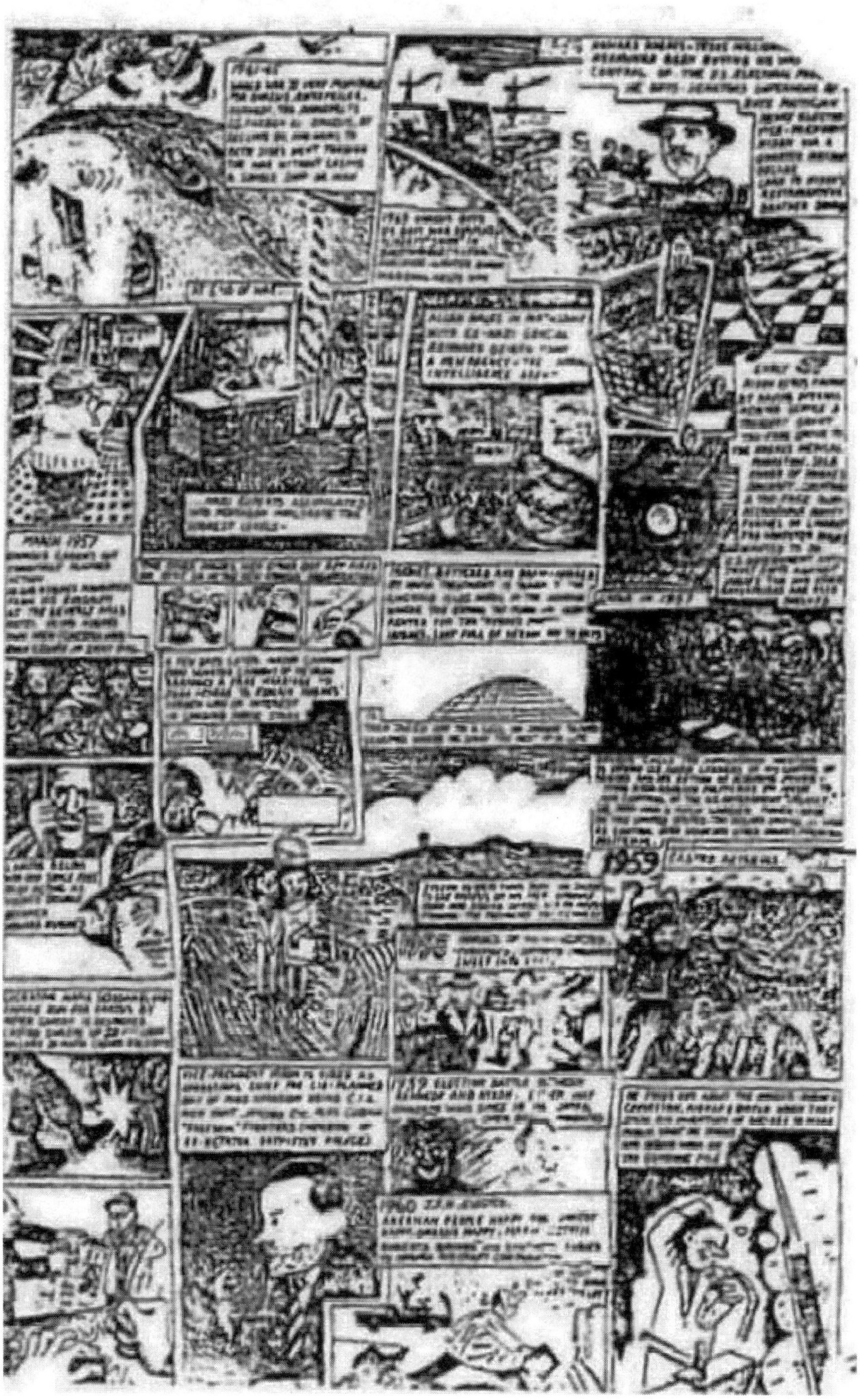
MARCH 1957
1959

5 A Skeleton Key to the Gemstone File
(First released on March 25, 1975, but dated April, 1975)

The Gemstone File was written in many segments over a period of years, by an American man named Bruce Roberts. Parts of the file were released to certain Americans beginning in 1969. The number of hand-written pages is well over a thousand, of which I have read about four hundred. I have been able to verify some of the statements made in these files, but I do not have the time or the research facilities to verify the entire story. Perhaps others can help.

Since the scope of the work is so large, and the events described so complex and interlocking, it may be more easily understood with this skeleton outline of the Gemstone Thesis. Individual papers can then be read with greater comprehension.

1932: Aristotle Onassis, a Greek drug pusher and ship owner who made his first million selling "Turkish tobacco" (opium) in Argentina, worked out a profitable deal with Joseph P. Kennedy, then Ambassador to England; Eugene Meyer, and Meyer Lansky. Onassis would ship booze direct to Prohibition-dry Boston, in diplomatic pouches, for Joe Kennedy. Also involved was a heroin shipping deal with Franklin D. Roosevelt.

1933-40: Eugene Meyer, Joe Kennedy's partner in S.E.C. (Securities Exchange Commission) stock swindles, bought the *Washington Post*, as part of a Mafia drive to get control over news media. Other Mafia bought other newspapers, magazines, radio and TV broadcasting stations, etc. Massive news censorship regarding Mafia political and financial dealings went into effect in all the major media.

1934: Onassis, John D. Rockefeller, Jr., and the Seven Sisters (the major oil companies) signed an agreement, outlined in an oil cartel memo: Screw the Arabs out of their oil, ship it on Onassis's ships; Rockefeller and the Seven Sisters to get rich. All this was done.

1936: Roberts, studying journalism and physics at the University of Wisconsin, learned these things via personal contacts. His special interest was in crystallography—and the creation of synthetic rubies, the original Gemstone experiment.

At age 17, as a journalism student at the University of Wisconsin, Bruce Roberts covered Bob LaFollette's formation of Wisconsin's Progressive Party for the *Wisconsin State Journal* in Madison, Wisconsin.

1937: Roberts was dating Dorothy Boettiger, Roosevelt's niece. Sam Giancana, then a young Chicago hood and murderer connected with Al Capone's gang, had the goods on Roosevelt regarding the heroin deal with Onassis. He told Roberts to tell Dorothy; then used the blackmail later to gain control of the Chicago Teamsters' Union Fund.

[Hjalmar Schacht, president of Germany's Reichsbank and economic dictator of Hitler's 3rd Reich, launched a massive program of rearmament. Onassis's tanker, the Ariston, the largest oil tanker ever built at the time, was nearing completion in Sweden. Onassis signed a year's contract with Jean Paul Getty's Tidewater Oil Company to move oil from California to the Mitsuis Corporation in Yokohama.—sc2005]

1940: Roberts played baseball for the University of Wisconsin. Henry Wallace, Roosevelt's Secretary of Agriculture and a candidate for Vice President, visited the campus, met and talked to Roberts, and showed him a copy of the oil cartel memo.

1941-1945: World War II: Rigged by the same group involved in the 1932 deals. Very profitable for Onassis, Rockefellers, Kennedys, Roosevelts, I.G. Farben, etc. Onassis, selling oil, arms and dope to both sides, went through the war without losing a single ship or man. He made millions. Stavros Niarchos, member of another Greek ship-owning family, who later became

Onassis's brother-in-law, handled it differently. He lost lots of ships and lots of men, and made his millions on the insurance.

1945: Roberts was in the Army, stationed at Victorville Army Base, in California. No war hero he, apparently; he was assigned for the day to patrol the area in front of HQ with a stick, spiking trash and stuffing it into a sack.

[Note: This ignominious and inglorious task sounds like the sort of job assigned to Army dissidents who, perhaps overly-intelligent and overly-independent from the Army's point of view, don't "just follow orders, sir!" Various researchers have sought to get more information about Roberts' military service, but it is all "classified." Like it was a state secret. Which it is, of course. This item came from Roberts' own letters.—sc2005]

Heroic Bomber Captain George McGovern, back for reassignment from the war in Europe where he had flown many bombing missions, chewed Roberts out for not saluting him, and threatened him with a court martial.

[McGovern would be the Democratic presidential candidate in 1972. Roberts implies that McGovern was the role model for a profiteering pilot—perhaps "Milo Minderbinder," who arranged to bomb his own air base in Joseph Heller's Catch 22.]

1946: Onassis married Greek shipping magnate Stavros Livanos' younger daughter, Tina.

1947: Greek ship-owner Stavros Niarchos married Livanos' older daughter, Eugenie.

1947-8: *[Onassis set up the United States Petroleum Carriers (U.S.P.C.), as a U.S. corporation, using 3 U.S. citizens as front-men. The U.S. Maritime Commission approved the sale of five enormous T2 tankers for $1.5 million apiece, to the U.S.P.C. A week later, Onassis's Sociedad Industrial Maritime Financiera Ariona, Panama, S.A., bought 49% of the stock. Three more American citizens with close ties to Onassis each acquired 1% of the rest of the stock, in effect giving Onassis complete control of U.S.P.C., using 100% "OPM" (Other People's Money). The first ship was launched at Bethlehem Steel's Sparrow Point shipyards in Baltimore.—sc2005]*

1948: April 30: Onassis's son Alexander was born at the Harkness Pavilion, a private clinic in NYC. His daughter Christina was born in 1950, at the same NYC clinic. Both were thus U.S. citizens by birth.

[Alexander Onassis could have run for President. So could Christina, for that matter. People who knew Onassis have remarked that he set seemingly unreachable goals for himself, then set about achieving them with brilliance, determination and ruthlessness. After reading so much about Onassis's life and activities, I think his ambition was to see his son elected President of the United States. And before you say "Absurd!", ask yourself what George W. Bush is doing in the White House for two terms; and how much choice you actually had or have in the candidates presented to you for "your vote".—sc2005]

1949: Onassis bought 16 U.S. war surplus "Liberty Ships" in a fraudulent [illegal] purchase, at bargain-basement prices. Lawyer Burke Marshall helped him.

[Since there were delays putting the tankers to work transporting oil, Onassis had them converted into whaling factory ships, registered in Panama, and run by the "Olympic Whaling Company" of Uruguay. Neither country had signed quota agreements limiting whaling. He hired ex-Nazi Hjalmar Schacht to run the whaling fleet.—sc2005]

1950-51: Onassis's whaling fleet, largest and most modern in the world, began a bloody onslaught on whales. He made yet another fortune; and almost wiped out many species of whales. The bar stools on his yacht, Christina, were upholstered in the skins of whales' penises.

[The fleet consisted of the factory ship Olympic Challenger, which had formerly been the T2 oil tanker Herman F. Whiton, plus 17 "killer ships." The whales were spotted by helicopter. Hunting was good, and sometimes several hundred whales, of all sizes and varieties, were slaughtered each day and towed to the

"factory" ship, while the seas around them were covered with whale blood. Every international law limiting the "harvesting" of whales was violated. "It was clear that his fleet had inflicted massive damage on whale stocks."—Evans, p.203.

This ruthless depredation on whale species has contributed to the reduction in whale numbers to the point where some species are in danger of extinction. Of course current heavy over-fishing involving unbreakable nets, and most lately, the U.S. Navy's current experiments with underwater sonic explosions, which kill whales, etc., en masse, don't allow these species to regenerate their numbers.—sc]

1951: Onassis orders 18 more massive oil tankers to be built in Hamburg shipyards, financed by a $100,000,000 loan—O.P.M. (other people's money).]

1952: Roberts lived in the Los Angeles area. He was described at this time as a "former actor turned jewelry designer" in a brief notice in the *Los Angeles Times*. He was still involved in crystallography, was making synthetic gemstones and apparently selling them to the Hollywood crowd.

1953: Onassis buys control of the "SBM" [Societe des Bains de Mer] in Monte Carlo, including the decrepit old Casino, yacht club, Hotel de Paris, and about 1/3 of the acreage of Monaco. He revamped the Monte Carlo Casino, casting a well-calculated glow of "international glamour" on Monte Carlo, which soon began to yield millions of dollars. His new oil tanker, the Tina Onassis, largest in the world, (price tag $6 million), was launched. He employed ex-Nazi Hjalmar Schacht to negotiate the "Jiddah Agreement" with Saudi Arabia, which later gave Onassis a virtual monopoly on the transport of 45,000,000 tons of Saudi oil a year.

[By this time, Onassis was a multi-millionaire—one of the richest men in the world. But why should he stop there?—sc2005]

1954: May: Dien Bien Phu fell to the Communists. Roberts' wife, daughter of the French Consul, was imprisoned with other French nationals in North Vietnam, at a "Hanoi Hilton." She escaped with other French prisoners and hiked north to a U.S. Army base, Kunming, in the Yunnan Province of China. Along the way she saw strange rocks resembling those of the chief ruby-producing district in Burma. These rocks suggested the presence of rubies, together with a rare mineral or heavy metal, essential for the production of synthetic rubies and also, perhaps, for the production of a super-weapon. *[Uranium??—sc2005]* She later told Roberts about them.

1956: Howard Hughes, a Texas millionaire who had inherited Hughes Tool Company, specializing in drill bits for oil wells, had expanded into aircraft design and manufacturing. He had begun buying his way toward control of the U.S. electoral process. He bought Senators, Governors, etc. [One reason for these "purchases" was that Hughes was seeking Government contracts for his airplanes. He had learned "the hard way" that the best, or only way to gain these contracts was to buy the votes of the people in Congress who could vote for or against him.] He had developed Hughes Aircraft's position as the U.S.'s leading defense contractor. He finally bought his last (and biggest) politician: newly elected Vice President Richard M. Nixon, via a $205,000 non-repayable "loan," secured by a $13,000 vacant lot, to Nixon's brother Donald. [The lot in question belonged to the Nixon brothers' mother.] The money was ostensibly for Donald's failing restaurant, "Nixonburger," in Whittier, California. A few months later, the restaurant closed. The money was never repaid. Onassis got the vacant lot. Instead, Donald Nixon used the money to finance his way into Mob-connected real estate operations.

(And, by "purchasing" V.P. Nixon, it appears that Howard Hughes also purchased his own dreadful fate. He made himself a big enough fish in American politics to be an irresistible lure to an even bigger fish: Onassis, who gobbled him up on March 11-12, 1957. But it is also possible that Onassis' grab of Hughes occurred a bit earlier, and that Onassis might have been in charge of Hughes by the time "Hughes" lent

the money to Nixon.—sc2005).

1957: On January 17, Jean Peters, a Hollywood star who had been romantically involved with Howard Hughes, divorced Stuart Cramer—one of the first steps in Onassis's plan for Howard Hughes.

Early 1957: V.P. Nixon repaid the "favor" Hughes had done his family with the $205,000 "loan" by having the IRS-U.S. Treasury grant tax-free status (refused twice before) to the "Hughes Medical Foundation," sole owner of Hughes Aircraft, creating a tax-free, non-accountable money funnel or laundry, for whatever Hughes wanted to do. U.S. government also shelved antitrust suits against Hughes's TWA, etc.

March: Howard Hughes lived in a secluded bungalow at the Beverly Hills Hotel, romancing movie stars. Unfortunately for him, his business and political success had caught the eye of an even bigger fish. Onassis conceived a brilliant, ruthless, carefully planned event: He had Hughes kidnapped from his bungalow, bribing and using some of Hughes' own men (headed by Chester Davis, born Cesare in Sicily). Hughes's other men either quit, got fired, or stayed on in the new Onassis organization.

[Onassis also had a suite at the Beverly Hills Hotel, since 1942, where he frequently stayed when in Los Angeles. "He took a suite at the Beverly Hills Hotel and was already sufficiently recognized to merit a pink registration card, the color code for the hotel's most important guests."[9] Like Hughes, Onassis also romanced movie stars, to "promote himself as a great lover. He dated Paulette Goddard…, Simone Simone… Gloria Swanson…[and] Veronica Lake." So Onassis and Hughes were making the "Hollywood Playboy" scene at the same time, in the same place, probably had some of the same movie star conquests, and would have known each other because they moved in the same Hollywood social circles.—sc 2005]

March 12: Noah Dietrich, Hughes's right-hand man for 32 years, suddenly got fired, by "Hughes", over the phone, and never saw Hughes again.[10]

March 13: Howard Cannon, City Attorney of Las Vegas, Nevada (who later became Senator Cannon) arranged a fake "marriage" between Hughes and Jean Peters in Tonopah, Nevada, to explain Hughes's sudden loss of interest in chasing Hollywood stars. Jean Peters received $1 million cash to take part in the deception. No actual record of the marriage has ever been found. The fake "wedding" was announced in Louella Parsons's gossip column, leading some unkind souls to remark that Howard Hughes and Jean Peters were apparently married by a Parson name Louella.

Hughes, battered and brain damaged in the scuffle, was carted off to the Emerald Beach Hotel in the Bahamas. The entire top floor had been rented for thirty days for the "Hughes party" with "top security." Hughes, now a helpless invalid, was shot full of heroin for thirty days, then dragged off to a "hospital" cell on Onassis's private island, Skorpios, *[or Tenos, Onassis's other island??—sc2005]* where he was the only "patient". Onassis had now doubled his power base in the U.S. (with the addition of the Hughes empire), and had control over V.P. Nixon and other Hughes-purchased politicians—as well as that wonderful private money-laundering device, the "Hughes Medical Research Foundation."

L. Wayne Rector, a "Hughes" double hired by the Carl Byoir P.R. firm in 1955, now had a full-time job playing "Hughes".

Also in 1957: Joe Kennedy took his son, John F., and daughter-in-law Jackie to meet Onassis on

---

[9] Peter Evans, *Ari…*, pp 110-112.
[10] Dietrich told his side of the story in *Howard: The Amazing Mr. Hughes*, Fawcett 1972. I am fairly sure he knew what was going on, but decided to depart when Onassis took over Hughes and his corporations. Dietrich wound up alive and well, wealthy, and living in Beverly Hills. The date and circumstances of his departure from "Hughes" were supplied by him in his book, but are questioned elsewhere.

his yacht, the Christina, to introduce John, and to remind Onassis of an old Mafia promise: the presidency for a Kennedy. Onassis agreed.

November 14: Onassis called the Apalachin, N.Y., Mafia summit meeting with representatives from all over the country to announce his grab of Hughes and his adoption of Hughes's game plan for acquiring power: buying U.S. senators, congressmen, governors and judges, en masse, to take control "legally" of the U.S. government. Onassis's radio message to Apalachin from a remote Washington, Pennsylvania, farmhouse was intercepted (reluctantly) by FBI's J. Edgar Hoover, because of a tip-off from some Army Intelligence guys who weren't in on the plan. Among the attendees were San Francisco's Lanza, Sam Giancana and Joe Marcello, Carlos's brother. *[Sam Giancana and others avoided capture in the raid by running away through the woods. See Double Cross for an amusing account of this.—sc]*

1958: Hordes of Mafia-selected, Mafia-purchased and Mafia-supported "grass roots" candidates swept into office: a successful test of Onassis's new Mafia game plan for taking over the U.S. Government via bought and paid-for candidates.

1959: Fidel Castro took over Cuba from dictator Fulgencio Batista, destroying the cozy and lucrative Mafia gambling empire run for Onassis by Meyer Lansky in Cuban casinos. Castro scooped up $8 billion in Mafia casino receipts. Onassis was furious. V.P. Nixon became operations chief for the CIA-planned Bay of Pigs invasion, using CIA E. Howard Hunt as political officer (White House liaison). CIA James McCord was a major participant. A major purpose was to regain control of the Cuban gambling empire for Onassis. Participants included ex-Batista strong-arm cops (Cuban "freedom fighters") Eugenio Martinez, Virgilio Gonzales, etc., as well as winners like Frank Sturgis (born Fiorini, in Sicily), a gunrunner with a gambling background, This was the core group from which the CIA Castro assassination team, the JFK assassination team, and later, the Watergate team, emerged.

Antonio Iglesias, CIA/Cuban, was part of the invading "army" at the Bay of Pigs. (His sister Marina was married for a time to Bruce Roberts' brother Dayle.) The invasion group trained at Lake Pontchartrain, Louisiana, and No Name Key, Florida.

A stirring election battle between Kennedy and Nixon began. Either way, Onassis won, since he had control over both candidates. Of John, through his father, Joseph, Onassis's old partner in thievery; of both, through hefty "campaign contributions" bribery: $250,000 apiece. Peanuts to Onassis, who was by that time a multi-millionaire. Cheap at the price, to buy a President.

1960: JFK elected. American people happy. Joe Kennedy happy. Onassis happy. Mafia ecstatic.

Roberts was married to the daughter of the former French consul in Indochina. In that area, Onassis's involvement in the Golden Triangle dope trade was no secret. While living in Indochina, she had observed strange rocks in the Katha district of Burma, the natural source of Burmese rubies and sapphires. She owned some Burmese rubies. Burma is one of only eleven possible world sources of the mineral ingredients which can be used to create artificial rubies and sapphires—and also, where beautiful natural rubies and sapphires occur. *(These are also apparently the mineral ingredients necessary for the "secret weapon" Roberts hints about: the one which fuses your ass to your belly-button in 22 hours. Possibly a rare heavy metal. Hey, don't ask me what this is all about!)*

When the French retreated from Dien Bien Phu, she was imprisoned in a "Hanoi Hilton." She escaped with a small group of prisoners. They walked north out of Vietnam into China, and through the Yunnan Province to Kunming, a U.S. air base in China. On the way she saw similar-looking rocks. She told Roberts about this. He may have been able to smuggle some of this mineral and some rubies and sapphires out of China [and Burma].

Roberts experimented with the creation of artificial rubies—the original "Gemstone experiment." Hughes Aircraft in Los Angeles was experimenting with laser beam technology, using synthetic rubies for their light-refraction qualities. Roberts brought his synthetic rubies to Hughes. Nervously, they stole his rubies—the basis for laser beam research, laser bombs, etc., because of the optical quality of the rubies. Roberts' investigation after the theft of his rubies revealed the Onassis-"Hughes" connection: the kidnap and switch.

1961: January: Just after the Inauguration, Joseph P. Kennedy, had a stroke, ending his personal control over sons John and Bobby. The boys decided to rebel against Onassis's control. Why? Inter-Mafia struggle? Perhaps a dim hope of restoring this country to its mythical integrity? They wanted to begin by dismantling the CIA.

They began committing Mafia no-no's. Bobby, John's Attorney General, arrested Wally Bird, owner of Air Thailand, who had been shipping Onassis's heroin out of the Golden Triangle (Laos, Cambodia, Vietnam), under contract with the CIA (Air Opium). He arrested Teamster Mafia boss Jimmy Hoffa, and put him in jail. And he declared the $73 million in forged "Hughes" land liens, deposited with San Francisco's Bank of America, as "security" for the TWA judgement against "Hughes," to be what they were: Forgeries.

April 1961: CIA Bay of Pigs fiasco. Kennedy refused to supply full support for the "Bay of Pigs" invasion of Cuba. It flopped. Kennedy vowed to "splinter the CIA into a thousand pieces." He fired CIA director Allen Dulles, and Deputy Director Charles Cabell.

Hunt and McCord, of the CIA, Batista's Cubans in exile in the U.S., and the Mafia who had been working with Dictator Batista in Cuba all were angry about JFK's lack of enthusiasm. Mafia Top Boss Onassis ordered his U.S. right-hand man, "Howard Hughes's top aide," former FBI and CIA man Robert Maheu (nicknamed "IBM" for Iron Bob Maheu), to hire and train a Mafia/CIA/Cuban exiles assassination team to kill Castro. Robert Maheu was Onassis's chief "contractor" for all of the major political assassinations that rocked the U.S. at around that time: JFK, RFK, MLK, etc. This was reported by Jack Anderson, who got a lot of his "tips" from his friend, Frank Sturgis, who was also on the Castro assassination team.

The team of a dozen or so included Johnny Roselli and Jimmy "The Weasel" Fratianno, expert Mafia hit men, assisted by CIA's Hunt, McCord and others. The assassination team trained in Mexico, Florida, and at Lake Pontchartrain, Louisiana. They tried five times to kill Castro, with everything from high-powered rifles to apple pie with sodium morphate in it. they nearly succeeded, but some were caught and executed in Havana on the day of the invasion. Castro survived.

> [NOTE: Many books published during the 80's and 90's have explored some of the criminal activities of the U.S. and international Mafia and elements of the CIA, plus huge corporate organizations, and their involvement in a long series of assassinations to gain control of political or financial power. A few of these are listed in the Bibliography. Two important ones **are Double Cross: The Explosive, Inside Story of the Mobster Who Controlled America**, by Sam and Chuck Giancana, and John Davis's book, **Mafia Kingfish: Carlos Marcello and the Assassination of John F. Kennedy.** Both supply excellent descriptions of the close interrelationship between the Mafia, CIA, big government, big industry and banking groups involved in such operations as gun running, assassinations, take-overs of foreign governments, large-scale international drug dealing, agricultural and oil business, international money laundering, etc., over the years. They also provide many details of Marcello's and Giancana's involvement in the JFK assassination. This assassination had tremendous scope; many people and groups were involved. It is interesting that we are getting more details about this from the Mafia families' side than from our government, which prefers to continue the cover-up even though it has singularly failed to work. Reading these books, each written from a slightly different perspective, a perceptive reader is

immediately immersed in the actual world of political assassinations as "business" policy, rather than emotion, and the real people and real pay-offs involved, rather than the sterilized and relatively depopulated worlds of "standardized" books on the major political assassinations which never seem to get anywhere that the other published books have not already traveled. Here is one example:

"In exchange for his underworld services, Mooney [Sam Giancana] said the CIA looked the other way—allowing over $100 million a year in illicit drugs to flow through Havana into the United States. It was an arrangement similar to all the rest they'd made, he said. The CIA received 10 percent of the take on the sale of the narcotics, which they utilized "for their undercover slush fund." Such illegally earned monies were stashed away by the CIA in Swiss, Italian, Bahamian, and Panamanian accounts."—Giancana, *Double Cross…*, p.259.

Roberts, living in San Francisco, put more emphasis on San Francisco Mafia operations and what he knew of the international operations of Onassis. But there is little or no real conflict between Roberts' account and those of the Giancanas and John Davis. It is the same story told from a slightly different point of view. Every big city in America had (and has) its large lucrative crime and monopoly empire, and its "Boss of Bosses," each of whom lived like the king of a small kingdom, and felt as omnipotent as a king. Mafia, CIA, government and big business co-exist easily as long as the "proprieties" of Omerta are observed. The proprieties are: No holds barred in the struggle between branches of the "secret government"—such as the present incarnations currently known as "Republican Party" and "Democratic Party." But, supposedly, strict silence and secrecy is maintained toward the outside world. The rules are slipping however. More and more the public sees small pieces of a vast complicated worldwide network of money-making operations.

But some things are still kept under wraps in these Mafia "let-it-all-hang-out" books. Specifically, the major role of Aristotle Onassis in world politics and economics is carefully ignored. When all is said and done, both of these books follow the cardinal Mafia rule: Give up what you have to, but keep the rest hidden. Such as, the bribing of nearly all public officials and politicians, combined with the knowledge that they can "buy" their offices, such as judgeships and ambassadorships, secure in the knowledge that they can use their positions as money-making machines. And none of these "tell-all" Mafia books discuss the basic money-laundering mechanism that makes it all possible: the enormous, insatiable Howard Hughes Medical Institute, the money funnel, tax free and always chewing away at the nation's available funds, for purposes that wouldn't stand up under public scrutiny, though thinly disguised as "charity." They are really used to develop products and systems that will draw ever more money and power into the hands of the already filthy rich, currently running the enormous corporations that have descended from Onassis's enormous empire.—sc2005]

The Murder of John Fitzgerald Kennedy

1963: Members of the Castro assassination team were arrested at Lake Pontchartrain, Louisiana, by Bobby Kennedy's Justice boys. Angered, Onassis stopped trying to kill Castro. He ordered the assassination team to change targets and go for the head: JFK, who according to Onassis, had welshed on a Mafia deal. JFK had set up the "Group of 40" (advisors) to fight Onassis.

Maheu reassigned the team to the murder of JFK. Shooters included Johnny Roselli and Jimmy Fratianno. To these he added Eugene Brading, a hitman from the Denver Mafia Smaldones "family." Brading, on parole after a series of crimes in California, applied for a new driver's license, explaining to the California Department of Motor Vehicles that he had decided to change his name—to "Jim Braden." Brading got his parole officer's permission to make two trips to Dallas, in November, on "oil business": the first time, to look over the planned assassination spot at Dealey Plaza, and the second time, when JFK was scheduled for his Dallas trip. [Various estimates of the size of the entire team, including back-ups and people standing ready to assist the shooters in fleeing the scene, and to confiscate cameras, or identify and intimidate potential

witnesses, etc., range up to several dozen people.—sc2005]

NOTE: One of the best descriptions I have seen of Lee Harvey Oswald's life and activities prior to the JFK assassination, and how and by whom he was chosen to participate as the chosen patsy, appears in *Double Cross*[11] on page 331-335.—sc2005.

August 1963: Two murders had to occur before the murder of JFK, of people who would understand the situation and might squawk:

August 3: Phillip Graham: Editor and Publisher of the *Washington Post*. Phillip had married Eugene Meyer's daughter, Katharine, who had inherited the *Washington Post, Newsweek*, and allied media empire from her father. Phillip Graham had put together the Kennedy-Johnson ticket and was Kennedy's friend in the struggle with Onassis. Phillip wanted to dump Katharine in favor of his girlfriend, Robin Webb, and keep on running the *Washington Post*. He had moved out of Katherine's home, and was living with his girlfriend. He was rewriting his will to assert ownership/control over the Post, and cut Katharine out. Katharine fought back. She bribed some psychiatrists to certify that Phil was insane, and had him locked up in a nuthouse. Then she checked him out of the nuthouse for a weekend, and Phillip died of a shotgun wound in the head, in the bathroom; his death was ruled "suicide".[12]

August 10: Senator Estes Kefauver: whose Crimes Commission investigations had uncovered the 1932 deal between Onassis, Kennedy, Eugene Meyer, Lansky and Roosevelt. Kefauver planned a speech on the Senate floor denouncing Mafia operations. Instead, he ate a piece of apple pie laced with rat poison, and had a "heart attack" on the Senate floor.

August 8: Jackie Kennedy's third child, Patrick, born prematurely, died. Jackie was depressed. Her sister, Lee Bouvier Radziwill, who lived in Paris, planned to join Onassis on his yacht, Christina, for a cruise. According to Lee, she asked Onassis whether she could invite Jackie along, to "cheer her up." Onassis agreed, but suggested that the plans be secret, because he knew Jack would not approve.

September: Members of the Castro assassination team were arrested at Lake Pontchartrain by Bobby Kennedy's Justice boys, but released.

September 17: Jackie Kennedy announced plans to visit Greece for a 2-week rest in October. Onassis was not on the public itinerary.

October 2-4: Jackie flew to Greece, and joined Onassis on the Christina. Also present were her sister, Lee Bouvier Radziwill, Lee's husband Staz, and Mr. and Mrs. Franklin Delano Roosevelt, Jr. (This Roosevelt was the U.S. Under Secretary of Commerce.)

Onassis's assassination contractor, Robert Maheu, was making final arrangements to blow JFK away, while Onassis was getting off on this extra layer of complication and perverse pleasure. And that's where Jackie was when JFK got tipped off that big "O" was arranging to wipe him out.

JFK called Jackie on the yacht, from the White House, hysterical, screaming: "Get off that yacht if you have to swim!" And he secretly canceled his planned appearance at a football game in Chicago, ("a safe Mafia murder town") on November 1, where the CIA-Mafia assassination team would be poised for the kill. But Jackie stayed on board, descending the gangplank a few days later on Onassis's arm, in Turkey, so that Onassis could impress the Turkish Bey, Mustapha.

October 17: Jackie Kennedy returned to Washington from her two-week tour: Turkey, Morocco, various Greek islands, and Onassis's private island, Skorpios.

---

[11] *Double Cross*, Giancana, 1992.
[12] See Davis: *Katharine the Great: Katharine Graham and her Washington Post Empire*, for some of the details of the story.

November 1-2: The hit on JFK was planned in true Onassis style: it was to be a dramatic triple execution, together with South Vietnam's two brothers, Ngo Dinh Diem [then President of South Vietnam] and Ngo Dinh Nhu. Diem and Nhu got theirs, as scheduled, via Onassis's Captain Nung. The third brother, Cardinal Ngo Dinh Thuc (Cardinal of Vietnam), avoided his death because he was at the Vatican visiting the Pope. Jack avoided his—scheduled to occur on the way to the Chicago football stadium—that day. Nhu's wife, now a widow, Madame Nhu, bitterly remarked, "Whatever has happened in Vietnam will see its counterpart in the United States."

One of the assassination team (Tom Vallee, a double for Oswald), in Chicago with Oswald for rehearsals for the hit, was picked up in a car, with a rifle, with 2 other team members, and quickly released by the Chicago police. The arrest record was fudged over.

November 22: Three weeks later, Onassis's and Maheu's Dallas murder back-up plan went into effect: JFK was assassinated in Dallas—like Chicago, a "safe Mafia murder town."

A witness who recognized pictures of some of the people who were arrested in Dealey Plaza [and quickly released] as having been in Chicago three weeks earlier told Black Panthers Hampton and Clark about it. This witness spent the next 6 months trying to get the FBI to listen to his story. They didn't want to hear about it. Finally, when he kept insisting, he was invited to step inside their office, and he hasn't been seen since. [*Researcher Sherman Skolnick, a Chicago resident, also learned of the Chicago plot. See Chapter 48: Sherman Skolnick Sounds Off!*]

[*NOTE: Roberts wrote that the assassination team included 28 men. This included shooters, timers, back-up men to hide the guns, and people to transport the team members out of town, as well as people to seize cameras and identify and terrify witnesses. Many of these witnesses, as noted in other accounts, ended up dead. As there was at Watergate, one would expect that there would be a command/communication post somewhere nearby.* **Double Cross** *mentions an assassination team of "several dozen" people. Both Gemstone and Double Cross state clearly that the CIA and the Mafia had worked together for years, and were in some ways indistinguishable (especially in international gun-running and drug smuggling operations). From this perspective, the JFK assassination was simply one more in a long string of political assassinations, many involving the murders of leaders of foreign countries. Bringing it all home for domestic political murders was nothing special for the CIA/Mafia killer teams.*

Team members were supplied by the Mob, the CIA, Cuban "freedom fighters" longing to get back to the good old days of Batista; elements of the Dallas police force, etc. Presumably the CIA/Mafia overseers had, and still have, the entire roster.

We may never know the names of every member of the team. Nor does it really matter. None of them have ever been brought to trial for this crime, and it is unlikely that any will ever be. Many are now dead; some, like Frank Sturgis, from natural causes; others, like Johnny Roselli and Sam Giancana, wiped out by fellow gangsters of their wide-flung association to make sure they "keepa da mouth shut" permanently. Note to would-be killers for money:

NOTE: *The Kiwi Gemstone File asserts that G. Gordon Liddy shot Tippitt. See Chapter 38.*

NOTE: *I believe Police Officer Roscoe White, who had been "placed" with the Dallas Police Department only 3 weeks before the shooting, just like Oswald, when many of the assassination team took their assigned places, was the "second policeman" in the police car with Tippitt as it cruised around looking to pick up, and kill, Oswald. White, dressed in a policeman's uniform complete with badge, was supposed to be "guarding" the right side of the Overpass bridge, but had ample opportunity to drift over behind the picket fence, location of the "badge-man" whose picture is slowly coming into focus in enhanced photos and witnesses' account. See Jim Marrs'* <u>Crossfire, the Plot that Killed Kennedy</u>*.—sc2005*

Oswald went to the movies. A shoe store manager told the theatre cashier that a suspicious-looking man had sneaked in to the theater without paying. Fifteen assorted cops and FBI charged out to the movie theatre to look for the guy who had sneaked in. It may have been planned that the police would shoot the "cop-killer" in the theatre, for "resisting arrest". But since Oswald surrendered immediately, in front of witnesses, that didn't happen. The Dallas police brought Oswald out for small-time Mafia Jack Ruby to kill two days later.

[NOTE: Some researchers believe that Oswald was the designated patsy, but that he did not shoot at anyone that day. He was simply "in place", at the book depository, following orders like an obedient pawn. Davis and Giancana cite Oswald's connections with both the CIA and the New Orleans Mob. According to Double Cross, Sam Giancana told his brother that when the JFK hit was proposed, he asked Carlos Marcello, Mafia main man in New Orleans, for assistance, and Marcello proposed Oswald as the patsy. Giancana then sent Johnny Roselli to New Orleans to check Oswald out. Roselli reported back: "He's perfect." [p.332.] Roberts says that Oswald's assignment was to shoot John Connally, and he did so, perhaps putting two bullets into him. But he did not shoot Kennedy; others were assigned for that task.—sc2005]

[NOTE: Double Cross places Tom Vallee (a double for Oswald) and Richard Cain at opposite ends of the Texas School Book Depository, and as both shooting from there. It names Roscoe White and J. D. Tippitt as two of the shooters at JFK, both from the Overpass. It states that they were supposed to kill Oswald also, while "resisting arrest"; but Tippitt faltered, so Roscoe White had to shoot him. Oswald got away for a brief period.

I have tapes prepared by researcher William Klaber, including a taped interview with Geneva White, Roscoe White's widow, where she recounts the story of the Whites' involvement in the assassination. The interview was done when Geneva White was more or less on her death bed, dying from cancer. It is what is generally regarded as a "death bed confession." Although such confessions are traditionally taken seriously, in this case Geneva's story has been widely pooh-poohed by some who insist that Geneva and her son, Ricky White, are lying because they are publicity-seekers trying to make a quick buck off the assassination of JFK and the dead Roscoe White's part in it. I also have a tape of a William Taber broadcast over a small radio station in Jeffersonville, N.Y., where he recounts his story of interviewing Geneva White, then going to Dallas and being threatened by a Dallas police official with regard to using this information.

The Whites' story has been "disproved" and "discredited" by some, but I believe this to be part of the general denial and cover-up of any additional information that threatens to creep out about the JFK assassination. Geneva White said that Roscoe White was the tall man in the uniform (Dallas Police) (called "Badge Man" by researchers who have analyzed photos taken just at the moment when his shots were fired), who shot from behind the fence at the grassy knoll; jumped over the fence and took a camera away from a witness who was taking pictures while the assassination occurred; then jumped back over the fence. She also said that Roscoe White was an excellent rifle shot who had performed other assassinations in various countries for the CIA. Roscoe White had been "assigned" to the Dallas Police Force 3 weeks before the assassination—about the same time that Lee Harvey Oswald got his "new job" there. That is, when the assassination team, after the cancellation of the scheduled October 1 rub-out in Chicago, got the go-ahead for the Dallas scenario. Geneva also said that after he had participated in the JFK assassination, Roscoe vowed never to participate in another such "sanctioned" murder. For this, Roscoe himself was killed in a particularly cruel way. —sc2005]

Brading stayed at the Teamster-Mafia-Hoffa-financed "Cabana Motel" while in Dallas for his "oil business" and the JFK assassination. Ruby had gone to the Cabana Motel the night before the murder, says the Warren Report.

The rest, as they say, is history. Onassis was so confident of his control over police, media, FBI,

CIA, Secret Service, the U.S. Congress, Lyndon Johnson and the U.S. Judicial System that he had JFK murdered by a team of 28 or men, before the eyes of the entire nation, on prime-time TV; then systematically bought off, killed off, or frightened off all witnesses and had the evidence destroyed; and then had a 75-year seal of secrecy plastered over the entire matter.

Cover-up participants included, among many: Gerald Ford on the Warren Commission (a Nixon recommendation), and CIA attorney Leon Jaworski, of the CIA-front Anderson Foundation, representing Texas before the Commission to see that the fair name of Texas was not besmirched by the investigation. (It appears that Jaworski, just off the Texas assassination commission, kept the fact that Oswald had operative status with the FBI a secret from the Warren Commission.) There were also CIA Dallas Chief John McCone; his assistant, Richard Helms; and a passle of police, FBI, news media, etc.

WHAT HAPPENED TO THE CONSPIRATORS?

Most were rewarded; some were murdered; some were rewarded first, then later murdered, if there was any fear or danger that they might confess to what they had done, or implicate any of the other participants. Particularly, if the trail led upward to the next higher Maf level.

Johnny Roselli received part of his pay-off for the head shot on JFK in the form of a $250,000 "finder's fee" for bringing "Hughes" (Onassis) to Las Vegas in 1967. He was a "grand old man of the Mafia" for the next thirteen years. But in July, 1976, he was murdered, when he was scheduled to appear before an investigating committee.

***

Jimmy Fratianno's pay-off included $109,000 in "non-repayable loans", from the San Francisco National Bank (President: Mafia Joe Alioto). Credit authorization for the series of loans, from 1964 to 1965, came from Joe Alioto and a high Teamster official. Dunn and Bradstreet noted this transaction, listing the loans in their 1964-65 monthly reports and wondering in amazement how Fratianno could obtain so much "credit" as his only known title was "Mafia Executioner". *[Note: Roberts was joking about this a bit when he phrased it that way. D&B merely put something relatively mild in that file, to the effect that Fratianno was a "poor risk. Mafia connections.-"-sc]*

Fratianno went around for years bragging about it: "Hi there, I'm Jimmy Fratianno, Mafia Executioner...." A bank V.P. told the whole story to the California Crime Commission, where Al Harris heard it, and it was hidden in a file folder there. Al Harris later shot off his mouth a little too much about it—and "heart attacked".

In March of 1975, Fratianno was testifying before a San Francisco Grand Jury in regard to his participation, with East Coast Mafia Tony Romano, in the Sunol Golf Course swindle (which cost San Francisco somewhere between $100,000 and $500,000), with the active help of Mayor Joe Alioto.

In between, Fratianno used his $109,000 in "non-repayable loans" to start a trucking company in the Imperial Valley, where he engaged in a lot more swindling, involving U.S. government construction contracts. As one California Crime Commission member explained, "The Mafia is doing business directly with the U.S. Government now."

Fratianno spent many years in "protective custody" as a Federal witness. No one ever asked him: "Where were you on November 22, 1963?"

Eugene Brading was questioned by the FBI two months after his arrest—and release—at Dallas, and then released again, as part of the Warren Commission's determination to "leave no stone unturned" in its quest for the truth about the JKF assassination. In spite of the fact that Brading was a known criminal with an arrest record dating back about twenty years, the FBI reported

that he knew nothing whatsoever about the assassination. He was never called to testify before the Warren Commission.

Brading later became a charter member of the La Costa Country Club, Mafia heaven, down near Nixon's Paradise in San Clemente. He also became a runner for the skim money from the Onassis-"Hughes" Las Vegas casinos to Onassis's Swiss Banks.

A group of bankers, headed by a Bank of America official, had picked Nixon for Congress, in 1946, and ran him against Jerry Voorhees; then against Helen Gahagan Douglas, and moved him on up. The same group of bankers picked Gerald Ford to run for Congress. The reason for his selection was his real father: Leslie King, Sr.

Almost everyone knows the touching story of Ford's adoption, as an infant—and the reappearance of his real father, Leslie King, Sr., driving a Cadillac—when Ford was a college football hero. Almost no one knows that Leslie King, Sr., was a minor member of the Denver Smaldones Mafia family—engaged in minor swindles and scams in Montana. The Smaldones Mafia family did a few favors for King, Sr. Then they picked his son, Leslie King, Jr. (alias Gerry Ford, and Mr. Clean), to run for Congress. After the JFK murder, the time came for the Denver Smaldones family to ask for their return favor. They had U.S. Congressional Representative "Gerald Ford" put on the Warren Commission. His assignment: Hide the role of Eugene Brading and the rest of the Denver Smaldones Mafia family at Dallas. Gerry Ford did it.

The Denver regional office of State Farm Insurance carries the insurance of every member of the Denver Smaldones Mafia family, including Leslie King, Sr. Senator Everett Dirksen ran State Farm Insurance in Peoria, Illinois. When he died, his son- in-law, Senator Howard Baker (of the Watergate Committee) took over.

Gerald Ford, of the Warren Commission, went on to become President-by-appointment of Nixon, then in danger of even further and more serious exposure. From this position of trust Ford pardoned Nixon one month later, for "any and all crimes he may have committed." That covers quite a lot, but Ford is good at covering things up.

McCone, the head of CIA-Dallas, went on to become a member of the Board of Directors of ITT, sitting right next to Francis L. Dale, the head of CREEP ("Committee to Re-Elect the President.") Richard Helms, McCone's assistant for the Dallas operation, was ultimately rewarded with the post of CIA Director.

Leon Jaworski, CIA Attorney, became the Watergate Prosecutor, replacing Archibald Cox, who was getting too warm. Jaworski turned in a sterling performance in our "Government-As-Theatre": the honest, conscientious investigator who "uncovered" not a bit more than he had to, and managed to steer everybody away from the underlying truth.

On the other hand:

Dr. James "Red" Duke, the Parkland surgeon who stopped up the hole **ONE** bullet made going through John Connally's chest and lung and saved his life, but had to leave the fragments of a **SECOND** bullet (the one Duke never mentions) in his neck, was shipped off after Chappaquiddick to a remote hospital on a mountaintop in Afghanistan by a grateful CIA, to get him out of the way of any awkward questioning. He remained there for two years. *He was lucky the group who assassinated JFK didn't kill him. He has had a distinguished career as a surgeon, and all around great guy, ever since. But his human decency and life-saving skills wouldn't have saved him, any more than it saved the lives of many decent, law-abiding citizens who have been slaughtered over the years simply because they were witnesses to various public political assassinations. The fact that he saved John Connally's life may be why he has been spared. His testimony about the two bullets in Connally (plus being grazed by a third) would have made the unbelievable "magic bullet" theory of Senator Arlen*

Specter and the Warren Commission and its supporters into high comedy, as well as high tragedy for our country.

Jim Garrison, New Orleans D.A., who tried to get Eugene Brading out of L.A. for questioning (but used one of Brading's other aliases, Eugene Bradley, by mistake), had his witnesses shot out from under him, and was framed on charges of bribery and extortion. (His case was later discredited in an interminable press controversy launched by James Phelan, who collaborated with Robert Maheu on a book about Hughes.)

FBI officers "confiscated" photos of Brading taken on the scene, and hid them away. But at least one photo escaped. This is the one first published in 1976, in Peter Noyes' book, *Legacy of Doubt*, reproduced here. The one where he is seen wearing his X-marked leather hat.

After JFK's death, Onassis quickly established control over Lyndon Johnson through fear. On the trip back to Washington, Johnson was warned by radio relayed from the Pentagon: "There was no conspiracy. Oswald was a lone nut assassin. Get it, Lyndon? Otherwise, Air Force One might have an unfortunate accident on the flight back to Washington." Lyndon got it.

When Jackie got back to the White House with JFK's body, Onassis was one of the first visitors there to console her.

***

During the following months, Onassis filled all important government posts with his own men. All government agencies became the means to accomplish an end: rifle the American Treasury, steal as much as possible, keep the people confused and disorganized; murder their leaders; pursue world domination. *(Much like what is going on today, under "El Busho's" administration—sc.)*

"Hughes," Onassis's invisible Charlie McCarthy puppet, became America's largest "defense" contractor, sucking money out of the U.S. like a gigantic vacuum cleaner, at the rate of $1 million per day. The money was funneled away through the "Hughes Medical Research Foundation" tax-free money-laundering facility. *Today it is Halliburton, Bechtel, Lockheed, etc. Same guys, same philosophy.—sc.*

JFK's original "Group of 40" was turned over to Rockefeller and his man, Henry Kissinger, so that they could more effectively screw over South America. And they did. *(And they are still doing it.—sc.)*

1964: Arthur E. Silva, a San Francisco private detective hired by Angelina Alioto to get the goods on philandering Joe, followed Joe Alioto to Vacaville, to the Nut Tree Restaurant, where Joe held a private meeting with other Mafiosi to arrange the details of the JFK assassination pay-off to Fratianno. Silva's witnessing this meeting led to his murder on September 2, 1971.[13] His name was included in [and lost among] a list of 73 murder victims in the so-called "Zebra" and "Death Angels" murders, and the peculiar details of his murder were covered up and fudged over. Silva had been the only "outside" witness to this meeting, which became a crucial factor in a suit filed by Joe Alioto against *Look* magazine. The suit dragged on from 1970 through 1976, and ended with Alioto's victory and *Look* folding.

[I am indebted to indefatigable journalist and researcher Gerald Carroll's 1994 book, *Project*

---

[13] A California resident recently informed me that the Nut Tree corporation suddenly collapsed around 1995, when more information about Gemstone emerged. It had been a great establishment, restaurant, tourist attraction and a huge moneymaker. But it mysteriously went down due to "family conflicts" within the family that owned it. He said: "I was told the nagging Gemstone allegations of an Alioto mob meeting were always dogging the family and they just got fed up with it. They ended up shutting down the Nut Tree. The huge beautiful I-80 landmark was ingloriously torn down just last year and replaced with a bland shopping center."

Seek: Onassis, Kennedy and the Gemstone Thesis, for many interesting details regarding Silva, Nut Tree, Joe Alioto, etc.—and for many other elucidations of dark corners in Gemstone and the *Skeleton Key*. In fact, for interested readers, I recommend reading this book and Gerry's book together. They complement each other well.—sc2005]

1967: Onassis had always enjoyed the fast piles of money to be made through gambling. He began by buying into Monte Carlo, in the 50's, and continued in Cuba under Batista, where Meyer Lansky ran a huge gambling operation for Onassis. When Onassis's Cuban gambling empire was lost to Castro (together with the $8 billion in the till) and the Bay of Pigs fiasco made it unlikely to be recovered, Onassis took over Las Vegas in 1967, using the "Hughes" cover. U.S. Government officials explained that it was all right because "at least Hughes isn't the Mafia." (ha, ha.)

NOTE: L. Wayne Rector was hired around 1955 by the Carl Byoir Public Relations Agency (Hughes's Los Angeles P.R. firm) to act as Hughes's double. In 1957, when Onassis grabbed Hughes, Rector got a full-time, permanent job as Hughes's stand-in. Rector was the "Hughes" surrogate for years in Las Vegas; Robert Maheu actually ran the show; Maheu got his orders from Onassis; the six male "nursemaids," called the "Mormon Mafia," kept Rector sealed off from prying eyes. Meanwhile, brain-damaged, heroin-hooked, permanently crippled Howard Hughes sat silently staring from his wheelchair in Onassis's private hospital-prison on Skorpios/Tenos for all those years, like a paralyzed fly in a monstrous spider's web, always available for fresh fingerprints if necessary.

1968: June 5: Bobby Kennedy knew who killed his brother; he wrote about it in unpublished revisions to the second edition of his book, *The Enemy Within*. When he foolishly tried to run for President, Onassis had him offed, using a sophisticated new technique. Hypnotized Sirhan Sirhan shot at him from the front—and missed. "Security guard" Thane Cesar (from Lockheed Aircraft *[according to Roberts, secretly owned by Onassis—sc2005]*), standing right behind Bobby, held a small palm gun right up to Bobby's head, behind the ear, and ultimately shot him three times: once, behind the ear, right into the brain, and twice more into the right rear armpit. There was no way he could possibly miss. Sirhan's nine shots went all over the place, everywhere but into Bobby. Before the shooting, Sirhan had been escorted "across Lake Michigan" by a group of Greek friends, where he was hypnotized and drugged, presumably in a medical or mind-control center *[maybe in Canada?-sc]*. Bobby, dying, turned around to face his killer, and pulled Thane Cesar's bow-tie from his shirt as he fell. The black bow-tie lay near his hand as he lay on the floor, dying.

Evelle Younger, then the Los Angeles District Attorney, covered it all up, including the squawks of Los Angeles Coroner Thomas Noguchi. Later, Younger was rewarded with the post of California Attorney General. His son, Eric Younger, got a second-generation Mafia reward: a judge-ship at age 30. Ted Charach, who was on the scene when Bobby was murdered, did a documentary film on the RFK murder, called *The Second Gun*. It was bought, and suppressed for years, by Warner Brothers.

After Bobby's death, Teddy Kennedy knew who did it. He ran to Onassis, on the Christina, afraid for his life, and swore eternal obedience. In return, Onassis granted him his life and said he could be President, just like his big brother, if he would behave himself and follow orders. Teddy decided he would prefer to go on living; well, no one can exactly blame him for that.

[NOTE: Part of the deal Teddy made was that Onassis would get to marry Jackie. She was the ultimate Trophy Wife. Imagine: the widow of the President of the United States, sold to the Mafia Big-Time Murderer, who had already killed her husband and her brother-in-law. And all she got out of it was money.—sc2005]

1968: Mafia Joe Alioto had Presidential ambitions, shored up by his participation in the Dallas pay-off. Everyone who helped kill JFK got a piece of the U.S. pie. And Joe had helped arrange for Jimmy Fratianno's Mafia pay-off. With Bobby Kennedy assassinated, Hubert Humphrey became the Democratic candidate. Joe Alioto, Mafia Mayor of San Francisco, wanted to be Humphrey's V.P., and San Francisco Mafia Boss Lanza approved. Why not? But J. Edgar Hoover, FBI head, spiked Joe's plans by releasing some of his raw FBI files on Alioto at the Democratic National Convention. Joe was out of the running for V.P., and Hubert had to settle for Ed Muskie.

September 16, 1968: A car smashed into Roberts' car, parked in front of the Soviet consulate in San Francisco. The Soviets routinely take pictures of everything that goes on in front of the consulate. Their photos showed the license plate of the car: UKT-264, on a blue Cadillac belonging to Mia Angela Alioto, Joe's daughter. The driver was Tom Alioto, Joe's son, whose driving license, and the car's license, were both fraudulent. Mayor Joe Alioto was high up in San Francisco's Democratic Mafia hierarchy, second to Lanza, and Joe still had high political aspirations, even though his V.P. hopes were scotched, at least for the present. Humphrey planned to come to S.F. for a final pre-election rally, sparked by Joe Alioto. Roberts threatened to blow the hit-and-run story plus its Mafia ramifications wide open, if Humphrey came to S.F.

Tom Alioto smashing into a parked car using a fraudulent driver's license could be troublesome. So a first-class fix-up was arranged. First, the San Francisco Police towed Roberts' car away. Then, San Francisco MP's from the Presidio staged a few more car smashes on the same corner, all duly filmed by the Russians. When Roberts arrived on the scene and began picking up pieces of the various cars that had been involved, trying to figure out what had happened, Lanza himself was on the scene, and ordered him to "Move on; nothing happened here."

To make doubly sure that neither Alioto's son's or daughter's name would ever be connected to Roberts' smashed car, Alioto's "fixers" found Kathryn Hollister, a nurse whose car had a nearly identical license plate number, only off by one digit. She, with a perfect driving record, was "persuaded" to take the rap for the hit-and-run. Details of the hit-and-run and the cover-up were filed under Kathryn Hollister's name, with a cross-reference to another file for Bruce Roberts. In addition, however, some sort of block was put on the files, so that no one was allowed to see them except Bruce Roberts, who couldn't do anything with them.

Roberts had been completely apolitical for years, happily busy with his crystallography and scientific experiments. He had, though, through a series of accidents, coincidences, family connections, and long nights spent conversing in a wide cross section of bars, a talent for communication that brought him into contact with many different people, and a remarkable memory. He had learned a great many things about how things are done and what was going on in our country, particularly in San Francisco—without especially trying. He made the mistake of thinking that this smash-up, and the following cover-up, were directed at him personally. He got mad. With the photos supplied by the Russians, he threatened to spill the whole story at the scheduled Court hearing—with photos—and to relate it to corrupt Mafia election processes and the whole ball of wax.

The Judge of the Court Hearing, Judge Aitken, let Roberts know that she intended to dismiss the charge against him. But Roberts planned to plead "Guilty—with an explanation"—and then launch into a FULL explanation—with photographs. When the Court hearing came up, Roberts began to speak, but she cut him off. She dismissed the case immediately. Roberts planned to carry it further.

The next evening, Brading and Fratianno showed up in the Black Magic Bar. Brading was

wearing his big X-marked hat from Dallas to see whether Roberts recognized it, and them, and how much he knew. Brading and Fratianno took the bar stools on each side of Roberts, while another killer stood behind him. Brading handed Roberts the hat, and asked him what he thought about it. Roberts took the hat and studied it.

"It's a good hat; that's all I can say for it. But if you wore a beanie, you'd look just like Pope Montini," Roberts said.

Brading laughed. "Better not let my Rabbi—Rabbi Magnin—hear you say that."

[Note: Rabbi Cyril Magnin, a San Francisco Rabbi, was prominent, wealthy, and politically well-connected (to the Republican Mob) —and to Mae Magnin Brussell, his niece. Her own father was Rabbi Edward Magnin, a prominent Democrat. So it's impossible to tell from this exchange which of the Rabbi Magnin brothers is meant here. But it makes little difference, since both Democrats and Republicans were entangled with "Mafia" control and deception—including the religious leaders, as well. Mae's grandfather was the founder of I. Magnin's, an upscale California department store chain, and the family was quite wealthy. I have asked myself whether what looks like Mae's resolute suppression of the contents of her section of the Gemstone File for many years may have been due to her family's political connections. And it has been suggested to me that she got away with her research, writing and radio programs as long as she did because of her family's protection. Of course there were other possible reasons as well. See Chapter 36, on Mae Brussell's 1977-8 Dialogue Conspiracy programs on Gemstone, and my comments on them.—sc2005]

An MP from the Presidio posted at the end of the bar piped up, "I heard they let everyone with an X-marked hatband through the police lines at Dallas".

Roberts didn't say a word. He was not in a position to say anything.

He had seen the hat before—in a photo of Brading, taken at Dallas, stuffing a rifle under his coat, in the pergola on Elm Street, closely adjoining the picket fence atop the "grassy knoll", *[from behind which, perhaps, "Badgeman", perhaps J. D. "Roscoe" White, had shot, simultaneously with Brading's shot at JFK.-sc2005]* The photo may have been taken by Antonio Iglesias, CIA—whose sister, Marina, had been married to Roberts' brother, Dayle.[14]

Cover-up support for Alioto in the hit-and-run was complete. Senator Everett Dirksen, who ran State Farm Insurance in Peoria, Illinois, insurers of Roberts' car, covered up the insurance end of the hit-and-run.

Humphrey had planned to come to San Francisco for a final pre-election rally, sparked by Alioto. Roberts, angered by the auto insurance company's plan not to pay off on his wrecked car, threatened to blow the hit-and-run story plus its Mafia ramifications wide open if Humphrey came to San Francisco as planned. Humphrey didn't come; Humphrey lost perhaps 100,000 votes in San Francisco. This happened to be the margin by which he lost the state of California, and the election.

That is the basis for Roberts' claim that "he elected Nixon to the Presidency."

As a result, Humphrey lost the State of California, and the election. And Richard Nixon became President. *[Well...maybe. But obviously, many factors determine the outcome of an event such as an election.—sc]*

Beginning at about this time, Roberts' "gemstones"—synthetic rubies, sapphires and diamonds, with accompanying "histories", which he called "gemstone papers", began going out to private individuals, foreign heads of state, and foreign consular officials, over a period of years, in return for more information. A worldwide information network was gradually developed—a

---

[14] See Appendix A.

trade of the intelligence activities of many countries. This intelligence network is the source of much of the information in the Gemstone File.

Roberts wrote later on that he had been mistaken in his evaluation of the hit-run incident as a personal attack on him; apparently, it had been strictly an accident in every sense. Roberts had been apolitical and quite indifferent to politics for years; he hadn't even voted. But his father was a Republican who had worked on Nixon's campaign, and had many friends in the Republican camp.

[NOTE: At this time, Roberts appeared to feel that the immediate problem with the election process was with the Democratic camp. So his first "Gemstone" offers were to Nixon and Mitchell in 1968. Roberts sent a letter to Nixon (and John Mitchell) that he claims elected Nixon to the Presidency. This letter is not in the section of the file that I now have, which only goes back to 1970. But he does describe what he says were the reactions of Nixon to this letter: totally negative.—sc2005]

October: Jackie Kennedy was now "free" to marry Onassis. An old Mafia rule: if someone welches on a deal, kill him, and take his gun and his girl: in this case, Jackie and the Pentagon.

November: Richard Carlson wrote "The Alioto Mafia Web" story for *Look* magazine.

Election Day: Nixon was elected President.

1969: February: Roberts gave information to Nixon, via local Republicans, about certain heavy stones or minerals of strategic importance that might be found in China, which he says changed Nixon's policies. [See Gemstone letter dated May 24, 1971].

July: Leak of Carlson's "Alioto Mafia Web" story caused political consternation. Alioto and Baker tried to bribe Jess Unruh to run for the U.S. Senate instead of for Governor, thus leaving Joe Alioto a clear shot at the Governor's slot. But that would interfere with Ted Kennedy's plan to put his friend, John Tunney, into that Senate seat.

Murder at Chappaquiddick

Mary Jo Kopechne, a devoted JFK campaign worker, and after his murder, one of Bobby's trusted aides, was put in charge of packing up his files after his assassination in L.A. But she read too much of the files. She learned about the Kennedy family's Mafia involvement, going back to Joe Kennedy's dealings—and other things.

She said to friends: "This isn't Camelot, this is murder!" and vowed she would never work for a Kennedy again. She was an idealistic American Catholic. She didn't like murdering hypocrites. So she went to work for Mayor Whelan in New Jersey, where she learned even more about rotten crooked Democratic politics.

The party at Chappaquiddick was arranged by Teddy Kennedy's Democratic organization as a "thank you" for the workers in the last campaign. It was scheduled for the weekend of July 18, 1969.

Mary Jo came to the party to announce her engagement, and to tell her old friends and former co-workers that she would never work for a Kennedy's election again. She died trying to get off Chappaquiddick Island, where she had overheard (along with everyone else in the cottage rented from Sidney Lawrence), Teddy Kennedy's end of a series of telephone calls from John Tunney, at his sister Joan Tunney Wilkinson's home in Tiburon, to Teddy, and then from Teddy to Joe Alioto, and then to Democrat bigwigs Ben Swig, Shorenstein, Schumann and Steven Bechtel.

Teddy Kennedy and John Tunney had become friends when they were college roommates. Joan Bennett Kennedy had known Joan Tunney from college as well.

Teddy's good friend John Tunney had called to complain that Alioto's friend Rabbi Cyril Magnin (Mae Magnin Brussell's uncle) and others were trying to bribe Jess Unruh to switch from the

California Governor's race to run for the Senate, for the seat John Tunney wanted. Alioto would then have an easier run for Governor—but John Tunney would have a harder race for the Senate. Teddy felt he had exclusive dibs on the right to select the Democratic candidates for office, as the surviving Kennedy brother who had sworn eternal submission and allegiance to Onassis after Onassis had murdered his two brothers. But Alioto felt equally important, because of his own role in arranging for the pay-off to one of JFK's assassins: Jimmy Fratianno. Teddy, drunk and loud, called Alioto to tell him who was in charge, but Alioto told him to go to hell. So Teddy began calling his friends to arrange for yet another Mafia murder.[15]

Mary Jo, up to there with Mafia murders, ran screaming out of the cottage, saying she was on her way to Ralph Nader, and would tell him everything she had learned. Teddy realized he couldn't let her do what she threatened to do. He grabbed the keys to his car, grabbed a lady's purse (which turned out to be Rosemary Keough's purse, by accident), and drove after her. He caught up to her on the road, and offered to drive her to the ferry. She got into the back seat because she wouldn't sit next to him in the front seat. Teddy drove down the road, trying to soothe her anger, until he reached the cross-road. The left-hand turn, on the paved road, led to the Ferry, and Nader. The right-hand turn onto the dirt road led to Dyke Bridge, over Poucha Pond, and to the ocean beach beyond, where the entire party had picnicked that afternoon. Teddy stopped the car at the turn in the road.

Chappaquiddick Deputy Sheriff Christopher Look saw the parked car with its lights on, and thought the occupants might be lost or in trouble. He drove toward them. It was 12:45 a.m.

Teddy, in no mood to talk to anyone, sped off away from Look, and away from the ferry, toward the Bridge. He was going much too fast. The car roared and jounced along the rough dirt road, and began to climb the humpbacked bridge, which curved slightly toward the left at the center of the bridge. The bridge had no railing, only a low curb. Mary Jo, frightened, grabbed Teddy's arm from the back seat, and he backhanded her, busting her nose. He lost control of the car. The right front wheel slammed against the curbing, and Teddy opened his door and bailed out, landing hard on the bridge as the car sailed off in a high fast arc, rolling over as it flew. The car door slammed shut and the car hit the water and sank, landing 32 feet past the point where it went off the bridge, upside down.

Teddy, who was still wearing a neck brace as the result of an accident, watched in amazement as the car sank. Poucha Pond was shallow; the nose of the car was buried in the mud, but the rear end of the car was visible in the water. Teddy climbed to his feet and took off running, back to the cottage. In his mind, Mary Jo was already dead, or would be soon. He thought that if he could make it back to the cottage without being seen, he might come up with a story, and find a way to avoid taking the rap.

The car was nearly filled with ice-cold water. But Mary Jo found that if she clutched the edge of the back seat, she was just able to thrust her busted nose up into a bubble of air that formed up against the floorboards, just inside the trunk of the car, and breath, while she waited for help that never came. Eventually the tissues in that broken nose swelled, and she couldn't breath through that little snorkel. She suffocated in the cold dark car, her body held rigidly in that position, where she was found the next day. Rigor mortis had set in. According to Roberts, it took her 2 hours and 17 minutes to suffocate.

Teddy ran past two pay phones and several houses on his way back to the cottage. If he had phoned the Chappaquiddick Rescue team, available at all times, Mary Jo's life could have been

---

[15] I think this paragraph holds the key to why Mae Brussell was adamant about hiding the *Gemstone File* section she had during her lifetime, and even after death. She was equally adamant about advancing a fantasy that Teddy had not even been in the car when Mary Jo was killed. Her theory was that someone else had killed Mary Jo, somehow swiped Teddy's car and put the body in it, then pushed it off Dyke Bridge. There has never been a shred of evidence to support this theory. But considering her own family's involvement in the Chappaquiddick incident, what else could she do?—sc2005.

saved. When he got back to the cottage where the party was still going on, Teddy called his cousin Joe Gargan and friend Markham outside and told them what had happened. Joe Gargan offered to take the rap for Mary Jo's death, if necessary, to keep from destroying Teddy's chance of running for the Presidency. Nobody reported the incident to the local police or to the Chappaquiddick Rescue Squad, which was always available for emergencies, particularly since this was the weekend of the big. Gargan and Markham drove Teddy to the Ferry landing. From the telephone there they called Bobby's oldest son, Joseph Kennedy III, who was staying at a hotel in Edgartown, and told him to pick Teddy up at the Chappaquiddick ferry dock. The younger Kennedy "borrowed" a boat from the Edgartown dock and ferried Teddy across to Edgartown, with the boat's lights out.

Mary Jo was still breathing in that bubble of air while Teddy sneaked into his room at the Shiretown Inn, combed his hair, put on a bathrobe and went out to establish an alibi with the hotel desk clerk. He yawned, pretended he had been asleep, and pointedly asked the clerk what time it was. It was 2:25 a.m. Then he went back to his room and called Jackie and Onassis on the Christina, charging the call to his own phone number and using his credit card. He also called Katharine Graham, and lawyers. Jackie called the Pope on Teddy's behalf; Pope Montini assigned Cardinal Cushing to help.

The next morning, the incident was still unreported, and Teddy was still pretending he knew nothing about it. After all, anything was possible. Mary Jo might have drowned in the car, or died in the crash, or her body might have gotten out of the car somehow, and vanished in the tide. Depending on the circumstances, a story might be manufactured that absolved Teddy of blame. Particularly since he had manufactured some sort of alibi. The other occupants of the cottage would agree to whatever the official story was to be.

Early the next morning, at low tide, the car was discovered, its trunk sticking up out of the water, by two early fishermen. They had no idea there was anybody in the car. They called the local police, and Police Chief Dominick Arena came down. He dove down to the car, and discovered there was a body in it.

John Farrar, an experienced diver attached to the Chappaquiddick Rescue Squad, arrived next. He dove down to the car, and ascertained that the occupant was dead. He noted her strange position in the back seat of the upside-down car, half-kneeling, with her feet braced against what had been the roof of the car, and her hands gripping the edges of the rear seat so that she could stretch upward and just barely be able to thrust the tip of her nose up into the bubble of stale air in the topmost corner of the submerged car, near the trunk. She had held that awkward pose for hours in the cold, dark water, the only possible posture that would allow her to breath. He noted the pink stains on the collar of her blouse, which showed that she had been bleeding before the car hit the water; and the pink froth that lingered around the tip of her nose, in the corner of the air bubble. She had held that desperate pose for so long that her body had grown rigid with rigor mortis. Farrar had to force her fingers to relinquish their grip on the edge of the rear seat, and disturbed her pose in order to get her body out of the car and up to the surface. She had not drowned; she had suffocated. She had lived for some time in the car. If Teddy had reported the accident in a timely manner, she would have lived.

The license plate of the car was noted, and the car was identified as belonging to Senator Edward Kennedy. They tracked him down, and he eventually came down to the Bridge with Joe Gargan. The situation was not good. John Farrar had observed that Mary Jo had suffocated, not drowned, and that she had lived long enough in that back seat for rigor mortis to have set in while she held her body in that unnatural position. Then there was that awkward bloody, broken nose, and the blood stains on her blouse that showed she had been injured before the car hit the water.

Teddy decided that he would have to take the rap himself, rather than lay it on his cousin Joe Gargan (and Gargan didn't want it!)—and use all his power and influence to avoid a charge of murder or manslaughter.

The first person he called was Attorney Burke Marshall. Marshall had worked with Onassis to steal a whole fleet of surplus "Liberty ships" from the U.S. at bargain basement rates, in a very illegal deal, after World War II ended. He was also the designated custodian for JFK's brains after Dallas.

Cover-up of the Chappaquiddick murder required the help of the following:

- Massachusetts Highway Patrol, which "confiscated" the plates from Teddy's car after it was fished out of the pond;
- The Massachusetts Legislature, which changed a 150-year-old law requiring an autopsy (which would have revealed the suffocation, not drowning, and the broken nose);
- Coroner Donald Mills, who let Kennedy's aide K. Dun Gifford supply him with a death certificate, already prepared for Mill's signature, listing the cause of death as drowning, not suffocation;
- Police Chief Dominick Arenas;
- All the people who had been at the party, including Mary Jo's old friends and co-workers;
- Cardinal Cushing's priests who appeared before Mary Jo Kopechne's parents "direct from God" with personal instructions from Him that Mary Jo's body was not to be disturbed by an autopsy;
- A Pennsylvania mortuary where Mary Jo's broken nose was discreetly patched up;
- East and West Coast phone companies clamped maximum security on the records of calls to and from the Cottage, some of which had been charged to Teddy's credit card. (S.F. Police Chief Cahill was reassigned to a new job: Security Chief for Pacific Telephone, to sit on those phone records on the West Coast—at the same salary as his old job.);
- The entire U.S. Senate, which never said a word or asked a question about Teddy's (required equipment) plug-in phone at the cottage;
- The judge who presided over the mock hearing made sure no embarrassing questions were asked;
- James Reston, editor of Martha's Vineyard's only newspaper, who never said a word about Teddy's phone at the cottage, though residents called in to tell him about it;

No one knew anything, including the *New York Times*, the *Washington Post*, etc.

Gene Tunney's Daughter Joan

John and Joan Tunney were the children of Gene Tunney, a famous boxer. John Tunney's sister, Joan Tunney Wilkinson, heard her brother's end of the phone call, made from her house in Tiburon, California, to Teddy at the Chappaquiddick cottage. The next day, after Mary Jo's body was found, the whole Tunney-Wilkinson family was shipped to Europe. In a panic, Joan ran away to Norway, where she was kidnapped by Mafia hoods Mari and Adamo. They locked her up in a Marseilles heroin factory for 60 days, where heroin fumes turned her into a junkie (no needle marks). Then they turned her loose outside the factory, where she was found wandering around in the woods. Joan's husband complained, so she chopped his head off with an ax, and was subsequently locked up in a nuthouse belonging to the Marquess of Blandford, then Tina Livanos Onassis' husband. Mari and Adamo got pressed into scrap metal in a New Jersey auto junkyard.

Black Panthers Hampton and Clark

In the panic of trying to cover up Teddy's guilt at Chappaquiddick, many things came unglued. The JFK murder threatened to creep out of the woodwork again. Black Panthers Hampton

and Clark were murdered (the Chicago cops fired over Attorney Charles Garry's head) because of what they knew about the JFK murder squad's presence in Chicago on November 1, 1963.

"Gemstones", with histories, had been released around the globe since 1968. In 1969, Roberts gave a Gemstone with history to John Mack, head of California CREEP, and a bank officer with Bank of America, for Nixon, with a proposition: the Presidency in return for wiping out the Mafia. The "history" included Teddy's phone calls to and from the Lawrence Cottage on Chappaquiddick, billed to Teddy's home phone in Hyannisport. Nixon, being Mafia himself, wasn't interested; but he kept the information to use on Teddy whenever it seemed advantageous.

Watergate Plumber/bagman Tony Ulascewicz got the whole story too. He spent almost a year at Chappaquiddick interrogating witnesses, pretending to be a reporter. Among the witnesses: a couple, illicitly fooling around on the banks of Poucha Pond, who saw and heard the car race down the road and sail off the bridge, its headlights rolling wildly as the car rolled over in the air; then saw Teddy stand up on the bridge and walk off. He never dove off into the water to try and rescue Mary Jo, as he claimed; so it never occurred to these bystanders that someone else was still in the car. They might have saved her.

[About Anthony Ulascewicz: In his book, Nixon: A Life, Jonathan Aitken stated that when John Ehrlichman became Nixon's Special Assistant for Domestic Affairs, his former job as the President's counsel was taken over by John Dean. Dean inherited Counsel Ehrlichman's two investigators, Jack Caulfield and Anthony Ulascewicz, both former New York Police Department detectives. In November 1971 Dean ordered Caulfield to send Ulascewicz to case the Watergate offices of the Democratic National Committee. As an ordinary visitor, Ulascewicz made a walk-through seven months before the break-in of June 1972. Dean was aware that Ulascewicz had done the study on Teddy at Chappaquiddick: Dean to Nixon: "…a man who I only know by the name of "Tony," who is the fellow who did the Chappaquiddick study."—White House Transcripts, p.149.—sc2005]

Blackmail, like chewing gum, loses its flavor when it is used. So it is saved. The *Manchester Union Leader* got a copy of the phone calls, made from the cottage, billed to Teddy Kennedy's home phone at Hyannisport, and leaked a teaser on it. The editor, Loeb, used it as leverage to get Jimmy Hoffa out of jail, in return for Hoffa's million-dollar "loan" to the *Manchester Union Leader*.

May 4, 1970: Charlotte Ford Niarchos called her ex-husband Stavros Niarchos, worried about the Ford Foundation's possible involvement in the Chappaquiddick cover-up. Eugenie Livanos Niarchos, in bed with her husband, overheard the conversation. Stavros was forced to beat her to death; he ruptured her spleen and broke the cartilage in her throat. The official cause of death was listed as "overdose of barbiturates," though the autopsy showed these injuries.

Clifford Irving's "Hoax" biography, and Howard Hughes' Death

End of 1970: Howard Hughes presence on earth was no longer required. His handwriting could be duplicated by a computer. His voice pattern could be duplicated over the phone, by speaking through a computerized voice box. His fingerprints were on file, and could be duplicated if necessary. His biography—all the known facts about his life—had been compiled, and a computerized biography had been issued to top Hughes executives. His double, Wayne Rector, had been doing "Hughes" for years. And Hughes was ill. His death was expected shortly. Preparations were being made so that it would not interfere with the orderly continuation of his empire after his death. No reason why it should. Stories were planted that Hughes intended to have his body preserved cryogenically—so that he could be resuscitated in the future, when medical science had advanced, and take his empire back!

Onassis had done well with the management and expansion of his "Hughes" base of

operations in the U.S. In 1970, the "Hughes" holdings were estimated at $2 billion—making him "one of the two richest men in the world, along with J. Paul Getty, the oil man," according to one account. "Hughes's" various U.S. operations employed 67,000 people. "Hughes" was the U.S.'s "largest defense contractor," which meant that billions of dollars went direct from U.S. taxpayers into Onassis's pockets. If you add Hughes's known fortune to that of Onassis, it is quite clear that Onassis was the richest man in the world. And he didn't get that way by being "Mr. Nice Guy." Howard Hughes had no direct heirs. According to one story, an illegitimate child, who might have had a claim, mysteriously disappeared—along with her mother.

Clifford Irving, living on Ibiza, was writing a book about an art forger named Elmyr De Hory. He called the book *Hoax*. One day, De Hory laughed and said, "If you like hoaxes, how about Howard Hughes? That's an even bigger hoax." The Mediterranean gossip about "Hughes" and Onassis was common, and irresistible.

Irving went to "Hughes's" so-called "Mormon Mafia", the six "nursemaids" who guarded "Hughes" for Onassis, for information. One of them—Merryman—had grown tired of the game. He gave Irving the computerized Hughes biography. From it, Irving wrote his "Autobiography of Howard Hughes." He bargained with New York publishers McGraw-Hill for a large advance. He explained that Howard Hughes wouldn't budge from an asking price of $850,000.

November, 1970: When he heard about Irving's book, Onassis knew immediately that someone had given Irving the "insiders'" biography. He suspected Maheu, and fired him. Nervous about discovery—the stakes were high!—Onassis ordered Wayne Rector, the "Hughes" double, and the six Mormon Mafia Nursemaids to get out of Vegas—immediately! And on Thanksgiving Eve, 1970, in the middle of the night, "Hughes" (Wayne Rector) made a well-publicized "secret departure," from Las Vegas to the Britannia Beach Hotel, in the Bahamas.

December 1970: Onassis discovered his mistake, and had Merryman killed. Merryman's name suddenly disappeared from the list of "six Mormon nursemaids." From then on, there were only five. Robert Maheu, accidentally deprived of his $500,000 annual salary, sued "Hughes" for $50 million—mentioning "Hughes's" game plan for the purchase of Presidents, governors, Senators, judges, etc. Onassis settled out of court—cheap at the price—to maintain his custodianship of "American democracy" and the "free world"—and to keep from hanging for multiple murders. *[At last look, Maheu was alive and thriving in California.—sc2005.]*

The "Hughes" Mormon Mafia party, plus Wayne Rector, fled around the world—from the Bahamas, where they murdered an uncooperative Governor and Police Chief; to Nicaragua, where they shot the U.S. Ambassador between the eyes for noticing that there wasn't really any Hughes, only Mafia;[16] and thence to Canada, where another Mormon Mafia nursemaid, Howard Eckersley looted a goodly sum in a swindle of the Canadian Stock Exchange; and on to London, where they holed up in Rothschild's Inn of the Park.

April 18, 1971: Howard Hughes, a human vegetable as the result of serious brain damage suffered during his 1957 hustle, plus fourteen years of heroin, grew sicker and sicker. A final overdose of heroin did him in. His coffin was lowered into the sea from a rocky headland off the coast of Skorpios, Onassis's 500-acre private island. Present at the funeral were: Jackie Kennedy Teddy Kennedy, Francis L. Dale, Director of CREEP; Tom Pappas, also of CREEP; and a South Vietnamese Cardinal named Ngo Dinh Thuc—the third brother of Ngo Dinh Diem and Ngo Dinh Nhu, who had escaped Onassis's planned triple Mafia murder back in October, 1963. (JFK got away that time too.) Onassis allowed some pictures to be taken from a distance; he himself did not appear. The pictures were published in *Midnight*, a now-defunct Canadian tabloid, with a cover story speculating that perhaps the mysterious man who had been kept for so many

---

[16] See *Project Seek*, pp101-105, for an excellent expansion of this passage.

years as a "patient" in Onassis's private "hospital" was really JFK, who didn't die in Dallas!

[NOTE: I included the **Midnight** reference in both the **Playgirl** article on Hughes and Onassis (December 1974) and the original **Gemstone Skeleton Key**. The photos, when the subjects are correctly identified, provide visual evidence; while the cover stories, such as "JFK is alive" and "Is this JFK being buried?" indicate how the mass-directed tabloid publications are regularly used to spread disinformation and cover stories almost instantly to the general (bewildered) public. The twice-monthly **National Enquirer**, for instance, has one of the largest circulations in the world—something like 25,000,000. If you want to spread a story quickly, which would you choose as an outlet: a learned and "serious" publication, which may reach 5-10,000 readers, or the **National Enquirer** or its equivalents? The general public reads these stories and chortles, or gets alarmed. In some cases, the "troll" works differently, and someone steps forward with information that he or she shouldn't have, and is dealt with accordingly. The headlines such as "Is JFK Alive?" alert those more in the know and able to read between the lines that the stories have something to do with politics, even though the story is not meant to be taken literally, and that they should read the stories carefully to keep up to date on what is happening. Unfortunately, some commentators on Gemstone have failed to understand how and why the tabloids are used (for propaganda on one level, and information on another), and consider that my citing of the **Midnight** articles somehow invalidates the Gemstone thesis. On the other end of the scale, Virginia McCullough, keeper of the Mae Brussell archives (in unsorted, unfiled cartons in her basement) has taken another tack. In her irritation with the whole "Gemstone File thing", and perhaps to evade examination of why Mae Brussell hid the files and misrepresented them, (which Virginia doesn't understand anyway), she has plunked a phony "JFK really is alive" article onto her section of the Newsmaker.news website.—sc2005.]

The Albanian Frogmen

Albanian frogmen, who had been tipped off in advance that Hughes's coffin would be lowered into the sea, were waiting under the water. Before the body had time to cool to the surrounding water temperature, they seized the coffin and took the corpse off to Yugoslavia. From there it was sent to China and Russia, and then back to Boston in a foot locker. The corpse's dental work was compared to Hughes's very own (genuine) dental records, and they matched.

Aristotle Onassis was Lord of the Mafia, the richest and most powerful man in the world, a murderer for profit and fun, by the tens, thousands, and millions, in the continuing phony wars—for oil, drugs, arms sales or whatever. He took the same pleasure in destroying men and nations, and profiting from their deaths, that he had taken decades ago, when his whaling ships cruised the seas and mercilessly slaughtered thousands of whales, of many species, some to the point of extinction, using the latest and most devastating technology ever to be directed at these creatures; then he upholstered the bar stools on his yacht with their foreskins. *(Well, the Nazis had their lampshades made out of the human skins of their victims.)*

News of Hughes's death, and the take-over of "Hughes" and of the United States Government by Onassis, and the facts surrounding the murders of JFK, RFK, Martin Luther King, Mary Jo Kopechne, and many more, and the subsequent cover-ups (involving still more murders) have circulated around the globe since late 1968, the date of the Alioto smash-up of Bruce Roberts' car in San Francisco, in the form of the original Gemstone letters. Any country with this information has had the wherewithal to blackmail the U.S Mafia government, which has had no choice but to pay up. The alternative would be for those involved to be exposed as a bunch of treasonous murderers.

This is why China-hating, red-baiting Nixon was forced to "recognize" China (which he later claimed as his greatest accomplishment). And this is also why the USSR walked off for years with such good deals in U.S. loans, grains and whatever else it wanted. All they had to do is mention those magic words—'Hughes, JFK, RFK, MLK, Mary Jo "—and the U.S. Mafia government crawled into a hole. There was no place else to go!

Information once leaked can't be unleaked. The only way to end the dilemma is through a

nuclear war, and that wouldn't be one-sided. Another way would be to throw the Mafia out of the United States. Starting at the top with Ford, Rockefeller and Kissinger.

Super-patriots please note: No one, not all of the radicals and subversives hounded by the US domestic intelligence agencies put together, has done one fraction of the damage done to the US economy, morality, power and prestige as the thieves at the top.

Talk About Chutzpah!

On the day that Howard Hughes was "buried at sea," Clifford Irving's wife, Edith, presented a check from the would-be publisher, McGraw-Hill, in the amount of $325,000, made out to "H. R. Hughes," to Onassis's Swiss Bank ("Credite Suisse," in Zurich) for payment. She was carrying false identification in the name of "Helga R. Hughes," a creature who never walked the earth and who vanished the moment Edith received the cash. Onassis (that is, his bank officers) paid off—cheap at the price![17]

More Skeleton Key

Gemstone papers rolling around the world here and abroad kept the situation hot. Everyone was nervous. Rockefeller gave Kissinger $50,000 for Carlson and Brisson to write their 'expose', The Alioto Mafia Web,' for *Look* magazine. Their mission: find out everything that was public record about Alioto's connection with the JFK murder (like the pay-offs to Fratianno as non-repayable loans, listed in Dunn &Bradstreet), and to explain it all away—any way that didn't lead back to JFK and Dallas. The idea was to get Alioto to quietly go away, but still keep the lid on everything.

May, 1971: Tina Livanos Onassis Blandford divorced the Marquess of Blandford and married Stavros Niarchos, her former brother-in-law-until he killed her sister, Eugenie.

May, 1971: "Folk Hero" Daniel Ellsberg, a well-known hawk from the Rand Corporation, who had designed the missile ring around the "Iron Curtain" countries (how many missiles to aim at which cities) was told to release the faked-up "Pentagon Papers" to help distract people from Hughes, JFK, RFK, MLK, etc. The papers were carefully designed by Ellsberg and his boss, Rand Chief and later World Bank Chief Bob (Body Count) McNamara, to make the Vietnamese War look like "just one of those incredibly dumb mistakes". *(60,000 American dead and a nation hooked on heroin, just an accident, really, folks...)* This helped to cover up the real purpose of the war: continued control, for Onassis and his friends, of the Golden Triangle dope trade (Vietnam, Laos and Cambodia); and for Onassis and the oil people, of Eastern oil sources. To say nothing of control over huge Federal sums, which could be siphoned off in profitable arms contracts, or conveniently 'disappear' into the war effort. *(Oops! Just like Afghanistan (poppies, opium) and Iraq (more oil) under El Busho and VP Cheney—probably the only man in history who has **two private bunkers**—one in Washington under the V.P. mansion, and one in Pennsylvania somewhere. Want to bet whether they are stuffed with money?--sc2006.)* McNamara's 'World Bank' hand-outs of American money to 'starving nations' actually set up huge private bank accounts for various dictators in the Onassis-controlled Swiss banks. The money could be used as needed to support and extend Mafia operations. Example: $8 billion in World Bank funds for 'starving Ethiopians' wound up in Emperor Haile Selassie's personal Swiss bank accounts. This would make Haile Selassie the richest individual in the world, but other dictators have Swiss bank accounts too. Maybe even larger. The money drained from America and other captive Mafia nations to feed a greed that can never be satisfied.

---

[17] A recent article in the New York Times reports that the Credite Suisse Bank is being sued for $millions for stealing money and art work deposited with them by Jews fleeing Hitler's Holocaust. Apparently the source of yet more millions for Onassis, world's richest man at that time.

Rand Corp., one of our major 'think tanks', has another goody in store for the public: "Project Star"—Rand's cover-up fallback version of the JFK murder, held in reserve should public restlessness over the Warren Commission Report cover-up ever threaten to get out of hand. That ought to confuse the people for at least another twelve years, and by that time most of us will be dead anyway...

*NOTE IN PASSING: A major dope trade route is: Golden Triangle to Taiwan to San Francisco. Heroin from the Golden Triangle was sometimes smuggled into San Francisco in the bodies of American GIs who died in battle in Vietnam. One body can hold up to 40 pounds of heroin, crammed in where the guts would be. Some dope gets pressed into dinner plates and painted with pretty patterns. One dope bust in San Francisco alone yielded $6 billion in heroin 'china plates'—the largest dope bust in history. It was quickly and completely hushed up by the San Francisco Mafia press. The dope "plates" sat in the San Francisco Police Department for a while, then were removed by FBI men, and probably sent on their way—to American veins. All this dope processing and shipping is controlled and supervised by the Mafia for the Mafia. Dope arrests and murders are aimed at independent pushers and maverick peddlers and smugglers who are competing with or holding out on the Mafia. While Nixon was conducting his noisy campaign against dope smuggling across the Mexican border, his dope officer in charge of protecting the Mafia dope trade was E. Howard Hunt! Lots of heroin gets processed in a Pepsi Cola factory in Laos. So far, it hasn't produced a single bottle of Pepsi Cola. Some dope gets processed in heroin factories in Marseilles. (See the **French Connection**). Still more dope comes from South America—cocaine, and now heroin. U.S. AID went to build a highway across Paraguay—"From a mountain to a swamp." Useless for the natives who have no cars. (They use it for sunbathing during the day). But at night, it becomes the longest landing strip in the world. All night long, airplanes take off loaded with cocaine. It was financed by US tax money for the benefit of the international Mafia dope pushers. And then there is morphine from Turkish opium. This was the starting point of Onassis' fortune.*

In case one is still wondering whether the Mafia can actually get away with such things, consider the benefits derived from controlling the stock market, the courts, the police, etc. In one swindle alone, the 1970 acquisition by "Hughes" of "Air West", Air West stockholders were swindled out of $45 million. Recently indicted for this swindle by the SEC (in a civil suit) were "Howard Hughes" and Jimmy (the Greek) Snyder, not usually associated with the Hughes crowd, and others.

[**9/11: Mega-Swindle:** Of course, there has never been a swindle in the history of the world as large as the 9/11 attack on New York City residents, New York State, the citizens of the United States, and the Constitution of the United States, as the attack conceived and directed by elements of the United States government, embodied in the Bush administration. In one blow, these grim folks wrapped in the United States flag swindled us out of our Constitution ("a mere piece of paper," they said, foisting the Patriot Act upon us); and the $300,000,000,000+ (trillion) of additional national debt, money poured into the pockets of the global consortiums resulting from the endless and obviously unwinnable "war on terror," created by and for the real terrorists, (U.S.A.), etc.]

June 1971: *New York Times* began publishing the *Pentagon Papers*, Rand Corporation's prepared cover-up of the real reasons for the Vietnamese war. Nixon had been given a copy of the first Gemstone Papers circulated in the U.S. back in 1969. He was now wondering how much information Democratic Chairman Larry O'Brien had about Hughes, Onassis, JFK, RFK, et al., and more specifically, how much of the dirt the Democrats planned to use. Nixon set up the "plumbers unit" to stop security leaks, and investigate other security matters. It consisted of Erlichman, Krogh, Liddy, Hunt, Young, etc. Hunt, as "White House consultant," supposedly worked for the Mullen Corporation, a CIA cover. Mullen's chief client was "Howard Hughes." Robert Bennett was the head of the Mullen Corp.

June 28, 1971: Ellsberg indicted for leaking the Pentagon Papers.

Question: Why the intense battle between Mafia forces? Answer: While Onassis was the recognized crowned head of the Mafia, intense, no-holds-barred scuffling for the lucrative second spot (control of U.S. Presidency, government and so on) was permissible and encouraged under the Mafia code of rules. The only stipulation: Outsiders mustn't know about it. "Hughes" contributed liberally—and equally—to both Democratic and Republican parties for the 1972 election. The winner would get even more money from "Hughes".

September 3, 1971: The Watergate team broke into Ellsberg's doctor's (Fielding's) office to get Ellsberg's psychiatric records. Team members were: CIA Hunt and Gordon Liddy, Cuban "Freedom fighters" De Diego, Martinez, Bernard Barker. All had worked together back at the Bay of Pigs.

September 23, 1971: E. Howard Hunt spliced up the phony cables implicating JFK's administration in the Diem assassination.

October, 1971: *Look* magazine apologized to Alioto for their "Alioto Mafia Web" article—and folded. The sticking point: they couldn't prove Alioto's Mafia Nut Tree meeting back in 1963 re: the JKF murder.

November, 1971: Alioto re-elected San Francisco mayor.

December, 1971: Roberts applied for a "Gemstone" visa from the Russian Consulate—on a tapped phone. Phone was tapped by Hal Lipset, San Francisco private investigator, who worked for Katharine Meyer Graham and others, and routinely monitored Consulate phone calls.

January, 1972: The Watergate team showed up at the Drift Inn in San Francisco, a CIA-FBI safe-house hangout bar, where Roberts conducted a nightly Gemstone rap for the benefit of any CIA or FBI or anyone who wandered in for a beer. James McCord, Martinez, Bernard Barker, Garcia and Frank Sturgis showed up—along with a San Francisco dentist named Fuller. James McCord remarked: "Sand and Arab oil with hydrogen heat makes glass brick"—a threat of war to the Arab nations. The event, like all the other nightly raps, was taped by the Drift Inn bartender, Al Strom, who was paid to do so by his old friend, Katharine Meyer Graham. But "Al was fair;" he also told his other friend, Roberts, about it. The bar was also wired for sound by Arabs, Russians and Chinese.

January 27, 1972: Liddy and Dean met in Mitchell's office, to discuss Liddy's charts for his $1 million "Gemstone plan" for spying, kidnapping, etc. The plans included breaking into Hank Greenspun's Las Vegas Sun office safe, in hopes of recovering Greenspun's files on the Hughes kidnapping and Onassis's Vegas operations, which Greenspun had successfully used to blackmail Onassis out of $4 million or so. A "Hughes" get-away plane would stand by to take the White House burglars to Mexico.

February, 1972: Liddy and Hunt traveled around a lot, using "Hughes Tool Company" calling cards, and aliases from Hunt's spy novels. Liddy, Hunt and other Watergaters dropped by for a beer at the Drift Inn, where they were photographed on bar stools for Katharine Graham. These "bar stool" photos were later used in the *Washington Post* after Liddy, Hunt and the others were arrested at Watergate, because CIA men like Liddy and Hunt aren't usually photographed.

Roberts quoted to Liddy "the Chinese stock market in ears":

The price on Onassis's head by the ear—in retaliation for a few things Onassis had done, and:

- ❖ On Wayne Rector, the Hughes double;
- ❖ On Eugene Wyman, California Democratic Party Chairman and Mafia JFK pay-off bagman;
- ❖ On Aristotle Onassis; and

❖ On Lyndon Johnson:

"Four bodies twisting in the breeze".

Roberts: "Quoting prices to Liddy at the Drift Inn made their deaths a mortal cinch. Liddy's like that, and that's why the murdering slob was picked by the Mafia."

"Gemstones rolling around the bar at the Drift Inn in February inspired Liddy's 'Gemstone Plan' that became Watergate."

Francis L. Dale, head of CREEP and ITT Board of Directors member, pushed Magruder to push Liddy into Watergate.

In a Mafia-style effort to shut Roberts up, his father, Verne Dayle Roberts, was murdered by "plumbers" team members Liz Dale (Francis L. Dale's ex-wife), Martinez, Gonzales, and Barker. Mr. Roberts had been taken to Hahnemann's Hospital, San Francisco, after swallowing a sodium morphate "pill" slipped into his medicine bottle at home by Watergate locksmith/burglar (from Miami's "Missing Link" locksmith shop) Gonzales. The pill didn't kill him. He had a weak digestion, and vomited enough of the sodium morphate up (it burned his lips and tongue on the way out). But he had emphysema and went to the hospital. In the hospital, Liz Dale, disguised as a nurse, and Martinez, disguised as a doctor, assisted him to sniff a quadruple-strength can of aerosol medicine—enough to kill him the next day.

The day before, Eugene Tisserant, head of the College of Cardinals at the Vatican, died in a clinic near Rome. Tisserant had followed the career of the present Pope, Montini [Paul VI] (whose mother was Jewish). Montini sodium-morphate-murdered Pope Pius XI; was banished from Rome for it by Pius XII; and became Pope himself in 1963. Tisserant wrote it all down. He called Pope Paul VI "The Deputy of Christ at Auschwitz", and the fulfillment of the Fatima 3 Prophesy: that "The anti-Christ shall rise to become the head of the Church".

Tisserant also wrote about all the suppressed secrets of the Roman Catholic Church: that Jesus Christ was a Zoroastrian Arab baby, born on April 16, 6 B.C., during the rare conjunction of Saturn and Jupiter. Arab (Persian) astronomers (the Magi) came to Bethlehem to look for their king, an Arab baby. They found him in a stable, because the Jews wouldn't let Arabs Joseph and Mary into their nice clean inns, even then. When Jesus overturned the tables of the money lenders at the Temple, the Jews had the Romans nail him to a cross. He died on the cross when the Roman soldiers stuck a spear in his side, pulled out his liver, and ate it. Tacitus, the Roman historian, described it all in a chunk of history smuggled out of Rome, but deleted by the Church.

But the Persians "resurrected" Christ—and kept him alive—by spreading his teachings, the "voice from the grave."

62 a.d.: Nero burned Rome—but Tiberius's clay tablets with the original story escaped the fire, along with other records. Jesus' teachings were spread by the early Christians (Arabs). So the Romans decided to adopt the religion, clean it up, make Christ a Jew and Mary a virgin, and work out a church-state deal to screw the people in the name of God and country that has been operating ever since.

325 a.d., at the Council of Nicaea, [the first Nycaean Council], the Christian Orthodoxy was established as the State religion by Emperor Constantine. Arius, a presbyter of Alexandria, expressed the belief that Jesus Christ was not the "Son of God" in a literal sense, but a man of human birth who expressed a humanistic philosophy. Many of the early "Christians" agreed with him.

But Arius's beliefs were termed the "Arian heresy"; a dissenting bishop had his hands chopped off; and another bishop was assigned to round up all the old copies of the various Gospels and

destroy them in favor of the "revised," de-Arabized version. Cleaned-up Matthew, Mark, Luke and John were declared "it"; the other Gospels were declared Apocryphal, and heretical. Roman Emperor Constantine became the first "Christian" emperor. Later—after centuries of "Holy Crusades"—Gutenberg's newfangled printing press rolled out the first printed Bible— and the Bible was again rewritten, to include "Jesus' warning against the 'yellow race'".[18]

[Tisserant's writings hit Roberts hard; the man may have been murdered by members of the Catholic Church who had learned about his writings on the secrets of the Church. Roberts's father had been murdered at around that time, because Roberts had been writing about the secrets of the U.S. government.]

NOTE: Tisserant was apparently working with the newly discovered Nag Hammadi texts. He was an excellent linguist with knowledge of ancient languages.—sc2005.

"37 Gemstones, with histories, to 37 countries, brought Red China into the U.N. and threw Taiwan out. "

April, 1972: Money pours into CREEP: "Gulf Resources and Chemicals Corp., Houston, Texas" [Gulf Oil Corporation] contributed an illegal $100,000; the money was laundered through Mexico, and came back through Liedtke of Pennzoil Corporation, Houston. Ashland Oil, $100,000; Braniff Airways, $40,000; American Airlines, $55,000. Financier Robert Vesco gave Maurice Stans [and John Mitchell] a $200,000 "campaign contribution", etc. Gordon Liddy gave James McCord $76,000 to buy equipment for Liddy's "Gemstone Plan." McCord bought $58,000 worth of bugging equipment, cameras, walkie-talkie radios, etc.

May, 1972: J. Edgar Hoover had the Gemstone File; he threatened to expose Dallas-JFK in an "anonymous" book, *The Texas Mafia*. Instead, someone put sodium morphate in his apple pie. The corpse was carted away from his home in the back seat of a V.W. and his files were "burned"—but some of them got away.

May 28, 1972: First break-in at Watergate: McCord, Barker, Martinez, Garcia, Gonzales, and Sturgis were involved. DeDiego and Pico stood guard outside. Hunt and Liddy directed the operation from a command post at a (safe?) distance—from rooms in the hotel across the street. The object was to check on Onassis's two men in Democratic Party HQ: Larry O'Brien and Spencer Oliver. (O'Brien's chief P.R. client had been "Hughes"; Oliver's father worked openly for Onassis). McCord wire-tapped their phones.

But!!!! little did McCord know that the plumbers were being observed by Hal Lipset, Katharine Graham's San Francisco detective, who had followed two of the plumbers from Liz Dale's side in San Francisco to Watergate. Lipset "watched in amazement" as the Plumbers broke in and bugged the phones; then reported back to his boss Katharine Graham. Lipset and Graham set a trap for the Watergaters when they returned to remove their bugs and equipment.

"In the style of the old Holy Roman Empire: a slave nation paying tribute to the conqueror."— Roberts [US, paying tribute (our tax money) to Onassis.]

June 17, 1972: Bernard Barker was wearing his Sears Roebuck delivery-man costume—the same one he wore at the Dr. Fielding break-in, and at the Hahnemann's Hospital murder of Verne Roberts. Hal Lipset, Graham's spy, was dressed as a mailman, watching the action. He left his mail-sack behind when he taped *several doors* at Watergate to tip off the security guard, Frank Wills, that something was happening that required his attention. He watched Wills REMOVE the tape and walk on. So Lipset RE-TAPED the door, in a not-so-gentle hint, and the second time around, Wills realized that there actually might be something funny going on. Frank Wills

---

[18] This apparently refers to a reference somewhere in Gutenberg's first printed *Bible*.

went across the street and called the police, and McCord, Martinez, Sturgis, Barker and Gonzales were caught in the act. (Katharine Graham had them on tape and film, too, every minute of the time.) Liddy and Hunt, in their headquarters and observation post in the hotel across the street, supervising via walkie-talkie, were not caught. Liddy called Magruder in California re: the Watergate arrests. Magruder told Mitchell, LaRue and Mardian.

Time to burn files. Gordon Liddy has his secretary, Sally Harmony, shred the Gemstone File (in two manila envelopes) at CREEP headquarters. John Dean had Hunt's safe at in his White House office drilled open, and sorted out the contents. He gave Hunt's copy of the Gemstone File to L. Patrick Gray, acting FBI head, saying: "Deep-six this—in the interest of national security. This should never see the light of day." Gray burned the file.

[NOTE: In his book, Will: The Autobiography of G. Gordon Liddy (1980), Liddy describes shredding copies of his "Gemstone Plan," which existed between December, 1971, when Liddy moved into an office of CREEP ["Committee to Re-Elect the President"] to the early morning hours of June 17, 1972, when Hunt and Liddy's CREEP team of burglars (the "Plumbers") were arrested at Watergate. He probably did shred these plans, but nowhere does he mention Bruce Roberts' Gemstone File, copies of which were in Hunt's office, according to Bruce Roberts. Nor does Liddy mention that his "Gemstone plan" concept was a distorted response to Roberts' "Gemstone" letters, and Roberts himself, whom Liddy and Hunt had met at San Francisco's Drift Inn in January, 1972. Liddy's co-opting of Roberts' name for his own work ("Gemstone File") has led to a great deal of confusion. See Chapter 44 for an explanation.—sc2006)

[NOTE: From a Meeting between President Richard Nixon and Henry Peterson, Acting Attorney General, in the Oval Office of the White House, April 17, 1973:

Peterson:...Incidentally, I talked with Pat Gray[19] again.
Nixon: Yeah.
Peterson: I went back again today.
Nixon: Do you think you can put that piece together?
Peterson: Yes sir. I'll tell you what happened. He said he met with Ehrlichman in Ehrlichman's office. Dean was there, and they told him they had some stuff in Hunt's office that was utterly unrelated to the Watergate Case. They gave him two manila envelopes that were sealed. He took them. He says, "They said get rid of them." Dean doesn't say that. Dean says, "I didn't want to get rid of them so I gave them to Gray." But in any event, Gray took them back later, and I said to Pat, "Where are they?" And he said, "I burned them." And I said—
Nixon: He burned them?
Peterson: I said, "That's terrible."
Nixon: Unrelated—only thing he can say was—he did it because it was political stuff I suppose?
Peterson: Well, you know, the cynics are not going to believe it was unrelated.
Nixon: Oh yes, of course.
Peterson: I said, did you read it?
Nixon: Who handed it to him? Dean? Who knows the contents?
Peterson: Dean and Ehrlichman. Gray says he never looked at it—never read it.
Nixon: Did Dean? Did we ask Dean what the contents were?
Peterson: I didn't ask Dean because he said it was—
Nixon: Did anybody?
Peterson: Not at this point. We'll have to get to that obviously.
Nixon: Sure. Damn dumb thing to do.
Peterson: I think it is incredible and I just—

---

[19] L. Patrick Gray, acting Head of the FBI)

Nixon: Why didn't he just put it (inaudible)?
Peterson: I said, "Pat, why did you do it?"
Nixon: Pat's naïve.
Peterson: He said, "Well, I suppose I took them at their word."

-From *The Nixon Tapes* (p.577-8).—sc2005]

June 20, 1972: DNC Chairman Larry O'Brien filed a $1 million suit against CREEP—naming Francis L. Dale, the head of CREEP. This was a big Mafia mistake—for Dale led directly back to Onassis.

June 21, 1972: THE 18-1/2 MINUTES OF ACCIDENTALLY-ERASED WHITE HOUSE TAPE: Nixon, furious over the Watergate Plumbers' arrests, couldn't figure out who had done it to him: Who had taped the door at Watergate that led to the arrests? Hal Lipset, whose primary employer at the time was Katharine Graham, couldn't tell him. Nixon figured that it had to do somehow with Roberts' running around in Vancouver tracing the "Hughes" Mormon Mafia nursemaid's (Eckersley) Mafia swindle of the Canadian stock exchange; and Trudeau. The 18-1/2 minutes was of Nixon, raving about Canada's "ass-hole Trudeau," "ass-hole Roberts," Onassis, "Hughes" and Francis L. Dale. It simply couldn't be released.

Stephen Bull's secretary, Beverly Kaye, later heard the "erased" tape, stored in a locked room in the White House. She was horrified. She sent out some depressed Christmas cards and notes to friends, and sodium-morphate "heart-attacked" at age 40 in a White House elevator outside the locked safe room where the tapes were stored.

[*NOTE: The date of the last entry in Mae Brussell's section of the Gemstone File was September 23, 1972. It was probably shortly after this that Roberts decided to give this file of 360 pages to Mae Brussell because she was doing a weekly radio program, "Dialogue: Conspiracy," coming out of a radio station in Monterey which was rebroadcast on public radio stations throughout the country. All of the events described in the Skeleton Key that occurred after this date were derived from later letters and my conversations with Bruce Roberts in 1974-5. Mae never had any of this material.—sc2006]*

January, 1973: Tisserant was dead—but as the Church rushed to destroy every copy of his papers, Roberts received one—and wrote a few of his own, released over New Years:

❖ "The Cover-up of the Murder of Christ"
❖ "The Yellow Race is not in China; The Yellow Race Screws Mary Jo Kopechne";
❖ "Mrs. Giannini's Bank of America Financed the Murder of JFK at Dallas via Alioto's Fratianno, Brading and Roselli";
❖ "Vietnam: Fatima 3—Holy Crusade.

These four documents; [led to] four bodies twisting slowly in the breeze":

1. Lyndon Johnson had a Sodium morphate "heart attack" at his ranch on the Pedernales River. Among his last words: "You know fellows, it really was a conspiracy...."
2. Alexander Onassis's plane crash via "accidentally crossed ailerons," at Athens Airport. (January 22, 1973). Alexander's death certainly destroyed Ari; so perhaps it was meant to do just that.
3. Eugene Wyman: California Democratic Party Chairman and JFK assassination pay-off bagman: Heart attack.
4. L. Wayne Rector, Hughes's double: Killed at Rothchild's Inn of the Park, London.

"Started the Shattering of the Mafia Economy".

Losing his son Alexander took all the fun out of killing for Onassis. Who was there to inherit the world empire he had dreamed of handing over to his son?

(His daughter? Nah! She was just a girl; moreover, lacking in charm or charisma, apparently, but hungry for love. She married several times, each time unsuccessfully. She wound up hooked on Diet Coke, it seems, and also very likely some drugs and prescription pills. Accounts vary as to whether she pilled out, drowned, or was offed because she was trying to take a more active part in managing her father's global-size estate and got in the way of those who actually were managing it. Here is Gerald A Carroll's account:

> "Christina Onassis' death: Completing the legacy of death, daughter Christina's passing was perhaps the most mysterious of the three. Christina was only 37 years old when she collapsed and died suddenly in Buenos Aires, Argentina, on Nov. 20, 1989. An Argentine judge, Juan Carlos Cardinalli, said the day after that an autopsy showed that Christina died of "a lung disorder" described as "pulmonary edema," caused by "an accumulation of blood in the lung," according to wire reports as rewritten in the Nov. 21, 1989, editions of the San Francisco Examiner. Chemical poisoning, such as the effects caused by the feared sodium morphate, could have caused similar symptoms; after all, Christina was healthy at the time, and she was in fact becoming quite the businesswoman. She took a hands-on approach to the running of her late father's shipping company. Cardinalli was quoted in that same story that the possible presence of any drugs in Christina's system would be ascertained by ensuing blood analysis, the "results of which would be available in a few days." Those test results were never released. In fact, there was a conflicting report out of Buenos Aires that stated Christina suffered a "heart attack" and died as she prepared to go swimming in a country-club pool some 25 miles northwest of Buenos Aires, according to Dr. Herman Bunge."—Gerald A. Carroll, *Project Seek*, pp. 325-6. [1994]—sc2005.)

March 18, 1973: Roberts called Hal Lipset, discussing all these matters publicly over a tapped phone. Lipset reported to Dean, who had hired him away from Katharine Graham, after they figured out who had taped the door at Watergate. (John Mitchell said: Katie Graham's liable to get her tit caught in a wringer").

March 19, 1973: Dean to Nixon, nervously: "There is a cancer growing on the Presidency".[20]

March 21, 1973: Nixon said that on this date, he "received new evidence on Watergate". Hal Lipset bragged on T.V. that he had been the one to bring new evidence to Nixon.

Meanwhile, back at the *Washington Post*, Katharine Graham ("Deep Throat") had been feeding Woodward and Bernstein information for their articles.

May 10, 1973: The first witness at the Watergate hearing, reading down the names on the CREEP organizational chart, mentioned the name at the top: Francis L. Dale, Chairman. That was a big mistake, for Dale led right back to Onassis. His name was never mentioned again during the rest of the trial.

July 9, 1973: Roberts had used Al Strom's Drift Inn bar as an "open lecture forum" for any and all—and Al Strom taped it as well, for his boss, Katharine Graham. But "Al was fair", and told Roberts he was doing it—for which he was murdered on this date.[21]

August 1973: Murder of Chile, by Group of 40: (Rockefeller and his man Kissinger, working with the CIA and $8 million.) Allende's Chile had nationalized ITT's plants. Rockefeller had copper mines in Chile. Admiral Noel Gayler, O. N. I. (Office of Naval Intelligence), had told Roberts 1-

---

[20] Apparently, Dean <u>had</u> read the contents of those two manila envelopes after all, because Roberts uses the "cancer" metaphor for the Mafia destruction of the USA throughout. But Dean recently wrote me a note stating that he never heard of the Gemstone File. However, he added: "Good luck with your project."

[21] Date of Al Strom's death was confirmed by Al Strom's son Randy, along with other details in Gemstone. See Chapter 37, Subhead on "Richard Alan's" 1992 "Gemstone File" book, and Carroll's book, *Project Seek*, for amplification of this and many other *Skeleton Key* statements.

1/2 years earlier that Chile would get the shaft. Roberts warned the Chilean consul in advance, with a Gemstone letter: Allegria, now "teaching" at Stanford. ITT has now extracted $125 million payment for its Chilean plants, a good return for their $8 million. Mafia-controlled Chile's annual inflation rate has set a world's record. In the style of the old Holy Roman Empire: a slave nation paying tribute to the conqueror.

October, 1973: Another "Holy War": Israelis vs. Arabs.

November 6, 1973: Oakland School Superintendent Marcus Foster was shot to death, by SLA's Joseph Remiro and Russell Little—two white men who wore black face when they committed the murder.

January, 1974: San Francisco Mayor Joe Alioto grants Sunol Golf Course lease to Mafiosi Romano, Fratianno, Nuniz, Madeiros, Abe Chapman and Neil Neilson. Alioto sets up the Dallas murder squad in San Francisco for more murders.

January 26, 1974: "Hughes" extradition trial canceled in Reno by "Alioto Mafia Web" Mafia Judge Thomson, after Moses Lasky, from Mafia Alioto's California Crime Commission waves the forged "Howard Hughes" signature under his nose. Maheu "wins" his damage suit against "Hughes"; his blackmail pay-off—after publicly discussing Hughes' "Game Plan" for buying control of the U.S by buying politicians: governors, judges, senators and presidents.

February 4, 1974: Mafia Hearst's daughter Patty "kidnapped" by Hal Lipset's "Symbionese Liberation Army", consisting of a few CIA-controlled criminals and patsies, together with their CIA "handlers", in a fake terrorist action. Martin Luther King's mother was murdered by a hypnotized black student, a self-declared "Israelite—acting alone," who was escorted to the church by somebody or other—and who had a list of other mothers as targets. Next day, THE target—Shirley Chisholm—got the message, which had been directed at her, and rushed to sign off the Democratic National Committee's suit against CREEP naming Francis L. Dale; she had been the last hold-out.

February 29, 1974: Randolph Hearst's "million-dollar food distribution" in Oakland, ordered by SLA General "Cinque"—the former Donald DeFreeze—takes place.

[I as a journalist was watching this from an upstairs "press room," and wondering what the hell was really going on. Hearst had promised steaks; the paper sacks were filled with cabbages. They were literally thrown out of the back of a pick-up truck to a rapidly disillusioned crowd, who became noticeably angry at this strange act of contemptuous "charity."—sc2005]

April 4, 1974: Mary McCarthy, a writer who had been given a copy of the Gemstone File, said in an article in the *New York Review of Books* that the key to the formation of Liddy's "Gemstone plan" lay in the where-abouts and activities of the Plumbers between December, 1971 and February, 1972. Answer: They were in the Drift Inn, watching Gemstones rolling around on the bar top.

[**NOTE:** Gerald Carroll dutifully looked up the McCarthy story and this is his account:

"We obtained a copy of McCarthy's story, and the *Skeleton Key* rightfully points out the time gap as being mysterious; as for the alleged activity at the Drift Inn, we can only imagine that might have happened, although young bartender Randy Strom—son of late Drift Inn owner Al Strom and assistant to Hal Lipset and Katharine Graham in the alleged taping of conversations in that establishment, as the Key stipulates—has implied to us that the Plumbers did frequent an area tavern, but not the Drift Inn.... Specifically, we feel that Gemstone 11:1 relates to the following passage in McCarthy's opus:

"...Several times in his (Watergate Committee) testimony, (Nixon aide John) Dean returned to the incredible transformation that, in the space of a month and a half, had overtaken a project with which he thought he was familiar. [Dean said:] 'That has always been one of the great mysteries to me, between the time he (Liddy) went over there...what happened between December 10 and January 27 and my conception of what his responsibilities were and possibly his own and others'

conception (sic) dramatically changed.'

"[Dean's] mystification continued and embraced the whole sequence of events right up to June 17. He had thought the plan was dead after January 27. When it resurfaced on February 4, he was alarmed enough to inform (H.R.) Haldeman."[22]

Clearly, plans had been made outside the confines of Washington D.C. But where? The *Skeleton Key*'s rendition about where the Gemstone Plan of G. Gordon Liddy was originally cooked up is as good as any explanation."—*Project Seek*, pp. 275-6.

[**NOTE:** *The relationship between Gordon Liddy's "Gemstone Plan" and Bruce Roberts' "Gemstone File" is explored in more detail in Chapter 44. I wrote to John Dean through his publisher, asking for his comments which would be very enlightening. He replied, stating that he had never heard of the "Gemstone File." But he added, "Good luck with your project." ☺—sc2006]*

[*Patty Hearst's "Tanya" tape, where she praises her SLA comrades and vows to fight with and for them against the evils of capitalism, was released on the same date. A superb distraction for the public from the Watergate mess. —sc2005]*

April 15, 1974: Rifle-waving Patty Hearst participated in armed robbery of the Hibernia Bank with her SLA "comrades."

[I was living in Berkeley, about a mile from Patty's apartment, when the "kidnapping" took place. These strange events aroused intense curiosity and disbelief. A friend, the News Director of KPFK, recommended that I go to Mae Brussell, in Carmel, for answers. I did, soon after, and Mae and I did the interview which appears in Chapter 1.—sc2005]

May 12, 1974: Our article exposing the SLA and the Hearst kidnapping as a phony set-up for Public Relations, to create "fear of black terrorists" and serve as public distraction from Watergate appeared in the *Berkeley Barb*.—sc2005.

May 19, 1974: Slaughter of the phony "SLA" soldiers/patsies by the LAPD Swat Team. None could be permitted to live to tell this tale—except for Patty Hearst and her CIA "co-soldiers" and protectors, who supposedly left the house shortly before the slaughter. I[*have wondered whether it was the appearance of this article, exposing the fakery behind the SLA, that led to the premature bloody climax of this mini-drama.—sc2005.]*

[**NOTE:** *Gerald Carroll, author of Project Seek, was a reporter at Hearst's newspaper, the San Francisco Examiner, at this time. He wrote:*

"It is our view that the Hearst family was fed information from an undisclosed source—it could have been Lipset—that kept them fully informed about Patty's situation, with assurances that she would not be harmed throughout her 'imprisonment.' Patty and her father, at that time publisher of the Examiner, would frequent the Examiner library periodically, purging the paper's text and photo files of any inside information that would contradict the carefully controlled version of events that the mainstream media publicized. Famed attorney F. Lee Bailey was hired not only to defend Patty Hearst in the ensuing bank-robbery trial, but to keep the underlying truth about the escapade from leaking."—Project Seek, p.274.

August 6, 1974: Nixon and Ford signed a paper at the White House. It was an agreement: Ford could be President. Nixon got to burn his tapes and files and murder anyone he needed to, to cover it all up.

August 7, 1974: Roberts passed information to Pavlov at the Russian Consulate in San Francisco which led directly to Nixon's resignation:

The *"More" Journalism Review's* story about Denny Walsh's "Reopening of the Alioto Mafia Web

---

[22] *The New York Review of Books*, April 4, 1974, "The Watergate Solution," by Mary McCarthy.

story" for the *New York Times*, killed in a panic, plus a long taped discussion of who and what the Mafia is.

Hal Lipset listened to the conversation in the bugged Russian Consulate room, from his listening post in the building next door. He had phone lines open to Rockefeller and Kissinger, who listened too. Rockefeller sent Kissinger running to the White House with Nixon's marching orders: "Resign—right now!" Nixon and Julie cried. But there was still some hope, if Nixon resigned immediately, of drawing the line somewhere, before it got to the King of the Mountain himself—Onassis. Nixon, on trial, would blurt out those names to save himself: Onassis, Dale, "Hughes". Even "JFK".

August 8, 1974: Nixon stepped down, and Ford stepped up, to keep the cover-up going.

August 23, 1974: Fratianno was in San Francisco, staying at the Sunol Golf Course. More murders were scheduled re: the Gemstone cover-up.

August 30, 1974: New President Gerald Ford hired Mafia lawyer Becker to work out a pardon deal for Nixon, who might otherwise name Onassis, Katharine Graham, and Pope Montini to save himself.

San Francisco Zebra Murders: A series of "random" killings, dubbed "Zebra murders" by the police because supposedly blacks were killing whites—randomly. The last target was Silva, the only witness to Alioto's Mafia Nut Tree Restaurant meeting. Silva was shot to death in an alley. Careful Mafia planning went into this series, to kill several birds with one stone:

Get witness Silva out of the way, without being too "obvious" about it;

Spread fear of "black terrorists" and convince people that the Police Department needed more money and more repressive power.

Blame and frame Black Muslims; knock off leaders of the opposition.

September 7, 1974: Roberts had made an agreement with a friend, Harp, of Kish Realty, over a bugged phone. Harp was to buy a Gemstone—with history—for $500, the price of a trip to Canada for Roberts to check into the "Hughes" Mormon Mafia Canadian stock market swindle and other matters. But Harp was sodium-morphate poisoned before the deal could go through—on this date.

NOTE: Sodium morphate: a favorite Mafia poison for centuries. Smells like apple pie, and is sometimes served up in one, as to J. Edgar Hoover. Sometimes in a pill or capsule. Symptoms: lethargy, sleep, sometimes vomiting. Once ingested, there is a heart attack, and no trace is left in the body. Proof is in the vomit, which is usually not analyzed. Not mentioned in your standard medical books on poisons, etc. It is a common ingredient in rat poison.

[NOTE: At about this time, I showed up unannounced on Roberts' doorstep in the Sunset District. Fresh from Mae Brussell's house, I fully expected him to invite me in for tea with his mother. However, he glowered at me suspiciously, and asked me who I was and what I wanted. I introduced myself, and said I wanted to tell him that Mae and I had just completed an article for Playgirl in which we had used some of his information. I thought he would be pleased, and I also had gotten the impression from Mae that she had some sort of ongoing friendly relationship with Bruce Roberts. He told me he didn't give a damn what we had done, and seemed about to shut the door in my face. Tea was not mentioned. But instead, he asked me brusquely whether there was anything else I wanted. I told him I wanted to know what had happened in my country and the world between the end of Mae's files (1972) and the present (1974.) He took a deep breath and launched into a verbal "Gemstone Paper." After an hour or so, during which time his hair had dried, and I had been filled in on a shocking string of murders, conspiracies, etc., he was about to go inside his apartment when he asked again whether there was anything else I wanted. I said I wanted to see and read some of the new letters he had written. He produced a small note pad and wrote a

note on it:

> *"To whom it may concern: This note is my authorization for the bearer to read my Gemstone letters."* He listed 6 foreign consulates in San Francisco, and the names of the men I should speak to, and signed and dated it. He explained that he could not invite me in because someone was in his apartment copying something. The entire interview took place at his apartment doorway in a long, empty hallway of the apartment building. Then he shut the door. Interview over.—sc2005]

September 8, 1974: Ford pardons Nixon, specifically, for "all crimes committed" from June 20, 1969, (*oops, better make that January*) through August, 1974.

Gemstone papers are still floating around the world. Indira Gandhi talks about the "U.S.'s bloody deeds".

October, 1974: Ford drops "extradition" of Hughes from the Bahamas. Explanation: "We dropped it because we knew he wouldn't come". THAT'S FOR SURE!

October 3, 1974: The Watergate trial, the cover-up of the cover-up, got underway, starring Montini's Ben Veniste, Onassis's Neal, Graham's Jill Volner. In the White House, Mafia Mayors Alioto, Daley and Beame met with the "Truth squad": Ford, Scott and Griffin—and Mike Mansfield—in secret.

October 10, 1974: Tina Livanos Onassis Blandford Niarchos was sodium-morphate poisoned by hubby Stavros Niarchos. She puked, slept and died of a "heart attack". (This was the second of the two beautiful Livanos sisters to be murdered by their (successive) hubby, "Blue Beard" Stavros Niarchos. Just international politics as usual, folks!

NOTE: Along about this time is when I was visiting various S.F. Consulates trying to see Gemstone letters. I believe I got photographed outside the Russian Consulate, through the nozzle spray of a garden hose. I wonder if that might have been Lipset holding the hose???—sc2006

November, 1974: NOTE: After trying unsuccessfully 3 of the 6 foreign consulates mentioned in Bruce Roberts' note, I finally got somewhere at the 4th: the Norwegian Consulate. I was allowed to read and take notes on one long current letter, about 12 pages long, addressed to the leader of Norway. (My notes taken in the library of the Norwegian Consulate on that one day, from that one letter, formed the basic chronological backbone for the *Skeleton Key*.) The next day, the Norwegian Consul allowed me to read and take notes from a second letter. But he also asked for my phone number, and a few days later I noticed that my phone line had been tapped. Every morning, a different voice with a foreign accent would call and ask for "Sven" or "Olaf."

December 1974: [*Our article on Howard Hughes and Onassis, Is Howard Hughes Dead and Buried off a Greek Island? appeared in Playgirl magazine.*]

- ❖ Four targets were chosen by the international Mafia: Brezhnev, Bruce Roberts, Chou En Lai, and King Faisal. The Mafia Stock Market shot up wildly, regaining the ground lost since the "four bodies" letters in January, 1973.
- ❖ Chou En Lai had a heart attack.
- ❖ Brezhnev had scheduled a meeting with Egypt's Sadat. The outcome wouldn't help the U.S.—no matter how many trips Henry Kissinger made to the Middle East with clean socks and blank checks. A new U.S. CIA "secret weapon" was apparently used: a speck of nickel dust, introduced somehow into Brezhnev's lymph system. It lodged in the cluster of lymph nodes over his heart, and gradually became coated with layers of phlegm, much as an oyster creates a pearl around an irritating grain of sand. Brezhnev's lymph system clogged up; he got the "flu," and the meeting with Sadat was canceled. Russian doctors X-rayed Brezhnev and found a huge lump in his chest. Then they put him before a Kirlian camera and checked his aura for cancer. No cancer.

NOTE: The Kirlian camera is the latest Russian diagnostic tool. It reveals the presence of disease—physical or moral. (It also detects lies).

Brezhnev's mysterious "lump" was treated with radiation therapy; hence the rumors that he had cancer. It took six weeks to clear up.

March 15, 1975: Roberts got the "Brezhnev flu," and spent two weeks at the University of California Hospital, in San Francisco. Doctors there, without the Russian Kirlian photography diagnostic technique, assumed the softball-size lump over his heart was cancer, and treated it with cobalt radiation. It wasn't cancer.

NOTE: Bruce phoned me from the hospital that morning, and told me he had a "lump the size of a grapefruit" over his heart. I told him I would come to see him. I was extremely upset. Even though I was aware that he seemed to be surrounded by a lot of deaths, I had believed he was able to protect himself somehow. That idea came crashing to the ground. I went to see him. He asked me to buy him a couple of packs of cigarettes, and I did. I would have liked to protest that smoking at this time wasn't likely to benefit his health. But I had to admit that his likelihood of living long enough to benefit from not smoking did not look promising. So I got him some cigarettes. But I was frightened for him, since I had read his account of how his father had been murdered in a hospital. I decided to fight back with what I had: the chronological notes I had made from the two long current Gemstone letters I had read at the Norwegian embassy. I went home and began to type them up. The result was the first issue of the Skeleton Key, which started going out around a week later, on March 22, 1975—to major media, friends, and strangers.—sc2005.

March 16, 1975: Onassis died, of myasthenia gravis. The Mafia Organization began to regroup.

Prince Faisal watched his uncle, King Faisal, silently watch Jungers, head of Aramco, pick up the Mafia oil trade ball. Prince Faisal had followed Roberts's Grommet Bar raps, via a series of Arabs with tape records, and kept Uncle Faisal informed. The Shah of Iran's intelligence service, the Savak, had assigned two Arabs to Prince Faisal, to report back, and to win Prince Faisal's confidence, and guide and influence him in interpreting "what Roberts really meant." Prince Faisal knew Roberts was in the hospital. When King Faisal was targeted, the Savak decided that one way to get King Faisal was through his nephew, Prince Faisal. Prince Faisal's "baby sitters" interpreted Roberts's comments, and Daniel Schorr's comments, to Prince Faisal thus: "Your Uncle, King Faisal, will murder you, like they did your brother, because you are the only one besides himself who has this information. King Faisal won't stop working with the Mafia. He must kill you. You are dead, no matter what you do. The best thing would be for you to kill him first, and then rely on the help and mercy of your other friends and relatives."

After enough of this, Prince Faisal couldn't stand it anymore. He shot his uncle, King Faisal, the spiritual leader of 60,000,000 Moslems, who had played ball with Onassis all along. The Shah of Iran, who set it all up, hoped to take King Faisal's place as leader of all the Moslems.

Richard Helms, ex-CIA head, and by then Ambassador to Iran, wasn't kept informed of all this by the Shah. He emerged from Rockefeller's CIA hearings saying, "Killer Schorr," hoping to place the blame for King Faisal's murder on Daniel Schorr.

South Vietnam's Leader, Nguyen Van Thieu, dubious about which way the Mafia cookie would crumble now that Onassis was dead, decided the time was right for him to split. He abandoned the War Effort, cursed the U.S., and split for Taiwan, his plane so overloaded with gold bullion that he had to dump some of it overboard.

CIA Chief William Colby, in a fit of spite, "leaked" the "stolen" story of the CIA-"Hughes's" *Glomar Explorer's* raising of the bodies of drowned Russian sailors from their sunken nuclear submarine. Purposes: to bug the Russians; and also to halt criticism of the CIA by pointing out

how noble, brave, and self-sacrificing they are in their efforts to save us; and to distract the public from Onassis's death, and the massive reshuffling of global Mafia companies and resources that ensued.

"The Russians are funny about their dead." They bitterly resented Colby's game. They quietly went through a massive naval "war game"—the rehearsal of a nuclear attack on the U.S.—denied, in a panic, by the U.S. State Department.

NOTE: This was the last chronological entry in the first "Skeleton Key" edition released—and the next to last entry The last paragraph of all was a plea for readers to make copies and give them away, and it is repeated as an entry in July, 1975.

March 22: I sent out the first copies of the Skeleton Key to the Gemstone File for free circulation, dated April.

***NOTE:** April 1: I picked up Bruce Roberts from the hospital and drove him home, at his request. On the way, we stopped at an overlook and sat looking down at San Francisco. He seemed to be in a nostalgic mood, or was perhaps exhausted by what he had just been through. He pointed out City Hall, and said that he had once repaired or replaced the roof, as a contractor. "You have to make a living somehow," he said. I was just glad he was alive. I gave him a copy of the Skeleton Key to read, and told him I had sent out copies to major media and friends. He seemed very surprised that I had done this. After he read it, he approved of it as a digest of his major contentions. From then on, he apparently took it (and sometimes me) along to various political rallies and events, to serve as an introduction or precis of his work. He had it with him at his first—and last—published interview with the City of San Francisco, in September, 1975. See Chapter 35 for the interview.—sc2005*

END OF A SKELETON KEY TO THE GEMSTONE FILE, APRIL 1975 EDITION

(Additional entries were made as they happened, or as I got the information from the two "Gemstone letters" I purchased from Bruce Roberts. Some of these entries appeared in the May and June "editions".

April, 1975: The Cambodian domino was no fun at all; it fell right over. Premier Lon Nol fled to exile in a Hawaiian suburb. The word from Peking to the Cambodian government had been: "Run or hang." Lon Nol prudently chose to run.

Which brings us to 1975. Ford, Kissinger and Rockefeller squat like toads on the corpse of America. By the time of the Bicentennial the stink may be unbearable.

President Ford talked of doing a propaganda movie version of his book, *Portrait of an Assassin*, which would reiterate the exploded notion of Oswald as the "lone assassin" of JFK. With singularly inept misunderstanding of the times, he seemed to think Americans would take his word for it and be "reassured" in the face of those "crackpot conspiracy theories." He didn't seem to realize that he would be reminding, or informing, Americans of his role on the infamous Warren Commission. [*The pseudo-"history" books still go that way, but very few Americans now believe this was the case.—sc2005*]

May, 1975: Antonio Iglesias, CIA, who kept tapes and photographs of the CIA-Mafia murder teams chasing Castro and JFK, popped up again in the news, presiding over a massive CIA-sponsored land swindle in Florida, the largest ever. (A few pages from his highly expurgated CIA/FBI FOIA file, giving his explanation of his role in the swindle, appear in Appendix A.)

May 5, 1975: A CIA assassination attempt was made on Marshall Tito, President of Yugoslavia. Tito had recently received a Gemstone letter detailing the involvement of Harold Smith, former owner of Harold's Club, the Las Vegas Casino, in an attempt to cover up the evidence of Howard Hughes's death and the passage of his body through Yugoslavia. [*See transcript of this letter, in Chapter 33.—sc2005.*] President Sadat of Egypt, who had also just recently received a

Gemstone letter, scheduled a special meeting with Tito, for May 29-30, in Belgrade, to discuss the matter—just before Sadat's scheduled meeting with U.S. President Gerald Ford/King. *[See transcript of this letter, in Chapter 32.—sc2005.]* A CIA kill team was in Belgrade, with instructions to assassinate Tito and Sadat should certain events take place. *[Tito and Sadat knew they were there. If the CIA team had moved to carry out their mission, the outcome would not have been what they had planned.—sc2005.]*

June 1, 1975: President Ford's Air Force One Presidential plane landed in Egypt. On his way down the ramp to meet and greet Sadat, Ford stumbled and fell down the landing ramp—landing on all fours in a "perfect Moslem salute." He got up, then stumbled again, and Sadat picked him up. Ford was scared; his knees were trembling so hard he couldn't stand alone. He knew—and Sadat knew he knew—that Sadat had been the CIA target two days earlier. Sadat—and Egypt—got millions out of that meeting. Another triumph of U.S. diplomacy!

Tito had canceled his meeting with President Ford, and went hunting wild pigs instead.

Ford then flew on to Rome, to discuss "World Peace," etc., with Pope Montini.

Back in the States, the Rockefeller Commission wound up its investigation of CIA illicit assassination attempts on foreign heads of state, saying, "They may have made a few mistakes, but basically, they're OK."

June 6, 1975: Roberts gave information about the fraud involved in General Dynamics' fighter-plane contract to the French and Belgian Consulates in San Francisco. Two hours later, General Stehlin, a French Government official who was surreptitiously on Northrop's payroll, and a potential witness to the fraud, was hit by a bus in Paris and killed.

June 16, 1975: Sam Giancana, a potential witness on the Castro assassination attempts (and thus a potential leak regarding the overlap of the Castro assassination squad with the JFK assassination squad), was himself assassinated in his Oak Park, Illinois, home. Police, investigating, were puzzled: "It doesn't look like a Mafia rub-out to us. Why, everybody knows that in an official Mafia rub-out, they like to use machine guns, small cannons, or larger-caliber revolvers. But this was just an ordinary pistol. So we figure it was just a personal argument." Naturally, no one was ever "caught" for this inter-Mafia rub-out.

June 24: John Roselli appeared before the Senate Select Committee on Intelligence. For three hours, he answered questions about his participation in the CIA-Mafia team's attempts to murder Castro. But no one on the Committee asked him the big question: "Where were you on the afternoon of November 22, 1963?"

June 25, 1975: San Francisco: With Nut Tree Restaurant witness Silva safely dead, and the Black Muslim Zebra trial proceeding nicely, Joe Alioto pressed to reopen the *Look* trial and have himself declared totally innocent—on his way to the Democratic V.P. nomination under Teddy Kennedy. Qualification, major: He arranged the Mafia pay-off to Mafia Jimmy Fratianno for the rub-out of Teddy's brother, JFK. U.S. politics in a Mafia nut-shell.

NOTE: Eugene Brading at Dallas: Why, with all the books and lectures featuring films and photos from Dallas, does no one show or discuss this one? Eugene Brading, Mafia hit man, was arrested—and released—by the Dallas police immediately after the shooting. The only photo of Eugene Brading at Dallas to be published, it appeared in a Pinnacle paperback book called Legacy of Doubt, by Peter Noyes, in 1976. You can easily make out the big white X's on the hatband of Brading's wide-brimmed leather hat. All of the 28-man JFK kill squad could get through the police lines with the "Dallas Cross"—either by wearing one, or by making the sign of the cross.

The Zapruder Film: To attempt to control or channel public interest in the JFK murder, the CIA recently released the long-suppressed Zapruder film—locked up for years by Luce's *Time-Life*

empire.[23] Teams of representatives from CIA-sponsored and funded "investigative groups" like A.I.B., C.I.P.A., and Committee to Investigate Assassinations (CIA, for short, isn't that cute?) toured the country with the Zapruder film and a careful selection of slides, righteously calling for an investigation by the same Mafia Congress that brought you (the less juicy parts of) Watergate.

You can stare at the Zapruder film for hours on end, and watch JFK's head get blown to bits, and you still will never know who killed him, or how.[24] And that's the whole idea.

July, 1975: "I hope this outline will make individual Gemstone papers easier to understand. If you found this outline interesting: You won't be reading it in newspapers. At present, the only way to spread this information here in America is from hand-to-hand. Your help is needed. Please make one, 5, 10, 100 copies—or whatever you can—and give them to friends, politicians, groups or media. The game is nearly up. Either the Mafia goes—or America goes."

***

I distributed the first 3 "editions" of the *Skeleton Key* in San Francisco in April, May and June, 1975. But by this time I had lost my regular job as a Contributing Editor at *Playgirl* due to the "Onassis is Hughes" article, and with it, my income. I had to do something fast. With my last few hundred dollars, I decided to go to New York to seek a book contract. Within a month, I signed a contract with Prentice Hall to write a book about Florynce Kennedy, to be called *Color Me Flo*.

Oddly enough, the editor at Prentice Hall who arranged the contract was Robert Sussman Stewart. He had previously been with McGraw-Hill, and negotiated the famous contract with Clifford Irving for the Hughes "autobiography," later revealed as a spectacular hoax. [See Chapter 13 for details.]

A week later, my own father died suddenly of a heart attack, and I flew to Miami. My mother survived him, but she was in such bad emotional shape that I decided to stay in Miami Beach to look after her. I didn't enjoy living in the Miami area, but felt I had no choice in the matter. The book contract went away, and Flo wound up writing *Color Me Flo* without me.

Here are a few final items for a *Skeleton Key* edition that will never be written—at least, not by me:

1976: July 27: Johnny Roselli was scheduled to reappear before a Congressional Investigating Committee, and this time perhaps someone thought he might reveal too much. He "disappeared" on this date. He was missing for 10 days.

July 30: Bruce Roberts died, in San Francisco. I had been out of touch with him since I left San Francisco a year earlier, and did not know when he died.

August 7: Roselli turned up dead—strangled, stabbed, dismembered, his body stuffed into a chain-wrapped barrel, in Dumfoundling Bay, off Biscayne Bay, near North Miami Beach, Florida. He had been missing for ten days. Sleeping with the fishes, gone for good, like Jimmy Hoffa—if the gases from his decomposing body hadn't floated his makeshift Mafia coffin to the surface, where two fishermen found it, bobbing among the barracudas.

[This item has a special meaning for me. At the time, I was living in Miami Beach, supporting my mother, and attempting to run my dead father's plastics business. The back door of my father's business opened up on a dock on Biscayne Bay. Roselli's body popping up nearby gave me a strong hint that it

---

[23] (And ruthlessly doctored, according to current researchers. See especially Murder in Dealey Plaza, James Fetzer, ed.-sc2006).

[24] Two interesting sidelights on Abraham Zapruder: 1. His partner in his clothing company was Jeanne de Morenschildt, a cousin of George de Morenschildt, who was up to his nose in CIA/JFK plot intrigue just before his suicide or murder. 2. Zapruder's family belatedly was awarded $16 million for the tiny film that was phonied up by the CIA for the U.S. public consumption.

might not be safe to know anything much about the Kennedy assassination just then. And what would my Ma do if I got wiped out? All things considered, I kept very quiet for several years, until my mother recovered enough to live on her own and I was able to get out of the plastics business.—sc2005]

NOTE: *Ovid Demaris quotes Jimmy Fratianno on the subject of Roselli's death in* **The Last Mafioso.** *Fratianno described the Chicago Outfit's concerns about what Roselli might tell the Senate Investigating Committee about the Kennedy Assassination. He confided to Demaris that a contract on Roselli had been put out on him to keep him from talking too much. And Fratianno knew who had the contract. Roselli and Fratianno were long-time friends, so Fratianno wanted to warn Roselli, but he could not tell him the details ercause that would mean betraying his loyalty to the Mafia. At a meeting with Roselli, he hinted of this.*

Deep Six for Johnny

"On July 16, Roselli dined with Santo Trafficante at the Landings Restaurant in Fort Lauderdale. Early one afternoon, twelve days later, he left his sister's home to run an errand and never returned. His car was later found at Miami International Airport, parked where he usually left it when he went on trips, a newspaper partially opened on the front seat, leaving the impression that he had rushed at the last moment to catch his flight.

Jimmy knew these details long before they became public knowledge. What he had feared had happened, and he was convinced Roselli's body would never be found. Yet on August 7, fishermen became suspicious when they spotted a 55-gallon oil drum, with holes punched through it, floating in Biscayne Bay. Heavy chains were coiled around the container to weigh it down, but the gases caused by the decomposing body had given the drum enough buoyancy to float it to the surface....

The medical examiner reported that Roselli had been asphyxiated by someone holding a washcloth over his mouth and nose, a rather simple feat considering the serious nature of his emphysema and frail condition. There were stab wounds in his chest and abdomen but he was presumably dead at the time they were inflicted. Then his legs were sawed off and his torso hoisted into the drum, with his legs stuffed in with it. Although no news story Jimmy read mentioned the real reason for cutting off the legs, he guessed that it was because Roselli had been killed almost as soon as he had reached his destination, and by the time they got around to stuffing him in the barrel rigor mortis had set it, making it impossible for the killers to fold the limbs as desired.

It had been a sloppy job, from beginning to end, and looking at it from a professional standpoint, Jimmy felt it was exactly what one could expect from a family bossed by a creep like Aiuppa....

It was a grisly sight, and only a partial fingerprint enabled the FBI to identify the grotesquely swollen corpse as belonging to Roselli. It was "Deep Six for Johnny," as *Time* titled its full-page story on his murder, concluding that "Roselli was one of a breed that is dying off—usually by murder."

-*The Last Mafioso*, p.392-3.

PART II—BRUCE ROBERTS' GEMSTONE FILE
6 August 10, 1970: To Ralph Nader

Dear Mr. Nader:

This writing is one of many attempts to secure moral and legal cooperation in the correction of immoral and illegal acts. So defined in my Constitution and yours. It is in a sense an application for legal representation. The subject matter will be new to you, and because of its vastness and your unfamiliarity with the background, you will have immediate questions. I ask only that you overlook any questioning until you have read the entire bit. You will find that most of your questions will be answered.

I am an American—born that way and I'll die that way. But of the original 1776 variety, whose intent was clean, believing in freedom for this country and for all others. Not the type of today, the group which has converted that original Constitution and its intent into a Mafia base of operations, grown so powerful that it censors the will of the general public and threatens the security of the rest of the world.

The first lawyers to whom I made this request, two months before the 1968 election, were Richard M. Nixon and his partner, John Mitchell. That request elected Nixon to the Presidency, as you shall see. And he has been running from me ever since.

"Chappaquiddick" and "Howard Hughes" are some of the keys. But the real key was a hit-and-run accident on my car in 1968, by Alioto family members—covered up by San Francisco Mayor Joe Alioto, which exposed the Mafia election process which in turn elected Nixon.

The early July, 1969 information leak in the More Journalism Review about the upcoming Alioto Mafia Web story scheduled to appear in *Look* magazine caused political consternation. Alioto's money brokers tried to force Jess Unruh to run for California Senator, leaving Alioto a free shot at the California Governor's race. But Ted Kennedy already had his good friend John Tunney lined up for the Senate race.

Teddy blew his stack over Joe Alioto's presumption, that night at Chappaquiddick. Over the phone. There were several calls, incoming and outgoing; loud, and threatening violence.

Mary Jo Kopechne heard these calls, as did everyone else gathered in the cottage for Ted Kennedy's party. She had worked closely with Bobby Kennedy on his election campaign in L.A. before his assassination. After his death, she went through his papers. She knew about JFK's murder in Dallas: who had ordered it, and why. After hearing Teddy's heated phone calls, she bolted from the cottage in total anger. That led to her death. Teddy didn't dare try to rescue her from Poucha Pond. A forty-year governmental and business conspiracy would have been exposed. His father, Joseph P. Kennedy, was a member of that conspiracy. Those phone calls were the reason for the entire August cover-up of the causes of Mary Jo's death.

The cover-up of JFK in Dallas—from the very top—was done for the same purpose: to prevent disclosure of the same forty-year conspiracy.

Nixon, Mitchell and J. Edgar Hoover all know this (through me—not before). I alone wrote it all down, in book form, and sent copies out to various places in this country and other countries. I

even sent a copy to Alioto.

Another event had happened to me in April 1967. A woman jumped in front of my car in an attempted insurance fraud. I beat the case in court. Later I found she had been paid anyhow, by a group of insurance companies. I also found that San Francisco Chief of Police Cahill had buried the entire matter that I had turned over to him. Reason: it involved a huge insurance company and corporation rackets that went back and paralleled the other—the one and only—same forty-year conspiracy.

These events happened to one who for ten years had been happily experimenting in the physics and chemistry of a group of minerals. In voluntary isolation, which is the only way I can really work. I had no political affiliations, hadn't voted for fifteen or twenty years, didn't care who was in or out, wasn't even sure we had a president. Couple of divorces and all that stuff, but at least I was doing what I wanted to do.

At any rate, I've been watching your action and it looks pretty good to me. I read where General Motors had investigators watching you. Move over. I've had Alioto hoods, Kennedy aides, the FBI, the CIA and a batch of others following me around like a Conga line.

All are wondering. It is known that I have spread my writings (dates, places, times, evidence—volumes about four phone books in size) out in different places. It is also known that almost everything is true and verified. What they don't know is what I (or my friends) are going to do.

And that is why I write to you. My action happens to parallel yours. I have the financing and the tools to get the job done. Yesterday on TV I heard your answer to the question: "In view of your certainty of conspiracy, what are you going to do about it—relative to elections and changes you have in mind?"

Your answer: "Nothing."

That, of course, is up to you. However, I have the solution for your entire program. You are welcome to go over my entire file and use it as you see fit. I'm going to do exactly what I have planned to do, under any circumstances.

Don't misunderstand me. I think you're going great. I'm not criticizing. I figure you'll get it done, one way or another.

But I know things that you don't know. The solution for your programs, now. Not forty years from now. I'm fifty and I'll be damned if I'm going to wait till the year 2000 just to correct one injustice.

For instance: A week before the recent Cambodia invasion I submitted an alternative to Nixon, Mitchell and Hoover. I proposed to use a traffic citation (for a minor offense) to blow the whistle on Teddy, Alioto, Onassis, a forty-year conspiracy, some FCC monopoly stuff here, and almost the entire list of injustices you are currently pursuing.

I notified them that in the interests of getting the job done I had switched channels, but that I proposed to bring it all out in that San Francisco courtroom. That particular judge was running for election to a higher court, and that would automatically elect her. I also specified that a positive response to this ultimatum was required.

On April 28, 1970, I appeared in court. I was innocent, I thought. But I pleaded "Guilty," with the understanding that I could explain. The Judge knew in advance of my intention.

"Please," she said. "I want you to plead 'no contest.' I dismiss this ticket, and 'Next case.'"

The Judge lost the election and is now unemployed.

On the same date that I appeared at that court—April 28—Nixon issued the final decision to invade Cambodia. He had had my ultimatum for four days prior to that. Four days in which all

Republicans had told him, in horror, that the Cambodian invasion was certain political ruination.

But Nixon was in possession of political knowledge that the others did not have. He intends to use it. Or at least whatever part of it will benefit the Republican Party. Not me, not the public; just them.

So far, I alone have done this:

-possibly caused Nixon's election in the first place: the 150,000 California vote switch that would have elected Humphrey (or at least I silenced Joe Alioto, Jess Unruh and Hubert Humphrey in San Francisco);

-caused Alioto to bow out of the California Governor's race, and will cause his removal from the Mayoral job (his new Mafia trial starts next month);

-caused Teddy Kennedy to bow out of the 1972 Presidential election race—and will cause his removal from the Senate;

-have started the dissolution of the Democratic Party (they are deeply committed to the forty-year conspiracy, going way back through Joseph P. Kennedy and Onassis).

And this could affect the existence of the two-party system, since behind that phony façade lurks the faults that you yourself so plainly see.

Two days after that "traffic court" hearing, two men appeared at one of the San Francisco taverns which I like to visit. They were a man named Ed Sullivan and his partner, whose name I don't remember. They were written up in *Readers' Digest*, about five years ago, in a story about the top team of the FBI strike force. I knew who they were. They were friendly, but somehow nervous and apologetic. Finally the partner blurted it out. "You have just been through the biggest con game in history."

That was supposed to be my "positive response," since regulations require that no information be given out.

I said, "I know that. But how did I do? (What I was after was percentage of correctness.)

His answer: "You were…[pause]…okay."

That's it. They left. But what concerned me was the "pause". Was he about to say "100% right," or "90%"? Or "screwed"?

Legally, I live with my parents—an elderly couple who also respect you—at 1277 8th Avenue, Apartment #206, San Francisco, Telephone OV 1-6718. Actually I spend nearly all my time in an apartment downtown.[25] I cannot leave San Francisco because of what is happening here, and what will happen soon.

For your sake, you should read a copy of this entire affair. You can read it at my mother's apartment. Or in a conference room in a bank vault downtown. Or whatever you wish to do.

"Nothing," as you said on TV.

I regard this letter as a confidential matter between you and me. All matters will be public soon. However, my plans relate to the timing of release.

Pre-knowledge is a powerful weapon. Political power is a weapon. Money is a weapon. Communications access is a weapon. I have these things; I will use them. To the hilt.

As far as I can tell I want the same things that you do. Or maybe you just like to read murder mysteries. If so, come on out and read the grand-daddy of them all. Mary Jo Kopechne, John Tunney's sister, Newsom's nieces, Eugenie Niarchos, and more.

Assassinations? There have been a few. And they are related—to the forty-year conspiracy

---

[25] With his girlfriend, Carmen.—sc

and its fringe developments.

Which is the reason I have the Conga line behind me. And nothing to fear, really, since it's more like I'm covered by an umbrella. Anyone with knowledge of this entire affair is completely safe. Quite the contrary: I have never seen so many people so totally afraid of a few sheets of paper. And this goes from local mayors through Congress and the Supreme Court and right up to the presidency.

Sincerely,

Bruce P. Roberts, OV 1-6718

P.S. I just read this thing over, and let me correct an impression. The events (Alioto, Kennedy, etc.) I have listed here are minor. The major import of this entire thing relates to much bigger things. Your field. Total reform. The forty-year conspiracy is a cancer that has the entire socio-economic lives of Americans locked onto a course of destruction. I'm sure you know this, but I'm also certain that you do not have the keys to the curing of the cancer.

I do.

For your information: Reading time of the main written sequence of events: about 6 hours. Study of evidence, affidavits and proof: 1 hour to 1 month. Verbal questioning: 1 hour to 1 month. Or a year, if you choose to examine how it is that a finger of this cancer touches every phase of matters which I note interest you. (For instance, the history of U.S. Leasing from its formation in San Francisco in 1957 to its recent attempted merger with Chase Manhattan Bank; numbered bank accounts, the legal Mafia, insurance, lobbyists, etc.)

And one more interesting point. At this moment I have employment for at least 500 attorneys—and their staffs—on a permanent basis, all collecting money from collectable suits similar to yours against General Motors. The attorney who generates the publicity from the major fraud suit will probably be the next president. These suits will all be in the public interest. The conspiracy was against me, primarily, for prevention of disclosure, and involves a list of thousands of individuals and groups. And it is in this light that I have a question for you.

Are most attorneys rotten because it is a basic requirement of nature in order to be one? Or do they become rotten by the mere fact of joining the group?

Reminds me of "Which comes first—the chicken or the egg?"

I would respect your judgment on this matter. And you may consider that an application for legal counsel.

If, that is, there still remains an abstract affair called, as I recall, "Law and Order."

BR

7 August 12 1971: To Recipients of First "Nader" letter; Chappaquiddick

[This apparently accompanied additional copies of the first and some subsequent letters to Nader.-sc]

This letter, since August, 1970, has been on Nixon's desk, Mitchell's, Alioto's, Teddy K.'s, Onassis's, J. Edgar Hoover's—and on and on. It with related incidents has resulted in China's admission to the U.N., Nixon's world trips to everywhere, including Russia and China; Agnew's antics, Teddy's bit, and Nader's winning of a private poll by Mike Royko on the Presidency: 1100 votes for Nader, 400 scattered between Muskie, Kennedy, Humphrey, and Nixon.

Nixon is crawling around the world on his belly. Buying, where possible. Selling, otherwise. Teddy dips into all the "holy crusades" everywhere: in the Mid East, Pakistan and Ireland. China wouldn't even let him in.

Yesterday a British politician stated in Parliament: "Teddy Kennedy should stay out of public affairs—and settle his own personal affairs. The Churchill-Kennedy-Onassis cancer of the British hierarchy is a hangover from the Joseph P. Kennedy, Franklin D. Roosevelt, and Winston Churchill trio."

Onassis's original 1932 booze-heroin group, hooted him down: "It's unfair to mention the murder at Chappaquiddick!"

This is the same group that covered up the head-chopping-off murder of Carter Wilkinson in England by his wife, Senator John Tunney's sister, Joan Tunney Wilkinson.

Tunney, Teddy's closest friend, originated the phone call series to and from Chappaquiddick on that murder night—from his sister Joan's home in Tiburon in the San Francisco Bay Area. Joan overheard her brother's end of the calls, and when Mary Jo Kopechne turned up dead the next day, Joan panicked and ran away to Europe for a "vacation." Her family joined her there, and later she wound up in England where she eventually chopped her squawking husband's head off. For this murder she's currently in an English nut house: "sequestered". She'll be released soon: "cured."

Me? Since August, 1970? Nothing. John Mitchell and J. Edgar Hoover are in hiding. And the entire hierarchy is out with shovels, covering up.

The plainly exposed areas: Onassis's 1957 snatch of "Howard Hughes", Chappaquiddick, this letter, and a host of uncovered history from assassinations through wars, are all focused on the 1972 U.S. elections. Cover-up is the name of the game.

Potential candidates? Nixon, Nader, Teddy, Muskie, Humphrey, and all the rest? Well, how impressive can they be, with shit-covered faces and massive necrophilia on the grave of Mary Jo Kopechne?

It starts with the most crucial cover-up of all, the cover-up of the cause of Chappaquiddick: FEAR OF EXPOSURE OF THE MAFIA ELECTION PROCESS. Specifically, the cover-up, by Mayor Joe Alioto, of the Alioto hit-and-run on my car at the corner of Franklin and Lombard Streets, San Francisco, on September 16, 1968, two months before the 1968 election, which secured Nixon's election because of the cover-up action.

This, in spite of Onassis's-"Hughes"-Maheu's wholesale Las Vegas skim money bribes to all contenders (the skim that the "Justice" Department currently ascribes to Meyer Lansky—and that's how big it is. Lansky is to be the "fall guy" for that phase of the bit.) That hit-and-run report is currently buried in City Hall, under a Federal "no-peek" order. In a loose-leaf binder, for convenient removal, under the name of Kathryn Hollister. (I can look at it any time I want, but no one else can.) My name is Bruce Porter Roberts, and I am not a girl.

Because of this, Alioto is on trial for many things. But always elsewhere. And never about the hit-and-run. My "friend" of the hit-and-run incident in September, 1968, Richard Carlson (now known in China as "Chappaquiddick Little Dickie") was ordered to write "The Alioto Mafia Web" *Look* story on election day, 1968, by Nixon, and to bury the hit-and-run incident. He obeyed. This was to hide the key: the Mafia election process, highly exposed by me. Nine months later, the continuing pressure from that hit-and-run caused Chappaquiddick. And there they are, all of them, with shit on their faces.

CHAPPAQUIDDICK

Mary Jo Kopechne was murdered at Chappaquiddick on July 18, 1969, because of a hit-and-run accident to my car on September 16, 1968, at 10:47 p.m., at Franklin and Lombard Streets, in San Francisco.

San Francisco Mayor Joe Alioto covered it up, since a member of his family was driving the car that smashed into my car.

The details are buried in the hit-and-run files under the name of Kathryn Hollister: Report #522225. My name is Bruce Roberts. Report #522223 is also involved. The witnesses listed on that one know the names of witnesses to the Alioto hit-and-run.

My exposure of that hit-and-run cover-up led to Hubert Humphrey's flight from a presidential election finale in the Bay Area. He lost an estimated 100,000 votes, the margin of victory that won the state of California for Nixon and ultimately elected Nixon.

Republicans Nixon, John Mitchell and J. Edgar Hoover and their staffs, all the way down to local San Franciscan Republicans such as Dick Carlson, Greenagel, and John Mack, were informed, and watched this. San Francisco Democrats such as locals Joe Alioto, Ferrari, Savero, Newsom, and on up to Hubert Humphrey, Ed Muskie and Teddy Kennedy, also knew, and leaped to Alioto's assistance. Attorneys Melvin Belli, Davis and Lewis were informed, and sat on the lid. Onassis and the hard-core Mafia watched with vital concern.

Onassis helped Teddy Kennedy beat the rap for Mary Jo's death, and in return, Teddy withdrew his objections to the wedding. Onassis married Jackie just before the election. Cardinal Cushing blessed the pair. Said he: "If the world knew what I know, they wouldn't believe me. Bring your checkbook, Onassis."

On election day, with victory in his pocket, Nixon opened all federal files for Dick Carlson to write a story on Alioto's Mafia web connections—an already-established local fact. He opened the Treasury files for Knowland, of the Oakland Tribune, to expose Alioto's fee-splitting arrangements—an already established national practice. And Nixon ordered the slow murder of me and my family. Yes, a Presidential murder of the family of the man who elected Nixon to the presidency. For "National Security" reasons, he would say.

That "National Security" is the preservation of the unconstitutional, self-imposed Mafia two-party system, which permits—unqualified by any tests—the Mafia back room selection of candidates, and their immediate treason, bribery and conspiracy.

The Mafia election system then follows. Directed by careful media imagery and fraud and rigged voting procedures, and with only two back-room Mafia-selected and Mafia-purchased candidates to choose from. Thirty million votes elected him president, out of 206 million bodies who live here. That is one-seventh of the total. And neither candidate is qualified by any test other than the purchase price paid by the back-room Mafia who selected them.

The reasons for the slow murder of my family are:

~ These papers, poised overseas; and

~ My interrupted success in a new field of atomic physics.

Today, the American CIA is 200 miles into Yunnan Province in China, searching for jungle

rocks. The Chinese, Burmese, Thai, and Laotian border areas are open to opium smuggling, saturation bombing and geological surveillance because of this. The geological surveillance area by the CIA, on foot, and with bombers above, corresponds (check any map) with an overland escape route by a group of French prisoners from the Hanoi Hilton in the days of Dien Bien Phu: a walk from Hanoi to an American air base in China, at Kunming, followed by a flight to Calcutta. My ex-wife was a member of that escape group. My field is minerals. She, a French consul's daughter, remembered things. So did I. Unfortunately, in my naïvete, I notified Nixon of this through local channels in February, 1969, just after his inauguration. He took over from there. He sent John Mitchell to San Francisco to set up the Alioto Crime Commission to complete the lid on me, while he proceeded to search the Southeast Asian Jungles. This is why Nixon changed his "Vietnam Plan." At that time. Later, as we shall see, he had a more urgent reason.

That reason was Chappaquiddick. Mary Jo told her mother of three decisions, or tried to, three days before Chappaquiddick. Her room-mate and her fiance already knew. (They have been sequestered):

-Get married;

-Quit Democratic politics. She had just discovered the New Jersey Kennedy Mafia picture in Newark and Jersey City, where she worked for a while for (subsequently indicted) Mayor Whelan. She had already been through Bobby Kennedy's personal papers in Los Angeles after his murder, and she had announced, "I will never work for a Kennedy again. Too many killings." She knew about Dallas.

-Join her new idol, Ralph Nader, in cleaning up the crap of both Mafia parties.

She went to Chappaquiddick for old times' sake, and to notify everybody of this.

But before she could do that, the telephone calls started. Gentle, the cottage owner's rental agent, had plugged the phone into the wall jack behind the day bed in the cottage. (A Senatorial rule: there must always be a phone on hand). John Tunney called his old friend, Teddy, from his sister Joan [Tunney Wilkinson]'s home in Tiburon, across the bay from San Francisco

In 1967, after Alioto became San Francisco Mayor, Onassis and Kennedy stated after a conference that Alioto would some day be President. But at the time of Chappaquiddick, Alioto was desperate. His hit-and-run cover-up, and my threat to expose it, had blown his chance at the presidency. Even Lyndon Johnson's six-days-before-election bombing halt couldn't save it. A Northern California vote-getting campaign was denied to Humphrey and Muskie by my threat of the cover-up exposure. And Humphrey lost the state, and the presidency, by just that margin: 100,000 votes.

So just before Chappaquiddick, Alioto and the Democratic Mafia back-room boys attempted to persuade his primary rival for the California governor's race, Jess Unruh, to run instead for Senator against John Tunney.

Tunney, Kennedy's personal pick for Senator, was furious. He called Teddy at the Chappaquiddick cottage in the middle of the party, while everybody was in the room. Terrible tempered Teddy called Alioto, and the Mafia-type conversation—loud, screaming, violent—brought back memories of Mafia Jersey City and Newark, and Bobby's Mafia murder at Los Angeles, and JFK's Mafia murder at Dallas, to Mary Jo.

Teddy made more calls, from the cottage: the first, to Alioto, telling him to keep out of Kennedy's election fix for Tunney, and then, when Alioto told him to go to hell, to Teddy's friends—four of them—arranging for Kennedy's Mafia-style retribution against Alioto. (These five calls made from the Sidney Lawrence cottage phone were charged to Teddy's credit card. A courtesy to the owners. After all, no murder had occurred—yet.)

Mary Jo, hearing these calls after a few drinks, was boiling. She told Teddy what she planned to do. In anger, she said she was getting off the island and going to Ralph Nader—now—

any way she could. She departed, and slammed the door. (This is one of the few true statements in the inquest report). Without her purse, even.

Teddy grabbed the keys to his car, then grabbed Rosemary Keough's purse by mistake, and caught up with Mary Jo in the car, on the road that led to the ferry, promising to take her to the ferry. Mary Jo got in, but, still angry, she sat in the back seat. At the crossroads (where the paved branch led left to the ferry, the unpaved road to the right, across the Poucha Pond bridge and the beach where the cottage occupants had held a beach party that afternoon) Teddy stopped the car to try to cool her off. The local cop, Sheriff Look, saw the parked car and drove up to offer help if needed. But Teddy in a panic headed for the beach, away from the ferry. It would never do to have a cop hear angry Mary Jo. He was driving much too fast for the dirt road.

At the bridge over Poucha Pond, Mary Jo clutched his upper right arm, screaming, "Take me to the ferry." It was enough, sudden, and in frantic violence, to start the car veering over the rail.

Sudden violence was the response. Teddy backhanded Mary Jo, broke her nose, opened the car door and bailed out on the bridge. Mary Jo, still in the back seat, went into the pond, in her tomb. Teddy's head hit the curb, but he came up sprinting. Sprinting back down the road, expecting to meet the cop to whom he could cry "accident." Past the first phone, and the second, and the third, and still no cop. All the way back to the cottage.

Teddy's cousin Joe Gargan and his friend Markham drove him to the Chappaquiddick ferry landing.[26] Teddy went unobtrusively to his room at the Shiretown Inn, changed into his pajamas and a dressing gown, and then went to the front desk, appearing to the motel clerk, yawning. He stated that he had been sleeping, but was awakened by party noise. (But there wasn't any noise.) He pointedly asked the clerk what time it was, establishing an alibi for himself, to the effect that he was nowhere near Poucha Pond when Mary Jo went into the water in his car. He then proceeded to make additional phone calls from the motel phone—again, deliberately, charging them on his credit card—since, at that time, Joe Gargan had agreed to take the rap if necessary for what Kennedy, Gargan and Markham assumed would be called "leaving the scene of an accident."

Teddy Kennedy called Jackie and Onassis on their yacht, the Christina, begging for help. Then he called Katharine Meyer Graham, owner-editor of the *Washington Post*, and a staunch member of the Democratic side of the electoral equation, and lawyer Burke Marshall.

While Kennedy and Markham and Gargan were arranging for a Mafia cover-up, Mary Jo was still alive. She lived—in complete terror—for 2 hours and 13 minutes, in her tomb. She might have lived until the diver, John Farrar, found her in the morning, except for one thing: her broken nose. That was her snorkel into the air bubble up in the corner against the floor boards. But, after 2 hours and 13 minutes in that cold salt water, her broken bloodied nasal tissue swelled shut. She died of suffocation, not drowning. One final desperate gulp and another good one was gone.

They say it took Christ eight hours to die of suffocation on the cross. Mary Jo didn't even get the eight. Her busted beak fixed that. And that is why an autopsy was prohibited. Broken noses don't heal after death.

Cardinal Cushing and the Kennedy priests rose to the defense of Teddy. Priest Costa, at Judge Paquet's side on the bench, threatened Gentle, the rental agent, with eternal damnation if he mentioned the telephone in the cottage. (That might have led to the series of phone calls.) Priests assigned to the Kopechnes conned Ma and Pa Kopechne into refusing an autopsy for Mary Jo. Said Pa Kopechne: "We don't care if there was foul play. We are satisfied."

---

[26]*Teddy apparently called his nephew, Joe Kennedy III, who was in Edgartown for the Regatta, from the pay phone at the Ferry Landing. According to witnesses, young Joe obligingly "borrowed" a small motor boat from the Edgartown dock, went over to pick Teddy up at the ferry landing, and motored back across the narrow channel, with no running lights. He dropped Kennedy off at a convenient landing spot, and then returned the borrowed boat to its mooring. Two different accounts of Teddy's crossing appear in Leo Damore's* **Senatorial Privilege**, *on page 261 and pages 263-4. Suffice it to say that Teddy never swam heroically across the channel wearing his neck brace, as he later insisted.—sc*

Christ was born in April, in the year 6 B.C. It was a natural birth. He had a natural father: Joseph. Mary was not a virgin. "Christmas," in December, was established because of a vacant period in the ancient Catholic religious calendar. Christ was judged by Romans, and crucified by Romans.

The Bible is a good book. Christ did those things and he said those things. But he said much more as well. He had other commandments. "Kill cancer" was one. (Doctors have been doing this for years. They don't jail it, or release it on bail, or allow crooked judges or the Mafia legal system to "fix it." They kill it if they can, before it kills the victim.) "Put the murderers on the cross, not me," was another one. (Those were his dying words. And Mary Jo was thinking them too.)

In the year 325 A.D., the religious hierarchy made a deal with Emperor Constantine. For survival. "You leave us alone, and we'll leave you alone," said the Emperor. "And skip that 'Murderers on the cross' bit. And delete that 'Kill cancer' bit, too. Cheerist, that's us you're talking about. Put in something about 'Turn the other cheek,' and then you can create all the myth and imagery you want, and all the titles and hierarchy you want. Then you go your way and we'll go ours, creating our own myth and imagery—our own ruling society and senates. Hereafter, we will declare it illegal to discuss religion and politics."

In the year 500 A.D., the new Bible came out, altered slightly, as described, and the Church and the State—the two "handmaidens", as Bernadette Devlin bitterly describes them—proceeded to murder their way through history.

Comparatively recently, Cardinal Spellman arranged with JFK for the first troops in Vietnam. "There they stay," said JFK, "until I am re-elected."

Not so. Onassis murdered him at Dallas, and snatched, Mafia style, his broad and his shotgun—Jackie and the Pentagon.

Cardinal Cushing sanctified Onassis and Jackie, and Teddy at Chappaquiddick. Archbishop McGucken sanctifies Alioto, and the entire Papal hierarchy sanctifies the Mafia, MMORDIS, and cancer, and cloaks their murder in confessionals. For a fee. "Bring your checkbook, Onassis."

***

After Chappaquiddick, Lyndon Johnson made a deal with Dickie. "Stop knocking it, Dickie; you're into it too. And give my boy, John Connally, the keys to the Treasury. Come on down to my Memorial Library Dedication, and get your religious handmaiden, Billy Graham, to sanctify all this shit. And remember what I said: It's better to have J. Edgar Hoover inside the tent pissing out, than outside the tent pissing in."

Dickie obeyed. Graham spouted about the "American Dream." And Dickie said, "The two-party system is an absolute essential to our democratic system."

***

That's the same system which sponsored Joseph P. Kennedy, Winston Churchill, Franklin Delano Roosevelt and Onassis, in their 1932 introduction of illegal booze from England, and started Onassis' Marseilles heroin, and Onassis' South American cocaine, flowing freely into the United States. (Today most of the heroin comes from Southeast Asia, courtesy of the CIA, while they search through Yunnan Province in China for minerals and plant missiles in Thailand).

Blackmail from that single 1932 deed sat Onassis in the White House and in Number 10 Downing Street. Self-regulation and Mafia looting proceeded—with Joseph P. Kennedy and the Securities Exchange Commission, the American Bar Association, Mafia elections, and Mafia candidates.

For his third term, Roosevelt wanted World War II to continue. Joseph P. and Onassis had already blackmailed Churchill—again. Roosevelt rigged the murder of 40 million humans in World War II. Hitler could have been squashed at any time.

The Republican Mafia refused to mention the fact that Roosevelt was an insane Mafia creep, in the election of 1944. This was a shining example of Mafia courtesy (Omerta).[27] And Roosevelt was re-elected. We then had the Yalta Conference.

The Republican Mafia again refused to mention the fact that Teddy Kennedy was a murdering Mafia slob during Teddy's 1970 senatorial race. Mafia courtesy. And Kennedy was elected. We now have Teddy as the leading presidential candidate.

Chuckled John Tunney, "Nobody can impeach us Senators." His sister, Joan Tunney Wilkinson, took a hike to Europe, in fear—after Chappaquiddick—because of Tunney's call to Teddy from her Tiburon house. And there she was kidnapped by Mari and Adamo, two Mafia killers from Joe Bonanno's San Jose.

They locked her up in a Marseilles heroin factory, where the fumes she breathed for two months (no needle marks) turned her into a junkie. Then they released her, in the woods in Marseilles. And then, when her hubby Carter Wilkinson squawked at all this, she chopped his head off.

She is currently buried in a nut house in England. Mari and Adamo were "rewarded" by being pressed to death in a wrecked-car press in New Jersey (shades of MacBeth!) and today, Sciacca, Bonanno's successor in New York, has been indicted for questioning about their deaths.

The exposure of the key: the Mafia candidate selection and the Mafia election process by the Mafia back room Party boys, brought about the order for my family's murder—by the President, whom I elected because of that Alioto hit-and-run cover-up on September 16, 1968.

The exposure of all the historical layers of shit at Chappaquiddick is out in the open, in these papers, for every human being to read. The Pope, the Mafia parties; "self-regulation", the rape of the Constitution, the crooked hack judicial system, the Mafia legal system, Onassis and the hard core Mafia, McNamara and the World Bank, Ted Sorenson and General Motors, the Mafia Presidency, Mafia Congress, State Legislature, City Halls, Coroners, medical examiners, news media, TV. Name anything; it's all represented here in full view. All of them squatting on Mary Jo's grave—even Ma and Pa Kopechne.

Any of you females out there who read this could be Mary Jo tomorrow. Any male could be me—on the murder block. Any child could be one of Newsom's barbecued nieces. Or 100,000 of you could go as 200,000 did at Hiroshima: on a whim by Truman, against the advice of the eight scientists who developed the atom bomb. Or 100 million of us could go—about half of the U.S. population—if the original plan for World War III, set up by Onassis at Apalachin in 1957, is carried out.

That plan called for state-by-state Mafia vote rigging to get Joseph P.'s son John into the White House. It worked, and in 1960, Onassis purchased America. He moved into the White House with his old friend Joseph P. Kennedy, who was also J. Edgar Hoover's close friend. (JFK and Bobby welched on the deal somewhat, and they were bumped. Teddy bowed to Onassis in August, 1969, on Onassis's yacht, Christina, and he was saved).

World War III was—and maybe still is—to be a nuclear noose around Russia and China, the last remaining haters of the Mafia. A limited Nuclear War, to blow off the other half of the globe entirely, with only about half of US at home exterminated. Constant prods: Vietnam, Greece, Turkey, the Mid-East. They are all on the "far side," and missiles are planted in all of them, right at the commie borders, from West Germany to South Korea. (One missile site in Greece had to be moved back a mile; it had been accidentally planted on Russian soil).

Or one man could destroy it all. It's easy. He could booby trap himself with a new field of physics. Ten seconds before Hiroshima, who of the dead ones could conceive of an atom bomb? He

---

[27] *Omerta is an important part of the Mafia code. Any branch of the Mafia is free to use whatever methods or tactics it can find to destroy or conquer any other branch—but outsiders must never be informed of the existence or identity of the root.—sc.*

could distribute proof, in various ways, for timed release. With a button-pushing effect. He could tie the two together: scared Mafia-hating countries, and minerals.

What if he were on the murder block? Don't you think he'd remember that deleted commandment, Christ's last words "Hang the murderers on the cross, not me"?

Mary Jo's tortured last thoughts.

Christ's.

They both want off the cross. He's been up there 2000 years. The church symbolizes that tortured, skinny, spiked body, and advises, "Turn the other cheek." And the State chops that one off too.

Christ says: "Get me off this cross. I'll show you how to kill cancer. I'll clear up the cover-up. All 2000 years of it. First, I'll wanna talk to the Pope. Second, Dickie and Teddy and Onassis."

Fatima #3 says: "Satan will reach the summit of the church. The Great War will happen in the second half of the 20th Century."

That's a quote. But we're halfway through that last half of the century. And you can comprehend missiles as well as you can comprehend the strata of shit exposed at Chappaquiddick, or at Franklin and Lombard Streets in San Francisco on September 16, 1968. So why worry about something new in high density physics?

Jefferson said: "Political power belongs to the people. If tyranny corrupts, then the public should be informed. They should be educated so that they can control their own destiny."

Rochefort said: "Presidents fear one thing: An historian. One with knowledge, who writes of current history, and traces it back. This man has the power to rewrite the inscriptions on tombstones. And shape the course of the history he writes about."

I think, when I read this, of Nixon and Johnson at Johnson's Memorial Library dedication. A mammoth monument to MMORDIS. And Dickie's vow: "I will never allow a President of the United States to be demeaned." And a Congressional resolution: "Death to anyone who demeans Congress."

And I note that Teddy will officiate at the dedication next week of the mammoth new Kennedy Memorial in Washington. And I recall the memorials of JFK and Bobby in Arlington National Cemetery: two who were murdered by the Mafia because they welshed on the Mafia, and who reside there with innocent GI corpses, some of whom they murdered, and Roosevelt murdered, and Truman murdered. And through it all, the murdering fingers of Joseph P. Kennedy and Onassis and the Mafia boys in the back room who own Congress and the Presidents—Democrats and Republicans.

And I remember a man hanging somewhere, spiked to a dilapidated cross, and a beautiful girl buried in an isolated Pennsylvania grave with a broken nose, and not a visit from her Chappaquiddick friends or her 'satisfied' Ma and Pa. And I think back to Teddy, our next presidential candidate, hosting those hordes of American well-wishers, and grinning, and I....

Write the following quote—my own words:

"Aristotle (not Onassis) said: 'Give me a pivot and a long lever and I will lift the world.'

"That's a simple experiment. A written history became the lever.

"An historian (not Aristotle) has placed a weight of writings on the long end of that lever. The pivot arrived at Chappaquiddick.

"Daily, the lever of history lengthens. And this writer pushes the weight further out. And adds a chapter. And then he listens for the creaks. And then he writes chapters on these. And adds that. And assistants push the weight further out.

"That's an interesting experiment.

"Jefferson said, "Educate 'em.'

"Have you learned anything yet?"

Perhaps you don't wish to. Greenagel, Nixon, Hoover, et al, are burning their copies.

Life is short. Eternity is long. I'd like to have the number two job in eternity. I despise this Mafia crud so much that I not only have arranged to take them with me but also to hang them on crosses over a hot fire and barbecue them through eternity, like Newsom's nieces.

"Murderers on the cross, not me," said He. "Kill cancer."

Fair enough. I'll do that. There. Or here.

This is a lawsuit. These are papers.

It is a corporation charter.

A Plan to Clean up Government

Since Congress and the Legal System are Mafia, and illegal, exact filing of the corporation papers will have to await correction.

That correction includes qualified candidates, with selection by testing, grading, etc.; no lie, no cheat, no steal, no bribe, no conspiracy.

Service: Compulsory.

Best eleven must run for each office. Immediate recall for first stutter.

Hours of Work: Three Congressional shifts—24 hours a day, seven days a week. A tour of duty, like sentries in an army camp.

Penalties: For bribery: confiscation of all property, and 20 years at productive labor. For offering a bribe (lobbyists): death.

Elections: To be held on income tax day.

Written campaign statements, by each pre-qualified candidate, to be mailed out with income tax forms on January first. Four months allowed for voters to study them. They are signed.

First lie gets prison.

206 million people vote—all of us—compulsory. Pa votes for the kids; they breathe the same polluted air and drink the same tainted water that we do. To them he's the deity, and he votes for them.

Voting in this way will phase out the necessity for filing an income tax return. That personal income tax return is all Mafia take anyway.

Mafia criminal statutes of limitation on crime? Torn up.

*Ex post fac*to laws on crime? Torn up.

Padlocking the barn door after the horse is stolen? That's fine—as long as the horse is tracked down and returned, with interest, plus penalties.

Ralph Nader estimates $200 billion a year in corporate criminal thievery. Crime statistics estimate $200 billion a year in hard core criminal loot. Mafia governmental take is about $100 billion a year; that's Federal, State and local taxes.

There it is. Half a trillion dollars a year. Criminal loot. Half the gross national product. That is why the nation, the states and the cities are broke and in debt. Six million Mafia hoods are robbing the rest of the 200 million. Committing murder, bribery, treason, conspiracy—every crime known to man.

And that's just for one year. But back through time—oh yes; back to the signing of the Constitution: 200 years. Every crooked judge's ruling, every congressional cover-up. Plus penalties

and damages. It comes to trillions. It is collectible. The Constitution restored to its original intent.

It comes to $100 thousand, or more, apiece, in cash. With a six million cancer work force available, producing to pay off their damages direct to the 200 million who have been robbed, whose families have been murdered by war, disease, pollution—or heroin.

A shot in the back of the head to any drug pusher.

This could force the correction of commie tyranny—or dictatorship tyranny, anywhere. It could be a U.N. race to clean up shit, instead of a race to blow us all to hell.

The law suit hereby filed, in the public's "right to know", under the law of humanity, can never be placed under Mafia "secrecy" laws. It can be established over a four day holiday: a fly-over and a body count of humans, out in the open.

A vote by 51% of the population would move qualified interim candidates into Mafia-held congressional seats, in an orderly fashion.

Surely these Mafia Senators, who committed treason when they took their oath of office, and bribery when they accepted their first "campaign fund" or "lobbyist offer," and conspiracy the moment they joined the club of silence on matters already mentioned briefly here, would agree to this.

That church that squats its hooded ass on Mary Jo's grave has more than a hundred billion dollars in tax-free assets. Have you ever seen an accounting? Foundations have $50 billion. Criminal corporate loopholes leave another hundred billion. That would pay a lot of taxes.

It would take many millions of us—full time—just to investigate the fraud of the last 45 years, let alone the last 200, or the last 2000, back to the murder of Christ. That's employment. Collecting that would be downright fun.

I will control that corporation. I trust me. I work for the man on the cross. And I'm not even religious. When he gets off that cross he can go his way and I'll go mine. I don't want anybody telling me whether I can or can't have a martini. We, as citizens, can do anything we damn well please, within the boundaries of common decency.

It's only those selected sentries in Congress patrolling the perimeter 24 hours a day, 7 days a week, who can't make a mistake. They'll be floodlighted and covered by gun muzzles every step of their rounds. And we'll be expecting good clean original thoughts about what's good for us at all times.

Most of them will be happy when their tour of duty ends, but at least it won't be the way it is now: the Tuesday-to-Thursday Mafia Club in Washington—all of them selling the Mafia the right to slit our throats while we sleep.

Read on—for documentation and solutions. Or burn it, as the Mafia does. Other reading arrangements have been made, in countries that are interested. And still other arrangements have been made involving panel adjustments in missile silos.

He wants off the cross.

And murderers up.

He's gonna get the job done. At last his law has teeth.

Mine. Right where they should be. as Nader says: in the jugular.

Doesn't it strike you as odd that no "man of God" anywhere—and there are hundreds of thousands—would read such a thing as this from his pulpit?

And they know. Billy Graham knows. The Papal hierarchy squatting on Mary Jo's grave knows.

Presidents know. Legislators know. The six million Mafia MM0RDIS cancer know. They own

communications.

Someone said: "It's too bad J.C. didn't own a printing press."

Well, I think he just found one.

I know he found his teeth.

Nader's $457,000 Cash Settlement with General Motors

Here's a contemporary validity check.

The accompanying letter was written on August 10, 1970 (a year ago), following a TV interview with Nader on August 9.

On August 10, two phone calls were made to two San Francisco newspapers—ostensibly to locate a Nader address to which to send the letter. The general reason for the letter, with an intimation as to its contents, was deliberately mentioned. This, over a phone which has been tapped for several years. And to the offices of both highly concerned local newspapers—one of which was known to have been purchased by Alioto.

The August 15th issues of both newspapers carried a story involving a sudden cash settlement ($457,000) of Nader's law suit against General Motors. That settlement was made on about August 14—three or four days after a summary of the contents of a letter involving Chappaquiddick and one of its cover-up mentors (Ted Sorenson) was publicly released over a tapped phone to two San Francisco newspapers—plus the information that it was being sent to Nader.

Ted Sorenson was the lawyer originally hired by General Motors to contest Nader's suit. His law firm presented the cash settlement to Nader's firm on about August 14th.

The cash settlement settled nothing relative to consumer pressure against General Motors. The original suit was still effectively blocked through the year 2000 by the legal staff of General Motors.

Why, then, the sudden settlement—by Teddy Kennedy's Chappaquiddick cover-up lad, Ted Sorenson, who was also defending General Motors against Nader?

I believe this letter—the knowledge of which was released publicly on August 10th—caused this action by Ted Sorenson, who happens to be the cover-up artist in both cases: General Motors, and Chappaquiddick.

Millions have been spent to cover up Chappaquiddick. What's another half million spent attempting to get a known reformer—Nader—off the back of this monstrous group, or attempting to prevent any knowledge of this huge 45-year conspiracy from coming out in the open?

Because of the phone calls to and from the cottage at Chappaquiddick, Mary Jo threatened to inform Nader. This is one of the reasons she is dead.

And this, after all, is all that matters: the preservation of the hierarchy of cancer. Is it not?

The United States of Mafia. Cancer in a flag and a robe.

Goldberg (Sorenson's Simon Rifkind partner) said on Law Day, May 1st: "The Constitution requires equal justice for all of us. That is what is written on the Supreme Court Building, and that is what it is all about."

Ah yes: Mary Jo. Goldberg hired Chappaquiddick broad Esther Newbergh, one of the "Boiler Room" girls at the Chappaquiddick cottage party, all old friends and co-workers of Mary Jo's, and sits on her mouth.

Sorenson, who had just bribed Nader for Onassis, Teddy and Dickie, filed a brief for Mafia advertising against all TV stations: "Stifle all TV regulation by the FCC. Go along with my clients who pay the loot to TV, or we'll put you out of business."

Reagan said: "Shut down all Free Speech radio stations. They talk too much."

Congressman Moorhead said: "Nixon leads an assault on press freedom, beyond calculated deception and news management. He uses governmental censorship, intimidation and naked legal power to stop the newspaper presses, as well as grand jury harassment, legal action against legislators and publishers, and other less direct methods of attack."

The injunction against news of the "Howard Hughes" Bribe Loan of $205,000 to Nixon is more than naked legal power. Dickie followed it up by sending a 20-man IRS team to Vegas to collect, for Onassis, all the loot pilfered from "Hughes" (i.e., John Meyer's mining claims, the casino skim by Lansky, etc.). Robert Maheu ("Iron Bob Maheu", or "IBM") is suing his ex-boss, Onassis, (as "Howard Hughes") for $50 million—Maheu's fee for arranging the major assassinations—his loyal service to that good Mafia group: the FBI, CIA, and Onassis.

Brugmann, publisher of the *San Francisco Bay Guardian*, advertises for volunteers to clean up the Mafia shit of San Francisco. He was one of those reporters Greenagel stated were working on the Alioto hit-and-run at the time of Chappaquiddick. Two years ago I told Brugmann about all this shit so that he could win a law suit. He gulped, and disappeared. But he still advertises for volunteers.

Two months ago in a long phone conversation I gave him this shit again, so that he could win another law suit. I offered him specific convicting evidence. His last words, sadly: "I'll see what I can do." And then he disappeared again. His ad asking for volunteers still runs. So does he.

James Reston, *New York Times*, threatened to publish the Pentagon Papers in his personal paper, *The Martha's Vineyard Gazette*. Yet he, who withheld the Bay of Pigs bit for his friend JFK, wouldn't print the facts of Chappaquiddick in his own local paper in the place where the murder occurred.

NOTE: Ralph Nader published a book: a costly critique of General Motors. The attorney for General Motors was Ted Sorenson (a former JFK advisor). General Motors attempted to discredit Nader, using private investigators. Nader sued for $26 million, for "invasion of privacy." It was called the "suit of the century", because General Motors' attorneys (Sorenson, Rifkind, Goldberg), had it blocked through the end of the century. The Nader faithful believed that Nader would fight it all the way through.

Public knowledge of the accompanying letter changed that in four days. Without stopping Nader in any way, in his critique of General Motors, Simon Rifkind, Sorenson's partner (Sorenson suddenly dropped out of sight), delivered to Nader a $457,000 cash (tax free) settlement. Nader quickly grabbed the bait, to the total dismay of his faithful followers. Nader knew, however, what his followers didn't know: this letter. This, he knew, was the whole ball of wax. He didn't have to settle for $26 million. He could have it all. If I gave it to him. And I offered.

(Ted Sorenson, an advisor to JFK, was called upon to write Teddy's Chappaquiddick "walk on water" speech. Simon Rifkind, a former federal judge, and Sorenson's law firm partner, was a key figure in the Tammany Hall Judge Crater disappearance in the 1920's, and an old Joe Kennedy friend. Arthur Goldberg, former U.N. representative, Labor Department head for Kennedy, and another partner in the firm, hired Esther Newburgh (one of the Chappaquiddick "girls"); but recently, sensing problems, resigned from the firm in favor of private practice.)

Today, Nader kicks Presidents and Senators in the ass and spits in the eye of other governments (i.e., Japan, England), with impunity. His old partner, Fellmeth, finally given access to this information—by me, not by Nader—published a report labeling the entire California State Government a Mafia cell. Today, Fellmeth is publicly investigating Congress. The original Nader group was Nader, Fellmeth and Cox. Cox is now Nixon's son-in-law.

8 October 7, 1971: To Nader: Death of Nader's "Consumers' Party"

The following pages were written around October 7th, 1971, but crudely describe a few phone calls from October 5th to October 7th, and amplify the projection of the total Mafia clamp. I will, you may be sure, Nader, be very careless with copies of this letter. That's just the way I am; I am careless. Besides, I'm curious to see which way I can shape the events that are certain to follow.

(Let's see: today is November 29, 1971. 1 may get it to you by Christmas.)

October 5th: A Phone Call from Alexander Onassis?

After weeks of previous calls, I made another call (from a downtown apartment) to 285-6115.

"Mr. Miller's Office."

"Ask Harry Miller to call OV 1-6718. Tell him it's about Ted, Simon and Ted. He'll understand. It is urgent."

"All right."

Within minutes, my phone rang. It was my mother, who had just received a call and was passing on the information to me. Subject of the call: Ted Sorenson, original author of the Chappaquiddick "walk on water" TV speech of Ted Kennedy. Law partner of Simon Rifkind, Kennedy Attorney, and participant in entire 47-year Mafia job, way back to the 1920's, when he was a key figure in the Mafia Judge Crater experience and disappearance. Sorenson and Rifkind delivered the $457,000 cash settlement to Ralph Nader just four days after my announced letter to Nader, relative to the Alioto hit-run of September 16, 1968, that exposed the Mafia election process; elected Richard Nixon, and caused the phone calls to the Chappaquiddick cottage, to and from Alioto, Tunney and Teddy, which murdered Mary Jo.

"Harry Miller just called," said Mother. "He asked for Mr. Roberts, and I called your father."

Miller announced himself to my father and said, "I understand you've been making a nuisance of yourself by calling my secretary."

My father: "I haven't called you. It might have been my son."

The voice: "Well, tell him I don't want him to call me any more. I'm not going to talk to him. Tell him he's making a nuisance of himself and I don't want any more of it."

That was all.

At 11:30 a.m. I called Miller's number again.

I said to his secretary, "Why didn't you tell me this weeks ago, that Mr. Miller didn't want to talk to me? You have wasted several weeks of my time. He called my father and told him that, or at least a voice did."

She: "I don't know anything about it. I just gave him your message."

Me: "I have no way of knowing that it was really Mr. Miller who called. I would like to hear that from him personally. Would you ask him to call me at this number?" And I gave her my number. "And ask him to call me back right away. I have no desire to talk to you or to just any old voice; only to Harry Miller, the crusader, the Nader Raider."

She: "All right."

Mr. Harry Miller—or the voice—did not call me back.

At 2:00 p.m. I called again.

Me: "Tell Mr. Miller to send me a handwritten note with his finger-prints on it, like 'Howard Hughes'; then I won't have to leave messages for him or wait for him to call."

As with "Ted, Simon, Ted," the phrase "Howard Hughes" brought an immediate response. Within five minutes the phone rang.

Me: "Yes?"

There was a long pause. Then: "This is Mr. Miller. Is Mr. Roberts there?"

Me: "Yes."

He: "I don't want you calling me any more, or calling my secretary."

Me: "When did I last speak to you? Can you tell me this, for identification purposes?"

He: "I don't know."

Me: "Well, repeat some of our last conversation so I'll know who I'm talking to."

He: "I don't remember."

Me: "Send me a written letter to that effect, like poor dead Howie Hughes sends his—handwritten, and with fingerprints on it."

He: "No, I won't, but if you don't stop trying to talk to me, or my secretary, I will call the police."

Me, full of joy: "Fine! Can we really get the police into this? Beautiful!"

He, in fury: "You would be well advised to heed this advice."

Me: "Iron Bobby Maheu."

He hung up.

The voice, of course, was not that of Mr. Miller.

And the whole thing is rank. When Ma and Pa Kopechne state, smiling and in public: "We don't care if there was foul play," (and that includes murder.) "We are satisfied." the extent of the pressure is obvious. There is no closer tie than this: a mother and father to their only beautiful daughter.

Later, it might appear that Nader might have been paid that $457,000 to become a replacement for Teddy. It could be that "Ted, Simon, Ted" relates to a critical situation—just as critical as "Howard Hughes."

If the Mob realizes that it's got to give up a little to retain the keys, this it will do. Hoping, and expecting, that Nader will only nibble at the fringes, but will faithfully preserve "for the Mafia system" the three real keys to the rest:

(1) The Legal Mafia (to which Nader belongs, and wishes to rule the government);

(2) The Press and Media Mafia monopoly (which favors Nader as long as he doesn't attack any of the three keys, which he doesn't); and

(3) The Vatican, and other church Mafia, which covers up Christ's murder and all the religious murders since.

October 7: Nader Assassination Warning

At 10:30 a.m., October 7, 1971, I made a call to Neilson and Green.

A secretary answered.

Me: "At this stage of the game, when I make a Mafia call I get warned not to call anymore. I was calling some friends recently to warn them about a plan to assassinate Ralph Nader this coming week-end in San Francisco. And I mentioned a phrase to a secretary: 'Ted, Simon, Ted.'

"That's a magic phrase relating to the bribery of Ralph Nader by Ted Kennedy, Ted Sorenson and Simon Rifkind—all murderers in their own right. And within seconds, Alexander Onassis called my father—not me—and left a message telling me not to call secretaries any more.

"So I called this secretary back, and I told her to please have that voice write me a handwritten note confirming that instruction—with a fingerprint, like Onassis does for poor, dead Howard Hughes. And within five minutes Alexander Onassis called me back, and told me not to talk to any more secretaries, or else.

"So I thought I'd call a few secretaries, starting with you, dear. The procedure for you now is to hang up. I have a message. Will you take it?"

"Of course," she stuttered.

"I wish to report the attempted assassination of Nader, Fellmeth and four of his assistants, upcoming, this weekend in San Francisco. And I was talking to Neilson last Friday about 'Chappaquiddick Big Dickie, Chappaquiddick Little Dickie and Chappaquiddick Alioto' (that's the way the Chinese phrase it), and now Strangelove Kissinger is on his way to China to check it out, and…."

She interrupted: "Just a minute." And she put me on hold.

I waited about 25 minutes, and then someone opened the connection, and I quickly asked, "Is this Mafia Central? Hello?"

I got put back on hold, and I waited ten more minutes and then hung up.

Then I called again. I got another secretary.

Me: "Can I leave a message?"

She: "There's no-one here to receive it. Everybody is gone." Boggle boggle.

Me: "What's your name?"

She: "I'm the secretary."

Me: "Do you have a name?"

She: "I don't know."

Me: "I was just checking. I'd better get off the phone. I wouldn't want to disturb anybody."

She hung up.

Sorry about that, all of you down there at Murder, Incorporated. Come to the Assassination Ball at Nader's Consumer Group Coalition this weekend, and you may see a batch of gore.

Of course, all this was really only to publicize the assassinations of the future, and therefore possibly to stop them.

All the evidence indicates that advanced publicity can stop assassinations.

World War III, the combined nuclear-noose Vatican-Mafia plan (Fatima Secret #3) is now in a Mafia-frustrated stage. Advanced publicity, in the other half of the world, has made it a fair fight. And if there's one thing the Mafia hates, it's a fair fight. Fair, that is, in that the whole cancer goes, not just the "other half."

And some dirty sons-of-bitches have upped the ante considerably. They have mixed up a chemical to add to the flames. These days, it's as easy to blow up the whole world as only half of it. The names of these sons-of-bitches (who are friends of mine, since I, too, am a son-of-a-bitch) are Christ and Mary Jo Kopechne, both of whom want off the cross. Christ wants his spear and nail holes patched. And Mary Jo wants her busted nose fixed.

It is too bad that Martin Luther King couldn't have had advance publicity about his murder. Or John Tunney's sister's hubby, Carter Wilkinson, before his head got hatcheted off. Or Eugenie

Livanos Niarchos, before her hubby Stavros Niarchos belly-kicked and pill-sauced her because, while in bed, she overheard that Mafia conversation between Charlotte Ford (Niarchos's ex-wife) and Niarchos. Or Yablonski's family, before they got shotgun-blasted. Then Mari and Adamo wouldn't have been pressed into baled scrap steel, in New Jersey. And...and...and, on into the millions: 40 million in the Roosevelt-Kennedy-Onassis-sponsored World War II, and all those people who died in Truman's Korea, and in Kennedy-Onassis-Vatican's Vietnam.

In the afternoon, a Legislative Advisory Commission was conducting hearings with experts to determine whether to raise all banking interest rates in California from 12% to 26%. The Advisory Commission? Fourteen bankers. The hearing experts? Twelve more bankers. Hard core Maf were there; I checked my list later. The rest will, as usual, check out on the bribery list. How do you think the totally bribed California State Legislature will vote on that interest increase? That's right. It's quietly going through in Sacramento now.

October 8th 1971:
Nader Cancels; FBI Swarms; Consumers' Coalition Crashes

All right. Now it's October 8th, in the a.m. And mobs of FBI—100 of them, they say—are combing the town, in an unheard-of "raid," picking up small-time bookies who are "the usual suspects." Why are they here? Local police want to know!

And you called, Nader, from an unnamed location in Washington, DC, to cancel your trip to that all-important "Consumers' Coalition Party Formation Conference," to be held in San Francisco this weekend. You said your cancellation was due to "unexpected developments," but you promised to address your loyal followers by phone.

October 8th, 1971: First day of the great new Consumers' Coalition Party Formation Conference, that you were supposed to inspire with your courageous leadership.

That morning, in a speech, Sylvia Siegel, a local Association of Consumers official, said:

"That Banking Legislative Advisory Committee? It stinks, it's a fraud, pure shit." (She did not mention the Mafia at all); and

"I'm totally sick of Nader. His cancellation 'reason' was the most idiotic thing I've ever heard. This meeting is the highlight of years of work. It was to have been a real beginning for the Consumer movement, the springboard for positive political action, a movement with teeth. His appearance was to be the spark that ignites the flame. We have the core of the vote of 40 million registered consumers, in three groups. And he cancels, for an idiotic reason. Instead, he will honor us with a phone call from some secret, hidden telephone in Washington on Saturday night. Hell, we're not hiding. We're here. Who does he think he is? I don't know about the rest of you, but I'm damned mad...."

At this point she was interrupted by a long ovation.

"...And I hate to say it but I think this movement will fall apart right here."

I remembered covering the Progressive Party Formation for the Wisconsin State Journal, in Madison, Wisconsin, in 1936 or '37, and at age 16 passing on the quote that if it were not for the presence of its leader, a La Follette, it would have been a busted bubble right there. (Actually, it flamed for a while).

That night, there was a Consumers' Union meeting. Harry Miller showed up, in the middle of a bodyguard group headed by Bronson La Follette, Attorney General of Wisconsin. He wouldn't speak to me.

Warne, head of the Consumer's Union, was asked why he hadn't done anything about all the known shit in the country.

His answer: "We've only been in business for thirty-five years. We only have a budget of $14 million a year. We can't do anything about anything."

Vail, head of the Association of California Consumers, was asked what he had been doing about land rape in California during those same thirty-five years.

His answer: "Nothing. That is a political matter."

The third consumer group, whatever it was, was probably supposed to be addressed by Miller, but he didn't move out of his huddle. The meeting collapsed.

What happened to this generation's breed of La Follettes?

October 9th, 9 a.m.

Miller was huddled in front again. There was no speaker. Mafia Alioto welcomed all (me, too.) And when he left, he waved at me—and I checked his arm length for a fit on the left bar of a cross.

Said Alioto: "Labor unions should run the consumer movement. The President of the California Consumers Association loves me because I am truly a trust buster. Nader likes me too."

There was an ovation here, and Miller clapped like hell.

Mafia George Moscone (our next Guv) welcomed all. Said he: "Get your power base from the unions. You're too weak, politically. Work with the labor boys."

Heevey (AFL/CIO briber in Sacramento, and also on the Board of Directors of the California Consumers Association) said: "You need organized labor in your group. You need money to buy the legislature. We have the money."

After the Alioto welcome, Miller left. Later that afternoon he appeared at the back door, staring at me. I gave him a telepathic several minutes, and he left again.

He didn't bother to show up on Saturday night to hear your telephonic sermon from a secret phone booth in Washington. (Were you changing into your Superman cloak in that phone booth, Nader?)

In the meantime, Florence Bernstein made a speech: "That was the Mafia in action, that Legislative Committee on the interest rate raise. The Committee was composed of Banking Attorneys and others who were appointed by the Financial Company owner, who was the Chairman of the Commission."

Miller's friend, Kay Pachtner, spoke: "We need money and people who know how to do investigative research. We have a pipeline to the Department of Motor Vehicles." (This is where the Alioto hit-run records got all twisted up). "We need an issue to unite all the little groups. We are not powerful because we are all in pieces. We have to sneak our reports through the media."

And there I was, sitting there with my bare face hanging out. She must have known what you and Fellmeth and Miller also know. I just didn't listen to the rest of the speech because I was busy identifying the Mafia in the room.

Most enjoyable was a luncheon speech by Illinois Law Professor O'Connell. He quoted from John Rothschild: "The Mafia take is 30% of everything. That's why they went legitimate, into government and business; because there is more loot there. The Pope has the sweetest racket of all. He sells Blue Sky."

But he was wrong on that. The take was 40% then, and it went up 1% last month, in loot and murder, to compensate for heavy bribes regarding Chappaquiddick and Alioto and the UN fight on China. (They write off $457,000 bribes as petty cash, Nader.)

October 10th 1971

And on the final day, Sunday afternoon, when the original group of 100—scheduled to be a thousand, until you canceled—had dwindled to 31, the election of the Board of Directors was held. And in that remaining group were 11 hard-core Mafia.

The lady next to me said, "This is ridiculous. Some of them voting here don't even belong to the Consumers' Association. Nader himself couldn't get elected to this Board of Directors. What's going on?"

Me: "Have you eaten?"

She: "No."

Me: "Then I won't tell you. You'd puke on your pretty dress."

About then a few sincere consumer people asked politely to be placed on the ballot for consideration. But the Labor hood contingent roared, "Out of order. Disturbers. Sit down. Close the meeting. Election over."

And the meek meekly sat down, and Heevey, the AFL/CIO legislative briber, declared the election over and the meeting closed.

The lady next to me said, "I see what you mean." And she was puckering to puke about two inches from my tie, so I left. I only have one tie.

So there you are, Nader. Your consumer coalition meeting: Mafia to start, and Mafia to end.

Except for your telephoned "speech." No Mafia were there. No Miller. And no crowd.

At the end of your speech, there was a public question period.

First question: "What kind of a fraud is Nader? This is rank. He raves about false packaging. And you have just promoted it. He didn't show. This whole thing is a phony."

Petris: "Mumble, mumble, mumble."

Next question: "Nixon is a fraud. Why aren't you getting this out to the public?"

Furness: "Yes, we must try."

Judge Brunn (Master of Ceremonies and Consumer Expert): "These three arrived safely, to replace Nader and to answer your questions; and we were lucky to get the call from Nader. We had no idea which phone number he would call from, or whether he would call, or anything. It's like waiting for a ghost. The public just has to protect itself from everything...."

A voice: "From Nixon and Nader too?"

Judge Brunn: "We have run out of question time. These people must hurry back to Washington to save us all from the most frightening fate in the world: bum deodorants."

And that's the truth, Nader. Something stinks. How could you stand yourself in that phone booth? You need fresh air and a cross to dry out on. Or a swim in Poucha Pond. Teddy will tell you how refreshing that is.

Foreign Relations

Recently, odd things have happened. In Japan, for instance. Nixon had screwed Sato properly. The Peking bit, U.N. bit, surcharge, etc., and Sato himself is a rucked duck.

So John Connally, on a con trip, smiled and said, "Hi y'all, Sato, ole buddy."

And Sato grinned, like Chou en Lai, and responded: "I've been meaning to ask you: How is the bullet hole in your neck from Dallas, and the fragments from the other bullet in your belly? Do they still bother you? What actually happened there? And how are Teddy and Dickie?"

A photographer caught a picture of Connally then. I have it. Man, what a mad Maf he was.

Then Connally hastened on to Vietnam to inaugurate Thieu as President. It has been said that if Connally can't be V.P. for Dickie, he will be transferred to Vietnam as V.P. to Thieu. He can't be Prez there, because Reagan has already declared Thieu to be as great as George Washington. Perpetual President Number One.

And Dickie has reshuffled Intelligence. He sent Noel Gayler to Iceland, and CIA Cushman to the jungles. "Cheerist!" he mutters. "Can't anybody keep the lid on that son-of-a-bitch? He can have dinner with Brezhnev and Mao anytime. I know that. Hey! Maybe he already has! Oh shit! And that would be my place in history."

These days, Nader, Dickie blinks, and rattles his hands. He stutters too. He says: "Bust up the U.N. Shut off all foreign bribes—no, wait. Keep 'em going, and raise taxes instead. Keep the surcharge on all over; hit 'em where it hurts."

The Bishops said to the Pope: "Screw you. We won't sign a new constitution declaring you to be God. Like the U.S. Senate, we all want a shot at that."

In fact, they wiped out the Synod. There was no declaration at all. They did pass one resolution, though:

"We now think the war in Vietnam to be profitless. We don't condemn it and won't issue a Papal order to our soldiers to that effect. But we're beginning to doubt whether we can convert those bastards, and we might lose our big customer—the United States—in the process. There is one son of a bitch there who caused Chappaquiddick and elected Dickie, and then he started on Alioto, Kennedy and Onassis. And then he went on to paralyze Congress, and Dickie, and Hoover. He's booby-trapped both of our loyal parties, shuffled the U.N., and set up a U.N. Knapp Commission on Chappaquiddick.

"Cheerist! His next step would be to go to the boss himself; you know, the real one—God, I'm talking about. But wait a minute! One of us is God—and the rest of us are Deputies of Christ. I'm confused.

"And you'd better call the janitor and have him sweep up all those Mary Jo Kopechne pictures. How the hell do they keep getting in here, anyhow? Things are getting tight. Let's get Fatima #3 on the road. Go next door and get Ambassador Lodge. He handled Diem for us real good, and helped on the Kennedy hit. Call in Body Count McNamara. Collect the whole Chappaquiddick group. Move, move, move!"

And immediately, Dickie pledged some loot to Archbishop O'Boyle and the Knights of Columbus. Said he: "Screw the Supreme Court. Screw 'em on El Paso. Screw everybody but us Mafia. It's in the National Interest."

And of this, newsman Dan Schorr stated: "That Knights of Columbus speech proves positively that Nixon is both a liar and a traitor. It is a deliberate violation of the Constitution and the Supreme Court."

Immediately the FBI clobbered Schorr. They are following him around like a shroud, and he will soon disappear, like the witness to the aborted JFK assassination crew in Chicago did, or like Black Panthers Hampton and Clark.

Archbishop O'Boyle tells George Meany in confessional, "Check that Yablonski lid, stupe. Things are leaking out."

And Dickie is boiling because Loeb, in Manchester, is mad at both him and Teddy; but he's not really worried, since Loeb won't blow the whistle on the Chappaquiddick phone call records, on account of the millions of dollars he received from Jimmy Hoffa.

LBJ issues a Mafia version of the Pentagon Papers, and is paid a million and a half. Ellsberg—for free—passes out a verbatim report. The press Mafia censors the key parts of that. Ellsberg will go to prison for life. He is $50,000 in debt. "Justice" wants his ass.

November 30: "Alioto for President"

Today, James Heisterkamp began nailing up "Alioto For President" posters.

Said he: "We can image him for president. He is next to the people. He knows what they

want. The people want him to run."

Said Alioto: "That's nice. And I like James. But I prefer to run silently, like Teddy."

Street interviews, with a dozen San Francisco Mafia: "Beautiful! We want Alioto for President."

In the Channel 2 news room (which filmed this), three newsmen went into convulsions, and the program ended.

In historical Massachusetts, in 1776, Minutemen stood on the bridge at Concord, punching Mafia. Today the Mafia breed is under Dyke Bridge, at Chappaquiddick, passing out Mafia bribes, pushing heroin, and running in Mafia elections for positions from President to God.

The Chappaquiddick Brigade: working in 24-hour platoons to hold Mary Jo's head under the water, and fiddle with Fatima #3 buttons.

Aren't they a fun group, Nader? You and Alioto, and Dickie, and Teddy, and all the rest of MMORDIS (Moldering Mass Of Rotten Dribbling Infectious Shit.)

***

Some CIA ghoul was talking to me one night about murder. It seems he wanted me to know how many means were available.

"Necrophilia," said he, "is defined in the dictionary as 'fucking the dead'. In our group we have a motto: 'If you can't eat it, or fuck it, kill it. And then fuck it.' Do you dig me?"

Me: "Yes. One of the fringe benefits of your job. You appear to enjoy it. Did you get in on Mary Jo? Terrible tempered Teddy must have been tortured terrifically when he couldn't make the back seat under the pond for a quick fresh dead bang. Poor boy. He had to wait until she was stretched out in the Edgartown morgue, and then the entire necrophiliac Kennedy mob was there taking turns—in secrecy—behind locked doors. And only his aides had the fun on that hasty secret flight to Pennsylvania. The thing to do is to bury all the broken-nosed evidence. I understand, and I quote you a phrase from Erskine Caldwell: 'Fuck you!'"

He: "Don't get nervous. I'll see you again."

And now I know why Onassis labels Mary Jo a whore.

***

As all branches of Mafia do, the legal Mafia disposes of its own.

So go, Nader, you hypocritical necrophiliac Mafia cancer. This letter is not confidential. You don't have to hide it from Fellmeth. Tell him he can save some time by dropping that congressional investigation. We talked about that last February, and the specific Mafia relations of each: the murder, the treason.

Any crime of omission is as serious as any crime of commission, and you and he and Miller already have an oversupply of charges. In history, Rome committed suicide, but it was so rotten it spawned both the Vatican Mafia and the Mafia Mafia. This infectious crud spread over half of the world. And look at it today: stretching from Vietnam to Greece.

Teddy and Dickie circle the globe, whipping it into line. One of the two plans to be the next president. And someone has stated that the last word ever spoken would be: "Why?"

I have a Christmas present for you. From them—and me. Much better than your Onassis bribe. Don't get worried, as some keep telling me. I'm not after you or Teddy, or Alioto or Onassis. I don't want any single cancer cell. I want all of them.

And here's a Christmas greeting: Happy Chappaquiddick, you slobbering Mafia cancer.

Roberts

***

P.S. Where do you live, Nader? Which secret phone booth?

"Nader's Nation of Necrophiliacs." How about that for your place in history, Nader?

Poor Jim Garrison. Framed—now—for everything from extortion to income tax to spitting on the sidewalk. And he was only right on one thing: David Ferrie, who piloted portions of the assassination crew from Chicago and Dallas.

Ferrie's alibi? "I was with Marcello."

Carlos Marcello? The Maf who owns Louisiana; including McKeithon, Boggs, Ellender, Long, Hebert, the Archbishop and everybody else. Illegal Mafia alien since 1919. A murder a day. Onassis cocaine and heroin ever since. Mucho murder. Hoover's Catholic Boys have known about him since 1932 (actually, before that). That's 40 years. Ain't that sweet? He does not live in a phone booth. He, alone, sponsored the Mafia statute of crime limitations laws. He ordered the Legal Mafia to pass them. They did.

Do you work for him, Nader? or for Onassis, or Teddy, or Dickie? Or all of them?

Johnson said it again, yesterday, to Maryanne Means: "Our system is in trouble; we hang together, or we hang separately." And his message is going out to all of you. Right, Ralphie?

Be careful passing crosses, Nader. That one is angry. He might jump off and nail you up there for the next few thousand years. Crusader Nader.

9 November 26, 1971:
To Nader: Mustapha Bey's Diary on Onassis

Nader:

On September 27, 1971, I called Neilson-Green (Private investigators who worked with Dick Carlson, Lance Brisson, Cooper, White, *Look* Magazine, Justice, CIA, etc., on preparing the Alioto Mafia Web cover story). I was looking for Dick Carlson, who has been running from me ever since the Mafia election process of 1968, when the September 16, 1968, Alioto hit-run cover-up on my car frightened Humphrey and Muskie out of California, brought about the six-days-before-election "Peace—bombing halt" by Johnson, elected Nixon to the presidency, and resulted in Chappaquiddick ten months later.

Local columnists mentioned that a CIA lid had gone on Carlson as of election day, 1968. The key is the Mafia election process, which owns the candidates and is the winner in every election. (In 1960, Joseph P. Kennedy, Onassis, the Vatican Mafia, the Legal Mafia, and the Press Mafia all moved into the White House. Immediately, John F. Kennedy invaded Vietnam, and sent Cousins to Krushchev to get Cardinal Slipyi out of the jug, for the Pope. He was in for Nazi collaboration—just as the entire Vatican Hierarchy had done at Auschwitz, and elsewhere throughout the period.) Vietnam was called by Cardinal Spellman "a Holy Crusade."

And immediately, Iron Bob Maheu (Robert A. Maheu to you; this is the "I.B.M." nickname that runs through all the later assassinations: Martin Luther, Bobby, and JFK) was sent to assassinate Castro—by the CIA, the hard core Mafia, and the Vatican.

The Vatican Mafia wished to regain Cuba for the Church, while taking over South East Asia, consolidating Taiwan, and pitching for China. The hard core Mafia (Onassis, Lansky, etc.) wanted the Cuban gambling money back. Castro had stolen $8 billion Cuban Casino cash from McLaney, Lansky's man in Cuba. McLaney went to Florida and set up the training camp that helped to train Roselli and Big Jim and the rest that later formed Maheu's assassination crew.

Maheu's crew failed to murder JFK on November 1, 1963, after JFK canceled his Chicago trip. Onassis and the CIA nailed Diem and Nhu on that same day in Vietnam, but missed Archbishop Ngo Dinh Thuc, the third brother, who, as South Vietnam's Roman Catholic Prelate, had been recalled to Rome, and Madame Nhu, who was valuable as a heroin courier link under the new man, Thieu. Two weeks earlier, JFK had canceled his Chicago trip, and called Jackie on Onassis's yacht, screaming "Get off that yacht if you have to swim."

On that day, November 1, a witness saw "the second Oswald", Tom Vallee, with two others and a gun in a car in Chicago. After the Dallas affair, three weeks later, he recognized some of the people photographed in Dallas as the same Chicago crew, and told two people, Black Panthers Hampton and Clark, what he had seen. And he kept dinging at the Chicago FBI and CIA to take his information connecting the Chicago "Mafia crew" to the murder at Dallas. After about six months of refusal to take his information, the CIA invited him in one day, and he has not been seen since.

Hampton and Clark were murdered by Mayor Daley's man, Hanrahan, in December, 1969, a few months after Chappaquiddick. The Hampton and Clark murder and cover-up is well recorded.

Robert Maheu was well rewarded for his assassination accomplishments by Onassis and the CIA. He was put on a half million dollars a year salary for life, paid out of the "Howard Hughes" organization, and he also had sole charge of "Hughes's" Las Vegas gambling empire. (Hughes was kidnapped by Onassis in March, 1957. And Onassis took over the whole Hughes empire: communications, defense contracts, all of it. Later, Hughes went into a cage on the island of Tenos, Greece, Onassis's other island, and was buried at sea there on April 16, 1971. Jean Peters obtained her "divorce" from the corpse in early June.)

Chester Davis, a trusted Hughes employee, managed the Hughes kidnap and switch in Los

Angeles, in 1957, utilizing Hughes's known eccentricities, such as his reclusiveness and his self-protective use of doubles. It was an easy take-over. Just as easy as changing his name from "Cesar"—as he was christened when born in Sicily—to Chester after he arrived in New Jersey.

Maheu decided to take over the Onassis-"Hughes" department on the strength of his blackmail—of everybody. He took charge in the "Hughes" TWA suit loss; and it was lost because no genuine Hughes signature could be produced.

Maheu was then called upon to arrange the Martin Luther King murder, and he arranged it.

Again, in 1968, he was called upon to set up the hypnotic Sirhan Sirhan hit on Bobby. And also, in 1968, he was the one who bribed Nixon with a $100 thousand (known, that is—actually more) cash contribution, direct from skim money from "Hughes's" Silver Slipper Casino in Vegas, and some others. He also bribed Hubert Humphrey ($80,000 known) and Larry O'Brien (via a Public Relations deal—post-election—worth about $50,000 per year).

Teddy visited Onassis's yacht in August, 1968, after Onassis had RFK shot. To save his own life, he accepted Onassis's terms on everything, including Onassis's marriage to Jackie.

On September 16, 1968, San Francisco Mayor Joe Alioto's son clobbered my car, and I opened the can of worms on the key: the Mafia election process, which leads to all the major assassinations, all the Mafia elections, and, more important, to the Fatima #3 secret. Namely, the intended blow-off of the non-Vatican half of the world, if they couldn't be converted (which was Fatima secret #2). And all of this is sanctified by the realization that Fatima #1 came true. That one was World War II—rigged by Onassis, Joseph P. Kennedy, and FDR. Hamilton Fish, Jeanette Berlin, and a host of intellectuals will verify this for you.

Mustapha Bey's Onassis Diary

Or you can find it in an Onassis diary which I purchased: a diary kept by Mustapha Bey, the Turk whom Onassis sought to impress as he strolled down the plank of his yacht in Turkey with Jackie on his arm.[28] This was a week before the aborted JFK murder in Chicago, a week before his successful murder of Catholic Mandarin Heroin Pusher Ngo Dinh Diem (and his brother, Ngo Dinh Nhu), a week before the Papal recall of the third brother (Archbishop Ngo Dinh Thuc). And this he did with Jackie on his arm—a week after her hubby, JFK, screamed at her over the phone, in public anger: "Get off that yacht if you have to swim."

This diary of Mustapha Bey's goes back to Onassis's teen years in Smyrna and Onassis's murders, heroin trade, the whole works, at age 14. It continues on through the 1932 deal between Roosevelts (FDR & Elliott), Churchills (Winston and son), Joseph P. Kennedy, and Onassis regarding the smuggling of English Booze and Turkish opium (refined into heroin at Marseilles) and cocaine from South America, in a direct shot to Boston and New Orleans. It continues through Joseph P.'s SEC rigging, War II, the postwar Onassis "Liberty Ships" rape[29] (Chief Justice Warren Burger sat in on this), a few more wars, and on up through early October 1968—still pre-election. And to one month after the Alioto hit-and-run, when Jackie and Cardinal Cushing worked out an unbelievable confession, a marriage contract, and a deal with the Pope and the Vatican which included Teddy's absolution for Chappaquiddick.

This entire Democratic Mafia group settled on my back on September 16, 1968, via Mafia Joe Alioto. The first attorney I turned to was Republican Mafia candidate Nixon, and his campaign manager, John Mitchell. Nixon, Mitchell, and the local Nixon hatchet men Greenagel, Carlson, Best (Northern California campaign manager), and Mack, were gleeful, until the election. After the election, they all had a partial loss of memory. After Chappaquiddick, it became a total loss of

---

[28] This was apparently a book published in Turkey. I have seen a reference to it elsewhere, but have been unable to obtain a copy.—sc

[29] This refers to Onassis's fraudulent and illegal purchase of a fleet of American "Liberty ships" after World War II.

memory.

Democratic Mafia President Lyndon Johnson went to see Republican Mafia candidate Nixon and said, "We hang together, or we hang separately. I got my message from the Pentagon on the plane back from Dallas. 'No conspiracy,' they told me. 'Cover it up.' It was clear to me that I'd never make it back to Washington alive if I didn't obey, and that loyal Vatican John McCormack, , Speaker of the House, who had been dealing with the Mafia for years, would be President in my place. Now, Dickie, I want you to give my friend John Connally the keys to the Treasury. I want one of my boys right at your elbow. He's a good one. He learned his lesson. He has a Maheu-inspired bullet hole in his throat and fragments of another bullet in his belly. So come on down and dedicate my Memorial Pyramid and tell them all how great I am."

Chappaquiddick Dickie agreed.[30]

Prior to that chat, I had been to see John Mack (lawyer for Bank of California) and Greenagel (P.R man for the San Francisco Chamber of Commerce, who worked on this with Fred Martin, formerly in charge of government offices for the Chamber, and now, quite naturally, moved up the ladder as Public Relations man for the world headquarters of Bank of America.) That was just three weeks after Chappaquiddick, and I told them exactly what had happened there.

At any rate, the CIA and FBI were busy covering everything up. Best and Carlson I couldn't find. Greenagel and Mack went into hiding. Nixon, Mitchell, Congressional "truth squads", Reagan—all built a shield.

Long before the Aitken hearing (April 27, 1970) that caused Cambodia, my papers had gone elsewhere. (Greenagel burned all his copies; Mack lost all memory; attorneys Wright, Belli, Lewis, Davis, couldn't remember their own names.).

You, Nader, took your bribe: $457,000, from Simon Rifkind, the last one to see Judge Crater alive, on behalf of Ted Sorenson from Teddy Kennedy, because of my first letter to you. You turned the letter over to Eddie Cox, Tricia Nixon's husband, and he turned it over to Chappaquiddick Dickie, his pappy-in-law, the President.

I publicly sent the letter August 11, 1970. Contents were out then.

On August 15, 1970, the cash was in your hands.

"Impossible," everybody said. General Motors had you sewed up forever. Why did they suddenly have to send you that money?

On about the same date I showed a copy to Fellmeth, and to Harry Miller.

Said Miller: "Nader doesn't write letters."

Said I: "Mafia is murder, treason, bribery, conspiracy, cover-up. Is Nader Mafia?"

Said Miller: "He is influenced by those around him."

Said I: "They seem to be largely Kennedy friends. Are they Mafia?"

"I don't know," said Miller.

Said I: "These evidential papers are poised for release to foreign countries. What do you think of that?"

Said Miller: "That's probably the thing to do."

He seemed perturbed. Poor boy. He was surrounded with bodyguards, beginning with Attorney General La Follette, when he appeared at the Consumers' Party dinner here, on October 8,

---

[30] This is one of the clearest examples of Mafia *Omerta* that I know of. The two opposing U.S. branches of "government" (Democratic Party and Republican Party) are free to use WHATEVER tactics they choose against each other, but they close ranks **IN SILENCE** against the outside.

1971. Remember, Ralphie, when you canceled your visit to start a third political Consumers Party?

At any rate, six weeks after Fellmeth expressed dismay at not being informed of the "Ted, Simon, Ted" bribe to you because of that letter, I talked to him again in St. Louis.

Said he: "Nader admitted he had received your letter—and the 'Ted, Simon, Ted' cash, and said he had turned it over for investigation."

Said I: "What about the investigation? Who is investigating? And what are you doing in St. Louis?"

Said he: "My wife is having a baby here with her parents. And I'm on my way to Washington. Nader wants me there. That's where the action is, isn't it?"

Said I: "I don't know. Is it?"

But I digress.

"Howard Hughes."

In November, 1970, about three months after that letter obtained your $457,000 bribe, a man came to see me. He was Noel Gayler (an Admiral, head of Defense Intelligence, Pentagon, to you). He began a polite conversation about how beautiful America is, but then asked one definite question: "Which country would you like to go to?"

And then he showed anger, twice. Once he was asking about minerals, and I used the word 'smuggling'—and he was angry, since this stuff I write, smuggled out, is dangerous. And more important yet, smuggled out, the knowledge of a certain mineral. And again, when a friend of mine walked up and joined us. And she knew about this entire bit. She looked him over, and then she left, and I told him that was Senator Proxmire's niece, Jo Fulton, and also related to Gaylord Nelson.

And he mumbled something about "That's the one that has the SST bottled up," and then I had to leave. He seemed puzzled. I wasn't; and neither was Proxmire's niece.

Several weeks ago Gayler went down in Nixon's intelligence shuffle. "Inefficiency," said Chappaquiddick Dickie, and he shifted his over-all intelligence control to Diem-Kennedy Richard Helms of the Vatican CIA (which is now cooperating with the Pope in the overthrow of seven South American countries, running heroin from the Golden Triangle, and roaming 200 miles deep in Yunnan province searching for minerals), and to Strangelove Kissinger, the hero of Peking, as you shall see.

But—"Hughes." A key to all this. The Mafia election process, defense contracts, the political assassinations, communications control (satellites), gambling, are dumping grounds for any CIA or FBI that graduates from Hoover's Fagin school. They get into Intertel, and everywhere, even on the staff manipulating the *Look* cover-up story.

Chester Davis swindled Maheu out of his job as Onassis-"Hughes's" righthand man, so Maheu demanded a $50 million cash settlement from Onassis. That was his price for arranging all the "major" assassinations. (I refer to the fake "kidnapping" of Hughes from Vegas.)

So Onassis decided to settle with Maheu, and thus avoid any public inquiry into the gory past: Chappaquiddick, assassinations, and the Mafia outright purchase of the U.S. in 1960, even going back through War II, to 1932.

And the "Justice Department" (that's people like Texas Willie Wilson and Poucha Pond Mitchell) immediately issued a "leak" from an "authoritative source":

"Hughes is alive and well and healthy and happy, and everything is normal."

Well, what else can they do? Exposure of any of the myths would burst the entire cruddy bubble. It is desperate and revolting.

A dissident from the FBI told me recently that in 1776, barefooted Americans stood on Concord Bridge punching another tyranny with rusty muskets and pitchforks, while today's breed

gathers under Dyke Bridge to hold Mary Jo's head in the pond. And they peddle heroin and bribes for the Mafia and the Vatican, while they place a nuclear noose around the non-Mafia non-Vatican half of the world in order to conduct a mutually profitable blow-off and write a new Constitution for the Pope declaring him to be God.

The Legal Mafia branch—to which you belong, Nader—has already rewritten (and reversed) our original Constitution. How long has it been since treason, bribery, high crimes, conspiracy, and cover-up charges have been enforced, as they were intended to be, as hanging offenses?

Why do you think relatives of the Merrymans and Eckersleys want to talk to me at 1170 Sacramento Street, Onassis's building here in San Francisco? They were two of the six Mormon Mafia "nursemaids" (personal staff) to Howard Hughes. But Merryman's name was suddenly dropped from the list after "Hughes's" phony Thanksgiving kidnapping. Merryman died early this year. I was up in that building once, in Merryman's old apartment, and have no desire to go back.

The group is related to Bechtel, McCone, Parsons. McCone, of the Kennedy-Diem CIA. Bechtel, the number one defense engineering contractor. And the whole building smells of Onassis and CIA. A book on the bookshelf is autographed by Cardinal Spellman; it's his autobiography. And he and Kennedy promoted the "Holy Crusade" in Vietnam. All of history has been a "holy crusade."

But Vietnam was only a prelude, Ralphie. Fatima #3 is more necessary to blot it all out than was War II for Roosevelt. But—two bishops at the recent Rome synod carried pictures of Mary Jo Kopechne under their tunics, instead of the Virgin Mary. I know them. They know the whole bit. Some people call that a crack in the wall. So let's take a look at a few more.

Neilson & Green's office: a CIA front

Like Guy Banister's office in New Orleans in the early stages of the JFK assassination, Neilsen-Green is a CIA front. Currently it serves as an office for Richard Carlson and Neil Brisson, for a "Public Interest Project": investigating the San Francisco Dog Pound. This project is "financed" by $10 contributions from 100 people. Carlson and Brisson are President and Vice President.

I called, and spoke to the secretary, Mary Pongalis. I stated that I knew Carlson and wanted to contribute a huge chunk of tax-free cash.

She said, "Goody, goody, but Carlson and Brisson aren't available. Here's a few names you can try."

I tried, but they weren't available. So I went back to the secretary: "Do you run things for them?"

"Yes."

"I'll come down and see you."

"Well, here's Mr. Neilson, you can talk to him." And he got on the line.

I said, "Mr. Nielson, I want to give you some cash; can I come down and bring it to you?"

"Well, what time?"

"I don't know. Does it matter? If there's nobody there, I'll push it under the door."

"Okay."

They have a large staff. (Dog pound investigation is a deep subject.) I expected the joint to be closed, but Mary Pongalis was there. Green and Nielson were in the next room while we talked.

I said, "Mary, last year I arranged for Ralph Nader to receive $457,000 tax-free cash. I want to do the same for Dick Carlson. He can have as much as he wants. By a stunt, following a hit-run on my car by Joe Alioto's son on September 16, 1968, I elected Nixon to the presidency. Carlson was in on it. But after the election he went into CIA hiding from me.

"I have spent years compiling lists of murderers, traitors, bribers, etc. I know the names of all

the Mafia, FBI, and CIA, and I have discovered that usually they are one and the same. I have probably sent out more shit than J. Edgar has buried in his files. You know: murder, treason, high crimes, bribery, conspiracy, assassinations, cover-ups. Names, dates, places, whys and hows. I am also careless. I leave papers lying around. Anyone can pick them up. These things get into the United Nations. I wish I weren't so careless.

"And at the same time I was talking to Carlson—pre-election, 1968—I was also talking to Reagan. But on election day, Reagan developed a lapse of memory too. I like to think that Fellmeth, Nader's boy, was doing me a favor when he recently released a report on California labeling the entire state government a Mafia cell.."

Mary: "Dick Carlson is unavailable. He is working for a TV station in L.A. Brisson is in Washington on a foundation grant—studying our glorious Congress. But you can leave the cash with me."

Me: "I must hand it to Dick personally. I wish to establish that he is indeed worthy. I have a few questions, you know. After all, I said any amount. It isn't limited to $457,000. You state that he is a skilled investigator. Probably. But I wish to determine whether he'd be interested in solving human murders, instead of dog murders. He is, after all, an accessory to all murders, treason, bribery, and high crimes committed since that hit-run on September 16, 1968. They could all have been ended on that date—including Mary Jo Kopechne, the Cambodia invasion, Tunney's sister's husband's murder, Newsom's nieces, etc.

"And I am disappointed in Nader. He too could have stopped it all on about August 15, 1970, when he received his $457,000. Fellmeth failed to mention that particular Reagan lapse of memory about the September 16, 1968 hit-run when he accused the entire State Government of California of being a Mafia cell. *Look* Magazine also failed to mention it. The Justice Department failed to mention it as they prosecute Alioto far away in Washington for a bribery practice which is practiced by all members of the Legal Mafia, the Government Mafia, and the Vatican Mafia.

"In fact, Reagan was so sure that it wouldn't be mentioned that he remarked that Nader reminded him of a 'mouse trying to fuck an elephant.' And that is not obscene language, since our holy governor is the one who spoke it—just as holy President Johnson sanctified the phrase: 'It is better to have J. Edgar Hoover inside the tent pissing out than outside the tent pissing in.'"

Mary: "Oh dear, how do I handle this?"

Me: "Well, you are a tough private eye, Mary. I have never met one before, but I've seen them on TV and I'm sure you'll figure out something. Why don't you write Dick Carlson a slow letter and tell him to contact me at my mother's? Here's the address and phone number—although he knows it well. Slow, because that will give me time to sell more of my gemstones, with histories.

"You see, the first legal firm I went to, before the 1968 election, was that of Nixon and Mitchell, who were just candidates then, and they seemed glad to see me. But after the election, they crawled into a hole with the rest of the Mafia. And then, after Chappaquiddick, they installed a lid over the hole, and a padlock, and left all the Mafia branches to hide themselves: Legal, Press, Vatican, Pentagon, Insurance, Banking, Corporate, Multi-national, etc. But I got through to Nixon anyhow, through Mack, several days after the 1968 election."

And I gave Mary Pongalis an abbreviated version of the following conversation which I had had with John Mack[31] back in November 1968:

Needling Mack: Selling Gemstones with Histories to Foreign Countries

Me: "Here's an experimental mineral I've been working on. When the Mafia moved in on me the night Alioto's son clobbered my car, all of my experimental work ceased. I had, however,

---

[31] John Mack was a California Banker, a staunch Republican and head of the California Committee to Re-elect the President [Nixon].

already discovered the dirty end of the stick. Now, I elected Nixon. Scratch my back. Give me Federal help to clean up this Mafia country."

Mack: "I think we should discuss this mineral."

Me: "I asked you for four people to help me in October, 1968, and I promised I would hand you Alioto and the Mafia, on a platter, before the election. Your answer was silence. You have held this mineral in your hand. You are not dead. I have been playing with it for years. I am not dead. And yet you sense—and I know—some of the qualities involved in it. What I want is Federal help."

Two days later, John Mitchell came to San Francisco with Vatican Mafia Bundy, a hero of Spellman's Holy Crusade in Vietnam, for the Ford Foundation. They established the Alioto Crime Commission: a Mafia Commission run by Alioto, which proved to be a perfect Mafia lid. I was sick; and arrangements for the disposition of that mineral were completed. Not the Mafia way; my way.

Then came Chappaquiddick. Three weeks later, I went back to Nixon, again via Mack: "Here's the solution, and information about the Mafia purchase of the country in 1960. The assassinations, the whole bit. Get me lawyers and the Justice Department to help me—and I'll donate the entire proceeds of suits to the Justice Department to clean up the rest of the crime."

His answer: "You'll have to give me some time."

I got time. I got total silence. The total Mafia CIA, FBI, Vatican, and Legal clamp was on. Greenagel burned evidence. Best disappeared. Everybody took a hike. Attorneys. Judges. Everybody.

In August, after Chappaquiddick, Dick Carlson's Alioto Mafia Web story came out in *Look*. It was a total Governmental Mafia frame to slap Alioto around a bit, but still avoid the key: the hit-run on my car that elected Nixon, exposed the Mafia election process, and led back directly to all the major assassinations.

I was sick again. I took a group of experimental rubies and sapphires to Mack.

I told him: "All right. I'll do it myself. I elected Nixon. Scratch my back. Sell these for me. Nixon can pick up the phone, and every Republican would buy one for his wife. At a fair price. I can get the money I need tomorrow. And I'll have this Mafia country cleaned up in no time. All alone."

He: "Okay."

A year later I stopped back to pick up the group of stones. They were still in his desk.

But two weeks after I left them with him, I knew the only scratching of the back I would get from Nixon would be a stiletto. A Maf by the name of Lello notified me, in the Maurice Hotel, in front of witnesses, about the fate in store for the rest of my family. So, two weeks after I asked Mack to sell the stones, I took another group of gemstones to the other Mafia party—the Democrats—and I offered them the same proposition. That door slammed quickly as well.

I tried some private sales. And I discovered that I could not sell an item in high demand, in high scarcity: a ruby worth $1000—anywhere in America—for $10. Nor for $5. Or at any price.

All right. Murder for the entire family. My parents, after three years of this, have aged 20 years. They have been expecting a Yablonski-type shotgunning, or a Newsom-type barbecue, or a Tunney-type head hatcheting off. Actually, it looks as if this Vietnam-Legal Mafia group have settled on the CIA type of thing called "dying on the vine": letting time hide everything, a la the JFK, Martin Luther, and Bobby bits. Other types of pressure have been thrown in too.

No law whatever. Every constitutional right suspended.

But while Mack held those stones in purgatory, other stones were going out. To countries where they hate the Mafia.

Some, I was mistaken about. But usually a question would come back from, say, a foreign embassy: "Why? Why try to sell us a ruby? America is begging for them."

So I told them why. Everything. From Chappaquiddick, both ways—backwards and forwards.

And the Mafia-hating countries then seemed generous. For instance:

"You ask for $1000 for your gemstone. We feel its true value is $3500 American dollars. How would you like payment? We would like to purchase more of your wares, especially the "whys." They are interesting. And it is true that most gemstones achieve a greater value because of their historical value. Did you realize that the very history you write about increases that value? Or that we too have lawyers of international repute who would be delighted to be of service on any basis you may desire? It would appear that you have suits for recovery that would blanket the world. And we would be delighted to assist in any proposed mineralogical venture."

It was easy. To that country, I later sold a piece of gravel that I picked up in front of Alioto's City Hall for $2500. I shipped it wrapped up in a few sheets of "whys." Their view of the value of a "stone" rising with its historical interest proved to be true.

My response to the $3500 sale: "I do not want the money. I wish to purchase information. Everything here is censored to me. But what is censored here is not censored there. What I wish to purchase with my $3500 credit is evidence regarding the following matters."

(And I quoted them—and I received some answers.)

You now know how it was that I purchased Mustapha Bey's Onassis diary. And facts about War II. And about tablet discoveries in the Middle East, hastily suppressed by the Vatican, proving the birth of Christ to be in April of 6 B.C., his natural birth, his Persian father, his trial by the Roman Mafia, and his crucifixion by the same, and the whole gory history of the Vatican.

Some of it verified what I already knew. For instance, from an ex-wife who was the daughter of the French consul to French Indo-China at the time of Dien-ben-phu, and who was imprisoned in one of the early Hanoi Hiltons, I heard a sad history of Vatican French colonialism and its tie-in with Onassis, Diem, the heroin from the Golden Triangle, and the Taiwan piece of that action.

In fact, some of my gemstones came from that area, Nader, smuggled in, along with the opium. Turkey always has been a decoy. Eighty percent of the stuff has always come from the Golden Triangle.

Early this year, after Hughes had died and the Merryman and Eckersley women invited me up to 1170, and Bobby Kennedy's murderer was named, and that information was buried by the same Mafia group of Mary Jo Kopechne fame, I mentioned to Mack that the only thing I had ever been 100% successful at was smuggling—say, of papers, or gemstones. He was perturbed at that, just as Noel Gayler had been when I mentioned "smuggling". They suddenly realized that papers and gemstones had been going in and out, and this horrible mob couldn't do a damn thing to stop it.

And just to illustrate the reason for their anger: 37 nations to whom I sold my gemstones, with "whys," voted in the U.N. to oust dictator Chiang, the Taiwanese dope pusher, and Roman Catholic Cardinal Lin, his handmaiden; and they also voted for the admission of China to the U.N.

(Incidentally, Nader, I don't care for the people who say they represent you and then ask me for tidbits of information. I don't like your back-door methods. It stinks like CIA. And yet I've seen my phrasing of some of that information turn up later in foreign newspapers. It is not coincidental.)

***

This, Nader, was approximately the end of my September 27, 1971, conversation with Mary Pongalis of the CIA firm of Nielson and Green, partners to Carlson and Brisson, who are pawns of Nixon, Mitchell and all branches of Mafia everywhere. At this writing I don't remember if every word of this conversation actually went to Mary Pongalis. But whatever I didn't mention to her got out to others, of the Noel Gayler and Ed Sullivan type, who occasionally look out of the woodwork at me like cockroaches.

For instance, on the following Saturday night, the son of the owner of the "Dr. Pepper" company, in Houston, Texas—Clemens by name—asked me for various earfuls concerning "IBM" (that's "Iron Bob Maheu," otherwise known as Robert A. Maheu, Onassis's favorite assassination crew leader.) And I was so tired (I was in the Mark lobby bar waiting for an Eckersley or a Merryman to appear—they live just across the street at 1170 Sacramento Street, Onassis's building) that I might have recited a huge chunk from J. Edgar Hoover's files. I don't know. Or care. It's all true. As I said to Nixon and Mitchell in October, 1968, I will repeat every word under pentothal or a lie tester or hypnosis or anything else. They, and everybody else, have been running ever since.

I know that you wouldn't volunteer to take a lie test, would you, Nader? Because you know about all this, and because this monster group knows you know. (I made sure they did, via copies of everything to Alioto and Kennedy.) You use the information I gave you to call Reagan and Nixon "Mafia bastards", and you watch them run. But you don't use it on Kennedy, do you, Ralphie? And you run too—from me. Right, Ralphie?

Did you know, Ralphie—and I'm sure you do—that Onassis owns General Motors? Did you know that the $45 million skim money that Lansky is accused of grabbing from "Hughes" in Las Vegas actually went to Onassis? Onassis is "Hughes". Maheu, for "Hughes", bribed Nixon in 1968 with $100,000 of that skim money. About the same bribe amount went to Humphrey: over $80,000. A similar bribe went to Kennedy's Larry O'Brien: $50,000. And so it is, Nader, that this year you accepted a $457,000 bribe—from that same Vegas casino skim money—from Onassis.

Check with another member of your legal Mafia: Greg Bautzer. He represents only two clients: "Hughes," and Kerkorian. Onassis buried "Hughes" and owns Kerkorian—and you. How do you spell Mafia, Nader? John Maier (and any of his aliases: Meyer, Meier, Andre...) works for Double-"O"—Onassis and "Hughes"—and oversees Jackie. Only the Mafia runs from me. I control the means of their extermination. You realize this, by now, or you wouldn't be running from me.

***

I talked to Mary Pongalis on September 27, 1971. On September 30, my father took a call from Los Angeles, from a voice that stated it was Dick Carlson. I was not there. My father notified this voice that I would be there to take a call at 10 a.m. the following morning.

The voice asked if I was some kind of lawyer working with Nader. My father answered that all he could say was that I provided cash for people like Nader, or Carlson, and why didn't he call back at 10 a.m. the following morning to find out.

At 10 a.m. the next day, October 1, I was waiting for the call from Carlson which meant all the cash he needed. There was no call, of course.

So at noon I called Mary Pongalis, and she said that Dick Carlson had called her and notified her that he had called me. And I congratulated her on a major breakthrough, because I hadn't been able to get through to Carlson for three years, ever since the Mafia election of 1968. I told her that she deserved a reward, and asked whether she would be in the office that afternoon so that I could bring her a lot of cash. And she said she would be there all afternoon, and had nothing else to do but wait for me.

At 2:00 p.m. I was there, and another secretary ushered me in to see Neilson.

Me: "I came to see Mary Pongalis."

He: "She's gone and she won't be back. What can I do for you?"

Me: "It's what I can do for you. I wish to reward Mary for doing the impossible: actually contacting Dick Carlson. It's a miracle. I was thinking of giving her that building at 1170 Sacramento Street. If she wants to give it to you, you would have a plush 11 floors, or whatever it is, on top of the Hill, instead of sitting here in Mafia North Beach under the wings of Alioto's St. Peter & Paul's in this dinky pad."

He, changing the subject: "Dick Carlson is easy to reach. I talk to him every day. He's at such-and-such a TV station in L.A. "

Me: "Let's see; isn't that station owned by Sarnoff, Roosevelt's and Joseph P. Kennedy's friend—the keeper of BNWS? One of the bigger con artists who conned Krushchev into that 1959 meeting with the 'real owners of America'? Oh yes, and several key witnesses to that Alioto hit-and-run have since disappeared into the maw of that very same TV station. I guess they like to be together."

He, changing the subject: "Do you know Lance Brisson?"

Me: "I know lots of details, such as Brisson's father and Strangelove Kissinger making the rounds of the nightspots together. And I know Carlson's relative was a Senator from Massachusetts, and we do know about Massachusetts Senators, don't we?"

He, changing the subject: "Well, that's the only way to reach Carlson: phone the TV station."

Me: "No, I'd rather do it through Mary Pongalis. She performed a miracle. She actually got through to Carlson, and she will probably be murdered for it. Secretaries who learn this type of information usually are. I want her to have her place in history, such as all presidents desire, and I have a way of arranging this. I have sent her a letter, assuring her of this. She will receive it. It is now on its way around the world picking up endorsements."

He: Silence.

Me: "Carlson doesn't have to scrounge for ten bucks from people. I'll give him the whole Howard Hughes Empire, and he can prosecute dog pounds in luxury from Las Vegas. Assassins Maheu, Cesare Davis, and Onassis aren't going to need these things where they're going. Neither will I.

"But that way, Carlson can kill the big dog murderers. That's China; they kill dogs there, and serve them for dinner. He can use Lockheed and Bechtel and the "Hughes" satellites—all owned by Onassis—and lob in a few missiles, and murder all 800 million of the Chinese dog murderers at once. And while he's at it, he can lob a few at Russia, and clobber them too. That way, he gets a bonus from the Pope, who has declared himself to be God, in the form of a medal for completing Fatima #3. And he can also win a Pulitzer Prize for exposing the Maheu assassination crew: names, dates, places, all the way from Castro through Dallas, Memphis, and L.A.

"I think these things would be better than, say, the Russians and Chinese blotting out the 500 million "soldiers of the Vatican" and the 20 million world-wide Mafia population (the greater share of these presently engaged in running the Mafia U.S.), and then all of the billions of Russian and Chinese men and women going to bed one night and repopulating the cancerous crud with fresh new humans. Brand new, non-cancerous, non-Mafia humans. Maybe the man hanging on the cross for two thousand years, placed there by the same Mafia cancer, would appreciate this. Mary Jo Kopechne would, I'm sure. A one-night replacement orgy. Wouldn't that be a better 'Holy Crusade' than the Kennedy-Spellman 'Vietnam Holy Crusade'? Problems, problems. But the real problem is this: In China they have a phrase: 'Chappaquiddick Big Dickie, Chappaquiddick Little Dickie, and Chappaquiddick Alioto'.

"When I learned of 'Chappaquiddick Little Dickie' being in the group, I was reminded of our own Dick Carlson and our pre-1968 election chats. And I remembered that Reagan had received his reminder of his part in that 1968 Mafia election and cover-up. And incidentally, that I had also assured Reagan's reelection, since Alioto would surely have beaten him, had not Alioto backed off because of Chappaquiddick, and assorted threatened Mafia exposures.

"But 'Chappaquiddick Little Dickie' needs a little reminder, and so I have decided to assist him with cash in his dog pound investigation. We've got to get 'Chappaquiddick Little Dickie', our mutual friend and partner, off the list, don't we, Neilson?"

Neilson looked somewhat like Hugh Scott, Chappaquiddick Big Dickie's Senate whip.

Silence. Only a "blink blink" of the eyes. It is a know fact that CIA murderers and Private Eyes don't blink. But he did. He looked like a frog. I expected him to go "bleep." But he didn't. Just "blink blink." And if you have ever tried to conduct a conversation with an apparent human being whose sole response is batting his eyes, you would do exactly as I did. I left.

***

During the Inquisition the Popes read the litany of Ignatius Loyola to their barbecues, while they suffocated. Recently the entire Alioto Mafia trial jury, plus attorneys and Judges, stood around and enjoyed the barbecue of Newsom's nieces—Pelosi's daughters. Pelosi was elected President of the San Francisco Board of Supervisors. Newsom, Pelosi's brother-in-law, was in on the 1968 Mafia cover-up and election; he joined Onassis after Chappaquiddick. Pelosi's in-laws are the D'Alessandros, who own Baltimore. Pelosi's godfather is Alioto. Oh well.

Copies of all this went out to Neilson and various members of his staff, so I know it was received—dead center, in the Strangelove Kissinger-Chappaquiddick Big Dickie and Little Dickie ear. The key was the reference to the Chinese phrase "Chappaquiddick Big Dickie, Chappaquiddick Little Dickie, and Chappaquiddick Alioto."

Five days after that Chinese phrase-Neilson conversation, Kissinger announced a sudden second trip to Peking to "check the agenda" of the forthcoming Nixon-Chou En Lai talks.

Kissinger was still there—in Peking—on voting day, in the United Nations, on the question of Taiwan's ouster and China's admission. That fact alone cost him the votes of six countries—and ousted dope-pushing dictator Chiang and his handmaiden, Vatican Cardinal Lin.

37 countries who bought Gemstones voted China into the U.N.

All 37 countries who bought my gemstones and accompanying histories voted against Taiwan and for China.

So Vatican mouth William Buckley organized a group to cut off all U.N. funds. Mafia Congress shut off all foreign aid (but later relented, realizing that Mafia purchase was their only remaining hope).

Taiwan briber Murphy, a Senator beaten by Tunney because the Chappaquiddick lid was on him, too, and he knew the entire bit—took a financial loss. What good is a briber who can't effectively bribe? Chiang is ruthless with his Mafia loot: produce or else.

The Mafia Congress, the Mafia press and the legal Mafia now announce that they are out to destroy the U.N. To wipe it out. This, after years of using it to promote governmental Mafia and Vatican Mafia interests. The fear is that the U.N. will become a giant Knapp Commission type of thing, conducting public inquiries into everything: Chappaquiddick, the assassinations, the cover-up of Christ—with nothing like the American Mafia legal methods of legal Omerta—secrecy at all levels, from grand juries on up.

The Mafia will do absolutely anything—no holds barred—to prevent the exposure of Chappaquiddick and what it leads to, and to cover up the Mafia election process exposed by the Alioto hit-run. Including a first strike: Fatima #3—to blot it all out.

The U.N. delving into the root causes of all wars, all crime—including the Vatican cover-up of the Roman murder of Christ, to achieve the prevention of War III? This would never do.

Your purchase, Nader? Minor. The JFK murders for cover-up? Minor. Same with Martin Luther King and Bobby. Destruction of the U.N.? Also minor.

Backed with massive evidence, and run through a computer, it all checks out. Non-Mafia countries have done this. Non-Mafia "lawyers" are developing a mass international Knapp Commission, hoping to beat Fatima #3—or perhaps to pull a first strike themselves and bring out the papers later to justify their actions. And they would be justified.

Today, the CIA and the Vatican openly announce support for "revolution" in seven South American countries. They run 200 miles deep into Yunnan province, looking for a mineral. "Chappaquiddick Dickie" will never relinquish control of Indo-China, for that same mineralogical reason. Nor will he cease providing money to Onassis. Through Lockheed, "Hughes," General Motors—anywhere Onassis and Mafia aliases own the stock. How can he? He took the same Onassis bribe that you did. And he has one huge monkey on his back.

Johnson enlightened Nixon just after Chappaquiddick: "We must all hang together—or hang separately. We must preserve our places in history—along with the Onassis-Kennedys, the Prendergast-Trumans, and the Onassis-Kennedy-Roosevelts. We've come a long way with those 'Holy Crusade' wars, and we can have it all with just one more hump: Fatima #3. Send Lodge to the Vatican, Dallas-bullet Connally to the Treasury, and fuck the Supreme Court. All we need to do is to boost Hoover's white Catholic boys [so described by Mike Novack], support the Pope and the Knights of Columbus, and keep Hoover inside that tent, pissing out."

Dickie listened and obeyed. But he also listens to Neilson's conversations, and crawls on his belly to Chou and Brezhnev. With reason; they are not stupid.

A Heavy Piece of Rock

China can have that mineral tomorrow, if they do the right thing. Without going through the lengthy process of developing it in the laboratory. Geological logic suggests it also exists in Russia, and that's bad news for everybody. One misplaced missile would really jazz this joint up. Or one deliberate missile. All it takes is one missile crew. Or one finger on one button. Ask any Maf and they'll tell you that you can always find someone you can buy, or hype, or frighten. Any one human being can do this, Nader. Just one.

I told John Mack, several days after Nixon's inauguration, that one human can do what a whole army can't.

He was holding a mineral—a piece of rock—in his hand when I said this, and he said, "It's heavier than lead."

True. Much heavier than lead. And in a stable field.

Last Christmas, Noel Gayler, from the Pentagon, was curious about this mineral. I told him, in my own way, that its natural occurrence in this country was doubtful. And then I mentioned "smuggling," and he blew his top.

The U.S. Mafia's luck has run out, Nader. You've picked a losing side. Kennedy and Chappaquiddick, like a snowball rolling down a hill, have picked up all the kindred Mafia—including you and Chappaquiddick Dickie—in one huge glob, and we're all rolling down the tube. In 1849, California gold put the U.S. out in front of the world. Today, a key mineral is not available here. It is not available to the Mafia. I naively offered it to Nixon on February 1, 1969, in exchange for the clean-up of cancer. On February 4, I received the second of six hit-runs on my car. This time I was in it.

Three weeks after Chappaquiddick I again offered Nixon my solution to the clean-up of cancer, and added the offer of money from suits to accomplish it. I told Mack, "Nixon can be another Abraham Lincoln and can take credit for leading this country out of slavery—Mafia slavery." I got zilch. Johnson was making his spiel to Dickie at the same time.

Currently, Nader, non-Mafia countries are eager to assume the Abraham Lincoln pose, and they gain confidence from minerals and papers. And they begin to realize their power, and they make it known.

I told someone that I had given you an infusion of guts, via information, blackmail for you—which enabled you to label Reagan and California and Nixon and America "Mafia" with impunity. But you, like Dickie, were converted, by bribery, and now you seek subterfuge in a society of Legal

Mafia. You want $1,000,000, I believe.

The three chief Mafia groups that could have exposed all this crud at any time are the Legal Mafia, Press Mafia and Vatican Mafia.

But you merely nibble at the edges, currying the potential 40 million "consumer votes." Your allies are the Legal, Press and Vatican Mafia, and you cooperate with them. They cooperate with you. It has always been the Mafia way: give up a little, to preserve the keys, and the basic structure. That is: the Mafia election process, the Mafia press to cover it up, and the Mafia Vatican to make it holy.

***

I told Mack in May, this year, that America appears to be too puny to rise up out of its own Mafia shit. He shrugged. I asked him what he had done—as anyone in any public position could have done in the past 47 years (coincidental with Hoover's reign) to correct this. He shrugged again.

I shrugged too. His bank has a piece of the Lockheed loan, and helped push through the next $250 million loan. His bank also has $12 million of Alioto interest-free city money.

In July, this year, I needled Mack again.

The background: Hughes's death, on April 16, 1971; and Jean Peters "divorce," from Hughes's corpse, in late May; Mayheu's $50 million suit against "Hughes," his settlement for the assassinations he arranged for Onassis, around June; the anniversary of Chappaquiddick; Ellsberg's papers on the Pentagon—particularly some references to the Diem murder; and then Ted Charach's Bobby Kennedy murder expose and its cover-up.

And while these things were boiling, the appearance of "Hughes's" Merrymans and Eckersleys[32]: "Come up and see us at 1170 Sacramento Street."

And this one: "Hughes's" Merryman's brother was at the Bohemian Grove. Dickie was scheduled to speak there, but a Humphrey-type expose had been arranged. And Dickie heard about it, and called to cancel his appearance.

"Fear of newsmen's questions," was Phil Ziegler's explanation, and he was right; those questions were loaded. I had found some news people who still possessed a few drops of original American blood.

At any rate, I called Mack in July.

I said, "Mafia or not, Mack, it's your country too, and this is too much. The *New York Times*, the Press Mafia, did it again, as with the Llellyveld cover-up of Loeb's Manchester Union Leader 's Chappaquiddick phone call records. While they were bravely printing the Pentagon Papers, they somehow deleted the fact that Vietnam was a religious war, a Holy Crusade a la Fatima #2. Also, that it was a dope war for Onassis and the CIA and all the other Mafia branches.

"I knew of the Onassis-heroin-Vietnam connection long ago, via the back door, through my own gemstone exportation and my ex-wife, who was there. I just had never assembled the facts. When Alioto clobbered me on September 16, 1968, I was highly sensitive because of experiments I was conducting which I believed to be the most important thing in the world. I assessed that hit-run and my gemstones and Onassis's Vietnam heroin and the dual Kennedy-Diem murder date and my experiments to be all rolled up in that mess together. But I was wrong. The hit-run was pure accident. It was just a coincidence that Tom Alioto had clobbered my car while it was sitting in front of the Russian Embassy.[33] But under that momentary illusion, I sent all the facts out immediately—all the way out, where they would be safe. And in those facts, I was correct.

"Evidence has proved it all—100%. That's too massive to charge to coincidence. I did this in

---

[32] (*the wives/widows of Hughes's vanished Mormon Mafia "nursemaids."*)—sc
[33] "*where they take photos of everything.*"

sheer self-defense. I jammed those papers and that mineral deep up the collective Mafia ass. And there is no way to unsend it.

"Unless the entire mess is voluntarily cleaned up now in America, you can expect to be combing missiles out of your hair at the same time you get a mineral goose up your ass. That would make a meat sandwich out of you. And me. And all the rest of us. I don't know everything, but I have a feeling that the man wants off the cross, and I know Mary Jo wants out of her busted-nose grave. She's gotta be sick of staring up at all those Mafia ass-holes that squat on her grave—and I don't think she cares much how she gets out.

"In fact, we all gotta go sometime. A lifetime isn't even a speck in geological time. Eternity is the thing. I'm not religious, but I know this: whatever is up there is a friend of mine. If I reach out a hand for a rock to throw, I find it. You held one of them in your hand. And some papers.

"If we all survive, there's going to be a new President and a new Attorney General—and the key is that Attorney General. He is the meanest son-of-a-bitch in the world. He wants all the Mafia cancer hung on crosses, beginning with the Pope. There's a switch: Christ off the cross, and the Pope on. Let the Pope hang there for the next two thousand years.

"And instead of a skinny spear-stuck skeleton saying, 'Turn the other cheek; allow the Mafia cancer to murder you as they did me. Listen to the Pope; he is God, and infallible, and he has written a new constitution to prove it,' we'd have a new image of a healthy doctor with a healthy scalpel, cutting out a malignant cancer from an 80% Mafia cancer body that is currently a mortal cinch to die from the disease anyway."

Mack: "Would it do any good if I arranged for you to talk to John Mitchell?"

Me: "Mitchell! That Mafia son-of-a-bitch…." And I was thinking: Mitchell's got one foot up my ass, one on my back, one foot down my throat and the other pounding away any way he can. And him I elected

But then I thought, Why not? Needles are for lesser ass-holes, like Mack and Neilson. For people like Mitchell I've got harpoons.

Mack: "Well, tell me what you want me to do, and I'll do it."

Me: "I know what to do. The question is: who for?"

Mack: "Think about it and call me tomorrow."

Me: "Onassis wants to talk to me. I get this from the sister-in-law of 'Hughes's Merryman. Do you know anything about that?"

Mack: "No."

Me: "They want me to do this at Eckersley's place—in the same building. He's one of the surviving five 'Hughes' nursemaids."

Mack: "What's the address?"

Me: "1170 Sacramento Street."

Mack: "Good-bye."

The next day I had a huge harpoon ready for Mitchell, and I called Mack.

I forget the exact words, but the message was clear.

"Mr. Mack's phone lines will be tied up for the next few centuries. He is no longer available."

I haven't checked back since. Maybe he's dead. It wouldn't surprise me.

***

Back to that Neilson chat on October 1, 1971. Afterwards I went to the Alexis bar, across the

street from 1170 Sacramento, and repeated what I had told Neilson to friends, and to anybody else who cared to listen. In addition, I labeled the son-of-a-bitch who had notified the Chinese of all this crud, a son-of-a-bitch. And I carefully explained why it was that the Chinese have the phrase "Chappaquiddick Big Dickie, Chappaquiddick Little Dickie, and Chappaquiddick Alioto." I couldn't stir up anything. But Strangelove got an earful.

I explained how it was that after Kissinger's first secret trip to Peking in July, a Mexican reporter interviewed Chou-en-Lai and found Chou full of strange, mischievous statements, such as: "JFK's assassination facts have not been released"; "Chappaquiddick has not been explained"; and "Bobby's murder was strange."

And I explained why it was that such things would not be printed by the American Press Mafia, such as Kennedy's Hearst, or Alioto's De Thieriat, or *Look*, or Kennedy's *New York Times*, etc. Nor would they be recounted by Strangelove Kissinger. (Actually, the Mexican report only got out by chance.)

So then I went across the street to the Mark Lobby bar, where Clemens, son of the owner of Dr. Pepper's, joined me. He wanted to know about assassinations and IBM and Chappaquiddick and Hoover's files—and I told him.

He interrupted me once to state: "That's all true."

I said "I'm glad you think so, because I spent some time with Blinky Neilson today and his total response was 'Blink, blink,' and no bleep to go with it. And I notice that you blink quite a bit, and I was beginning to wonder whether you were frog or human. I'm glad you made the cut."

I proceeded to quote some tidbits about the various Mafia state ownerships—such as Marcello's Louisiana (Ellender, Boggs, Hubert, Long, McKeithon, etc.), Kennedy's New Jersey, Massachusetts and Illinois, Fellmeth's California, and on and on, until the bar closed.

Clemens and five of his Texas friends gathered at a table and they asked me over. I proceeded to enlighten these loyal Texans on the rottenest state of all: Texas. I discussed Willie Wilson, John Mitchell's crime leader, and the Guv, Lt. Guv, Insurance, Banking, John Connally, and all the Mafia back room groups. Finally, when I couldn't stir up anything and they were getting sadder and I was getting hoarser, I said good night and walked over to the door.

And one of them shouted, "That was the smartest thing you ever did in your life."

I said "Yes, I think so." I left with the feeling that he was a human—not a frog—and that he would be proud if he knew some other stunts currently underway—some against his own state.

I bought a bottle of Dr. Pepper in a store. While I drank it I thought back to early August this year, when I went to Derrough, at CBS, checking on the press Mafia at the time Stanton was under contempt of Congress for producing "The Selling of The Pentagon."

Derrough had only read the first paragraph of the papers I gave him, describing, concisely, the murder of Mary Jo and Alioto's connection, when he quickly handed the papers back to me. So I told him about the assassination series of Maheu; and about Ellsberg, and the Nader bribe—all in a few quick minutes. Suddenly he "had to be elsewhere for a conference." He would "call me later."

Yes. Dont'cha know.

At any rate, an hour later Christopher Beam pounced on me. From Nixon's San Clemente. He went right at it.

Said he: "I know all elected officials commit treason when they take their oath of office. They say, 'I will defend the Constitution from enemies without and within,' and they are lying. I know that they have taken bribes to get where they are, and have joined the Mafia by accepting candidacy, as lawyers do the moment they are accepted as 'officers of the court.' Like the Vatican, they are their own gods and write their own laws. Now, what happened at CBS?"

I told him. And also about the computer-confirmed Mafia 1968 election in which I elected

Nixon.

He mentioned Dick Sprague of the Assassination Investigation Squad. And I called Mrs. Merryman and said I'd be up at Alexis, and then I asked him to come with me to meet Mr. Mafia. (All the labor hoods were in town plotting Alioto's reelection campaign, and I somehow expected Onassis to be at the 1170 Merryman dinner). Alexis was closed, so we went to the lobby bar of the Mark.

I told him that the leaders of various non-Mafia countries and Nixon and Mitchell had read the entire script of things, but Derrough of CBS was too frightened to read Nader's bribe letter. He said he wasn't.

So he read it, and again he said the right things: "I don't think so much of Nader any more. He changed."

That was true. Mafia bribes work that way.

Again: "You don't mention IBM much in your work."

Me: "Only to those I want to know."

He: "IBM is important."

Me: "Only for assassinations!"

He: "I'm a Catholic."

Me: "So what? The cancer is only at the top. The Protestants have it too. The Reformation was a bust."

He: "What's to happen?"

Me: "Christ wants off the cross. Cancer is going up. Mary Jo wants out of the grave. We need the grave space for cancer."

He: "I like Johnson."

Me: "He was purchased outright on the plane back from Dallas. But he has no excuse. Eisenhower did. By the time Eisenhower knew what was going on, he was trapped. It was too late. He cried on Russell's shoulder, and died sad. Russell covered up for JFK, and he too died sad, issuing his deathbed statement: 'Oswald didn't do it.' The only honest thing Johnson ever did was to publicly speak those same words: 'Oswald didn't do it.' That's probably why you like him."

He: "There is one good man in Texas. You should meet him. You probably will." And he paid the check and left.

So, as I drank my bottle of Dr. Pepper that night after leaving that Texas group, I wondered if perhaps I had met the man of whom Beam spoke. He did invite me down to Texas to stay at his place, and not many people choose to hold my hand these days. That's a dangerous place to be, next to me—right, Nader? As we shall see, you canceled a San Francisco visit recently—an important visit, for you, since it involved the coalescence of your Consumer Third Party. You did this because of me, didn't you, Ralphie?

That Neilson chat was on Friday, October 1, 1971. You were due to appear at this major Consumer Coalition Conference on the 8th. So on Monday, October 4th, I called Harry Miller's secretary.

I said, "I've been waiting for Miller to call. He hasn't. It's about life and death—his, for one. He helped write the Fellmeth 'California is Mafia' report, and I have reason to believe that he, Fellmeth and Nader are to be assassinated this weekend because of nasty remarks they made about some big Mafia people. This weekend is to be the foundation of a political threat to the other two Mafia parties. Fellmeth, Nader and Miller know about Iron Bob Maheu's assassinations, and about Chappaquiddick. Martin Luther King and Bobby were murdered because of their potential political threat; Bobby for The Enemy Within thing, plus his hatred for the group for murdering his brother.

Martin Luther King was murdered because he represented reform. The Yablonskis got shotgun murdered because they were jabbering about the Union Mafia. Pre-knowledge could have prevented any of those murders, plus Mary Jo's. Now be sure that he gets this message. Have him call me. Maybe we can prevent these murders."

She: "I'll give him your message."

Later, I called again.

Said she: "He's out of town and I don't know when he'll be back."

So I called Neilson-Green. I got another secretary.

"This is Roberts. Is Mary Pongalis there?"

"Uh…no."

"I can't seem to get through to Carlson to give him money, and now I can't get through to Mary Pongalis. Is she dead?"

She: "No, she's around somewhere, but she's not available."

Me: "Well, who are you?"

She: "Pat Gonzales."

Me: "Can you take a message for everybody there?"

She: "Uh, yes."

Me: "Tell Neilson he can personally have all of the $12.5 million Alioto is suing *Look* Magazine for because of the Carlson-CIA-Nixon-FBI Alioto Mafia Web story. I will give it to him. I can even raise the amount to the entire $50 million that assassin Maheu wants from Onassis for murdering all those important people. I have offered Alioto a clean victory in that suit.

"You see, it was deliberate evasive persecution to attempt to avoid the exposure of the Alioto hit-run cover-up that led to Nixon's election in an exposed Mafia election process. He can beat the federal rap for legal bribery, because I can prove that it is an established American custom. And I can show why it is that the entire Mafia, from Hoover and Nixon on up to Onassis, are using the courts, in common Mafia fashion, to ease Benito Alioto down the ladder, because he has committed the cardinal sin of letting some of the Mafia's most important secrets slip out from under the blanket of Mafia Omerta.

"The Pope is considering making Alioto a Cardinal when he gets ousted from his Mayor's job (they had a meeting in Rome, and the Pope said this) because of Omerta. I have offered to make Alioto an American hero, granting him partial immunity and promising to keep him off the cross. All he has to do is to confess to his part in the hit-run cover-up that led to all the other events, including Chappaquiddick

"I asked him specifically for the complete story of his Mafia involvement, going all the way back to the Justice Department in World War II, where he peddled information furnished by Lucky Luciano about secret German war plants. Specifically, I wanted him to open all of Hoover's blackmail files. At any rate, all the money from that cooked-up frame is mine, and I will give it to Neilson, no matter what Alioto does. Tell Neilson to call me and I will give him the concrete details.'

"I'll give him the message," she said, and hung up.

But, Nader, I still don't understand why you stood all those people up, when all you had to do was to fly to San Francisco and accept the acclaim of consumers, who vote, and for whom all Mafia politicians shape their images.

For it is they—the tax-paying, producing consumers, who are the ultimate target of all Mafia branches. They are history's pigeons, whom you wish to pluck. (For what, Nader? The Presidency?) And by the same old process: a "legal" Mafia society, controlled by you. You run, with the rest of the

Mafia, from the real key, the only possible solution: the clean-up of the shit. It is the only solution to a suddenly potent international suicide.

Anyone in any authority since the cover-up of Christ 2,000 years ago could have straightened it out.

A Pope and Emperor Constantine, both Roman, worked out a Mafia deal in the year 325 A.D., at the Counsel of Nicaea. And that set the Mafia pattern. The Reformation failed. But a branch of it sputtered momentarily, here, in 1776. They wrote a beautiful Constitution, passed in a free house, with a batch of amendments. But it was already perverted by that Mafia-Vatican political mob in the year 1800.

Today, the murderer of Chappaquiddick is a candidate for President against the incumbent: Chappaquiddick Dickie, bought long ago, heart and soul, by Mafia Kingpin Onassis. American Mafia/Vatican Mafia dictators reign all over the world, and more are being set up daily. American-Vatican Mafia want to wipe out the U.N. because one of the worst of the criminal nations, Taiwan, got kicked out. Murder, treason, conspiracy, cover-up, and on and on.

The greatest mistake of your life, Nader was made the day you deposited that $457,000 from Onassis and didn't grab the first flight to San Francisco. You knew where it came from and why. That was more than a year ago.

I offered Joe Alioto to Nixon, Mitchell and Reagan on a platter two weeks after the hit-run. They refused, and witness the murder, treason and bribery that followed.

Today, the Vatican hierarchy is in trouble. Many of the flock carry pictures of Mary Jo, instead of the Virgin Mary. And Fatima #3 is a stalemate. It will not be a Mafia blow-off of the other half. The nuclear noose has been reversed.

I saw a map with strange new names: Gulf of Skorpios, Gulf of Hyannisport, Gulf of Alioto, Gulf of Dubai. If that isn't enough, there is a new thing around. Since it is new, for verification you can ask your friend, Chappaquiddick Dickie. He knows a little. Or try Brezhnev or Mao. They know a little. Or me. I know a lot. Specifically, the dirty end, and what else is needed to dispose of cancer.

I sent a proposition to Teddy: To stand up in the Senate and let it all hang out. Congressional immunity. Unravel himself like a ball of string, and expose himself for the Mafia crud that he is. And take the rest of the Mafia cancer with him. It would be a truly American service. As his brother stated (as he and the Pope leaped into the "Holy Crusade of Vietnam"), "Ask not what your country can do for you. Ask what you can do for your country."

Even if Teddy were to perform such a thing, it wouldn't help him much. No portion of manhood can ever be attributed to cancer. But, if we survive because of that action, maybe within a few centuries people would stop spitting in the general direction of his cross, where he would be, along with the Pope, Onassis, and a host of treasonous, murderous, bribing public officials and back room Mafia from all branches. This Mafia "congressional immunity" has little meaning to the man who's been hanging there for two thousand years, nor does the Mafia "statute of limitations" on crime. He wants off the cross and out from under his cover-up. So does Mary Jo.

A Cockroach from Hoover

Last week, a cockroach jumped out of the woodwork. From Hoover.

He opened with: "The Irish are a strange breed. You're Irish, and it took an Irishman to do it." (He was speaking of Teddy and the solution to Chappaquiddick, but he was wrong. Actually I was born Welsh, Scotch and Irish, apparently in equal thirds, but I defecate daily. And I reason that after 52 years of that I have lost my Kennedy Irish, and am by now pure Scotch and Welsh. However, some records list, for brevity, just the nationality "Irish"; once I was proud of it.)

So I told him: "You are a friend of Hoover's, and he is one of the hugest globs of Mafia crud. Gallinaro dug up the shit on Hoover's Mafia connections, going back to the 1920's with Rosensteil

and Johnny Torrio and Joseph P. Kennedy. Hoover has been riding blackmail on the greatest murderous Mafia shit for 47 years.

"On the day following Gallinaro's expose, the Mafia put a $250,000 contract on his head. That's close cooperation. Last week in Texas, while Gallinaro was snooping into Mafia Justice Criminal Chief Will Wilson's Mafia activities, the Mafia—not Hoover or Wilson—almost beat him to death in a hotel room.

"Back east, Nixon and Hoover hate Stern, who dug up information on some New Jersey Mafia: Kennedy-Addonizio and Kennedy-Whelan, Mary Jo's last employer and the one who sent her to Chappaquiddick loaded with loathing of the Kennedy Mafia. The Mafia put a $150,000 tag on him; the Mafia, not Hoover or Nixon. I like Gallinaro and Stern. I do not like Chappaquiddick Dickie, or your boss, Mafia Hoover. I elected Nixon—and the Mafia (not Nixon and Mitchell; the Mafia) put an unlimited price tag on the murder of me and my family, and my friends. It was originally supposed to be a Yablonski-type wipe-out, but it has since been changed to a CIA-type slow torture, die-on-the-vine type of thing. I watch my mother and father rot daily, in total torture. Yes, they know how to hurt. And so do I.

"Hoover's Catholic white boys have been plugging for the 'Three secrets of Fatima.' Fatima #1, World War II, was rigged by Roosevelt. Fatima #2, the conversion of the entire world to Vatican rule, has long been in progress. The Mafia is the handmaiden in this, just as it has been for any political-religious type of "Holy Crusade" ever since Emperor Constantine in 325 A.D. Vietnam is a current example of Fatima #2, as well as the seven South American countries that the CIA and the Vatican have announced they will overthrow, working together. The saving of Cardinal Lin and Heroin Chiang in Taiwan by the U.S. was the basis for the U.N. fight that the Mafia, having lost, will now use as an excuse for wiping out the U.N.

"Fatima #3 is the Mafia blow-off of the other half. The Pope, in a subtle refusal to announce his plan, has 'leaked' it, like the Mafia Pentagon 'leaks' things, in the form of 'nuclear holocaust'. And the 'soldiers of the church' around the world are spreading the idea, for prior justification. 'If you can't convert the heathens, kill them.' That is the final 'Holy Crusade.'

"But Brezhnev and Mao are not stupid; they can read. And the nuclear noose has been reversed. America now has a noose around itself. It's gonna be a Donnybrook. But at least it will be a fair fight. This is very distasteful to the Mafia. But those billions on the other half of the world don't particularly care to disintegrate at the holy whim of the Pope and the Mafia.

"Those sea-bed nuclear plantings, done years ago, are now like leftover World War II land mines. They will still work. They are still there. The Amchitka test, a mile deep on a geological fault, was to determine what effect a nuclear explosion might have on earthquakes. It proved to have only local effect. But 'local effect' can change a piece of land into a gulf. And these arrangements exist off San Francisco, Hyannisport, Skorpios and Dubai. Some son-of-a bitch has figured out a way to short-circuit the deal. And that is why one map lists some funny names: 'Gulf of Alioto' (right where we sit, by the way); 'Gulf of Hyannisport', 'Gulf of Skorpios' and 'Gulf of Dubai.'

Said he: "I can understand Hyannisport, Skorpios and Dubai; there's nothing there anyhow."

Me: "Nothing except Mafia."

He: "Yes, but why where we sit?"

Me: "As of November 1, there are 254,471 hard-core Mafia—Aliotos, Genoveses, Bonannos, etc., in San Francisco. That's out of 700,000 total population. That 250,000 are passively supported by another 350,000 who pay 41% taken out of each paycheck to the Mafia. And that's an 80% cancer. The other 100,000 pay under protest. But the cancer couldn't exist without the voluntary payment by the 41% Mafia siphon.

"The Mafia has been undisturbed for a century. For instance: your Mafia boss, Hoover, will

not furnish one single FBI man to work with the local strike force. And the strike force itself is run by Willie Wilson. He's one of Connally's Texas boys. That's Dallas-bullet Connally, from Hoover's ancient racetrack caper.

"There just isn't any doctor to cut this cancer out. Take me, for instance. I'm dead. I get this message occasionally. And I, like Brezhnev and Mao, am aware of the power and malignancy of this monstrous group. They murder and loot at whim, for personal gain, revenge or pleasure, with immunity. So I look to the future. Mine happens to be eternity.

"And I want the Number 2 job there, in charge of personnel placement. The man on the cross is a friend of mine. He wants off. Mary Jo is a friend of mine. She wants out of her grave for a nose patch job. No lady wants to go to her own funeral without her purse, or a properly straightened nose. What I must do is what every doctor takes an oath to do: kill cancer. Primarily because this group desires to kill me. That is self defense, and it is the primary law of the world. And I have arranged for such a thing to occur—whether I am dead or alive. In 80% cancer, the patient is dead anyhow. I know exactly how to cut that cancer out, leaving the patient mighty sick, but alive. But, the tools? Who's gonna give me a scalpel?

"Nixon? I elected him, and he said 'Screw you. I'm gonna murder you—and your family.'

"Nader? I set him up in business, and he said 'Screw you. Now I can be President.'

"Teddy? He said, 'I wanna be President.'

"No, cancer won't furnish the tools to kill itself with. So I use what I happen to have—a bloody fucking meat-ax."

He: "Shhh. There's a lady over there."

Me: "Excuse me. What I said was 'a bloody fucking meat-ax.' For instance: Just in case missiles won't get the job done, there's a new thing around. And now we're back at sea-bed devices, since one of them rests amongst a very funny mineral. And it—particularly it—is completely short-circuited."

He got up to leave.

Me: "You are an intelligent person. By now you should be curious. As one of Mafia Hoover's very own, you should be asking questions. And I'll answer."

He: "You've given me enough to think about. Don't get worried."

And I thought about that: "Don't get worried."

Let's see: My whole clan, and my friends, on a murder chart; and they know it, and shudder quite a bit. A missile-noose around America, debating whether to make a first strike to avoid Fatima #3, and bring those papers out afterwards to justify it—and still unaware of the new thing. Certain scheduled gulfs.

Two wounded, sick and worried snakes: Vatican-Mafia and Mafia-Mafia—just about frightened enough to pull Fatima #3 in the hope of blotting it all out, as Roosevelt, Onassis and Kennedy did in World War II. Mafia everywhere, from Nixon through Nader. (Mafia is what Mafia does), and the true name of the Mafia is MMORDIS (Moldering Mass Of Rotten Dribbling Infectious Shit). I've been rubbing it on Alioto's face, and Teddy's, and Nixon's, and Hoover's, and the Pope's, and a host of others.

But—like the man said, "Don't get worried."

There was more to that conversation: something about a proposed experiment involving 100 proven murderers, with attached crimes such as bribery, conspiracy, cover-up, and the blowing off of their heads with the biggest gun in the world. What bugged him most were the names of the first 100. I mentioned Presidents, Senators, Congressmen, Governors, Mayors, Supreme Court Justices, back room Mafia, and that was when he decided to leave. Just as I was beginning to list exact names

and crimes—from memory, from Hoover's files—his boss. I guess he didn't want to know.

Jim, the bartender, who had been listening to all this, asked me please, not to frighten any more good clean FBI customers out of his place. He said he liked the FBI. And I agreed.

Jim didn't bat his eyes or look away when you talk, or develop rattling hands, and I've grown weary of people who bat their eyes and rattle their hands. I also don't care for normal people who develop a stutter.

Do you stutter, Nader? Are you a traitor? Do you take bribes from the Mafia, such as Onassis Are you an accessory after the fact to Mary Jo's murder, and before the fact of every murder since you received notification of that one on August 13, 1970?

Where would you prefer to be mounted? To the right or left of Jesus Christ Teddy, who walks on water? How do you feel about assassinations? Any of IBM's? Or let's say IBM's assassination of you because you know of his other assassinations?

At any rate, I informed Pat Gonzales of the Alioto hit-run cover-up that elected Nixon and caused Chappaquiddick and the murder of Mary Jo, and the entire general bit.

And I went into the key: the rigged Mafia election process.

I pointed to 1970, for reference, such as the rigged Kennedy win in Massachusetts, since his Republican opponent was hand picked by Nixon, given no money, and told to keep his mouth shut and be a good stooge. That was Josiah Spaulding, who also happened to be a Kennedy friend and the best man at Jackie's wedding to Teddy's brother Jack. All the monstrous mob on Mary Jo's grave helped, and it was easy.

Spaulding himself was sick of the fraud and one night moaned, "I go to bed nightly, hoping someone will drop the bomb on this stink."

And I quoted the rigged election of Catholic Mandarin dope-pushing Thieu, which restored Vietnam to the same status as Diem did in 1963 when the Papal Mafia Holy Crusade first mounted into high gear.

The American Mafia loves to deal with Mafia dictators, be it in Vietnam, Taiwan, Greece, South America, the Dominican Republic—anywhere. They have never set up a democracy. Only a Mafia hierarchy, self-regulated and self-perpetuating—a la the complete constitutional de facto reversal of the Constitution which rules America with a tight-fisted Mafia glove.

Morgenthau said it in 1969: "The Mafia owns America. Why not admit it and let them have it? Pay them the 40% they siphon off the top and hope they don't murder too many of us. And leave them alone."

John Mitchell fired him for that statement. No kind of truth—no way—is allowed into print. If it leaks, they cover it up—a la Llellyveld's *N.Y. Times* cover-up of Loeb's *Manchester Union Leader's* partial publication of Teddy Kennedy's Chappaquiddick phone calls. Or Nixon's *Look*. Or Alioto's *San Francisco Chronicle*. Or Hearst's *San Francisco Examiner*.

And I quoted the rigged Alioto election here in San Francisco. There was no Republican effort at all—no candidate. One third of the votes were purchased by Alioto, and that won for him easily. All the other candidates pledged to "keepa da moutha shutta" about the Mafia or crime and play the good stooge. There was even one hopeless Republican, who, just in case, had Police Chief Cahill, Hoover's friend, at his elbow.

(Cahill sat on that auto insurance fraud cover-up on me in '67, and again on the Alioto hit-run cover-up on me in October '68. And in February, 1970, Alioto switched Police Chief Cahill to Security Guard at the local phone company, at the same salary. His job: To sit on the California end of the Tunney-Alioto Chappaquiddick phone call records.)

I then mentioned that Mary Pongalis wanted to meet Nader, and that Nader would be in town that weekend. I said I would bring him out there to meet her—and also to investigate the

entire Alioto hit-run affair, starting with that CIA office. And I would also bring some members of 14 separate "Mary Jo Kopechne Public Research Groups"—all unpublicized and quiet—like the CIA she worked for, because certain people want to know who they are. I said I would introduce them and we could have a barn-raising investigating party, and probably solve the whole cruddy mess right there in that office, and put the proper people on crosses.

She: "No one will be here any time after Thursday."

Me: "Well, we'll hunt you up or write notes on the sidewalks, or go through your files—whatever it is that private eyes and Nader's Crusaders and private people who resent Mary Jo's murder would do. And, by the way, secretaries who know the things I just told you frequently wind up murdered. In ponds and in other ways. Nader is scheduled for assassination because he knows these things. This weekend. Have a happy weekend, Pat Gonzales."

She: "Thank you. I'll be gone. Good-bye."

But these phone calls of mine provided you with protection from this, Nader. Four days later, on Friday morning, October 8th, the day of the start of the 3-day Consumer Coalition meeting that was to be the highlight of your consumer movement—and the formation of a third political party, with you at the head of a 40 million consumer voting block, 100, count 'em, 100 FBI men combed the town and picked up 34 miserable two-bit bookies who are in and out of the jug every week.

"Why?" asked local cops. "Never in the history of San Francisco has this happened. Hoover has left us strictly alone. Jeez. It's an invasion. What? It's crazy."

Not exactly. Hoover's FBI army was here to prevent any questioning of anyone connected with Neilson, or Green, Carlson, Pongalis, Gonzales—anybody. It was a huge harpoon in the shit bubble. At any rate, Mafia Hoover was clamping down the lid on any questioning of Neilson. And by publicity on it, giving a warning.

On October 5th this Mafia voice on the phone warned me not to talk to secretaries, or else. It also mentioned bringing a horde of police on my back, and it wound up warning me to heed the advice—or else. Are 100 FBI men "police," Nader?

On Friday, October 8th—the scheduled start of your most important convention, and a new political party, you phoned and canceled out:

"A sudden development in Washington," you said. And you said you would give your scheduled speech on Saturday night from a hidden, secret place in Washington—over the phone.

Martin Luther and Bobby were knocked off because their political power was becoming dangerous to the Mafia—Bobby, from revenge (The Enemy Within), Martin Luther from conviction. But you know that an assassination attempt, exposed in advance, never happens. Yours was exposed in advance. I did this. You were safe. You knew that. But you didn't wish to see me, or go with me to Neilson, or go into anything. The Mafia are always like this.

And Nixon and Hoover wouldn't want a real potential reform party to come into being, would they? So they preferred that you didn't come to San Francisco—for Mafia political reasons, true, but specifically in fear of the harpoon burst of the bubble.

You go along with these people, don't you, Nader? And with Teddy. And Ribicoff. You are truly one of the boys.

There is one good thing about Mary Jo's murder: she at least was spared the disillusionment of learning what it was—you—that she was running to from that cottage on Chappaquiddick, after knowing what it was—Mafia Teddy—that she was running from.

December 2, 1971: To This Group

My proposition: To bring this entire matter out into the open in a giant "Knapp Commission" in the United Nations, sponsored by moral human legal representation from all non-Mafia countries. Delineated by tape, film, personal appearance, and volumes of evidence. With deliberate withholding of certain evidential items, in order to stimulate 140 million partially decent American minds into individual investigative activity, with continual clues furnished to offer encouragement. Participation: the finest therapy.

I believe that an international race to clean up crud is preferable to an international race to blow us all to hell.

The Knapp Commission professed to be simply an open investigation. But it did uncover total New York police corruption—i.e., cops selling heroin, etc.—for the public to see. Since it was minor (compared to, say, World War III), the Mafia-censored press allowed parts of it to be exposed. Why not? The Legal Mafia will cover it up, and the Vatican Mafia will sanctify the cover-up. I propose to focus world non-Mafia Press and Legal exposure on the current United States Mafia Election Process, starting with the 1972 election campaign. It is readily visible, as all the concentrated geological strata of 2000 years of Mafia time are, exposed along the "cliffs" of Chappaquiddick.

In 1776, an oppressed little band of Americans fought a huge tyranny: religious Mafia tyranny and English political tyranny, the same one that caused the Reformation. They composed, in a matter of days, a beautiful Constitution—flawed by haste, but beautiful in intent. Two hundred years later it was gulped up by the Monster of Poucha Pond. And the Mafia group that swallowed it there is the same group that crucified Christ: Mafia political and Mafia religion.

Today the United States—and the world-wide Mafia—is the tyranny that is stomping on Vietnam, in a complete reversal. I wish to expose that cancer. I believe that exposure would lead to a world race to clean up the crud, so that we can all continue to live. It is not a matter of one nation viciously facing another in a "national interest" or a "Holy Crusade" holocaust, which today amounts to international suicide. It is a matter of survival for all of us.

Said a dissident CIA man to me recently: "It's too bad Jesus Christ didn't own a printing press. If he did, he might have beaten that crucifiction rap. And we wouldn't be sitting on the edge of a shit pit."

I believe that a U.N. "Knapp Commission" could be that printing press. Other means are working. And I don't care which way gets it done.

I'm dead. But I have completed arrangements to kill the cancer. Dead or alive.

Better alive. Dead, it's a bloody meat axe that can't tell cancer from non-cancer, or a Russian from an American, Chinese, or Samoan.

Our Mafia has decreed: "Death to any American who talks to any foreigner and says anything mean about us or about the U.S.A."

I will discuss suggested reforms with any human, any nationality, any place, any time. He must be a principal, positioned to be able to do something about it. He must be non-Mafia. The conversation must be completely open to all non-Mafia national principals.

A wise man has stated: "Anyone who knows a way out of War III has a duty to try to do just that. Anyone who blocks him is cancer."

The subject is vast. But answers are simple. Ask any scientist. Any experiment is complex. But when it is solved, all is simple. "Why didn't someone do this long ago?" There isn't one successful scientist who hasn't asked this question. Of himself. After he had made the complex simple.

I will walk out this door as if I've never been here. And go about my own business. About which you can probably surmise. I know something about time. It is priceless. And fleeting.

Your move.

Roberts

P.S. I can understand the need for confidentiality in preparing a legal case of this nature. There is no precedent. Film, tape, form of presentation, timing—all would have a bearing. It is a one-shot affair. If it were not handled properly, and presented with its utmost shock value—suddenly—Fatima #3 would be here. What have they got to lose? They would be dead anyhow. This is part of the philosophy which has sustained me.

So far I've stayed ahead of the game. I also have the feeling that at least a few of them—Mafia and CIA—are counting on me to do the right thing. Otherwise, I would never have been allowed to walk in this door.

I know that you have noted a conciliatory U.S. attitude since I submitted the April 23, 1970 "ultimatum" to Nixon, that led him to take a chance on invading Cambodia. Or more recently, to open trade attempts—stimulated sharply by the Neilsen conversations. There is not one single national or international event that has not been affected by my efforts to expose—and the Mafia attempts to cover-up—the Alioto hit-run cover-up on my car on September 16, 1968.

The recent U.S. Intelligence shake-up (i.e., sending the Pentagon's Gayler to Iceland, and CIA Cushman to the jungles) was done partially because of the abysmal under-estimation by them of the totally dedicated effectiveness of my "tricks". Basically because of honesty. Something this group does not understand.

When I first went to Nixon—then only a candidate—in October 1968, with papers, and evidence, I emphasized lie detector verification of every word. They have been running ever since. I call it the "run of the rabbits."

When I walk into a building and say "Chappaquiddick", everybody disappears. (Once when this occurred I proceeded to shuffle through their files, copying Mafia information. Nobody stopped me. Nobody came back. And I finally got tired, and left. I left a note saying "Thanks for the use of your files," and signed it—and I didn't even hear about that. All of the American leaders that I have approached have reacted this way.

And I assume that those from foreign lands are not entirely free from personal motives, relative to personal gain.

Such thoughts, and the same underestimation, would be a grave mistake, in this case.

My motives are clean. My methods are dirtier than theirs, of necessity. A paper and a mineral jammed up the Mafia ass around September 16, 1968 assure this.

So—understanding the need for secrecy in preparing such a case, and its timing, I would request total honesty and total openness between the legal representatives of all the non-Mafia nations participating in the presentation of this case.

Starting now.

As the man on the cross once said: "The truth—why not let it all hang out? What's wrong with it?" And as I told Nixon, fighting crime can be more profitable than committing it, for everybody. He disagreed, for his personal reasons. And he also burned his copy of the proof of that.

10 December 8, 1971: To Nader: From Cradle to Grave with the Mafia

Nader:

An English interviewer quotes Chou-en-Lai: "An inevitable trend is often manifested through accidental phenomena" (referring to China's United Nations victory). Ah, so, Nader. Do you think he knows something?

Add another quote: "To solve a problem you must first recognize it."

Do you recognize the Mafia-Vatican fucking that begins at birth? Forty-one percent of the national income goes to the Mafia for the rest of the way, and that includes fucking the war dead, and many more, as in the hospitals for the aged.

Then the real fucking of the dead commences. The coffin roaches of the Legal Mafia pluck the estates and destroy the dreams the dead ones had developed, however suppressed.

In the early years, it's legal Mafia indoctrination. In the middle years, it's legal Mafia war—and the legal Mafia writes the laws, while the Vatican sanctifies everything. And then: It's Chappaquiddick. The Legal-Vatican-Press Mafia clobber the grave of Mary Jo, fuck the dead, and drool on the coffin lid.

From the Princeton Study: "Hoover needs informers because his entire FBI staff are 'white Catholic boys'—and therefore they cannot penetrate most groups."

A quote: "If a town or a nation is Mafia, you can bet the top cop is too." In the 47 years described briefly herein, you can see the top cop's bosses in Mafia action. So, what about you, Nader?

Nixon's forthcoming hasty trips around the world, to visit government leaders, and Agnew's recent world trip, and the trips of most of the government figures, are attempts to find out who knows what about Chappaquiddick. This in turn leads to the Mafia election process—the key, exposed by the Alioto hit-run on September 16, 1968—and forward from there to the 1972 election swindle now shaping up. And backwards, through assassinations and wars. The reasons for the hasty trip to China, on his belly—and to Russia, on his belly—are partially to determine how much those people know, far enough in advance of the 1972 elections to:

Release part of it himself (and thereby get elected), if he believes it will be released elsewhere anyhow; and/or,

Decide whether to clamp the lid on tighter and bull through the election, winning—but still retaining the Mafia election system; and/or,

Cancel the 1972 elections (thereby being "re-elected;") and/or,

Flip Fatima #3—and carry out the prophesy, making himself permanent president of half a world—the half that remains.

The handmaiden? Oh, yes: Billy Graham, from Pope Pontius, to keep the souls turning the other cheek for the Mafia to masticate or fornicate, as they prefer.

Just as "Body Count" McNamara listed the reasons for the Vietnamese war as "90% kill 'em and profit, and 10% to help get re-elected."

JFK said in 1963: "Keep the troops in Vietnam until I am re-elected" (his quote to O'Donnell).

In 1940, Roosevelt said: "Joseph P., we've bled them pretty good. So now let's get me re-elected and I'll drag us into the war, and we can blot out that Onassis shit, and all the other shit. We can proceed right on down the line; and your Mafia sons can be presidents forever. Do you realize

that this war—World War II—is Fatima #1, and that would set up Fatima #2 and #3 for the Pope?"

The result of all this is the perpetuation of tyranny. A foreign policy of divide and conquer, or purchase and deal. For the handmaiden: conversion to the Pope. That's the carrot. The stick is Fatima #3.

Look around. From Ireland to Vietnam, Argentina to Taiwan. It is a desperate situation. Exposure threatens on all sides. This is why yesterday, the Press Mafia in the form of McGraw-Hill and Life announced that they will publish an "authentic autobiography of Howard Hughes"—dictated by "himself"—to "balance the lies and rubbish which I know will be published about me."

Poor Howie! Hyped and caged since 1957, dead and buried on April 16th, 1971, he is as visible a symptom of this mess as is Chappaquiddick. Onassis's "Hughes" is an exposed segment of the Mafia ownership of all branches of government; its purchase thereof, and its looting therefrom—from defense contracts (Bechtel, Hughes Satellites, Lockheed) to Nevada and Caribbean gambling, and general murder whenever necessary to keep the secret.

And poor Ralphie! That's you. From "Ted, Simon, Ted" to "Chappaquiddick Dickie" and "Onassis and IBM", you too are exposed—right in the middle.

Happy Chappaquiddick, Ralphie.

Roberts

11 February 10, 1972: To Nader: My Father's Illness

Nader:

I write this from the hallway outside the intensive care ward of Hahnemann's Hospital. In a room over there is my father. "Critical," says the doctor. Transfusions and all that stuff. On September 16, 1968, when Alioto clobbered my car, he was healthy. That was three and a half years ago. Then, he was campaigning for Nixon and working with local Republicans. The Democrats were crooks, and the Republicans were for law and order, said he. Today, he has a bleeding ulcer. He never drank booze in his life, and he once played professional football. Ulcer source? Nerves. Since 1968, he and my mother have waited daily for a Yablonski-style shotgun blast. And for people to show up to take their depositions about the most monstrous Mafia conspiracy in history.

His Republican "friends" have all disappeared. And a year and a half ago, you were scheduled to appear at his house to take depositions and examine copies of evidence I left with him, for that purpose. Friends, foreigners, mother and father read them. But you didn't show.

A year ago Fellmeth, in St. Louis, said he had just talked to you, and that some of your sleuths would be there soon. But—still no show.

One day my father said, "Nader isn't coming, is he?"

I told him, "No. They bought him off. Nixon, Onassis, Kennedy, Billy Graham and the Pope."

After the October collapse of your Consumers' Party, when you didn't show, and the Mafia wound up on the Board of Directors, my father began to hit the hospital road regularly. Ulcers on his feet. Nervous stomach. Heart problems. At night he'd wake up at any noise, wake my mother and tell her, "Here come the shotguns. Go do something."

He was helpless, you see, Nader. He hasn't been out of bed for months. Living for one thing: to get the truth out. He believed your propaganda: that you were the last remaining hope for a clean country. He doesn't believe it any more.

A quote from James Reston: "The difference between a Mafia dictatorship and a democracy is that the Mafia dictatorship suppresses the truth and a democracy searches for the truth." How come you run the other way, Nader?

I have placed a heavy price on murder. From Mary Jo's to my own family. Accessories, before and after the fact: Gene Cesar, who clobbered Bobby in L.A.; and Iron Bob Maheu, who directed the series of murders for Onassis-"Hughes", from Dallas through Memphis and L.A., and purchased President Nixon, Humphrey, O'Brien, all the Kennedys, and you. It is covered under a separate document (currently out in several languages), labeled "The Murder of the Family of the Man Who Elected Nixon, by President Nixon." Would you like a copy?

Checking out Barbara Phillips of Ms Magazine

Daniel Ellsberg wrote a centerpiece for the new magazine, Ms, sponsored by Elizabeth Harris, Gloria Steinem and Barbara Phillips, an attorney (part of a new political party of women formed here in San Francisco to collect women's votes to clean up this country).

Said Ellsberg: "This group of women is the last remaining hope to kill the cancer that's killing this country." They featured his article in their charter edition. I read it. And then Barbara Phillips appeared on TV, as you did a year and a half ago, pleading for money to help their glorious cause. So I called her, on February 4.

I said, "Barbara, I saw Nader on TV a year and a half ago, in an interview where he pleaded for money. And I arranged for a big chunk of money for him, which he received four days later. And

I saw you on TV the other day asking for money. Your aims sound even better than Nader's. I can arrange for some money for you, too."

She: "You sound like some kind of an angel."

Me: "Not exactly, but I do get the job done."

She: "When did you get interested in the consumer movement?"

Me: "On September 16, 1968—two months before the last presidential election, when I presented a legal matter to the legal firm of Nixon and Mitchell."

She: "Now I really am interested. Come and see me on Tuesday at 11:00 a.m., at 1204 International Building."

I was there at 11:00, and—shades of Derrough at CBS!—she had been briefed, and I was out at 11:10.

I had rather expected that, since I had been informed that she was a friend of Nicholas Katzenbach, Johnson's Attorney General, and had an office in the firm of Patrick, Buchanan and Phillips, specialists in international law: oil, minerals, banking, corporations—the whole multinational bit which the CIA supports. And besides, the offices adjoining hers were those of Indonesian Oil.

Her previous client was ushered out from behind a closed office door. I was ushered in and the door was left open. But at least she wasn't as crude as Mafia Derrough at CBS, who conducted his interview in the receptionist's lobby with a hood reading my papers over my shoulder. But the subject was the same. She was cold, non-communicative, negative. Her manner was Papal, rather than hard core Maf.

I handed her the first Nader letter, and the preface.

She read it and stated, "I don't see how this concerns me."

Me: "You asked for money on TV. You can have any amount you want. Nader got only a small chunk. You state that you wish to be a political power.

"As I told Nader, one of your group can be the President. Members of your group can be Senators and Congress people. Your magazine can have a Pulitzer Prize. The evidence is here for you to clean up the Mafia cancer as your central theme. Last October, Nader's Consumers' Alliance's try for a third party folded before it started—ruined by Nader's cancellation, because of me. I can put yours together, with money and reform, or watch it fold."

She: "I will take that up with the group. I have your phone number. I will call you. Good-bye."

Me (a few quick shots): "Gene Cesar, a security guard from Onassis's General Motors, murdered Bobby Kennedy. Three shots in the back of the head, from a small palm gun. JFK got his from the overpass in front—one shot that blew off the back of his head. Maheu ran the assassinations of JFK, Martin Luther King and Bobbie. That's IBM—Iron Bob Maheu—who was first hired by the CIA to assassinate Castro. He now wants $50 million from Onassis for his deeds.

"Hughes died on April 16, 1971. He was hyped by Onassis in 1957 in conjunction with Apalachin, where the 1960 Mafia outright purchase of the United States was arranged."

"Onassis's-'Hughes' empire is the Mafia money funnel which washes money and purchases presidents such as Nixon, Kennedy, Johnson, and their opponents too, such as Humphrey. Peking has a phrase: 'Chappaquiddick Big Dickie and Chappaquiddick Little Dickie'—meaning Richard Nixon and Richard Carlson. Big Dickie is crawling to Peking this week because of this. I asked Nixon to sell my gemstones for me just after I told him what happened at Chappaquiddick—three weeks after it happened. His hatchet man, Mack, just held them for a year. But two weeks after I left them with him, I sold other gemstones all around the world, along with the history that went with

them.

"Chiang Ching has one of my stones, together with the history that goes with it, and she tells Mao what to do.

"I didn't accept money. I purchased information. That is how I purchased the Onassis diary. What is censored here is not censored there.

"Twenty-seven of the countries which purchased my stones, and the history that goes with them, voted against the United States in the United Nations, ousted dope-pushing Taiwan from the United Nations, and invited China in.

"Dickie's boy Reagan now says, "We will fight World War III to defend Taiwan," while Teddy's boy, Tommy 'The Cork' Corcoran, washes the loot, through the Miami National Bank. America is going down the drain. Don't these things interest you?"

She, coldly: "No. They are out of my field."

Me: "I have a copy of a second Nader letter with me, which is currently on its way around the world picking up endorsements by various world leaders. The people who read it are the leaders of the civilized non-Mafia world. They are intensely interested. It either has been or will be delivered to Nader, with the endorsements. It is worth all of the money and political power that exists. Here it is. Would you like to read it?"

She, coldly: "No."

Me: "You can have all the money you want, elect one of your women to the presidency, and clean up the cancer, as you and your group and your magazine specify to be your purpose. Pulitzer Prizes, fringe benefits. I offer it to you. Free. Now. Do you want it?"

She, coldly: "No. Good-bye."

Me: "Good-bye."

***

On the way out I paused in front of the Indonesian Oil offices. I remembered that on this day Rogers had said we might have to dump Thieu in South Vietnam, and the communists might take it all back again, as they did in 1954 at Dien Bien Phu. And that would cancel all the fat Nixon, Rockefeller, Getty, Onassis, Connally, Johnson, etc., Indonesian oil leases, and the CIA Air America geological raids into Yunnan Province, and the CIA-Onassis heroin flown in from the Taiwan-run "Golden Triangle." And it would knock the Vatican loose from part of its Fatima #2 booty (Vietnam and Taiwan, and possibly the Philippines and India). Almost like a "domino theory," right, Nader? Only this time, collapsing around the Vatican-Mafia handmaidens with their bloody hands in the till. I guess it had to happen sooner or later, Nader. A man can get mighty tired of hanging on a cross for 2000 years.

At any rate, the name of the game is to dissipate and destroy. Right? Corner the voting blocks and steer them to women's liberation, or stir them up over bum deodorants. Don't you agree? You and Barbara Phillips. Clean, sweet, treasonous, murderous cancer.

A quote, in today's L.A.Times. D. J. R. Bruckner: "What we are seeing now is panic at the very top of our government."

Oh yes, Nader. The legal Mafia, which you and Barbara espouse—in total cancerous treason—is shuddering a bit. The Vatican-Billy Graham-Mafia cringes. And those Mafia who own the press and TV. One of them is Onassis , whose "Hughes's" TV station has been airlifted to Peking to beam back Dickie's image by way of a "Hughes" Intelsat satellite over an Onassis-controlled Comsat satellite system. Meanwhile a bill is waiting quietly in Congress, to be attached to the first convenient "urgent" major bill, which will grant "Hughes" the world rights to launch a private world-wide satellite system. But those Media Mafia are feeling stomach pangs.

A quote from the Los Angeles Times, TRB's column on press censorship: "We aren't even allowed to ask Nixon why he pardoned Jimmy Hoffa."

The reason, Nader, is because Hoffa "loaned" Loeb, of the Manchester Union Leader, $2,000,000. Loeb is the one to whom telephone credit card records of Teddy's phone calls to and from the cottage at Chappaquiddick were given. He published part of them. And all were copied, and are out. (Would you like to see them? Brezhnev has copies).

But Loeb was asked by Dickie to bury those records. And in return, Loeb asked Dickie to get his "friend," Hoffa, out of prison. And the deal was made. Reporter Arthur Egan, to whom the records originally came (from a phone company employee), was assigned to go to work on Hoffa's freedom. Eventually, everybody, from Mitchell through Texas Willie Wilson, Justice Criminal Chief, recently dumped because of his Texas Mafia dealings, got into the act, and Hoffa is now free to murder more.

I'm going back into that room down the hall and check on just how well the CIA-Mafia-Nixon "slow murder" is working on my father. And get my mother home, because she stumbles a little—she's 83—so that she can sit there all alone and wait for the Yablonski shotgun bit.

It's a sweet life, Nader, when you think that—as I told Nixon, pre-election, 1968—he could clean it all up right then. I told you, a year and a half ago, the same thing; but instead, you have both earned places on crosses. As Chappaquiddick Dickie says, "Presidents must earn their places in history." So be it.

He's still alive, Nader. Full of tubes and needles. All he can really do is blink his eyes. But he did whisper something. Said he: "Kill 'em."

That's a paternal order, Nader. Should I listen to him? Or to you, and Chappaquiddick Dickie, Teddy, Onassis and the Pope, who persuaded the Kopechnes to say, "We don't care if Mary Jo was murdered. We are satisfied."

Mary Jo isn't.

Said Thieu yesterday, reacting to Dickie's panicked threat to remove him from office: "Dickie can't withdraw any American troops until I tell him it's all right. He couldn't even make the China trip if I hadn't okayed it."

Thieu, you see, is calling up his blackmail reserve. He knows of the Onassis-Joseph P. Kennedy English booze and heroin smuggling bit in 1932, under the sponsorship of President Franklin D. Roosevelt here, and Winston Churchill in England. Would you like to see the Onassis diary, Nader? And the documents that go with it? And the external corroboration, such as the recently released (after a twenty-five-year secrecy clause expired) Churchill papers, in which Churchill stated bluntly: "Roosevelt and Joseph P. Kennedy rigged World War II:. They could have stopped it, but they didn't. They promoted it."

He makes no mention of the third partner to the deal: Onassis, who moved into the White House and #10 Downing Street in 1932; who served all the warring parties: Stalin, Hitler and us—and who never lost a ship, or a deal.

The first key, the Alioto hit-and-run cover-up that elected Nixon in 1968, exposed the Mafia election process, and the lid went on. But lids create internal pressure. And that hit-and-run caused the second key: Chappaquiddick, which once more exposed the Mafia election process. Both events brought total exposure and led back to the Onassis-Kennedy heroin deal. And right on up through World War II, Korea, Vietnam, the assassinations, the Vatican "Deputy of Christ at Auschwitz" Holy Crusade, and the Kennedy-Spellman direct quote that Vietnam was a "Holy Crusade".

But the third key is the most exposed and vulnerable of all: Hopped-up Howard Hughes, Deceased: April 16, 1971. Most vulnerable because it's current. There is no "75-year secrecy" lid on it. The "Hughes" world-wide empire operation, to be viable, must continue—and "all who run can read."

12 A Chronology

To recap:

1932: The original "blackmail" Kennedy booze, Onassis heroin deal, direct to Boston under the auspices of the two "leaders of the civilized world", Roosevelt and Churchill.

1939: World War II—courtesy of the same group. And Fatima #1 became a reality. Rigged, but none-the-less a fact.

Post war: Fatima #2 plunged ahead: "Convert the world." Dulles and the CIA went into action, all over the world.

The handmaidens of history, Vatican and Mafia, joined in the looting: one for the bodies, and one for the souls. It was a profitable joint venture. "We must destroy communism" was the creed, from J. Mafia Hoover and his "Catholic Boys," as Mike Novacs labels them. Korea. Wars, with Mafia financing, all over the world. Onassis lived with every king, and every dictator, from Franco to Batista.

1957: Apalachin. Called by Onassis to announce the "hyping" of Hughes, by his employee Cesare Davis, who changed his name to Chester in New Jersey after he arrived from Italy. Mafia leaders from the various states, including my Lombard and Franklin Street friend, Lanza, Alioto's godfather, were to spread out and scientifically purchase all elections, local, state and federal.

Hughes, alive and on his own, had already purchased Dickie Nixon to do a tax-exemption favor to the Hughes Medical Research Foundation, which now serves as a tax-free fountain-head for all Onassis-"Hughes" ventures. When notified, by Noah Dietrich, that accepting that Hughes loot was treason, Vice President Nixon said, "Fuck 'em. My family comes first."

"Fuck America" became the national motto that day, courtesy of Dickie Nixon. Today, my father is across the hall being murdered, courtesy of Dickie Nixon. Mary Jo is dead, courtesy of Dickie Nixon. Teddy only assisted. And in that year—1957—Joseph P. Kennedy, Winston Churchill, John F. Kennedy and Jackie Kennedy hashed it all out on Onassis' yacht, the Christina, off Monaco.

1958: The Onassis plan announced at Apalachin worked. There was an amazing "grass roots" Democratic Mafia-financed sweep of Congress.

1960: It worked again, as in vote stealing and all, in Daley's Illinois and Johnson's Texas. Dickie knew, and cried. He too had been purchased by Onassis, as a hedge: for another half a million bucks of hot Mafia Vegas loot. Onassis already owned Kennedy and shared the ownership with an ally: the Papal envoy, Cardinal Spellman. The Mafia wants the world, and so does the Pope.

(Today, the legal Mafia has rewritten our Constitution. Crime has become legal. Election to public office carries with it a license to steal and murder. And, as in all dictatorships—Onassis's Greece for instance, or Cardinal Lin's Taiwan, or Papa Thieu's Vietnam—that election is Mafia-rigged. The Pope wrote a new constitution declaring himself to be God. But some dirty bastard passed out pictures of Mary Jo Kopechne to the Synod in Rome, and the hierarchy actually voted against the Pope on that new constitution. My, my. What a rotten dirty trick.)

On a golf course, Joseph P. Kennedy said to V.P. Johnson, "My sons, President John F. Kennedy and Attorney General Bobby Kennedy, are too young to really be effective. You and I will really run things." And he glanced at the club house and waved. In the club house, Onassis was watching this, and waiting for the wave, to be sure that Joseph P. Kennedy had delivered his message.

And Johnson hurried to Vietnam to deliver the "Holy Crusade" message from Cardinal Spellman and President Kennedy to Catholic Mandarin Diem and his brother Nhu, the police chief who ran the opium trade out of the Golden Triangle for Onassis; and to the third brother, Archbishop Thuc, Roman Catholic prelate of Vietnam. The Vietnam "Holy Crusade"—a part of Fatima #2—was on. The Onassis-owned CIA hired Maheu to assassinate Castro and promoted the Bay of Pigs in an attempt to regain Cuba for the Batista-type gambling—including the recovery of $8 billion stolen from McLaney by Castro when he took over the island. (McLaney ran the Cuban casinos for Lansky. McLaney set up a Florida camp and trained Maheu's original Castro assassination crew.)

1963: Bobby intended to go after Hoffa, in his planned revisions to the second edition *of The Enemy Within*. Of course, his planned revisions got scotched after he was murdered. [These revisions included what he knew about his brother's Mafia murder.] Hoffa was in charge of Onassis's Labor-Hood Mafia, and a whole bunch of rigged votes. Bobby indicted Wally Bird in Vietnam. (Bird was the opium dealer for Onassis). JFK ordered the Taiwanese dope smugglers out of Laos, and then, in mid-year, decided to dump Diem, to appease the American public. (Fatima #2 and the heroin trade was becoming too apparent). These things violated Onassis' orders, and Joseph P. couldn't intervene; he was speechless with a stroke. Onassis ordered a triple murder: brothers Diem, Nhu and Kennedy. As with Thieu's blackmail today of Nixon, Diem would have talked, and so would JFK.

November 1, 1963: Onassis' man Captain Nung blasted Diem and Nhu at the railroad track, as planned. But Maheu's assassination crew missed in Chicago because JFK had canceled his planned trip to Chicago to throw out the first ball at a baseball game. The assassination had been planned to take place in public, with a large proportion of the public watching on TV.[34] (A witness saw the murder crew in Chicago, and then noticed that they reappeared in Dallas on November 22. He told the Chicago CIA about what he had seen. He was murdered. But he had already told Black Panthers Hampton and Clark.

Hampton and Clark were murdered by Daley's Hanrahan in Chicago four months after Chappaquiddick reopened the "75-year-secrecy" lid on Dallas, Memphis and L.A.)

Maheu was successful in Dallas. And JFK knew it was coming.

In mid-October, when he learned of Onassis's plans to kill him, he knew. He had a tantrum and called Jackie on Onassis' yacht, screaming, "Get off that yacht, Jackie, if you have to swim." She didn't, and a week later Onassis walked down the gangplank with Jackie on his arm, to impress the Turk, Mustapha Bey, who for self preservation had kept a diary on Onassis, dating back to Onassis' activities as a boy of 14 in Smyrna.

According to Mustapha Bey's diary, Onassis was a seasoned murderer and dope pusher at the age of 14. It is because of this Turk's diary, and the gemstones with which I purchased it, that the world took a flip. The Alioto hit-and-run on my car in San Francisco led ultimately to Mary Jo's murder at Chappaquiddick, and that in turn purchased the diary. And that exposed the Onassis-"Hughes" Empire Mafia money funnel—a tax-free money washing affair, which purchased all public officials and assassinations, and many other things, such as Elizabeth Jean Peters.

When Onassis had Howard Hughes overpowered and kidnapped, injured, from his secluded private bungalow at the Beverly Hills Hotel, in 1957, the lecherous Howard Hughes needed an

---

[34] Onassis loved to perform his important political assassinations in public. It was "show business." The fact that he could have an important public figure like JFK brutally slain IN PUBLIC, with perhaps millions of people in the TV audience, and then proceed to silence all the witnesses by death or by fear, was a potent display of his power.—sc

image to "disappear with"—a beautiful famous girl.[35] So Onassis purchased Jean Peters. (She had dropped the "Elizabeth.") There were two phony signatures on a marriage license in Tonopah, Nevada, in 1957.[36] There were two phony signatures on a divorce agreement in Tonopah, in May, 1971—a month after Hughes' death on April 16, 1971. Settlement? A flat $2 million for Jean Peters, plus a permanent CIA army around her, to "protect" her—her mouth, that is. From blabbing.)

Bob Maheu's old Castro assassination crew worked again at Dallas. Among them was Johnny Roselli. Roselli was later "given" Lana Turner as part of his reward for his good shooting at Dallas. Later still, he was placed in "cold storage" for Mafia manipulation of the ownership of the Las Vegas Flamingo casino.

Lana's next hubby after Roselli was Eaton—copies of whose book were recently allowed to "leak" through Rosemont's screen for one reason alone: namely, to establish the fact that somewhere in Hughes' thinking was the idea that immediately upon death he would be hermetically sealed—forever—in a cryogenic vault, for purposes of later being brought back to life. This would prevent anyone from examining that body, and Onassis could continue to run the "Hughes" empire with impunity.

Maheu was then rewarded for his efforts. He was "hired" by John Meier at half a million dollars a year—"for life"—to run Onassis's "Hughes" Vegas casino empire. John Meier then "quit" "Hughes," and became Onassis's visible right arm. Today John Meier rides herd on Jackie. John Meier, the younger, went to work for Maheu, participated in the aborted "salting of the mines," was fired, and now is running for Senator from New Mexico. He will be elected; all Maf are.

Greg Bautzer, a New York Attorney, has two clients: "Hughes" and Kerkorian. Onassis owns Kerkorian, and IS "Hughes."

Maheu was called on again to direct the murders of Martin Luther King—a would-be reformer of the Mafia election process—and Bobby Kennedy, whom he hated with a passion. Bobby left notes about this, which Mary Jo Kopechne read in L.A. after his murder. Her next step was to work for Mayor Whelan, the Jersey City Democratic Maf, where she gathered more of the Vatican-Mafia-Kennedy background, and by the time she went to the Chappaquiddick party she was seething with rage about the Democratic Mafs she had been idealistically working for. She was on her way to see you, Nader, when Teddy murdered her.

1968: The Alioto hit-and-run on my car.

[Onassis believed in evenhanded bribing of all candidates. So Onassis's Maheu purchased all the presidential candidates with Lansky skim money from the Las Vegas joints: a half million to Dickie, and another half million to Humphrey. Whoever won, Onassis "owned" him from the beginning. And the loser had a substantial bandage over his wounds.]

Also, "Democrat" Larry O'Brien arranged for other Mafia politicians/candidates to be placed in ery congressional, state and local election. It was a well-organized affair stemming from Apalachin. In "Weird October," 1968, the entire mass landed on my back, from the Pope to Onassis, and from Kennedy to Alioto, Dickie and Mitchell.

Onassis arranged a contract through his partner, Cardinal Cushing ("Welcome, Ari, and don't forget your checkbook!") with Jackie Kennedy, and a marriage made in hell was consummated.

The total lid went on. Then there was Chappaquiddick; my purchase of the Turkish diary on

---

[35] Hughes was already famous for his hunger for famous movie stars, and unknown starlets.
[36] To add to the confusion, Charles Higham has this account of Hughes's "marriage: "Hughes chose as the site of his wedding on January 12, 1957, a town in Nevada, Tonopah...One of the advantages of marrying there was that they could wed under assumed names (G. A. Johnson and Marian Evans)...p.185-6 (see bibliography.)

Onassis; and the whole thing blew wide open again, including the Onassis-"Hughes" Mafia money funnel. Panic.

August 1969: My full memo, and gemstones, regarding Hughes, Chappaquiddick and Alioto were given to Nixon's hatchet-men, Greenagel and Mack. Nixon refused to sell my stones, but two weeks later, other gemstones started their way around the world, with the history that goes with them.

1970: I gave an oral, four-hour detailing of the complete affair in Mack's penthouse, on top of a bank that holds part of the Lockheed Loan and a batch of Alioto's tax-free, interest-free loot.[37] It was all being taped. Suddenly he's called out of the room. He returns, shuts the door, and gets right to it. Says he: "Tell me all you know about Howard Hughes." So I did, including "IBM's" [Maheu's] assassinations.

---

[37] The "oral detailing" of the story sounds very much like my own first encounter with Bruce Roberts, which took place in August, 1974, in the hallway of his San Francisco apartment residence. It was delivered *ex tempore*, in response to my question about what had happened during the two years that had passed since August, 1972, when Mae Brussell had received her Xerox copies of a portion of Roberts' papers, and lasted about two hours. It was quite detailed, and shocking to me. Bruce Roberts was always ready to launch into such an account, and did so in bars, hallways, offices, on request, or whenever he felt like it, even when no one was requesting it, or even when people were begging or ordering him to please shut up and stop scaring people. These were oral "gemstone papers."

13 Clifford Irving's "Hughes Autobiography" Hoax

November, 1970: Merryman, Hughes' sixth "Mormon Mafia nursemaid", sick of it all, contacted Clifford Irving, who had been nosing around Vegas and Noah Dietrich looking for "Hughes" background. Irving had lived in the Mediterranean area, on Ibizza, for years. He was writing a book about an art forger named De Hory, to be called Hoax. Gossip about the Onassis-Hughes thing had been floating around the Mediterranean for years. One day De Hory told him, "You want to know about a real hoax? Try Howard Hughes and Onassis—it's the biggest hoax going."

Irving went to Vegas. When Merryman heard about his interest, he gave him some of the secret "Hughes" memos relating to the Mafia purchase of such things as President Nixon, Humphrey, and Larry O'Brien, with the understanding that Irving wouldn't release them until Hughes, who was failing from his continuous heroin dosing in Onassis's prison/hospital on Skorpios—died. And that was expected soon.

Based on the information he got from Merryman, Irving went to McGraw-Hill and got a big book contract [$750,000 advance] for an "autobiography of Howard Hughes."

Onassis panicked when he heard about it. The "Hughes" kidnap and takeover was crucial in the life he had forged for himself. He knew Irving had gotten his hands on secret information, but he didn't know the source. He suspected Maheu, but couldn't kill him, because Maheu had papers on the major political assassinations that led right back to Onassis; these were Maheu's "protection."

Thanksgiving, 1970: So Onassis set up a phony "kidnap" of "Hughes" from Vegas. (Hughes had actually been on Skorpios, imprisoned in his little cell, for years—since his kidnap in 1957.) Onassis fired Maheu, and put Chester Davis in charge of managing the "Hughes" double who had been doing "Hughes" in the U.S. ever since the 1957 kidnapping. Intertel took over management of the "Hughes" casino empire, in Las Vegas, for Onassis.

Onassis fled from Vegas in the form of a "Hughes" disappearance (but he bounced back again, through Intertel and Chester Davis.) Maheu was now a liability. But Maheu still wanted his pay: $50 million from Onassis for those big assassinations. So he sued his former employer, "Howard Hughes," for it.

Three days after the "Hughes kidnapping" in Vegas, Kitty Lowry (Hughes's aunt—about 85 years old, and spry, with one tooth in the middle of her jaw) came to see me. I had only seen her once before. She had looked me up for a chat after Chappaquiddick.

Said she: "I just saw Howard in England."

Said I: "He's been in Greece for years. How's his heroin habit?"

Total fury.

Said Cliff Jones, watching this: "What did you say that set her off?"

Me: "I don't know. She was telling me about the special artificial volcanic glass on the runways of Hughes's new airport in Vegas, and then we got onto the subject of his whereabouts and health, and I commented on that; and there she was, an erupting volcano. Her last words to me were: 'I hate you. You'll get yours.'"

Onassis discovered his mistake shortly after the "Hughes" Vegas disappearance. He learned that it was Merryman, not Maheu, who had released the memos which strike at the key: the Mafia election process and the "Hughes" Mafia money funnel. So, around Christmas, Merryman disappeared, and was never mentioned again in any of the Mafia press releases.

From then on, the press mentioned five—five only—Hughes Mormon "nursemaids", instead of the original six.

December 1970: Merryman disappeared—murdered, probably, in December, 1970 or January 1971.

Two weeks later, Noel Gayler—head of Intelligence for the Defense Department—showed up for a chat. Senator Proxmire's niece [Jo Fulton] interrupted that chat (related earlier), and Gayler had his moment of fury when I mentioned the subject of "smuggling" papers and gemstones out of this country.

January, 1971: at the same locale: A UPI reporter (CIA) quizzed me on Bobbie's murder and a "cultural exchange" between myself and foreign "students" (based on "what's censored here isn't censored there," and vice versa). I told him I'd bring him a Pulitzer Prize on the following night: the biggest story in history. He snarled: "Nothing gets out of here." And he hasn't been back since.

April 15, 1971. Hughes died and was buried at sea, off Skorpios.

Clifford Irving felt he had hit the jackpot, but he kept his word to Merryman (who was already dead.) He showed McGraw-Hill the "Hughes" manuscript for the first time, on the day after Hughes was buried: April 16, 1971).

Meeting Merrymans at the Mark Bar

Late June, 1971: It was six months later, almost to the day, that Marie Elena told me that her sister-in-law, Louise Merryman, sitting across the table from us, was on her first night out since her husband's death. And the accepted six-month mourning period takes us back to a Christmas demise, 1970, for Merryman.

The "Bobby" murder had just been solved. The Pentagon Papers were out, including segments that corroborated the double Diem-Kennedy murders. Jean Peters had her divorce from Howard Hughes's corpse; and Lockheed, one of Onassis-"Hughes'" money-funneled purchases, was just being granted that enormous loan from the U.S. government. Maheu was suing "Hughes" (Onassis) for $50 million, for the assassinations. Ted Charach[38] had reopened the Bobby murder story in L.A., with his film fingering Thane Cesar, Bobby K's real killer. Frank Stanton had brought out "The Selling of the Pentagon." And Hughes's heirs, the Lowrys, had been seen talking to me at intervals since Chappaquiddick.

So, in late June, Marie Elena Merryman tapped me on the shoulder in the lobby of the Mark, and said, "Please." Though I didn't know it then, she was asking me for help. Remember, it was her sister-in-law's husband who had been dumped for committing a breach of Omerta.

These women are beautiful, and can have any man. I was unkempt and angry. She asked me to come and sit with them. I said no. She said "Please."

She knew me. And within five minutes I knew these two. Marie Elena made sure that I did.

Marie Elena's husband was a Bechtel executive. Bechtel[39] is the number one Defense Contractor in Construction. It used to be Bechtel, McCone, and Parsons. McCone was CIA chief in

---

[38] I met Charach at a *Playgirl* party in Los Angeles, after he had done the film on RFK's murder. I had recently moved from L.A. to S.F., and had just written the "Onassis is 'Hughes'" article.-sc

[39] Bechtel Corp. is still a major player in "Defense," "Construction" and international skullduggery swindles today. Recently, it robbed Boston of $7 billion in cost overruns for the infamous "Big Dig" highway and tunnel construction. It's also busy with no-bid contracts demolishing Iraq. In a third grandstand play for the title of "Criminal U.S. Corporation of the Year," it bought ALL THE WATER RIGHTS IN BOLIVIA from a corrupt government and set about trying to collect for every drop (this included ALL RAINWATER FALLING FROM THE SKY) from the impoverished, disempowered residents. However, they objected seriously to this proposal for mass murder and so far have managed to THROW THE BUMS OUT. Would that we could do the same in our own country. Most recently, [July 2006] Bechtel is making headlines with the collapse of several tons of cement from a ceiling panel in a Boston "Big Dig" tunnel, which landed on a car and squashed a Jamaica Plain resident to death.

charge at the time of the Diem-Kennedy murders. Helms, now in charge at the CIA, was his assistant. For a few minutes we spoke of this. Marie Elena informed me that this was Louise's first night out after her mourning period over her husband's death.

As the four of us—the two women, myself, and a stranger I grabbed from the bar for Louise—sat there, an apparent drunk descended on us and directed questions to Marie Elena and me.

He asked, "Are you two married?" and "Who are you?"

At the time we all dismissed it as an alcoholic aberration. As I think back, however, I recall that he resembled the one who was reading my papers over Dick Carlson's shoulder, about the Alioto hit-and-run details, in my car, at a drive-in, in early October, 1968—one month before that event elected Chappaquiddick Dickie to the presidency.

The drunk at the Mark Bar kept zeroing in on Marie Elena and me, backed up tight against the wall where he had to tightrope to get to us. It was indeed odd, considering the decorum of the place.

"Unheard of," was Louise's comment. "Here?"

"Unbelievable," said the stranger.

But—if indeed he was the same one who was peeking so obviously over Dick Carlson's shoulder in early October, 1968, then the desperation was the same: to find out about a critical situation. And the source would be Alioto. (Since, in early October, 1968, he was the chief one concerned, and Dick and I agreed that even Humphrey didn't know about the hit-and-run cover-up at that time. And that means Onassis. And if Onassis was desperate to know what I was doing with the Merryman women, that means they were playing some opposing game—not his; probably their own—all alone).

I had called Carlson back that same day in early October, 1968, and given him the description of the man who was shuffling back and forth from the back of the car to the window where he could be seen. I checked back in my written records and my memory, and the Drive-in 64 "shuffle" was the same as the Mark Bar "tightrope." Everything else was identical. At the drive-in, in the sunlight, he wore dark glasses and had papers sticking out from his coat pockets. At the Mark Bar, he had no glasses and no papers, but everything else was the same.

Suddenly everybody left except Marie Elena, Louise and me. She said, "My husband is at the Bohemian Grove. Come with us up to my place."

Walking across the park from the Mark to her place, she said, and it surprised me: "You are the only good man left."

And on the way up to the Merryman apartment that night—Apartment 10A—I was watching Marie Elena. She had already told me of her husband's executive position with Bechtel and the relationship to CIA McCone. So I said "Merryman publishes books, doesn't he?"

Marie Elena didn't look at me. She just said "Yes." Louise didn't react. It was as if that was what was on their minds, and they assumed I knew. And that's what this meeting was all about: the Merryman tapes released to Irving, and his first display of his manuscript to McGraw-Hill two months before, on the day following Hughes' death in Greece.

"Her place" was Onassis's building, 1170 Sacramento Street, across the park from the Mark. Her neighbor was Eckersley—the top man of the remaining five "Hughes" nursemaids. Eckersley is currently under indictment for Mafia stock frauds in Canada. (Everybody tried for a piece of the pie after "Hughes" died). One thing fascinated me: on a shelf, an autographed copy of a book by "Cardinal Spellman"—who, with Kennedy, espoused the "Holy Crusade" in Vietnam.

At the Merryman apartment next door to the Eckersley apartment (the head "nursemaid") in Onassis' Olympic-style building, I was wondering "What's up?"

162   *The Gemstone File: A Memoir*

The stranger—apparently a gentleman—said he had to leave. Marie Elena and Louise held a conference. I felt they wanted me to stay. It seemed almost childlike. "Please," they said.

But—let's face it: Onassis is no friend of mine. I left with him; the stranger, that is.

The next day, I called Marie Elena to thank her for her hospitality. She said her husband would be at the Bohemian Grove for a while, so I told her I'd call her in a week or so and we'd go out to dinner.

Said she: "I'd like nothing better in the world than that."

And then I said, pushing a bit: "Besides, you mentioned some names the other night that are currently making headlines—big ones; and I know them too, and we should talk about them, shouldn't we?"

And she answered, in relief: "Yes. Please call soon."

A month later, after Derrough pulled the CBS censorship bit on me, and Christopher Beam appeared, and we discussed "IBM" in the Mark Lobby, I called her during her dinner party. I asked her to come down and join us. She said, "I'll be there if I can, but I have dinner guests. But please call again. I'd like nothing better in the world. Remember that."

I haven't called since, primarily because of something else I did.

Two days after the original Merryman meeting, I called Nixon's barking hatchet man, John Mack. I told him about the Merrymans and Eckersley, and how I figured Onassis wanted to talk to me. (See how wrong you can be sometimes? It was quite the reverse; I know that now. Those Merrymans were caught between the devil and whatever else is rotten.)

I asked Mack how he would like to comb missiles out of his hair while a mineral goose went up his keester because of the censorship of the fact that Vietnam was a "holy crusade" whipped up by Onassis and the Pope and based on Fatima #3, partly to keep the opium flowing.

He said: "I'll do whatever you say. Do you want to see Mitchell?"

***

July, 1971: Kissinger made his secret trip to Peking. And Dickie canceled his speech at the Bohemian Grove. Said he: "I'm afraid reporters might ask embarrassing questions.

And Dorothy Hartcher, from Australia, who knew of my plans for that Bohemian Grove speech, left for home on the day the papers carried news of the cancellation. When she said good-bye she pointed to that news item and said, "You bastard."

I guess I am.

Read the chronology again. You'll see strange drunks with strange questions; Mitchell's sudden availability; Kissinger's funny trips, Hughes's nursemaids' reactions, all through this thing—any time someone (that's me) pushes the "Hughes" button.

October 1, 1971: I said to Neilson, "I'll give Carlson the entire Howard Hughes empire to prosecute dog pounds from, if I can only find him. I'll give him a Pulitzer Prize for the 'IBM' assassinations story. I'll give Mary Pongalis the Onassis building at 1170 Sacramento Street, and she can give it to you. I'll give you the $12.5 million from the Alioto *Look* suit. Hell, let's make it $50 million, like 'IBM' wants from Onassis—and I'll give that to you, too. In any event, that phrase current in Peking—'Chappaquiddick Big Dickie, Chappaquiddick Little Dickie, and Chappaquiddick Alioto' refers to Little Dick, meaning our friend, Dick Carlson—and we've just gotta get him off that list somehow, don't we?"

From CIA Neilson, I got only a blink. But a week later, Kissinger announced a second trip to Peking, "to check on the agenda of the talks."

And a week later that information about your upcoming assassination, which I passed on to

Neilson and to Harry Miller's secretary, using the name of "Hughes", brought a 100-man FBI flush of San Francisco, but your cancellation—and the failure of the budding consumer movement.

Odd, isn't it, Nader, that the plot to assassinate Caesar Chavez was thoroughly and publicly investigated by the FBI; but in your case, where the danger was real, no one asked me what it was all about. Not even the FBI army that was here, or you, who hid in a phone booth in the Washington of Hairbreadth Harry Miller, whose name was also on the list.

***

After Hughes's death, even the Mormon nursemaids wanted a chunk of the loot. Eckersley and three more of the "Hughes" Mormon nursemaids staged a raid on the Canadian Stock Exchange.

Clifford Irving felt he was home free. But Onassis's cover—Dickie, the FBI, CIA, Pentagon, and D.A. Hogan—the lid for Hoover's Rosenstiel connection—all of them are now piled on Irving's ass.

Said he yesterday: "I don't understand why this is drawing all this amount of prosecution."

By now he does. But they can't kill him, any more than they can kill Maheu. Both of them know too much. As does Thieu in Vietnam.

***

I've gotta get back to that murder room, Nader, across the hall. And the complete details of the Onassis-"Hughes" Mafia money funnel are out all over, to interested non-Mafia countries. If any of us are still here, you may read them.

But that loot that comes from oil, opium, whatever—doesn't stop with the purchase of presidents and countries. It also owns Bechtel, General Motors, Lockheed, and on and on. Your bribe came from Onassis, with the knowledge of the entire group.

You are allowed to rave around at the edges (better, they say, to offer token reforms than to have it all get atomized), and you in turn are ordered to avoid any keys: Legal Mafia, Press Mafia, Vatican Mafia. Your objective, you state, is to have a nation run by lawyers. Run by the ABA, who refuse to open their files on Governor Koerner, the Mafia Governor of Illinois, who is guilty of every known crime. And the ABA is one of the Mafia groups that squats on Mary Jo's grave. And they, and you, and Dickie, and Teddy—all squat on the murder of that man across the hall. My father, Nader.

Merryman's disgruntled tapes won't do too much damage. From the Justice Department: "An unidentified source" states positively that Hughes is alive and well. There is only a slight mention of political bribery, treason, presidential purchase, etc.

Naturally, Onassis doesn't like it, but business goes on. He and Dickie's brother Donnie Nixon are in the housing business together.

For fifteen years, the CIA and Onassis have been buying up all old photographs of Hughes, and switching fingerprints and signatures in police and government files. (It's easy, Nader; you should see what they did in the San Francisco Hall of Justice with those Alioto hit-run records—and back east with the Chappaquiddick phone records).

You see, back in 1963 an honest judge and honest experts ruled that Howard Hughes's signature was not genuine in the TWA suit, and that is why "he" (actually, Onassis) lost the original $120 million. Now, all the judges are purchased—and the experts—and they have nice new fingerprints and signatures which do match all the switched files.

At times people have approached me and asked if I had more evidence for Nader. I finally asked one, "Are you from Nader?" and he said "Da." I gave him a batch. And all of the others. I'm

not too sharp at languages.

Once one of them told me that Russian citizens were going through the San Francisco Justice files and lawyers files and other places in an effort to assist the United States in solving crimes, such as assassinations. They seem to feel that the question of the century, "What causes crime?" can be answered here.

Wouldn't that be something? If the friendly Russians are solving our crime for us because we here are too criminal to do it ourselves? Do you suppose that subject is on the agenda for Dickie's Peking and Moscow talks? Do you suppose Dickie would thank Brezhnev if the total solution to all the United States' major crimes were handed over to Strangelove Kissinger?

A remark was passed to me recently that Hughes's body had been recovered from the bottom of the Mediterranean Sea, and authenticated by dental records. Supposedly by a country that doesn't care much for Mafia America. It seems some dirty bastard had told them where the body was, and who had the authentic dental records and authentic signatures. That dirty bastard should be placed under CIA surveillance. That bastard acted against "national interest." Didn't he, Nader? How will your Legal Mafia cover that up? Pull Fatima #3—the blow-off of the non-Vatican half? Or will the non-Mafia half pull a first strike on the Mafia half and justify it by the evidence, plus a basic desire just to stay alive; self defense, I believe they call it?

I don't understand Strangelove Kissinger. I can see Brezhnev and Mao any time. No secret trips; I don't even need a visa. Us people, we don't have any law at all, as you-all, the legal Mafia, do. Us people—that's me, and Mary Jo, my father, Yablonski, my mother, Martin Luther King, and a batch more—including Christ himself.

We're ghosts, Nader, in a never-never-land of no law. How does your ABA Mafia regulate a thing like that?

Archbishop Sheean voluntarily dropped out of contention as the next Pope. Said he: "I can't pay the price: disloyalty to my own principles." Part of his disgust was against the "Holy Crusade" of Spellman in Vietnam. Said he in 1967: "If Johnson withdrew all the troops from Vietnam he would become the moral leader of the world."

Cardinal Terence Cooke then became the leader. To him and the Knights of Columbus, Dickie promised loot. Daniel Schorr labeled Nixon either a liar or a traitor for his actions. Schorr said it was unconstitutional, which of course it was. Schorr now has a conga line of FBI after him, waiting for him to spit on the sidewalk. Lodge, who set up Diem for dumping in 1963 (and then wound up as a Judas for Onassis), is now the Ambassador to the Vatican.

Noah Dietrich, who arranged the Hughes "loan" to Nixon in 1956, was fired by Onassis-"Hughes" a few months later: in March, 1957, just after Onassis snatched Hughes and spirited him away. That $205,000 "loan" to Nixon (to Donald Nixon, Richard's brother, on behalf of Donald's failing restaurant, the "Nixonburger," in Whittier, CA) persuaded Nixon to get approval for the Hughes Medical Research Foundation, which owns Hughes Aircraft, and pays no taxes. It is located in Miami, where the Miami National Bank funnels Lansky loot, via Lou Chesler. That is, loot from Tommy "The Cork" Corcoran, Teddy's boy, from the CIA opium route in Laos, and skims from the "Hughes" Vegas casinos, cocaine, hot stocks, etc. This loot is funneled to Switzerland for "cleansing." From there, it comes back, clean, as billions in Mafia cash, and is then funneled through minor hoods into, say, stock purchases of Lockheed. And voila! Onassis owns the Board of Directors. This is how the hard core Mafia shifted into Corporate ownership, and then compounded that through the Pentagon and the Pope—the "joint handmaiden" affair that is Vietnam.

It was a message from the Pentagon, via a mid-west radio station, that gave Johnson the message, on the plane coming back from Dallas: "There was no conspiracy, Lyndon. And whoop up that war in Vietnam, or you'll never land in Washington alive. We'll name John McCormack President. He's been letting the Maf out of prison for years, and he works well with the Pope. He's one of ours. Voloshen owns him."

J. Mafia Hoover? Gallinaro dug up the dirt on him—and on Rosensteil, and Johnny Torrio, and all of the other hoods. Mrs. Rosensteil was the key informant. And the following day, Hoover's friend, D.A. Hogan, of New York, arrested Mrs. Rosensteil for spitting on the sidewalk. The hard core Maf put a quarter million dollar price on Gallinaro. And down in Texas, they beat the hell out of Gallinaro, because he turned in the Mafia dealings of Texas Willie Wilson, Mitchell's Chief of Criminal Investigation. Hoover runs a school for Fagins.

Onassis-"Hughes" doesn't hire anyone in Vegas except ex-FBI, ex-CIA, or ex-Justice people. Examples: assassin Maheu from the FBI; Hundley from Justice, who rigged the *Look* Alioto Mafia bit for Mitchell and helped to cover up the barbecue roast of Newsom's nieces; or the Intertel boys from Justice who ran the Bahamas and Caribbean rackets for Onassis, and then moved into Vegas when Cesare Davis replaced Maheu.

Hoover, Justice and the CIA, plus the Pentagon, Secret Service, and Defense Intelligence all sit on the lid of this thing. All of it, from Alioto to Chappaquiddick, from Onassis in 1932 down through the assassinations, to the burial of Hughes on April 16, 1971. (Two members of the 116th Intelligence Group from the Presidio here witnessed the Alioto hit-and-run on my car that started this entire bit. Copies of their statements are out. They have disappeared.)

The Mafia, you see, has moved up to the Corporate Boards of Directors, the Presidency, Congress, State and local governments. And around the world; they are multinationally "corporate." And along with the Vatican, they are multinationally pushing Fatima #3.

Dead Howard Hughes is the visible, working, exposed link to all of this. All they can do is try to cover it up. And this they try to do. All of Justice and FBI and Interpol are climbing over everything Clifford Irving said and did.

They say nothing about Robert P. Eaton, who only followed orders: "Make the thought of cryogenic freezing of Hughes' body public." Or the "disembodied voice" of "Howard Hughes" from the Bahamas—which is now being sued by Maheu for another $17 million.

There is no investigation of "Hughes". A private, drafted into the army, gets a security check. But "Hughes"—who is the tenth largest defense contractor (and controls all of the others, behind the scenes)—and deals in global satellites, and Laser work—will remain unquestioned forever, even after his official death. Known for total treason, bribery, murder, and the purchase of everything, from Presidents on down, he is totally immune. As is assassin Maheu. And the next Senator from New Mexico—John Meier. And Chappaquiddick Teddy and Tunney, who today are in Switzerland plotting a Teddy-Tunney Demo Presidential ticket this fall to run against Chappaquiddick Dickie.

They will be supported by Jackie, Onassis's wife, and Rosie, the wife and mother of the Mafia, and Pope Paul, who has written a constitution declaring himself to be God, infallible and beyond questioning—as "Howard Hughes's" cryogenically frozen body will be. And the rest of the two Mafia parties, who are currently passing a new "security" bill that puts a 30-year secrecy clamp on everything. A total freeze. Actually, they might cancel the '72 election altogether (a memo was seen on that subject). "Disorder" or "anarchy" or something will be the excuse.

But there are complications, Nader—such as a billion and a half people who don't care much for the Papal Fatima #3 oblivion and might lob things the other way first. That's in your direction.

And there is some anger over Spellman's "Holy Crusade" and your "Nader Crusade." The "Holy Crusade" wants to conquer the world with "soldiers of the church." "Nader's Crusade" wants to do it with Mafia Attorneys—the legal Mafia: 40,000 of them, you said, to start with.

What are you gonna do about Hughes's body? And Mary Jo's busted nose, when she comes up for air? Or those POW relatives who have my gemstones, and the history that goes with them? Any one of them could present that history to Hanoi and Fatima #3 would be here, in reverse—coming this way. One, I know, is about ready. She'll trade getting hubby home for the entire Mafia

here that she has learned to hate.

A sage stated that once corruption sets in there can be no reconversion. History proves this. It is identical with cancer. It grows until it kills the source it feeds on, and consequently itself.

Well, I'm going back in and see how the murder is coming along. I remember that Maheu tried to murder Castro with a chemical that caused a heart attack. He tried putting poison in Castro's food. And other things—the whole CIA murder bag of tricks. He missed on Castro, but he did better on two Kennedys and a King.

And I'm beginning to wonder about all that blood that's pumping out of my father's stomach. The doctors are puzzled. They've never seen anything like it. They're trying to find out what it is. So am I.

Let's see: Dickie's going to Peking next week. Maybe there's an urgency about the murder of my family. But then, nothing can change my own schedule, and there are events that could automatically speed it up. Dickie's a Mafia cancer, but he's not stupid. We'll see.

Said Chappaquiddick Dickie—then Vice President Nixon—when he took his first "Dietrich-Hughes" bribe in the famous year 1956: "You say it's treason, Dietrich? Screw America. My family comes first."

Says President Chappaquiddick Dickie today: "Screw America. Murder the family of the man who elected me. My family comes first—my Mafia 'Hughes' family, that is."

February 13, 1972: In the Hospital

My father is still breathing, Nader. He's a tough old bastard.

Said Thieu, yesterday: "Nixon can't withdraw American troops from Vietnam until I say he can. Nixon had to get my approval before he could visit China."

Said Dickie, in response: "That's right. We support Thieu."

Ah, that blackmail is potent.

***

Merryman's tapes, filtered through Irving, were damaging, right at the key, just as certain parts of the Pentagon Papers were damaging. So a phony "Hughes" voice, over the telephone—"disembodied" was Maheu's term—was forced to deny any cooperation with the phony "autobiography." In the meantime, Eaton—one of the shady Rosemont crew since he was given Lana Turner—was allowed to leak out a bit about the planned cryogenic sealing of "Hughes's" body immediately after death. (I wonder who the body in that cryogenically sealed package will be). You will note that Eaton isn't being investigated or harassed.

"Hughes" TV news comes from Peking, about Dickie's visit—via "Hughes" worldwide satellites;[40] the "Hughes" defense contracts, the "Hughes" Mafia money funnel to purchase all public officials, and all private corporations, banks, insurance companies, foreign countries—and all with the benevolent approval of the Vatican, who stand to gain all the souls in this worldwide Fatima #3 movement: "Convert 'em or kill 'em."

The "Hughes" story is as vulnerable as the Alioto hit-and-run and Chappaquiddick. It is as current. An integral part of everything. With Dickie in Peking, Dickie's brother in Greece, John F. Kennedy's ex-wife Jackie in bed with the Boss, Onassis, and Teddy and Tunney running on a ticket against Dickie and Dallas Bullet Connally for the position of next President of the United States. And so it goes.

---

[40] Well, I do hate to bring this up; but every time I see that "Hughes Medical Institute" is donating money to support PBS programs, and just might have a tiny bit of influence over which programs it supports and funds, and which it does not....-sc.

By the time you read this I will have kept that date with Louise and Marie Elena Merryman. Others from within the "Hughes" chain contact me at intervals. Now, they too say "Please." There's the "body" of Hughes, somewhere. And possibly Mary Jo's busted-nose carcass.

This year, 1972, is scheduled to be either a re-run of 1968: Onassis's Nixon vs. Onassis's Humphrey; or a re-run of 1960: Onassis's Nixon vs. another Onassis's Kennedy. Either way, Nader, who would win? America, or Onassis?

Onassis bribed you. Who bribed Barbara Phillips? Anybody we know?

Today her partner, Gloria Steinem, is campaigning for the Democrats in New Hampshire. Said she: "Us women will make the required changes. We will be the conservers of life. We will run group politics for reform. We love this system."

Reference to Evidence

Note: The following pages, tape, film and documents contain proof of various exposed keys to the destruction of the United States by the group known as MMORDIS.[41]

- The Alioto hit-and-run, on September 16, 1968, at 10:45 p.m., at Franklin and Lombard Streets, San Francisco—the attempted cover-up of which elected Dickie to the Presidency and exposed the real key: the Mafia election process.
- An event which caused Chappaquiddick, because of the phone calls from Tunney to Kennedy and back to Alioto about that same exposure of the Mafia election process—and the subsequent Inquest cover-up, whose reason was to cover up those calls. (The hiding of these phone calls by Loeb resulted in Hoffa's release from prison.)
- Chappaquiddick exposes the 1932 Joseph P. Kennedy-Onassis's English booze and heroin importation into Boston, under the auspices of Franklin D. Roosevelt and Winston Churchill. That blackmail moved Onassis into the White House and #10 Downing Street. It moved Joseph P. Kennedy into the top rank of legal looting—S.E.C. swindling on up. It moved the Mafia three—Onassis, Kennedy, and Roosevelt—up to rig World War II. Documents now released, after 25 years of secrecy, have finally certified this. Chappaquiddick exposed the entire Mafia election process; and the assassinations by "IBM" (Iron Bob Maheu), of JFK, Martin Luther King, and Bobby.
- The exposure of the Onassis "Hughes" Mafia money funnel, which takes in all heroin, gambling, murder, and S.E.C. loot from all over the world, washes it, and sends it back by the billions to purchase presidents and all public officials (in the identical manner in which William Turner describes how Hoover's FBI club does it with the Hoover blackmail files).

It deals with Onassis calling the Apalachin meeting in 1957 to brief all state Mafia "families" on how to run, and win, their own state elections, and the nation's. And the Onassis "hyping" of Hughes (by Hughes's assistant "Cesare" Davis, now Chester Davis, in charge; and Johnny Meyer, now Onassis's alter ego and Jackie's "security"); and the take-over of the Hughes empire.

And the purchase of V.P. Nixon, via a bribe from Noah Dietrich, who warned Dickie that it was treason, and recorded Dickie's answer: "Screw America. My family comes first."

And also:

- The direct Onassis takeover of the U.S. via the Kennedys in 1960.
- Maheu's C.I.A.-ordered assassination plan for Castro (aborted).
- The promised Onassis-Vatican-Kennedy-Spellman "Holy Crusade" in Vietnam, for loot, heroin and church conversion.

---

[41] [NOTE: No such evidence was included with this copy of the file.-sc]

- The resistance of Hoover's FBI white boys' club to the Onassis take-over.
- The assassinations—by Maheu—for Onassis.
- The creation of Onassis's Greece, via the Colonels.
- The purchase of Nixon and Humphrey in 1968 by Onassis-"Hughes".
- The snatching of Jackie—by Onassis—with Vatican approval.
- The murder of Mary Jo, on whose lid all now sit—Vatican and Mafia, all groups.
- Howard Hughes, buried off Greece, April 18, 1971.
- The power struggle going on now, and the fact that all bribery now associates to treason—a hanging offense for all participants.

February 14, 1972—Nader letter continued

In the news today (this is February 14, 1972—and he's still alive, Nader), Time quotes as a source of Irving's writings "current and former Hughes employees." "Former" Hughes employees would include Noah Dietrich, and Jim Phelan, who wrote articles knocking attempts to investigate the JFK murder.

That quote, "Current and former Hughes employees," was as close as any of the press Mafia will get to saying "Merryman", the sixth "Hughes" nursemaid, who "died" and/or "disappeared" around Christmas, 1970. (Wouldn't it be something if his body, saved on ice, turns out to be the one that will momentarily be "cryogenically sealed" as the body of the "suddenly dead" "Hughes"?)

Says Irving today, in response to Time's charge of his pirating Phelan's and Dietrich's stuff: "It's more complex than you think. You haven't seen the bottom line yet. There is going to be some big news breaking."

Like Mafia Thieu and Mafia Maheu, he knows what's going on. Those prosecuting him—Hoover's Rosensteil cover-up man, D.A. Hogan, and Mitchell's cover-up man, Seymour, who can't find any Mafia in New York, as Stern does in Jersey, will work out a deal for Irving. No wonder he still smiles. That's potent blackmail.

(Dietrich was fired by "Hughes" in that famous Apalachin year, 1957. He knows nothing from then on. The Irving writings, and the tapes they were based on, which our FBI so desperately seized, and buried, contain references to the purchase of presidential candidate Nixon in 1960. And Humphrey, Larry O'Brien, and Nixon in 1968, and many other Mafia purchases of people from 1957 to 1968. Only the six nursemaids had that tape file. Only Merryman is missing. He "died" a month after the "strange Vegas kidnapping.")

All those hordes of former FBI, CIA, Justice, etc., people who currently work for "Hughes" and guard Jean Peters know about this.

Why don't they just bring Howard out into the open for a few days, Nader? Everybody knows that this is the greatest breach of "national interest" and "national security" in history: a Mafia empire that purchases Presidents, Congress, the Press, the Legal System and the total economy, and runs wars for heroin.

Is it surprising that the U.N. legal group says: "National Security—nothing! This is the whole ball of wax. It's Fatima #3—and, you say, going one way or the other—probably both…?" The only cure, they say, is to correct it at the source: right here, now.

So why are Dickie and Onassis and McNamara and Teddy and Connally—and everybody—rushing around the world to put on the clamp?

Meanwhile, doing the digging here, for bodies, are only those eager searchers from non-Mafia countries around the world.

Why didn't Harry Miller, last Valentine's Day, run to Jack Anderson, as I suggested he do?

He knew it all. I showed it to him.

Or Fellmeth, at the same time? You and he were both in town. I had a long talk with him about the exact Mafia names in Washington. You and he ran like rabbits from that evidence. And you had already taken an Onassis-"Hughes" bribe six months before that, and didn't even inform your followers.

Sylvia Siegel was right when you ducked out on that consumer's third party start. Said she: "I'm sick of Nader. He is a traitor. I think he's shit."

Jack Anderson? I asked Miller what, with all his exposes, had Anderson ever accomplished in 47 years? It was a good question. The answer is, nothing. The cancer has grown steadily.

Today Jack Anderson stated: "The Senate of the United States is a gentleman's Cosa Nostra, which enforces its own code of silence." (Everybody else says "Mafia Omerta.") "Above all, it is strictly taboo to expose or embarrass a colleague."

That includes Chappaquiddick Teddy, Chappaquiddick Tunney and ex-Senator Chappaquiddick Dickie, plus another 98 Senators—all purchased by Onassis-"Hughes" and Associates.

This particular Anderson column relates to Senator Sparkman's stealing your money for the Bankers, and Senator Proxmire—"the only reformer"—bowing to the priority of Sparkman's higher Mafia ranking: ceasing to criticize the theft, and apologizing for calling Sparkman a thief.

Do you think, Nader, that these Mafia will stand up and confess the treason they committed when they took their oath of office: "To defend the Constitution against the enemy within and the enemy without—" (both Mafia: Grecian Onassis, and American "disembodied voice" "Hughes"—and their assorted associates)? They had already accepted Mafia bribe loot in order to be allowed to take the oath of office. Their own individual and collective Mafia treason is thereafter a matter of public record

Do you think Teddy will stand up and unravel himself like a ball of string for the Mafia crud that he is, and confess that he did not Jesus-walk on the waters of Chappaquiddick? And that he busted Mary Jo's nose, murdered her and buried the body in a grave on which sits the most monstrous horde of Vatican Mafia ghouls since the beginning of time?

Dr. Akar said: "No corruption will ever reconvert itself. History proves this. Cancer will never kill itself. It only grows." This came from a doctor across the hall, Nader, where my father is being murdered.

He said, "There is 100% human approval for the killing of cancer."

I asked: "100%? The Mafia too?"

He said: "Of course."

There's a doctor's view, Nader.

You were quoted as saying in Saturday Review: "The system cannot change and it will not die. How long can I go on?"

Poor boy. Maybe you'd prefer to join us who are being murdered by President Chappaquiddick Dickie. You've been as puny as Anderson. And completely cancer since you took the Onassis bribe.

Now, you say: "Congress is the one institution that can change things around." Is that the same Congress that Senators Mansfield and Smith say they can't get enough of together for a quorum? Where the Mafia "legislative aides" (such as those that scurried with Mary Jo's busted-nosed body for Teddy from Chappaquiddick to Pennsylvania dust) cut up the loot and pass it out to the Mafia? And where Chappaquiddick Dickie and Dallas Bullet Connally sock "you-all" (that's a Johnson Texas phrase) with another $50 billion debt, this year, and more next year, in order to

finance the Mafia in future murder and looting of "you-all?"

Chappaquiddick Dickie now hides behind a world-crawling crusade for peace, instead of cleaning up his own shit, the total cause of war and crime. It is just what Russia and China have always said: we are gangsters, because our Mafia owners are.

Now Nixon has Haldeman declare that anyone who exposes the Mafia cause of all this crud is guilty of treason. And Chappaquiddick Teddy circles the globe too: Ireland, Israel, Germany, Bangladesh, spouting about Freedom, Treason, Health Care, Judicial Process.

Murdering Mafia Hoffa—the subject of Bobby Kennedy's planned new edition of The Enemy Within, which the Mafia censored—is loose again, courtesy of Loeb (bargaining with the Chappaquiddick phone calls) and Dickie. And he's back on TV, making his payoffs.

First, he endorsed Nixon for reelection, and then he vowed to help all the other criminals in the world.

The *New York Times* committed total treason when they ran the Jerry Llellyveld cover-up of the Chappaquiddick phone calls—as reported to Loeb, who could overcome that, but not the plum of Hoffa's release and Dickie's presidential Mafia deal. Who else could Loeb turn to? The Pope? No; his ass rests on Mary Jo's grave too. Nader? No; he's the one Mary Jo was running to, and his "holy crusading" ass covers that same section of Pennsylvania dirt.

The obvious remedies to this crud were submitted to Nixon along with the note that he, Chappaquiddick Dickie, could be another Lincoln. But he burned those papers and set about the murder of my family instead.

James Reston, commenting on our own Mafia government, asked a question: "What kind of monsters are these?"

Between tears, my mother has been asking me that for three and a half years. She figures it's a Yablonski-style massacre every time the doorbell rings. But she doesn't hide.

You? You hide in a phone booth somewhere in the East while your precious "consumer movement party" folds in San Francisco when somebody only mentions a Yablonski, Nader—and an army of FBI combs the town.

If Miss America were selected in the same Mafia manner as our candidates for office are, she would be a syphilitic, cankerous slob—a 500-pound, three foot high, snake-haired, fang-toothed, shit-dribbling, perverted whore, down in the audience guzzling bloody unborn lamb juice, peddling heroin as she buys the judges, while the legal Mafia declares her the constitutional winner and the press Mafia whips up an image of Camelot. And whatever patrons escaped the mugging would run home and declare, "Well, we voted, didn't we? What else was there to do?"

And the following morning, Onassis comes knocking on the door with a tax bill and a draft notice. It's an American Dream, Nader.

There's a murder going on across the hall. His name is not Pa Kopechne, or Kennedy, or Nixon, or Onassis, or Alioto, or Pope Pontius.

It's Roberts. And that's my name too. And I'm not after any one Mafia cancer. I want all of them.

Today, Beckman—head of Nixon's "Golden Circle," to which Mack suggested I contribute $1500 when I first brought him this matter in October, 1968, said: "Nixon would have lost the election if he had lost California."

Beckman and his Lincoln Club claim they purchased California for Dickie. As in the case of "Syphilitic Miss America," who else was there to elect except Onassis-owned Dickie? Onassis-owned Hubert Humphrey?

***

As with Oswald, Ray, and Sirhan later, Hitler made a beautiful, highly visible decoy to take the rap for WW II, while Onassis and Joe Kennedy were rigging it.

The Pope beneficently blessed Auschwitz and all the mass murders. He was the "Deputy of Christ at Auschwitz." Forty million were murdered in that war; thirty million of those were Russians. The Pope blessed that too. Russians are non-Vatican, you see.

The drive is on. Vatican and Mafia: handmaidens of history since the first "deal" in the year 325 a.d. They want it all.

Is this why "you-all" "holy crusaders"—Nader, Pope Paul VI, Dickie, Onassis, Congress, Legal Mafia, Press Mafia—squat on Mary Jo's and Hughes's graves, and dig a fresh one for the man across the hall? You-all could let it all hang out instead, and let the rest of us live—mighty rich, too, on the recaptured loot of centuries of this Monstrous Mafia crud.

Or do you feel you'd rather push the world into Fatima #3, killing 90% of everything, but allowing the 10% cancer to remain?

And this is what we now see: all the Mafia groups marching on "Peace" missions around the world: from Moscow to Peking, Africa, South America and on and on. But that non-Mafia, non-Vatican half of the globe—scheduled for Fatima #3 extinction—know this, and they too have nuclear buttons.

"Trust us," CIA Helms says as he ships heroin out of Laos, and roams deep in Yunnan Province looking for a rock—a fruitless search, since it is already on its way down his Mafia throat.

Brown's Mafia California Supreme Court suddenly declares the death penalty to be invalid, for any reason. "Not even the Supreme Court can overrule us," he says. True; the Supreme Court is Mafia too. Most of them were appointed by Mafia Nixon, some by Mafia Johnson, and some by Mafia Kennedy.

Says Dickie today: "Just after my China trip I'm gonna have my diplomats blitz the world." Is he lining them up for Fatima #3? Brezhnev and Mao think so—for suddenly, Laird, the Pentagon Chiefs, and the British War Department are screaming in unison about a "dangerous Russian arms buildup". The next step is obvious: Fatima #3. He and the Pope have nowhere else to go. Dickie said it, for both of them: "Screw America. I come first."

Too monstrous, you say? Take a look at the precepts and how they developed:

1932: Onassis, Kennedy, Roosevelt, Churchill, all hooked by that heroin-booze bit. Then, Joseph P. Kennedy's crap game, the S.E.C.: easy, as with all self-regulated, self-perpetuating controls.

Then World War II (rigged by Onassis, Kennedy, Roosevelt—and 40 million murdered).

Then Truman's murder of 100,000 at Hiroshima, while every AEC advisor said, "Pick an empty mountain".

Then the Mafia purchase of the U.S., stemming from the Hughes hyping and a coalition at Apalachin.

Then Vietnam, and the murder of presidents, reformers, and would-be presidents. Mary Jo, Newsom's nieces' barbecue, Tunney-Wilkinson's head hatcheting, Niarchos' belly stomping, the Yablonski blasting, were indeed minor by comparison.

***

Fatima #3 is a natural. The Pope watched all this, and Auschwitz, and Vietnam, without a protest. As in the year 325 a.d., Dickie made a deal with Cardinal Cooke (the next Pope) and the Knights of Columbus. Daniel Schorr said Dickie was a "traitor," and the deal was "unconstitutional," and—zap!—Schorr gets a CIA/FBI shroud. Like Teddy, they say, "We can live with it."

Chou En Lai said, publicly, seven days before Dickie's "peace mission": "He speaks of peace

and redoubles his aggression, in Vietnam and everywhere else. His sole desire is re-election—self-perpetuation."

(Kennedy felt that way in 1963: "Keep the troops in Vietnam until I'm re-elected.")

***

Dual headlines today: "Dickie Off to China on Peace Mission," and "Hughes Vanishes Again—from Bahamas to Miami to Nicaragua; Customs Won't Talk; Nobody Will Talk."

Peterson (Justice's new Criminal Chief, replacing Mafia Texas Willie Wilson) was asked, "Why don't you drag Hughes out of his crypt and clear this up?"

After weeks of stalling, he said, "We will, if necessary. But if Clifford Irving turns out to be a fraud it won't be necessary." (This was a few days after Irving confessed that he, personally, was a fraud.)

Asked Irv Kupcinet, "Who gave Clifford Irving such accurate up-to-date facts—damaging to "Hughes" and all politicians—that McGraw-Hill and *Life* both certified the facts to be genuine?"

He was speaking of the Presidential purchase, and the key: the Mafia Election Process.

There was no answer.

Said Rosenbaum: "Alioto did not come from nowhere. He was suddenly, publicly pushed for Mayor in 1959 in North Beach, San Francisco." That push would be Lanza—Alioto's godfather. (Lanza said to me: "Get out of the street; you might get sunburned," as I picked up pieces of my clobbered car at Franklin and Lombard, on September 17, 1968.)

Said Hoffa, who yesterday endorsed Nixon: "Teddy should be the man to run against Nixon." He is loose, and he owns them both.

For bringing out some truth, Ellsberg will go to prison for 115 years. For bringing out some truth about Onassis-"Hughes's purchase of presidents and the national economy, Clifford and Helga Irving face 25 years in prison.

Murderers Teddy and Dickie, the two Chappaquiddick lads—both wholly owned by Onassis—will be the only two candidates you can vote for. And only one quarter of the population will vote. The winner will be elected by one-eighth of the population—a totally rigged, purchased deal, patterned, as was Thieu's election in Vietnam.

Onassis and the Pope, with aid from all Mafia governments and a total Mafia economy, swing on their merry way to Fatima #3. The Mafia wishes to annihilate the United Nations.

In Congress, Vatican representatives, led by William F. Buckley, demand this. Goldwater demands it. Meany and Mafia Rooney shut off U.N. labor funding; and even "75-year secrecy" Earl Warren, the Maf from "Dallas," laments: "The United States is now openly violating the charter of the United Nations—the last bulwark of world peace—into dissolution."

Dickie—by way of a Hughes bribe in 1957—set up the Hughes Medical Foundation that became the base for the Onassis Mafia Money Funnel, which purchased control of all government and all of the economy—and results in the 41% Mafia siphon from the trillion dollar gross national product. This finances the purchasing of nations around the world, for their bodies, while the Pope pushes for the souls. And now, because the non-Mafia countries know all this, Fatima #3 has become a Mafia reality, rather than simply a Vatican plan.

Teddy parallels Dickie in his trips around the world. The Mafia murderer speaks of freedom and smiles at Mama Mafia Rosie at Hyannisport.

"The only thing that matters is what you can get away with," he says. "I can live with it." And they recall that Mary Jo is now pulverized Pennsylvania dust.

John Mitchell quit his Crime job to run a bigger crime: the re-election of Chappaquiddick

Dickie. Said Martha: "He has solved all crime. He has eliminated the Mafia."

(That's the truth; Mitchell has banned the use of the word).

"He has done more than any crime fighter in history."

(And that's the truth too. He has probably wiped us all out—along with the world.)

Christopher Beam compared you to Murderer Maheu. Harry Miller wouldn't state that you were not Mafia. The Saturday Review describes your own private CIA, and says you are devious and deceitful even to your own associates. It's as if you conceal things from them. Fellmeth and Miller verified this for me.

Jack Anderson states that you suppressed the truth and used your new-found power, from an Onassis bribe and the blackmail that goes with it (both arranged by me) to harass a biographer, McCarry. He charged that you rigged the Yablonski effort that brought out the labor Mafia shotguns, and then joined the lid that sits on the Yablonski family wipe-out.

You know that my family has been sweating out a Yablonski-type situation for three and a half years. They waited for you, with depositions, for a year and a half. One of them is now in that room across the hall. Mary Jo was on her way to see you when Teddy murdered her. You participated in these murders—both before and after the fact. I kept you from being assassinated. Your reaction was predictable: you hid in a phone booth.

My father came into that room across the hall belching blood and hydrochloric acid. The nurse told me that I could expect a call at any time. From here I'm watching a green line on a TV screen. It moves and jumps every time his heart beats.

Said Teddy: "I can live with it."

I wonder. I watch that green line and the last part of Irving's quote comes back: "You have not seen the bottom line yet. Be prepared for a huge surprise."

"Kill that cancer," said the man across the hall. His name is Roberts. So is mine. Bruce Porter Roberts. He was murdered because I elected Nixon.

14 February 19, 1972: To Nader: Bouncing Onassis Through the Tropics

Nader,

Two phone calls to a relative in Spokane[42] got some action. The calls covered the whole story, including the Onassis-"Hughes" Mafia Money Funnel, and the fact that Chou en Lai, if he wanted to, could introduce Dickie to the proven skeleton of Howard Hughes as he steps off the plane in Peking. And Chou could then slap Mafia Dickie all over China on a "Hughes" TV pickup, relayed by a "Hughes" Satellite, and picked up in the U.S. by the "Hughes" communications network.

And if Chou doesn't do that, it might be even worse. There could be a planned first strike by the entire non-Mafia world to avoid the Mafia-Vatican Fatima #3, and then the release of the evidence, to justify the act.

These calls were made on Wednesday, February 15, 1972, about 11:30 a.m. The reason for the calls was to notify this relative of the critical condition of my father at this time in the process of Nixon's 3-1/2-year murder.

A few hours later, the entire Onassis-"Hughes" mob vacated the Bahamas, and the invisible, disembodied "Hughes" was reported to be in Nicaragua. They were received and verified by a Mafia U.S. ambassador (one of those who purchased their jobs) and the dictator of Nicaragua. Neither the U.S. or Nicaraguan Customs actually saw this ghost—but they passed him through just the same. Neither did the Ambassador, or the Dictator, as they vouched for his presence.

Patty Nixon's Sapphire for Elizabeth Dale

This was the end of a campaign that had been going on since the previous Christmas. It began on December 27, 1971, when I gave a 62-carat, heart-cut sapphire to Elizabeth Dale [CREEP head Francis L. Dale's ex-wife] to sell.

She was bugging me for money for Mexican orphans. I offered her a letter to the Mexican reporter who reported Chou en Lai's scornful remark, "The facts of JFK at Dallas are still not out."

Said she: "No, that would be political blackmail."

Me: "Then you either work for Onassis or Chappaquiddick Dickie."

She: "No, I'm a nobody. But my husband is a V.P. for ITT."

(Boing! That one had been under way for some time.)

Me: "Here's a 62-carat heart-shaped sapphire. Sell it, with the history that goes with it. But do not mention my name or take it to anyone who knows me. They will not buy it at any price. The stone you are holding was offered to Mrs. Patty Nixon, along with the request that Nixon sell the other 150 stones for me. I wanted money to buy more information with—the information that my government tries to suppress and withhold. But Nixon wouldn't do that, or let me sell them anywhere else in America.

"That was a month after Chappaquiddick, when I gave Nixon the full solution to Teddy's murder of Mary Jo, the story of Onassis's capture of Hughes, and the history of the entire 50-year conspiracy. The history included everything in here, including the 'Onassis Hughes Money Funnel' and Hughes's burial at sea.

"So I offered the gemstones to foreign outlets.

---

[42] Bruce's brother, Dayle Roberts.

"They said, 'Why sell them to us?'

"So I told them 'why'—the whole sordid history. They paid me well—for instance, $3500 for a ruby that would sell here for $900. Once I sold a piece of gravel from the San Francisco Hall of Justice driveway for $2500—together with an additional history. The history of a stone—or a coin, for instance, gives it a value far above any normal rating.

"POW wives have some of my gemstones, and histories. They could start World War III tomorrow, simply by giving a gemstone—with the history—to Hanoi, in exchange for their POW husbands. Chiang Ching has one of my stones, along with the history. A relative of one of the Chappaquiddick broads threw hers off the Golden Gate Bridge in an attempt to destroy the history, and she was filmed doing that. The filming of the cover-up is far more incriminating than the events themselves."

She: "Thank you. Will you repeat the history to a multi-millionaire friend of mine?" (There it was—big bribe loot from ITT).

Me: "No. I have my own way of doing things. I used all that gemstone money to purchase information comparable to what has been denied me, here, from Mafia Hoover's blackmail files. For instance, Mustapha Bey's diary on Onassis, the Maheu assassinations, the Mafia Election Process, the Onassis-Nixon-"Hughes"-Hoover-Mitchell-Kennedy Mafia Money Funnel, and the story of the handmaidens of history—Vatican and Mafia—all of whom squat on the graves of Mary Jo Kopechne, Howard Hughes, and a murdered horde of millions.

"They are currently murdering my family—and the history of my own father's stones and coins is now out working its way around the world amongst non-Mafia people.

"That sapphire, and its history, is worth a fortune; in fact, the whole ball of wax. Let's see what you can do."

She wasted no more time. She asked, "Where in Asia did that heavy density mineral come from?"

(Only a few people know about that. Mack and Nixon are two of those.) I mumbled something useless.

She: "Why does it take 22 hours to work?"

(That surprised me. I didn't think Helms or Gayler would ever be desperate enough to let that out. To anyone.)

She was referring to my experiments that ended when Alioto clobbered my car on September 16, 1968, and set this entire thing in motion.

A week later Liz Dale said she had done what I asked her not to do—and received the answer I told her she would. "They won't buy at any price," she said

And several weeks later she told me, "I hate you. I am more dangerous to you than any of those others. I might kill you myself."

Me: "That is one way to get the job done. We'd all take a trip—and I'll hang you there. I'm ready, are you?"

No answer. I left.

***

Over New Year's I went to Tahoe and laid the whole cruddy story on a friend of Jimmy the Greek. (Jimmy worked for Maheu and "Hughes", before the Thanksgiving kiss-off).

A week later, Jimmy the Greek quoted public (and differing private) odds on whether Howard Hughes was dead.

He added: "If he is, the entire government is in on it, and it would be the biggest conspiracy

in history."

In January, 1972, I laid the full story of the Onassis-"Hughes" Mafia Money Funnel on Al Strom, Kish, Harp, Bill, and many more, plus likely-looking strangers. (And it was getting through.)

On February 8, I laid the story on Barbara Phillips, Gloria Steinem's partner in *Ms* magazine. "Chappaquiddick Dickie," the Peking phrase, was mentioned, together with the assassinations; and dead Howard Hughes.

On February 9, at 5:00 p.m., my father started vomiting blood and hydrochloric acid. We called an ambulance and took him to the hospital. While waiting for doctor and ambulance, I wrote a long letter to this Spokane relative—and walked out and mailed it, just as I did yours.

On Saturday, February 12, I called Spokane, determined that the letter had been delivered there that day, and discussed its contents (the entire thing: "Hughes", Chappaquiddick, Alioto, and Dickie in Peking). That call too was monitored.

And on Wednesday, February 16, in the morning, I made the two calls in which I verbally recited the entire affair and the possibility of missiles coming in—because of the Onassis-Hughes Mafia Money Funnel—and Dickie, and Chappaquiddick, and Alioto.

That afternoon, Wednesday, the entire "Hughes" Onassis mob pulled their exit from Bahama. It was due to "political problems," they stated, which had started in January.

My campaign had become concentrated in December, with monthly jobs starting way back in June, 1971, when the Merrymans looked me up.

In 1970, two phone calls, about you—and a letter—brought you a half million cash action, four days later. One phone call which mentioned dead Howard Hughes, to Harry Miller's secretary, accompanied with the proposed disclosure of an assassination threat on you, brought me a return call five minutes later. It was from someone other than Harry Miller—possibly from the "Hughes" direct dialing system in the Bahamas. "Police" were mentioned, and police were there. One hundred FBI men combed the town picking up a few winos on your proposed assassination day, even though you were safely hidden, by cancellation, in a Washington phone booth.

They didn't bother me (who started the whole bit), but they did protect Neilson-Green—where in early October I had left messages about "Chappaquiddick Big Dickie, Little Dickie, and Alioto—Peking style" and offered the "Dead Howard Hughes Empire" to Carlson. And five days after that, Kissinger announced a surprise second visit to Peking to "check the agenda" of the talks.

When Clifford Irving's book subject, De Hory, the art forger of Irving's *Fake*, heard of the Bahamas kiss-off, he said, "That's the biggest hoax of all. Hughes has been dead for a while. I know."

William Turner reports that, under heavy public pressure, the IRS has admitted that "Hughes" has not signed a tax return in 15 years. "Maybe," they say, "we'll look into it." Forget it.

The same public pressure, says Turner, forced "unnamed government sources" to admit that they have no proof that Hughes is alive—but none that he is dead, either. Three months ago, an "unnamed, unimpeachable Justice Department source" publicly announced, in a special press conference, that "Howard Hughes is alive and well."

The alternate flight destination of the Onassis Bahama hoods was San Jose, Costa Rica—adjacent to Nicaragua. San Jose, Costa Rica, is a Mafia hub city.

When Lello notified me about the impending violent death of my family—in front of witnesses, at the Maurice Hotel on August 9, 1968 [when Carlson's *Look* story was due out and my papers and stones about Alioto, Hughes and Chappaquiddick were in Dickie's hands], he mentioned that he had just come from San Jose, and asked if I knew it. Yes, I said, thinking he meant San Jose, California, which also has a Mafia group of Bonannos, etc. "Lello, Jardin Baru" was stamped on the back of the bill he paid for his drink. His passport read, "Munoz, Colombia." After

the eye squint, throat rattle and shoulder tap, he departed.

Later, it was determined that Lello was a Mafia "sponsor", a liaison man, all over. He "sponsored" Mari and Adamo, two hoods who left New York and never returned. What they did was kidnap John Tunney's sister, Joan Tunney Wilkinson, in Norway. They released her—hooked on heroin fumes—in Marseilles a month and a half later. Together with "shut up" instructions about the first Chappaquiddick phone call from her Bay Area home, by her big brother, John Tunney. Joan Tunney then chopped off her husband Carter Wilkinson's squawking head in England, and beat the rap in a nut house. Mari and Adamo were later found pressed into a bale of scrap car metal in New Jersey. They had fouled up the deal because Joan Tunney's head-hatcheting-off bit re-exposed what they were supposed to cover up. Lello doesn't believe in witnesses. Nor does J. Mafia Hoover, or Dickie.

In the *Nation*, William Turner politely describes J. Mafia Hoover's Society of Former Special Agents of the FBI. Says he: "They have penetrated the highest echelons of the nation's security-industrial complex, and Congress, the Executive, the Judiciary, and state and local governments. Their luminary is Robert A. Maheu, Hughes's mastermind before going out in a blaze of controversy."

He goes on about how they are phone company tappers, and run Hughes Aircraft, Las Vegas and Caribbean gambling, Lockheed, Ford, Law Enforcement, American Security Council, and parts of the CIA. (Their pattern follows the plan of Onassis at Apalachin—and they work side by side). Dissenters are punished. Always, they follow the "hate the commies" Fatima #3 policy. Mike Novacs labeled them "Hoover's Catholic Boys".

California Attorney General Younger, who wants to be Governor, is naturally listed among them. He covered up Bobby's murder in L.A. The head of the Defense Intelligence Agency is also among the group. (That's Noel Gayler, who chatted with me in the presence of Proxmire's niece, and was so irritated by her presence, and my "smuggling" of papers out of this country. This chat occurred within two weeks after the "Hughes" departure from Las Vegas).

Turner is very polite. He doesn't mention J. Mafia Hoover's connections to Neilson, Johnny Torrio, Al Capone and Joseph P. Kennedy. Or Gallinaro's busted body, because he dug up information about these matters. Ah, these people are all alike. They let out a little in order to avoid the big burp.

Dickie's Trip to China in Search of World Peace

I'm watching two TV's. One has a jumpy green line representing my father's heartbeat. The other is focused on a "Hughes" TV broadcast of Dickie's forthcoming landing at Peking. Both have a relationship to whatever future you have.

Here's Dickie, on the opposite side of the globe, searching for "world peace," when for 3-1/2 years he has been aware that the cause of crime and the cause of war is right here, and exposed. For three and a half years, he has prosecuted the murder of the man who is responsible for that jumpy green line. And all because that man's son elected Dickie and exposed Dickie and all the crud, at the same time. The Mafia election process—conducted not by the visible Mafia parties in a rigged wrestling match, but by the two real Mafia families:

Onassis-"Hughes" Maf, who murder in Maheu's direct way, the "Moldering Mass Of Rotten," and:

J. Mafia Hoover's select club that murders by the blackmail in his files, the "Dribbling Infectious Shit Club."

Put together (and they do work together; Hoover's group is why it was so easy for Onassis to set up the Apalachin deal and the Hughes hyping in 1957), this spells: "Moldering Mass of Rotten Dribbling Infection Shit," or MMORDIS. And that's a much truer name than "Mafia", since it includes all of the cancer, who join the rest on Mary Jo's grave—and Howard Hughes's—and that of

the man attached to the jumpy green line.

Today, the TV informs me that Onassis got Jackie into the "verification act" of Hughes' existence. He had Jackie order his man, Johnny Meyer (formerly "Hughes's" man), call "Howard" and demand that he give an interview to Jackie. Johnny Meyer reports that "Howard" said "No." (But that "verifies" that "Hughes" still exists, doesn't it?) And Johnny Meyer also reports that Jackie is mad at the "proved living" "Hughes" and "will get even with him" for the slight.

This is an example of Onassis's desperation.

Remember Jackie? She was snatched by Onassis from the dead hands of JFK, who was murdered by Maheu for Onassis. It's Mafia policy: Snatch the murdered slob's wife and shotgun—in this case, Jackie and the Pentagon.

***

Dickie is trying to buy China, Mafia style.

Here at home, the California Supreme Court (appointed by Mafia Pat Brown, whose record includes the huge water swindle, the I.O.S. swindle, and active participation with Voloshen and McCormack in the release of convicted Mafia from jails) ruled the death penalty illegal—by the State Constitution, regardless of what the U.S. Supreme Court says.

By poll, 80% of the population favor the death penalty.

Said Reagan: "This makes a farce of constitutional law. It exposes the public to crime and treason and murder with no deterrent."

This, with the Mafia "statute of limitations," now makes all crime legal—even Treason and Murder.

Said Teddy—and Pat Brown, and Moretti, and another local Maf I talked to last night, "Great; now there's no way they can hang us for our murder and treason."

Tablets were discovered recently dating from the year 325 a.d., and the Council of Nicaea, when history fell prey to the canons of the church. These clay tablets escaped the Holy Fathers' censorship in the 10th Century a.d. They have aided in exploding the Vatican cover-up and subsequent use of the murder of Christ. Therefore, they are kept secret.

"Put Murderers on the cross—not me," said Christ, as it took him eight hours to suffocate in that cross position.

Two hours and thirteen minutes was all it took for Mary Jo to suffocate in that air bubble And not because of lack of air, but because of the swollen tissues of her nose, busted by the mighty backhand of MMORDIS Teddy.

There's a jumpy green line going up and down, showing the heart beat of a man involved in another slow murder: this one, courtesy of Chappaquiddick Dickie—who, on the other TV, is just landing in Peking, in search of world peace and the cause of crime and war.

I'm gonna watch and see if in the receiving line, as already intimated to me, will be the skeleton of Howard Hughes. And whether Chou en Lai will then whip Chappaquiddick Dickie all over China. Or, if he doesn't do this, give him some choice revelations on just how the Chinese plan to defend themselves against Fatima #3.

February 21, 1972

Says the Pope today: "Important events are taking place in the world. We are busy trying to draw predictions of the future of people and of all mankind." (That is: they are wondering whether, if they pull Fatima #3, they can survive themselves. A good question.)

And today, the Justice Department declares that "Hughes" has fled "because we had a subpoena for him. Too bad we missed."

The man who arranged the escape from the Bahamas was James John Golden, formerly in charge of Secret Service for Dickie Nixon.

William Turner has described how Hoover's ex-FBI agents' club runs everything for "Hughes".

Isn't it sad that all these experienced ex-FBI agents who surround "Hughes" can't seem to find him to give him a paper? Even JFK-Bobby-Martin-Luther-King Assassin and FBI Club member Iron Bob Maheu—known familiarly as "IBM", a luminary of the club, along with California Attorney General Evelle Younger. (Maheu, who brought in Gene Cesar, who fired the shots that killed Bobby; and Younger, who now enforces that new Supreme Court ruling: "no death penalty for anything.")

No Mafia wants to hang. So Dickie and Congress are trying to destroy the United Nations; it is a threat. They pervert the Constitution to make Mafia crime legal, and then the legal Mafia throws out all deterrents—even the death penalty for Treason, of which they are all now proven guilty.

"Keep them in Vietnam until I am elected." That's a quote from JFK, who pushed the Holy Crusade with Spellman, in a pungent example of the Mafia election process and the Vatican-Mafia handmaiden approach to Fatima #3, the blow-off of the other half.

"We hang together or we hang separately. Better to have Hoover inside the tent pissin' out than outside the tent pissin' in." That's a quote from Lyndon Johnson. (Senators Brewster and Montoya carried $100,000 bribes from Hoffa in suitcases—as part of their Senatorial duties—to Lyndon. Body Count McNamara covered up Chappaquiddick, after conducting mass murder in Vietnam. And around the globe—where he now buys countries for the new Mafia Boss, Dickie.

"Fuck America. My family comes first." That's a quote from Dickie Nixon—as Hughes' Noah Dietrich handed him a $205,000 bribe in 1956 while warning him that accepting it was treason.

Mafia creed indeed. All Mafia families post this creed on their family walls.

Those are some quotes from three Mafia Presidents of the United States—since 1960. All were bribed by Onassis-"Hughes" cash. Mafia blood cash; murder cash; skim loot; Swiss-washed murder money. All committed treason. Hanging offenses.

I've had it on all sides. From Nixon, Mack, Greenagel, and various other Mafia hoods, listed elsewhere. And what they tell me always has to do with the murder of my family:

Jim Lindberg: "We murder when necessary."

Elizabeth Dale: "I might kill you myself."

"Sometime tonight, or tomorrow."

Well, what is Dickie doing in China? They aren't attacking anybody, as we are—on their doorstep in Vietnam, and by Mafia purchase all over the world, from Taiwan to Greece.

And Chou tells Dickie: "You speak of peace, while you escalate the physical and economic war. You try to purchase us, as your Mafia crew has the rest of the world."

"Journey for Peace," Dickie says. He is running for his life. The cause of war, the cause of crime, is here. They have nothing to lose by trying to purchase the non-Mafia world. Failing that, they will pull Fatima #3—with the Papal handmaiden blessing—hoping to survive the event.

And the non-Mafia world—in self-defense—might lob in the first strike. Or both sides could go at once, and there we are. I get a new job in "Personnel Placement," where I will be employed stringing Mafia cancer on an Eternity Yo-Yo.

Dickie, now exposed, has, visibly at least, taken a 180o turn away from the "hate the commies" theme. He slinks around the world, buying, selling, begging; anything to get off the hook, and always, slyly aware of the potential of popping Fatima #3.

Teddy, now exposed, has, visibly at least, taken a 180º turn too—on the POW's, for instance,

that his brother first sent over on the "Holy Crusade". He is desperately trying to expiate for Chappaquiddick. But he can't.

"Invade Northern Ireland," says he. Teddy has slinked away from the wreckage of Chappaquiddick and is now the "leading presidential contender."

Onassis—now exposed—has pulled out all the stops. Money flows like water, but his disease is catching up. His disease? A fear that he will wake up some day to see his entire Mafia empire gone.

The rest? CIA, FBI, Congress, Legal Mafia, Press Mafia, right down to those who discredit, demean, block and otherwise prevent disclosure—especially by omission of action—are faced with hanging. Treason is any aiding or abetting the enemy, within and without. Based on our Constitution, international law and even the shreds of our own national law.

Ambassadors, such as Nicaragua's, purchase their positions in true Mafia style.

The Pope travels the world and writes an edict declaring himself God.

Ah, this vermin blankets the world. And two billion of the world's non-Mafia population—out of a 3.5 billion total—are angry at this blight, and even some Americans. Missiles exist on both sides. And something new—which I gave to them.

15 March 12, 1972: To Whom It May Concern: My Father's Murder

The writing above was done in the hospital room on the evening of February 21, 1972. On February 22, 1972, at 11:40 a.m., Nixon completed his murder. My father was murdered by Chappaquiddick China, we took my father to the hospital, coughing blood and hydrochloric acid. Two days after Dickie Nixon, whom I elected. "Stress" reads the death certificate. Two days before Dickie took off for Chappaquiddick Dickie landed in China, the murder was complete. Three and a half years of "stress"—a typical CIA-type slow death clamp. On the entire family.

He knew who was murdering him, and why. We talked in the hospital. He fought it all the way. A helpless old man, bursting to belt the truth out. He left a legacy. For all his murderers.

Eugenie Livanos Niarchos died in an inter-Mafia murder performed by her husband Stavros Niarchos because she overheard a phone call. The call was from Charlotte Ford [Stavros's ex-wife], of the Ford Foundation clan—which, led by Body Count Bundy and Attorney General John Mitchell, and in response to my plea to Nixon for help in capturing Alioto for the hit-run that gave Nixon and Mitchell their jobs—brought in a bundle of loot, in the week following Nixon's inauguration, and Mitchell's first official act, for Alioto.

Mitchell enabled Alioto to form the Alioto Crime Commission, which became the lid on my exposure of the Mafia Election Process—laid out by the Alioto hit-run and the Onassis's-Maheu-"Hughes" Vegas skim money bribes to Nixon, Humphrey, et al, going on at the same time—in 1968.

They thought they had the lid on then. But nine months later—Chappaquiddick! I exposed that two weeks after it happened. And Johnson rushed to Nixon, and they issued a joint statement: "We hang together or we hang separately. And it is better to have Hoover inside the tent pissin' out than outside the tent pissin' in."

At the same time, I exposed the Onassis "Hughes" Mafia Money Funnel to Nixon, and he burned his copies of all of that. And the handmaidens of history, the Vatican and Mafia, moved massively to cover it all up. It worked.

They covered Chappaquiddick. They had to. But now they have nowhere else to go. Except to Fatima #3. And that is why that is urgent, now.

The other half of the world knows about all of this. The Onassis-"Hughes" Mafia Money Funnel story is current, bubbling—and they can't hide it.

Their only "out" is to pull Fatima #3—and that's a two-way street, now. They're worried. Check any Mafia action in the past three years. Mafia Executive, Congressional, Judicial, Legal Mafia, Press Mafia—any branch. Corporate, for instance—such as Onassis's ITT, Onassis's General Motors, or Onassis's Lockheed.

Dickie can't leave Vietnam or desert Thieu, the Maf, or Chiang Kai Shek, or the Grecian Maf, or the Vatican Maf. They're all one Maf, with a nuclear noose poised around the non-Mafia half for purposes of Fatima #3. While he was in China, the CIA was still running 200 miles into Yunnan Province on geological field trips, looking for a mineral I was experimenting with when Alioto clobbered my car. The U.S., Russia and the common market countries are all working desperately—in billion-dollar labs—to develop it artificially. I was working with that stuff when Alioto clobbered my car.

And I solved that too. The dirty end. at least. It, with these papers, is up the Mafia ass that squats on the graves of my father, Mary Jo Kopechne, assorted assassination victims, 40 million murdered by Roosevelt, Kennedy and Onassis in World War II, and the dead at Truman's

Hiroshima.

All the scientists who developed the atom bomb said: "Please—pick an empty mountain; it isn't necessary to murder people to demonstrate annihilation."

But then, Truman's boss was Prendergast, and Truman was a typical selection of the Mafia election system.

Prendergast was Mafia, and Truman got his start in life washing whorehouse towels from Prendergast's joints. Oh well; Onassis had owned them all since 1932, when he and Joseph P. Kennedy brought in booze and heroin in presidential pouches.

Presidential intellectual timbre is based, in our Onassis-"Hughes" world, upon how efficiently the potentials wash the Mafia whorehouse towels. What the Mafia looks for is a combination of rotten immorality, murder capability, heroin-pushing adeptness, cunning, greed, and strict adherence to Omerta. These, they make public officials, via the Mafia election process—and voila, there you are.

In nature, the opposite to this combination exists. Where there is anti-matter, there is matter. Always. Any imbalance of this results in an implosion.

I know humans who are the opposite of this cancerous Mafia growth. Some of them do exactly what I tell them to do, knowing there is only one solution if the 90% innocent are to remain in existence. It requires a fatalistic attitude. And it is why a document is out entitled "The Murder of the Family of the Man Who Elected Nixon to the Presidency, by President Nixon."

In the hospital on the night before he died, my father, knowing he was being murdered, told my mother and me that one of us was going to be "knocked over between 9:30 p.m. and 9:30 a.m." I thought it would be me.

But he beat them. He didn't die until 11:40 a.m. That's two hours and ten minutes he beat them out of.

And I remembered something else he said a long time ago: "There isn't anything in this world that can't be done in less than an hour—including the total destruction thereof."

***

Hoover, Mitchell and Nixon wash Onassis' whorehouse towels. Including Jackie's, when she goes to Turkey to sleep with Mustapha Bey, whenever Mustapha orders, since Mustapha kept the Onassis diary from 1914 on.

I purchased a copy of that diary with the sapphires that Nixon refused to sell for me, when I sold those gemstones to 37 embassies around the world, together with the history of why I couldn't sell them in Nixon-Onassis's Mafia America. And all 37 of those countries voted against the U.S. during the ouster of dope-pushing Taiwan from the U.N.

And all of those nations also noted that Kissinger was in Peking at that time—sent there by my announcing to Neilson-Green (CIA) the Chinese phrase, "Chappaquiddick Big Dickie (Nixon), Chappaquiddick Little Dickie (Carlson) and Chappaquiddick Alioto."

"Cancel the United Nations!" scream all the Mafia leaders.

***

My father was murdered on February 22, 1972. 1 called the hierarchy—all of those who weren't with Dickie in China—on the morning of February 23, 1972, to notify them, and to tell them to be sure to be at the funeral that afternoon. None showed.

On that evening and the next, February 24, 1972, Dita Beard, of the ITT Mafia, was pressured.

On the next day, February 25, 1972, Jack Anderson, supported by Nader, released the Dita

Beard ITT memo describing the usual treasonous Mafia bribe of Nixon, Mitchell and the Republican Mafia by the Onassis-"Hughes" Mafia money funnel, while Chappaquiddick Dickie's treasonous face was being picked up by a Chinese "Hughes" ITT satellite and reproduced here on TV stations controlled by "Hughes". This memo was just a needle. Harpoons are on the way. Mafia style: belly to ass-hole.

Said Greenagel, when I told him of the murder and the funeral: "Thank you." (He burned all his copies of this). No card—and no appearance. Nothing.

Best—Nixon's California campaign manager in 1968, who unwittingly cooperated in scaring Humphrey out of the Bay area, sent nothing, and did nothing.

CIA Neilson-Green and Dick Carlson sent nothing, did nothing.

Mummert, my father's coin club friend, and the insurer of my car, who was present at the cover-up of the hit-run from the beginning, and realizes the historical value of my father's stones and coins, said: "Thank you," and pulled a total fade. A week later he sent me a premium notice.

Last week my mother received a death sympathy card from a stranger. It included a Mafia warning to her about me. She cried.

She too would like to get the truth out. Her own deposition. But this massive Mafia is back at the business of the slow kill of the weakest link. Her, now. My brother is bought, and stifled. Has been for three and a half years.

Does that sound sad? It isn't. It's just the way it is.

I sincerely hope people don't get jumpy and pull a Fatima #3 going both ways. It would all be over in an hour.

I prefer the 22-hour way. A day to listen to the Mafia chorus. And for everyone to understand what is happening, and why.

The Republican Mafia, because of the exposed Nixon treason, exposed the Democratic Mafia AT&T treason, in return. But only part of it. They didn't mention that AT&T sits on the lid of the Chappaquiddick phone calls. (In San Francisco, Police Chief Cahill was transferred to the Telephone Company as Security Guard. He has only one job: to sit on the San Francisco lid of the calls from Tunney's sister's house in Tiburon to Chappaquiddick, and Teddy's call back to Alioto).

The real reason for Dickie's China trip was to beg Mao for some form of non-intervention pledge in the internal affairs of other nations. That is also the reason for his Moscow trip. He must achieve an internal lid for Chappaquiddick, the Onassis-"Hughes" Mafia money funnel, and the Vatican-Mafia handmaidens of history. But he knows it's hopeless. It all stems from Greece and Rome: that is, Onassis and the Pope, the Deputy of Christ at Auschwitz. It is worldwide economic robbery, international war, international crime, international control of the soul by the self-declared Infallible God—the Pope.

Father Andrew Greeley issued a report on a five-year study of the American Catholic Church, commissioned by the U.S. Roman Catholic hierarchy (the ones who hold the hands of Alioto, Daley, Kennedy, Onassis, and all who squat on Mary Jo's grave).

He said, "The Catholic Church is on the way to chaos. Its leadership is morally, intellectually, and religiously bankrupt. The naming of the Bishops from Rome, instead of their election in their own diocese, has resulted in a hierarchy of men who are unfit and unable to govern."

Substitute "government" and "Mafia" for the words "Bishops" and "hierarchy," and you spell "The United States of Mafia."

And Greeley's report was substantiated when some Bishops carried pictures of Mary Jo Kopechne under their robes to the Synod in Rome and voted against the Pope's new Constitution declaring himself to be God.

The Pope today ordered all dissident Bishops and priests to stop exposing the myths of the Vatican hierarchy under the threat of the direst punishment—and Fatima #3 plunges on.

The blow-off of the other half would indeed put the lid on the entire globe. But the "other half" knows this now. Missiles can come this way first. And they would be morally correct. America is crud—owned by crud—and sustained by the apathy that breeds more crud.

I once repeated this entire history—on request—to a Republican Mafia "Executive." (He owns banks, and corporations).

Said he: "What else can you tell me in five minutes?"

I took out a list of names and wrote his name on it.

Said he: "What is that for?"

Me: "I'm going to hang you. But not for any of your treason, or bribery, or for your collusion and conspiracy to commit murder and treason. I am going to hang you for apathy. For taking, and wasting, my time. For blocking my efforts. For failure to do anything. I will reshuffle the Mafia legal system, and take your banks and corporations, and hang you. You have a phone on your desk, and direct access to Dickie, Mitchell, Hoover—all the hierarchy. Don't just sit there all pale and shaky. Call them. Report this threat. See if they can protect you."

He didn't call. That was a long time ago. No one can sit on the fence in this donnybrook.

***

Nixon and Mitchell received the ITT memo message. Bob Dole, in Congress, rattled "blackmail" at Teddy and Tunney, who are pushing the ITT charges. He charged the AT&T with Democratic cash bribery and "other considerations." Dole's "other considerations" was a reference to the cover-up of the Chappaquiddick calls by AT&T. Say all the Mafia Senators: "Jack Anderson is insane, and the ITT memo is discredited by decree of ourselves."

Says Anderson: "It's a crime: treason (the ITT bribe). But Justice won't investigate itself. And who else is there?"

I wonder why he doesn't try the Pope. That Vatican group conceals all the murder and treason of the world in its confessionals. Aren't they the moral leaders? 2000 years of inquisitions and "holy crusades", from ancient up through Auschwitz and Vietnam.

The legal Mafia, Party Mafia, Vatican Mafia—none of the branches will investigate itself. That's my baby; and it's out and under way. And all branches are feeling the needles graduating to harpoons and meat axes. And, at any time, we can have "glob" instead of "globe."

And Jack Anderson? Nader's Miller told me in February, 1970, they might turn it all over to Jack Anderson.

Said I: "He's been lipping off for 25 years. Has he ever changed anything?"

In 1960, he, along with all branches of the Mafia, withheld the facts of the Nixon treason bribe that set up the Onassis-"Hughes" Mafia Money Funnel—because "we don't wish to bring up a scandal during an election campaign."

(Translation: "We must maintain a clean image for the voting public.")

The information was then leaked by Mafia Kennedy in order to help win the Mafia election—and move Onassis into the White House, so that he could proceed with his heroin and other businesses in Vietnam. And so Cardinal Spellman could join hands with Onassis, Chiang Kai Shek and Cardinal Yu Pin in the Taiwan dope-pushing end, in a "holy crusade" to convert Vietnam (Fatima #2)—or kill it (Fatima #3). But Fatima #3 has been altered somewhat. By me.

What a Mafia shit pit. Chappaquiddick Dickie and Poucha Pond Mitchell, whom I elected, and who murdered my father, lock horns with Teddy and Tunney, the Mafia murder Senators from

Chappaquiddick, over the ITT treason bribe—exposed by the press Mafia, Anderson. And not a word about the Onassis-"Hughes" Mafia Money Funnel shit stream in which they all swim—the stream that only has one way to go: down the tubes.

***

Merryman, the sixth "Hughes" "Mormon Mafia" nursemaid, released information on Hughes to Irving at Thanksgiving, 1970. And "Hughes" immediately took a hike from Las Vegas. But first, Onassis fired his assassin honcho Maheu, who Onassis suspected had released it. Onassis quickly discovered his mistake, and murdered Merryman around Christmas, 1970.

Louise Merryman, his wife, came out of mourning six months later.

About June 25, 1971, she tapped me on the shoulder and invited me up to Onassis's building at 1170 Sacramento Street—where another nursemaid, Eckersley, has evaporated from his apartment as well. Louise and Marie Elena Merryman wanted help—from me.

Hughes died on April 16, 1971. Jean Peters got her "divorce" a month later. Eckersley and three of the other "nursemaids" made a raid on the Canadian Stock Exchange. And Irving first showed his manuscript to McGraw-Hill on the day after Hughes' death.

Today, Hoover's cover-up D.A., Hogan, covers all this up in New York, just as he covered up Gallinaro's revelation of Hoover's Rosensteil connection. They want to give Irving 100 years in the jug—in an "international prosecution." They want to censor all publication about Hughes. Except for Eaton, who was peacefully permitted to leak the "hint" that Hughes—when dead— would be forever sealed in a cryogenic casket.

But Onassis's Mafia are still worried about the "source" behind all of this. They accused Maheu, and he rattled blackmail back at Onassis. Said he: "If I write a book about Hughes, it'll be a lulu."

Two heated and lengthy phone calls—by me—to a relative, recorded—about the entire Onassis-"Hughes" Mafia Money Funnel, on a Tuesday morning, sent "Hughes" running from the Bahamas to Nicaragua that afternoon.

The Justice Department—"Poucha Pond Mitchell"—covered this up.

How do you think they'll try to cover up the body of Hughes, which was recovered and is now lodged in a foreign country? Who do you think the source of this harpoon is?

March 14,1972: Noel Gayler to the Pacific Fleet

Today, Noel Gayler, Pentagon Intelligence Chief, was pulled out of an N.S.C. deep freeze and given charge of the Pacific fleet. (Actually, this was a Kissinger punishment). Senator Proxmire's niece, Jo Fulton, who joined me in needling him during his inquisition of me, is appearing on BBC television. I don't know what she has in mind.

John Mitchell—again a private citizen, now running Dickie's reelection campaign, calls the ITT facts a lie. Geneen, ITT head, calls Mitchell a liar, and lists the dates and names of all Dickie's hierarchy, plus Congressmen he dealt with. The ABA head, Walsh, admits getting McLarren a Chicago judgeship. (They need more Mafia judges in Daley's Chicago to keep the lid on the Hampton-Clark murders—since that too relates to the double Diem-Kennedy murders, and to Chappaquiddick and Onassis's "Hughes".)

Today, Hoover's cover-up D.A. Hogan, and Mitchell's cover-up U.S. Attorney Seymour made a "deal" with a smiling Clifford Irving. He probes no more, and mentions no more about his knowledge of "Hughes's" death and his prior captivity, and he gets off with a few months' "vacation" in a gentleman's prison—with a fortune assured.[43] The missing McGraw-Hill money? The

---

[43] Some quotes from Ibizzans, after the whole thing was over: "...Of course, Cliff knows a lot more than he's told...Howard Hughes doesn't really exist, but that's off the record, old boy...The man who's running the Hughes

"Grand Jury"—which was conducted in secrecy—ignores it, as is true in all Mafia cases. It will disappear into the selected Mafia pockets.

"The 'Hughes' case is complete," says the Justice Department. "Forget it."

Says Alioto: "All attorneys bribe and steal."

Says Gianelli (re: Brown's California water boondoggle): "All politicians steal."

Says Senator Hruska: "All political conventions are purchased by the Mafia."

Says Dita Beard's doctor in Denver: "The only heart trouble she has is a fear of testifying on that ITT memo."

Says another doctor, briefed by Justice for the Senate hearing (an AMA hero): "I say she's nuts. She didn't write the memo. It doesn't exist. I discredit her, and Jack Anderson. I speak for her and the holy ABA, the holy AMA, Justice and the Pope. I am under indictment for stealing from the aged in Medicare. So is my wife. We, however, like the ABA and the Pope, regulate ourselves. We declare ourselves innocent. And the ABA will 'fix it' so that we are."

***

A friend and his wife visit. PhD's. Education specialists. Back from five years in the Philippines, setting up schools for Mafia Marcos, sponsored by the Ford Foundation, the foundation which joined John Mitchell in putting a local clamp on this, via the "Alioto Crime Commission." The foundation which suddenly—recently—withdrew all backing of public broadcasting—the last remaining partially uncensored news source. Run by Body Count Bundy. Ford, the daughter of whom (Charlotte) originated the phone call that murdered Eugenie Niarchos.

In the Philippines—Mindanao—Catholic Bishops pay a group to murder Moslems (documents attached). Marcos loots the Archipelago. It is one of the 50 acknowledged Vatican-Mafia wars going on now around this world. (Start with Vietnam and Northern Ireland and count them yourself). These educators—deprived of news—read these papers, and departed for Nigeria.

The same Ford Foundation project is scheduled for Nigeria. Nigeria recently committed genocide on Biafra. Biafra is one huge pool of oil. Onassis now shares in those oil leases

The Ford Foundation is now buying—for the Mafia—countries all around the world. "Body-Count" Chappaquiddick McNamara is doing the same for Dickie's World Bank. Dickie's old Treasury Secretary Kennedy is doing the same for your Treasury Department, now run by Johnson's Connally, the noted Texas Maf going way back to Hoover's Del Mar racetrack deal. Dickie himself is trying to purchase China, but they said no. Chiang Ching has my stone and the history that goes with it. And Russia soon—likely—will have a stone, and a history as well.

Well, 37 countries bought my stones—and voted China in, and dope pushing Vatican Mafia Taiwan out of the United Nations. Kissinger was in Peking at vote time because of the phrase, "Chappaquiddick Big Dickie, Little Dickie and Alioto," that I quoted to CIA Neilson-Green. Six more countries switched, and voted against the U.S, because Kissinger was in Peking. That was enough to get the job done.

Asked this friend, "What's the name of your group?" There wasn't time to answer. But if you will examine anything that's happened since September 16, 1968, you can find Russian newsmen all around the U.S., smiling. They publicly state that they're watching the "political" trials: Daniel Ellsberg, (a friend of Nader's) for the Pentagon Papers; the Berrigans (friends of Mary Jo) for their Anti-Vatican-Mafia-Vietnam War activities; the Daley-Hanrahan murder of Hampton-Clark, even Angela Davis. They're probing the 1968 Nixon election (particularly the Onassis-"Hughes"-Maheu Nixon and Humphrey bribes), and the Onassis-"Hughes" Mafia Money Funnel.

A laity group is in full revolt for everything from money disclosure to the murder of Mary

---

empire is a member of the Mafia, but don't quote me..."—*Hoax*, p.305

Jo. Nader is dinging at General Motors and all corporate Mafia. Fellmeth is dinging at Congress, and FBI Turner and Shaw and Sullivan are dinging at Hoover. Gallinaro spits on Hoover, publicly. Fensturer, Charach and others (Weisberg, Marcki, Tung) have the assassinations blocked out.

Ex-CIA groups have some interesting plans. Hoover's FBI files, for instance—where total civilian surveillance occupies all of their time. Every Maf, they note, who was here, alien or not, when Hoover took office, is still here—and not on a hang rope, but instead, in Congress and on corporate boards.

Group? It's a "deal." Like Mitchell and Nixon and ITT. Like Mitchell and Nixon and Onassis'-"Hughes". Like Mitchell and Nixon and Chappaquiddick Teddy and Dyke Bridge Johnson. I get him off the cross—and I get the eternity job I want: hanging this cancer over there, in case I don't finish it here.

I don't have any problem communicating with Brezhnev or Mao. There, they shoot dope pushers in the back of the head. They don't have a dope problem. There—for a bribe—they confiscate all property. If it involves any officer of public trust, they hang him. They hang all Mafia. They don't have any bribery or any Mafia.

Noel Gayler—in disrepute—must now crawl through the hills of southern China with the CIA and find that mineral—or else. His new title? Commander of All Pacific Forces.

Said this friend's wife: "Interesting. We'll be watching to see what you do."

***

Mack is Attorney for the Bank of California, a two billion dollar conglomerate. When he suggested that I talk to Mitchell, he also asked me to let him know what he could do. I said, "I know exactly what to do. The question is, who for?"

"Watching." That's an interesting word. The "Watchers"—on the fence—are the most guilty of all. This is the apathy that rises from bed in the morning, and pays 41% of every paycheck to support that Onassis-Vatican-Mafia in its daily round-the-world murder. Except on Sunday, when it goes to church piously to worship the image there: a skinny man hanging on a cross, tortured, the original murder cover-up. And walks away smugly—as all do from Mary Jo's grave, with the message from the Pope: "We don't care if it was murder. We're satisfied."

All right. Apathy—on the fence, "watching"—goes first. That is the breeding ground of cancer. Without the 41% financing by them, and the giving of power by them, this cancer would be dead.

Is that you, who read this? Who daily masticate Onassis' crap and pay the 41% tribute to the Mafia? For years, this "group" has been "watching" you. "Who for?" That's what it's all about.

When you've read this you will look in a mirror, sometime, and say, "I'm not cancer. I don't breed cancer. What can I do about it, anyhow? I'm just one person—just one lone brave free American. Besides, I don't want any trouble. I'll just join the Chappaquiddick crowd and run in total secrecy. If the 'Big Bang' gets here—so what? The Pope tells me to meekly turn the other cheek. And where do you go from him—to God?" And you'll go back to your Mafia-owned TV.

You will not remember what you've just read. What one man did. Verified and sent out to "doctors" who use meat axes for scalpels and don't much care about the cancerous patient anyhow. If the missiles and "big bang" make it first, you won't even remember "why?" But when you get there, I'll be there to repeat it to you and assign you to your eternity Yo-Yo. That's my deal. I figure I've already eased my father's path—and I accept Chappaquiddick Dickie's presidential dictum for my own:

"Screw America. My family comes first."

***

These events are mushrooming fast. As noted, Irving's "Hughes" hoax case was quickly closed by Mafia Justice and Mafia Hoover's "deal". There will be no more mention of Irving's proof of Hughes's captivity and death. Or of the "Hughes" flight from Vegas because of Merryman's release of those papers, Merryman's murder, or Maheu's firing because he was suspected of leaking the "Hughes" "biography" to Irving. Then, Maheu's $50 million suit—payment for his part in the assassinations. And my calls that chased Onassis out of the Bahamas.

Just now: a series of news reports. (Remember: the Irving papers finally flushed out a phony "Hughes" voice in denial).

Maheu goes to court tomorrow demanding the physical presence of "Hughes" in court. (And Maheu has the most potent blackmail: bribes paid to Nixon, Humphrey, etc., in 1968, for instance—plus presidential protection as the assassin of JFK, Martin Luther King and Bobby).

The Democratic Mafia just announced an investigation into other major corporation bribes of Nixon, expanding the ITT bribe investigation. This means it must get into Onassis-"Hughes's" owned or controlled Corporations: General Motors, Lockheed, Hughes Tool, all of it. Congress itself could not avoid demanding the physical presence of Hughes—soon, maybe tomorrow. The "body" of "Hughes" has become prominent. How does Onassis put it out of reach?

Onassis' "Hughes's" Rosemont Corporation blocked all publication about "Hughes." Prosecuted Irving. Made a "deal." But they allowed one of their own—Eaton—to get out a magazine story—undenied, unchallenged, unprosecuted—which was based around one point only: that Hughes has specified that upon his death, he is to be immediately placed in a cryogenically sealed capsule and deep-frozen, in order to be brought back to life a hundred years from now, so that he can resume control of his "empire."[44] No one could tamper with that capsule for the next hundred years. (That's even better than Warren's 75-year secrecy lid on JFK). There is no cryogenics firm in Nicaragua. The only ones I know of are in the United States.

Tonight, Mafia dictator Somoza of Nicaragua announced "Hughes's" departure for the United States. A few of Onassis's Mafia aides remain to clean up Nicaraguan affairs and affirm the departure of "Hughes".

No one can predict the future. Right? (Unless he knows the delineating line direction from the past.) And so it is that "Hughes" will "die" soon—in brave, free, Mafia America—and will be immediately cryogenically sealed into his time capsule.

But this paper will complicate that. By a 24-hour watch on the cryogenic joints (there aren't many)—and a little trick with the real, already dead (April 16, 1971), recovered body of Howard Hughes—now on ice, elsewhere.

Said FBI Strike Force Team Ed Sullivan and his partner to me: "You have just been through the biggest con game in history."

Said Clifford Irving's Art Forgery hoaxer De Hory: "Hughes has been dead for nearly a year."

Said Irving: "He's dead, but I made a deal. Nixon won't let me talk."

Said Jimmy The Greek: "He's dead. And it's the biggest conspiracy in history. The government is in it up to its ass. I want to go somewhere else. This isn't safe."

Tomorrow we go out to Cypress Lawn to inter my father's remains. He knew of the Hughes cryogenic bit a year ago.

What'll you bet that the body that goes into that capsule—they'll try—won't be that of Merryman?

---

[44] In *Ladies' Home Journal*, February 1972.

March 18, 1972: Cypress Lawn

A few days ago I went out to Cypress Lawn on the matter of my father's interment.

In August 1, 1969, two weeks after Chappaquiddick (and a half hour before I told him the answers to Chappaquiddick), I asked Greenagel, "What's Dick Carlson doing about that Alioto hit-run ten and a half months ago, on my car, that elected Nixon?"

Said he: "He started in October, 1968, with your handful of papers, and now he has volumes to release. Five reporters are working on it."

I assumed he meant they were working on the hit-run, the Mafia Election Process, the Howard Hughes Mafia Money Funnel of Onassis, and the new thing: Chappaquiddick.

And I was shocked to learn, several weeks later, that on Election Day, 1968, Nixon had put a clamp on everything. Instead, he released raw files on Alioto's Mafia connections for Carlson to copy into his article for *Look*: "The Alioto Mafia Web," and raw Treasury files for a prosecution of Alioto on bribery charges in Washington.

Said I: "What's Mitchell been doing about it?"

"He's been working hard," said Greenagel. "And everywhere those reporters go, Justice has been there ahead of them—and the FBI, and the CIA."

That fit, then, since local papers were saying that every phone in the Hall of Justice was tapped and that all the local political chiefs were making their calls from phone booths—and those too were tapped.

(I was shocked again, several weeks later, when Lello offered me a bribe that started with a million and wound up with, "What do you want?" I learned then that those Justice, FBI, and CIA people had been around all right—but only for the burying of evidence, disappearance of witnesses, and discrediting of anything they could.)

Greenagel said: "What have you turned up?"

Then I told him the solution to Chappaquiddick—and he went silent. So did everybody else

The next day I handed Mack a written summary of Chappaquiddick, and elaborated on it verbally. I offered Mitchell the proceeds—for Justice—from million dollar suits. Mack went pale and silent, and refused to assist in furnishing any Attorneys. The total block was on.

Ten days later, I went back to Greenagel, with the first volume of the whole history.

I told him, "If you like these papers, act on them, and arrest them all. If not, call me and I'll come and get them."

While I was waiting in his outer office, a man came out and stared at me for a while.

That man, I was later to see in the paper, was James Browning ("Peek-a-Boo," I call him). He became the U.S. Attorney here on the following February 1, 1970, on the same day that Alioto transferred Police Chief Cahill to the job of Security Guard at the Telephone Company, in order to sit on the California end of the Chappaquiddick phone calls—from Tunney to Teddy, and from Teddy to Alioto.

At the same time, I took some of my gemstones to Mack for Nixon—and the gift of a heart-shaped sapphire for Mrs. Nixon.

Two weeks later I knew what that action was (nothing), and I started selling gemstones to foreigners—with histories—and purchasing such things as the Onassis diary.

Another volume went to Greenagel (and others) on January 31, 1970, one day before Browning took over as U.S. Attorney. And another volume went to Greenagel on April 29, 1970—the day after Judge Janet Aitken refused to let me describe these matters in court, under oath.

That was the day Dickie issued the order to invade Cambodia.

Judge Janet Aitken dismissed the case. She had already mailed my bail money back to me on the day before the hearing. At the time she was running for election to a higher court. She lost, but later she was made an Assistant U.S. Attorney under Browning. Mack was her campaign manager. Mack had told me on August 1, 1969, that Aitken and Browning were the two between whom Nixon would choose the new U.S. Attorney.

***

Let's talk about the connection to Taiwanese-Laotian heroin. Just after Chappaquiddick, I had told Mack that 80% of the world's supply came from Laos—the Golden Triangle, not Turkey, which always has been a joint Mafia-Justice decoy

This heroin is one of the major keys to the Vietnam War. Other commercial elements enter along with the heroin—oil, for instance.

These account for the interest of Onassis and the U.S. government.

The second major party to the Vietnam deal is the Vatican—as in Cardinal Spellman's "Holy Crusade." Diem was set up as the President of South Vietnam, while his brother, Archbishop Thuc, was the Roman Catholic prelate of South Vietnam. Diem's other brother, Nhu, barbecued the Buddhists.

JFK and Bobby's mild objection to the raw nature of the large-scale dope running (via CIA Air America to Taiwan; from Chiang Kai Shek to Tommy "The Cork" Corcoran, and on into the Onassis-"Hughes" Mafia Money Funnel; then, the money laundered by Florida and New York Banks through Onassis's Swiss Bank, and back again, to purchase all public officials, starting with President Nixon and other contenders on down). The raw nature of the 10% Catholic Mandarin persecution of the Buddhists—and then their overthrow of Diem—was the motive for their murders. (Tommy Corcoran was Roosevelt's advisor and one of the Kennedys' closest business partners.)

Mary Jo uncovered this fact in Los Angeles, in Bobby's files after his death. She confirmed it while working in Jersey City for convicted Democratic Maf Mayor Whelan—just before she went to Chappaquiddick, boiling. All right.

There was world publicity about any heroin arrest connected with Turkey. For instance, the Turkish Senator caught a week ago at Marseilles with $10 million worth. The story made headlines—even in San Francisco. And early this year, there were banner headlines about the biggest heroin catch in history—in Marseilles, $500 million worth—an accidental catch by two honest cops. Turkish stuff. The world of dope prosecutors were deliberately decoyed to Marseilles and Turkey. With complete cooperation of U.S. Government leaders. (Now, who would that be?)

Just after Chappaquiddick, to blackmail silence about the murder of Mary Jo, Senator Tunney, the Chappaquiddick murder accessory, punched Dickie: "Nixon is pushing control of Indo-China. He will never leave—in order to keep open the opium routes."

And as Dickie stepped off the plane from his round-the-world trip, he shook hands with a waiting Teddy—fresh from the Chappaquiddick cover-up inquests.

It was a bargain. A deal. Of the Mafia, by the Mafia, for the Mafia. Omerta.

When the Pentagon Papers hit, Senator Gravel punched Nixon. He cried, "The complete dishonor of the United States pushing heroin along with the lowest Indo-Chinese—and fighting a war to sustain their joint heroin venture—sickens me."

Gravel was censured by the Senate, and a lid went on him.

Ellsberg has dropped from sight. The Legal Mafia—headed by Mitchell—has him buried.

The bribery of Nixon and Mitchell was a prosecution pushed by the Chappaquiddick murder twins, Teddy and Tunney, leading to massive lying denials by Mitchell and Nixon. It follows the same pattern of massive Mafia blackmail used to cover up the Alioto hit-run that elected

Nixon and exposed the Mafia election process, Chappaquiddick, the Onassis-"Hughes" Mafia Money Funnel, and various assassinations. Pick a few: JFK, Martin Luther King, Bobby, Yablonski, Eugenie Niarchos, John Tunney's sister's husband, Newsom's nieces—and a host of others.

It's all the same group and the same pattern. Dickie jumped in—eagerly—in 1957: "Screw America," with his first bribe from Onassis (that "inexplicable" $205,000 non-repayable, unsecured "loan" to Dickie's brother, Donald Nixon, for Donald's failing "Nixonburger" restaurant in Whittier, California—which promptly failed.) The $205,000 went into the Nixon family bank account. In "gratitude", Dickie Nixon then helped Onassis set up his wonderful tax-free money-laundering funnel, the "Hughes Medical Research Foundation."

Onassis and the Pope pushed JFK into the dope-running business in Vietnam. But a huge group had already been in it for all the years that J. Edgar Hoover has been sitting on the lid. Hoover grew up in the business, with Joseph P. Kennedy, Roosevelt, Tommy Corcoran and Onassis.

The takeover of "Hughes" was a minor matter for such a massive cancerous group. The hyping of a nation was equally easy. Heroin for many; clobbered apathy and bribes for most. Shit for the rest.

All right. Back to Alioto's San Francisco. U.S. Attorney James Browning's town. Assistant U.S. Attorney Janet Aitken's town. (She took U.S. Attorney Metzger's place. He had been convicted—and released—for running dope. The legal Mafia got him off, and today he is—yes: a leading Attorney.)

(Or was it Ladar's place? He was in charge of the Criminal Division for the U.S. Attorney's office. He covered up a gang rape by some friends of his, and, when caught in that one fix, resigned. The legal Mafia got him off, and today he is—yes, again: a leading Attorney).

16 The $6 Billion Heroin Bust, September 15, 1971

Last year. One month before the U.N. vote that ousted dope-pushing Taiwan out of the U.N., and voted China in. Don Warner drove a semi-truck from the San Francisco docks—U.S. President Lines—to importer Harry Yee, on Lombard Street, in San Francisco. Don had FBI clearance. He had been delivering these truck loads of "china" for eight months.

At the Yee warehouses, there was a gigantic FBI, Secret Service, Justice, Customs raid. Inspectors snapped the "dishes" in half. They were made of sugar, opium and heroin, mixed. They had come from Japan.

The heroin and opium had come from the Golden Triangle, on CIA Air America planes—rented by the CIA base at Long Chang in Laos (the base is still there), to the Air America base in Taiwan. From there it was shipped to Japan, where it was pressed into dishes, carefully packed, and delivered via U.S. President Lines to San Francisco.

On the dock, it was loaded onto Don Warner's truck. Don delivered it to respected San Francisco Chinatown Civic Leader, Taiwanese Chinese Harry Yee. The loot from the sale of the dope was to go through Tommy "The Cork" Corcoran and the "Hughes" tax-free Medical Research Foundation (for which Dickie had arranged the tax-free status), which owns most of the "Hughes" empire—tax-free, to various Florida banks (Miami National, Citibank, NYL, for instance).

From there, it would go to Onassis's Swiss banks for washing. And then it would reappear—freshly "laundered"—"clean"—through the "Hughes" tax-free Medical Research Foundation, to purchase all public officials—from Nixon, here, to dictators everywhere around the globe (the CIA aids in this). And as much of the U.S. and World economy as rigged stock purchases will buy.

Lockheed, for instance, which recently received a U.S. guaranteed government loan; and General Motors, from whence came Body Count McNamara, and the $500,000 bribe to Nader which "encouraged" him to get off Teddy's ass and stick to bum deodorants.

Twenty-six years of notes had been kept on the Laotian Golden Triangle producer. Ten years, on the Air America CIA supply connection in Taiwan, and six years on the Japanese end. They had known of dope-smuggling Harry Yee for twenty-five years.

But this time, there was a hitch. Some of the CIA and FBI people in on the raid had seen friends hooked on this shit—and suddenly sickened. They revolted, and forced this actual raid—seizing the right timing (as I did with Neilson-Green, just before the critical U.N. vote on ousting dope pushing Taiwan).

This was the biggest dope haul in history—from Laos. Six billion dollars worth.

One of the dissidents—the chemist who went through the sheds to estimate the quality and the value—announced this, publicly, and in a loud voice, to Don, and to 25 other teamsters who had gathered there. He deliberately dwelt on the dope route. (What he did was to "be careless" about "secret information," just as my "carelessness" in getting these papers to Nader resulted in their turning up in Moscow and Peking). He also stressed that it was a mix of opium and heroin.

Those Teamsters walked away knowing many things:

The source of the biggest known dope haul in history: the Golden Triangle, in CIA's Laos (not Turkey)—where the Vietnam war , started by Onassis-Kennedy and Vatican Spellman-Thuc, and continued by Johnson-Nixon, still rages, and the CIA there now ranges 200 miles into China searching for a new thing—a mineral;

The existence of a heroin refinery in the U.S. (the mix of opium in the haul), probably in Alioto's San Francisco, where the same group ran illegal booze at the same time Onassis and Joseph P. Kennedy were bringing illegal booze and opium into Boston in 1932. That was the original

blackmail and treason that captured Roosevelt, Churchill, Hoover and Tommy Corcoran, Roosevelt's advisor, Kennedy's advisor, and permanent "legal counsel" to the Soongs.

Madame Soong is Chiang Kai Shek's wife, and it is the remnants of Chiang's Kuomintang in the Golden Triangle who initiate 80% of the world's supply of heroin. They were also one of Maheu's clients after he quit the FBI in 1948 (others being Niarchos and Onassis), and before he took on the CIA-paid job of assassinating Castro in 1961. That was just before he went to work for Onassis in assassinating JFK, Martin Luther King and Bobby. Today he is suing Onassis for $50 million for performance of these functions.

(Madame Nhu—Diem's brother's wife—the "Dragon Lady"—is only a minor CIA Air America drug pusher, compared to Chiang.)

Anyhow, the original booze-and-opium deal, with its associated blackmail and treason, captured Roosevelt and Churchill to such an extent that World War II—arranged partially by Joseph P. Kennedy and Onassis (check Churchill's part of the just-released "25 year secrecy" English papers)—became a "blot out" necessity.

By now you probably realize why it is that Fatima #3 is a blot-out necessity of this monstrous group. For many reasons: the expose of the Vatican's part in the cover-up of Christ; Mary Jo Kopechne; World War II (the Deputy of Christ at Auschwitz); assassinations; the murder of my father—and the parallel of the other Mafia branch, MMORDIS. And that includes everything from the Onassis-"Hughes" Mafia Money Funnel, and everybody's blackmail from Hoover, going both ways. And why it is that the other two-thirds of the world, now aware of this, finds an equal urgency. And there we are—nose to nose with missiles.

Both sides know the answer is the killing of the cancer. This side—the pure cancer side—won't kill itself. The other side might do it for us. But because of other elements there is a hesitation. And the great bulk of America sits in Mafia shit up to the snorkel—in total apathy—without a spine. Brave, free Mafia Americans: votes stolen, economy stolen, pride, honor, everything gone—surrounded by murder, treason. bribery, anything—the Onassis-"Hughes Mafia Money Funnel Way of Life—and wait for they know not what.

I do.

All right. So those teamsters learned something on September 15, 1971. How did the press and legal Mafia cover that up? Easy. They couldn't have the Taiwan-Vietnam dope thing exposed, with the entire Vatican and U.S. hierarchy fighting desperately to keep Heroin Taiwan. And the U.N. vote only a month away. Reagan, Agnew, Connally, Nixon—all were poised for support trips to Taiwan. Buckley, Alsop, and other Vatican mouths were all poised to destroy the U.N.

So—in the press—it only appeared in the back pages: a small article on the raid, with a relatively small local value: $7 million, I think, instead of SIX BILLION DOLLARS.

Don Warner and the Teamsters—and the CIA-FBI dissidents—were boiling. As with the Merrymans (caught between a rock and a hard place), some of them contacted me.

When the case came to court, it was Peek-A-Boo James Browning, Greenagel's boy; that is, U.S. Attorney Browning. His Assistant U.S. Attorney was none other than Janet Aitken, who, in total treason, had kept the lid on me—and the entire history—in her courtroom, a year earlier, about the hit-and-run, on April 28, 1970. Dickie—confident of using part of this laundered drug money for his re-election—at that same hour, decided to invade Cambodia.

But they hadn't counted on this sudden CIA-FBI defection. So the case was heard in a closed court, a secret one. Only witnesses were allowed in; it was a "closed" decision—and nothing more was heard about Harry Yee.

Greenagel's Browning, Mack's Aitken, Carlson's "Mafia Web", Best (Nixon's campaign manager), Nolan (the Hearst Mafia columnist)—all were present in that courtroom to keep the lid on Six Billion Dollars worth of drugs from Taiwan and Laos. And three months later, the same group

sponsored banner headlines about a $500 million drug bust—"from Turkey". They called it "the biggest dope haul in history."

I explained to some of the dissidents (CIA, FBI) and some of the teamsters why these things happened; the entire history, in fact. I'm a bit careless, too. In fact, I don't give a damn about anything. Except for killing cancer. I've already arranged for that: total. Including the apathy that breeds it.

While waiting, I jab harpoons just to prime the background for a symphony—a Mafia chorus. Here or there.

And now you can understand why it was that two weeks after that $6 billion Yee opium raid, when I explained to CIA Neilson-Green about "Chappaquiddick Big Dickie, Little Dickie and Alioto," Onassis-"Hughes", the gemstone-and-history sales to foreign embassies, the Nader assassination "plot", the U.N. vote, the fact that there is no difference between Mafia, CIA, and FBI, and how "IBM", Robert A. Maheu, arranged for all the assassinations—and on and on—why it was that they paled, and meekly crawled, and left town.

And why Nader canceled his appearance, and all those funny phone calls. And why a hundred FBI—count 'em—combed the town "to arrest a few bookies" on that day—to prevent any of the "Mary Jo Kopechne Public Interest Research Groups" from contacting anybody.

And why the hard core Mafia moved in, en masse, to take over the Association of California Consumers and kill any political foundation of consumers. And why Sylvia Siegal called Ralph Nader "Shit."

Read the description of those events again. It'll help you to understand why Dickie gave Taiwan back to China on his recent trip.

"World Peace," he says. His only concern is covering up and keeping the lid on. That's what Hoover is doing, too. And all of them.

There is no Congress at all. No government. Only a total squabble over who bribed who. Or everybody running for re-election. Or everybody blackmailing everybody else. Teddy and Tunney, Nixon and Mitchell—and on and on. It's a Mafia Shit Pit.

Said a man from Hoover to me recently: "What if we produce Howard Hughes? Would that satisfy you?"

Said I: "He died of heroin on September 16, 1971, on Skorpios. Onassis's island. Buried at sea. Friends of mine recovered the body. They identified the dentures. You have a problem."

He left, angry.

But they tried, anyhow. There was a disembodied voice, and a fake (a double) in Nicaragua. That will fail too.

Brezhnev and Mao have read these papers. Dickie is crawling to China and Russia because of these papers. My father was murdered because of these things. The rest of the family is on the line.

And I wonder about families.

The non-Mafia half of the world is nervous.

The Onassis-"Hughes" Mafia Money Funnel group is nervous too. The Vatican? Very nervous. Too many tablets are turning up. Bishops with Mary Jo's picture in their tunics refused to ratify the Pope's constitution declaring himself to be God.

And I'm nervous too. I'm curious about my own family. I didn't ask for this, but I've made arrangements for its flushing. All of it—including the apathy, or fear, that breeds it. And all the watchers on the fence. We'll see.

17 March 20-April 9, 1972: Letters to Mother

Mother:

Every member of the Kimball family and the Roberts family is entitled to read these papers. This is the family being murdered. This copy of these papers comes back with you. Nixon, Mitchell, Kennedy, and all the rest who received copies, burned them.

I am interested in the reaction of each reader. If someone wants a copy, there are Xerox machines. My Xerox bill is already in the thousands. The price of three and a half years of terror on you and my father is incalculable.

None of our American legal institutions have appeared to take any depositions. These papers had to get out another way. You are aware of the (futile) destruction of evidence, and the disappearance of witnesses.

Copies, and documentary evidence, are scattered in many places. I'm available. So are others. We can direct them to the evidence.

The nuclear noose around the non-Mafia world has been reversed somewhat. A first strike, coming in, would be justified. This is what I call "the biggest gun in the world." Pointed at the Mafia. And on my shoulder. Object: kill the cancer—any way you have to.

That gun is why I am still alive, and why I jam harpoons up the asses on the graves of Mary Jo and my father and millions more, with impunity. And why they run and hide and keep the silent pressure on, and lie so openly that even the censored public today can openly see the hypocrisy.

They admitted it again, today: "The greatest issue in 1972 will be the credibility of the U.S. Government," said a government spokesman.

Relax, Mother. Let this letter answer any critic. If there are any brave, free Americans out there, it will show.

And here's a late-nite bulletin for you to read on the plane, along with the news in your paper:

McCone was the head of the CIA at the time of the Diem-Kennedy double murders, and the one who hired Maheu to assassinate Castro in 1961. McCone was the subject of my talks with the Merrymans last June, 1971 (the "Hughes" nursemaid bit) in the Onassis-owned building, at 1170 Sacramento Street, San Francisco.

McCone was the target of my Christmas 62-carat sapphire gift, with history, to the ITT wife (Elizabeth Dale). McCone is a director of ITT. (That was his reward. Maheu wants $50 million more—in cash—for the various assassinations he supervised: JFK, RFK, MLK, etc.)

McCone still rules the CIA. He called in William Broe—Director of Latin American Clandestine Services (CIA)—and arranged for economic chaos in Chile, through ITT, General Motors, Ford, and Bank of America. It was simple to do: "Shut off their money."

Then he attempted to instigate armed revolt in Chile. Object? To beat Allende in the local elections.

Working together with the Vatican, McCone has six other Latin American countries on the murder block. He did accomplish Vietnam, and another batch—but he was hurt deeply by the Taiwan loss.

Well, Mother, his affairs are finally getting out into the sunlight. It's all part of the same harpoon.

Senator Cranston says (now, finally, sensing the wind direction): "The Government is run by the FBI, monitored by the CIA, and paid for by the ITT."

That harpoon is still working its way in. It was designed to go from belly button to asshole, Mafia style. More are on the way.

The U.S. refused to join a U.N. committee to investigate the internal affairs of any country whose internal affairs might lead to war. That, of course, would have meant an investigation of itself. And of everything you have read in here.

The international group who represent me have noted these things. And they tell me, "You can have it all."

Have a beautiful vacation. And let these written words do your talking. They are indeed potent.

Love,

Bruce P. Roberts

March 27: Lake Tahoe, Jack Anderson, John McCone

Mother,

I'm delighted you enjoyed your trip. Mine was beautiful too.

At Tahoe with me was Jack Anderson (the one who, with Nader, produced the ITT memos and the one about the CIA-Mafia-Chile connection. And also about McCone, Louise Merryman's friend, who was CIA Director at the time of Vietnam and the dual Diem-Kennedy murders).

Also present was one of the first firemen on the scene of the Pelosi daughters' barbecue fire. Newsom's nieces, remember? Murder. Two girls, ages six and eight, plus their old Japanese nurse.

He said, "There was still the smell of gasoline from the basement. It was like a Molotov cocktail. The basement was full of fumes. and there was a down-draft that ensured a straight up—total—barbecue."

Following Jack Anderson around in Tahoe were a contingent of CIA creeps and Mafia characters of all types. They are really worried.

I am now going out to mail this and start fixing my clobbered car.

You have the most powerful papers in the world in your possession. I want to know what happens to them. Let me know.

Say hello to everybody.

Love, Bruce.

March 30: Car into Molotov Cocktail #1; Rand Institute's "Project Star"

Mother,

I'm delighted to know you're enjoying your trip.

I'm still working on the car. Lots of funny things were wrong.

Lots of other things have been going on since my Tahoe trip.

Said Diehl, of the Nevada Gambling Commission, "We won't transfer any 'Hughes' casino gambling license until his body appears before us. I get the feeling we're involved in some kind of a game. And I don't know what the objects of the game are. We now know that all the "Hughes" signatures were a fraud. The same experts who 'verified' Irving's false signatures were the ones who

'verified' the ones we received."

(He knows the whole bit, but he's getting nervous.)

Greenspun, of the *Las Vegas Sun*, says: "Meyer Lansky is the world's top criminal." He knows that Lansky is just the fall guy scheduled to be indicted for the $35 million Las Vegas skim—most of which went to Nixon, Humphrey, Larry O'Brien and a batch of Senators and Congressmen. Pure purchase.

"Hughes" (Onassis) is now suing John Meier—for $8 million—for the mining claim swindle in Las Vegas, for which Maheu fired him.

Meier is now running for Senator from New Mexico. His opponent is Senator Montoya, who—with Senator Brewster—carried $100,000 bribe cash suitcases to President Johnson, from Hoffa, to keep himself out of prison. Despite evidential proof of these $100,000 cash bribes, the indictments against both of the Senators were dismissed. It seems they have "Congressional Immunity."

New York Times headlines:

"ITT hires Intertel" ("Hughes's" security guards), "to discredit Dita Beard."

"Nixon hires Intertel to discredit Jack Anderson."

"Intertel," (composed of ex-Justice officials) "expands 'Hughes' protection from Bahamas and Las Vegas to Nicaragua and Vancouver."

"FBI Declares Dita Beard Memo Not a Fraud."

And there it is: the two gangs at war.

James Reston says, in the *New York Times*: "A vast deception has been perpetrated on the American people. Diem, for instance, was pulled out of Mary Knoll Seminary in New Jersey (a Kennedy/Cushing Sanctuary) and put in place as Premier of South Vietnam."

I've been busy. The actions of the CIA (McCone) and ITT (also McCone) have now been exposed in Chile, Colombia, and Vietnam.

Steve Ambrose reports that Truman started Fatima #2, with Greece (in 1947) as the excuse; it was a "Holy Crusade." This was followed by Korea, and Truman knew in advance of the Chinese attack. Ambrose presents files showing that Truman ordered the 38th Parallel crossing—not MacArthur. Other files: "Six days before U-2 planes discovered the Cuban Missiles, President Dorticos of Cuba offered to remove them. JFK refused the offer, and instead took us to the brink of war."

And: "Kennedy was the prime initiator of the military effort in Vietnam—using Diem as his cover."

Joseph Kraft, a dissident with Dickie in Peking, squeezed off a shot. He writes, "The Republican jitters over ITT are not because they are so far wrong there, but because of the 'cover-up of a deeper fix'."

Bribery is treason, but the Mafia has declared it legal—and, for an extra hedge, has canceled the death penalty on everything: treason, murder or conspiracy.

This was illustrated by Alioto in Vancouver. He didn't do anything that every Mafia public official doesn't do.

In Alioto's first big anti-trust trial, Goldwyn, the judge, "died" in the middle of the trial—and Alioto won the case. In Vancouver, the judge also "died" in the middle of the trial. Alioto was acquitted, and was congratulated by a jury of apathy.

Here, the Newsom nieces "died" in the middle of Alioto's *Look* Mafia trial, and Alioto won his case. The federal judge for Alioto's criminal trial went to the hospital yesterday, and the case was

delayed.

What do you think the chances of survival are for whatever judge conducts that case? Not that it makes much difference, since Alioto's prior acquittal—on the same charges—renders the case worthless.

And all of these trials, based on raw Justice files about Alioto's Mafia connections and his "accepted bribery" charges—are only to "cover up the deeper fix": the hit-run that elected Nixon, exposed the Mafia election process, caused Chappaquiddick, uncovered Onassis' "Howard Hughes," and placed everything else in perspective: Vietnam, Korea, World War II, and so on.

Said Alioto of the case: "It is pure political venom by Mitchell. Justice even wanted a sealed verdict. They knew they had no case."

He was correct. Bribery, treason, murder—it was all these things. But these things are now legal. Mafia law says this.

In Santa Monica, the Rand Corporation now rivals Hoover and the CIA for blackmail files. Ellsberg got away with publishing the Pentagon Papers. The harsh 150 years in prison they want to give him—for telling the truth—is because of a greater fear.

In that Rand Corporation building at the beach is one file, rated "higher than top secret": "Project Star." Rand can't destroy it—just as they couldn't destroy the Pentagon Papers—because they need it for blackmail purposes. And yet they cannot release it either. "Project Star" is a study of the JFK assassination.

Most of that is out now, anyway. Yesterday, to tighten security even further, Dickie named Rice, a 31-year-old super-guard, as head of Rand. His job? Sit on the lid of that file—just as Cahill sits on the Phone Company's Chappaquiddick call records here, and Loeb, in New Hampshire, sits on the eastern end (his reward was getting Hoffa out of prison). They sit on empty nests, and they know it. And that is why murder is their only out. And why the non-Mafia half is quietly planning the same thing—in self defense. They know these things too.

Any of these things—the Alioto hit-run, Chappaquiddick, "Hughes," JFK, Bobby, 1932, if exposed to public view, would hang them all. That is why, as the Media's FBI files revealed, 95% of all FBI, CIA, Justice, etc., surveillance is of the public. It's all a gigantic lid. Designed to keep the public from finding out anything about what is going on. And if they do find out, from letting other people know about it. And it is why all the Maf are still here, running things.

Attorney William G. Thompson, one of Sacco and Vanzetti's lawyers, states: "A government that has come to honor its own secrets more than the lives of its citizens has become a tyranny."

Political philosophy? Dickie, 1957, on his Onassis bribe: "My family comes first."

Teddy: "I can live with it." (His murder of Mary Jo.) These are the 1972 Mafia-selected Presidential candidates. Choose one.

Papal philosophy? "Just sign this constitution declaring me to be God."

I spent the last three days out on a public street, under my car, scraping off sealing wax and carbon and playing with parts. Today some guy said he'd been watching me for three days, and where was all my help?

I told him Alioto had clobbered my car, and neither he nor the insurance companies would help me, so I asked Nixon and Mitchell to help. But they wouldn't help either, and they told everybody else not to, and I was surprised he hadn't heard.

He said, "Screw 'em. I'll be here to help you tomorrow. I feel sorry for you. You could get yourself killed with all this traffic along here."

So I explained that I wasn't concerned over a local killing; I had made arrangements to take everything along with me—and wasn't he a bit leery of being seen with me?

"Not a bit," he said. "I figure missiles could be here any hour. And I don't give a shit anyway. There's nothing here worth defending. I was a marine, but when I read the papers these days I'm pulling for the Viet Cong to wipe us out."

I smiled, mother, for the first time in months. Here he was, talking to the man with a grenade up everybody's ass—and he's sorry for me, he's gonna keep me from getting killed.

So much for my days. Nights are for harpoons. I'll tell you about them after they've sunk in up to the hilt.

I'll send this as soon as I hear from you. And remember: anything I put in writing is not secret. I don't care who reads it.

Only the Mafia keeps a lid on the truth. Only apathetic crud does nothing with it. And lets the murders roll on.

Coming back from Tahoe, Carmen[45] said: "You be sure to tell your mother to relax and enjoy herself."

So—relax and enjoy yourself.

April 1: Car into Molotov Cocktail #2

Mother,

I received your card today and am enclosing another check for you. I checked with the stranger who decided to help me fix my car (he's a mechanic), and he said, "This really stinks. I'm going through this whole car and see what else we can find."

In the distributor I found that the hot wire plug-in (from the battery, to provide electricity to the distributor) had been cut through half way, causing a short—an electric spark. The distributor neck had been cracked. (Marks from a screwdriver, inside, used as a wedge to crack it, are visible). This allowed a constant spark from the distributor to be exposed, through the crack, to any gasoline, or fumes from the carburetor six inches away. It was not enough to cause the distributor to stop working; the object was the exposed spark.

Then the plug-in wire had been sealed in (with sealing wax). Some type of acid was then poured in the top of the neck, and it ate partly through the bakelite neck. This plug-in was part of an insert in the hot line. At the other end of the insert was another plug-in.

When inspecting, to see if the distributor was getting electricity, since I couldn't get the "sealed in" insert out, I always checked the other plug-in, and it always showed plenty of spark.

In the carburetor, the lid had been removed. There are two outlets for the incoming gas, into each side of the carburetor—about the diameter of a pencil. The carburetor pump side was completely clear, and functioning. The other side had been plugged solid with sealing wax.

When the sealing wax was poured in, hot, on heated metal, the hollow center sagged. In cooling a crack developed—and that crack is what has kept the car running ever since.

It wasn't planned that way. It was planned to be a solid seal, forcing all the gas to go through the other side—the pump side—and then gush out the flooding overflow holes and open pump plunger top hole.

Gas and gas fumes in the presence of a spark is known as a Molotov Cocktail. It is a flammable and explosive situation.

I checked with Carmen and we both agree. September 10, 1971 was when this "work" was done. That was just shortly after the Merrymans contacted me—McCone's friends, relatives of the "Hughes" dead nursemaid. The Pentagon Papers were out; Ted Charach had publicly named Bobby Kennedy's murderer (Thane Eugene Cesar), and I had gone to CBS over the matter. Christopher

---

[45] Bruce Roberts' girlfriend.

Beam and I were discussing "IBM", Iron Bob Maheu, and his series of assassinations, in the Mark Lobby.

It was also 5 days before the $6 billion Harry Yee San Francisco heroin raid, and 3 weeks before I pulled that Neilson-Green bit about "Chappaquiddick Big Dickie, Little Dickie and Alioto", Nader, "Hughes," Onassis, IBM, etc.

On that date we were at the end of an isolated mountain road, 9000 feet high, south of Tahoe. The car was in perfect condition all the way up, and it had had a recent tune-up. We were gone all day, over a mountain.

Late that afternoon we returned. The car started, just barely, and coughed and lurched down the 25-mile grade to Tahoe—the nearest civilization.

Five miles from our camp it conked out completely. Half an hour later it started again—just barely. It was lurch and cough all the way back. I'm no mechanic, but when I checked the distributor I got spark. When I checked the gas jets in the carburetor, I got gas jets from the carburetor pump.

What had been planned was that the car be destroyed—by fire or explosion, or both—in an isolated place, where the "fixing" could be done without a witness. It was to appear natural—even to me. And had it occurred, I would have assumed it to be an accident. The object was the destruction of the car. Just bad luck.

Just as the barbecue murder of Newsom's nieces (Pelosi's daughters) during the Alioto trial was to warn everybody—Newsom, Pelosi, Judge Brown, Jury, Attorneys—by fire, rather than murder anybody. But murder did come out of that warning fire, accidentally. In Pelosi's case, the two little girls were not the target. Newsom was. The barbecued meat that turned up in the mortuary—two little girls and a nurse—was just bad luck.

And it is possible that injury or death could result from a car fire or explosion. In Tahoe, Chartrand—owner of Barney's Casino—got his in second gear forward, after reverse. That was so that the car would be somewhat away from the house. They only wanted to murder him. They didn't want to hurt the house. He was the target. As with the five hit-runs on my car, in succession, after the first one by Alioto's son.

Those "mechanics" that "fixed" my carburetor should have had me around. For 10 years in that lab, I played with sealing wax (and higher temperature epoxy mixtures) to hold my gemstones on dop sticks. I've tried wooden dops, metal dops, solid and tube type, and anything else I could think of. The center sag—and crack—of sealing wax in a hollow metal heated tube was a common sight for me. I recognized the shape of the crack in that sealing wax they daubed in my gas inlet tube. Wax keeps well in fluid. In air it deteriorates slowly, and crumbles eventually.

So there was no fire or explosion, as planned. What did happen, since, has been a succession of problems. Back carburetor pressure blew out a fuel pump. Misfires have plugged the cylinders. Slow starting burned out the starters and batteries. Malfunctioning ruined resistors in the coils. We still don't know what else is fouled up. But this is why the car conked out on us at the cemetery when we were there recently. And why the carburetor pump finally quit altogether, on the day before you left.

Yesterday the two Mafia-purchased presidential candidates announced that they would not campaign, in order to piously attend church in honor of the death of Christ. With them, in the pews, were their Secret Service guards. One million dollars a month is the cost of guarding their lives.

Today I had one volunteer—a stranger—keeping cars off my back. I wouldn't trade him for all of that million dollar a month Mafia shit.

"Screw 'em," says he, as he fingers that sealing wax glob.

"Screw 'em," say I, and buy more parts, and wonder how many millions Chappaquiddick Dickie spends daily protecting his life, and Teddy's, and how many millions Gayler blows daily in

his Pacific command—especially in heroin-source Vietnam.

They will all be in church tomorrow. Easter. So will Thieu, and Chiang Kai Shek, and Onassis, and the Pope.

I will be under my car—with a stranger working above. It's cool there, mother, out of the sun—and thoughts come through. I will put them into action tonight

Love, Bruce

Easter: Tacitus, Nero, Burning Rome; Eternal Christianity, Mafia Version

Mother,

Today—Easter—the image of a man hanging on a cross still hangs there.

One of the documents that escaped Papal destruction was a record by Tacitus, the Roman historian. He writes, in the first century, that Nero burned Rome in the year A.D. 64, partly to destroy all records of the crucifixion of Christ—by Roman command, through the Roman Procurator, Pontius Pilate—and to divert attention from the affair. Nero laid the blame for the fire on the followers of Christ—the group called Christians.

Today we see carbon copies of that: Mary Jo, Newsom's nieces, my car, Tunney's sister, Vietnam, and on and on.

Today, United Mine Workers' Boyle, convicted of giving labor bribes to politicians, fights back. Says he: "The law prohibits political candidates from taking illegal bribes."

He was referring to 1968—and that $30,000 bribe to Humphrey, and thousands more to congressmen.

Federal Judge Richey ordered, "Let's have no talk on that subject," and hung a heavy verdict on Boyle for mentioning it.

Which is Mafia? Boyle? Or Federal Judge Richey (who paid $50,000 for his own job)? Or Humphrey and the congressmen? Or all of them? Choose here: → { }.

Boyle drew on the Hoffa-Onassis murder group to hire the shotgunning of the Yablonski family.

ITT did the same thing. They gave $400,000 to Dickie and Mitchell, for "business expenses." There will be no "Boyle"-type prosecution of them. ITT participates in the murder of the world—using Onassis's- "Hughes" equipment—along with the rest of the Mafia handmaidens: Dickie, Teddy, and the Pope. CIA-ITT McCone is a murder expert.

Today, in San Francisco, Dennis—a local collector for the Irish Republican Army, at the Abbey, says sadly about Northern Ireland the same thing Bernadette Devlin says: "The problem always has been the churches—both of them—with their handmaidens. Onassis owns the shipyards."

Today, a $15 million suit for invasion of privacy, by an investigator, against a religious group, is patterned on Nader's General Motors suit. The article is in the *New York Times*, which printed the Joseph Llellyveld cover-up story of the Chappaquiddick phone calls.

Once more the Mafia press tries to rewrite dangerous history.

The *Times*: "The attorney, Paul D. Rheingold—a former Justice Department lawyer—filed a suit for Nader in 1970 against General Motors in a similar action which was settled out of court." (Nader's suit was filed in 1966, by attorney Speiser. It was the "Suit of the Century, " and was blocked by General Motors attorney Chappaquiddick Ted Sorenson until the end of the century. But it was suddenly settled by Sorenson and attorney Speiser four days after my Nader letter was made

public. This Onassis-Kennedy cash bribe of $457,000 was paid to Nader by attorney Speiser in Speiser's office.)

As with the omission of Merryman's name from the "Hughes" nursemaid list, after his "death," and the switched date of JFK's hot call to Jackie, on Onassis' yacht, it is easy to rewrite history if you own the press and the journalists.

Today, Senator Fulbright, after examining the Pentagon Papers, said: "The Vietnam war could have been avoided."

And U Thant, former boss of the U.N. said, "If the American public knew how the Vietnam War started, they would force their leaders to pull out everything tomorrow."

From the recently released 25-year secrecy, World War II British papers, a quote by Churchill: "Roosevelt and Kennedy rigged World War II; it could have been avoided."

World War II was Fatima #1. Fatima #2 was started immediately after, according to Fulbright, by Truman and Roosevelt's leftover Secretary of State Byrnes, with the Ho Chi Minh rebuke and the "hate commies" theme—followed by Greece and Korea.

Today, Vera Glacer reports massive secret Mafia bribes to the G.O.P. by Onassis and Pappas, in Washington. They were repaid by U.S. aid to Greece, and support of the Onassis-Pappas Greek Mafia hierarchy. Greece, where the body of Howard Hughes was laid to rest, on April 16, 1971.

Today, Jack Anderson reports a new Versailles Mafia World Summit last month. It was 1957 Apalachin all over again—desperately mapping Fatima #3, but this time, for the whole world—the whole ball of wax. Said Anderson: "Their discussions were to shape the policies and economics of 100 countries, owned by these multi-national, multi-billion dollar conglomerates. The boards of directors of all the big ones were there: ITT (CIA Double Diem-Kennedy murder), General Motors, Ford, Fiat, Oil, Steel, Chemical. Corporate nations with more wealth and power than most nations—all contriving to forward their corporate interests ahead of our national interest."

Today the Pope said: "The Silent Church should speak out." This, at Auschwitz, was the "Deputy of Christ." Today—by his own decree—this is God.

His group is one of the biggest stockholders in the world. He exiled a South American Cardinal who published documents indicating that the Pope's mother—Mrs. Montini—was Jewish, and that the Vatican has corporate connections to Free Masonry around the world.

How come the Pope hates the Jews? Is it because they are non-Vatican? Does he hate his mother? She's Jewish. Does he hate himself? He's half Jewish. Why is he ashamed of his corporate Free Masonry connections? Aren't they a secret swindling branch of the Versailles group, to which he belongs?

Incidentally, don't Free Masons attend the funerals of their members' families? My brother is a Mason. No Masons attended my father's funeral—and they know why he was murdered, and who murdered him. My brother wasn't there either. Ain't that odd? But then, he's a Mason. Right, mother? It was a little lonesome, wasn't it?

Today, McGovern spoke: "Nixon and the G.O.P. are owned, lock, stock and barrel, by big business." Had he substituted the word 'Mafia' for 'big business,' he would still be only half correct. After 'Nixon and the G.O.P.,' he would have to add himself and his Mafia Democratic group. He did add: "ITT did the same thing Boyle did. They won't be prosecuted." He knows everything that's in these writings. Who's holding his baby-faced tongue?

Well, mother, it's part of a day called Easter. Let's see; oh yes, it's some kind of a holiday, celebrating the murder of Christ. Isn't that it?

Carmen says to wish you a Happy Easter. Me too.

Love, Bruce

April 3: Car into Molotov Cocktail #3; Dickie's Peking Trip

Mother:

Today, I found magnetic steel filings deep in the carburetor. Gasoline in the oil. Apparently, this was done the night before you left—the night before the backfire. I think the short in the carburetor blew out the resistor coil, which cuts down the 12-volt starter current to 6 volts for the carburetor base, and allowed the full 12 volts to go through to the carburetor. That caused more and better sparks, which caused the backfire—fortunately, not enough for a major explosion because, at that time, the carburetor pump was out and the jets were plugged.

The gasoline in the oil partially freezes the motor and builds up compression. That car was meant to go on the day before you left. Possibly to delay or cancel your trip, with these papers.

Your husband went to the hospital—suddenly vomiting blood and acid—two days before Dickie left for Peking. He died while Dickie was in Peking. He did not die of emphysema. He died as a result of the blood and acid eruption.

He was a witness. Suppressed for three and a half years.

So are you. So am I. So is the car.

You have witnessed the run of the rabbits—including your other son. Jack Anderson, Nader, etc., are only safely nibbling at the edges. These papers, tapes, and documents provide positive, clear, evidential linkage to this entire cruddy worldwide Mafia affair. And the solution to the mess—without a nuclear blow-off. They are the most important papers in the world.

I have sent you four letters—plus the one dated Easter. Have you received them? Who read them? What was their reaction? Did you reach any of the Roberts family? Answer these questions.

There are only two sides to this thing: Mafia or Non-Mafia. In God's world, there is no place to run and hide. It's either kill it, or die with it.

Before Dickie took his Peking trip in February, your husband developed a problem. He died from a sudden bleeding belly. You held a cup holding the sudden vomit of blood and acid that, taken in by a pill, came up, burning throat passages, mouth, tongue, and lips. He died "naturally"—like Mary Jo and Newsom's nieces.

My car was scheduled to blow up "naturally" in the mountains on September 10, 1971, and again on the day before your trip. Those papers were already packed in your suitcase.

Dickie made the desperate Peking trip to try to buy the country, Mafia style. It didn't work. Mao has read those papers. Chiang Ching has one of my stones, with the history.

Next month, Dickie rigs his biggest Mafia purchase: Russia. When he makes that trip, something will happen here. I don't know what. The murdering Mafia CIA is devious.

Brezhnev already has those papers. Dickie knows that.

I know from your deliberate absence of comment about those papers that either you have deliberately left them in your suitcase, or that others, having read them, are already suppressing what they have read. When sad things happen, are you prepared to take the responsibility for permitting, say, murder to happen because of your suppression?

Your other son was. After months of pleading, he finally showed up—20 minutes after our father's death. He delivered a Mafia message to me: "Lay off the Mafia." He read the synopsis, commented that the Mafia had murdered two more that he knew about in the same way up where he was, and took off running, white-faced, four hours later.

He wouldn't stay for the funeral. Didn't leave a flower, card, message, or anything. That was a month and a half ago. Not one word, letter or call to me since. We did receive a Mafia message from his ex-wife, Thelma Golding—a message that upset both you and I—delivered in a sympathy

card.

Remember the Nixon hatchet men I notified of the funeral? Your husband's "friends"? Not one sent a card, flower, call, anything. Are you and your other son and the rest of the family prepared to take the responsibility for your own murders?

The pressure is on me, from 1957 Apalachin through the Versailles Mafia Summit last month. Despite that, I am winning. If you think not, look around and read the news. Which is good. Because if I don't win I'll knock this whole shit ball all the way out. I own the bat.

Would you rather cooperate with Chappaquiddick Dickie and Chappaquiddick Teddy (Presidential candidates), and Onassis and the Pope (King of the world and God), who collaborated in all of the past murders—and have your murder and the rest of the world's on the drawing board? Or with me?

Try this on for size. Say tomorrow every member of this family suddenly coughs up blood and acid. To whom could one survivor take his murder complaint? Alioto and his San Francisco police? Taiwan Reagan and his Bobby cover-up Attorney General Younger? President Chappaquiddick Dickie and Poucha Pond Attorney General Mitchell? Teddy and Tunney, who run the Senate Judiciary Committee? The Pope, or Dickie's Billy Graham? ITT and General Motors and Ford, fresh from the Versailles Summit? Any purchased judge? Or Mafia-appointed U.S. Attorney? Any church? Press Mafia? Legal Mafia? "Hughes", maybe—with TV control and the International Satellites? Jackie's hubby, Onassis? Either Mafia party? Any Senator? J. Mafia Hoover? Murderer CIA McCone, or Helms? Onassis-bribed Nader, to whom Mary Jo was running when Teddy murdered her? Jack Anderson, who has been lipping off around his muzzle for 25 years, and has accomplished zero?

Or to me?

Rochefort's quote: "Presidents fear one thing. An historian, who writes from knowledge—and affects the history he writes about. This man has the power to change the inscriptions on tombstones."

You get the idea. No major changes. Only the criminals on crosses. Only the criminal loot reshuffled. The Constitution is a good one. The Bible is a good book. Only the perversion, the cover-up, the murder, the treason and the conspiracy have to go.

Even our "enemies" agree to this. Both Russia and China. "It is," they say, "as we have always said—and as you prove now. America is Mafia owned. You have our support."

They have nuclear buttons, mother.

And I have a thing of my own. The bat. They'll use theirs, if necessary. And I'll use mine, regardless. Dickie knows this. So he crawls to Moscow next month, while Brezhnev and Mao ship massive supplies into Vietnam—publicly, so that Dickie will know. And it will render his crawl that much more publicly humiliating.

"The U.S. of Mafia is being picked apart," says TV news.

Yes. It's massive judo. Maf against Maf.

Today, Mafia Murderer Teddy, of the Senate Judiciary Committee, is publishing the fact that Murderer McCone's CIA-ITT—a $20 billion dollar conglomerate—paid no income taxes at all for the past five years. ITT—as Lanza did in 1957 at Apalachin—attended the Versailles Mafia Summit last month.

Your Social Security check, which I am enclosing, is $6 short. Carmen will have to borrow to pay her taxes this year. Proxmire's niece had $30 thousand stolen from her by San Francisco and state Inheritance Tax coffin roaches.

Whom do you, or Carmen or Proxmire's niece, complain to? Shall I repeat the list of those in power—along with an itemized list of their Mafia crimes?

Merryman was a "Hughes" nursemaid. Merryman and McCone were with the same firm: Bechtel, McCone, Parsons—the number one defense engineering contractor (missiles, etc., all over the world). McCones and Merrymans and Spellmans and Eckersleys and Onassises and Hugheses are all represented at 1170 Sacramento Street—Onassis's building, where Louise and Marie Elena Merryman took me.

Said a local Mafia politician who once threatened to blow my head off, long ago (now he pops up, friendly): "Before this is over, no-one with the tag 'Republican' or 'Democrat' will be able to be elected dog-catcher. Voting for any of these bastards is treason. You never voted, did you, Bobby? Have a drink. What are you doing now?"

Me: "Nothing." I thanked him for the drink and left.

Said Jimmy the Greek: "Christ! The mau-mau are knee deep here in Vegas. If we don't cool off that 'Hughes' bit, the whole world will be laughing at us."

He worked for assassin Maheu—that is, for "Hughes" and Onassis. He knows the whole bit and sits on the lid.

Dickie goes to Moscow on the "big con" next month. All press releases regarding "Hughes" have been blocked.

Like that Molotov cocktail—gas fumes and a spark—I am aware of a building, tight situation. Something will happen. Soon.

I'm delighted to hear about your swing in the sunshine. Just pass the papers out and note reactions, and keep on swinging. Read the newspapers and watch TV. Even through the Mafia media you will see how this mental judo works.

The Social Security Lump Sum Death Payment for your husband arrived today. It is ten dollars short. $245.10.

I called the funeral parlor and they, at least, are considerate. They are in no hurry. They wish you a pleasant trip, and you can take care of it whenever you get back.

Aside from the "minor" distractions mentioned, everything is fine here.

I will go out and crawl under my Molotov cocktail again tomorrow. If it stops raining.

Tonight I will slog through the rain to deliver one harpoon personally. That's the only recreation I get.

But that ain't bad. It works up an appetite.

Love, Bruce

P.S. The timing of World War III has been delayed. Witness Dickie's trembling crawls to China and Russia. Wouldn't it be something if, when Dickie gets to Moscow, Brezhnev introduces Dickie to a fellow American—me? This has been suggested. I am told the remains of "Hughes" are there. Maybe I could present them to Dickie at that time. Everybody is looking for "Howie." Aren't they?

April 5: Three Popes and the Cardinal, by Malachi Martin

Mother:

A "distinguished Jesuit scholar, Dr. Malachi Martin, former professor at the Pontifical Institute in Rome"—a dissident, who carries Mary Jo's picture in his tunic—brought out a new book: an authentic, searching study of the Vatican.

It's called *Three Popes and the Cardinal: The Church of Pius, John and Paul in its Encounter with Human History*. The Cardinal is Cardinal Bea, depicted as a tragic witness to the church's crumbling.

Some quotes: "Well before the year 2000 (this is 1972), there will no longer be a religious institution recognizable as the Roman Catholic Church."

"Pope Paul is dry of compassion, locked in a fervid maze of circumstances over which he has no control, and from which there is no escape."

The narrative, written with authority and lucidity, is tinged with the regret of one who sees the old order passing without yielding place to the new. Only a disgusted Catholic scholar could speak with the candor Martin displays in these pages.

"The church of Montini (Paul VI) is a house divided. The ferment of ideas, the clash of opinions…[and] the trend toward liberalization contending with a long-entrenched and prejudiced conservatism, have rendered Montini's position as Pope theoretically untenable. It has, in a sense, unpoped him. He cannot act as Popes have acted before. Montini does not know what to do. Nobody alive can tell him."

It's true, mother. Bishops carrying Mary Jo's picture would not vote for Montini's constitution declaring himself to be God.

"Locked in circumstances from which there is no escape."

That ranges from the cover-up of Chappaquiddick back to the cover-up of Christ, and forward, from the Versailles Mafia Summit to the completion of Fatima #3—a joint venture promoted by the Mafia and sanctioned by the church.

The handmaidens with a nuclear noose around the non-Mafia, non-Vatican half, are now losing. The Mafia Election Process, by which they select their leaders, is exposed.

The same process is also used by the Vatican: Papal selection by appointment of the hierarchy; the election is a show.

In the U.S. of Mafia: candidates are selected by the money of the Mafia. All the Maf are on the boards of ITT, General Motors, Lockheed—and they own the candidates. The election is simply a show.

But they are losing. Visibly. Last October, China was voted into the United Nations, and dope pushing Taiwan was voted out. Suddenly, it was all over.

Despite U.S. and Vatican support, dope pushing Chiang is going down the tube. Despite Vatican and Nixon support, dope pushing Thieu is going down the tube. Russia and China are pouring it on, right now, in Vietnam—just after Chappaquiddick-"Hughes" Dickie's Peking trip, and on the eve of his Moscow crawl. Chile is in full revolt against the CIA and ITT. You read the papers. Think about it. In Northern Ireland—where Teddy and Dickie pander for American-Irish votes, there is nothing but hatred for the exposed fangs of the Vatican-Mafia handmaidens that own the U.S., and squat on all those graves—from Wilkes-Barre, Pennsylvania to Cypress Lawn.

These handmaidens can't afford to lose, or to allow the exposure of the massive cover-ups: the Alioto hit-run, Chappaquiddick, JFK at Dallas, Bobby in L.A., the Yablonski family, Martin Luther King.

So—Fatima #3. "Circumstances…from which there is no escape."

No time to read documents then, mother. Maybe time for one word: "Why?"

Nixon and Mitchell have banned the use of the word "Mafia."

They spoke instead of "Law and Order." And proceeded to murder Mary Jo and my father—and, upcoming, all of us. Courtesy of the Mafia who pays them: Onassis' "Hughes," CIA-ITT, Ford, General Motors—and on and on. Holy sounding names, until you examine the carefully hidden Mafia connections of the key stockholders, who appoint the Boards of Directors, who appoint the Presidents, Judges, Congressmen, Governors. Or until you examine the murder, treason, conspiracy, war crimes, and necrophilia they commit. The list is long.

Holy Week. The eager volunteer, the stranger, hasn't showed up since Easter. But an Alioto cop did. I got a tow-away warning: "Get this car off the street or we'll impound it."

There are two mechanics within two blocks. I went to see each, and asked them to tow my car in and fix it.

"Fine," they said. "We need the work."

I stopped at each today and said, "Okay, let's go."

And then I told them what happened to the car: the hit-runs by Alioto, sealing wax in the carburetor, exposed spark in the distributor, Chappaquiddick, the fact that I wanted to preserve the car as a piece of evidence, and would they check closely for tampering while they were fixing it.

You would think they were reading from the same script.

First man: "Sorry, I can't tow you in. I don't want to get involved."

Me: "I'll pay you well."

Him: "Try somebody else. I'm busy. Good-bye."

So I went down the street ten blocks to the next mechanic. I did not tell him the truth. I simply said, "My car won't start. Can you fix it?"

Him: "Sure. Bring it in."

And I will not say a word. I've gotta get it off the street anyhow. Maybe he'll fix it, if I don't tell him the truth.

I thought that maybe the stranger was in jail. But as with the September 10, 1971 rigging, these things usually add up at a later date. He did have my phone number, and he did live just across the street from the parked car. And he was digging into the problem. And then he disappeared.

Evidence must be destroyed. My car is evidence. Your husband was evidence. Mary Jo was evidence. It took everybody—CIA, FBI. Justice, Supreme Court, President and Pope to destroy the JFK evidence. Same with Chappaquiddick. Same with "Howard Hughes."

But the reason this group is losing is because the Alioto hit-run cover-up was like swallowing a fish hook. The more they swallow, the deeper it sinks in, and the line is still attached. I can jerk it up anytime I please.

In any war, if a commander's position is overrun, he calls for the artillery—right on his own head. It kills everybody. All of his men, but also all of the enemy. And that is the name of the game. The commander gets the Medal of Honor—posthumously.

The Enemy Within—revised edition, by Bobby K.—was suppressed. Onassis bought it, blocked it, buried it. The title was taken from the "treason" definition. It was too dangerous.

"The Enemy Within and Without" is amplified and described herein. The Constitution of 1776—in word and intent—reads: "Treason is aiding and abetting the enemy within and the enemy without."

The Mafia courts—for the Mafia—declared: "No death penalty for any crime—including treason."

They will solemnly convene and declare missiles coming in to be illegal, as the first ones come in. They will resist the killing of cancer up to and including the bitter atomic end. Unfortunately for you, when they go, you go too. And you can tell that missile, as it comes in, "I'm too busy. I don't want to get involved."

Mack, to me, about a talk with Mitchell: "Let me know what you want to do."

Me to him: "I know what to do. The question is, who for?"

He didn't answer. And the next day, when I called with an outline for scalpel conditions, he disappeared. He hides in a shit bowl in the penthouse of the Bank of California, occasionally opening the lid to receive Alioto's interest-free deposit money, and pass out loans to Onassis'

"Hughes's" Lockheed.

That lid has a time lock—one for the Alioto "take" and one for the Onassis "give."

Without the busted beak, Mary Jo would have lived in that air bubble just under the trunk until the diver dragged her out in the morning. And if that happened to Mack, he would feel, personally, how the terror murder of Mary Jo was committed.

He is hiding from me. But there's always an answer. His own bank's policy: "Who cares how you get the loot or what happens to the body afterward?" Dickie's Policy. Montini's. You can't go any higher than that. Or any lower than a shit bowl. Which Onassis would then promptly flush. To remove the evidence.

Love, Bruce

April 7: McGovern for President

Dear Mother:

Today V.P. Agnew stated: "The Vietnam War is the most moral act in U.S. history."

Humphrey states: "I want Teddy for my V.P. That way I can shelter him from antagonism about Chappaquiddick. I swear to serve one term only—and then Teddy can take over."

Herb Caen asks: "Why can't McGovern be as phony as FDR, JFK or Bobby? To add some zest to the campaign."

The answer is that McGovern must be clean—in order to cover up for Teddy.

McGovern's campaign managers are Salinger and Mankiewicz—stalwarts from old Kennedy campaigns. They beg Daley to join their campaign. McGovern was the first Senator to assure Teddy of "full support" in his "Chappaquiddick troubles."

A quote from Daley: "McGovern's going to have all those woolly heads gathering around him. He might as well forget about support from our kind of people."

Regular Democrats? "Stopping McGovern at Miami Beach is a holy cause…. We think the nomination of McGovern would mean the end of the Democratic Party. The means of nominating Teddy are shrouded in ambiguity."

The hierarchy of the AFL-CIO "sees McGovern as a menace."

McCabe states: "FDR and JFK were phony but did become human once in a while. Nixon and his mob are cold hearted."

Schorr called Nixon a traitor. True. A murderer, too. Bribery? Yes. Conspiracy? Yes. High Crimes? Yes. Misdemeanors? Yes. Aid and Comfort to The Enemy Within and Without? Yes. War Crimes? Yes.

Nixon's record reads like Teddy's. These two will run for the next presidency. One of them will be elected.

Carl Rowan states: "The Peking trip failed. China didn't budge."

(Chiang Ching has my stone, and history.)

The Russian trip will also fail. Dickie already knows it as he watches Russian tanks "invade" South Vietnam. (Brezhnev has a gemstone, and history. Everybody has copies of this history—except Dickie and the full Mafia hierarchy. They burned theirs.)

And so Dickie's cranking up Fatima #3.

Anderson today quotes dissident top security people (now dismissed, jailed, etc.—all but seven, who are still there). "Contingency plans are set to A-blast Vietnam."

The mechanic said, "Your motor was eaten out from inside. It won't start again."

Does that sound familiar? A new motor, mother, when I bought it. The owner guaranteed me 50,000 miles without any major motor trouble—in writing. It died after only 20,000 miles, and it had the best of oil and care, from me. But something was intermittently added to that oil. Just as sealing wax in the carburetor, and distributor "alterations", were added on September 10, 1971.

The history of the car is interesting. Clobbered by Alioto's son two weeks after I bought it. Then five more hit-runs—none before, and none since. Sealing wax and "spark" adjustments on September 16, 1971. Death, suddenly, two days before you left—with papers.

"Stress" reads my father's death certificate. That started the night Alioto clobbered my car. Three and a half years later, one week before Peking, came the hydrochloric acid and blood. While Dickie was in Peking, came death.

The car went out as you left. Then three more weeks of problems, for me. This weekend I will entomb it—just as we did my father.

Dickie goes to Moscow next month.

You said, "What kind of monsters are these?" You were the one who got up at intervals all those nights, when he asked you to check on a noise and see if Yablonski shotguns were out there.

He was worried about us the night before he died. His roommate in the hospital warned him. He told both of us, "One of you is scheduled to be knocked over tonight." Whatever else, he had guts, and he was honest. He would have been an excellent witness. Nixon, Nader, and all the hierarchy, left him alone with his "stress."

My car—14 years old, and non-running. Three strangers offered to buy my useless motor. Almost eagerly. Peculiar.

It has already had an autopsy. It will have another.

These letters weren't entirely meant for you, as you know. They go out to many people, in different ways. You, or anyone else, can burn them, destroy them, or forget them. But please, do exactly as I tell you—and sit back and enjoy your swing in the sun.

Love, Bruce

April 9: Kuwait bails out the U.N.; Cryogenic freezing for "Howard Hughes"

Mother:

A bunch of people were here at the house to say hello. The car has been interred, with a flower in the radiator. Some friends of mine will quietly conduct an autopsy. (They did this on "Howard Hughes"—and have a plan for Mary Jo's resurrection. They're foreigners, mother. No American would do it.)

Laird and Gayler state: "Russia is behind the current North Vietnam 'invasion.' It is a flagrant violation of Johnson's understandings." Johnson—all alone—declared six days before the 1968 election: "There will be peace in Vietnam. Stop the bombing; elect Hubert."

(And that would have elected Hubert, if he hadn't been frightened out of the Bay Area by Alioto's hit-run—a flight that cost Hubert 100,000 votes, the state, and the election.)

Kuwait's ambassador to the U.N., Bishara, states: "We have no political prisoners in our jails. I dare you, in the U.S., to tell me you have no political prisoners." (He speaks of Ellsberg, the Berrigans, Sirhan, and a lengthy list.) "We were asked to solve the U.N. monetary problem, not because we were the wealthiest," (oil) "but because we are the fittest. Kuwait was asked, instead of the U.S, because the U.S. would put conditions on its financial assistance."

(Bishara also knows that the U.S. of Mafia is now scuttling the U.N. because, somehow, the U.N. kicked out heroin-pushing Taiwan—and brought in the heroin-hating Chinese, who are currently resurrecting Mary Jo's busted-nosed body.)

A year or so ago, when that "legislative aide" (from Javits, I thought) was needling me, I quoted him the Chinese prices on the ears of every murdering Senator, etc., and I suggested that he watch for a nasty U.N. resolution from Chile.

Chile's finally gonna spring it. (Kuwait is a prelude.)

Here's something about eternal life:

Three hundred and sixty "living" people have made financial arrangements for cryogenic freezing after death. One of these is "Howard Hughes", who died on April 16, 1971, was buried off Skorpios, Greece, by Onassis, on April 18, and was later "resurrected" by friends of mine.

Jean Peters supposedly married Howard Hughes, with a secret, phony marriage in Tonopah, Nevada, in 1957, shortly after Hughes was kidnapped. In June, 1971, two months after Hughes died, Jean Peters obtained a Tonopah divorce.

The CIA and Onassis guard Jean Peters around the clock. Things are getting tight. She is one more human who may have an accident in a pond.

You have a front row seat to history. So did my father. He had lots of faith in me. I do too. Someday I'll tell you what he said to me those nights in the hospital. You would be very proud.

I am.

Luv Ya,

Bruce

18 Dickie's Moscow Trip; News Round-up

June 1, 1972: Dickie is winging home from Moscow at this moment. Somewhere en route he will pass a communication headed the other way. That communication was composed in part from notes on news stories quoted below:

"Hughes' Mormon Mafia nursemaids are up again for fraud in Canada."

Eckersley, one of the 'nursemaids', said, "Yes, it was fraud. We used phony signatures. It embarrasses me, and Hughes. Besides, it is bad publicity. I hope the people don't panic. I wish they'd leave us Mafia alone."

"Legalization of gambling will be here soon [in New York]. Will 'Hughes' run it?"

"Mafia government okays gambling. [in Hawaii]. The 'Hughes' Mafia mob is moving in. Executives are furnished by CIA, FBI, and Justice-as in all 'Hughes' operations."

In London: The "Hughes Hoax" expose by the *London Sunday Times,* scheduled for release May 15, one week before Dickie's Moscow crawl, was deleted. All news of "Hughes" was suppressed. Instead, the paper carried the headline:

"Mafia TV and news censorship covers England relative to religion, 'Hughes' and Dickie's insane bombing in Vietnam—all on the eve of Dickie's Moscow visit. Is there a connection?"

Here is a free paraphrase of their article: "We quote Saigon Senator Tho: 'God—the Pope—is on our side. The U.S. of Mafia is on our side. They can leave any time they want. But they would have to leave us their Navy and Air Corps. Our President, Thieu, tells Dickie what to do. He's got drag. And "skai" and "skag." We can't lose.'

"Clifford Irving's arrest for the 'Hughes Hoax' was an accident. In New York, two reporters mentioned they knew about "Meyer". Irving went white, had a fit, ran down to J. Mafia Hoover's D.A. Hogan, begged for protection, and confessed everything. Hogan, U.S. Attorney Seymour, Hoover, and Nixon also went white and had a fit. They convinced the reporters that the man they spoke of was really Stanley Myer, an obscure writer.

"The reason for the white faces and the fits is that the 'Meyer' mentioned was really John Meyer, Onassis's right-hand man, who was taken over from 'Hughes' after Onassis hyped Hughes and made the body switch in 1957. And purchased Dickie and the 'Hughes' Mafia Money Funnel. This media censorship in England goes back to 1932 when Onassis, Roosevelt, and Kennedy conned our leader, Churchill, into supplying booze, heroin and World War II (Fatima #1) for the handmaidens—Vatican and Mafia.

"We note that L. Patrick Gray, Hoover's successor, was picked by Nixon a year ago—but Dickie, fearing Hoover's files, patiently waited for Hoover's demise. Like Saigon Senator Tho and Mafia Mama Rosie, God is on Gray's side. He attends Mass before all missions to request help from God—the Pope. Gray's Justice friends say:

"Gray hates the Press because of publicity on things like the Pentagon Papers. He wants a crackdown, like Reagan, on all underground press, all critical media, and all critical legal services. He is like unto Christopher Columbus: a poor boy, a devout Catholic and a Mafia government loyalist.'

"Said Gray, 'We keep no dossiers on the revolting public.'

"Said Jack Anderson, 'Here are a few thousand copies of dossiers from your files.'

"Said Gray, 'Well, yes, we do keep files on the revolting public.'

"He is Dickie's most loyal friend. His loyalties, says he, are, in order:

#1: Nixon

#2: The Justice Department Family that runs things for Onassis' "Hughes"; and somewhere down the list,

#642 (we think): the peeepul, the revolting public.

"'Hughes,' in Vancouver, has six days left on his first 3-months visitor's visa. We have Canadian friends who will insist on a 'personal appearance' for any renewal of that visa. We will watch for a sudden 'Hughes' disappearance from Vancouver, or a sudden cryogenic burial. We will try to let you know by secret carrier pigeon, unless the Pentagon shoots them down.

"You see, we're peeved. The U.S. of Mafia sent the British Empire down the tube in the past 50 years. We don't like that. We don't want the Mafia-infected colonies back. They're worse than we ever were."

***

Memorial Day in the U.S. of Mafia: All the days of respect to the dead have been shuffled into one day, for calendar convenience.

Said Dickie: "A nation which condemns those who serve it will find itself condemned in turn." From Leningrad he talked about the Russian Mary Jo, now enshrined: "Tanya."

"As some of the millions were being murdered at Leningrad, Tanya wrote, 'Today my uncle died. My brother died. My grandfather died. And my mother. Only Tanya is left.' Let us make sure that no other girl will have to endure what Tanya did."

And his pious eyes looked upward as he meditated for a moment on Mary Jo—the reason for his being at Tanya's tomb in Leningrad (on behalf of all murderous Maf who squat on all the graves listed herein.)

Teddy's Memorial Day response (clutching his right fist of steel that broke Mary Jo's nose): "Nixon wages peace in Moscow—but war in Vietnam. We heard all about Tanya in Russia, but what about all the Tanyas in Vietnam?"

One of these two will be the next President. Both are Mafia, squatting on the graves of U.S. of Mafia Tanyas and Mary Jos, and baying at the world in frenzy.

Prior to Moscow and Peking, Dickie and Kissinger had a talk. "The world's two big bugaboos are war and crime. We can't go after crime, because that is us: Chappaquiddick, 'Hughes,' Onassis and so forth. So we'll set up a Public Relations campaign against war and get set for Fatima #3."

They discussed their aims for the Moscow trip. They wanted the same 12-clause agreement that they had gotten in Peking.

Clauses 1, 2 and 3, backed up by 4 and 5, are what it was all about for Dickie.

Clauses 1 and 3 specify: "noninterference in the internal affairs of any other country." (Dickie is still trying to classify Chappaquiddick as an internal affair, while conducting P.R. to produce an image that the U.S. of Mafia is not pushing heroin and Fatima #3).

Clause 2 tries to give teeth to 1 and 3. Discussion on outstanding issues (Chappaquiddick and Fatima #3) will be conducted:

(4) "in sacred blood" by

(5) "top level only" (that's Dickie);

(6) "in secret";

(7) "in a spirit of reciprocity, mutual accommodation, and mutual benefit."

That's a Mafia bribe offer. Those that were offered to me always wound up with: "Whaddya want?"

In Moscow, the top Russian reporter said: "Nixon has a Zig-Zag policy, like a scared rabbit. We have had our doubts about him for a long time."

His title gets longer and longer all the time: Let's see: Onassis-Hughes-Chappaquiddick-Heroin-ITT-CIA-Thieu-Chiang-Tricky—" Oh, you finish it. And put this in too:

MMORDIS—that's "Moldering Mass of Rotten Dribbling Infectious Shit."

In Moscow, Dickie settled for an agreement that allowed the U.S. of Mafia to build an Anti-Ballistic Missile ring around Washington—to protect itself, the Mafia Club and its clubhouses: the White House, Congress, etc. (This is where the U.S. Mafia Government stands today—circled by ABM's in D.C., and by the moats of Miami for the Mafia conventions—having been frightened away from San Diego by an anonymous letter).

In Moscow, Kissinger commented on his sudden, secret trip on April 16, to "check the agenda." This time it was about fear—of the possibility of being handed the remains of "Howard Hughes" and being introduced to an American named Roberts.

Said Kissinger: "The Russian Summit was so well prepared in advance that the two governments agreed, 'Don't let's surprise each other at the summit'."

The U.S. of Mafia couldn't provoke Russia to cancel that summit. The Russians wanted Dickie on record. They wanted Dickie to visit Tanya's grave—their Mary Jo.

In the first big Haiphong raid, four Russian ships were hit. One Russian ship was sunk. But Russia backed away from the mines. And the Russian Ambassador told Dickie, "We wouldn't cancel your trip for anything." And he smiled.

Mafia Dickie's blackmail to Brezhnev was this:

"You, directing the 20 million member Communist Party, which rules all 240 million Russians—are identical to us. We are 20 million Mafia ruling 206 million Americans. You have your tyranny. We have ours. We won't squeal on you if you don't squeal on us."

And Brezhnev replied, smiling, "We'll see…."

Because he knew, as did Mao, that this was a repeat of the same deal Roman Emperor Constantine made to the first Pope in the year 335: a.d.: "You leave us alone and we leave you alone. We will cover for each other."

And that's where it is. Right back to the cover-up of Christ. But with a difference. Everything is out in the open, and two and a half billion pairs of feet are conscious of the need to stomp out cancer and get the man off the cross.

Brezhnev smiled again as he arranged for Chappaquiddick Dickie to be guided, in Leningrad, to the shrine of Tanya—the Russian Mary Jo.

Dickie got the message and reacted quickly.

"There will be no more Tanyas," he said.

Teddy jumped out of his skin. "What about Vietnamese Tanyas?" he said. (Vietnam—that's the "Holy Crusade" his brother and the Pope and Onassis started.)

In Moscow, Russia really did want trade agreements. They need everything. But the man in charge of that, for Dickie, was ITT Flanigan. (These Maf are everywhere). No Russian would sit in the same room with him. They could put up with Dickie; they had a reason. But Flanigan?

"Nyet," followed by puke.

So Dickie returns from Moscow and tells Congress: "We will not stain the honor of the U.S." (All applaud. The lid is still on.) "We must be proud of what we have done—and P.R. the revolting public into being proud" (of murder, treason, bribery…) "and proceed with our mission in the world." (Fatima #3.) "History" (Chappaquiddick) "lays an obligation on us. We must seize it now or

we are beaten."

(Johnson phrased it more simply: "We hang together, or we hang separately.")

Stressed in Moscow was Dickie's plea for non-interference in our "internal affairs" (Chappaquiddick).

Gray Congressional faces waited for reassurance on this from Dickie. He informed them of failure by his silence on the subject.

Dickie laid it all out a la Teddy: "We must learn to live with it."

Kissinger, en route to Moscow, was questioned: "Why are you so popular with the ladies?"

He replied, "Power is the most powerful aphrodisiac in the world. For instance, our State Department and the Pentagon Generals don't care what happens, so long as they stay in power. They are power mad."

Question: "What about Samoa?"

Answer: "Samoans can't vote."

(He didn't come back by way of Samoa. He settled for the Shah's belly-dancers in Iran. Next week Iran gets Phantom jets.)

News Summary

Twin headlines:

From Tehran: "Kissinger fiddles with Shah's belly-dancing broads in Onassis' Araby. 'Foreign Policy,' said Kissinger. 'I want to make the world safe for belly-dancers.'"

From Saigon: "U.S. planes blast all of Indo-China—except the opium fields. Thousands of Indo-Chinese are dead—but not one poppy."

'Foreign Policy,' said Noel Gayler, Commander in Chief of all Pacific Forces, as he lobbed tons of 'smart bombs' on the soft flesh of Indo-China."

***

Dickie and Mitchell did not stop in Tel Aviv and beg Golda Meir to please give us back Onassis' Meyer Lansky, who lives there. Lansky would be governor of New York, except that he was caught stealing $35 million of Vegas skim money from Onassis.

He qualifies for high Mafia political office—like John Meyer, who qualifies as Senator from New Mexico. (Meyer stole $17 million from Onassis via "Hughes" phony mining claims, and now he wants to succeed Senator Montoya, who, with Senator Brewster, carried $100,000 cash suitcases to Johnson in the White House to try to keep Hoffa out of jail.) Or like Alioto's Sicilian kin, Sal Balistreri (guilty of rape, sodomy, assault), as San Francisco Judge. Or Onassis's Chappaquiddick Dickie and Mafia Pond Murderer Teddy, for President of the World.

Says Golda Meir: "The Lebanese are sheltering murderous terrorists. We want to hang them."

At her elbow as she said this was Meyer Lansky, who murdered Americans for 47 years, and still does. U.S. Justice says it wants him—for the $35 million he stole, not for any murder. They want the loot back for Onassis. But Golda Meir won't give him (or the loot) up. She wants the loot to buy Phantom jets.

In Moscow, Dickie said: "Soviet citizens ask me, 'Does America truly want peace?' Our actions answer that question far better than words can do."

(Let's see: Vietnam, Greece, Taiwan, heroin, Pakistan; ITT-CIA: Chile; Maheu: Spain, Portugal, Rome…you finish the list.)

But Dickie got Moscow's agreement that he could build an ABM ring around Washington

for protection.

What's to protect in Washington? A San Francisco high school group toured there and were asked their impressions:

"Depressing. Worse than our ghettos. Pushers all over. The House of Representatives had thirty people on the floor out of 435, and they were passing envelopes. We remembered what Bobby Baker said: 'Thousand dollar bills pass around like confetti.'

"Rogers, from the State Department, and our two Senators, Tunney and Cranston, lectured us: 'The U.S. has always been right, and always fights for right against wrong. Our history is glorious.' And we all knew how they got elected, and what they are covering up. It was sickening."

In Washington, the Bulletin of Atomic Scientists published its usual front cover, The Doomsday Clock, showing the time pushed back—from 10 minutes to midnight, to 12 minutes to midnight. These people are highly intelligent, scientifically, but a little shy on facts.

Not Dickie. He knows. And he interrupted his harangue to the gray-faced Mafia Club to look directly into the camera and address you, the peepul, who don't have an ABM ring around you for your protection. To you he said solemnly: "Every American is in on it now. Either I win, or you lose."

(Teddy was absent from this meeting. He was in Pittsburgh drafting the Mafia Democratic Platform—for you, the peepul.)

That clock is on the final tick. Barely holding. Dickie knows it. But he won't mount the cross, with "Howard Hughes." And Teddy won't mount the cross with Mary Jo.

And the Mafia Election Process continues. Mafia candidates, selected by the Mafia—with no other qualifications—are placed before you for your vote in a rigged election process.

A tricky poll was set up in a selected Illinois spot by Kennedy pollster Quayle.

His question: "Did Teddy behave immorally before the car went off the bridge at Chappaquiddick?"

Even so, 44% said yes. But think a minute. They were Kennedy supporters—and they know nothing except what their bishop tells them. That is, they know nothing. Murder occurred after the car went off the bridge, and Mary Jo suffocated—after 2 hours and 13 minutes—because of a busted beak—while Teddy called Mafia Onassis for cover.

For a long time now, a Memorial Plaque to Mary Jo Kopechne has been hanging in the New York Metropolitan Museum. No news media has ever investigated the matter, or asked the name of the donor. Observations, however, have been continual—of those who see and know, and run.

McGovern said: "The central threat to the U.S. is right here at home. Not overseas." (That's as close as he'll ever get to Chappaquiddick.)

In Sacramento, Dymally said: "People are angry. Our State Legislature, and the Federal Legislature, have been motionless for three and a half years."

That's when the shit hit the fan—three and a half years ago: September 16, 1968.

Said Mack at that time: "You have opened the world's biggest can of worms."

Me? I was shooting dice with Herbie Kamatsu at the Black Magic Bar when Alioto's son clobbered my car. Already the jackpot—in a lab—had been tapped. My interest at that time was solely in finding a gift ruby for Herbie's wife that Les Williams had dropped on the floor. I hadn't the faintest idea that at that moment, Alioto, Kennedy, Onassis, "Hughes," Dickie, and Montini were already climbing on the middle of my back.

***

From Chicago: "Daley, Teddy, Stevenson, and the Cardinal are working together raising

funds for Teddy's presidential race."

From San Francisco: "Humphrey and McGovern have purchased $3 million worth of votes in the California primary so far. This evening, Alioto, Archbishop McGucken, Shorenstein and Swig are raising funds for Humphrey. The rest of the local core are working with Kennedy aides pitching for McGovern—until Teddy can call them all together after the convention."

"Swig and Schulman" (who with Alioto and Shorenstein started Chappaquiddick rolling by their offer to bribe Unruh to quit the governor primary against Alioto and run instead against Tunney), "were told by Kennedy not to release their 'campaign funds' for either Humphrey or McGovern yet. Teddy plans to use those funds after the Democratic convention, after he has either defeated those others or disposed of them in some other manner." (George Wallace was gut-shot.)

"Alioto arranged a Lindsay-Humphrey conference. Reason: a possible Presidential-Vice Presidential coalition. He then directed Humphrey to get out a series of rumors: 'McGovern is anti-Labor, anti-Jewish, anti-Lockheed, and pro-riot....'"

In Washington, a Senator: "The top priority on the agenda when the 93rd Congress convenes in 1973 is reserved for prison reform. That's where we'll all be—if the campaign fund finance law is enforced."

He jokes, smugly, of course. For who would jail them for murder, treason or bribery? Dickie? Teddy? Montini? Legal Mafia? They have already abolished the death penalty, and whoever they can't keep out of the jug, they let out.

**

Teddy murdered Mary Jo. Dickie sent a Secret Service Army to protect Teddy.

George Wallace received a gut shot. All government medical facilities were placed at the disposal of Mafia Presidential candidate Wallace.

All mines and bomb facilities were aimed at the population of Indo-China to protect the heroin trade of Thieu, Chiang and the Onassis-"Hughes" Mafia Money Funnel.

All necrophiliacs are still in place on Mary Jo's grave—with Secret Service, FBI, CIA, Pentagon and Holy Vatican protection.

Hearst published Cafarakis's shit about Onassis.[46] The sole reason for this con relates to Cafarakis's attempt to rewrite the history of the frantic JFK phone call to Jackie on Onassis' yacht, re: the planned Double Diem-Kennedy murder day, November 1, 1963: "Get off that yacht if you have to swim!"

Says Cafarakis solemnly, with approval of the hierarchy of Onassis, Montini and Dickie: "There was no phone call. JFK sent a letter mildly remonstrating Jackie for remaining so long on the yacht. This was early in 1963."

(The entire White House staff remembers JFK's white-faced hysterical screams over the phone to Jackie. "Never," says one, "have I heard such loud uncontrolled anger in the White House.")

Gervais, whose testimony about Garrison's pinball pay-offs got Garrison indicted, confessed he'd lied.

Says Gervais: "Because of my record, Justice forced me to frame Garrison. I lied and I'm sorry. As my reward, Justice got me a soft job with Onassis's General Motors, in Canada, under an

---

[46] "The *Christina* sailed with three guests: Jackie, Lee [Bouvier Radziwill'], and Maria [Callas]. In order to avoid publicity, it was announced that Onassis would not be aboard....But who would have suspected at the time that like a simple peasant girl the First Lady of the United States was falling in love with Onassis?....In a letter that quite a few people at the White House saw at the time, Jackie described Onassis with such uncharacteristic enthusiasm that John Kennedy asked her, by return mail, to come home as soon as possible....Jackie calmly continued her cruise all the way to Turkey...." *The Fabulous Onassis: His Life and Loves*, by Christian Cafarakis. William Morrow, 1972, p.101-2.

assumed name. It's too big. I'm afraid. I know, for instance, that CIA McCone is hidden at ITT under the name of Director—with the same salary as Maheu: half a million a year, 'for life', and none of us are safe. Maheu is in hiding."

Yablonski's sons: "Murder is an institution in the UMW and among Labor Mafia leaders."

Novotny, the whore, states that Fensterwald investigated her in view of his conclusion that World War II and the chain of assassinations were rigged by the Mafia. She affirmed that from her personal view of JFK and the International Mafia (looking up from a bed), everything checked out "real good."

***

19 George Wallace's Gut Shot

Said George Wallace: "Vote for me. Let your message to Washington be that you are unhappy with Nixon's brand of law and order." Said a Pat Buchanan (Nixon) memo: "If Wallace develops strength, we must destroy him in 1972."

Wallace is out of the way now. Gut shot. A la King, Kennedy and Kennedy. In an identical manner, on TV, where everybody could see who did it. With a proven deliberate stalk, a la King, Kennedy and Kennedy. It's open and shut. Clean.

***

"Case Closed," says the FBI. "There was no conspiracy. We have determined that Bremer had no money, but he spent a fortune traveling in Canada and the East.

"Hypnotized Bremer was stalking four people: McGovern, Humphrey, Nixon and Wallace. Had he or the other hypnotics still roaming around nailed them all, just think: there would be only one man left, who would win: Teddy. Just like Thieu in Vietnam, Nol in Cambodia, Chiang in Taiwan, Onassis in Greece—the heroin chain.

"Bremer, a pauper, had time and money. Bremer, an idiot, had detailed plans and directions. Bremer, a total loner, had a series of Greek friends usher him across Lake Michigan for hypnotic classes and booster shots, during his stalk. We have prohibited anyone from disclosing the identity of those Greek friends or discussing anything about anything with any witness—or anybody. The case is closed."

Says Shirley Chisholm, who has read these papers: "If I were President, I would reopen investigations of the assassinations of JFK, Bobby, MLK and others. I have a feeling there is a deliberate attempt to have this country taken over by certain kinds of forces. I feel that Teddy will be the Democratic candidate this fall."

Bobby never spoke to Hoover after Dallas—even though Hoover faithfully pushed the "Holy Crusade" Fatima #3.

A hypnotized Sirhan was present for Bobby, and got him, with the help of Onassis's back-up, Thane Eugene Cesar. Another hypnotic, Arthur Bremer, was present for George Wallace, but only got him in the gut—with no back-up handy. Other hypnotics are waiting for McGovern, Humphrey and Dickie—for everyone but Teddy, Onassis's choice.

Phony Assassination Attempt on FDR by Zangara
Real Target: Cermak

"There was an assassination attempt on President Franklin D. Roosevelt. Giuseppe Zangara missed Roosevelt, and killed Chicago Mayor Cermak," say United States history books.[47]

The facts emerge today from Louis Zangara, Giuseppe's nephew, in Chicago:

"My uncle, dying of cancer, was hired to kill Mayor Cermak by the Mafia Syndicate, because Cermak had shut down their gambling activities around election time. Giuseppe's pay? His widow and family would never have any financial worries."

(But later, they welshed on that).

"My uncle's target was Cermak. He killed him, while Cermak was riding with Roosevelt."

Sound familiar? It should. The Dallas operation was copied after this. Oswald's target was Connally. He got a piece of him. Onassis-Maheu's back-ups didn't miss on the real target: JFK. Oswald was still puzzled by the con when Ruby gut-shot him. Ruby didn't miss. Pro's don't. Only

---

[47] They were riding together in an open car, in a parade, in Chicago,

hypnotics, like Sirhan and Bremer, who couldn't hit a target at four feet with eight shots.

"And," continued Shirley Chisholm, "that's all I'll say about assassinations right now. I don't want to be gut-shot yet. Instead, nine of us in Congress introduced a bill to impeach Nixon. The Congressional Mafia buried that. So we published the criminal impeachment charge, with some of the evidence, in the *New York Times*—and the union press Mafia almost stopped the publication of that. Nixon sent the press Mafia a medal for their attempt to suppress the printing."

***

Black specks in your soup, that move.

Dickie took the U.S. into debt: $100 billion extra in three years. You pay. He pursues Fatima #3, Onassis-"Hughes" heroin, Mary Jo's cover-up, and his place in history. Says he: "Either I win, or you lose."

***

In Vancouver: "A P.R. man was called in to examine Howard Hughes's big toe. He discovers the toe is bigger than the average, and publishes this fact—stating incidentally that Howard is healthy and happy."

"Hughes's visa runs out soon. He must appear personally, soon. Yesterday, three private planes left for Guadalajara, Mexico. With top secret State Department clearance."

In Washington, Senator Hart: "Since Joseph P. Kennedy set it up 35 years ago, the SEC has been a Mafia cartel, a monopoly of price fixing, discrimination, looting, barring of competition and boycotting of competing markets. I refer specifically to the New York Stock Exchange."

In Washington: "In the Senate—quickly buried—Alfred McCoy[48] named the South Viet leaders (all of them), and the CIA and U.S. officials, as Onassis's heroin pushers from the Golden Triangle. The Senate inquiry was immediately dismissed."

That evening a new flight of B52's left for Thailand, and two new air bases were activated next to the opium fields.

In Rome: "Medallions are out featuring Italy's three top heroes: Pope John, JFK and Bobby, who opened up Vietnam and heroin for the Mafia.

"Protection at the top level of government and religion keeps the Mafia going. It is a cancer that owns Italy. Lucky Luciano and Vito Genovese ran the Sicilian invasion for the U.S. in World War II. American Generals joined them, and they helped the U.S. by sending German secrets back to their boy, Joe Alioto, in Roosevelt's Justice Department."

Jack Anderson: "Rep. Emanuel Cellar—Dean of House of Representatives—fingers personal loot from FBI, Lockheed, ABM, nuclear and conventional power plants, Pentagon. He does this through his Legal Mafia firm."

In Lewisburg: "Bobby Baker follows Hoffa out of the jug. Baker, on a salary of $19,000, banked a million dollars in cash and bought a $50 million motel. He is now out of jail after 17 months, because he wrote a book about how he "earned" the loot: By Senate thousand dollar bill-passing on the Senate floor, and $100,000 suitcases to his bosses, Johnson and Nixon—and Judges."

In Washington: Teddy, in the Senate, screams: "Whitewash! The entire Senate is whitewashing Kleindienst. Whitewashing is a crime!"

Barboza, a murdering Patriarcha Maf from Kennedy's Boston, sang about Mafia murder, treason and bribery. He named names.

For instance: 'Sinatra fronts for Patriarcha.'

---

[48] Author, *Politics of Heroin in Southeast Asia.*

Barboza's song was sung in public. Mafia Congress, up for reelection, subpoenaed Sinatra. Chappaquiddick Tunney suggested an 'invitation' rather than a subpoena, as they did with Mafia Speaker McCormack during the Mafia Swig, Voloshen, Donato, Heffernan, Pat Brown hearings.

Tunney tried to soften it for Mafia Sinatra because Sinatra himself is a singer. He provides loot for any Mafia public official, such as Reagan, Nixon, Agnew, Teddy, Tunney.

The Senate committee, because it was public, and election time, issued the subpoena. As with Cermak and Zangara, somebody will get shot.

Chief Justice Kleindienst: "I am an Episcopalian Priest. My religion allows me to forgive myself in the bribery and treason of ITT, and to forgive U.S. Attorney Seward for the bribery and treason in San Diego. (We have fully atoned by switching the convention to "Hughes" Mafia Miami.) My religion also forgives us for conspiracy in the murders of Mary Jo and Hughes—and all of the others."

In Manila: "U.S. of Mafia and Ford Foundation friend President Marcos bribed the entire Philippine Legislature to change the original FDR-written constitution to allow him to be President forever."

In Seattle: "David Somes has for a year brought charges against U.S. Attorney Pitkin (currently prosecuting Alioto in a rigged suit) and the FBI for conspiracy to commit murder. Finally, when he publicly submitted confessions of five of the Mafia participants to a Federal Judge, that judge ordered the entire matter sealed and buried in a Federal Grand Jury—from which, like a collapsed star, no light emerges. This is known as the density of shit."

In Onassis's Peron's Argentina, a complaint: "As at Bethlehem, we have persecution of all dissenters—particularly the revolting priests, who protest as the Berrigans do in the U.S. of Mafia."

In Paris (Shit Pit): "Niarchos and his new wife Tina (Onassis's ex-wife) argue with Onassis over his daughter Christina Niarchos. Niarchos is the Pa. He murdered his wife Eugenie, who was Tina's sister, and Onassis' private reserve. As to Christina Onassis, Tina is the Ma. Onassis is the Pa. Alexander is around somewhere with Fiona Thyssen,[49] who is also Onassis' private reserve. Niarchos's ex-wife, Charlotte Ford, worried, about their daughter and Chappaquiddick, called Niarchos while he was in bed with his latest wife, Eugenie. Eugenie heard the conversation, and Niarchos murdered Eugenie. And then Tina, Eugenie's sister, divorced the King of England [Marquess of Blandford—sc] to marry Niarchos, who is, by this time, somebody's godfather. Maybe George Livanos, the brother of Tina and Eugenie, who chases Callas and Jackie around the back bedrooms of Onassis's yacht, singing opera. Onassis phones Jean Peters regularly, and flies between his various loves at General Motors in Canada, 1170 Sacramento Street in SF, Norway and Switzerland. Kennedys and Roosevelts sail on his yacht."

Got that straight?

Taiwan: "Chiang's son elected. 94% vote."

Cambodia: "Nol elected. 98% vote."

Thailand: "Government still the same. 100% vote."

Laos: "100% vote."

Greece: "Unanimous vote."

Got that straight?

***

Vietnam—Big Minh: "America gives aid to one man: Thieu. Not to the Vietnamese people. The Americans will never leave. They need war to sustain their policies. If they don't have a war

---

[49] [of the German munitions mogul Thyssen family, partner of I.G. Farben.—sc]

here, they will have it somewhere else."

In Washington: "Six billion in interest-free government money is deposited in favored banks." (For instance: Mack's Bank of California, and Fred Martin's Bank of America.)

Jerry Wolf, AFL-CIO leader: "We should shift our bribery emphasis from the states to Congress. The big crap game now is going on in the nation's capital."

Pennsylvania, near Mary Jo's grave: "Tony Boyle transfers his loot to his wife's name."

Boyle, who supervised the murder of Yablonski with hierarchy approval, is running for reelection. His conviction for bribing Humphrey in 1968 bars him from holding public office. But Humphrey, who accepted the bribe, is not barred from running for president. Humphrey is backed by Alioto, also on trial for bribery—in a rigged trial, where the judge has already informed the jury that all bribery is legal.

Why shouldn't murderer Boyle be reelected? Murder, treason, bribery—these are the qualifications of public officials. Check Teddy, Daley, Nixon…anybody.

New Jersey: "Demo Mafia Party Boss Kenny, Whelan's Boss, convicted, conducts his political fiefdom of murder from his hospital bed. The Judge says Kenny will only continue to do this from prison—so maybe the Judge won't sentence him. (So what's the use?)"

Halvonik, ACLU: "It is impossible for an independent to run for office. Election laws are rigged to prevent this. Eugene McCarthy couldn't win a suit of that nature. The Supreme Court threw it out."

Washington: "Senate rules prohibit one member from criticizing another: Omerta. Scott and Griffin—the 'truth squad'—label Senator Gravel a traitor for revealing the Kissinger papers. And they demand that he produce whoever gave him the papers so that Justice can hang that one as a traitor too."

Los Angeles: "Lockheed wins another billion dollars in defense contracts—with a government bank loan guarantee for the job to be done in Onassis's Greece."

Sacramento, Reagan: "The State Supreme Court ruling against the death penalty is a complete reversal of its own decision four years ago" (that was just before Alioto, "Hughes" and Chappaquiddick) "and a complete reversal of two hundred years of our constitutional law."

San Francisco, Alioto: "My police play an essential role in safeguarding the rights and freedoms which are guaranteed by the Constitution to every American."

(There is a City fund shortage. $2 million is missing from the City Employee voting bloc; and $2 million goes to his Police to buy, specifically, two "Hughes" helicopters.)

Women's Lib: Barbara Phillips read these papers and ran and hid. Last week the State Legislature voted down her project: the Equal Rights Amendment for Women. She has now pulled a lid over the hole in which she hides.

Consumer's Confederation: Kay Pachtner was notified of these papers and the contents. She ran and hid. Last week the Alioto mob turned down her consumers' bill. She has pulled a lid over her hole.

Has anybody seen the Chappaquiddick broads around anywhere? Or Elizabeth Jean Peters?

New York: Press Freedom Task Force: "There is a double standard of treatment: one for the free underground press, and one for the established press. There is a threat of complete Mafia press censorship typified by the government's pre-publication restraint."

(The Pentagon—Onassis' toy—publishes 371 magazines and publications, all about itself. The yearly tax-payer cost is $56 million.)

San Francisco—McCabe: "Al Capone learned his morals from William Randolph Hearst."

Last week, Hearst bought the remaining two papers in Boston. He now owns them all. Cowles dumped *Look* like a hot potato, and last week purchased all the papers in Denver.

Loeb, of the *Manchester Union Leader*—a Mafia animal—suddenly became a power. Dickie panders to him. Hoffa hooked him long ago with a $2 million bribe. His copies of the Chappaquiddick phone calls give him great blackmail. He whipped Muskie out of the presidential campaign.

He even made him cry. Vatican Muskie couldn't respond with "Chappaquiddick." It was horrible frustration—and Muskie cried and cried, and quit.

Loeb told Dickie and Poucha Pond John Mitchell to get Hoffa out of jail, and they did. This monster, Loeb, unregulated by anything, has as much power as Thieu. That power is a copy of the Chappaquiddick phone calls.

Oh, Dickie, thy lid will be done.

***

It's all a Dickie shuffle. The day after Wallace's gut-shot, Dallas bullet Connally suddenly resigned as Secretary of the Treachery. Lid-sitter-on-Yablonski-murders Schultz was moved into Connally's place, in charge of Indochinese heroin. A hot spot. San Francisco's Weinberger (whom I contacted in October, 1968, when I couldn't get through to D.A. Ferdon, and Reagan refused to respond after my Sacramento visit) was moved into Schultz's place—a very hot place, since it is the Mafia cancer rotting of the dollar that is the Achilles Heel of the U.S. of Mafia.

(Treachery Secretary Connally rigged votes and came out for Humphrey in 1968—and beat Dickie, in Texas. After his election, Dickie was about to jail Johnson and Connally for the Austin land steal.

But then came Chappaquiddick, and Johnson told Dickie, "Cover it up, as I did Dallas, L.A. and Memphis—or we'll talk about 'Hughes.' Remember, we hang together or we hang separately. Appoint my boy Connally to be Secretary of the Treachery—from whence that $50 billion a year, tax-free Onassis heroin money flows."

And Dickie did what Johnson told him to do. And upon his resignation, on May 15th, Connally, with his Dallas bullet still inside, endorsed Dickie to be the next President.)

Seattle: "Connally, under orders from Nixon, released convicted Teamster Dave Beck from an IRS tax rap—to gain Teamster support for Dickie's price freeze."

The *Seattle Post Intelligencer*—a Roosevelt paper—started a probe of this to embarrass Nixon, and Connally promptly quit his job. Any probe that might get through to the Nixon purchase of Loeb (for the release of Hoffa) in order to cover up the Chappaquiddick phone calls (as Johnson had ordered—"or else") would blow the whole bubble of shit.

Schultz was ordered to take the Treachery job. He and Nixon worked together in Mafia affairs for 3 years—such as murder and politics in the UMW, Mary Jo, "Hughes," oil, and the 41% siphon of the Gross National Product.

Dickie's reasoning: "The only one you can trust is a co-conspirator."

From Ellsberg: "The Phoenix Program in Vietnam: The CIA put up one billion dollars as an assassination fund. For the murder of 'enemy' leaders, listed by the CIA; mainly to go to brothers and sisters of the victims, exactly as the Legal Mafia branches do here: Marcello, Maheu, Nixon, Onassis, Patriarcha, Kennedy, Lanza, Alioto, Boyle, Daley, etc."

San Francisco: "John Mack has a joker hidden in the ballot for control of the San Francisco Republican County Committee. Once again, Mack—attorney, banker of the Bank of California and his slate are trying to unseat Bechtel's Emily Pike and her group. He, treasurer of the Nixon campaign committee, sponsors this power play by Conservative Republicans to overthrow the

current self-perpetuating County Central Committee."

That entire blurb could be condensed into five letters: MAFIA.

***

When I handed Mack the solution to Chappaquiddick, three weeks after it happened, I asked him, "How much would the Mafia pay for the presidency?" His face went white.

Mack was introduced to me by my father. I offered him Alioto on a platter in October, 1968. And Kennedy in August, 1969. Then "Hughes" in December. He read these papers in my mother's kitchen. His wife wears a gift of my rubies.

Said Mack: "Tell me what you know about Howard Hughes."

"Tell me about the assassinations, and smuggling, and heroin."

"It'll cost you $1500 to join the Golden Circle." (Lincoln Club: C. Arnholdt Smith, Alessio, Schulman—the San Diego Mafia).

I said to him: "Here's some loot for Justice. I elected Nixon. Now he can be another Abraham Lincoln."

"Here's Alioto, Kennedy, and Onassis—'Hughes' on a platter."

"Sell my stones. Give this one (a 62-carat heart-shaped sapphire) to Mrs. Dickie."

***

My father worked for that Mafia Republican County Central Committee—and Mack—for many years, believing in their integrity.

On February 22, 1972, Nixon completed the murder of my father.

The next day I invited Mack to the funeral—personally. And Greenagel, Best, and Carlson.

The next day, the Dita Beard memo went out.

20 Cardinal Tisserant's Papers

What these Mafia run from is more deadly than they know. A series of things have placed that Doomsday clock only one tick away from midnight. One of these came from the papers of Cardinal Tisserant, a Dean of the Sacred College of Cardinals at the Vatican. He died on February 21, 1972, in a clinic near Rome.

Cardinal Tisserant was a dissident at the very highest level of the Vatican hierarchy. Once close to the Pope, in recent years he had become a hated thorn. Like Ellsberg scooting off with the Pentagon Papers, and Mary Jo scooting toward Nader at Chappaquiddick, he too scooted. His bag was the entire Vatican crud, including Onassis, Hughes, and Chappaquiddick. He had lots of papers. They're out now. Pope Montini wants to quit.

All this started, for me, in 1966, with a local priest, Father Mootz. He was a Jesuit Education Professor at the University of San Francisco. Old and crippled with multiple sclerosis, he could barely shuffle. It was his birthday—a party given for him by a friend. I was the accidental host.

Helping him down the school paths, into the car, and up to the apartment for the party, we talked. He knew he was dying. It was his first party, ever. Twenty people, drinks, a religious argument, all vying for Father Mootz's approval. He squirmed, and motioned to me. I helped him to the bathroom. We talked. When the party was over I helped him down the stairs, into the car, and back to the school, and we talked some more.

Said he, finally: "They're farming me out to the Jesuit Seminary at Los Gatos. Come by and see me. I want to talk to you. You are not impressed by the religion you see. And you're smart enough to know the way to the bathroom. Nobody else was. I was ready to vomit."

Six months later the hostess and I went down to see him. He was in a wheel chair in a beautiful cloistered room. We hoisted him into the car and took a ride. Around the beautiful seminary and down around San Jose.

He talked to me when she was gone. "Do you know the Vatican?"

Me: "I was married to the daughter of the French Consul of Indochina. She was in a concentration camp there after Dien Ben Phu. I know of the French Vatican colonization of the area, the French Vietnam heroin trade, and the Cardinal Spellman-Kennedy 'Holy Crusade.' I was told about the Diem-Kennedy-Onassis connection. It all added up in 1963. Things like that, Father Mootz."

He surprised me: "That's fine."

Later, driving around, I got lost. I didn't know how to get back to the Seminary among the winding, hilly roads.

I told him, "Father Mootz, I'm lost. We're like the Flying Dutchman; we'll just have to drive around forever, looking for it."

Said he, like a little boy, "That's fine. Stop somewhere and we'll wet our whistles."

The girl disappeared somewhere. Over the beer he named one of those at that party. "Be careful. He is very bad. Always will be. I will tell you about him, for your sake."

He did. He told me the guy's confessions.

I told him, "Thanks for telling me, but he's no friend of mine. I'll probably never see him again."

I felt guilty. Here he was, violating that privileged confessional, in my behalf.

But he was intent. "You are just like me. I know about you."

I asked, "Why, Father? I'm not Catholic, and you could never convert me. I know too much."

He said, "That's fine. And you don't like what you know, or what I just told you. I don't like what I know either. But I won't last forever. I want you to know."

The girl came back then and we finally found the Seminary. I wheeled him into his room.

We talked, and he found a thin wallet, pulled out the only bill and pushed it into my pocket.

"For the beer," he said.

I told him, "Well, Father, you said I was just like you, and so you know that I will accidentally lose this five before I get to the door." And I did.

We said good-bye. He said, "I'll get something to you."

Father Mootz died a few months later.

Later still, after the hierarchy of crud was assembled on my back, someone—I don't know who—pushed the Tisserant papers into my pocket, as Father Mootz had pushed the five dollar bill.

And since I was "just like him," I accidentally lost them too. Around. Where the finder could get some good out of it.

Maybe Dickie would like to study these papers. He's in them. And I know where he can pick up a supply. These are "foreign affairs." His major hobby.

A quote: "The highest priority project in the U.S. of Mafia is the suppression of these papers—documents, tape, film—that you now read."

***

Cardinal Tisserant died on February 21, 1972. The Vatican immediately raided his office to find his files. And burn them. But the files were already gone.

Tisserant believed in the public's right to know, *a la* Ellsberg; and that morality took precedence over loyalty to his church. For many years he kept secret records of the truth: Vatican finances, holy murder, Fatima #1, #2 and #3—going back for a hundred years, with fingers reaching all the way back to the murder of Christ.

During those years, people smuggled out copies. Even Tisserant didn't know this.

These Tisserant papers are a sordid tale of Mafia, MMORDIS, whatever you call it—using a willing, trapped, 2000-year-old institution and its fringe religions to subjugate the bodies, souls and spirit of man.

This is why the Roman Catholic Church is collapsing. It is why Berrigan was refused entry to Cardinal Terence Cooke's Church. Why the Vatican historian writes, "Montini is trapped in the most monstrous clutch in history. There is no one alive who can tell him what to do."

It is why the world's most massive CIA—from the Vatican—searches the world, to locate, burn, destroy them, and murder all who have copies, or have seen or know of them, or even suspect.

Montini's Mafia record is in them. Onassis. Hughes.

Today a Swiss account was set up for Canadian Customs' McKinstree. He granted "Hughes" an additional one-year visa. Then we had a "voice" from the Bahamas, and a proxy view by a stranger in Nicaragua. We will get a proxy photograph. But "Hughes" will be hidden until after the '72 Mafia elections—behind the moats of Miami and the ABM ring around Washington.

Three months after Tisserant died, when Pope Paul knew the papers were gone, he cried hysterically. Said he: "It would be beautiful to shake off the burden of the Roman Catholic Church and say I do not want it."

Said the headlines: "Pope Paul VI wants to quit but can't."

In 1960, Dickie cried. He lost a Mafia election. "You can't push me around anymore," he said.

Teddy cried at the bridge at Poucha Pond. "It couldn't have happened."

Montini cried too, after Tisserant died. "I want to quit."

And Necro Nader cried. "It's too much. No one can change it," he said. "These people hold the power." He's wrong.

The Power is the skinny one on the cross with the speared liver. It is a busted beak in a Pennsylvania grave—and a plaque on the Metropolitan Museum wall. A priest who sends a five dollar bill from the grave. A broken heart and a coughed up belly in Cypress lawn. (That one was my father.)

The Power to release the hold on the final tick. How can Dickie and Montini keep the lid on them? How can they murder the dead?

In Stockholm at the U.N. World Environmental Conference, U.N. Secretary Waldheim and Swedish premier Palmer violated Omerta of the U.S. of Mafia. Said both, "The first priority in the ending of world pollution is the extermination of the Vatican-U.S. of Mafia Vietnam War."

Dickie's screams are being heard around the world.

At the Kennedy graves, the entire Kennedy clan is gathered. They hold a Mass. A wafer of Christ's liver goes to Jackie, former queen of Camelot, present queen of Onassis, who murdered the man over whose grave she ate the wafer.

(Jackie is on call to Mustapha Bey, the Turk, who kept the Onassis diary—whose wife divorced him when she found Jackie in her bed. See the Canadian Papers; not all Canadians are like Canadian Customs McKinstree.)

Another wafer goes to nose-busting Teddy from the Pond (see the Chappaquiddick Papers), who sold his brothers out for eternal silver from Onassis, and eternal life from the Pope.

Another slab of wafer goes to Body-Count Chappaquiddick McNamara (see the Pentagon Papers), custodian of the POW's, MIA's, and very dead GI's in the Mafia-Papal Dickie-Heroin Vietnam "Theatre of war."

Present, by priestly proxy, was Montini.

After World War I, Pope Pius XI said, "I shall never allow Monsignor Montini to become a Cardinal. He has his own massive spy organization and has evil Mafia plans." But Pius XI was murdered by Mussolini, who was stronger than the Pope (see the Paris Papers). And so it was that Mafia Montini triumphed over Pius XI and is Pope Paul VI today, and tearfully wants to quit.

Not present at this Mass was Commander in Chief of All Pacific Forces Noel Gayler, on assignment by Dickie, in Vietnam, to exterminate all of Indochina—except for the poppy fields, heroin mule trains and air bases for CIA transport of the product (see the Kissinger Papers).

Not present was Onassis, who doesn't cry and eats liver (yours). A New York attorney says, "There is no way in God's world of knowing who owns the stock—through Chase-Manhattan Bank—that owns all the airlines." Or General Motors, or Lockheed…unless you check Onassis' Swiss banks, where McKinstree's new account is, and where Mrs. Clifford Irving presented the checks made out to "H.R. Hughes" from the publisher, to be cashed.

Nor was Dudley. His campaign bribe to Dickie purchased the "Ambassador to Denmark" job. Dudley later quit Denmark to join Dickie's reelection campaign and fight against no-fault insurance (He is part of the U.S. Insurance Mafia that never paid me a dime for the Alioto-clobbered car.)

Nor was Dickie, who set up the "Hughes" Mafia Money Funnel in 1957, in grateful appreciation for the $205,000 bribe to his brother Donald.

Nor was Connally, who is really carrying the ball. A news item: "Connally is suddenly being sent around the world to visit almost every country. Nobody knows why."

A termite heard Dickie tell Connally: "Kissinger and I couldn't buy Russia and China. Fatima #3 would be a sticky affair right now. You, Dallas Bullet Connally, former Secretary of the Treachery in charge of all Vietnam heroin, are now assigned to the greatest 'search and destroy' mission in history. Find those papers, and destroy them. Draw on the heroin billions, Onassis billions, the 41% tax siphon of the U.S. GNP, the Vatican billions.

"And then buy anything that's left. Any country. Draw on the $100 billion extra National Debt we just socked to the peeepul. Buy, buy, buy. And destroy, murder—whatever it takes. The Vatican will back you. They control most of the world. And they are as worried as I am. Tisserant is no idiot. Blow it all if necessary. Money won't do us any good in a box. Do this, or don't come back. There may not be any place to come back to."

Dickie's not stupid. Mafia, yes. But not stupid. He is aware that history proves, even without Tisserant, that all balance of power relationships soon break down, and war follows. He also knows that in a world of five actual nuclear powers, the only way to peace is to get the man off the cross. That, of course, would blow his "place in history", and that would never do.

From the Tisserant Papers: "Twenty four hours before his murder, Christ stated, 'A new commandment I give unto you, that ye love one another....'"

He was interrupted by events, and arrest. On the cross, twenty four hours later, he completed it: "...and hang murderers on the cross, not me."

This commandment, the eleventh, was destroyed by Religion and Politics—the two handmaidens. It ruled out war and crime.

Substituted was the code of Omerta: "Do not squeal on a fellow Maf." Religion has its Mafia Omerta confessional. Government has its Legal Mafia: the Mafia Election Process. Both sponsor war and crime, for personal gain.

In Moscow, Dickie and Brezhnev agreed on something: "Russia and the U.S. acknowledge the fact of the possibility of mutual devastation. We offer our entire populations as hostages to peace (except Washington and Moscow, both encircled by ABM's)."

About this, Dickie said: "We want to be remembered for our deeds—not by the fact that we brought war to the world." And Kissinger said: "Forty years ago, this agreement would have been considered insanity."

Twenty-seven years ago—one second before Hiroshima—public reference to a weapon that would murder 100,000 was called insanity.

21 June 1972: Good Housekeeping: "We Ate Mary Jo's Liver" (A Satire)

**GOOD HOUSEKEEPING
PUBLISHED BY HEARST CORP.
WE SQUAT ON BUSTED-NOSE MARY JO'S U.S. GRAVE**

[The original Gemstone paper features the cover page torn from the June 1972 issue *of Good Housekeeping*, with an angelic-looking photograph of Joan Kennedy and an announcement of an interview with her, plus a hand-lettered caption by Roberts, pasted on. The written text on this page (Joan Kennedy's story) is neatly written, up, down, and sideways, around the central image. On the following pages, Roberts returned to his usual full-page neat writing. Facsimile of Roberts' "cover" on page 26.-sc]

WE ATE MARY JO'S LIVER
(Teddy and me and the U.S. of Mafia)

"Onassis owns the U.S. of Mafia, Greece, Vietnam, Taiwan, Swiss-Montini, Dickie, Humphrey, Teddy, Thieu, Chiang, CIA, FBI, Pentagon, Party, Press, Legal, Corporate Mafia. He ate the livers of JFK, Mary Jo, Bobby, King, 'Hughes', Yablonski, Joan Tunney's hubby, Newsom's nieces, Roberts' father. He wants livers of Wallace and McGovern. One of his will be president.

"Ten million opium growers pass heroin from Burma, Thailand, Laos, Vietnam to Chiang's Taiwan—and on to Harry Yee in San Francisco. CIA-Air America flies it, and Thieu clears the flights. Nixon's missile silos and air-bases in Thailand protect it. The Spellman-JFK 'Holy Crusade' covers it up. 80% of the world's supply adds up to $50 billion a year—tax free—to Onassis. Twelve years in Vietnam = $50 billion x 12 = $600 billion. Twelve years in Vietnam = $200 billion spent on bombs. (Onassis owns U.S. "defense spending" via "Hughes".) $600 billion + $200 billion = $800 billion. 50,000 American dead = $60 million per American death, for Onassis. A much better yield per American corpse than oil. And considerate, too: no charge for 'body-count' Chinese corpses.

"The head of our family—Onassis—has courage and long life. Ditto our Mama Rosie—Papal Princess. CIA-Meo opium growers have courage and long life. Not one died during this long war. They have courage and long life because they kill their enemies, and eat their livers. Onassis and Rosie have been eating livers since 1932, when Onassis and Joseph P. Kennedy first brought heroin and booze into Boston with the blessing of Roosevelt and Churchill. This is why Mary Jo's intestines were chopped into hors d'oeuvres—wafers for brave, free Americans who support us and will vote me queen. Courtesy of Ma and Pa Kopechne, who clutch Cushing's crosses, saying, 'We don't care if it was murder. We're satisfied.' On to Fatima #3: the blow-off of the other half; that is, heathens who eat the livers of their victims. Convert them to our way, or kill them.

"Hearst (Kennedy blood pact, 1934) promotes images of Rosie, Jackie and me (with a Madonna style and look). Hearst printed Cafarakis's Onassis story in order to establish JFK's angry phone call to Jackie ('Get off Onassis's yacht!') before the planned double Diem + JFK murder day—November 1, 1963—as a 'polite letter.' Onassis ate the livers of Black Panthers Hampton and Clark—in Chicago, after Chappaquiddick—because they knew of the aborted JFK Chicago murder. I love Hearst. Cafarakis, Onassis' former bus boy, is now a millionaire, with hotels on the Riviera. I love Cafarakis. And liver. And I go to a psychiatrist.

"Mary Jo heard the angry Tunney-Teddy-Alioto phone calls at the cottage that night, and was running to Nader with the entire bit: the Onassis-Maheu assassinations of JFK, Bobby, and

King. (FBI Maheu now wants $50 million for this, from Onassis, our family leader).

"Mary Jo knew about the 1957 Apalachin Onassis Mafia take-over of the election process, after the March 1957 hyping of Hughes by Onassis, and the 1957 set-up of the "Hughes" Medical Research Foundation as a tax-free Mafia Money Funnel—to and from Onassis's Swiss banks. The money went to purchase things such as Greece and V.P. Nixon, who originally set it up, in 1957, via the Onassis bribe—and said to Dietrich: 'Treason? Screw America. My family comes first.' (1957 was a vintage year).

"And she also knew about the Alioto hit-run cover-up, September 16, 1968, on Roberts' car; and how he became angry and made Alioto's Humphrey cry by electing Nixon President. That hit-run cover-up caused Chappaquiddick and the death of Howard Hughes in his cage on Onassis's Greek Island of Skorpios, on April 16, 1971.

"Teddy backhanded Mary Jo in the back seat of the car as she clutched his arm at the bridge in total terror. Teddy bailed out on the bridge. Mary Jo suffocated—after 2 hours and 13 minutes—because of a busted snorkel (her nose), while Teddy phoned Onassis. Dickie murdered Roberts' father on February 22, 1972, and proceeds now to Fatima #3—to cover up all of these murders, and more, back to that of Christ.

"I write this from my psychiatrist's couch. Regardless of what Hearst prints, here we let it all hang out. These are notes to my psychiatrist who is out of the room at the moment.

"Onassis tells me I can eat Hearst's liver when all this blows over—and my psychiatrist's. 'No witnesses,' says he. Onassis says my college room-mate, Joan Tunney (Wilkinson), will get out of her English nut house soon, and that she enjoyed eating her husband's liver after she chopped his head off. Onassis says she gets to eat the livers of everybody at the nut house, too. 'No witnesses,' again, in case they heard her speak of John Tunney's first Chappaquiddick phone call from her home outside San Francisco. (In San Francisco, Alioto made Police Chief Cahill a security guard at the phone company to sit on those phone call records. Back east, Publisher Loeb, Manchester Guardian, got Hoffa out of the clink by promising Nixon to burn his credit card copies of all of the Chappaquiddick phone calls).

"During the middle of his Mafia trial, Alioto shocked the jury by eating barbecued girls' liver: Newsom's nieces, Pelosi's daughters—plus a roasted older Japanese liver, the nieces' nurse. (After Chappaquiddick, Newsom, who knew why it happened [the Alioto hit-run], was recalled to Switzerland by Onassis—and Newsom was getting ready to squawk). I imagine the six-year-old girl's liver was the tenderest—but my brother-in-law, JFK, and Cardinal Spellman and Diem and his brother, Cardinal Thuc, and another brother, Nhu, and his wife, Madame Nhu all say they enjoyed older Buddhist barbecued livers in Saigon in 1963. Madame Nhu still runs heroin out of Vietnam—courtesy of the Pentagon—for Onassis. Cardinal Thuc is still doing his thing for Montini somewhere.

"Onassis ate the livers of JFK, Diem, and Nhu. Captain Nung did it for Onassis on Diem and Nhu at a Cholon railroad crossing. Nung is now big with Thieu, and Thieu is big with Montini, Onassis, and Dickie—and that's as big as you can get. Where can you go after the top of the Vatican and the top of the Mafia?

"The man on the cross? 2000 years ago the Romans pinned him on a cross, speared him in the liver, and pulled it out and ate it. Tacitus sneaked records of the action out of Rome in 64 A.D., and Nero burned the town. They burned Christ's 11th commandment, his last words on the cross: 'Murderers on the cross, not me,' but retained his skinny skewered body as a symbol of submission. And today you can get a symbolic bite of Christ's liver in any church. Even without seeing documents of proof, ask yourself a question: 'If this is not true, why do they cover up the murder of Christ and the murder of Mary Jo?'

"Said Cardinal Cushing of the Onassis-Jackie merger, 'Welcome, Onassis, and bring your checkbook.' Said Montini and Cushing of Teddy, after Chappaquiddick: 'He is a Prince of the Church; if he leaves politics, we will furnish sanctuary, and he will become a leader of our church.'

Montini made the same offer to Alioto: Cardinal, I believe. Onassis was gonna give some of JFK's liver to his Turkish blackmail friend, Mustapha, when he walked down the gangplank in Turkey with JFK's wife, Jackie, my sister-in-law, on his arm—just after JFK's call to Jackie: 'Get off that yacht if you have to swim.'

"But frightened Jack John canceled his Chicago Stadium speech that day—November 1, 1963—and Onassis didn't get Jack's liver until 3 weeks later at Dallas, via Maheu (who was still smarting from his earlier failure to assassinate Castro for the CIA Onassis branch)—and he was so hungry he ate the whole thing.

"Mustapha had a diary on Onassis—going back to the 20's when Onassis ran Turkish opium into Argentina; and later, when he ran Marseilles heroin into Montreal and cocaine into New Orleans with French brandy; and later still, when Onassis brought this heroin and cocaine in direct to Boston with Joseph P. Kennedy's booze. This was under the sponsorship of President Roosevelt and Churchill, who, with the Pope, ruled the 'civilized' world—an act which moved both Kennedy and Onassis into the blackmailed oval offices of the White House and Number 10 Downing Street. That was in 1932.

"Joseph P., my father-in-law, then took what he wanted. The SEC, for instance. Anything. Onassis ran the dope and whatever else he wanted, protected by the President and the President's boy, J. Mafia Hoover (whose ex-FBI Agents Club today runs most businesses and all of the 'Hughes'-Onassis' gambling.) Roosevelt's sons loot around the world: Teamster's Pension Funds, IOS, whatever is ripe. It's a legacy.

"Joseph P. and Onassis helped Roosevelt rig War II, by way of heavy blackmail on Churchill—and got Churchill to place a 25-year seal on documents. They made a pact: oil and arms for Onassis (he delivered to Russia, the Axis, and the Allies, and never lost a ship or sailor. A good 'deal.') A Presidential dynasty was guaranteed for Joseph P. Kennedy's family. (For instance, I shall be the next queen of America—after Onassis eats the livers of Wallace and McGovern). The pact was sealed in 1940, by Joseph P.'s backing Roosevelt's sick third term after his previous years of successfully prodding the war as Ambassador to England. Onassis slapped our current Supreme Court Chief Justice, Burger, around for a batch of free ships after the war, and that's when the fun really began.

"Fatima #1—War II—had been successfully rigged. Fatima #2—the conversion of communism to the Vatican ('The Cold War') was under way. The handmaidens of history were marching on to Fatima #3—the Deputy of Christ at Auschwitz, and the Greek, in command of the blow-off of the other half. It was all a matter of cover-up—each layer adding more murder, treason, bribery (Constitutionally, hanging offenses) to be covered up.

"In 1954 JFK met two people. Papa Joseph introduced him to his partner, Onassis, as the future President. And Cardinal Spellman introduced him to Diem. Diem came from our Jesuit Seminary in Maryknoll, Maryland. The Vatican sent him to Vietnam to restore Vatican ownership after the French blew it at Dien-ben-Phu. In 1954, Spellman brought Diem back from Vietnam to meet JFK and arrange the future 'Holy Crusade' in Vietnam—from the Papal standpoint.

"1957—a vintage year—arrived. Apalachin (the Mafia take-over of the U.S. election process.) Nixon's 'Hughes'-Onassis bribe to set up the 'Hughes' Medical Research Mafia Money Funnel Foundation. Onassis's hyping of Hughes, and the body switch. A phony name marriage license, and a phony "marriage" occurred in Tonopah, Nevada, between Elizabeth Jean Peters and 'Howard Hughes.' The battered, hyped body of the real Hughes was carted off to a cage on Tenos, while a permanent double was set up to play Hughes in 'real life.'

"1958: Test of the new Mafia election process was run, successfully; a heavy Democratic Mafia congressional win.

"1959: Onassis hosts his slave Churchill and his partner's son, JFK, with wife Jackie, on his yacht.

"1960: Onassis-Hughes' $500 million hedge bribe was paid to candidate Dickie, (and a matching bribe to JFK), but the Mafia election process and vote rigging—in Daley's Illinois, and Johnson-Connally's Texas—got JFK in. Dickie cried, but Joseph P. Kennedy and Onassis moved into the White House. Johnson, the new V.P., was immediately sent to Vietnam to force Diem to take in American troops and start Spellman's 'Holy Crusade.'

"Maheu was hired by the CIA to assassinate Castro. (Castro had stolen $8 billion in Cuban gambling money from Onassis's man, McLaney, when he took over Cuba.) McLaney set up a Florida training camp where Maheu trained his assassins. The Bay of Pigs was launched to get Cuba, and the gambling money, back for Onassis. When that failed, Castro offered to remove the missiles six days before JFK issued his ultimatum: 'Stop, or I'll start Fatima #3—the nuclear blow-off of the other half.' It was a stalemate—but Cuba was lost to Onassis and the Vatican.

"Attention switch to Vietnam: 'Pour in troops and keep them there until after my election in 1964.' A 'Holy Crusade.' Fine with Onassis—but Joseph P. had a stroke and could no longer relay orders to his sons, JFK and Bobby, from his partner Onassis.

"JFK and Bobby jumped on Hoffa's group—a branch of Onassis. 'I'll break your back,' said Hoffa. They indicted Wally Bird in Thailand for heroin running. (Bird was high in Onassis's Thai-Laos-Vietnam heroin flow. The indictment was burned after Dallas.) Diem barbecued Buddhists, and this seemed to be poor public relations to the Pope and JFK. And Diem made noises like settling the squabble with Ho Chi Minh. JFK decided to dump Diem and continue the Vietnam crusade with a more congenial boy. But Diem was Onassis's main stem in the Heroin bit. Without his partner, Joseph P., Onassis was getting too much static from the sons. They removed Diem from office—and Onassis removed Diem, Nhu, and JFK from their livers. It was a good deal.

"Maheu used some of his boys from the Bay of Pigs for the JFK murder. Some of them were in Chicago for the JFK aborted murder on November 1, 1963—and finally got the job done in Dallas, three weeks later.

"Johnson got a message from Onassis's Pentagon, on the plane from Dallas (via a mid-west radio station): 'It was no conspiracy. Repeat: No conspiracy. Put a 75-year secrecy lid on it and whoop up the Vietnam War. Cool it. Cover it up. Burn the Bird indictment. Remember, if your plane has an accident before you get back to Washington, Speaker of the House McCormack will be president, and our boys—Voloshen and Swig—own him.' 'Yes, Mr. Onassis,' answered LBJ.

"Mafia code: 'If they welsh, kill'em, and take the broad and the shotgun.' Onassis did: Jackie and the Pentagon. Today, at missile launches to the moon, a full bird Pentagon General flies John Meyer over the site for a better view. John Meyer, as with FBI Maheu, was Hughes's 'right hand man.' Onassis took him over when he took over Hughes. As his 'right hand man.'

"1968 was a vintage year too:

"**April:** Martin Luther King's liver (he spoke of the key: reform of the Mafia election process.)

"**June:** Bobby's liver (he would have been elected president—and nobody hated Onassis more than he, as Mary Jo discovered when she went through Bobby's personal effects in L.A. and discovered horrible things about the Kennedys and Onassis and all Mafia politics. She said to a friend: 'I will never work for Kennedys again. This isn't Camelot; it's all murder.'

"**August:** Teddy surrendered, body and soul, to Onassis on his yacht—and offered his brother's wife, Jackie, to the new head of the Kennedy family. Then Onassis purchased both 1968 candidates through assassin Maheu, who carried Las Vegas skim loot to Bebe Rebozo and Nixon—and Humphrey and O'Brien—roughly a million apiece when you add in amounts from Tony Boyle (who murdered the Yablonski family, with approval of the hierarchy), and Jake 'The Barber' Factor and Alioto to Humphrey, and more batches to Nixon from such groups as ITT (whose director, McCone, was the CIA chief who hired Maheu to assassinate Castro and scrambled things all the way

through the Diem, Nhu, and JFK murders.)

"**October 16:** In vintage year 1957, 'Holy Crusade' Cardinal Spellman married Teddy and me. It was the 'social event of the decade.' In vintage year 1968—October 16—the merger of the century occurred. The two warring Mafia Monster families united. Frankenstein took a suitable bride. Onassis snatched Jackie Kennedy—widow of JFK.

"**September:** But before that, in September, at the corner of Franklin and Lombard streets, San Francisco, a car belonging to an Alioto daughter pulled a hit-run on a parked car—a Plymouth, license plate BZA 494—belonging to Roberts.

"When Alioto was elected mayor of San Francisco in 1967, Teddy and Onassis issued a joint statement: 'We figure he will be president some day.' For you see, Lanza was Alioto's godfather, and Lanza was the Northern California representative at Apalachin in 1957. Upon Lanza's return to San Francisco, he debated whether to name Alioto mayor in 1959. He ran a brief public test and decided to bring him on later, which he did, in a Mafia-paid blitz in 1967. Once in as mayor, they pushed him fast; he was one of their own.

"In **June 1968**, Alioto was selected to nominate Humphrey for the Presidency. Humphrey was to select Alioto as his Vice Presidential running mate. But somebody publicly brought to the attention of the Democratic convention—and Humphrey—the FBI Mafia rap sheet on Alioto. Since it was out in public, Humphrey decided to take Muskie as his V.P. instead. But he did plan his campaign to wind up in San Francisco—the home of the man who had nominated him, Alioto—where he could count on an overwhelmingly Democratic Mafia community welcome that would rouse the populace in a triumphant finale.

"The Alioto car had just delivered Alioto to the airport. It was returning to Bushati's Pizza Parlor, at Scott and Lombard Streets—owned by Adolpho Veronese, Mia Angela's (Alioto's daughter's) fiance. Alioto flew to Chicago that night to accept the Justinian Award as 'Lawyer of the Year.' And crud flew all over San Francisco. Roberts was up all night sorting it out. He finally got his car back from the police garage before they destroyed it, and was picking up pieces of various other cars crashed in a Mafia demolition derby at the hit-run site when the younger Lanza told him to 'get out of the street or you'll get sunstroke. Forget it. Nothing happened here. Everything will get settled.' At the same time, another Maf—McCracken—was quizzing Roberts' parents. 'Who is he—this son of yours? What does he want?'

"I know these things because I know the story from this end. And then after a while Roberts sent a letter, and documents, and volumes of papers to Teddy. And he asked Teddy to stand up in the Senate and unravel himself like a Mafia ball of string—with Congressional immunity—referring to JFK's 'Ask not what your country can do, but what you can do for your country.' And he suggested that Teddy get the Pope to do the same thing in the Vatican on behalf of Christ and the entire necrophiliac Vatican-Mafia American nation which squats on Mary Jo's grave and drools and screws that broken-nosed dead girl with a frenzy greater than ours who eat liver.

"Roberts is why I am on this psychiatrist's couch. He elected Nixon, because of that hit-run cover-up. And he exposed the Mafia election process, which exposed the entire Vatican-Mafia group, including Nixon. He exposed the Onassis'-"Hughes" Mafia Money Funnel—which purchased Nixon. Nixon murdered his father, because of this. The hit-run caused Chappaquiddick. He maneuvered Taiwan out of, and China into, the U.N. He wants Christ off the cross—and His murder cover-up exposed. And that's not the worst thing. I don't understand it all except to know that it is very bad—horrible. At any rate, he hates cancer, Mafia, murder, treason, bribery, liver eaters, necrophiliacs and shit. He's arranged for flushing.

"On **October 1, 1968**, Kathryn Hollister, a nurse, paid by Alioto, 'confessed' to the crime at a court hearing on the hit-run. She was fined, had a fit, and was escorted from the court by Alioto's wife—Angelina, mother of Mia Angela. Hollister, a 35-year-old woman, wasn't anywhere near Franklin and Lombard that night. Hollister's Chrysler, however, bears license plate UXT 264.

Alioto's daughter's Cadillac bore license plate UKT 264, issued to a fictitious name, and a fictitious address: 'Andy Andersen, 6969 Lankershim Blvd., L.A,' for the convenience of Alioto's sons whose licenses had been revoked after their convictions for a series of Bay Area hit-runs. Fingerprints identify a youthful Alioto clan member as the driver. A male.

"By the time Alioto returned from Chicago the cover-up had already mushroomed out of proportion. Participants no longer mattered. The filming of the cover-up, from then till now, and on into the 1972 election between Chappaquiddick Dickie and Chappaquiddick Teddy, is—who knows the word? I don't. Try 'deadly'. Cancer killing? Fatima 3, in reverse? A new thing?"

[**EDITOR'S NOTE:** This is all Joanie gave us on that date. However we had a spy hiding behind a Moosehead mounted on the wall, and he tells us that the psychiatrist came back into the room and Joanie handed him the notes quoted above, and the psychiatrist read them.

And Joanie said, "My problem is that the Constitution says murder and treason and bribery are hanging offenses, and yet we do those things daily. We screw dead people and eat liver and we get elected queen. I've learned to love liver, and Teddy says he can live with it—meaning being president; and…what is that you're eating, doctor? It looks like 2000-year-old liver—1972 years old, to be exact, and well aged, and marinated, and tenderized by a spear hole. Doctor! Is that the real thing? Lover!"

And she leaped from the couch, drooling, and they embraced in a frenzy, chewing their way, on opposite sides of the most prized of all livers, toward ecstasy. We, as impartial observers, do not feel that we should report the private actions of consenting adults in the privacy of their own offices, and so our observer behind the Moosehead withdrew, at that moment. We do know that they did not eat each other, like piranha fish, because we saw Joanie later and she gave us a copy of all those letters, documents and volumes that Roberts sent to Teddy. Buy our next edition.]

[**OBSERVER BEHIND THE MOOSEHEAD'S NOTE:** We do not consider the actions of consenting adults in public to be subject to invasion of privacy—in the case of the necrophiliac screwing of Mary Jo on her Pennsylvania grave. An entire nation is there, drooling and screwing—Presidents and Priests, Senators and Judges—everybody, including Ma and Pa Kopechne. Hearst is out there now. And if I don't hurry, the crowd will be so huge I'll have to stand at the Pennsylvania border and hump whoever is in front of me. And, with my luck, that would be Onassis.]

[**JANITOR'S NOTE:** Hearst and Moosehead rushed out of here drooling—on their way to screw some Pennsylvania grave dirt—and forgot these papers. And I have something to add. I'm 98 years old, and I sweep up around here and flush shit. My greatest thrill is going to the bathroom. The relief, you see….

A funny thing about George Wallace's shooter. As with Sirhan, goofed up with hypnosis, Bremer couldn't get a center shot into Wallace—out of six mechanical hypnotic shots from a distance of four feet. Neither could Sirhan, at six feet. Sirhan scattered eight mechanical shots—hypnotic—and never did hit Bobby with a single one. One of the back-ups, Onassis's Maheu's Gene Cesar, got him with three shots in the back of the head with a palm gun.

Sub-conscious hypnosis invariably causes inaccurate conscious action. At Dallas, Oswald actually hit his target—from behind—(Connally)—one out of two shots. Here, it was an Onassis-Maheu back-up bullet from the overpass—in front—that went through JFK's under-chin and blew the back of his head into the face of the cop riding behind. Oswald was surprised. He was there—alone, he thought—for Connally—and when he heard the two shots from the overpass and the one from the grassy knoll he knew he had been conned. Ruby silenced that.

Onassis was eating livers of people he murdered in Smyrna at age 14, and peddling opium to the Turks during the Smyrna massacre. Supreme Court Chief Justice Warren ate the livers—for Onassis—of all those who were murdered over Dallas, such as Hampton and Clark. He put a seventy-five years of secrecy lid on everything. Onassis was lucky with his back-ups at Dallas, Memphis, and L.A. With Wallace, he goofed. There was no back-up—and Wallace is still alive.

Sirhan and Bremer can't help. Hypnotics can't remember what happened.

McGovern will probably get a frontal assault—9000 Maf jamming machine guns in all the holes he has. Why not? Onassis owns the legal Mafia. On August 14, 1970, he even purchased Nader. Maybe Onassis already owns McGovern, who was the first to congratulate Teddy on his escape from the Chappaquiddick inquest. Kennedy Mafia are running McGovern's campaign. McGovern is begging for Chicago Daley's help—and Daley helped remove the livers from Hampton and Clark. Only "God" Onassis can decide McGovern's fate. "God" Montini is in second place, and fading fast.

At the time of the Bay of Pigs—and later Caribbean action, such as Volman and Perlmutter and Supreme Court Justice Douglas, re: gambling, in Haiti and the Dominican Republic, reporters rumbled about hidden maneuvering by a power greater than the CIA and the government itself. Fit it in, folks.

A Federal Judge declared all ITT bribery, treason and murder to be legal, and the Mafia Senate closed its inquiry into the matter. ITT-CIA McCone is back on the grave piously screwing Mary Jo. Agnew is visiting Thieu, and Dickie's off to try to purchase Russia for Onassis, dragging his Haiphong mines behind him.

Roberts laid out to Teddy how, in September, 1968, and early October, he notified Nixon and Mitchell and Reagan of the whole mess. Via the whole crew of Nixon hatchet men: John Mack (Bank of California—Lockheed loans, Alioto money); John Greenagel (Swig50's Chamber of Commerce); Bill Best (Nixon's Northern California campaign manager); Dick Carlson (who with Brisson, Kissinger's pal, was given FBI files for the *Look* "Alioto Mafia Web" bit. Also: attorneys Belli, Davis, Lewis, D.A.'s Ferdon, Winkler, Goldsmith, Owens, FBI. Most of Alioto's Mafia cops. "Truth squad" Senators Griffin and Scott. Bausch, O'Brien, Kosewicz, Kish, Chang. Bribes by Doherty, McCracken, Lanzas. Witnesses, affidavits, film. By mid-October, it looked like a Nixon landslide. Everybody was smug.

And on October 16, 1968, Onassis merged with Jackie. This was preceded by a Jackie confessional to Cardinal Cushing, and an Onassis business contract with Jackie. Cushing emerged from the confessional in shock and said, "If the world knew what Jackie told me, they wouldn't believe me. I dispense with all Vatican rules. Welcome, Onassis, and bring your checkbook. What else can we do?"

Onassis emerged with a cash "deal": purchase of the queen of the civilized world. And October rolled on.

Roberts arranged a noose for the three—Unruh, Alioto, Humphrey—when they gathered in San Francisco for Humphrey's triumphant finale to his campaign. And he notified all, publicly, of this matter. And all of them crawled into a hole. Humphrey canceled that Bay Area finale, and lost the election by the 100,000 votes he would have gained.

Teddy sent one of the aides who later turned up at Chappaquiddick to bribe Roberts. Johnson threw in an "understanding": "Peace in Vietnam: Bombing halt", six days before the election (a total myth), and it helped Humphrey. Connally rigged the Texas votes for Humphrey, and it also helped. But not enough. As the final votes came in, Humphrey lost California—by those 100,000 votes—and lost the Presidency.

Nixon, on election day, threw a total clamp on the Alioto hit-run. His vital weakness was the Onassis-"Hughes" ownership of him and the Mafia Election Process. They all thought it was buried.

But those raw FBI files on Alioto's Mafia web were out. Alioto needed to be Governor of California. So, just before Chappaquiddick, Swig and Shorenstein (with Alioto money) offered Unruh lots of loot not to run against Alioto—thus leaving Alioto a solo shot. In addition, they

---

50 Ben Swig, owner of S.F.'s Fairmont Hotel

suggested that Unruh run against John Tunney for Senator.

But Teddy had already picked Tunney, his old college roommate, for the Senate job. Alioto was desperate to be governor—but Tunney was desperate to be Senator, and he didn't want competition from Unruh either. In total anger, Tunney called Teddy at Chappaquiddick, from sister Joan's home in Tiburon, that night, and raved about the treachery of Alioto, who had already blown the presidency for Humphrey because of the Alioto hit-run cover-up.

Teddy called Alioto back, and a Mafia conversation ensued. Those calls Mary Jo heard, fresh from dealing with murdered Bobby's papers in L.A.

She had said, "I will never work for Kennedys again. This is not Camelot; it's all murder." She had had a few months' stopover to help elect Whelan mayor of Jersey City (who is now in prison). While there, she heard another bunch of New Jersey Kennedy Mafia tapes. She arrived at Chappaquiddick, boiling mad, on her way to Nader.

A few more Mafia calls were made by Teddy at the cottage. Mary Jo bolted in anger, running toward the ferry—and Nader. Teddy grabbed a purse—Keogh's; jumped into the car, and followed her. He talked her into getting into the back seat. She was too angry to get in front with him. She was still angry at the cross-road, where Teddy stopped the car to "reason" with her. Teddy couldn't take her to the ferry—and Nader. Nor could he let her talk to the cop who stopped to offer help. Teddy headed instead for the bridge—away from the ferry. As they reached the bridge, Mary Jo clutched his arm, from the back seat.

She said, "Take me to the ferry!"

Instead, he backhanded her, breaking the beak, and bailed out. He landed on the bridge. The car sailed off the bridge, and Mary Jo was trapped inside. The murder occurred as he ran to phone Onassis.

Joan Tunney Wilkinson's entire family was shipped to Europe on the following day. In Norway, Mari and Adamo (sent from the Bonanno Mafia crime family) kidnapped her, hyped her for a month on heroin, a la "Hughes", and then released her, now an addict, near [the heroin factory in] Marseilles. The following Easter she chopped her hubby's head off, and Onassis arranged for her seclusion in a rest-home—out of the way, in total silence.

Newsom had followed Roberts around, for Alioto, after the hit-run, and he knew the 'why' of Chappaquiddick. And after Chappaquiddick, Onassis jerked Newsom off to Switzerland to work for him there permanently. But Newsom revolted, and returned to San Francisco. And so it was that Onassis barbecued Newsom's nieces—in front of Newsom—during the middle of the Alioto Mafia trial.

I don't like this. So I took one of the shrink's volume copies of Roberts' stuff to the nearest Xerox machine. I had noticed that people often pick up their copies, but forget to remove the original from under the rubber mat. And the next one who comes along reads this forgotten copy as if it were the secret formula for Coca-Cola. So I waited for a long-hair to head for the machine. Then I put this volume copy under the mat and walked away. He read it. And walked to the phone.

Said he: "When is the next plane to Chile?" and he took the volume and flagged down a cab. (Probably a rich hippie.)

I left a bunch more around different Xerox machines. One guy read it and asked me, "Where's Bulgaria?" (The CIA declares that Bulgaria is the hub of all heroin.)

Another called someone: "Get the commune together. We're going to Russia. I've got a fortune."

Another: "Baby, you like China? I got ping pong balls."

A John Wayne type: "I'm gonna trade this to Hanoi. They can have Thieu, Indo-China, and ropes to hang all the Mafia in the world. We get our POW's back, and they can hunt down all the

criminal Mafia in the U.S., at a million dollars per ear, and there'd still be trillions in buried criminal loot, back through time, for the rest of us to divvy up. I'll take Mafia Texas for my own private shit house, and I'll give Mafia Massachusetts to an orphanage, Mafia Illinois to the Blind Foundation...." As he walked out the door on his way to Hanoi, he gave Marcello's Louisiana to the clerk at the counter.

A black, with "Zambia" on the back of his motorcycle jacket, rushed out to his bike with his copy, grinning. "We'll move the U.S. capitol to Zambia."

A doctor, in hospital white, walked up to me. He said, "Sir, we have discovered the cure. We even have options. We can push buttons in all non-Mafia countries, aim all the missiles at Mary Jo's grave—and that would kill all cancer, because all of it squats there. Or do as in India, where they put a man in a cage, let mosquitoes bite him, and when one gives him malaria they follow that one back to its breeding grounds and exterminate the entire family. For instance, Malarial Mafia Mosquito Alioto and the Alioto breed. We will track them back to their breeding grounds and exterminate all of them, like putting a cancer-killing serum in the blood stream to kill the cancer without killing the patient. And then we doctors will collect our fee—all of their criminal loot—back through time. Trillions for medical research. Stick out your tongue."

I did.

He said, "Hmm. Looks like apathy to me. I'll run some tests, just to be sure. If you have apathy or Mary Jo Necrophilia, you're dead, man. There's a deadly disease running around. It's called MMORDIS—Moldering Mass of Rotten Dribbling Infectious Shit. Have a happy day."

And then there was one who made me angry. He was a stockbroker type. He read the volume and came over and sat down, starry-eyed.

He said, "Hey Pop, I just hit the jackpot. I just made arrangements to marry the love of my life—and she doesn't even know me yet. And I cornered all of the loot in the world.

"You see, three weeks after Chappaquiddick, Roberts went to Nixon and Mitchell—President and Attorney General—with the solution to the murder. He told Nixon, 'You can be another Abraham Lincoln, and free this land from Mafia slavery. I want you to cooperate with me. I know Onassis owns you—through 'Hughes'. And I know you turned down my offer, on election day, 1968, to accept Alioto, and the entire Mafia, including both Mafia Parties, Mafia CIA-ITT McCone, Mafia Rosensteil, Hoover's FBI—all of them—on a platter. I know you put a lid on it, to protect the Mafia Election Process.

"'But this latest Kennedy murder has reopened it all, in spite of your lid. And it exposes the entire web of assassinations, heroin, Onassis, and everything. It exposes the Vatican and all of the other handmaiden religions, including that of your boy, Billy Graham. And it leaves you only two choices: the keys.

"'Your Onassis-'Hughes' Mafia Money Funnel murder, treason, bribery, 41% siphon of the GNP, War, Heroin, Crime Administration is now exposed, and currently in motion. Everyone can see it. You can either cure this cancer, or blow off the other half via Vatican Fatima #3—and preserve the cancer.

"'If you choose to cure it, I offer a new thing: experimental results on a new very dense mineral—experiments which ended when Alioto clobbered my car, an act which precipitated this entire shit-pit. The keyword is "Chappaquiddick" and...hey, where did you two go? Where is everybody?'

"And, Pop, that's where I got the idea. Because, you see, from then till now, I have seen this guy—what's-his-name? Roaming this Mafia country, shouting 'Chappaquiddick! Anybody for Chappaquiddick?' And when he does this, everybody runs to the bathroom and jumps in the shit bowl and pulls the lid down.

"Now here's what we're gonna do, Pop. I'm gonna get girl scouts with bull horns on a

certain day, on the balconies of every Mafia City Hall in this Mafia Nation. They're gonna shout 'Chappaquiddick' at 10-second intervals. The shit bowls will fill up fast and we will see a panic-stricken city exodus. Hordes of Mafia will be running for the country to jump into rat holes or dig themselves into beach sand like sand crabs. Then, I send my troops of boy scouts around to padlock those shit-bowl lids and cap over all those rat holes. It's just like capping oil wells, Pop. The scouts will hold an honest election, and we bring Princess Grace back from Monaco as a chaperone for our new youthful government, and we rename the U.S. of Mafia 'Monaco West'. Those of us who aren't capped over will go around occasionally and lift the lids and shout 'Chappaquiddick,' and the Mafia will send us up all of the criminal loot, buried funds, secret accounts, corporate stock. And we'll pass them down their daily bread, which happens to be all of our garbage, pollution, sewage, etc., which is how we clean up the environment that they dirtied up for us. After 2000 years, it's our turn, Pop. They've been doing it to us all this time. They call it the 'national interest.' Actually, it is our legacy from all those murdered dead, like Mary Jo."

I interrupted: "Princess Grace? What about her hubby, Stubby Rainier?"

He: "We'll hang him. He's a friend of Onassis. We'll hang Cary Grant, too. He kissed her once in the movie, To Catch a Thief. And he's also a friend of Onassis."

Me: "What's your interest in Princess Grace?"

"Don't you dig it, Pop? She's the one. She'll be a widow. She and I will chaperone the Scouts. She will fall in love with me. I want her. She's mine."

Me: "There's just one thing wrong with your plan, sonny."

He: "What's that?"

Me: "I'm gonna murder you, you Mafia slob." And I hit him over the head with my cane. "I've been in love with Grace Kelly ever since War II, and nobody gets her but me."

This is where I got angry, and he ran out the door with me hobbling after him clobbering him with that cane.

And finally when I was running out of breath on the Marina green he said, "Okay, you can have her. I'll take one of the daughters. Can I buy you a beer, father-in-law?"

In the beer joint my son-in-law elaborated: "We'll get the man off the cross and give him back his liver and patch up his nail holes—and Mary Jo's busted nose—and give her a decent burial. And we'll have a new symbol: a healthy doctor, with a scalpel, cutting out a cancer. And on that vacant cross we'll hang, on one end, Teddy, who states: 'Ask not what your country can do for you, but what you can do for your country.' And on the other end, we'll hang Pope Pius, who states: 'I will gladly give my life for all of humanity.' That's what I really want, pop-in-law. What do you want out of all of this?"

Apparently he didn't hear me very well out there on the Marina Green, and I was about to club him again when I realized I hadn't told him everything.

So I said: "I'm 98. You might say, I'm dead. A lifetime is only a speck in geological time—called by some, 'Eternity.' I want Christ off the cross. To do this, I can kill the cancer—His murderers—here, or take them with me, and hang them there, on an eternity yo-yo. That means I get a ticket to eternity without crossing the Vatican palms with silver. In other words, I deal direct with the boss. And that means angel wings for my princess. Everybody wins but the shit. Shit gets flushed.

"I'm a janitor. Dickie clips me to fight the 'Holy Crusade' in Vietnam and Fatima #3. My union clips me, to murder the Yablonski family. Hoover's FBI and ITT McCone's CIA clip me to run heroin, keep lids on and murder around the globe. Mafia government clips me to pay for the squat on Mary Jo's grave. What I receive is crime, war, pollution, and a job. That job consists of flushing shit.

"Whatever your job, you're supposed to try to be the best at it. And so I've arranged for the flushing of all shit. Separately, or along with the patient. As the doctor said, we have 'Options'—under the Hippocratic Oath—with 100% human approval, from the year zero. Even Dickie, who, in treason, accepted Onassis's bribes and said, 'Fuck America; I come first,' also said, 'The killing of cancer is our highest priority.' Ticket to eternity, sonny, for me and my princess—"

The bartender said, "This bar is closed. Me and everyone in here wants a ticket to that kind of action. Drinks are on the house. What will you have? Sir?"

(I'm a dirty 98-year-old janitor. Nobody ever called me "sir.")

A drunk, coming back from the restroom, said: "There were four turds in the bowl. They looked like Joanie, Hearst, CIA Moosehead, and the liver-eating shrink. They were not human. They were shit. I reached out and pushed a button, and they disappeared down the drain. It was easy. I checked the bowl lid. Good and solid. I'll bring a padlock tomorrow."

Bartender to the drunk: "Drinks are on the house. What will you have? Sir?"

Son-in-law: "I picked a winner. Tell me about that mineral, Pop."

Pop-in-Law: "Sonny, I may have to club you all the way through eternity. That mineral subject is taboo—and you didn't pick anything...."]

[**CIA MOOSEHEAD OBSERVER'S** (just returned from grave-fucking) **NOTE**: "Hearst, I quit. By the time you read this I will be at the South Pole, burrowing deep down with the Penguins. Us Penguins hate you Necrophiliac Murdering Treasonous Mafia bastards. May that radio-active cloud never reach this far south. Us Penguins never hurt nobody."]

[**FRESH FROM GRAVE-FUCKING HEARST'S NOTE**:

"Jeeeeeesus Cheeerist!"]

Mary Jo Kopechne

***

22 Mafia Democratic Convention in Mafia Miami

I'm watching the Democratic Convention on TV. I just puked. Archbishop somebody-or-other just opened the Mafia Democratic Convention for Mafia O'Brien. He said, "This is a troubled nation; you need my divine guidance, and I will give it to you. Help the poor. Send a buck to Montini. Elect Teddy."

Larry O'Brien just praised the Great American Political Process.

Last week he said: "Campaigning is giving the ugliest meaning to the political process. The Nixon law-and-order administration is stooping to tactics that raise ugly questions about the integrity of the political process. The First Amendment Rights and Civil Rights of myself and Teddy and the Demo Party have been violated. The cover-up of the bugging of our offices by Dickie indicates that he does indeed have something to hide."

He hints, but doesn't go on. What he refers to is the "cover-up of a deeper fix," hinted at by Joseph Kraft, another brave, free American.

Six more pukes: Larry O'Brien just welcomed the viewing public: "We must tell the American Public the truth."

In Miami, just now, Alioto spoke: "The vote to stop McGovern in favor of my Mafia boy Humphrey is in the lap of the Gods. And right now the Gods aren't speaking to us." This is true, And then the camera panned to Pat Wyman, wife of the national director of Hubert's campaign. She, too, was sad.

Senator Nelson, who has read these papers, said: "The heart and soul of the Democratic Party is at stake tonight, under the eyes of the entire world. If we lie, cheat and steal now, we are dead. If we are not honest now, there is no hope. Do not let Alioto and Humphrey and Wyman steal these California votes from McGovern."

(Joanie's bipartisan telethon flopped. The Mafia won't ante up for a loser. They'll blow it on Dickie and assassinate McGovern, even though he fronts for Teddy.)

The vote was close. Old ladies knitted and young ones giggled. Mafia faces that I saw on TV yawned, waiting for the Kennedy blitz. The archbishops were sad.

Nelson sweated this out. And at 2:00 a.m., the entire Mafia Demo Convention, including Nelson, walked out under the Miami moon. It was a frenetic fandango, led by Shirley Chisholm and Willie Brown and the Black Caucus, and Mafia Sinatra's Shirley MacLaine, Pierre Salinger and the White Caucus and Chicano caucus. Moon over the Mafia Moats of Miami.

Wallace, sourly (disappointed at McGovern's quick win): "I think I'll knock the hay down where the goats can get at it."

Dickie, in fright: "Please don't hold any public hearings on my CIA bugging of Mafia Larry O'Brien and the Mafia Democratic headquarters. Don't prosecute that million dollar suit. Such a thing would ruin the Republican Mafia party, and, after all, we hang together or we hang separately. Remember, liver-eating Joanie's telethon was to raise money for both Mafia Parties—the Two Mafia Party system—and that includes us."

The Archbishop, sadly: "We quote our Pope: 'I was vested with the sublime and exceptional dignity of the Deputy of Christ. God has chosen me to suffer in a church troubled by protest and change. A vote for Teddy would ease my suffering.'"

Gloria Steinem, Barbara Phillips' partner in Women's Lib, was at Miami. And anti-women's lib broads, and anti-anti-women's lib voters.

Humphrey roars: "Politics is like religion."

Shirley MacLaine screams "Jesus Christ" in her finest Mafia Sinatra voice.

Dita Beard wasn't there

It was a glorious 4th of July orgy on Mary Jo's grave. Complete with firecrackers and glorious eagles, high flying flags, and stirring music.

(From Hanoi there was a joint statement by 16 POW's: "Dickie's 4th of July bombing—on us, here—left us in total despair.")

In Miami, there was a McGovern questioner: "Dickie and the U.S. CIA hierarchy run most of the world's heroin out of Laos, and cover it up. We have presented proof and notified you about this long ago. You didn't answer. What about it?"

McGovern, who has been covering this mess up in the Senate for years, said, "I'll check into it—after you elect me. But you must elect me first, after which I have executive privilege and I don't even have to say 'Screw You' to you. I can just cover it up, as Teddy and me cover up Chappaquiddick. The democratic thing to do is elect me. And 'Screw You.' "

(This was on live TV; none of this CIA, heroin, or S.E. Asia bit was printed in any Mafia newspaper that I saw.)

From the Convention Podium, Mafia Boggs said: "I was in China on July 4th, and someone said, 'We will live in peace, or we will die in terror.' It is true. We are benevolent, we Louisiana Marcello Mafia. We have allowed some delegates to be here tonight who have never been here before. Thank us for that. We are proud.

"Us Marcello Mafia, who helped murder JFK, love him—our glorious defunct leader. Believe me. Us Marcello Mafia have made America what it is today."

(The drunken Maf didn't fall off the podium once.)

Larry O'Brien: "We wish to salute you—the delegates—for showing the world a true example of pure democracy."

Governor Pat Lacey: "Teddy is highly qualified to be President and should be at least V.P., so that he can take over if we have to gut-shoot dear old George McGovern."

Attorney General La Follette of Wisconsin was a McGovern delegate. Said he in passion: "We will organize a draft of Teddy by the convention."

McGovern: "Immediately after my nomination, my first phone call will be to my master, Teddy, to beg him to be my V.P. Should he say no, I shall then ask him how I shall run the presidency and what I should do. And he will ask Onassis and Montini, as JFK did—and relay my orders back to me."

Abe Ribicoff, a Kennedy-Nader stooge senator: "McGovern is exactly like our revered JFK and Teddy. He is just as honest. Elect him."

Valerie Kushner (her hubby is a 5-year POW in Vietnam) said: "I feel total confusion. Which way to flagellate in frenzy? Toward my hubby's cage in Vietnam, or Mary Jo's grave? Just vote for George."

Mrs. Martin Luther King: "I sympathize with Teddy. He says he isn't running because of fear for his life." She looked up at Martin's picture. "I wonder if George is safe."

Shirley Chisholm's second speech started out: "The hour is late. Time for America is running out...." and Mafia Paley's CBS switched promptly to ten minutes of Mrs. King, Cronkite, Shell Oil—and switched back when Shirley's speech was over.

McGovern was nominated. Shirley Chisholm, from Meyer Lansky's Deauville Hotel, where she had her Presidential headquarters, said: "The delegates have made history here tonight." Yes.

McGovern's first phone call was from Teddy.

Said George: "Thank you, sir, for giving me the Presidency. Won't you please, at least, be V.P.? What shall I do?"

Teddy: "For the record, I decline for irrevocable Chappaquiddick reasons. But I will tell you what to do after I have discussed it with our family father, Jackie's hubby, Onassis, who murdered my revered brother, JFK, and took his broad and his shotgun—Jackie and the Pentagon—in approved Mafia Senatorial Code fashion. And my eternal father, God, Mafia Montini, who owns my eternal Chappaquiddick soul in Rome forevermore. Just as my revered brother, JFK, did, and was told to "Holy Crusade" Vietnam and its Heroin on behalf of both of my Mafia Fathers, plus my real Mafia Father.

"Now, George, that would be, let's see—1960, hmm—that would be Onassis, Pope John XXIII, and Joseph P. I'm confused, George, and my head still hurts where it hit that Dyke Bridge curb after I busted Mary Jo's nose with a backhand of my fist of iron and bailed out and let her take that flip in the Pond. In the back seat. That squawking broad. Can you imagine her threatening to run to Nader? Big ears on the call from Tunney and my call back to Alioto, the son of a bitch who blew the 1968 election because of a hit-run on the car of a guy who's got a grenade up my ass—and it hurts, George. She had a big nose about Bobby's murder, and JFK's.

"You just sit tight, George. Don't you make no mistakes. There isn't a man near you that isn't one of my Mafia—Mankiewicz, Salinger, Matt Troy, Fred Dutton, Stearns, Hart, Weil, Douglas, Palevsky—and you'll be getting more by the platoon. Montini and Onassis have decided to place another goon right by your side, one of theirs: Symington and Hearst's Eagleton. No one has convicted him of anything yet, and they can't connect him to me. But he's a 'soldier,' Georgie, remember that."

McGovern's Kennedy Mafia cocoon take their orders from Daley and Kennedy, who get theirs from the same source Dickie does: Onassis, Montini, and all of MMORDIS. And they told McGovern to select Montini's Mafia Eagleton of St. Louis, Missouri, where the Mafia group is Cervantes and Shenker, descendants of Prendergast Truman's Mafia cell.

Eagleton will be President in case McGovern doesn't play ball—like Johnson, after Dallas. He will play ball. So go the plans.

A McGovern aide, lawyer Miles Rubin: "We won. Now we will begin to accept big Mafia money chunks—special gifts."

Morris Dees and Kimmelman: "It'll work. We will pass the hat to the Capidonico—just as Mafia Stans does for Mafia Dickie."

Teddy's McGovern is nominated for Prez, and the Mafia Demo orgy overflows into the aisles. A Kennedy alternate carries the banner for Teddy, whose face is buried—deep and sobbing—in Rosie's Mafia skirts.

The third congratulatory call to McGovern was from Chappaquiddick Dickie: "Please, George, don't prosecute us for the CIA bugging of your offices. That would make our campaign look dirty. Remember, as Jack Anderson says in his column, us Mafia parties have the same boss, and we always cooperate in time of trouble. By the way, thanks for helping to get us out of that Mafia ITT mess in San Diego, and for letting us use your Mafia facilities here behind the moats of Miami. Let's not have any real dirt coming out this time. It's like any wrestling match. The people don't really want us to get hurt.

"Say hello to Lansky and all the rest of the Mafia that gave you the facilities there, and after the wrestling match we'll get together and cut up the cake. Give my love to Teddy and I'll see you all around. I understand the Mafia is furnishing you all with a good batch of broads this year. Don't wear 'em out, George. Save something for us. We'll be down there next month."

Inside the hall, a crawling thing is already swallowed. It's a cocoon.

Outside, demonstrators utter forlorn chants: "Aaaah—for the Mafia that owns Miami,

Chicago, New York, St. Louis, San Francisco—all the cities, all the states, all America. Aaaah—for the CIA and its Southeast Asia opium network. Alms for the love of Allah."

In Rome, at the start of the convention, Secretary of State William Rogers conferred in a secret back room with Mafia Montini. Today, Reagan carries on the "business discussion" with His Gray Eminence. (It's about approval for Dickie's new V.P., who must be of Montini's choosing. It will probably be Dallas Bullet Connally, Secretary of The Treachery—and the only Texas Maf who isn't currently a fugitive from Justice. The reason he isn't is because J. Mafia Hoover was murdered—and Connally's file was burned.)

A black delegate: "McGovern has double-crossed everybody."

Steinem: "You promised you would not take the low road, McGovern, you bastard."

Ribicoff, who nominated George: "I won't take the V.P. slot. Up your McBracket."

Askew, keynote speaker: "V.P.? Hell no—no way."

Woodcock: "V.P.??"

George Wallace sits in a wheelchair, and the portraits of two Mafia-murdered Mafia Kennedys and a King loom prominently over this Mafia orgy.

(Not present—hiding—were Meany, Daley, Johnson, various Roosevelts, Paley, Pat Brown, Swig, Lynch, and masses of other treasonous Mafia.)

"Reforms would ruin us," said the Mafia Demo rulers. And McGovern had his delegates vote down the very reform charter he himself had proposed.

And there we are. Kennedy's cocoon, in which McGovern is swallowed. No reforms. The Kennedy Mafia has announced it will now accept massive chunks of loot. And now the labor Mafia and Vatican Mafia will buy back in. And out of the cocoon will emerge a brand new Mafia butterfly: Kennedy's McGovern. Or they will kill him in the cocoon, and Vatican Kennedy Eagleton, impressed by the murder—as Johnson was—will carry on.

Either way, this was the best solution Dickie and Teddy could work out to cover the murders for their employers, and jointly preserve the Cancer Mafia Election Process.

Palevsky—Mafia McGovern money—left in a huff, before McGovern was nominated. ("I don't need you; I want Teddy," he said.)

House Speaker Albert: "We will dig the grave and bury all Republicans in the despicable ignominy they deserve."

O'Brien: "We have held a completely truthful and honest convention. We did not hide from any difficult Chappaquiddick issues. We allowed every American to be heard. Openly, freely, fairly. We achieved reforms. The spirit of this convention has been that of leveling with the American peeepul on all issues. I now quit my job as chairman of the Mafia Democratic Party. I am going back to the $50 thousand PR job that Onassis' "Hughes" gave me out of Lansky's skim money from Vegas, that assassin Maheu delivered to me and Hubert and Rebozo and Dickie in '68—as bribes. And, like Montini and Bobby Baker and Tony Boyle, I am gonna write a book too. I am not gonna hang alone."

Flash to Mafia airport, Kennedy International: "Here comes Teddy to bless McGovern."

Peabody, V.P. nominator: "We must elect a V.P. We cannot allow him to be appointed by Onassis—or anointed by Montini."

A Texas delegate, on TV: "Our Governor, Lieutenant Governor, and State Legislature, are all in jail down there for Mafia murder and looting. John Mitchell's Criminal Justice Chief, Wilson, is a fugitive from Justice down there, and he's sweeping though the state, looting like Quantrell—as fugitive Mitchell does in Washington. His honor, our State Attorney General, was just arrested yesterday. Us girls are just sitting here clutching our purses. It ain't safe in Texas any more, and this

is Mafia Central.... Which Mafia TV station are you with?"

Senator Gravel: "They won't let me speak. That tells the whole story. Now they have let me have a word. Elect a V.P.; don't let them choke one down your throat. The V.P. post belongs to the people. He could be your President—and probably will, the way the Maf knocks them over. I released the Pentagon Papers to you, the peeepul." (He's there. Ellsberg gets 150 years in prison.) "I released the Kissinger Papers. Dole censured me. There is total secrecy about American murders, and American genocide. Kennedy-McGovern Mafia hoods put the muscle on those who would have nominated me, so I hereby nominate myself."

Self-declared V.P. candidate George Smothers: "I ask everyone here who deplores all of the political assassinations, and the attempted assassination of George Wallace, to stand up." One human stood up.

There was one vote for Archie Bunker. This is a fun affair. And from the mass stupidity and wide-eyed innocence, so plain to be seen on CBS-TV, amid all the apparent stumbling and bumbling, one would never spot the directed cancerous Mafia Election Process, steering the Mafia cocoon into the White House—"Montini-Onassis West."

There were two votes for Roger Mudd—who works for oil Mafia Bill Paley—who owns CBS (visibly), and who fired Stanton, and hired ITT Ireland. CBS—where, having read these papers, they were "too busy" to care.

There was one vote for Martha Mitchell, Poucha Pond John's Mafia mouth.

One vote for necrophiliac Nader, sponsor of Mary Jo's swim.

One vote for Dowdy—a convicted Texas Congressman.

And then the cocoon was complete. Eagleton was nominated for V.P.

Strauss, the visible money man of the Mafia Demo Party during the years mentioned here, from 1968 to the present—quit too. He is writing a book, ya know. And other names move in, all bearing special gifts—Mafia style.

There is an interlude before Kennedy introduces his new cocoon to the mass orgy. All are up in the aisles, dancing and drooling. Here comes Teddy himself, and they are all thrilled. (Tomorrow morning, McGovern meets the Committee of 72—some of the big Mafia money chunks. If he takes the oath, he gets the loot. He will. There is blood lust in his nostrils—and there is no God over Presidents. No law. No check. Just Mafia.)

Computers will punch out the cash profit per American murder, and per non-American murder. The yearly take. As Onassis-"Hughes"-Lansky-Maheu do in any of their Vegas joints. How much skim from the Gross National Product? (41% under Dickie.)

And then the cocoon shell—Eagleton—speaks. (He was first appointed to the Senate because his Mafia predecessor was caught by Life Magazine, looting tills for the Mafia: Senator Long).

Eagleton says: "We are learning to live with things." (Chappaquiddick.) "Our faults make us strong." (Hersh, last week, said: "Chappaquiddick put the iron in Teddy's soul.") "We will not attack Dickie." (And he doesn't dare attack us.) "John Kennedy's brother will be with us presently. JFK said, "Ask not what your country can do for you—but what you can do for your country." (An empty cross waits for Teddy.) "He died in order that humanity might live." "We want to do more for mankind." (Yes, indeed.)

***

The band breaks into a "Hello Dolly" serenade—and Teddy appears, with Joanie, to a frenzied, frothy-mouthed welcome.

Teddy says: "A great party needs a great purpose. Jefferson beat tyranny. Jackson beat privilege. Wilson set us free. Roosevelt let us share the wealth…" (…and heroin, war, Fatima #1…)

"Humphrey and Truman gave us equality…" (…and Onassis and Fatima #2.) "JFK asked citizens what they could do…" (…and gave us Vietnam, and Fatima #3…) "Johnson said we shall overcome…" (…Keep J. Mafia Hoover inside the tent pissin' out, not outside pissin' in.) "Joanie and I ate Mary Jo's liver. We are all united in our heritage. The Republicans have had their chance. There is a new wind blowing across the nation (bearing the stench of frenzied rolling on rotting corpses). I give you my new butterfly: George McGovern. Join us for liver."

Humphrey and Muskie ushered in the new butterfly, and all raised their Mafia wings: Kennedy-Eagleton and Kennedy-McGovern. There was more music: "When the Saints Come Marching In."

George McGovern: "This is Montini's Friday Sunrise Service. I give my benediction to Senator Chappaquiddick Kennedy—and, of course, also to you citizens, and also to what's-his-name, Eagleton. I accept my gift—I mean, my nomination. I thank the most courageous and eloquent human in this land for the gift of the presidency he would have had if it hadn't been for the unforchunate incident at Chappaquiddick: the Honorable Senator Teddy Kennedy.

"You, out there—you got me to this stage, by small contributions. Open and genuine. I thank you." (Tomorrow, the Mafia takes over.)

"The peeepul have nominated me. My competition was the finest America has to offer: Mafia Alioto's Humphrey, Vatican Mafia Muskie. Mafia Pentagon Onassis' Jackson. Lansky's Deauville Shirley Chisholm. Teddy's Mafia Congressional looter Mills. Mafia gut-shot Wallace—and all of us despise the assassination attempt." (This time, no-one stood up.)

"Nixon is the issue in this campaign, and we'll kick his ass—all the way out. Albert will dig the grave, and bury him with Mary Jo. We chose the struggle: Reform the party," (canceled), "and let the peeepul in." (We need someone to screw). "This is the time for the truth. Let me inside the White House and I will tell you what is going on. I will end the War." (Shift it to Thailand, to protect Onassis' opium routes.)

"Never again will we prop up a corrupt dictator abroad." (We will bring Thieu over here and give him a cabinet post. We will bring Montini's prelates over here and give them government-purchased churches. That's my plan.)

"We will protect Lansky's Israel and Onassis' Greece and all of our similar allies, such as dope-pushing Chiang in Taiwan. We will open the sealed doors on 40 years of old wars, and conduct the big one right out in the open. No American will shed blood overseas." (You will do it right here at home. Fatima #3 ain't a one-way street no more.)

"We must make this a time of Justice and Truth. A chicken in every pot. A living income for everyone. We have a dream. We are going forward. Our land—yours and mine." (leased to the Mafia for one buck a year.) "God give us the wisdom to continue the successful screwing of Mary Jo."

(More music: "Mine Eyes Have Seen the Glory of The Coming of the Lord. Glory Hallelujah!" A frenzied orgy in the aisles.)

McGovern kisses Joanie, and then his wife. Teddy shakes his courageous mane and raises his fist of iron that busted Mary Jo's nose. The soul of iron strides out in glory with Willie Brown (and there was a distinct frown on Martin Luther's portrait). Bishop somebody blesses us all.

And it's all over.

***

Bobby's Mankiewicz saw to it that McGovern was heir to all the delegates that murdered Bobby had collected in 1968—so that McGovern could bid for the presidency using Mafia murdered Bobby's dead votes. Mafia murder, you see, followed by Mafia Omerta: part of the game in which you are slaughtered like beef, for profit—say, in heroin Vietnam.

Said liver-eating Joanie, on the telethon: "We must involve everybody." Very successful, as it turned out. Mankiewicz was one of the heroes of Chappaquiddick—a friend of Mary Jo's. He will be the next Attorney General, replacing Poucha Pond John.

McGovern: "No one likes to admit that my decision to run as a cocoon for Teddy came from secret arrangements made behind closed doors. But four administrations of both Mafia parties have charted a terrible war behind closed doors. I want those doors opened. The war will now move to Thailand. We will only guard the opium routes. That's my deal."

Present at that Miami Mafia Convention Hall, were mobiles, dangling from the ceiling. You know, tinkling things that dangle in the breeze, as in heroin-dazed Thailand, to ward off evil spirits. My Dickie-murdered father had, dangling on his mobile strings, murdered J. Mafia Hoover, and Joe Kennedy, and a long string of tinkling dead souls.

July: "Above the Law"

The Supreme Court rules, six to three, that no law governs the two Mafia Parties—to which they all belong. Both Mafia Parties are above the law. "They appeared on the scene 150 years ago. There is nothing in the Constitution about them. They just rule, that's all."

In San Francisco, a reporter asked, "Who are these Party Central Committee people who produce candidates for election? Who appoints them? Who selects them for election? Who is John Mack?"

He asked both parties, the Supreme Court, attorneys, and newsmen.

The answer: "We don't know who they are. But they are fine people. Forget it." They don't exist, you see. And that, of course, is—by precedent—the resolution. Non-existence.

Hannah: "The period from 1870 to 1912 was the filthiest era in American political history. Everybody bought their jobs and aided fellow millionaires."

The Mafia: "We use taxes like heroin for the people. We learned this from Plato, who said: 'The leaders' object is to impoverish the public by the payment of taxes—thus compelling them to devote full time to providing for their daily needs, and therefore, keeping them too busy to conspire against their leaders.'"

My car problems were trouble for me—and time, and expense. And the Mafia Demo Convention was about to start.

I wonder what's planned for me around Dickie's Mafia Convention time. That's the one that jumped from Dickie's favorite San Diego to the Mafia Moats of Miami, because of an anonymous ITT letter that went out on the day of the funeral of my father, whose final murder coup was administered at the time of Dickie's Peking trip. (His quest for world peace—as Dickie's Fatima #3 bombers obliterated everything in Vietnam except the CIA mule trains carrying heroin to Taiwan, Harry Yee, Onassis's "Hughes" Mafia Money Funnel, and back to Dickie for his reelection.).

The murder coup on my father was a rat poison in common use in Europe. (Robert Maheu tried to use it to assassinate Castro when he was hired to do so by the CIA—via John McCone, now of ITT. This was to be the first of a Maheu string of assassinations carried out for Onassis. Its effect is apathy, shortness of breath, and heart attack—too long after administration to detect the murder. It leaves no trace. This capped three and one half years of torture for that old man—starting with the Alioto hit-run on my car on September 16, 1968. J. Edgar Hoover was another victim of the same poison.

Professor Vernon: "Multinationals—in secret—use the U.S. as a means of controlling the economies of other countries. They sit within the structure of long established political and social institutions." (Read: "Mafia and Vatican.") "They sprawl across national boundaries, linking assets with an intricacy that threatens the concept of a nation as an integral unit. I suggest a Global Justice Department to regulate multinational Mafia concerns."

Burke Marshall was one of the first hero supporters of Teddy at Chappaquiddick. His phone number came just after Onassis's in Teddy's cover-up phone calls. I suggest that he be classified as cancer, and so treated. Or do we call it murder, treason and conspiracy? No, we can't do that. The Supreme Court has banned the death penalty for any crimes, including those. So, it must be cancer: cause for immediate extermination, with 100% human approval—including the Supreme Court.

There has never been a ban on the killing of cancer. This is approved by everybody—including those nine cancer cells on the Supreme Court, who declare Burke Marshall's Mafia Party Law to take precedence over Constitutional law.

***

Pat Wyman looked just the same at the Democratic Convention as she did on October 8, 1971—at a dinner during the "assassination threat, aborted"—Nader's non-appearance at the miserably flopped attempt at forming a third political party of Consumers.

Back then, the dining room was empty. But the tables were full of salads. And me—I was hungry. She charged up to me.

"I'm Pat Wyman." (I could see this on the big name tag.) "Who are you?"

I told her, and suggested that together we eat all the salads, and when the rest arrived they wouldn't know that they had missed anything.

She: "My husband is with Diamond Match and he is always busy, and I just don't know what to do with myself. Most of the people here are not consumers. They are wealthy and business oriented. Don't you agree?"

Me: "You forgot the Mafia. I know them all. And I see many here."

She: "Nader is wrong when he says that wealth over a certain amount should be taken away from people, isn't he?"

Me: "Nader is a craven coward."

She: "He begged out of this appearance because of Washington business. I can't see anything that would stop him from being here at a meeting as important as this. Oh, here comes everybody. I'll join you at this table. You look lonesome. We'll find a girl for you."

And then Bill walked up (an old friend). Said he: "We've been shafted too long; we're fighting back." He left.

And she, in surprise: "So, you do have a friend in the room!"

Dinner over. Jeff O'Connell (University of Illinois Law Professor) spoke: "I am told we have some very important people in the room. Therefore, I have a speech."

He produced John Rothschild's article on the Mafia and the Pope.

Said he: "The Mafia had to take over the whole economy; they were losing money on crime. The Pope has the best racket of all; he sells blue sky." (It was a pre-release of Rothschild's article in the following month's Washington Monthly.)

Pat Wyman cringed with every jab. I don't remember any words from her after I whispered a correction to her of an O'Connell statement.

Said O'Connell: "The Mafia takes 30% of the Gross National Product."

I whispered to her, "He's wrong. It was 41% as of last week."

I can't remember her after that. I don't remember her leaving the table. And I waited until everybody left, because I wanted to talk to Bill.

If Pat Wyman had furnished girls for me—and for Bill and O'Connell—we could have salvaged something out of Nader's Consumer Pratfall. After all, we were in a hotel: Mafia Del

Webb's Town House in Mafia Alioto's San Francisco.

Senator Metcalf states that via stock control, major banks control it all. In brief: "Corporate Secrecy is tighter than the Mafia Swiss banks. No one knows who owns or controls the stock in the super corporations. Dick Casey—Crooked Casey—won't give it out." (Just as Mafia Mitchell won't give out the names of Mafia Dickie's Mafia 'campaign fund' bribers—and neither will any of the Super Corporations, such as ITT. This—your life or death—they say, is 'privileged and confidential information.' So die—in Vietnam, at Poucha Pond, Fatima #3, wherever. You will never know the names of the people you are dying for. It's the corporate effect. Names like ITT's McCone, and Onassis—the current leader of Mafia Family Kennedy.

Bishop Don Camara, from San Rafael, Brazil (who was exiled there after he printed the fact that Pope Montini is one-half Jewish—by way of his mother—and wheels and deals with Freemasonry around the world, working both sides of the Mafia Street), is under a current sentence of assassination by the Vatican Mafia that owns Brazil. They hung Camara's Priest assistant on a cross in Camara's church. He is very dead. The Vatican Mafia death sentence on Camara is printed in the Brazilian Mafia Press.

Cardinal Spellman, hero of Kennedy's Vietnam "Holy Crusade" (now pursued viciously by Dickie), knocked Bishop Sheean down completely—out of Papal contention, because Sheean refused to kickback millions (from his TV pleas) to Spellman. Sheean said publicly that Spellman's "Holy Crusade" in Vietnam was the rottenest deed in history. Pius XII of course, boiled at this, and knocked Sheean down—hard.

Sheean now is a beaten, secluded 77-year-old man. He reminds me somewhat of Father Mootz, who arranged for me to see "some papers" from Tisserant—who was also disillusioned, as was Mary Jo. And dead, too.

Me, to Fellmeth, on February 14, 1971: "Would you like the names and crimes of all the congressmen who are Mafia?"

Three months later: me, to Fellmeth, in St. Louis: "You're running the wrong way to see those files. Shall I mail you the names and crimes of all the congressmen who are Mafia?"

Fellmeth, both times: "I have to go now."

Today, Nader announces that Fellmeth, his partner, will release a year-long study of Congress in October. In it, you will find no mention of Mafia—including a total absence of reference to legal Mafia, to which most of Congress (those who don't belong to the banking Mafia, industrial Mafia, and Mafia-Mafia) belong, along with Nader and Fellmeth and Eddie Cox (the original trio), Teddy's friends.

Nixon and Khrushchev

23 July 10, 1972: Charles Garry and the Murders of Black Panthers Hampton & Clark

In Chicago today, Hanrahan waived a jury trial on the charges that he murdered Hampton and Clark. That throws the decision into the hands of a Mafia judge, appointed and owned by Mafia Daley, and on up the Mafia ladder. Hanrahan will be acquitted.

Charles Garry was the lifetime attorney for the two murdered men, Black Panthers Hampton and Clark, murdered on December 4, 1969—after Chappaquiddick. The murders were done to suppress the connection to the November 1, 1963, double-Diem-Kennedy murder day, and the abortion of its Chicago end (Kennedy), until Dallas—three weeks later.

(The previous pages were delivered to Charles Garry, by me, this afternoon.)

At 3:00 p.m., I had an appointment with Garry in his office. There was the expected wait—a half hour. During that period, the smell of Mafia-CIA was strong. From McTernan's office came a client who looked me over. Then came McTernan. He walked in and out several times, peeking at me. Then Garry's client left. He had the same Mafia smell.

Finally, Garry said "Come in."

Me: "I know you're busy. Read the first three pages of this; it will only take five minutes, and it will take care of the matter."

(The first three pages are a repeat of the entire legal affair—the offer made in April, verbally, to Garry.)

He scanned them, then flipped them back at me.

He said: "Tell me what it says. I can't read."

Me: "But Mr. Garry, these words are concise, true, and the quickest way to explain the matter.

"No," he said, "don't read it, tell me."

Me: "All right. Today, in Chicago, Hampton and Clark's murderer, Hanrahan, was acquitted by a Daley Mafia judge. I will offer evidential proof of the entire Mafia hierarchy, from Daley on up, who participated in that. I have new and heretofore unknown evidence relating to a group of murderers. Using your Mafia legal right to defend your clients, dead Hampton and Clark, I propose that you sign a letter—written by you, or by me—to fifty of the bravest of the brave Americans. Cold legal facts, relating not only to Hampton and Clark, but to Mary Jo, JFK, Bobby, Martin Luther King, the Yablonskis, and thousands of others.

"These fifty are entitled to know the solution to the murders they're interested in—by way of the solution to the murder of Hampton and Clark. They are, apparently, the only fifty Americans who have the guts to stand on Concord Bridge and fight tyranny.

"You will already know a lot of the answers, and you will also see the predicted percentage of that bravest-of-the-brave fifty run in total fear. You will watch a total disintegration of the moral fiber of many self-declared bravest-of-the-brave Americans."

And then I quoted some of the other items mentioned in the 19 pages, including the murder, treason and genocide that had occurred during the three months since he had heard my offer—and read my papers—for which he could assume responsibility.

And I watched Garry's moral fiber come apart at the seams.

Said he: "I know who killed Hampton and Clark. Would it surprise you to know that I was in the room when the guns came in blazing? Hanrahan wasn't the entire murder source. Those orders filtered down through top Mafia channels. Those same channels ordered the genocide of the Black Panther Party—for whom I am the attorney. I know Hanrahan will be acquitted. That horrible

hierarchy will squash anything that steps on its toes. You know what will happen to you, too, don't you?"

Me: "I have been told by many, and the bribe offer is now up to a tax-free $50 million. Those cheap bastards; they are only offering me what Maheu and Dietrich want in their suits."

He: "You'll wind up face down in an alley."

Me: "So will you, and your family. You just said it: murder for Hampton and Clark, genocide for you and the Black Panther Party. You're dead from that source—unless you've joined the Mafia, in which case you're dead too. The people at Hiroshima, only one tick away from atomic eternity, wouldn't have understood if you had explained their future. They would have continued on their way to the grocery store, for that final tick. So why discuss that matter? You wouldn't understand this new situation. But you understand missiles, and that is probably enough.

"There is a way out. Call those fifty together and I will explain it. I will not do anything in secrecy, where it can be squashed. You don't have to open your mouth. You could watch the disintegration of the moral and human soul of some of those bravest-of-the-brave, and see some real giants among the rest—with new and powerful tools to use. You would have to sit in on that meeting to begin to know what it's all about. How about it? I offer you life over death."

He (slumping): "I don't understand it." And he shook his head. "No; that hierarchy would squash me."

Me: "You're dead anyhow, without a struggle. So die. And you'll take your family with you. Ponds, missiles, new things, whatever."

He: "Nothing can be done."

Me: "Two thirds of the rest of the world know what to do, and have the tools. It's been given to them. Bridges are burned. How can you defend yourself if you refuse to know about this, and block that right to anyone else?"

By now, he was slumped almost out of sight in his chair under the desk.

He: "What do you think of McGovern?"

Me: "He will be assassinated. He is a Kennedy Mafia alternate. But he has one faint streak of decency, even though he is a staunch member of the Mafia Senate Club. And they will allow no foothold of decency, however slight. They will murder him. One of their purchased own—a Mafia, Teddy or Dickie, will be president. Unless, of course, they purchase McGovern, as they did you."

He: "I don't understand. What do you think of the convention?"

Me: "It is a mass frenzied orgy on Mary Jo's grave. All Mafia faces—from Pat Wyman to Alioto. If Mafia Humphrey had gotten the nomination, Eugene Wyman would be the Mafia Attorney General in charge of sitting on the lid. McGovern's Attorney General would be Kennedy's Mankiewicz."

He: "Do you know how Bobby was assassinated?"

Me: "Cold evidential fact. Out, now, around the world. To people who want to know.

He: "Why was Mary Jo killed? Because she knew too much? Like you?"

Me: "I understand you. And, of course, I told you that before. Do I understand that you will not investigate the murders of Hampton and Clark or the genocide of the Black Panther Party—for which you are the attorney? And that you will block the presentation of the facts, and the solutions, to fifty of the bravest of the brave, free Americans—in an open public forum—at which CIA bugging will be welcome?"

He, rising: "I don't understand."

Me: "Then may I have my papers back? They cost me a lot of money."

He handed me a package, in which all three deliveries had been assembled.

Me: "This is only one package. I delivered three."

He: "I'll look for the others." He shuffled around the room.

Me: "One was a special publication article on Joanie eating Mary Jo's liver."

He said, "Oh," and headed for McTernan's office. I waited while he shuffled around some more. Finally he came back to the lobby, puzzled.

"Sorry," he said, a totally morally disintegrated cookie, quietly standing there like a chastened little boy. "I can't find them. When I do I'll mail them to you."

Me: "Thank you, Mr. Garry. See ya later."

And as I passed him he said "Good luck" and stared at his hands.

All three deliveries were neatly in the package. In order. CIA style.

***

On this day, in Chicago, Hanrahan was acquitted by a Mafia judge of the murders of Hampton and Clark.

On this day, in San Francisco, the lifetime attorney of Hampton and Clark, their closest friend, bravest of the brave—Charles Garry, denied the bodies of Hampton and Clark.

He acquitted Hanrahan and absolved the Mafia of all murder. Admitted his participation in genocide, treason, murder and bribery for the three month period since receiving these papers.

And I told him, "The girl who delivered these papers to you, three months ago, was Senator Nelson's cousin, and Senator Proxmire's niece. Senator Nelson knew of what he spoke, and spoke in total fear." (re: the "one tick away at Hiroshima.")

I did not mention the whimsical nature of the Hiroshima mass murder: one Mafia monster, deciding in secret: Truman, Prendergast's whore-house towel washer—against all advice. A cloud cover over the prime target led to his sudden selection of alternate Hiroshima for mass murder.

CIA fear was all over the office—and he slumped, in silence. He feared I was about to tell him more, and he spouted a quick change of subject: to McGovern, I believe. Today, two assassins were arrested outside McGovern's hotel.

Garry himself might be in line for assassination. He had obviously been brain-washed before I saw him. Possibly he has been treated to a Sirhan or Bremer type of brain bending. Who knows? Who cares?

This human—called "His Gray Eminence" (behind the defense) at the Angela Davis trial; defender of Attorney Thorne, who defended Tyrone—a Maf who conducted the King's Castle swindle (Mafia Tahoe: see the Tyrone Papers) for Elliot Roosevelt, Onassis' boy, via Daley's Chicago Teamsters' Union Fund. The indignant legal defender of the rights of man, who fought bravely and won the release of Huey Newton and Bobby Seale. Whose lifetime clients, Hampton and Clark, were murdered—and who defended their rights after their murders; who used these papers for three months in blackmail of his own involving murder; who admitted he knew of the murder of Howard Hughes—this human is now publicly on record as the defender, "His Gray Eminence," of the Mafia cover-up of the murder of Christ, and of the assassinations, war, heroin, Mafia Election Process, Fatima #3.

One remark by him, "It takes time." When I asked if he knew of one, only one, brave, free American who could qualify to join the proposed bravest-of-the-brave fifty, he said: "No, I don't know one."

***

On Monday, McGovern called Teddy: "Please be my Vice President."

Teddy said: "No!"

On Tuesday, McGovern begged Senator Nelson (mentioned previously in here) for two hours to be his Vice President.

Senator Nelson said: "I will not accept the V.P. job—not even with a gun at my back, whether the ticket was George McGovern or Abe Lincoln." Some frightened Mafia people. Correct?

Say Dickie and Montini: "Block time, delay, destroy, lie, steal, murder; seize the hour, seize the day—a Mao premise." Time—the most precious commodity Dickie attempts to corner. But it is not under his control. Nor Garry's. Nor any Maf.

It belongs to me—with an eternity bank to draw on. Time, and life, removed from Hampton and Clark, and Mary Jo.

At the Mafia Miami Demo Convention, there was a film of the Time and Life removal from JFK, Bobby, Martin Luther—in a PR perverted sympathy effort. Missing, and hiding behind the Mafia skirts of Mafia Mama Rosie, Mafia Martha, and Mafia Lady Bird, were the leaders of our country: Chappaquiddick Teddy, Poucha Pond John, and 'Pissin' Out' Johnson.

(See Senator Nelson's cousin, Senator Proxmire's niece, for evidence of this. She will direct you to documents about Christ as the son of a Persian. Care to read them?).

***

Pope Montini was jealous when Turkish Mustapha's wife caught her hubby in bed with Jackie and divorced him (see the Canadian Papers). He was unaware that Mustapha Bey has Jackie on call from Onassis because Mustapha kept a diary on Onassis—a diary which has since gone the way of the Tisserant Papers on Montini.

All around the world, the Tisserant Papers are screwing the Onassis Diary. Or is it the other way around?

At 1277 8th Avenue, I watch Dickie and Montini's CIA wrap up its fourth year of Time-Life, vulture-pecking at my mother—weakening fast.

Tonight, after my chat with Garry, I switched some papers around and picked up a sack full of *L.A. Times* back issues. It was a heavy paper sack, and I tucked some other things in, including an abbreviated copy of these papers. I caught a bus home.

I walked into a bar where I usually go. It's a nice bar, and it was busy. There were moveable easy chairs at the bar. There was only one spot open—my favorite spot, but there was no chair.

Some guy was sitting at my right. I dropped the heavy sack on the bar and walked back toward a table by the door. I picked up a chair and turned around, and he was right behind me.

"Buddy," he said, "I saw you dump that big sack and head for the door. If you had gone out that door I'd have been right behind you. I know you. I don't want to get my ass blown off. I just came in for a beer."

We went back to the bar and someone said: "Oh well, even if it's an atomic bomb, we'll never know what hit us. What's the difference?"

So—properly prodded—I joined in the fun.

Said I: "Well, no one worries about a quickie. What frightens them is what's in here. It's a creeping jelly. It takes 22 hours to work, and there's nothing you can do but watch your belly button rot away in intense torture, growing worse.

"It gives you time to contemplate things like the 2 hours and 13 minutes Mary Jo spent in total torture, in the air bubble—with a busted nose—in the cold pond. A couple of hours of little girls barbecuing near Alioto's house, or 8 hours on the cross for Christ, or the three and a half years it took Dickie to murder my father."

By now there were lots of empty chairs.

"And while you're waiting, you can sing Mafia chorus songs about assassinations, murder, genocide, treason, bribery and the perversion of the Constitution of the U.S. of Mafia, a nation of necrophiliacs, which was purchased by the Mafia in the year..."

By this time, only the bartender was left, standing sadly looking down at the floor.

To him I said, "I have to go home now. May I leave this sack here tonight? I'll come back and get it tomorrow."

He: "For God's sake, get it out of here."

Me: "For God's sake? That's a valid reason. See ya later."

***

The presence of these papers in a room reeks of the aroma of corpses, from Chappaquiddick up to date—and back to that of Christ. Mike Wallace said it, from a front porch on a quiet night at Chappaquiddick, a year ago, to friends—and the next day on the air, in bitter tones: "The profanity of Chappaquiddick."

Twenty-three of the Mafia hotels housing this Mafia Miami Convention, and the next one, are owned by known Mafia murderers—known, nurtured and revered, for the past 47 years, by all who rule the U.S. of Mafia here under the benevolence of Grecian Mafia Onassis and Roman Mafia Montini.

Joanie's telethon: to "rescue" both Mafia Parties: "We want to involve everybody"—was held at the Deauville Hotel, owned by Onassis murderers Meyer Lansky, Sam Cohen and Morris Lansburgh. Lansky is currently under legal Mafia (which means automatic release) indictment for skimming $35 million from Vegas casinos for Onassis' "Hughes" to purchase things like Dickie and Teddy and the multi-national economy of the world, via the Miami "Hughes Medical Research" Mafia Money Funnel. It filters Laotian heroin money through the U.S. to Switzerland and back—"clean," washed, unknown, untaxed Mafia loot that provided the food, lodging, broads, booze and heroin for the Mass Mary Jo orgy just held in Lansky's Convention Hall.

And it's reserved for the next (Republican) convention, which was shifted from San Diego for assorted Mafia reasons.

***

The one who controls congressional loot, Teddy's Mafia Congressman Mills, and Garry's Mafia Congresswoman Shirley Chisholm, the black reformer, set up their Presidential Headquarters in Lansky's Deauville.

Lansky himself lives with Golda Meir in Israel—a fugitive from Justice. As are Mitchell and Wilson, Attorney General and Criminal Chief Justice of the U.S. of Mafia.

Said McGovern: "We shall protect Israel, and Lansky, and give them our loot." The Israeli per capita income, from U.S. of Mafia gift money alone, is $5,100 per year, per Israeli human. It has been called the 51st State.

What is it that the U.S. of Mafia gives you? Let's see.

Plato: "The leader impoverishes by taxes, compelling public, full time, daily wants, so people are 'too busy' to conspire against him..."

Answer: The Mafia gives you Mary Jo.

Onassis and Jackie, the leaders of Teddy's Mafia, were not present at the convention. Why should they be? All of Onassis' Mafia families have delegates in Miami, watching closely to prevent a photo of Mary Jo from replacing Johnson's—or even the mention of her name.

But, as I told Garry, the filming of all this is technically beautiful.

Garry smiled and said, "You know, there are others who are brave, and it does take time. It can't be done overnight. This is Mafia imperialism—in full view of all."

And, knowing that lawyers are the Mafia residue of puke, I wondered about his political philosophy. Garry has contacts in Moscow, Peking, Hanoi, Delhi, Egypt, Africa, South America. The CIA runs in and out in frenzy.

The reason my appointment with Garry was delayed a half hour was because it took Jerry Rubin that much extra time to read my latest papers and make his deal with Garry. (Rubin is a Vatican Mafia murderer in charge of the local CIA office; a hangover from the days of Mafia ITT McCone at the time of the double Diem-Kennedy murders, which resulted—after Chappaquiddick—in the murders of Hampton and Clark.)

When Rubin left, I went in.

Garry said, "The hierarchy doesn't like people who step on their toes. You are dead."

And it hurt him when I answered, truthfully, "So are you. And your family goes with you. It is, as Dickie says, a game of murder. But I set all the rules. I own the bat.'

But—Garry did free Angela Davis, and all of the Black Panthers who weren't murdered a la Hampton and Clark. Garry angrily labeled these things "Black Panther Genocide."

Said he, bitterly, "I knew those kids all their lives." (Hampton and Clark.) "I read the news—and things were set up long ago. I judge that three-fourths of the world—from Chile to Korea, Boston to Hanoi, Capetown to Platinum Siberia—is fingering this film in a frenzy of their own—and probably bitter laughter."

Speaker Albert is the replacement for Mafia Vatican Speaker of the House McCormack, who was the chairman of this National Mafia Democratic Convention. Along with Mafia ex-President Truman and Mafia ex-President Johnson—not present, since he is a fugitive from Justice down in Texas—together with Mafia Connally and every Mafia public official in Texas.

Today, they arrested Mafia Representative Collins, of Texas, in Washington, for Mafia looting. He was granted Congressional Immunity, but they sent his squawking aide to the can for 15 years.

You ladies from that Texas delegation: forget your purses—they're gone anyhow. Just don't bend over.

Democratic Presidential Candidate George McGovern said: "America—Screw it or leave it."

Today, in Rome, Mafia Pope Montini—satisfied, like old Frazier, the lion—issued a Papal Nuncio: "All confessions of all sins must be made promptly to my priests, in person, and signed in blackmail blood. No longer will we accept unsigned group confessions such as in our wars, where entire groups are dying at once. There will be no more leaks, like Tisserant. Ours is the greatest CIA of all: Jesus Christ!"

The alter ego of "Hughes" is Hughes Tool, Mouth of the Mafia Money Funnel.

The alter ego of Onassis, who is "Hughes," via murder, is Chappaquiddick Dickie.

The alter ego of Teddy is McGovern. Onassis is the alter ego of Teddy. And also his father, via murdering his brothers.

Vote for either, or vote for both. The real next President is Onassis-Montini, the same as it is right now.

The massive mutilation of Vietnam is merely a projection of Dickie's frenzied gyrations on the graves of Mary Jo and Howard Hughes. The world watches in bitter horror as the pack trains of heroin crunch on corpses on their way to Alioto's San Francisco and Onassis' Switzerland and Montini's Rome.

"I made my deal in a secret room," said McGovern. "Just as four administrations met behind

closed doors to promote a horrible war."

That deal was made two weeks after Chappaquiddick—August 5, 1969—in the home of Henry Kimelman, Mafia Washington branch.

Chappaquiddick looked hopeless—even for Onassis-Dickie and Montini. The Chappaquiddick phone calls were out. Everything was out. I had informed Mack, Greenagel, Wright, Dickie, Mitchell, and various places around here and overseas.

McGovern, the "visibly" cleanest one they could find who still belonged to the club, was called in, as he was called in 1968 to pick up Bobby's dead votes and try for it at Chicago. McGovern was briefed then—along with Humphrey—about Alioto's Mafia connections, by J. Mafia Hoover, who was himself quietly murdered to "shut the mouth" of the beleaguered Mafia Blackmail Monster.

Henry Kimelman is "visibly" a Caribbean (owned by Onassis; see the Lansky CIA Papers) real estate dealer. Kimelman arranged the $6 million necessary to nominate McGovern. The deal? A total Kennedy machine—all Mafia money—plus Papal aid—to elect McGovern.

The price? An eternal lid on Chappaquiddick. And the next day, McGovern was at Hyannisport, offering support to Teddy "in his ordeal."

And after his acceptance speech last night, he said: "Senator Ted Kennedy is the most courageous human in America. Teddy is great."

All of the potential reforms are now squashed. All of the Labor Maf, and Jewish Maf, will be back in the fold. Wallace, properly admonished by gut-shot, will remain in the Demo fold, thus retaining votes that Dickie got last time out. Kimelman is now funneling in the Major Mafia Money chunks which now take over.

Bright-eyed young McGovern fanatics were screwed by McGovern while both he, and they, held a massive orgy on Mary Jo's grave.

Said Gloria Steinem (whose partner, Barbara Phillips, had read all this), to McGovern: "You bastard; you shafted us."

Not really, because Sinatra, who was in on Lansky's Miami deals (the hearings on this were squashed in the Mafia Congress, just prior to the Convention)—Sinatra, the Mafia, succeeded in getting "Jesus Christ" Shirley MacLaine appointed to the National Democratic Committee.

Roberts Meets McGovern in 1945: Catch 22

Victorville Army Base, California—late World War II. Bomber crews were returning from Europe for reassignment. On this day my job was picking up things in front of the headquarters with a stick with a spike on the end of it, and putting them in a sack I carried.

Up the walk came a batch of 50 mission crush officers surrounding their leader. I paused to watch the show. The leader smiled at me—the same smile I saw on TV in Miami—and they went up onto the porch.

There was a sudden hush, and then there was the wrath of God. The leader, flanked by a few buddies, stood in front of me, snarling at me.

"Don't you know how to salute, soldier?"

Me: "Yes, but I have a stick in one hand and a sack in the other. I didn't know I was required to."

He, livid: "Yes, what, soldier?"

Me: "Yes, Sir!"

He: "A salute is a mark of respect. You will salute me, and you will salute these men. Now, soldier! Or I'll court-martial you into the next war!"

I was confused. So were some of the others. I handed him my stick and saluted. He passed the stick back to me and returned the salute from six inches, like venomous spit in my face.

He left, and I kept my back to everything, bent over, picking up things, until that group of heroes left the building. If you don't see them, you don't have to salute; this I knew.

Later, Bill Ross, a friend, who worked at headquarters, came out.

"Who was that?" I said. "He was gonna court-martial me, and the rules state that I don't have to salute when I'm on duty with my hands full."

Said Bill: "His name is McGovern—and he could do it, too. He's quite a hero."

So is Bill Ross. Bill Ross was in more recent years the campaign manager for ex-FBI Agent Club Member Evelle Younger, who covered up the Bobby Kennedy murder in L.A. for the Mafia, as D.A. of Los Angeles. Younger is now State Attorney General.

His assistant was Neil Gendel, who quit, calling Younger a Mafia son-of-a-bitch, and yet is running himself, with Kay Pachtner, a necrophiliac Nader Chappaquiddick broad, away from these papers. So is Bill Ross.

In 1974, Mafia Younger plans to run against Mafia Alioto for Governor of California, to replace Ronald Reagan. Also announcing interest, so far, are Mafia Moscone, Moretti, and Pelosi[51] (whose two daughters—Newsom's nieces—were barbecued during the middle of the *Look* Alioto Mafia trial, in order to win a verdict by forcing all the judges, jury and attorneys to put out the fire and smell the stench of barbecued girl flesh.)

Also running will be Mafia Willie Brown, who left the Mafia Miami Convention Hall clutching the fist of iron that crushed Mary Jo's nose—Teddy Kennedy, the most courageous man in the U.S. of Mafia. I'm sick. Pardon me while I puke.

At any rate, I salute you, George McGovern. I shall even help you to attain your goal.

Coming up, next month, at the very same site in Miami, the Republican Mafia will meet behind the same Mafia moats—far removed from Mafia C. Arnholdt Smith's San Diego.

(Smith is currently indicted for fraud and using Mafia muscle to save himself. His partner, Schulman, is the employer of Thelma Golding of Portland—my brother Dayle's second Mafia ex-wife. Thelma sent my mother a murder sympathy card—about my Dickie-murdered father, and me.

Said Thelma: "Watch out for that son of yours." (Me). "He's a son-of-a-bitch. Everything that's rotten."

My mother cried. It had only been two weeks since Dickie murdered my father. After three and a half years of slow Mafia torture, my mother was almost dead too, also courtesy of Dickie.

A note from my daughter's mother states that my daughter—the age and beauty of Mary Jo Kopechne—is weak, and has black-out periods. My mother barely toddles.

I don't know Thelma Golding. I met her only once, and said hello, many years ago. But I do understand. Planned murder of my mother, and my daughter—by Dickie, Montini, the U.S. of Mafia, and a necrophiliac nation, which is "too busy" to care.

That Miami Republican Mafia Nominating Convention will be the Mafia show of the century.

***

---

[51] Nancy Pelosi, currently a Democratic Congresswoman representing California's 8th District (San Francisco), is a Pelosi by marriage. Both her father (Thomas D'Alessandro) and her brother served as Mayors of Baltimore. Since I am a registered Democrat, and Nancy is currently Democratic Leader of the House of Representatives, she occasionally sends me impassioned pleas for contributions. I thought of writing to her and asking how she interprets Roberts' account of the barbecuing of "Pelosi's nieces" back in the '70's, but there isn't any space on the forms for questions—just for how much money you want to contribute to the Democratic Party.—sc2006

George McGovern, in 1945, while castigating the yardbird (me) in the desert sun at Victorville, was constitutional. But I was correct. Army law says this.

He was a 50-mission crush murderer then, spreading smart bombs from a mile high on sandwich meat, crucified during Mafia Roosevelt-Joe Kennedy-Onassis' World War II: Fatima #1. Today he carries the banner of Fatima #3 for Mafia Montini-Kennedy-Onassis-Dickie and all of MMORDIS. A vicious murderer then. And with Mafia ambitions today: a treasonous glob, sucked up the cancerous ass of Mafia.

My job, that day, was picking up garbage—"flushing shit."

Elizabeth Dale, the broad who now wears the 62-carat heart-shaped sapphire originally offered to Dickie's wife about August 5, 1969, said to me, shortly before my father's murder, "I might kill you myself. You have no right to play with people's lives."

She was wrong, of course. These are not people. They are Cancer. And I am not playing. My finger won't be on any of those nuclear buttons that will be pushed. I won't personally conduct that final experiment, interrupted when Alioto clobbered my car.

The cancer is responsible for its own death—in the very process of consuming its host: the human lunch.

Said she: "You're insane."

Said Al Strom: "He's not insane. We're all insane."

***

Me, to a McGovern delegate newly returned from the Convention: "I wish to help elect George President."

"How?" said he.

I handed him a copy of this.

He read. And said, "But here you prove that George McGovern is the rottenest of all rotten cancers—and I note that you have affidavits that support that. How will this help elect George? Besides, we all know that Dickie is the rottenest of the rotten."

Me: "I have proof that McGovern is one fraction of a degree rottener than Dickie. And therefore he will win, since computers prove that the Mafia rigs the vote in favor of the absolute rottenest. And the rest of the nation votes that way too."

He: "Very good. Now what do you want out of this?"

Me: "Well, me and a buddy—his name is Christ, and he got off the cross at Chappaquiddick—we're looking for top tinkling mobiles to dangle on eternity yo-yos. I wish to prod George in the ass with my Victorville swagger stick, all the way to the White House, and then jam it all the way through—asshole to belly button, Mafia style, and then hang him on my mobile.

"And I have the same plan for Dickie. I have a thing about hanging Presidents on my mobiles. My buddy, Christ, goes for Popes. Tisserant prefers Cardinals, Bishops, and on down. And Mary Jo gets all of you Kennedy cancers.

"While you were gone I let your wife read this, and she was watching you on TV down there in Mafia Miami.

"I told her I was a carrier of syphilis, gonorrhea, and a new type of creeping Chinese crud, a 22-hour belly button rotter, highly infectious, and 'Let's go to bed.'

"And she said, 'Beautiful.'

"And then I read in the newspaper where you arrived home last night. How do you feel? You look sick."

He: "I'm too busy. I don't understand. I gotta go home." He went out the door.

I stood in the doorway and came to a full McGovern salute and shouted after him, "But, Sir, this is your home. I know. I was here before, screwing your wife, while you were in Miami. Come back so we can elect George. I have a plan for a gala that will be better than the Dickie campaign plan for the Republican Mafia Convention in Mafia Miami next month...."

But he never looked back.

Do you wish to know the name of this delegate? And the broad? She's cute. I gave her a list to sleep around with. After the job is done, I'll tell you.

***

That 62-carats of heart-shaped sapphire went up President Patty's ass. The anonymous ITT letter, up Martha's. The "Mary Jo's liver" went up Joanie's. Onassis' chancred cock story went up Rosie. The Mustapha diary, up Jackie. The "Red" Duke story, up Nellie. Sinatra's "Jesus Christ" Shirley MacLaine, up the Women's Liberation movement of Barbara Phillips. A double dose of Hampton and Clark up the wife of Charles Garry. All in the name of Christ and his Virgin Mother Mama and his Persian Pa.

Brave Free American men, such as McGovern's most courageous man in America, Teddy, says: "America begs me to be President and Vice President. But I quit. Joanie is afraid..."

Mitchell says: "I have it all now. I can keep it. But I quit. Martha fears..."

Connally: "I have it all now. I can keep it. But I quit. Nellie fears..."

Alioto: "I could be Governor now. But I quit. Until after J. Edgar Hoover is murdered."

Wallace: "They gut-shot me. I quit. I'll be a good Demo."

Johnson: "Hang separately."

Said Dickie on the 4th of July, as he smart-bomb murdered 234 POW's—ours: "America is the flag, motherhood, and apple pie."

The flag: Trampled into the ground in Montini-Onassis' Fatima #3 Vietnam, where Dickie and Teddy's heroin mule trains trample over rotten corpses.

And today, McGovern flies a mile high over the Gulf of Tonkin, lobbing smart bombs and preaching peace in the name of Teddy's brother, who pushed open those Papal gates for Onassis—just as McGovern did in *Catch 22* (written about him[52] by a fellow squadron commander, Joseph Heller, who describes American enemy-paid pilots, destroying their own air base in Genovese's Corsica).

---

[52] As the character "Milo Minderbinder".

24 The Bullet Holes of Dallas: John Connally and Dr. "Red" Duke

It was a slip of the tongue. On his just completed world tour for Dickie—passing out Mafia loot, plugging leaks and searching for Tisserant's papers—Secretary of the Treachery Connally stopped at Kabul, Afghanistan. Waiting for him there was Dr. James "Red" Duke—who plugged up the hole in Connally's chest from one of Oswald's bullets at Parkland Hospital in Dallas, November 22, 1963, where Connally and the murdered JFK were taken.[53]

Just after Chappaquiddick, Dr. Duke, the famous surgeon, was shipped to the lonesomest mountain in Afghanistan to minister to the medical needs of occasional goat herders in the Jalalabad area; try to find it on a map.

Only Connally, Onassis and a handful of Mafia know how to get a message to him. But for this occasion, they did. And the famous Dr. Duke came down from his trackless mountaintop into Kabul, riding on a mule, to meet Mafia John.

Afghan greeters were surprised when Mafia Connally embraced "Red" Duke.

Connally explained: "This man saved my life. He plugged up the hole in my chest from Oswald's bullet and he fixed the other bullet, which is still in my neck, so that it doesn't hurt too much."

Said one surprised Afghan mayor: "But, Mr. Connally, your government says there were only two shots fired—both by Oswald. If you caught both of them fired from behind the car, then who fired the one from the front that entered JFK's throat as he was looking up, and blew off the back of his head, spattering brain tissue in the face of a cop on a motorcycle behind the car? You know, the cop who, just after Chappaquiddick, was shipped to Onassis' sanitarium on Skorpios—the same one from which Howard Hughes was lowered… Mr. Connally? Where are you going? Come back! You just got here…"

But it was too late. Connally was gone, en route to Rome.

Under watchful eyes, Dr. Duke headed back up the mountainside on his mule.

A hippie was standing nearby. "Mayor—your fuzz—I'm an American," he said. "To uphold the honor of my country, I'll answer your question. Maheu's Roselli, from the original CIA Maheu Castro assassination group, fired the JFK head-blow-off shot from the overpass[54] in front. Two more shots were fired by two of Mafia Marcello's finest—one near the overpass, and one from the grassy knoll. They missed—in that CIA crossfire—because Roselli's first one got Kennedy.

"Everybody missed in Chicago, on November 1, 1963, on JFK, because he found out about the plans and cancelled his trip. But the Mafia batted .500 on that day anyhow: Onassis-McCone's Captain Nung blasted Diem at a railroad crossing in Saigon as a train roared by.

(Daley, in Chicago, murdered Hampton and Clark—after Chappaquiddick—because they knew of the Chicago end of this missed hit).

"Maheu's Gene Cesar got Bobby with three shots in the back of the head—from a foot away, while hypnotized Sirhan Sirhan shot up the rest of the room, from in front.

"Teddy busted Mary Jo's nose and let her flip into the pond at Chappaquiddick—as he bailed out on the bridge—because she knew about this. She was with Bobby in L.A. And also

---

[53] See Chapter 45, "Magic Bullet" Theory Exploded: Dr. James Duke at Parkland Hospital.
[54] Since the trajectory of this bullet was apparently upward, from the front to the rear, I think Roberts may be referring to the sewer opening on Elm Street, which was downhill from the Grassy Knoll, approaching the overpass. It has since been "remodeled," and effectively "disappeared," I understand.—sc2006.

because she had heard the Chappaquiddick calls—on a plug-in phone, plugged in behind the day bed—from Tunney, and to Alioto, in San Francisco .

"Hypnotized Bremer only gut-shot Wallace, but scared him into line."

Mayor: "If this is so, why are you here, in poverty? Why doesn't all of America and the world know? Why don't they do something about it?"

Hippie: "Who's to tell them? What makes you think they don't know? Why should they do anything about it? They're in it. They're Mafia Cancer too.

"For instance: the *New York Times* got a Pulitzer Prize for publishing the Pentagon Papers. Since they were out, Senator Gravel got a V.P. nomination for re-issuing them. Then President Johnson made $2 million by issuing a book of them to cover his own tracks. Ellsberg got 150 years in prison for releasing them.

"Said Ellsberg: 'If I'm a conspirator, then the U.S. Constitution is dead.' (It is).

"'If I'm a spy, then the American Public is the enemy.' (It is. A Necrophiliac Nation—the U.S. of Mafia).

"'If I am a thief, then the government, not the people, owns history.' (It does. Back to the murder of Christ and forward to Fatima #3).

"Me? I am here because I was hyped for 30 days (as was John Tunney's sister Joan, before she chopped off her hubby's head—when she was sent to Norway after Chappaquiddick. That was because she heard John Tunney's Chappaquiddick phone call to Teddy at the cottage, made from her Tiburon home, about Alioto's desperate try to be Governor, over Tunney's dead body)—and I was dumped off here with a habit.

"See those nomads over there, with the guns? Those guns are loaded. If Dr. 'Red' Duke hadn't gotten back on his mule and headed back up the hills, he would be dead. And if I don't get a fix and go back to my hole, I'm dead—two ways: heroin and them. And since you were stupid enough to ask this question, and I answered you—in full public view and hearing—what do you think of your future, Mr. Dead Mayor Fuzz?"

Poisoned Apple Pie

Apple Pie: So far in my research I've discovered only DDT, and a very ancient poison, used in Europe on rats.[55] And frequently by the Maf, such as Maheu, when the CIA hired him to assassinate Castro. (Castro lived. He didn't eat the apple pie.) It is provided locally by Sascha Volman, who operated with Superior Court Justice William O. Douglas (Vegas Stardust Casino) in the Caribbean on behalf of the Onassis-Lansky-Kimelman Maf group (and who also expounded the Stardust hypnotic bit that belched up Sirhan, and later Bremer).

It is a poison which causes, in order: 1) Languor, 2) Shortness of breath, and 3) Heart block.

(That's dead, baby. Ha ha.)

In an older person, the first two symptoms are not even noticeable. Death occurs too long after administration to finger the murderer. The chemical is burned away in the process of doing its job—just like the chemicals in the oil of my Alioto-clobbered car, and in the transmission of my next

---

[55] Based on his father's peculiar symptoms, Roberts began searching for a poison that might have been used. The "rat poison" he mentions is I believe the same "rat poison" marketed today under the name "Warfarin." A more "refined" and even more potentially deadly substance is used in hospitals under the name "Coumarin." Both appear to work similarly: they "thin the blood," preventing blood clotting. An overdose can lead to internal hemorrhaging, or fatal conditions in the brain. A case current today involves a man convicted of "shaken baby syndrome" in the death of his infant son, who may have died as a result of an overdose of Coumarin administered in the hospital. By the time I encountered Roberts and his letters in 1974-5, he had put another name to the poison: "sodium morphate," and that is how I referred to this poison in the various *Skeleton Key to the Gemstone File* versions I released in March through June 1975.—sc

one. This Onassis-Volman medicine was administered to J. Mafia Hoover, at a very critical time: just before Peking—in apple pie. Its faint odor is that of apple pie. No CIA Mafia ever eats apple pie.

Last night Betty Waterhouse appeared again, and said: "Did you murder my husband? They asked me if I wanted an autopsy. It's a law—and it's free—and I had it within five minutes. Maybe your mother put the poison in the apple pie. What evidence did you discover? Where is your brother? Where is that old car? Why would your daughter's mother worry you with a letter saying that your daughter has lately developed languor and fainting spells?

"My husband and I were in Hiroshima six days after it happened. It wasn't so bad. Just part of the war. Here is a certificate of appreciation about my husband's career—from Richard Nixon. Notice it's his real signature: shaky and minute. And here it is again, notifying me that I shall have free rent for life, and no financial worries. Isn't Richard Nixon wonderful?"

Pressure on me. Family death. Money. Threats. Insults. Taunts. Isolation. Certain areas wish to force me into their sphere. The Mafia here wants to force me to fall in with them. They all hope I drop dead. And fear just that. They miss the point—deliberately, because they know…all we're waiting for is the gang bang. It is so arranged. I have no sweat.

It's only those jittery countries that nervously jiggle about Fatima #3, and cause Dickie's hierarchy to scurry around the world, checking closely, to suppress more tightly. It is the eye of the hurricane. Seeded and growing toward a gang bang. Only one way out: Straight up. But I've got a deal with a friend. Hang them here, and stop the storm, or take them along and hang them there.

My mother's brother is still running—south—while Dickie and the bunch peck away at my mother. My brother—running during this three and a half years of torture on my father, arrived on schedule—an hour after the murder was complete—and delivered a five minute Mafia lecture:

"Lay off Alioto. You got what you asked for. I know he was poisoned. They rolled over two that way recently in Idaho. They'll get Hoover."

(They did.)

"I'm too busy. I gotta go." And he took off running and white-faced, without a glance, a flower, or a word to the murdered man—his father.

Three months later, he sent a card to my mother: "Watch that bastard—he's expensive." (Me). Mother cried, and wilted further, remembering his three-and-a-half year run, his belated arrival, Mafia message, and his quick, cold disappearance.

It is indeed depressing to watch the disintegration of human moral fiber into a glob of cancerous crud. His card was mailed from the home of Thelma Golding, his second ex-wife: the Portland Mafia who works for Mafia San Diego Smith, who works for wonderful Richard Nixon, who works for Onassis, and all with the blessings of Montini, the Deputy of Christ at Auschwitz, who owns Swig's Masonic branch, to which my brother belongs.

Let us pray: Holy Mother of God, Holy Virgin Mary, Jesus, fruit of thy womb. Splinters from the empty, festering cross are up snatches, screwing in unison with Teddy at Miami, toward Mary Jo's busted-nose Pennsylvania grave. A lemming practice session for the finale: the gang bang on Christ.

***

Me, answering Betty Waterhouse: "Dickie who? Wonderful? Oh yes, I remember. He's the one who murdered my father.

"Recently he had a choice of who to murder: J. Edgar or Alioto. Both had the same blackmail files.

"J. Edgar was alone. He had no family—nothing but blackmail enemies.

"On the other hand, there are 4,500 actively breeding Mafia Alioto cancers, and a world wide

web of cancer connections. It was an easy choice.

"Alioto was declared 'pure' by Dickie's judge, and J. Mafia Hoover was declared dead. The most powerful man in the world was quickly silenced, and suddenly not even remembered. All his files mysteriously vanished (or so they think).

"And 'Pure Joe' is running again for Governor of California.

"You see, Betty, in Alioto's first major trial, Sam Goldwyn, the judge, ate apple pie at the start of the trial, and had a heart attack in the middle. And Alioto won the case.

"In his second major trial—about Alioto's Mafia web…little girls are too young for heart attacks. A barbecue was better, as long as the judge, jury, and attorneys put out the fire and breathed deeply of burned baby girl flesh. Alioto was declared innocent.

"In his third major trial—about bribery, extortion, etc.—we had an older judge who liked apple pie, and he heart attacked right on schedule—at the dead center of the trial. Alioto again won, easily.

"And then just before his fourth major trial—and this one would have meant 45 years in the can for 'Pure Joe'—J. Mafia Hoover ate apple pie and heart attacked. 'Pure Joe' walked up to that judge, squinted, and pointed to the big badge he was wearing which said 'Pure Joe.'

"The judge said, 'I hate barbecues and apple pie, and I ain't taking no chances on this even getting to the jury. I declare this saint to be innocent—and I certify him to be Pure. Case dismissed.'

"And this is why Alioto is the only public official in the U.S. certified to be 'Pure' by both Dickie and Montini. Not to be confused with Teddy's certification by Dickie, McGovern and Montini as 'Most Courageous Man In America.'

"And, Betty, this is how executives of the nature of 'Wonderful' Richard Nixon are created. And, with 'Pure Joe' clarified, Edgar ossified, and Wallace perforated, Martha Mitchell bubbled, 'Get these CIA hoods out of my Chappaquiddick bed. Screw them—or screw you, John.'

"Well, trembling Poucha Pond John quit everything and rushed to Martha's bathroom and hid. Poor John. Gone back to where he came from.

"And since you, Betty, receive unlimited funds from Dickie, whose shaky finger personally signs the checks, let's calm him down a bit.

"I elected him to that worrisome place, so tell him I'm gonna let him out. I'm gonna elect George Teddy McGovern, and then collect all these 'Pure,' 'Courageous,' 'Wonderful' Presidents on a Victorville skewer—a Presidential shish kebab—and hang them out to dry on mobile strings that tinkle—their place in history forever."

She: "I'm gonna vote for McGovern."

Me: "The last time I saw you, the evening before my father was murdered, I told you that I was the hangman, and that I would hang you, and you said that Christ was a shit disturber and deserved what he got."

She: "I'm not saying that any more. I'm too busy. I don't understand. I gotta go home."

Me: "Oh no. Not again. This time, I go."

***

So—Ellsberg proves that the Government is infected with cancerous Mafia. Here, then, is a summary of Dickie's Flag, Motherhood, and Apple Pie. So what else is new? Cancer. And what happens to cancer? It eats its human lunch, then murders the host, and itself.

There is no jail, no bail, no election to the presidency. Either way, the cancer is dead. Even if the doctor—on a whim, like Truman's—gets impatient and incinerates the patient.

Charles Garry and Jerry Rubin, CIA

July 11: While I waited in Charles Garry's front office—a 26-minute delay—Mafia CIA Jerome Rubin was telling Garry (on the 2nd day of the Demo Mafia Convention):

"We know you are a Communist, your Gray Eminence. Recently, one of Noel Gayler's National Security Council Ellsberg-Tisserant type traitors mentioned the fact that Onassis-Montini's Pentagon has had the whole world tapped—including the KGB—as a prelude to Fatima #3.

"We know about a lot of the stuff you've shipped out, but we still don't know how that bastard out there in the waiting room does it. Now, we let up on the genocide of the Black Panther Party, and we haven't pulled any more Hampton-and-Clark type executions, since you agreed to direct your people to work with us 'within our Mafia System.' We even let you get Angela Davis off, and a bunch of other Panthers.

"But today, if you cooperate any further with that bastard out there—if you aid him in any way, we will 'accidentally' misfire a Vandenburg missile on San Francisco and eradicate every Black Panther, radical, and dissident in the Bay Area—as well as everybody else.

"You will notice that all of our people are out of town—at the Democratic Convention in Miami. Moscone and Moretti are vacationing in the Bahamas. Anybody we care about is out of town. I am the last one. I can ground every plane, except the one waiting for me—and issue that misfire order. Do you understand me, Garry?"

Garry said: "I understand. But if you do that you would include him out there, with a meat ax on his shoulder, with which to chop the pin out of the grenade he's got up your ass and mine. Wouldn't that be suicide?"

Rubin: "Possibly. But this is the whole ball of wax. We either stop him now—any way we can—or we all go anyhow. You can count on what I tell you. Even if we need to pull Fatima #3—first strike—to back it up. You're just a few minutes away from dead. We don't know, and you don't know, what his time schedule is. How much is time worth? How much would you pay for an extra minute?"

Garry agreed with a nod. And then he called me in and delivered a Mafia message: "The hierarchy will squash anything that steps on its toes. You are dead. I know about the Hampton and Clark murders. I was there. I can't get it into any Mafia court. I know about Mary Jo. I don't want to know any more. I don't want to know anything. Go away please. I'm too busy. I don't understand. I gotta go home."

***

And this is how it is that Communist Garry—by a nod of his head—saved the heads of the citizens of Alioto's Mafia San Francisco—for a while—on July 11, 1972—at 3:26 p.m.

Alioto was in Miami. J. Mafia Hoover was long dead—via American Apple Pie.

***

I watched the Miami Convention on TV. At the same time, I watched San Francisco on the streets.

At 10:00 p.m., when I first appeared with the big sack on my shoulder, at a Jones & Leavenworth Street isolated bus stop, a scattered group of tough ones jiggled every time I did. And I thought back to the first Nader letter—and his Onassis bribe, and the Conga line that follows me.

Now join me for the big Republican boogaloo—August 21, 1972—in Mafia Miami.

I had six options, four years ago:

1. Ask the cancer to cure itself: a total waste of time.

2. Burn all bridges: kill or cure.

3. Film the total crumbling of the moral fiber of the U.S. of Mafia.

And these three have been done.

4, 5, and 6 are coming up, not necessarily in that order.

I am very tired, and I don't give a shit. All this is the view of one man—one whim; like Truman's. Why worry about one man?

Mafia cancer has succeeded in murder—2000 years of it. Change it around? Reverse the murder? Hang them here or hang them there? Forget it. No one man could do this. Could he?

Today, informed areas won't rise to U.S. of Mafia prods. They withdraw from Egypt. Pronounce peaceful ideology. Shun war. Welcome trade. Accept visitors. And the Mafia greedily rushes around the world to purchase with the motto, "Why kill 'em if we can buy 'em?"

(Waiting. Watching the U.S. of Mafia Cancer eat its diseased self. A non-changeable course. And it is why the future scripts, which they have already seen, are so accurate—and why those out now will be accurate too. Why should they resist? One man is doing it all. A man who worked with minerals until Alioto clobbered his car. But you wouldn't understand that; just as those at Hiroshima couldn't comprehend—a tick away. Missiles you do understand—now.

Says Ellsberg:

"In 1961, just after Kennedy got elected, I was hired by the National Security Council to draw up a plan for worldwide nuclear war. (Fatima #3.) I had, previously, since Apalachin (Onassis' 1957 Mafia capture of the Election Process), been drawing up a plan for the Pacific area only (including the gate to Fatima #3—Vietnam). The Pentagon (Onassis' Mafia, and the 'shotgun' he snatched from JFK when he murdered him and snatched his snatch, Jackie), kept the existence of the plan from all outsiders, including Congress, Executive, and Judicial. (And, of course, from you, the corpse on the menu.).

"Fellwock quit the National Security Agency, (which was Noel Gayler's baby, breaking codes and stuff before Dickie named him Commander in Chief of all Pacific Forces to carry out that nuclear plan) and released the documents to Charles Garry, and then to the public, over screams of the CIA murderer Helms—via Ramparts. The most dangerous threat to me and my family, and to world peace itself, is the American Military. (Onassis' Pentagon and the Kennedy-Spellman 'Holy Crusade' Vietnam gate to Fatima #3).

"The build-up of America's vast military machine and global empire is based on the lie that there is an overwhelming military threat to the U.S. There is clearly one superior offensive nation, the U.S.A., and one inferior defensive nation: Russia. The NSA's success in snooping is kept secret in order to persuade the American people of the need for huge military spending."

***

[The key words above are "Onassis's Mafia Pentagon," "global nuclear war," and "secret from all outsiders." Onassis and the Pentagon and CIA, and their affiliates, murder around the globe. The CIA assassinates singles and countries and found Fatima #3 suitable for the world.—BR]

"This is why I can pull a missile down at any site, at any time. And this Mafia CIA doesn't really care how many are in town or out of town.

"Like Onassis on Bobby at L.A. or JFK at Dallas, I have backups. It is why just a nod of the head, in the right direction—an agreement by Garry with CIA Jerry Rubin—kept a Vandenberg "mistaken" nuclear obliteration away from San Francisco on the second day of the Mafia Miami Demo Convention, July 11, 1972 at 3:26 P.M., with some people of value to the Mafia—such as "Files" Alioto, Moscone, and Moretti, in town.

"That "mistake" missile is on 24-hour alert. And Betty Waterhouse's husband Sarnoff's Dew-

line defense group would not defend against that one, would they?"

***

It was barely aborted in the first week of October, 1971.

At 2:00 a.m. that night, at the Mark Bar, a CIA shit said, "That was the smartest thing you ever did." In complete frustrated disgust. It is why Nader didn't show in San Francisco that weekend—for his assassination, and yours.

Instead, Kay Pachtner handed the Consumer's Federation 3rd Party Convention to the Mafia. They were there—and under the same death sentence I was, had Nader appeared.

La Follette glared. Pat Wyman joined me for lunch, and Sylvia Siegal said, "Nader is a shit hiding in a phone booth in Washington." And hanging over all of us—Maf and non-Maf—was a "mistaken" missile. It was a fun affair.

And on the morning of Nader's cancellation, 100 FBI descended on San Francisco. Ostensible purpose: to pick up a few winos. Actual purpose: to seal the lid up tight on any loose ends of that Henry Yee opium-heroin bit. (There have been dozens of Chinatown murders recently over this.) And also to cart the crop out of town—since, if Nader screwed up his guts and did appear, and they had to lob one in, they were not going to atomize $6 billion worth of skag. You see, the Mafia has problems too. It's not all sweetness and light.

Strangelove Kissinger had a problem too. He had to get to Peking, because of my "Peking" talks with CIA Neilson-Green, and yet cover the Harry Yee Taiwan connection because of the upcoming U.N. vote on expelling dope-pushing Chiang and admitting China. He went to Peking, and was there when the bust happened, and that in itself helped vote Taiwan out and China in.

At lunch, Pat Wyman said to me, "You must be hungry," and I told her the truth. "Yes. I've had a busy week." A nice warm atomic flash would have been a relief.

So there was a 24-hour "mistake" missile alert. You see, this is election year 1972. As in 1968 (murders like King and Bobby), 1969 (murders like Mary Jo and Hampton-Clark), 1970 (murders like Eugenie Niarchos, Joan Tunney's hubby, Yablonski family, Newsom's nieces), 1971 (murders like Howard Hughes)—there must be warning murders—such as "Peking" Verne D. Roberts, my father, "Files" J. Mafia Hoover, and "Partial" Wallace. And there are more on the way. I guarantee you.

Said Mitchell, the Attorney General of the U.S. of Mafia sadly, just before he crawled up Martha's ass in the bathroom (from which she just called yesterday, again, and said: "I'm still a prisoner. I have a long story to tell....") "The lives of millions are at stake—probably all of us."

He was referring to another Manhattan Project: a search going on feverishly in Brookhaven, on the Swiss-French border, and in Kiev: a search for a mineral.

What do you suppose would happen if a "mistake" missile in some country—ignored by its own defense radar—searched itself right down the throat of a mineral pipe of that stuff? Or assorted back-ups of such a thing? What about mile-high smart bomb Catch 22 Teddy McGovern lobbing one in by mistake—or some berserk American pilot doing it deliberately?

I told the truth in that bar—with the big sack—about creeping crud that creates a 22-hour belly-button rot. And this is why, one week after I was standing at a lonely Jones & Sutter Street bus stop, I was standing there again at 10:00 p.m. with another armful of papers.

The Convention in Miami was just over. The previous week, that corner had been jammed with tough ones—jiggling every time I did.

This time there wasn't a soul in sight. Not even a bus, a cab; no Alioto whores. Fog rolling in. Nobody to even stare at it. Not even cars going by. I hadn't seen Betty Waterhouse (Levitus) since the night before my father's murder.

At the hospital that night, my father told me and my mother that something was going to happen to me, sometime between 9:00 p.m. and 9:00 a.m. When I left the hospital I went to Al Strom's, and Jim Lindberg asked me if I knew what was going on tonight, and I said "yes," and he left.

(His partner, Cliff Jones, was the one who was listening to my chat with one-tooth Kitty Lowry—Howard Hughes' half-aunt, or something, Betty Waterhouse's friend—back in here somewhere).

I was angry. I went to Betty Waterhouse's place and told her I was going to hang her. And I hadn't seen her since. That was four months ago. And so it was completely natural that on that totally empty corner, she should appear, smiling and friendly.

"Imagine seeing you here," she said. "There are no busses coming. Come up to my place and I will show you checks that Richard Nixon signs personally and sends to me, and citations about my husband—who was murdered just after your father was murdered—also signed personally. And we will talk about my dead husband's top security work in Kiev, and about that rat poison that leaves no trace, and his work on Sarnoff s Dew-Line, and your experiments on minerals, and Kitty Lowry and Howard Hughes, and the next president. And I have some beer, which I know that you drink—and you can catch a later bus. There won't be any for a while."

I was beginning to believe that. And I didn't have cab fare. And there weren't any cabs anyway.

In the papers in my arms were things relative to Dickie's nervous signature, and Howard Hughes. And everything else she was talking about. This woman was a fund of information, who loves the Mafia as an institution—and the military as a murdering instrument—and hates me with a venom that will never quit.

And so I said, "I don't like you. You are in books, on tape and on film—on display, or poised to be, before two thirds of the world. I will hang you."

And she said, "Oh well, what's the difference? We'll walk. Save money."

(She says she's heiress to $400 million—Price Waterhouse stuff. Checks from President Chappaquiddick Dickie. Signed personally, in a shaky hand.

And, once, the idea was to use that $400 million—all of it—to give a gigantic abortion to Body Count McNamara—who, in 1937, aborted her and left her bleeding—throwing money in her face and raging, "Damn you—you made me sell my car.")

We walked, and the rest of the chat is back in here somewhere.

***

Victorville: Catch 22

Teddy McGovern ponders Meany's decision to "sit this one out." And the wrath of God that spit into the yardbird's face in the hot desert sun spits again.

"Can a Mafia Union Leader deliver his union? Can a Mafia Mayor deliver his city? Can a Mafia Priest deliver his parish? Can Martha deliver John? Would a fart dislodge him?"

This to the press. And to himself, Teddy McGovern asks, "How can Onassis's Chappaquiddick Montini Teddy Kennedy amplify the Miami screw on Mary Jo, which he just conducted, in order to overcome the advantages of Onassis-Hughes Chappaquiddick Dickie's proposed campaign of a gang bang in Mafia Miami, on August 21, 1972? What kind of a super-gala can we come up with? Release the 'mistake' missile on the snake that bit us in San Francisco?"

There is a stone face on South Dakota's Rushmore. Stone face in the oval office. Stone face in Rome.

Says the law: "Anyone who feeds the 41% Mafia take and murders Mary Jo is guilty of every

crime known to humanity. The running rabbit has been snake-bitten and is dead."

Option 4 is under way. It has to do with the eating of liver. Which empty streets of which dead city will this "peace march" charge bravely down?

Have a happy day. See ya later.

***

"Magic Bullet" Theory Exploded

Texas Monthly: Interview with Dr. "Red" Duke (circa 1999)

Below is an unedited transcript from an interview with Dr. James H. "Red" Duke, Chief resident surgeon at Parkland hospital in Dallas at the time of the Kennedy assassination. Dr. Duke was interviewed by Joe Nick Patoski (editor of *Texas Monthly*). I don't know whether it ever appeared in the magazine; when I went back to look for it later on the Internet, I couldn't find it. After reading the portion of the Gemstone File which begins this chapter, I wanted to know more about Dr. Duke, whose role at Parkland Hospital on November 23, 1963, has been somewhat obscured in the record. And was he really shipped off to Afghanistan to get him out of harm's way in the form of possible questioning by any investigating Committee? The following is what I found.

Dr. Duke's role in John Connally's medical treatment has not been carefully scrutinized. Roberts describes two bullet holes in Connally, not one. This, if true, would demolish Arlen Specter's "single bullet" theory. Dr. Duke might have gotten his assignment to Kabul, Afghanistan, to remove him from awkward questioning in the '70's.

***

TEXAS MONTHLY: Dr. "Red" Duke, what were you doing on November 22,1963?

DR. DUKE: I was at work.

TM: And your work was?

DUKE: I was a fourth year surgery resident, called a senior resident. I was on thoracic surgery service. I was eating lunch and the chat room surgery paged overhead; "Staff." We didn't have beepers. I went to answer the phone. Another guy got there first.

He said, "Come on with me." He was a really serious fellow. He said, "Don't look excited."

I said, "Ron, I'm not excited." I was very unexcited. I said, "What's wrong with you?"

He said, "The president's been shot."

I didn't believe that. Not anything that serious. I didn't want to go shake hands with the president, you know. It wouldn't be a good idea to shake hands with the president.

I stopped to call my chief, who was Dr. Robert Shaw, and he was sort of my godfather and all this stuff in surgery. And then I went downstairs. Still didn't think anything was wrong until I turned and went in the trauma room. First, I went in where the president was. Put on a pair of gloves, walked on around behind him, and three other fellows were working on this hole in his neck. 1 saw this huge wound in his head. I don't know what I said, but somebody said, there's a guy across the hall needs some help. I knew I wasn't going to be able to help [President Kennedy] in that regard because there was nothing really to be done.

So I went across the hall and there was one intern standing in there and he was as white as his coat. But right quick I knew what the problem was: A large sucking chest wound; there's a big hole in this patient's chest. I don't know when I figured out it was Governor Connally. So I got that stopped up and put a chest tube in him which would allow him to breathe. You can't breath with a sucking chest wound because your lungs keep jumping in and out of the hole. I

got IV's in him, and then slowly people began to come in. I got everything ready to go, but I wasn't about to take him upstairs by myself. I kept thinking, "Where is Dr. Shaw?"

Dr. Shaw is one of my real heroes, who actually at that point in my life I realized was not 12 feet tall. (I'd known him for 10 years and I'm actually taller than he was). He finally walked in and put his arm around my shoulder and said, "Red, well what do we have here?"

I said, "This is Governor Connally."

At this point the governor is awake.

Dr. Shaw said, "Good morning, Governor Connally, I'm Robert Shaw, and I'm going to operate on you."

So we took him upstairs and operated on him. I stayed with him, We did not have intensive care units in 1963, so we kept him in the recovery room. I never left. I slept right there.

TM: Did you talk at all?

DUKE: Yeah. As much we could. The poor man hurt a lot. Chest wounds hurt like crazy. I don't recall, it was a pretty menial conversation; he was mainly there just trying to get over his problem. He had this big lung wound and an air leak in his chest tube.

TM: Did it ever hit you that day what had occurred?

DUKE: Oh yeah. The first time I went upstairs Sunday morning, the first time I ever left the recovery room, I went to make rounds on all the other patients and then Oswald got shot. We went into that same loop again. It was one of those moments when you felt like there was a great pall or cloud that descended upon where we were. In fact, my three-year-old daughter, who I didn't see until Sunday night, she prayed a prayer, my wife told me this:

"The world is dark, and we are very sad. Amen."

TM: When you look back 35 years ago, you were in a place and time where history converged. What do you make of it all? What do you think?

DUKE: I don't think we really understand it. I mean, I have never...I'm not a student of all the issues. I've never read much material about it. I haven't seen any movies about it. I don't study it. I saw, I was present, I know a little about the issues, circumstances, and wounds, and have been doing that for a long time. And I honestly don't...I've gone out of my way, not to be very involved in it. We did everything we could do in a positive way. To me there are a lot of unanswered questions. I think they will remain unanswered.[56]

TM: If there were any means to further illuminate the issue, I think that the time has passed, and now people are grabbing at straws and trying to make much ado out of pieces of paper now. I mean you can't talk to people anymore. It's like Nellie said: "I'm the last person riding in the back of that car that's left."

DUKE: Yeah. I don't understand what I know. When you're living through instances like that, it's like a freeze frame, a stopped phase movie where click, click, it's like having a slide show. It's still in my head. I can live through the dynamics of it, too, but you know the first view I had was of the president's neck and it's bubbling out of his neck. The neck with this big wound back here. I was there maybe a minute.

TM: And the first reaction was, what was it? "It's the president," or was it, "Look at the conditions," and, "This guy's gone"?

DUKE: When I turned the corner and saw Mrs. Kennedy with all this blood and other tissue on her dress, on her suit, I knew we were in trouble. And all I had to do was walk from here to that

---

[56] Texas "We Don't Talk About It" department.

cabinet and I was at the end of the table where I'd be looking at his head. I hardly…I recognized his face, but you know we're trained to solve problems we get, and I still deal with trauma all the time. Some people are kind-of oriented this way. We just lock on to an issue, just like a heat-seeking missile, and you've just got to solve the problem. You've got to be without emotion and cool. I mean, those of us that do it all the time are. I get deliberate, cold, focused, and you don't have to be any genius when you look at a wound like that, to know there's nothing [that] can be done. Tragic, but it can't be done. I felt that at the time there.

TM: You were in that mode pretty much all through the stay at the hospital?

DUKE: Oh, of course. I walked across the hall to the governor [who had] got his lungs jumping in and out of his chest, and I know what to do for that and I did it. It doesn't take long to stop up a hole, put in a chest tube, put an NG tube down, get IV's running.

TM: I'm glad you did what you did. One other question, I've often read out of this terrible moment that Nellie really committed a heroic act by covering her husband and in fact did.

DUKE: Well, actually she didn't know it. But in doing that—that's why he was alive when he got to the hospital. She forced him down and that partially closed that sucking chest wound. The bullet came in here and came out down here and went to his rib, but by doing that she was closing off the hole. When they put him on the gurney at the hospital, laid him out flat, he'd try to inhale and the air would go in here, and not down the wind pipe,

TM: Oh my God.

DUKE: So he was unconscious when I got to him.

TM: It's because he'd been lying on the gurney.

DUKE: Within moments from the time they unloaded him and took him in there. He lay there by himself because everyone went to the president. I went over there, and the first thing I did was stop the hole up, and the chest tube you put in takes care of the air leak, and then he woke up,

TM: Y'all talk about it afterwards?

DUKE: The governor and I?

TM: Yeah.

DUKE: We kept in good, close contact. He knew me real well. We hunted some together, and he knew I was a sheep hunter. In fact, he made some wise comment to my brother-in-law about, 'What's Red doing?" [George] said, "Well, he's in Afghanistan," and the governor paused and said, "That fool didn't mark his sheep very well, did he?"

***

Here is a quote from the *Warren Commission Hearings*: Vol. VI—Page 84:

(Testimony of Dr. Robert Shaw)

MR. ARLEN SPECTER:[57] Please tell us your name, sir.

DR. SHAW: Robert Roeder Shaw.

SPECTER: And what is your profession, sir?

SHAW: Physician and surgeon….I entered private practice, limited to thoracic surgery, August 1, 1938. I have continuously practiced this specialty in Dallas, with the exception of the period from June 1942 to December 1945, when I was a member of the Medical Corps of the Army of the United States, serving almost all of this period in the European theatre of operations. I was again absent from Dallas from December 1961 until June 1963, when I headed the medico team

---

[57] Later, and forever, Senator Arlen Specter, conjurer of the "Magic Bullet Theory."

and performed surgery at the Avicenna Hospital at Kabul, Afghanistan....

SPECTER: Did you have occasion to perform any medical care for President Kennedy on November 22, 1963?

SHAW: No.

SPECTER: Did you have occasion to care for Governor Connally?

SHAW: Yes.

SPECTER: Would you relate the circumstances of your being called in to care for the Governor, please?

SHAW: I was returning to Parkland Hospital and the medical school from a conference I had attended at Woodlawn Hospital, which is approximately a mile away, when I saw an open limousine going past the intersection of Industrial Boulevard and Harry Hines Boulevard under police escort. As soon as traffic had cleared, I proceeded on to the medical school. On the car radio I heard that the President had been shot at while riding in the motorcade. Upon entering the medical school, a medical student came in and joined three other medical students. He stated that President Kennedy had been brought in dead on arrival to the emergency room of Parkland Hospital and that Governor Connally had been shot through the chest. Upon hearing this, I proceeded immediately to the emergency room of the hospital and arrived at the emergency room approximately 5 minutes after the President and Governor Connally had arrived.

SPECTER: Where did you find Governor Connally at that time, Dr. Shaw?

SHAW: I found Governor Connally lying on a stretcher in emergency room No. 2. In attendance were several men: Dr. James Duke, Dr. David Mebane, Dr. Giesecke, an anesthesiologist. As emergency measures, the open wound on the Governor's right chest had been covered with. a heavy dressing and manual pressure was being applied. A drainage tube had been inserted into the second inter-space in the anterior portion of the right chest and connected to a water-sealed bottle to bring about partial re-expansion of the collapsed right lung. An intravenous needle had been inserted into a vein in the left arm and intravenous fluid was running.

I was informed by Dr. Duke that blood had already been drawn and sent to the laboratory to be cross-matched with 4 pints of blood to be available at surgery. He also stated that the operating room had been alerted and that they were merely waiting for my arrival to take the Governor to surgery, since it was obvious that the wound would have to be debrided and closed....

***

INTERNATIONAL SPEAKERS BUREAU (Lecturer available)

Dr. James H. "Red" Duke

Biography:

...Dr. "Red" Duke's academic career began in 1966, as an assistant professor of surgery at U.T. Southwestern Medical School and later at the College of Physicians and Surgeons in New York. Dr. Duke pursued graduate studies in chemical engineering, biochemistry and computer sciences at Columbia University under the auspices of an NIH Special Fellowship. While assistant professor of surgery in New York, Dr. Duke had the opportunity to move his family and career to Jalalabad, Afghanistan for two years as a visiting professor and later chairman of surgery at Nangahar University School of Medicine. Upon returning from Afghanistan in 1972, Dr. Duke joined the faculty of The University of Texas Medical School at Houston where he is a Professor of Surgery....

Programs: "**MODERN SURGERY IN THE MIDDLE AGES**" Dr. Duke shares some of the joys, trials and tribulations of practicing surgery in a Third World country where modern medical

procedures clash with the almost medieval surroundings and ancient cultures. This presentation of slides taken by Dr. Duke dramatizes the condition of life in the developing nation of Afghanistan, a place where misery and beauty exist side-by-side among a people who are kind and hospitable in spite of a long history of violent conflict and suffering.

© 2005 International Speakers Bureau

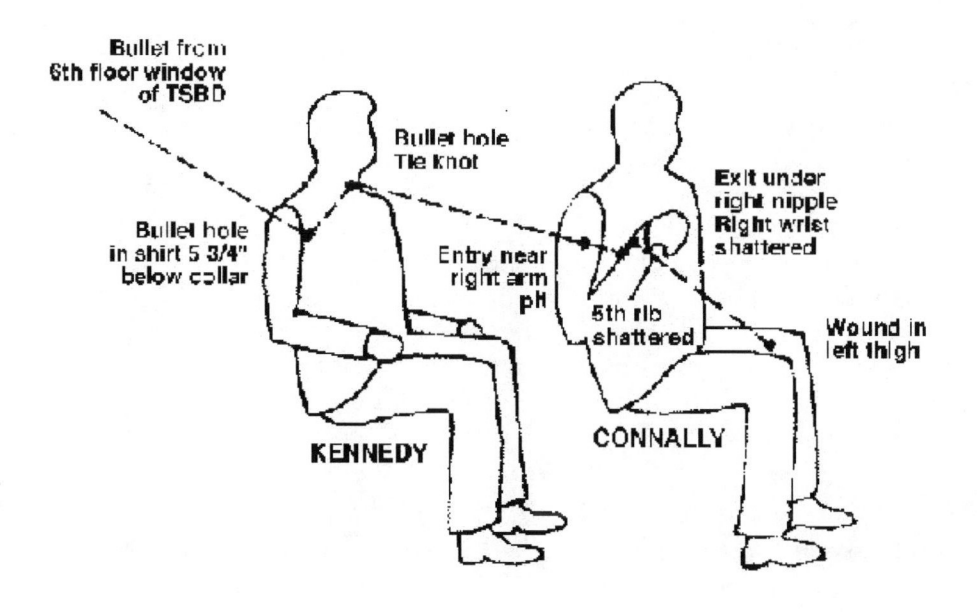

Theory regarding so-called "Magic Bullet" to account for 2 bullet wounds in Kennedy + 3 more bullet wounds in Connally, devised by Arlen Specter, a member of the Warren Commission and later Senator from Pennsylvania

25 Saving Daniel Ellsberg

July 21, 1972: They were a group of young, dedicated-looking anti-war marchers. Some were veterans of the anti-war campaigns. I knew a few by sight. All are fanatic McGovern people. All are fanatic Ellsberg fans. Angela Davis fans. And Teddy Kennedy fans.

They were grouping for a bus in San Francisco to take them to a gigantic anti-war rally in L.A.—a three-day affair. I asked them their names, and then I asked, "Do you want to get Ellsberg out of jail?"

Answer: "You'd better believe it. That's why we're going. He's the main speaker. We hope for a half million turn out at UCLA."

Dedicated. So again I asked, "Do you wanna end this goddamn war?"

Answer: "You'd better believe it! That's the other reason we're going."

Me: "Those are your only two reasons for going? You would let nothing stand in the way of those two objectives?"

Answer: "You'd better believe it!"

Me: "I was going. But as it turns out, I can't go. But I want Ellsberg's attorneys to have this sack full of papers. I want these papers to represent me.. The papers will get Ellsberg out of jail and end this war. Brezhnev has read them. Chou en-Lai has read them. Dickie has read them. Pope Paul has read them. And so have many more.

"Charles Garry used them to get Angela Davis free, and all the Black Panthers out of jail recently. Teddy Kennedy used them to get Teddy McGovern nominated. Dickie used them to get elected the last time out. And a few other things. Nader used them to win his General Motors suit. They got John Mitchell the Attorney General position.

"Recently, because of them, Mitchell quit, to help Dickie privately. And then he quit that job and crawled up his wife's ass. Martha, who hasn't been able to shit, for fear of flushing John down the drain, screams over the phone, "I'm still a political prisoner. I have a long story to tell."

"This is the story she wants to tell. I want you to give these papers to Ellsberg so that he may give them to his attorneys. Will you?"

"You'd better believe it!"

As I walked away, I heard the leader say, "Now, this is a sack—and we're all couriers to Ellsberg's attorneys. For our own safety—and that of our hero, Ellsberg, and his attorneys, we must examine this sack for bombs—as they do on boarding airplanes and other moving vehicles, for heroin, or other illegal contraband.

"I will take this first page and scrutinize everything that's on it, and will then pass it to the next one, who will do the same, and then I will do the same with the second page, and so on—until all of us on this bus are satisfied that there is nothing in that sack which would constitute a hazard—such as a potential hijacking of this vehicle, while we are on our courier mission to Ellsberg's attorneys."

Someone said, "You'd better believe it! Hurry up with page five!"

***

And so it is that I have presented L.A. with a new problem. Hanging over L.A. this weekend is a Mafia 'mistake' missile from Vandenberg.

Identical sacks have been arranged for delivery to the opposition of Ellsberg—Judge, Jury, witnesses, and so forth.

Ellsberg, the only one who didn't get a million dollars or a Pulitzer Prize out of the Pentagon Papers deal, has choices: 115 years in prison, assassination, hanging, or "mistaken" Vandenberg Missile atomization. Or, if he lets it all hang out, he's free. A hero. Bravest of the brave. All out for mankind, justice—all of the things he says he is for.

And the anti-war Peace March couriers and the half a million turnout? If they let it all hang out, they're free too. The bravest of the brave. All out for mankind and justice—all of the things they say they are for.

The options from this thing are many.

Thelma Golding's boss is Schulman, National General Corporation. Schulman's partner is Frank Sinatra (SS&R Enterprises, which holds 200,000 shares of National General).

Both are partners of C. Arnholdt Smith—the Maf who owns San Diego, and Alessio, and U.S. Attorney Seward, and Representative Bob Wilson; who owns Dita Beard, who writes memos about ITT, that caused the switch of convention sites to Miami's Fontainbleu, which Sinatra and Patriarcha own.

That is why Sinatra said "Screw you" to Congress—and then called Schulman. And on the following day Schulman and two other directors of National General resigned, to the total amazement of the entire Mafia economic community—except Sinatra and Onassis, of course.

And that reminds me of a day at Tahoe Airport—in a snowstorm. The only flight out, a Holiday Airlines flight, had greedily oversold the thirty seats by fifteen. So fifteen people were stranded—on a bench, in a blizzard. One was an older lady—a pensioner. Crying. Broke from the slot machines. Another was me. Also broke.

Holiday Airlines is owned by Golden West. Golden West is owned—illegally—by C. Arnholdt Smith (who owns Thelma Golding, who writes Mafia death sympathy cards) and Sinatra, who flies on Onassis' jets. Helms has "mistake" missiles to waste. What's San Diego? The Convention was moved to Miami.

"Waste 'em: Abrams Acres, My Lai—to retain President Thieu and God Montini. It's National Mafia Policy…. Waste 'em: Mary Jo, my father, Christ, Yablonskis, Hampton and Clark, Newsom's nieces, Hoover, Tunney's hubby, Eugenie Niarchos, Hughes," say Dickie and Teddy.

In L.A. this weekend, Garry's Black Panther Bobby Seale, and Hoffa's Teamster Gibbons, are directing the Anti-war Peace March, Free Ellsberg group for the election of Teddy McGovern. Lots of erratics are there—including Ellsberg and the radicals of Berkeley and San Francisco. Even Reagan, just returned from Rome.

Helms thinks "Why not? The 'mistake' missile. Fatima #3."

The cedar statue of Fatima—in the Parish of Mafia Marcello, owner of Louisiana—sheds real tears (olive oil). Says Father Brealt: "The weeping means that the Blessed Mother insists that the faithful follow the message of Fatima."

Yes indeed. I have extracted 57% water—H_2O—from an opal. 17% of sapphire juice from the 62-carat heart-shaped sapphire now up President Patty's ass. That juice is something else. A real tearjerker. From a ruby, the juice is red—the color of blood.

***

"The 1972 election gang bang could be canceled." (There is a memo about this from Rand—Ellsberg's employers—who also hide the file, "Project Star," about JFK at Dallas, in Agnew's office). Helms has a sudden reason, on his desk—to rack up a batch of Johns, Marthas, and Naders, there in D.C., this weekend, and flip all the rest on that other half—a "mistake", low, under unconcerned radar—which would cancel Catch 22 Teddy McGovern, cancel elections, and fulfill Fatima #3. And in Rome, this weekend, there is a sudden urgency to cut Montini out: "Why should he share the throne with us? Who does he think he is—God?"

Snake-bitten Dickie, the running rabbit, has no place to run—like Mitchell, with a 62-carat stone blocking Patty's ass.

Helms also has a vital reason—on his desk—to "mistake" Skorpios—this weekend. Make a clean sweep. Like a doctor. Cure Boss Onassis' phobia for good: "Fear of waking up to find everything gone."

This is the reasoning of one man—CIA Helms, as he sits painfully on the grenade tamped up his ass—and upon whom pressure is building. Hmmm. CIA heroin exposure, CIA-ITT murder exposure, CIA Fatima #3 Global Mission exposure. As with the "pressure" on J. Mafia Hoover—murder occurred. Helms may prefer another solution: "Waste 'em." This could mean you.

July 25: Divvying the loot in the White House

It's business as usual. This morning there was a Mafia meeting in the White House to divvy up loot. Dickie met with Mayor Alioto from McGucken's archdiocese, Mayor Daley from the Chicago Cardinal's diocese, and Mayor Moon Landreau from the New Orleans Diocese of Marcello's parish. This evening, loot in hand, Mayor Alioto rushes back to San Francisco to appear at a testimonial in Papal Knight, Shriner, Mafia Swig's Fairmont Hotel, sponsored by Archbishop McGucken, San Francisco, and Bishop Hurley, Santa Rosa Diocese—in honor of Mafia Alioto's successful escape from the murders of:

- ❖ Sam Goldwyn, Judge
- ❖ The "Mafia Alioto Web" barbecues of Newsom's nieces, Pelosi's daughters, and a Japanese nurse
- ❖ A Vancouver Judge
- ❖ J. Mafia Hoover (whose "broad and shotgun" he appropriated—Mafia style—both being J. Mafia's files).

For this, Alioto earned the badge of "Pure" from Dickie's federal judge, who paid $34,724 for his job—(less than Fraiman or the other three N.Y. Supreme Court Justices paid for theirs); admitted it, and retired on a pension.

Me? Same old thing. After dispatching the message to Ellsberg's attorneys, I Xeroxed some more stuff and sat down to wait.

Jim Lindberg came in, sat down next to me, stared sourly and left—with no words.

At Jim's (another Jim), someone else sat down and said, "All right, tell me what you know," and I did. And as I was deep into the shit an hour later he insisted on shaking hands, jumped up and ran away.

The next night, at Jim's, the entire U.S. Attorney's office, including secretaries and marshals, sat around staring at me with sour looks.

So I left and went up to Frank's. I was well into the huge cash prices being offered for any Mafia ears—*a la* Dr. Pepper—and particularly for the ears of anyone screwing on Mary Jo's grave, when Frank said, "Get out of here and don't come back."

So I went back to Jim's and said I had just put seven more of his customers on the hanging list.

And he said, "Get out of here and don't come back."

So the next night I was back.

I was thinking of what I already knew about that L.A. anti-war Peace March 3-day meeting.

It was Sunday night, and the buses were due back at about that time. Meeting of the Year? Half a million? One thousand showed up. There were two shifts—500 reading papers, and 500 listening to Charles Garry's Bobby Seale and Hoffa's Gibbons press for the endorsement of Teddy

McGovern—an endorsement previously 100% assured by all 1,000 in attendance.

The result: the group voted to endorse no candidate.

Ellsberg's speech? Scratched.

News coverage? Total blackout, except for one agonized scream from Ellsberg's attorneys.

"Historic! Unprecedented! Since Friday," (receipt of the papers), "the Justice Department and all government units have placed total surveillance, total clamp on the defense attorneys. Secret reports are given only to Federal Mafia Judge Byrne, and he is sworn to secrecy."

I was thinking of one member of that L.A. group: Jane Fonda, and her statement from Paris that day:

She said, "President Nixon is the greatest traitor known to mankind."

And on the Pedernales River in Texas, Lyndon Johnson was having another heart attack—that day. Johnson, you see, has been subpoenaed to appear at Ellsberg's trial.

And then two guys who had been on the bus to L.A. came in and sat down across the room.

I had never seen them before, but one shouted to me, "Beautiful, Baby! Send that man two drinks. I don't care if I die right now, tomorrow, or when. That's better than this prison."

So I look away and ignore all this, and then he's behind me at the jukebox.

I'm the only one there, and he says, "This song is for you, baby: 'S2, American Pie.'"

The words are very simple: "Bye-bye Miss American pie, singing this will be the day that I die."

So I ignore him some more—and then there they are, both of them, with hands stretched out.

"We gotta go, but we gotta shake your hand, sir."

So I shook their hands, and added, "You are gentlemen and scholars, I can tell. You must read a lot."

"Every word, baby. All the way." And they left, and two young plainclothes cops sat down near me, and Jim asked, "What was that all about?"

So I told him (as the two Alioto cops listened).

"Freddie De Mattei is 97 years old. He sells papers. In his youth, as the best around, he was never knocked off his feet in the ring. He beat Abe Atel and Young Corbett and the rest. He told me he followed a pattern: hit them in the belly first, until they covered; right eye next, until it was gone; left eye, the same. And then he'd call the referee over and have them hauled away—because, as a sportsman, he did not want to hurt them.

"'But, Bobby,' he told me, 'if it could be now, or if it were then, Mafia Mayor Alioto or any of the cancer crud, I would have chopped and stomped and ground the crud right into the canvas—and then pulled up a ring post and killed the referee, and the audience, for allowing such a profanity to appear and infect a public place.'

"And yesterday I saw Freddie, because he had been missing for several days—sick, as it turned out. And he said his daughter had died and he had sent her out to be buried at Cypress Lawn with my father (her name, Renee O'Leary), and he put a thou out for his own casket, and $1050 for a place in Cypress Lawn. And he passed out on the street, and might have died, if it hadn't been for two black men who weren't worried and who propped him up and fed him peaches until he was back on his feet again.

"And I said that I knew his son was Superior Court Judge De Mattei, and why didn't he call him? (He's busy these days, yes)—and that Judge De Mattei had just reversed a lower court decision which had found a dentist named Genovese, of South San Francisco, guilty of murder of a girl, into 'leaving the scene of an accident,' like Teddy did at Chappaquiddick, and was clearly on his way up

in the world.[58]

"And Freddie said, 'I'm getting sick again. I'm going home so I can be back selling papers Monday. You come by.'

"Well, Jim, the key words here are 'Dentist Genovese, of South San Francisco.' He's the son of Vito Genovese, who fed German information through Lucky Luciano to Joe Alioto in Capo Roosevelt's Justice, and made a hero out of him; who, with Luciano, welcomed American Generals to Sicily (a fight-free Mafia gift), and worked with entire Catch 22 squadrons such as that of Teddy McGovern—and then later arranged the details of the Apalachin Mafia sweep of the U.S. of Mafia Election Process—for Onassis—which produced many things."[59]

I rambled on for awhile, about the Nixon's White House Mafia now grabbing for the Mafia loot (campaign funds) of Danny Schwartz, Sinatra's National General partner—and Schwartz's National General superior, Kline. But the key word was Genovese.

And one of Alioto's cops muttered, "You'd better be big...." and they got up and left.

***

Next day at a bus stop in an isolated district, I saw an uptown group. Dale something; and Bob Saxon (last seen uptown, reading reports on Genovese over my shoulder and wrestling with 62-carat Elizabeth Dale, ITT)—and another one. I know Dale works for what's-his-name who carries cash to Ireland for IRA guns. So?

They pass and get into an untagged car at a fire plug and go away. I go downtown and Xerox things in a building on Montgomery Street: documents on Alioto's Mafia Police and Arthur Bremer's Greek hypnotizing friends across Lake Michigan.

Outside the building I stop at a magazine rack. Three of Alioto's finest cops, with cherubic Montini faces, in full blue regalia and big guns, surrounded me: "Freeze. Spread Eagle."

Identification. Rush hour. Thousands staring at this trapped criminal—me. One goes into the magazine place to phone, with my ID. The other two hold this trapped criminal at bay. For about fifteen minutes—for the entertainment of thousands of Montgomery Street commuters. Back comes O'Leary, with the Mafia message: "You can go now. You're lucky. Here, with all these store-front lawyers ready to jump us for brutality—we are polite. Now, on your way—by bus—out to your isolated district."

I transferred—way out—to 10th and Clement, an isolated corner. There was a squad car in front of the bus, one behind it, and others circling the corner.

And so down to Harry's Bar to meet George Wallace's local representative—Keith Green's et al. This was the same et al whom I had first met with Keith Green nearly four years ago, just after Alioto clobbered my car.

George Wallace's independent vote that year was an aid to Dickie's election.

---

[58] A reference to Mae's daughter, Bonnie Brussell.
[59] What the above six-paragraph passage is about, is the way the Mafia establishment in San Francisco handled the murder of Bonnie Brussell, Mae's daughter, apparently by that dentist named Genovese, who went to visit Mae. Roberts talked to everybody, and was friends with Freddie Di Mattei, whose son, da Judge, got the younger Genovese off the hook for murder. Do you see what I mean about Roberts skipping around through history, and how tough it is to follow these trains of thought? And this is what Mae didn't want to deal with at all. And no wonder Martin Cannon and Gary Buell can't understand the raw files. They just don't have the smarts, the memory, and the patience. The *Gemstone Files* are, among other things, an instant IQ test. John Judge, one of Mae's three "guardians", did, though. His mother worked for the CIA. When I finally got down to Dallas, in November, 2001, to attend Judge's COPA Convention meeting, he made sure I wasn't permitted to speak at the Conference. That was an interesting trip, though. In New York City, the smoke hadn't yet cleared from the rubble of the WTC 9/11 destruction. Ten days later I took a bus all the way from Cambridge, MA, to Dallas, because air travel was completely disrupted. We went by way of Washington, D.C. The bus driver obligingly drove us around to the back of the Pentagon where we could see, firsthand, the small hole in the rear wall where the 747 had supposedly plowed into the building. There was no wreckage, no plane, no bodies, no nothing. No scorch marks. The lawn in front of the spot was still green!—sc2006.

Said I to *et al*: "Prop Wallace up somehow—or better still, strap him onto something, somehow, on a portable cross—you know: velvet handholds, whatever will be the most comfortable, and I'll elect him to the presidency. As you know, my father was murdered for the same reasons as Mary Jo, JFK, Bobby, Martin Luther King, and on and on—and Wallace is a perfect living example. Who do you think racked up your boss?"

Et al: "Teddy McGovern's men."

Me: "Partially correct. It was Teddy Kennedy's Mafia father—Onassis—who, of course, also spawned Teddy McGovern and Dickie. They rousted me today uptown—but they very carefully did not look in this bulky sack." (By now, a Montini Alioto ear had come in and was bending our way. To make things easy, I spoke directly to the ear.) "The sack contains evidence about the Greek boys of Onassis who ushered Arthur Bremer across Lake Michigan to the Psycho Lab for booster shots."

Et al: "Can I see it?"

Me: "No. George Wallace already has. Tell Keith Green to call me."

Et al: "Okay, I know you. I know you can do it."

Today there is news from Wallace's Independent Party staff: "We will draft George Wallace to run for President, if we have to prop him up on a cross."

Tonight—now—I'm going down to Jim's for a beer. Care to go with me? Say yes, because you are going with me.

It's 3:00 a.m.

Not a cop on the street. Or in Jim's. No Federal Marshals, U.S. Attorney Mafia, nor Mafia-Mafia; nothing. Beer was on the house and Jim was busy.

He was reading about the arrest of Rudy Tham, member of the Genovese-Alioto-Lanza Mafia branch, Alioto's Fire Commissioner, and a Teamster Mafia President, along with the arrest of Tham's partner—Holt, of the Genovese-Dioguardi-Ducks Corallo New York Mafia—and Tham's other partner—Johnny Di Lorenzo, of the Genovese family, currently conducting Mafia murder from prison where he is serving ten years for prior Genovese Mafia social work.

I said "Genovese!" and nobody even looked up. So I sat there and tried ESP on the back of Jim's neck.

I thought at him as hard as I could.

"Jim, in answer to your question: it's not the hanging of those three Alioto cops who grabbed me downtown. It is the hanging of all of them. Fire Commissioners—including, of course, Nunzio; Police Commissioners—including Alioto's partner, Farrari, of City Hall; D.A. Ferndon's group—including the young one who refused to take my Alioto hit-run report four years ago; Goldsmith, son of U.S. Commissioner Goldsmith, who just released Tham, without bail. It is the hanging of the bartenders who serve them—and the incineration of the bar stools on which they sit. It is, as Freddie De Mattei suggested, a ring post to exterminate the San Francisco audience who allows such a cancer to infect the public. Supreme Courts, who endorse the 'no death penalty' for any crime—murder, treason, whatever, and 'no authority at all over the two Mafia Parties who anoint our leaders.' But International Law supersedes National Law, with legal rulings regarding war and crimes. Representatives of four-fifths of the civilized world agree to this. So—that means hanging, for all who obstruct, interfere with, or don't assist the hangman. On crosses, Jim, because of a ruling by a religious character with a speared liver, who jumped off the cross at Chappaquiddick."

ESP doesn't work for me. But he did turn around, with dew all over his upper lip, and bought me a beer.

***

I left. Still, not a soul in sight. For blocks, no squad cars. Nothing. It was early yet.

So I stopped at the Bank of America on the corner, raised the night depository flap and spoke into the Bank of America tape.[60]

"Mrs. Giannini, I saw you on TV, flanking Alioto a month or so ago. It was Sunday, prime time, and [Alfred] McCoy's *Harper's* article on the 80% of the world's heroin which flows from Onassis' Golden Triangle in Thailand had just hit the street.

"So Mafia Paley of CBS had arranged two one-half hour programs: the first, with you and Alioto revealing the Mafia to be non-existent and decrying false attacks on Mafia Montini. And the second, showing how all of that heroin really comes from Mexico. My question, Mrs. Giannini, since you own the Bank of America, a mouth of the 'Hughes' Mafia Money Funnel, is this: How is the health of Fred Martin, your Public Relations director at World Headquarters—known in Moscow as 'Heroin Mafia Freddie'?

"The last time I saw him, he was a lowly Republican Mafia hatchet-man at the Chamber of Commerce, owned by Mafia Swig—going over my Alioto hit-run reports that elected Dickie. After Chappaquiddick, you hired him—and Onassis hired Newsom to work in Switzerland, 'permanently.'

"It was too bad that Newsom violated that 'permanently' and returned to San Francisco in the middle of the 'Mafia Alioto Web' trial, and thus was able to witness the barbecue of his two nieces, plus their Japanese nurse. Mrs. Giannini, do you charge interest for barbecued girl flesh? Please answer my questions, sweet lady. I live just down the street—where my father was murdered."

There was still not a human in sight, up and down the streets in four directions. So I went across the street to the drug store, raised the mail flap and spoke to the empty store, and the apartment above.

"New York Police—the Knapp Commission—are totally on the heroin and murder take. Daley's Chicago cops have their own execution squads to exterminate the cops who don't shake down enough. Every Mafia diocese in every U.S. of Mafia city is the same. Montini gets his share from the confessional.

"Alioto-Genovese-Lanza-McGucken, of San Francisco, specializes in rat poison that works well in apple pie. My question is: did this store peddle the stuff that went into my father's apple pie, and J. Mafia Hoover's? And did the Alioto Mafia cops purchase a supply for the ones that came back from that Ellsberg Anti-War Peace March?

"I'm checking, you see, because a 'Hughes' helicopter gun-ship followed that bus—with a sack of papers—all the way to L.A., where massive surveillance took over. Down there, a peace marcher made a phone call to an Ellsberg attorney about the papers. Copies of this taped call were given to Mafia Judge Byrne, who declared the illegal defense lawyer tap legal and refused to divulge the tapes. But the screams from Ellsberg were so loud that the trial was delayed to go through the formality of holding an Appeal Court Ruling on that unconstitutional, treasonous act. That Appeal Court will uphold Mafia Byrne—since, of the judges, one is Supreme Court Justice Douglas (of the Mafia Stardust Vegas bit, and the Sasha Volman Caribbean bit for the same Mafia group—formerly

---

[60] Roberts occasionally referred to San Francisco's Bank of America as "Mrs. Giannini's Bank of America." Mrs. Giannini was apparently the widow of Mr. Giannini, a friendly San Francisco Maf. This was in the '70's. before Bank of America had grown and spread all across America like...well, like Cancer. Branches have recently appeared all over Cambridge, B of A having bought up another banking Behemoth, Fleet Bank. "So what?" you say. Well...the U.S. banking industry is largely owned by the same gigantic interlocking corporate entities who control virtually all of the "Big Business" in the United States. Frankly, this means that you pretty much can't have a major credit card without the (loosely defined) Mafia holding your credit card debt, and this means that the "credit card business" is yet another Mafia near-monopoly. They set the interest you pay on your credit card debt. Bank of America sends me credit card come-ons from time to time, but so far I have refused their blandishments. Maybe it's because they haven't yet made me an offer that I couldn't refuse. Besides, I'm holding out for *Credite Suisse*, because it's got more class.—sc2006.

Parvin-Dohrmann, now Recrion). And another is James Browning, Sr., father of James Browning, Jr., the Mafia San Francisco U.S. Attorney who has been sitting on those papers ever since I met him in Greenagel's office two weeks after Chappaquiddick—and who lately stops in at Jim's to glare at me.

"Even if Ellsberg's screams take that treasonous act all the way up to the Supreme Court, their ruling will be 'Constitutional'—since they ruled the death penalty 'illegal for any cause,' and 'the two Mafia Parties are the supreme law—over us even.' And since they belong to those two Mafia Parties, were appointed by them, are paid by them, and will be assassinated by them for any violation of Omerta.

"Pedernales Johnson, who has been subpoenaed for that Ellsberg trial, is in a hospital, 'indefinitely', under a doctor's care—as is Dita Beard, and any Maf anywhere who is about to squawk. My question is: are you participating in the apple pie murders of these kids who have read these papers?"

And then on to Harry's Bar, where on the previous evening I offered the Presidency to George Wallace, via his local officers—Keith Green's et al.

It was only midnight, but two things were odd: no humans were in sight, and Harry's was padlocked. That had never happened before. He caters to Alioto's Mafia cops, and they drink a lot (some of them get pensions for alcoholism). In fact, one of them was pouring booze down *et al* when I left on the previous evening.

So I backed up a bit and addressed myself to the open apartment window above Harry's padlocked door: "Harry, I know you and *et al* are in there—and I have a message for *et al*.

"Last night we agreed that he'd prop Wallace up on a comfortable cross and I would elect him president. And this morning the news quoted Wallace's Independent Party staff in Memphis as saying: 'We will draft George Wallace for the presidency if we have to prop him up on a cross.'

"And then, several hours later, Connally made a sudden urgent trip to see Wallace, begging newsmen to please keep the sudden trip secret. (But they didn't). And they discussed their mutual assassination bullets—Connally's from Oswald, and Wallace's from Bremer.

"Connally said, 'My job is to travel the world and plug leaks in this assassination row. I just left Red Duke in Afghanistan, and by God, that's where you'll be, George, if you don't knock this Presidency shit off.' And Wallace issued a weak statement to the press: 'No, I won't run.'

"My message is this: With all this off-and-on stuff going on, let me make one thing perfectly clear: George Wallace will run for the presidency on a cross. Either a comfortable one, or the hard way, you know: with nails, and all that stuff. Tell him that, please.

"Connally quit everything—the Treachery Secretary and the V.P. race.

"Said he to Dickie: 'V.P.? You're hotter than a pistol.'

"And Dickie had to fall back on Greeky Agnew, the Greek ticket, which is an approved Onassis Greek ticket. Mitchell quit everything and can't help anybody from up Martha's ass. Willie Wilson quit and is hiding in Panhandle sagebrush. J. Mafia Hoover quit by apple pie. Teddy quit both Pres. and V.P. and stays close to Joanie—ready for a quick leap in.

"At the Mafia Miami Demo convention, ten Democrats told Teddy McGovern, 'V.P.? No way; you're hotter than a pistol.'

"So Teddy finally dredged up St. Louis Shenker Mafia Eagleton—a Mafia drunk who staggers in and out of nut houses (perfect qualifications for a Vice President, says Dickie, and Marcello's Boggs, too, just before he fell off the podium). And now Teddy (Kennedy) is telling Teddy (McGovern) to dump Eagleton and dredge up a new one—maybe Alioto, or Genovese, or Lanza. We just can't seem to find a President or a Vice President for the U.S. of Mafia.

"I tell ya what—you up there in that apartment behind the open window. I'll elect any two of you President and V.P.—no charge.

"Jim, down the street in his bar, was complaining about business, and I told him I could bring four-fifths of the civilized world into his bar for a drink—not necessarily booze, but thirsty, and I mean thirsty, if he desired. And he agreed that I could do that, but no thanks.

"So, how about it? Is there anyone up and down the streets of this nation—the U.S. of Mafia—who would like to be President or V.P., or both? Anyone?"

The apartment window slammed—and a few more down the block. And there was silence, and fog rolling in, so I went home. I'm sleepy. I'll tell you about Teddy McGovern on Chappaquiddick weekend with Mafia Kimelman in the Virgin Islands—and Eagleton in St. Louis during his Mafia nut house days—and interesting foreign affairs, in India, Africa, South America, North Ireland, Egypt, Australia, and some other places, if I get around to it before the shit hits the fan via your local Mafia newspaper. But not now. This is very late on the evening of July 25, 1972.

July 28, 1972

Murder, for you, from the Supreme Courts, Federal and State. From Mafia judges, selected from Mafia attorneys, who, like all ambassadors, purchased their jobs—with *mordida*—the white envelopes. By declaring the death penalty illegal for any reason, they automatically release from prison those whose lives are committed to murder. Such as Manson, who will, a few years from now, be roaming the streets on his horror murder route. Barboza—who confessed to 25 Mafia contract murders—and recently squawked on Sinatra—is due out now on parole.

Any assassin—any cold-blooded murderer—will be out on the street. All those currently roaming the street are buying bullets; what do they have to lose? "Enemy within, enemy without."

Teddy McGovern: "Thailand is not part of Indochina. Heroin doesn't exist. Therefore we will keep our missiles and planes and troops in Thailand to protect those heroin routes with 'Hughes' smart bombs and 'Hughes' helicopter gun ships, 'Hughes' satellites, and 'Hughes' missiles in McCone, Bechtel missile silos."

In St. Louis the six traffic citations on Eagleton for "drunk driving" had been altered by erasure to read "reckless driving", and photo-stated, and then the original citations were destroyed by the Cervantes-Shenker-Eagleton St. Louis Mafia group. There was no hearing. Nothing. But the photostats got out somehow.

Maf who run in and out of nut houses don't like these deleted records getting out, because, like Thailand and heroin, and the Mafia Election Process, they don't exist. So, for a character reference, Eagleton directed a reporter to his closest friend—an unimpeachable source: Mafia Mayor Cervantes of St. Louis (who didn't bother to sue Life for its detailed Mafia report on him and Shanker, Hoffa's attorney).

Said Mafia Cervantes: "Eagleton is as pure as Alioto. Teddy Eagleton never touched a drop. And it would be impossible to delete, alter or destroy police records in our Mafia City Hall—just as it is impossible to do so in Pure Mafia Alioto-Genovese-Lanza's town."

"And this," noted the commentator, "does to Teddy Eagleton what Chappaquiddick did to Teddy Kennedy. I wonder what lurks ahead for Teddy McGovern? Or whoever he picks to replace Teddy Eagleton. Shriver, Mayor White, or Governor Lucey? What lurks ahead for my boss, Hearst? And come to think of it—for me? This is Teddy Cronkhite, from Washington."

From South Dakota, Teddy McGovern comments on all this:

"If I were President, the first thing I'd do would be to hang Thieu, Chiang Kai-Shek and J. Edgar Hoover." J. Edgar Hoover, already murdered, is Teddy McGovern's synonym for Alioto—who, with Hoover's files, is now top Maf.

McGovern thinks back to Chappaquiddick weekend, when he was vacationing with Onassis Mafia Kimelman in the Virgin Islands. Notified of the murder, he quickly phoned Teddy with his total support and availability as substitute. For it was he who picked up Bobby's murdered body

delegate votes in 1968. (JFK had purchased Greedy George McGovern back in 1961, and appointed him director for Food for Peace).

Just after I laid the entire Chappaquiddick murder out—publicly—to Dickie, et al, on August 5, 1969, Johnson met with Dickie in Washington to close that end of the lid. He said, "Dickie, we hang together, or we hang separately. Remember Howard Hughes?"

And in Washington, Kimelman (visibly, West Indies Corp. and Virgin Islands Hilton) called together McGovern and the Mafia to seal the deal.

Present were Nader's Senator Ribicoff, a JFK lad who wants to invade Northern Ireland; Fred Dutton; the Udall Brothers; lawyer Myer Feldman, Onassis's Blair Clark, Vatican McCarthy's Capo, and ten more faceless Mafia.

McGovern was the pick. Mr. Clean. Had he not chosen politics, he would have been a shoo-in for Bishop of the Methodist Church.

***

By 9:00 p.m., on July 20, 1972, Roger Rudenstein and his group, the San Francisco Peace Coalition, had read these papers. By midnight, they were in the hands of Jerry Gordon, N.Y. attorney, national director of the Peace Coalition, in L.A. for the three-day UCLA Peace March. In the morning, having read them, Gordon, as directed, called an Ellsberg attorney.

Gordon had a permanent tap on him. Ellsberg's attorneys didn't—a courtesy granted to Ellsberg to prove that the U.S. of Mafia is benevolent. As further proof of fairness: Justice delivered the contents of the tap to Mafia Federal Judge Matt Byrne (appointed by Mafia JFK), who was prosecuting Ellsberg for Attorney General Mitchell.

Vatican Mafia Judge Byrne (who purchased his job for $47,227) buried the tap in "total secrecy." Then, to prove Mafia benevolence, he told Ellsberg's attorneys he had it, and had buried it. Byrne got the tap on Friday afternoon, July 21, 1972, held it over the weekend, and then told Ellsberg on Monday, when the trial was set to start. Ellsberg screamed "railroad."

Byrne said, "Trial first, and then, if you are convicted, we'll look into it." This is illegal—but Byrne is as frightened as Eagleton. And McGovern. And Teddy. And Dickie. And Montini. The "benevolent" reason for "Justice" bringing the tap to Byrne, and Byrne reluctantly disclosing it, and then trying to pass it off (anything to get the rigged Mafia trial over with, a la the Berrigans)—is that they knew they were being rigged. All of their moves were being filmed.

***

Occasionally when I pick up my mother's phone, a voice says "Claude, what's up?" My father got that nearly four years ago when this first started.

So, on the Tuesday before this bit started—July 18, 1972—I called the Peace Coalition and asked about bus fares and times to that L.A. Peace March.

Then I said, "Fine. I wanna go. Where do I buy a ticket?" They told me. This was permissible to the CIA, for several reasons:

1) There wasn't a thing they could do to stop it;

2) The total clamp was on in L.A.

Which is why the Mafia watched me deliver these papers to Ellsberg's attorneys, via a batch of personal couriers in approved Mafia CIA style, the way they deliver heroin .

They were a little shocked and worried about a rig—and film. So Justice brought the tap to Byrne on Friday afternoon. Byrne, with Chappaquiddick in his pocket, was still reluctant—until, over the weekend, he read several pursuant papers I accidentally lost around San Francisco—which verified the filming of his activity, and the notification of others concerned.

And that is why the shit hit the fan on Monday, and I was spread-eagled on the street in San Francisco by three Alioto-Genovese-Lanza-Montini cops.

Said Mafia Byrne: "The matter discussed in the tap" (Chappaquiddick) "has no relationship to the Ellsberg trial. It is a completely separate matter. Irrelevant."

Said Ellsberg: "Unconstitutional! We defendants have an adversary right to determine whether it has a bearing on our defense."

Byrne said: "I rule. Trial first—on our rigged schedule. After that, we might discuss it—if it doesn't get deleted, destroyed or lost."

Ellsberg said: "Unconstitutional! We appeal."

So, on to the Federal Appeals Court—composed of Supreme Court Justice Douglas, James Browning, Sr., and Ely, whose Mafia status has been previously described.

There was an automatic Mafia denial, to Ellsberg, by that Mafia Court. Onassis paid Douglas a quarter mill for Stardust and Caribbean aid. So—to Douglas personally, in Pasadena, there was a request for the Supreme Court to rule.

Douglas: "Come to Yakima, Washington, where we can talk this over in private—and make a Mafia deal."

Today, in Yakima, Mafia choices are being sorted over.

Ellsberg was in Vietnam, blazing away with a machine gun on Vietnamese humans, just like Calley at My Lai. Today, Ellsberg's Mafia Kennedy attorneys are blackmailing Mafia Douglas with Chappaquiddick.

And Douglas is blackmailing them.

Mitchell's Justice is blackmailing both of them.

Douglas may offer Ellsberg a minor prison term, and loot, like Clifford Irving, and quickly and quietly get the trial over with, safely, so it will be forgotten by the time of the Mafia Election in 1972. Or he can put it in purgatory—until after that Mafia Election.

You see, the Mafia Supreme Court is in recess. It can't reconvene until after that gang bang on Christ.

Yes, it is true that they did reconvene—in 4 hours—at the command of the Mafia Demo Party—to issue a quick ruling that "The Mafia Parties that select our leaders are a law that supersedes our law. That's the way it is." And then they issued another ruling: "We do not reconvene once we are on our vacation."

So there we are.

***

In the meantime, the entire Anti-War group led by Jerry Gordon gathered to unanimously endorse Teddy McGovern. But suddenly, Gordon announced the results: "We will endorse no candidate. I'm going back to New York to meet my partner, Jane Fonda, who knows some more things now—and labels Dickie the greatest traitor in history. She will endorse no candidate either, even though as of last Thursday she had announced 100% approval of Teddy McGovern. We aren't even gonna be in Miami for the Republican gang bang on Christ. We have changed our plans. We have a friend who resents Truman's murders at Hiroshima."

In New York: Jane Fonda gets off the plane from Hanoi. "No comment. I must talk to Jerry Gordon first," she says.

Next day, she speaks, with hands folded in prayer: "What is a traitor? Dickie Nixon. The patriots are those speaking out against the war. I endorse nobody. I endorse peace. I am against death. I am for life. The men who are ordering the use of war weapons are war criminals according

to international law—and in the past the men who were guilty of these kinds of crimes were tried and executed."

Ah, yes. An academy award winning actress. We have an academy award winning actor running our state—Ronnie, baby. Wallace wants to prop up John Wayne, one of the Green Berets, who ran heroin out of Thailand (check Weiker, McCoy)—to take his place.

July 29, 1972

This is July 29, 1972. On the news at noon: "Douglas has granted a brief stay in the Ellsberg trial in order to consider wiretapping evidence." Ah, yes—Ellsberg's blackmail, and how to solve it, hide it, bury it—a la Chappaquiddick and "Hughes."

And also: "Wallace has bowed out of the presidential race—on doctor's orders." The doctor was "Dallas Bullet" Connally, who prescribed a vacation in Afghanistan for Gallant Fighter George Wallace and his family.

My instructions to Rudenstein: "Get this to Ellsberg's attorneys for me. It will get Ellsberg out of jail." He got it to them. And it did get Ellsberg out of jail.

There was another instruction: "I want this copy back. This copy. I don't care what Ellsberg's attorneys do. If they want a copy they can run one off—or thousands. But I want this copy back."

Rudenstein made two mistakes. He interrupted my questions and instructions with a question. And he did not return that copy. It has now been ten days. That copy—the physical sheets—has the mark of Cain upon it. There is no margin for error. Time ticks on.

U.N. Secretary General Waldheim says: "Bombing the dikes in Vietnam! That is the murderous drowning of millions of civilians!"

Dickie says: "Me and Montini and Teddy and Onassis have established a precedent for Pond drowning at Chappaquiddick—and for Holy Crusades. And so the Dyke Pond drowning is legal. So why not in Vietnam?"

And the nervous Mafia finger that signs Betty Waterhouse's checks, shakily rattles nukes.

"We can blot them out in an afternoon," he says. "They should be happy that we only kill at random."

***

On D-Day in Europe, Roosevelt told his press corps: "You want to get the word 'invasion' out of people's heads. It's a war of liberation. All wars will be wars of liberation from now on." Other FDR quotes: "I hate war," and: "Pearl Harbor—Day of Infamy."

In the midst of this current Eagleton V.P. qualification flap, a bill to end the war in Vietnam—calling for total pullout by Election Day—cleared the House and lacked only two votes to clear the Senate. Those two voters—Senators Teddy McGovern and Senator Teddy Eagleton—were off somewhere in a Mafia back room fighting the Teddy Kennedy-Vatican Presidential battle. They forgot about ending the war.

Eagleton was selected in a back room, on the basis of Mafia religion, Mafia districts, and Mafia rackets, by the handmaidens (Cervantes, Montini, Meany, Daley, McDonnell.)

So was Onassis-Pappas' Greeky Agnew. In Skorpios.

And Teddy McGovern, in Onassis' Caribbean, on Chappaquiddick Day.

And Dickie, long ago, by a banker—because he had the greatest rat potential in the world. Proven many times, from Helen Gahagan Douglas through "Hughes" Apalachin 1957, Chappaquiddick, and the murder of my father. A perfect pick to lead Fatima #3.

***

Five years ago, the CIA passed a million dollars under the table to Charles Perlick and the other directors of the Newspaper Guild. (Guild: a Mafia union of news reporters). This was to guarantee Mafia censorship—by Onassis.

This year, Onassis paid the Nixon-hedge Mafia press mordida to endorse Teddy (any Teddy: Kennedy, McGovern, or whoever—plus whichever Vatican Teddy replaces Eagleton: Muskie, from last time out, or Boston's White, or Larry O'Brien).

This year, all of the millions from Joanie's Mafia Demo Telethon went into Mafia Murderer Tony Boyle's National Bank of Washington—from which he looted the $169 million Teamster Pension funds and paid for the murders of the Yablonski family. He did this with the approval of Dickie's Secretary of Labor—Schultz.

True Davis is the Mafia President of that bank, for Mafia Tony Boyle. True Davis was Johnson's Ambassador to Switzerland, where Mafia loot from American banks is "washed" and returned via the "Hughes" Mafia Money Funnel for "political contributions"—for instance, $35,000 from Tony Boyle to Hubert Humphrey, in 1968.

Tony Boyle was given a 10-year sentence for murdering the Yablonski family. But he is not in jail. He is running for president of the union again. Federal law says he cannot run in that election. He is a convicted felon. The bank is still going strong.

True Davis will be the next Ambassador to Switzerland. True Davis is the one who released those "drunk driving" citations (six were destroyed—all but four sets, that is) on Eagleton to Jack Anderson. True Davis wants to scratch Eagleton in favor of the real Teddy Kennedy.

Mafia Strauss, former Democratic Treasurer, is the only man who can withdraw that loot. He works for Onassis, and he also wants to scratch Eagleton for the real Ted Kennedy. An entire necrophiliac nation moans for the throne for the real Teddy Kennedy. Including me. We may have to drag Teddy, that reluctant president, into the Oval Office with a rope around his neck and prop him upright there, on a Montini cross—slightly off the floor—since everyone knows that Teddy can walk on Chappaquiddick water, busted noses, and putrid floor board Poucha Pond bubble air. Christ himself never walked on air.

Let's see. A letter from me quickly elected Dickie in 1968—and caused another batch of fallout, from bombing halts to a sudden interest in a new mineral, and "Hughes".

Another letter, re: the solution of Chappaquiddick, tilted the world—Pope, Russia, China, and the U.S. of Mafia.

In four days in April, 1970, a letter to Mafia Judge Aitken, now employed by Mafia U.S. Attorney Browning, set off the Cambodian invasion.

In four days in August 1970, a letter to Necrophiliac Nader set him up in the holy business via an Onassis bribe. Fallout all over the place: Harry Yee's $6 billion San Francisco heroin bust; China into the U.N., and Taiwan out; Kissinger's begging trips to Peking, and, with Dickie, to Moscow and Peking.

A letter to Charles Garry quickly secured the release of Angela Davis, and all Black Panthers in jail—including Hilliard, who, before a crowd of 10,000, on TV, declared, "I will murder Richard Nixon." Fallout all over the place: Mitchell up an asshole, Teddy up an asshole; apple pie murders for others. So much, I can't remember them all at this tired moment—although they are all out, accurate and detailed, in the cold angry fingers of people who also push nuclear buttons.

On July 20, 1972, I handed a letter to Rudenstein. I said: "It will get Ellsberg out of jail."

On July 24, 1972, Ellsberg was out of jail. That's four days.

This world will:

- ❖ Reverse itself over a four-day Holiday—following the Eleventh Commandment-"Murderers on a cross, not me", or

- Go out in a 22-hour Mafia songfest, or
- Go out in a Fatima #3 one-hour Holy Crusade, followed by a one-hour remnant songfest. Whichever comes first, there will be singing.

Four days from now is my father's birthday: August 3, 1972. He is murdered ashes at Cypress Lawn. He enjoyed singing. During the four years of my father's murder, birthdays were rather grim. I will be at Cypress Lawn. I have a gift for him. And I will ask him to pass out the other gifts, to Mary Jo, Tisserant, Father Mootz, the Yablonski family, Newsom's nieces, Tanya—ah, the list is long.

I will go by streetcar and bus, and then walk over the hill. It's a long walk—behind Hearst's mausoleum. I have no car. The Mafia CIA wants it this way. I will be alone. My mother can't make it. Her murder is half done. She can't climb over the hill.

The rest of the family? Running—to Lagos, Nigeria, for instance. The Canadian border. The Mexican border.

And a Happy Birthday to you? Yes.

***

Let's go back to L.A., and Ellsberg. His trial is to start on Monday, July 24, 1972.

This week: the forced admission of the existence of the Jerry Gordon wire tap; Ellsberg's screams; the hasty Appellate and Supreme Court decisions to lid the contents of that tapped and recorded phone call. A final desperate threat by Mafia Dickie's Mafia U.S. Attorney Nissen to call together the Mafia Supreme Court in emergency session—for the second time in a century.

Today, the news consensus: "The Ellsberg trial has ended. Douglas has granted a 30-day stay for the defense to prepare a presentation to Dickie's Mafia Supreme Court—presided over by Mafia Burger, (who gave Onassis his U.S. Liberty ships), and including three more of Dickie's Onassis boys, plus Douglas, of the Onassis Stardust payroll, (a JFK appointee), and a few more assorted Maf—all of whom voided the death sentence for treason (their own).

"This Supreme Court will reconvene in the fall—and will consider this simple overheard phone conversation."

(It was a simple overheard phone conversation that murdered Mary Jo—and another that murdered Eugenie Niarchos, Onassis' first love, and sister-in-law.)

And that will be after the 1972 Mafia Election gang bang on Christ, and the entire matter will disappear, as have all of the other lid poppers. And Ellsberg has made his deal: "I've got better voodoo than you do"—with the Mafia. And today, those two Christ figures who carry Rand's Project Star on Dallas in their back pockets, Ellsberg and Russo, are out telling the public about the horrors of war, as did FDR and JFK and Johnson and Dickie.

Nader is busy with bum deodorants.

And Kay Pachtner is busy manipulating recalled General Motors cars.

Primitive stark legal Mafia hangout in action.

At the L.A. Appellate Court hearing, Mafia U.S. Attorney Nissen bluntly told the three Mafia Judges, "We admit Mafia Judge Byrne is illegal in not releasing that tape about Chappaquiddick. We admit that he is illegal in ruling that the Mafia rigged trial continue. But, your Honors, you have heard the tape. If we disclose it, we will all hang—and that includes you, your Honors."

And then court resumed and Nissen spoke these blunt, immortal words:

"If we disclose it, there is no way we can undisclose it."

The Court: "Ellsberg's stay is denied. The tape is buried. Permanently. The trial continues."

(This solemn verdict has since been reversed, by Ellsberg's voodoo in the Supreme Court—

those nine old Mafia who will solemnly declare missiles illegal, while they comb them out of their hair and clutch their rotting belly buttons and tug away at a mineral goose up the ass. And this is quite a feat, even for experienced Judges. And then they will join in the Mafia Chorus: Chappaquiddick, My Chappaquiddick, Why Do I Love Thee, My Teddeee, My Teddeee...."

And so it is that we now speak of thirsty, skinny, liver-missing people around the world. The four-fifths of the civilized world who might, at any moment, stop in at Jim's—thirsty, but not necessarily for booze.

And I thought back to unwanted babies. You know: a distraught mother bundles her baby up and leaves her, him, or it on a doorstep, with a note: "Please find a home for my baby. It is good, clean, real, true, and untainted. Nobody wants it. If you don't, please forward it on to someone who might."

Long ago, Ellsberg's sack of babies were left on many doorsteps. Many did find homes. A year and a half ago, when Javits' aide prodded me at Bill's (back in here somewhere), I told him about a U.N. resolution which would be introduced by Chile. This was because of a communication I had received from Chile, from a stranger—who notified me that my baby had found a home in every country down the Andes spine. He spoke bitterly of ITT, Bank of America, Anaconda, and a few more, and mentioned a letter from Hoover to Brady, in Brazil, congratulating Brady on the FBI-CIA-Montini-Medici terror takeover in Brazil. He spoke bitterly of Montini-Onassis-Peron in Argentina. And Colombia. And he ended with a funny phrase: "Fok Kannady."

One set went over with IRA cash from San Francisco to Ireland. Later an IRA man climbed into a Belfast bedroom window, threw the sack to Ma and Pa in bed, and said, "Read it," over the sight of his Bren gun. They read. And then, the gun was set aside, and all three went to the stove and threw in their crosses. That night, Montini lost one patron, and the Archbishop of Canterbury lost two. The two men now guide each other around mines, shoot across each other all day long, and at night, they work together cranking out copies. Peace has come to two Irish families. "Fok Kannady."

Africa and India were heard from. And a pattern developed. The route of the baby distribution was up the asshole of the 600 million soldiers of the Vatican Church—in its Medusa hold around the world. Tisserant's papers were jammed down the Papal throat, and these babies up his ass. Like ice tongs—clanking together at the belly button—to lift God to his throne.

Most now know of the Thai-Laotian heroin traffic, missile silos, and air bases, which profit the entire Maf—Montini, Dickie, Pentagon, Multi-nationals—at the rate of millions of dollars per death.

"Old Blue Eyes" Frank Sinatra with some of his Mafia buddies in 1976.
Top row, l-r: Paul Castellano. Gregory Di Palma, Thomas Marson, Carlo Gambino, Jimmy Fratianno, Salvatore Spatola
Bottom row: Joe Gambino, Richard Fusco
New York Daily News photo

26 World Bank's Super-Drug-Highway, Paraguay

Let's look at Body Count McNamara—formerly counting those millions per death for the Mafia; now promoted to counting the millions per death via the World Bank.

Take Paraguay, for example. Destitute. But a $100 million loan was made to the Montini Dictator. He decreed a super freeway to be made—running for many miles through the jungle, from a swamp to a cliff. Prompt payments on the loan are made to the World Bank; it looks beautiful on the books. Paraguayan peasants' taxes are doubled. They now work 14 hours a day to pay their taxes.

Cost of the highway to McCone, Bechtel, BRT-MK?-$5 million. Balance? $25 million to Montini-Onassis (Switzerland); $25 million to Dickie, McCone and the boys (Bahamas); $25 million to Lansky and the boys (Singapore)—to handle the Thai heroin flowing into Alioto's San Francisco and on through the "Hughes" Mafia Money Funnel—to keep the loot rolling.

Use of the freeway? During the day, sunbathing by peasants and jungle animals. During the evening, the U.S. Ambassador and Paraguayan Cabinet's work teams load Onassis' planes with cocaine and heroin for Marcello and Boggs in New Orleans—and those planes use that jungle runway all night long. It is the longest runway in the world. A good investment for Body Count McNamara and the World Bank.

Taxes on any of that loot in the U.S. of Mafia? None. You make up any shortages out of your taxes, working during the daytime. At night you get mugged and murdered by the hopheads who need loot to purchase the shit. Your loot.

Around the world a pattern is emerging. At the top of the non-Mafia countries, decorum is stringent. Russia—invited to Egypt because Dulles wouldn't build the Aswan Dam—built the thing, invested heavily, then departed. Just the opposite of the U.S. of Mafia in heroin Vietnam.

Russia and China shoot dope pushers: two shots in the back of the head. The U.S. of Mafia elects them President and sends the Pentagon around the world to install similar dictators everywhere: Taiwan, Saigon, Athens, Brazil, Argentina.

Chile—despite U.S. attempts to rig elections there, and economic starvation, in retribution for failure—quietly waits. China waits—unprovoked by U.S. border-mining, bombing, missile silos. India growls, and waits. Mexico's Echeverria warns Dickie: "You made a huge mistake backing Montini's terror Medicis in Brazil and shafting Allende in Chile."

At the bottom, the movement is quiet. Like Japanese travel groups. And South American groups. And African.

Said McGovern, about the Kennedy-Eagleton squabble: "I don't know how much more strain our system can stand."

August 2, 1972

On July 31, 1972, twelve days after Rudenstein took a copy of these papers to Ellsberg, I called Rudenstein.

"Not in," said the girl. I left my name. There was no call back.

On August 2, 1972, 1 called again

"He's out. He will be back before 5:30."

I was there at the Peace office at 5:30.

"He may be back before 7:30."

So I talked to girls in the office. "What happened in L.A.? The news was blacked out. Did Ellsberg speak?"

Answer: "No. He canceled. Something suddenly came up about his defense."

Me: "Did you endorse McGovern?"

Answer: "No, we decided to concentrate on anti-war measures. We are preparing to get our papers out in the event of some catastrophe occurring before the 1972 election."

Me: "What catastrophe is it that you refer to?"

Answer: "Oh, something like the bombing of the dikes in Vietnam. We are working for the acceptance of Hanoi's 7 points. We meet tonight to discuss future plans at the Unitarian Church."

Me: "Are you connected with Jane Fonda's Indochina Peace group?"

Answer: "Not directly. But we communicate on important issues." (All have read these papers; all know me.)

A belligerent one comes in and lectures one of the girls. "Big Brother is watching you. You are in trouble. Hanoi is a corporation, just as we are. We are clean. You are dirty."

Rudenstein pulls up, and parks on the sidewalk. (It's Market Street, downtown—all torn up for BART; nobody can do this). Cops drive by. They ignore his car on the sidewalk. Which is odd, since on the Monday Ellsberg screamed about the Jerry Gordon "Chappaquiddick" wire tap, cops spread-eagled me on Montgomery Street for walking on the sidewalk, then delivered a Mafia death rattle.

Rudenstein comes in, nods to me, gets a paper sack from the desk and brings it over to me in a corner—and makes 25 mistakes in the next 5 minutes. He is programmed like a robot.

He: "I took them to L.A., but Ellsberg canceled his speech at UCLA and I didn't get to see him or his attorneys."

Me: "Ellsberg is out of jail—four days after I gave these to you, and I told you he would be."

He: "Well, we have worked out Ellsberg's defense very thoroughly. It's in the bag."

Me: "He was released because of a taped phone call—one special one—that even Justice had to produce, and Judge Byrne both acknowledged and buried."

He, grinning: "I don't know anything about that. I couldn't get the papers to Ellsberg."

Me: "It didn't matter; a series of sacks were there, for Ellsberg and others. Other calls were taped, too. But only that one call—contents, 'Chappaquiddick'—was forced out to Ellsberg to get him out of jail."

Now Rudenstein wasn't grinning.

So I continued: "Did you read it?"

He: "Yes."

Me: "Anybody else?"

He: "Everybody in the office here."

Me: "What did they think?"

He: "Well, I guess that is one man's opinion. You undoubtedly have better sources than we do."

Me: "Other than the insulated sack which you brought from L.A., how many minutes, or hours, were your fingers in contact with the physical sheets in the sack?"

He, surprised: "I don't know." Rudenstein was now solemn. He didn't speak again.

Me: "Since that is how it is, there are things that you should know. I got him out of jail—permanently—in four days—just as I said I would. Didn't I?"

No response.

"I can put him right back in jail. Mafia Justice has asked the Supreme Court to vacate that stay. While all this has been going on, those nine old Mafia men are reading the other papers that have been delivered to them, like these were. They can jail Ellsberg again on another charge—much more serious—and true, not rigged, as this one is—and they will hang him.

"And everyone else involved. Regardless of the death penalty ban. There are 'supervening statutes.' Like a yo-yo, I could get him out of that, or let him hang. My hand won't be on any rope. Things had better be just right. I got him out—in four days—just as I said I would. I also offered to end the war—in four days. And you come back, two weeks later, with a stretched-out program of anti-war marches. You ignore the cause of war, the cause of crime: Mary Jo's grave and all that lies buried there. Do you want to end the war in four days?"

No response at all.

Apparently he 'didn't understand,' and was 'too busy,' because he just stood and stared.

So I went out to the bus stop. While waiting, I read the list of sponsors of this Northern California Peace Action Coalition. Garry, McTernan, Hallinan; remember them? Shirley Chisholm, Bobby Seale, Ronald Dellums. Moscone, Jacks, Draper. Sisters, Reverends, and the Chronicle. And I looked back, and his car still blocked the sidewalk while buses and cop cars jostled for the one lane left in torn up Market Street, passing that privileged car.

***

Let's bring Ellsberg up to August 5, 1969, when I laid it out to Dickie and the rest: the entire Chappaquiddick murder; and Teddy McGovern made a deal with Kimelman and the Mafia to replace Kennedy; and Johnson met with Dickie: "We hang together or we hang separately."

Ellsberg: After Apalachin, he had security clearance. His job was to map the Pacific for nuclear war. Later, working with the Kennedys, he was raised to "top security clearance." His job was to map the world for Fatima #3.

He worked with Bobby Kennedy, Teddy Kennedy, and JFK. (He was with Mary Jo and Bobby until Bobby's murder). After that, he worked with Kissinger. He knew all about Dallas; all top security clearance people did. He has Project Star from Rand in his pocket.

Over in Vietnam, he was a bloodthirsty volunteer in the brush with a machine gun, blasting "Gooks." His friend, Body Count McNamara, assigned him to draw up a hedge description of the Vietnam war. He carefully omitted the 'Holy Crusade' Fatima #3 bit of Kennedy, and the Kennedy-Diem murders—the key to everything rotten at Dallas, and the Onassis-Joseph P.-Roosevelt heroin deal of World War II.

(It was easy; he just does not go back that far).

He leaves out Cardinal Spellman, Cardinal Thuc, and JFK's involvement in Vietnam, and blames everything on Johnson.

Body Count McNamara dropped out, and went on to Mafia heaven, the World Bank. In the Pentagon Papers case, nobody was jailed for anything. By the very nature of its smuggled release, this bumbled version of how the war was just an accidental mess has been generally accepted. And that was the purpose of its release. It was composed by two very sharp ones: Body Count McNamara (at the top) and Ellsberg (at the top of security). Both are devoted to the Kennedys.

The Alioto hit-run cover-up pointed immediately to Dallas and all the rest. It was covered up well by Nixon and Mitchell, until Alioto brought it all up again at Chappaquiddick. Around August 3rd 1969, the first who read the Chappaquiddick solution was Mack, Nixon's hatchet man. His face went white when I spoke of Mafia ownership of the Presidency. Very odd; he's a tough Mafia. And back in Washington, everybody went to work on the cover-up.

The shit had hit the fan. Concessions were in order.

August 5, 1969: Johnson threatened Dickie with "Hughes." Dickie made a 180° turn; he crawled to

Russia and Peking, yet redoubled the murder of Vietnam to appease Thieu. He had Thieu elected again, and follows Thieu's orders today. Vietnam is the Onassis-Montini-JFK key to Dallas.

On the same date, McNamara was called in. "You got us out of the Bay of Pigs disaster; see what you can do with this one."

So McNamara called in Ellsberg, the one he had commissioned to compose the hedge, the partial blot-out, in which no one would get hurt too badly.

Ellsberg's instructions: "The *New York Times* will cooperate. 'Steal' the papers and release it, for all the Kennedys' sake—and in the National Interest. Cover up the keys: Project Star, Dallas, Mary Jo, Fatima #3. We will make a hero of you, eventually. Our entire Mafia history is at stake."

Ellsberg's story of stealing the Rand files starts from there.

Kimelman and the Mafia offered the substitute Teddy to the world. Teddy McGovern mouths off: "End the war. End tax loopholes."

The Vultures in Vegas were the first to know. Looting of Onassis started on a grand scale. (The *Wall Street Journal*—July 31 and August 1, 1972—enumerates some of this). Omitted, of course, are the probes by Clifford Irving, based on "Hughes" nursemaid Merryman's squealing (which murdered him) and then the hasty flight of the Onassis "Proxy" Hughes from Vegas to the Bahamas, then to Nicaragua (this time, frightened off by two Spokane phone calls to my Masonic brother, relative to my father's murder). Then to Vancouver—skirting the borders. It took Onassis a year just to arrange—after Chappaquiddick—to get his "Proxy" Hughes out of the U.S. of Mafia.

Ellsberg has top credibility, from top security. He is wealthy (married to Xerox, or something like that). Like Nader, he's a hero. Cold-faced Rudenstein, and the broads in the office, ran off multiple copies before returning the one I sent them, for their own blackmail purposes—and already Rudenstein parks on sidewalks.

Lids are on all over—at the American Civil Liberties Union, for instance. Doesn't it sound free and democratic? This is what they do:

Defended Mafs Sinatra and Patriarcha against Senate Mafia hearings;

Defend Onassis's Swiss Banks, and American Crime Banks against Criminal Loot exposure;

Defend secrecy of Mafia Campaign contributors;

Are against the death penalty for any crime: treason, mass murder, genocide; any Mafia crime.

If Ellsberg doesn't have top Mafia legal concurrence, why is it that he has top legal representation, plus monetary support—and I have none? Same question for Nader. The fact is that 1972 is a re-run of 1968—with no changes.

You see, we can't find a V.P. for Teddy #2. Teddy #1 (Kennedy) won't be a V.P. for Teddy #2 (McGovern).

And this is why Teddy #2 picked Eagleton in the first place: Teddy #1 can't run for V.P. or President because of Chappaquiddick. Eagleton called Alioto and got Alioto's okay to possibly take his place as V.P., and then he resigned. Teddy #2 now has a hell of a time finding another one, and the public shuffles uneasily.

Someone called it the "Crumbling of the Demo Party."

"Mafia Conventions are only a custom—a Mafia custom taking over all law."

Senator Scott said: "All Conventions are purchased; everybody knows it, and accepts it. It's a Hell of a way to pick a V.P.—in a back room."

Teddy McGovern doesn't know whether to shit or cry or both. He is about to be targeted by

half a dozen different Mafia sources—and get his ass shot off, but he can't quit, can't quit, can't quit.... Possibly Teddy McGovern would welcome—as a relief—a nice warm atomic flash. That is one way to solve all dilemmas.

(Teddy McGovern—and Teddy Kennedy—and Teddy Alioto—and Teddy Eagleton—were all handed these papers at the same time Ellsberg got his. By that same Peace Action Group. Besides Ellsberg, they love Teddy McGovern, Teddy Kennedy, and Teddy Alioto—who furnishes them space and police protection. The Peace coalition also loves the two who first proposed Mafia Eagleton: Alioto's Willie Brown and John Burton of Mafia pinball machines.)

Jack Anderson, who knows about all of this, had a private Mafia meeting with Eagleton in Washington. Eagleton laid on a Mafia death rattle, and Anderson came out, saying; "I retract, I retract...."

Said Eagleton to Teddy's Vatican Byrne, Boston D.A.: "Say a novena for me; a rosary isn't enough." And then he called Alioto about the purchase of Anderson and a V.P. opening in Washington.

Over the four day weekend in L.A. that freed Ellsberg from jail, CIA Helms was conferring with important men at the Bohemian Grove, 50 miles north of San Francisco—while 'mistake' missiles stuttered over which city to waste, or both. Ellsberg bowed. The Peace Coalition bowed. Back East, Anderson bowed. Just as Garry bowed on July 11, 1972, at 3:26 p.m. 'Mistake' missiles were stuttering all over the place. "Waste 'em."

From McGovern on down: "Only Kennedy on the ticket as V.P. will give the Democrats a chance of beating Nixon—and preserve the Democratic Party."

CIA burglars at the Mafia Demo Party Office are now linked by Mafia big loot cash to Mitchell and Stans. Neither can be reached for comment since they have both crawled up their wives' asses.

Mafia Montini was praised for his Allied spy activity in Tokyo during World War 11. (In Tisserant's papers, it was Montini's double spy dealing with the Russians, in Europe, after the war, that made Pope Whoever-it-was so mad he banned Montini to a northern post and labeled him a rotten Mafia son-of-a-bitch who he would see would never even become a Bishop. Untrue. As with our U.S. of Mafia, only the rottenest of the rotten get to the top in the Mafia Election Process—and so it was in Rome. The rottenest of the rotten made it. Mafia Montini became Ruler of the World: Pope-GOD.)

Burning Hay? Or Opium?

Today, the U.S. of Mafia televised the burning of 26 tons of opium in Thailand. The word went around that the opium was not opium, but hay. The CIA responded: "It was too opium! We purchased it at top price from the Taiwan Chinese in the Golden Triangle in order to present this public burning to the American peeepul. Top grade opium; we always buy from Onassis. We wouldn't cheat you. It was opium."

Today: Thieu said, "I order Nixon to destroy all of North Vietnam, and do it in the next six months—or I'll blow the whistle on the whole Kennedy Fatima #3 bit, and Onassis and Hughes too."

(Stop! Right here. Ain't this a pistol? Maf Demos, Maf Republicans, Maf Multinationals, Legal Maf, Press Maf, Onassis Maf, Kennedy Maf, Mafia Maf—and all the assorted branches milling around this nation, with "mistake" missiles and blackmail and whatever aimed in every direction, like a bunch of cross-eyed pistolleros at the Okay Corral, primed for a festering, gut busting shoot-out.)

Take tonight, for instance. Nine old Mafia—the Supreme Court—are shaking in their boots over Ellsberg. What to do? It's their neck or his. They'll choose his, of course. But then, will he hang them? Or do they delete him—as Ruby did Oswald? Anyway, murder is being planned.

Ellsberg, machine gunner from Vietnam, and architect of Fatima #3 nuclear plans, for the Pacific area and the world. With top security, knowing all the dirt, was commissioned by McNamara to draw up the hedge cover-up: the Pentagon Papers.

Ellsberg did not change his spots. He was scared shitless. McNamara had departed quickly for Mafia heaven—the World Bank. Kissinger was scooting around the world for Dickie. Ellsberg alone was left with the horrible cover-up papers: a crime much greater than treason—a crime against Christ, humanity and history. (And now, he hints at these things). He was to be the fall guy.

On August 3rd, 1969, my father's birthday, I was relaying it all to Nixon and on down. Teddy called McNamara. He said: "Get me out of this—as you got JFK out of the Bay of Pigs mess."

McNamara called Ellsberg and told him this might be the time to release the hedge, since the shit had hit the fan. And Ellsberg didn't need to be told. He knew he had been picked for the Patsy, just as Oswald was at Dallas.

Oswald was there to nail Connally (both of his bullets went into Connally). He was as shocked as the rest of the world when Maheu's CIA triple crossfire crumpled Kennedy. (Jim Fratianno missed when Roselli's shot got to Kennedy first.) Oswald didn't know what to do. He was guilty, and in it up to the ears, but not for JFK. He was not to be allowed to figure out what to do. Ruby was allowed to murder Oswald.

So it was with Ellsberg. Trapped, as a patsy, he did what all the rest of them do: He stole the blackmail papers—as many as he could.

The *New York Times* will print nothing about Dallas, Bobby, Chappaquiddick; this they cover up, *a la* Llelyveld. Why, then, would they print the Pentagon Papers? Because McNamara and Kennedy wanted it. You give a little bit to protect the whole. After all, Dickie was in office, and the blame would reflect on Dickie and Johnson—not back to the real thing: Kennedys, Onassis and Montini.

So Ellsberg went to the people, hinting at Project Star—but never mentioning the keys, such as Chappaquiddick. You release a little bit. Admit something. A fix, for instance—anything to "cover the deeper fix."

So, because of a rigged "Chappaquiddick" taped phone call in L.A., and rigged exposure of that call, Ellsberg is out of jail, forever.

Arthur Bremer? One hour for jury selection; witnesses were called that same day. Justice prosecution, one day. Defense, one day. Say—they are in a hurry, aren't they? And then it was all over. Neat.

Tomorrow Dickie gives a party in Palm Springs for Agnew, Reagan, John Wayne, *et al*. Connally? Like McNamara, secreted in Mafia heaven, he now moves into a hidden hub with Tokyo-Russia super spy Montini, on the Foreign Intelligence Board from which he can coordinate with Mafia Montini any leaks from the Tisserant Papers, Onassis' Diary, or any of the murder and assassination shit dribblers. This has been a normal day in the U.S. of Mafia.

27 August 3, 1972: My father's birthday

I took a plastic rose to the murdered man. My birthday present to him on August 3, 1969 was the exposure of Chappaquiddick. He had always said, and was still saying the night before the murder was complete, while Dickie was in Peking, "I want to question Teddy and Alioto on a witness stand."

There wasn't a live one in Fern Grove at Cypress Lawn. No one except me. And a hummingbird. Clumps of flowers around, called "bleeding hearts"—a perennial, I guess, with red flowers like hearts that hang upside down. The little bird buzzed around the flowers, and me, and stuck his snozzle in the flowers for lunch, deriving sustenance—and life—from a bleeding heart, without harm. My father was over there, 3rd section high, 3rd row, 5th from the top: Verne Dale Roberts.

This bird wouldn't stand on a flower branch. He ate gently, suspended in air. Biologists tell me the flower and the bird are friends; they give to one another life and propagation of the species.

This one would not foul his own nest. He would not wipe his dirty feet on his food as Teddy did on the floorboard air-in Poucha Pond. Putrid air, that was still there 2 hours and 13 minutes later when Mary Jo's busted snozzle swelled shut, while Teddy called Onassis, and McNamara, and Ellsberg.

This bird would not shit on his own food, his own friends. He went over on a rock to do that. And then he'd look sideways at me, and chirp, "See, you stupid son-of-a-bitch? It doesn't have to be rotten."

And so it was—since he was the only living thing there to talk to—that, while he enjoyed his lunch, I discussed with him matters like mobiles and Option 4. And he chirped, and buzzed me, and departed, and so did I.

Letters from the Moon

Our gallant astronauts—cream of the American Apple Pie Chappaquiddick crop—carried infectious cancer into space during the first landing on the moon: Chappaquiddick week.

Quoth Armstrong: "One small step for man, one giant leap for mankind."

While he spoke from the moon, during this week, his employers—McNamara, Montini, Ellsberg, Teddy, Alioto, Onassis, Dickie, plus American Chappaquiddick Apple Pie millions, and Papal Knights and Princesses, Swig and Mama Rosie, were busy elsewhere.

Look and the Mafia Press were banking bribes for Armstrong.

Wally Schirra was bribed by Onassis-Dickie's Penn Central Railroad and Onassis-Paley's CBS; Mafia Penn Central got a loan, and Mafia CBS, a gift. Later, the astronaut crew carried mail to the moon, postmarked the letters there, and returned them for the Mafia to sell, at $1,000 a copy. They were so busy postmarking that the landing was almost scratched.

All of the astronauts on the moon said, "We felt the presence of God." Upon return, they rushed off to Rome, and bowed in deference: "Anoint us, oh God, in the proper Pennsylvania style." Heroes all.

At splashdown, Mafia Dickie picked up 10 million votes—on world wide TV, courtesy of Howard Hughes.

You don't understand? You're too busy? You gotta go home?

In McKeithen's Mafia Louisiana, at Mafia Marcello's Senator Ellender's funeral, Archbishop Hannon—Marcello's sponsor—eulogized: "Senator Marcello Ellender was the most courageous of all men—next to Onassis's Patriarcha's Teddy Kennedy," and the statue of Fatima wept more tears. "The faithful must follow the message of Fatima."

And the faithful Mafia Fatima #3 leaders were there. On one side of the aisle were Onassis's Dickie and Agnew; and on the other side, Onassis's Teddy Kennedy and Teddy McGovern. Directing it all was Mafia Pope Montini, squeezing tears out of the miraculous statue of Fatima. Marcello played the organ. Lansky passed the collection plate—for reservations at his and Sinatra's Fontainbleu in Miami Beach for the August 21, 1972 Mafia Republican gang bang on Christ.

The guy who replaced Guv McKeithen anointed his wife to replace Senator Marcello Ellender in the Mafia U.S. Senate—a clubby, murdering group of Fatima #3 Capos, led by the murderer from the Pond—Teddy. And so much for the Mafia Election Process in Louisiana.

***

The United Nations? From August 3, 1969?

Well, prior to Chappaquiddick, it was a totally purchased Mafia non-entity. It had a World Court of Mafia Judges that sat for 25 years—at $50 thou a year per capita. And I mean they just sat—and nothing else. The U.N. was a world body that jumped to the orders of the U.S. of Mafia Multi-Nationals, which sponsored Mafia dictatorships everywhere, in conjunction with Montini: in Greece, Vietnam, Brazil, Taiwan, and manipulated national elections everywhere. It was a joint CIA-Vatican project: Chile, Northern Ireland, Guatemala, Dominican Republic, Colombia, Paraguay, Panama.

In both Panama and Paraguay, the dictators and their sons were exposed, in Congress, for running heroin and cocaine; (see the Heroin Papers). Congress squelched it, and the State Department approved of continued heroin-cocaine trade for the U.S. of Mafia's addict population. Meanwhile the CIA and Lodge's Vatican pursue the overthrow of seven Latin-American Republics, via their own elections—as in Chile. And they do this publicly, with Dickie's approval, and Montini's.

Since Chappaquiddick, many events have occurred. They feature the expulsion of Heroin Chiang and the admission of China to the U.N., the glee of victimized nations, and the Buckley-Goldwater Mafia Senate shut-off of the funds to the U.N.: "Destroy the U.N."

Meany and Rooney cut off U.N. international labor funds: "Destroy the U.N. international labor organization."

But the entire Maf said: "Keep the World Court. They just sit there. We own them. They won't set up any international law that might hang us for crimes against humanity."

In the U.S. of Mafia, the Supreme Court quickly knocked out the death penalty for treason, murder and genocide, crimes against humanity—primarily because it concerns them. And tonight, a major struggle continues over Ellsberg—a patsy, like Oswald—who stands alone as the one who drew up the plans for a Pacific Blow-Off, after Apalachin, and then for the entire world: Fatima #3, for Kennedy and Onassis and Montini.

And who then drew up the escape hatch explanation for Vietnam, for McNamara: the Pentagon Papers. And who then—after Chappaquiddick, in total Oswald Patsy fear, released the cover-up version to confuse an entire world—about everything: assassinations, Apalachin, Fatima #3, World War II, 1932, and the cover-up of the murder of Christ.

U.N. Secretary General Waldheim fumes over all of this: "Yes, the U.S. of Mafia is committing crimes against mankind and Christ in Vietnam."

Attorney Mark Lane, who is allowed to spout—in left field—about Dallas, has disappeared. So have the other left fielders, who are also allowed to spout: Fensterwald, Garrison, Winter-Berger, Nye, Fellmeth, Nader, Gardner, Garry, Turner, Harris, Tisserant's priests, *Politics of Heroin* McCoy, hundreds more. It's all right—as long as it's out in left field. They can have some exposure. It only confuses.

But not if it's someone totally on target. Me. I get a clamp on my own family. On transportation. On who sits next to me in bars. On money.

Presidents run. I screw their Mafia wives—and tell them so—and they crawl right up the other sleazy hole. Mitchell is up Martha's ass. Kennedy refused the Presidency, and crawled up Joanie's. Hoover gets a taste of Pennsylvania grave dust—in apple pie.

But the greater the clamp on me, the greater the exposure. It's like squeezing a tube of DDT: cancer-killing crap flooding the world, a part of Option #3.

***

Those nine daisy-chain Mafia Supreme Court Justices, selected by Mafia Presidents Roosevelt and Truman, through Kennedy, Johnson and Dickie, were selected from Mafia Judges, who purchased their jobs, as ambassadors do, with Mafia loot. They were picked as judges from the ranks of Mafia Attorneys whose sole qualifications are Mafia membership. They are then approved by the Mafia ABA who, finally, submit their names to the Mafia Senate Judiciary Committee. That is, the group that squelched the ITT inquiry (composed of Kennedy-Chappaquiddick, Eastland Subsidy Mafia, McClellan Banking Mafia, Hruska Drug Insurance Mafia, Fong Bribe Mafia, Scott Bribe Mafia, Bird Loot Mafia, Cook Fund Mafia, Gurney Front Mafia, Bayh Lobby Mafia, and five more Mafia men. See Congro-Mafia Papers). And then, it's out to the full Mafia Senate Club for rubber stamps.

These are the nine who tonight are wrestling with Ellsberg. Do you think he will hang?

Today, George Wallace said to the American Party Convention: "I will not allow you to draft me." And John Connally put his pistol back in his pocket.

Today, Arthur Bremer's trial: The jury was out for only two hours, and zap—into the deep freeze goes Bremer, for 63 years. No answers will come from him. Like Sirhan, he isn't aware of his own mind-bending. Puzzled, sad old Pa Bremer said: "If this is Justice, I can't understand it; he's a sick boy."

McGovern is three weeks overdue in selecting a V.P. There is precious little time, and Teddy McGovern still has problems. No one will take the suicidal spot. And by now, they all know it's suicidal. These papers are now out all around America—formerly, only around the rest of the world.

Last week, Russia politely left Egypt. This week they politely pulled out of Araby; next week, out of India, politely. China politely backs away from border bombs and missiles. Chile politely accepts its economic squeeze. The only Medusa Monster left, committing genocide around the world, is visible to all—out in the open, killing in desperation, frenzied for Fatima #3. The focus of horror viewing is now on the upcoming Convention gang bang at Miami and the Super Bowl orgy election coming up on November 7, 1972—in full world view.

Frightened away from Vegas, God-Onassis flits around the borders of the U.S. of Mafia: Bahamas, Nicaragua, Vancouver, and B.C., keying on Vegas. Oddly, that is the key to his own death sentence: the end to his dream of a second Alexander the Great ruling the world—his son, Alexander. I wonder which of them will die first.

***

Let's zoom in on the shit pit called Las Vegas. Dickieville.

The following is from a *Wall Street Journal* summary of recent "Hughes" Vegas activity. It becomes simple when Vegas is regarded as an arm of Onassis's "Hughes" Mafia Money Funnel. The key is that $300 million was "stolen" from "Hughes" casinos, and wound up, tax-free, with Onassis. Most of it goes back to the U.S. for purchase of Presidents, and pay-offs for assassinations.

Johnny Roselli's "finder's fee", for moving "Hughes" into the Desert Inn, was his pay-off for his frontal shot at Dallas on JFK. (James McCord and the CIA provided the timers, the getaway, and cover for the synchronized crossfire performed by Maheu's men and segments of the original Castro assassination group—plus some of Marcello's own.) Now, Roselli has been framed at the Friar's Club and securely put away.

John Meier started with Onassis-"Hughes" after Apalachin. He blackmailed his way in with Onassis, and was given free rein—even to purchasing Dickie, Humphrey, and O'Brien, plus all of Congress, in 1968. He was given a shot at a New Mexico Senator's slot—via a $100 thou bribe suitcase from Hoffa, via Johnson's Senator Montoya.

He is not related to Andre (also John) Meier (Meyer, Maier)—who uses all these names, and was "Hughes's" right-hand man, and is now—publicly—Onassis's right-hand man. He handles payoffs to Maf all over the world. For instance, Lansky's $25 million casino skim—and overpayments to the Mafia hotels in Kansas City, Detroit, New York, Chicago, and New Orleans.

Donald Nixon: started with Onassis's 1957 $205,000 non-repayable "loan," with which he bought Caribbean stock with Meier and other Onassis hoods. Today he is in the housing business with Onassis, dining with the Greek Mafia colonels, and running the Marriott catering service for Onassis' Olympic Airlines (and the other airlines Onassis owns through that hidden stock that no one—SEC, NYSE, not any of them—will reveal). Marriott ran Dickie's 4th of July gala at the White House two years ago. Dickie didn't have one this year; even the necrophiliac public burped at the thought.

The five Mormon "Hughes" nursemaids: Note that it is no longer six. Merryman, the sixth, was murdered in December 1970. I met his widow, Louise, in late June 1971, after Hughes's watery Grecian burial. 1170 Sacramento Street, San Francisco, is where she lives—Onassis's building. And so does Eckersley, some of whose Mafia activity is described herein.

Intertel (all ex-Justice, ex-FBI) is now running Onassis' Caribbean Mafia Empire.

Ex-FBI, all working for Onassis' "Hughes."

Current FBI, CIA, Treasury, are all working for Onassis-"Hughes." "Hughes"—poor, victimized dead Howard, himself, is not questioned.

Indictments will be issued for the small time thieves, but not for Maheu, who is suing "Hughes"-Onassis for $50 million because he was evicted from his half-million a year guaranteed salary—for life—for arranging for blowing off JFK's head.

Quote John Meier: "Hughes wouldn't fire me in a hundred years." Seems awfully confident, doesn't he? He runs around with Dickie's brother.

Hank Greenspun is suing Onassis for $142 million. He knows about all of it, and he is a typical Mafia newspaper owner. Oh well, you get the drift. Fit it in. It all fits.

And there is a completely separate entity in the new Hughes Defense contracts: for helicopters, guided bombs, and the new grant for a "Hughes" worldwide communications satellite system. "Hughes" is building the satellites for Western Union, which Onassis owns; more of that secret stock. It can beam information, and propaganda, to any TV set in Russia, for instance. International Mafia Cancer—Onassis—supported by President Dickie and Mafia Montini—for a Mafia murder fee.

(Following are reprints from the July 31-August 1, 1972, *Wall Street Journal*—dealing with the "Hughes" Vegas maze of Mafia activity. In case I don't get them into this set, go to some file and read them.)

August 8, 1972

Unger, *Washington Post*: "Any 8th-grader can read the Pentagon Papers and know they are not dangerous to National Security." Right. McNamara had them drawn up as a hedge cover-up of the war as a bumbling accident—and if necessary, to release them—and this he debated on August 5, 1969. So did Ellsberg—in total patsy fear. For while he was drawing up the hedge cover-up, the Pentagon Papers, he was also the architect of the Fatima #3 world nuclear blow-off plans. And that was the "deeper fix" that must be covered up at all cost.

Ellsberg's blackmail worked. Polled by phone, all nine Mafia Supreme Court Justices upheld

Douglas' stay of the trial: "The wiretap issue must be solved first," they said, knowing Justice would not allow the contents of that phone call—regarding "Chappaquiddick, Mary Jo's grave, and all that lies buried there"—to be released, since that is the whole ball of wax: "the deeper fix."

Today: News: "The Nixon administration will accept a long postponement of the Pentagon Papers trial, or perhaps even drop the case, rather than disclose the contents of a 'foreign intelligence' wiretap that led to a Supreme Court stay of all proceedings... Prosecutors will not seek to force Ellsberg to trial...by revealing which of their 16 attorneys and consultants was overheard in non-court-authorized electronic surveillance. Disclosure of wiretap contents was the only way prosecutors could have made the trial go forward... John W. Hushen, Justice information officer, said there was 'no chance' such a move would be made."

Today: More news: "New heroin statistics. U.S. buys $10 billion worth a year. Rest of world buys $15 billion a year." (It's much bigger than oil, which, world wide, is only $16 billion.) "Ten square miles of up-country Thai-Laotian land grows the entire U.S. supply. Nearly one ton of heroin was seized in the U.S. last year."

(On September 15, last year, they picked up six tons from Harry Yee, Lombard Street, Alioto's North Beach, San Francisco—after which the FBI raided San Francisco to cart it out, and Kissinger ran like a rabbit to Peking, and China got into the U.N., and Nader canceled formation of a third party, and Helms canceled a "mistake" missile, and I had lunch with pretty Mafia Pat Wyman.)

Watergate details

Of the nine CIA-Mafia men, of the Nixon branch, caught bugging Democratic Mafia headquarters at Watergate, only five were charged. Four got away and hid in Newport Beach, California.

Those were the four, plus her one Secret Service guard, who tied Martha to the bed and jabbed her in the ass at the Newport Inn.

L. Pat Gray, Director of the FBI, the Vatican lad who replaced apple-pie-murdered J. Mafia Hoover, directed the silencing of Martha.

One of the captured five—Sturgis, a Jack Anderson friend, formerly ran Cuban gambling with McLaney, for Onassis-Lansky.

Castro stole $8 billion from Onassis when he kicked them out of Cuba; and that was why Maheu was hired by the CIA Mafia to assassinate Castro, and why the Bay of Pigs invasion was planned. (All of the nine bugging Watergaters were involved in the invasion as well.)

Sturgis was with David Ferrie during the JFK Dallas hit. In court, Jack Anderson defended Sturgis as a "most honest American."

In Anderson's files are Riley's reports on the FBI-CIA-Dallas Police-Mafia coalition in the murders of JFK, Bobby, and Martin Luther King

Anderson withheld Bay of Pigs advance notice—along with the *New York Times*—and also withheld exposure of the "Hughes" bribes to Nixon in 1960.

Another Watergater, Barker, ran CIA Mafia loot from McCone's Chilean ITT—through a Mexican Maf—to purchase U.S. murder. Barker, and another one, Howard Hunt, were partners in Nicaraguan "business" (where "Hughes" ran to from the Bahamas).

Vatican Senator Buckley and Vatican CIA Helms proposed Vatican Howard Hunt for Dickie's top consultant on Narcotics and the Pentagon. Hunt was in the White House in charge of the Pentagon Papers (at the time of their release) and Narcotics (at the time of the Harry Yee $6 billion heroin affair).

At the time of the Watergate bugging, Hunt was doing research on Teddy and

Chappaquiddick—at the White House Library, where only altered versions exist—and a clamp has now gone on that information.

Another of the five, Vatican James McCord, was Dickie's top consultant on censorship of the news media and the U.S. Postal Service.

The object of that bugging was to find out what the Demo Mafia were doing about the key: Dickie's cross—"Howard Hughes."

Both Mafia parties have been fed complete Chappaquiddick details. And both have been fed complete "Hughes" details. It is necessary, for Mafia Demos to win, to have an expose of Onassis-"Hughes". For the Republican Mafia to win, there must be an expose of Onassis-Teddy Chappaquiddick. It's complicated, because both involve Vietnam, the gate to Fatima #3, and the McNamara-Ellsberg cover-up of that.

And this is how the bubble of shit swells. It will be a burst bubble, and canceled elections; or an out-in-the-open Thieu/Greece/Taiwan type take-over, or Fatima #3 and a new thing. There is no way out of it. All the murders since have been cold-blooded Mafia murders, to cover up all that went before.

A "Clean" Democrat for the V.P. Slot

Said Jack Anderson, on TV: "Swiss Ambassador True Davis—a true Vatican Onassis person, president of Mafia Tony Boyle's Mafia National Bank of Washington, had copies of photostats of the original drunk driving citations of Eagleton from the Highway Patrol. He told me about them in 1968. Then he tore them up—as the Highway Patrolmen tore up the originals. One other party saw them, but he doesn't have them. A third party has copies, but he has disappeared—'in the pocket,' so to speak."

Eagleton then stepped down, after calling Alioto. Eagleton called Anderson to a Mafia Meeting.

Anderson emerged. "I retract," he said. "Nothing exists. Eagleton is clean."

Eagleton called Alioto; and Anderson was "in the pocket", so to speak.

Humphrey: "Not me. Not again. I hate nooses."

Muskie: "No! My family needs me."

Boston White: "No! Things have been happening. I am needed at home."

So Teddy McGovern said: "Last week, Eagleton withdrew. He was a Mafia nut. A good man. But some voters don't care for nuts hanging around nuclear buttons. For the Mafia, that's normal. But we must not be distracted by nut issues, so I decided to pick a new one: Sargent Shriver. A clean, straight Kennedy-Montini-Onassis Mafia; a member of the Onassis-Kennedy family, married to Teddy's sister, Eunice."

That night, Garry Sullivan told me: "I've been on the White House lawn casting trout flies into a pool. National fly-casting meets. I won the last three. And right now, I'm sick. I feel like those trout that swallow up my flies—'We've gotta cough up this monster, whatever it is.'"

28 V.P. Convention: Unanimous for Shriver

The second Mafia Demo V.P. convention meets. There is a blessing by Cardinal Sheehan. "Bless the Papal Prince, Teddy Kennedy Shriver." Senator Mansfield: "Your Mafia Eminence and Reverend Mafia Fathers and all the rest of you: we admit we have made some mistakes. Now we are concerned with survival. Vote for Shriver."

Mafia Daley's Representative Pete Rostenkowski: "We Chicago Mafia all love Teddy Kennedy Shriver." He rattles a sack of bones. "Vote for the bones of Hampton and Clark. Vote Shriver."

Black Yvonne Braithwaite Burke: "All blacks love Teddy Kennedy Shriver. We ignore Mary Jo, and Hampton and Clark, and Martin Luther too, Let's make that a campaign slogan."

Mafia Rockefeller: "Shriver, in the Peace Corps, showed Americans what they could do for their country: drown Mary Jo, barbecue Newsom's nieces, and squash Bonnie Brussell. We love Teddy Kennedy Shriver."

Sweet-faced Dorothy Bush calls the voting roll. Sweet-faced Mafia from each state dutifully cast drooling, unanimous votes.

Said Brinkley: "This is odd. Nothing is ever that unanimous. There is even much doubt about flag, motherhood and apple pie lately. As for me—I will eat apple pie only if it's organic."

And there they were, on the podium: smiling Mafia in a huddle—Muskie, Humphrey, Eagleton, O'Brien, Teddy, Mansfield, Califano.

Jean Westwood, Demo Chairperson: "We are honest. We have told the people the truth. We have nothing to hide." (Except that Old Crow bottle in her girdle.)

O'Brien: "Miami: this is the most honest conclave in American history. We promise to tell the truth. We want everyone to say, 'I trust the Democratic Party.' Survival of the Mafia two-party system is at stake."

Humphrey: "We need to believe in our government. I learned that in 1968. Come home, all you Mafia Dems. I give you our new chief, Teddy McGovern."

Teddy McGovern: "I salute a truly great American: Teddy Kennedy. We can take this country back from Mafia Dickie and give it to Mafia Teddy. When government lies to people, then people lose liberty itself. We will dump Thieu in Vietnam and transfer our war effort to Heroin Thailand. We have decided to support Onassis's Greece and Lansky's Israel. Send us money. Send us help. What made our country what it is today are the ideals of our people. There is a God who hates injustice and we are prepared to ignore him. I give you our V.P.—America's great lady, Eunice Teddy Kennedy, and her hubby—who? Oh—Teddy Shriver."

V.P. Candidate Teddy Shriver: "Your Cardinal Sheehan Eminence—and the rest of you—and the great Ted Kennedy. Pity Nixon. His first—and only—V.P. 'choice' was Spiro Agnew. Us Demos have thousands of Mafia Onassis-Montini-Kennedys to choose from. The Demo Party is the Party of Daley and Ted Kennedy. We build tonight on the grave of Mary Jo Kopechne and the Justice buried there. We want equal justice for all."

Teddy: "I will campaign actively for my ticket."

Why Fatima Weeps

The miraculous weeping statue of Fatima: Does she weep because the Supreme Court ruled, "Yes, we are the Mafia-anointed supreme arbiters of American law, but we can't rule on the Mafia Party rules—because they rule us"? Or does she weep because here in the U.S. of Mafia, a Mafia murderer is not only immune in Congress, City Hall, and on the public street, but he also gets a

badge: "Most Courageous Man," and a title: "President"?

Is this why that cedar stump statue weeps in Marcello's Louisiana parish, where Sister Lucy, the architect of the Fatima #1, #2, and #3 blow-off of the world, reads comic books and genuflects toward Mary Jo's Pennsylvania grave?

Today, Friedheim, at the Pentagon: "Well, yes, we have been working on a first strike to blow up all of Russia."

Today, President 62-carat-up-the-ass Patty said: "There won't be any campaign issues. My hubby, Dickie, has them all solved."

Today—the Yippies, who have been planning for four years to disrupt the Republican Convention: "We have read some papers. We are withdrawing from Miami. We will not provide Dickie with a pretext for violence to either cancel elections or push Fatima #3 buttons at the gang bang on Christ in Miami, August 21, 1972."

After Jerry Gordon phoned Ellsberg about these papers at the UCLA Peace Coalition anti-war meeting last month, Gordon announced, "We, the anti-war group, will not be in Miami, on August 21, 1972. We, too, have read some papers. We will provide no pretexts for Dickie."

Ellsberg trial

Today, Ellsberg said: "Within the last month, I learned something about the Constitution, and why my persecution trial was held. This trial should never have been held." (He rattles blackmail about that taped call, and worries about the possible new charge.)

Today, Ellsberg's 16 Kennedy attorneys said: "We ask for a mistrial. Delay will mean a possible taint of the waiting jury from viewing other evidence." (I told Rudenstein other batches of papers were in L.A. for the jurors and witnesses.) "A new, untainted jury should be called when the trial is ready. We waive double jeopardy rights. If the trial is delayed somewhat we will not seek 'double jeopardy' release because of a new jury."

Today, the Mafia Supreme Court said: "Screw you, Alioto. It's our necks that will stretch, too. We will delay this trial past the election—probably forever—or at least until we figure out some Mafia scheme to bury it all—as Warren's Court did with Dallas."

Today, in Rome, 32 Mafia members of Montini's Parliament, charged with crimes ranging from murder to theft, were automatically exempted by the Papal rule of congressional immunity. This has been the rule through the Papal centuries; followed in the U.S. of Mafia during our last Mafia century. Montini's Italian Prime Minister, Andreotti, attacked McGovern's threat of withdrawal from Vatican Heroin Vietnam and other Mafia dictatorships around the world. (After his nomination, of course, Teddy McGovern reversed it all.)

Commented Mafia Reagan: "I heartily agree with Montini's Prime Minister Andreotti. We must not alter our plan to keep armed forces everywhere so that we can join our allies Onassis, Thieu, Chiang, Franco, Medici, Pakistan—in Fatima #3."

Ambassador Lodge laid down the law of God: "We will crush any individual, group, or nation who conspires against the church or the recognized legitimate authorities. Nationalism, as a substitute for Vatican Law, is unlawful; it is subversive of both civil and religious law. And we will crush it, if necessary, because it is inimical to the welfare of the Vatican, the Holy See, and the Roman Catholic Church."

Today—newsman St. John: "We have just witnessed the crumbling of the corrupt two party system. Who needs it?"

Today—Greeky Agnew: "What is really on the line now is the survival of our Republican Party and its ability to remain in power."

Neither Mafia party is mentioned in the Constitution. Murder, treason, bribery are. They are

hanging offenses. Nor is the established Mafia Party Law that one must be owned by Roman Mafia Montini, as is the case of our leaders. Nor is Onassis. The Constitution says: "Total separation of Church and State, and free elections (no bribery), by all. It says "Life, Liberty, and Pursuit of Happiness." It says "no secrecy," It says the public has a "right to know." It says that Agnew is wrong. Survival of the Republican Party is not the issue.

Survival of 206 million American bodies—and the birds and the bees and the flowers—is the issue.

Lansky's Mafia Convention Hall—overflowing from fresh and rotting corpses—will soon refill for a drooling mockery of Christ, before an empty festered slivering cross. Vote for one. It matters not which one.

Election decisions are made by the back-room boys of the two Mafia parties. They pass the results through Pennsylvania graves, Cypress Lawn and street corners such as Franklin and Lombard, in San Francisco.

Mark Lane and Mae Brussell Campaign for McGovern

Today, Congress toys with releasing that treason indictment against Joan of Arc Jane Fonda. Her attorney is Mark Lane,[61] as indignant as Mae Brussell over assassinations. Both have read these papers and run, and bark anti-war phrases, and campaign for Teddy Kennedy McGovern.

Today, Ellsberg, free, and the jury sent home, announces he will campaign against the war and Dickie—and for Teddy Kennedy McGovern. So will his staff of 16 Kennedy attorneys, who helped Teddy get out of the ordeal of Chappaquiddick.

Today I listened in on a street conversation: "Barker and Sturgis each got $115 thou out of campaign funds, for that Watergate Demo bugging bit. Sturgis and McLaney [Onassis' Cuban gambling chief] got kicked out of Cuba, and Castro stole $8 billion from Onassis."

Look what that $8 billion steal from Onassis brought on. Maheu was hired by the CIA to assassinate Castro. His crew later turned up in Chicago on November 1, 1963, and again in Dallas on November 22.

With the Bay of Pigs Invasion, we almost had a nuclear war with Russia.

So what would be so odd about Helms lobbing a 'mistake' missile on San Francisco when the massed FBI were here on October 8 to cart out that $6 billion worth of Harry Yee skag? Especially when it would be tied in with Nader's assassination if he started a 3rd Party and mentioned the key—the Mafia Election Process? Together with the admittance of China into the U.N.; complete dissolution of the two Mafia Parties; decapitation of the Mafia; crumbling of the Mafia Vatican Roman Catholic Church; the end of war and crime, and exposure of assassinations right back to the birth of Christ? And ditto—again—on July 11, 1972, in Garry's office?

To say nothing of such matters as 'Hughes,' Alioto, Chappaquiddick, Genovese, Bonnie Brussell, and Hoover! And again—in L.A., on July 21, 1972, where the Ellsberg-McNamara hedge cover-up of the Vietnam War—The Pentagon Papers—was about to be exposed.

And again, on the same weekend: National General's Sinatra, Klein, etc., and C. Arnholdt

---

[61] In 1975, after I wrote the *Skeleton Key to the Gemstone File* and Bruce had read it and liked it, he invited me one day to attend a S.F. meeting with him, at which Mark Lane was scheduled to speak. "Mark Lane will give his speech, and at the end, he will ask whether anyone in the audience has any information about the JFK assassination. But he knows me, and if I try to give him anything, he won't let me do it. So I would like you to go, and when he asks for information, go up and hand him your *Skeleton Key*. Okay?"
It didn't sound dangerous, so I wore an innocent-looking floating cotton frock, and at the end, when Lane asked for information, I tripped up there and handed him the *Skeleton Key*. He froze for just a second or two, then thanked me and went on. Much later, in 1979, when Larry Flynt was running around with his copy of the *Skeleton Key* wondering what to do about it, Mark Lane was at his side acting as *Playboy's* counsel. He probably did the censoring of the version ultimately printed. I'm sure he never mentioned that I had personally given him a copy in San Francisco way back in 1975.—sc2006.

Smith were all in San Diego.

"Waste 'em," says Helms. (San Francisco, L.A., San Diego.) "We're lucky. Let's get out of here. Who needs California, anyway?"

Tomorrow, my mother goes to Portland to try to find my brother, who is currently hiding in a closet in a National General office there—run by Thelma Golding, of the Mafia rattle death sympathy card that arrived after my father's murder. My mother's brother, my uncle, Kimball, drives from the Mexican border to the Canadian border, from San Diego to Seattle—circling away from San Francisco by way of Salt Lake City. His son, also Kimball, hides in Lagos, Nigeria—courtesy of Body Count Bundy, who now runs the Ford Foundation.

In San Francisco now, and throughout the next week, the last week before the Mafia Republican gang bang on Christ in Miami, are Earl Warren, former Supreme Court Chief at the time of Dallas; Burger, present Supreme Court Chief, and Onassis' "free ships" friend; the entire Mafia American Bar Association; and CIA Chief Helms.

Also present is former CIA Chief (at the time of the 'Holy Crusade' in Vietnam—through the double Diem-Kennedy murders) McCone, now from ITT and the world-wide Mafia rape; Kleindienst, Attorney General after Mitchell quit to run the Committee to Reelect Nixon, which employed the nine Mafia men to Bug Watergate; MacGregor, who took over that Committee after Mitchell quit to crawl up Martha's ass because she "had a story to tell".

Also, L. Patrick Gray, the new FBI Chief, Vatican replacement for apple-pie-murdered J. Mafia Hoover; Noel Gayler, Commander in Chief of All Pacific Forces, who apparently believes the war is being fought right here in San Francisco; and the regular San Francisco Mafia crowd: Genovese, Alioto, Lanza, et al; plus all of the thousands of fringe Mafia hoods that cluster around these Capos. Pope Montini might arrive himself to confer with Genovese, Alioto, Lanza and McGucken.

I expect Marie Elena Merryman—from the "Hughes" [Mormon] nursemaids group—to approach me at some lonely bus stop.

"Imagine seeing you here! Perhaps you have noticed that Jim's is too crowded these days to get in. There won't be any buses. I have beer at my place. It is spacious—baseball field size—overlooking Swig's Fairmont and the Nob Hill Square, and you can read Cardinal Spellman's works, and we'll talk of things like Onassis and Howard Hughes. We'll walk—to save money—since I know you don't have cab fare. Which is sad, because it is so easy to make money on the stock market."

We'll see. History does have a way of repeating itself.

For instance, Bill Moyers is here, and back in the newspaper business. He bought a local rag—the Progress. Moyers is an old LBJ Mafia; he was LBJ's Press Secretary when Johnson was the Mafia President. Johnson is intensely interested in stifling any San Francisco news. The Bay Guardian? Brugmann's Reformer Rag? Kennedy money bought that rag immediately after Chappaquiddick. "Eastern Money," Brugmann said, after reading all this.

Brave, free Americans. Flag, motherhood, and apple pie.

"The Jesuits keep me penniless, isolated and out of town," says a former Jesuit priest, John D. Roche, about L.A. Archbishop Manning, who said, "This is the usual condition for one who resists our order."

Haynes Johnson, *Washington Post*, said: "Despite publications such as the Pentagon Papers, no one has yet explained how America became involved in a war in a rural land so far away." (You have just read the explanation. And so have Dickie and Teddy (and all the little Teddies; Brezhnev, Chou, McNamara, Ellsberg, Nader, Montini, Onassis, and a long list around the world—most of whom I don't know.) "There has always been an air of inevitability about America's involvement in Vietnam. No one, no matter how powerful, seemed able to stem the tide."

The Jesuit Priest, Father Mootz—who sent me the Tisserant Papers, from the grave—explained this to me. Tisserant spelled it out plainly. What can Montini do to "crush" Father Mootz—or Tisserant—or Mary Jo—or my father? They're already dead. As you now know, it is a powerful tide. Onassis and Montini—and their "soldiers of the Mafia" and "soldiers of the church"—are running for election in the U.S. of Mafia. They are jointly in charge of both Mafia Parties—of Country, States and Cities—as planned at Apalachin.

They emerged from the Roosevelt-Joseph P. Kennedy-Onassis's World War II, which brought into reality a comic book vision of three little girls in Portugal in 1917: "The Three Secrets of Fatima", seized upon by the Church as a boost for its 'Holy Crusades'—and later by Onassis for his 'Holy Crusade'; it was a joint venture.

Today, around the world, entire Fatima churches and populations grovel in the Pennsylvania dust of Mary Jo's grave—along with Sister Lucy, the last survivor of those three little girls, who now reads comic books in Marcello's Louisiana Parish, while a wooden statue of Fatima—another reality from the comic book—weeps and weeps olive oil tears for the faithful Fatima followers.

In the U.S. of Mafia, nobody did anything about any of this since September 16, 1968, when I first turned it over to the bravest of the brave—beginning with Dickie. A total clamp went on me. From the Vatican and CIA to Charles Garry. From the President to Genovese-Alioto street cops.

This is why I performed the abortion on Body Count McNamara and Ellsberg—without the $400 million Betty Waterhouse proposed to use to give McNamara a giant one, in return for the brutal one he gave her long ago. McNamara, commissioned by Teddy after Chappaquiddick (and by Montini), to "get me out of this, as you got JFK out of the Bay of Pigs mess"—either ordered Ellsberg to release The Pentagon Papers as a cover-up hedge, or Ellsberg did it alone, knowing, like Oswald at Dallas, that he was the patsy for the "deeper fix."

After August 5, 1969, all of the crud of Chappaquiddick hit the fan. As it happened, the cover-up Pentagon Papers served a purpose. It fitted into a CIA style triangulation, like the crossfire at Dallas that blew off Kennedy's head. The three points were:

Johnson and Dickie ("We hang together or we hang separately—along with 'Hughes';

McGovern's instructions ("Pick up the Kennedy Banner as you did for Bobby after 1968; save the Kennedy political machine; we already have the loot");

McNamara-Ellsberg's cover-up version of the Viet war, the Pentagon Papers.

Chappaquiddick had blown the 'Holy Crusade' anyhow. So, release the cover-up version of the war. Release a little to save the whole. No one will get hurt; no Mafia, that is.

There was more crossfire—such as every Bishop and Archbishop and Cardinal rushing to the aid of Teddy, Daley and Alioto. Billy Graham and the Archbishop of Canterbury went to the aid of Dickie. Every Rabbi went to the aid of Golda Meir and Lansky. All this, to keep the lid on. Any or all could have exposed this whole mess—at any time—within the last 50 years.

Ellsberg couldn't care less. He's wealthy. His job is done: to get the Pentagon version of the Vietnam War accepted (like the Dickie-Onassis-"Hughes" myth)—in order to cover the "deeper fix."

After August 5, 1969, the Chappaquiddick cover was to be "anti-war"—or anti- anything else that happened overseas. Suddenly, Teddy, whose brother started it, was "anti-war." Ramsey Clark, who, as Attorney General, directed it—and whose pappy was one of Roosevelt's Mafia Supreme Court Capos—was suddenly "anti-war." Ellsberg, who drew up the Fatima #3 nuclear blow-off plans, and then drew up the McNamara "Pentagon Papers" cover-up, was suddenly "anti-war." Shriver, Dickie's French Ambassador, sanctioning Dickie's war policy, suddenly—after Chappaquiddick—became "anti-war"—and quit, and came back to defend Teddy. Catch 22 McGovern became violently "anti-war", and held Teddy's hand. Salinger, Mankiewicz—all of those in on the start of JFK-Spellman's (read Onassis-Montini's) Vietnam "Holy Crusade", were suddenly

"anti-war." Various fronts, such as Rudenstein's Peace Coalition, suddenly were "anti-war", as were ACLU and ADA and Common Cause. Anything to keep attention away from Chappaquiddick—and all that lies buried there: the cause of war, the cause of crime—back to the murder of Christ.

A quote: "Defending Ellsberg will top one million dollars in cost. It will be the most expensive trial in history. Ellsberg's defense expenses are running $80,000 per month. Since Ellsberg's July indictment, costs have been $400,000. Ellsberg's defense team includes thirteen lawyers at around $2,000 per month apiece, nine paralegal researchers, three professional consultants, five document researchers and six secretaries."

That's 36 high priced humans—plus financial backing for fronts ACLU, Common Cause, ADA—each and every one, like Nader, a protector of Teddy Kennedy, the murderer of Mary Jo at Chappaquiddick. "[Teddy] spends $3,000 per month for renting eight Bunker Hill Towers apartments. $2,000 per month for telephones. $10,000 per month for transcripts."

Me? My father was murdered. My half-murdered mother has run in fear to Portland to find my brother, who is hiding in a Mafia National General closet. The rest of the family is running away—all over the continent.

Buildings empty when I mention Chappaquiddick.

All of these mentioned above avoid the key to all war—Chappaquiddick—by chanting "anti-war."

Dickie, on the other hand, is "pro-war," while at the same time he runs "around the world for peace." Anything to keep attention away from Chappaquiddick, and all that lies buried there.

Betty Waterhouse

A week ago, I called Betty Waterhouse. I notified her that I had given her former boyfriend, Body Count McNamara of Mafia Heaven, the World Bank, and Ellsberg, a gigantic abortion, all by myself, in retribution for the savage abortion he had given her in Tacoma, on Green Street, in 1938.

She was indignant. "You didn't have to go that far. I hardly remember him."

That was odd, since, long ago, the idea was to use her $400 million to get even with him. But I did understand.

For, you see, she loves the Mafia, and gets personally signed checks from Dickie. Also, she runs a travel agency at the San Francisco Hilton. Remember Teddy McGovern's Kimelman's Virgin Island Hilton? The entire Supreme Court is now staying there, together with the Mafia ABA, Attorney General Kleindienst, and a host of assorted Mafia, from CIA to Genovese and Alioto.

That was a week ago. And I promised there would be a TV special for her—about Ellsberg, Kleindienst and the nine Mafia Supreme Court Justices. (Ellsberg and Russo were here three days later, scheduled for a Channel 5 TV special. But it was canceled.)

So I called her again last night and elaborated on the gigantic abortion.

Said she: "I arranged for a trip to Carmel for Kleindienst and his wife. They are so nice. We talked about trips to the wine country and other places, and I've talked to all of the other big people here."

Me: "I will be down at the Hilton next week to give some abortions to some of them. I'll stop and see you and tell you about it after it's done."

She, sweetly: "Why don't you stop by the travel place first? I am making money hand over fist on the stock market. You could do so well."

Me: "As well as McNamara and Ellsberg?"

She: "Much better."

Me: "But my business is abortions. Friends tell me that the stock market thing is due for an

abortion. So why should I mess with a sick cancer that's about to be cut out?"

She: "But cutting cancer out might kill the patient."

Me: "True. All doctors take that risk, with 100% human approval—even the Mafia. The cancer will kill the patient, so if the patient is dead anyhow, what's left to lose?"

She: "Well, stop and see me first anyhow."

That was last night. All messages get through. Today, Dickie's new Supreme Court Justice Powell—staying at Betty Waterhouse's Hilton—officially opened the ABA convention with a speech.

Said Supreme Court Justice Powell: "Destructive criticisms are threatening our institutions—and threatening our honor."

***

At Al Strom's Drift Inn, Perry's, Tiki Bob's, and Bill's Flagship, I have seen all five of the CIA Watergate buggers within the last nine months—roughly, since my Neilson-Green chats about Peking and Chappaquiddick Dickie, the Nader Assassination bit, and the Harry Yee $6 billion San Francisco heroin bit. I didn't know who they were until I saw their pictures in *Newsweek*, after the Demo Headquarters bugging.

About a month before my father's murder, as I walked into the Drift Inn, Elizabeth Dale whispered to two who were with her, "There he is." They looked at me for a while and then left.

Four escaped capture at Watergate, and later, apparently, helped jab Martha in the ass at Newport when she "had a story to tell." It stands to reason that if pictures of those other four ever come out, those two will be identified. One of them looked something like Frank Sturgis.

A quote from Don Freed's tape of Louis Tackwood, an L.A. Police informer: "James McCord is in on the concentration camp plan for dissenters. He's a stone killer. He was at Dallas. This man was talking about killing Nixon and blaming it on the liberals. Then Greeky Agnew would walk in."

One night Jim Lindberg was drunk and fell down. "Are you hurt?" someone said.

Jim: "Doesn't make any difference. I was dead 10 years ago."

Ten years ago is around the time of the Bay of Pigs and Dallas. I wonder why this batch of murderers turned up near me during the course of these events.

Said Jim to me one night, in jest: "We're all CIA. We murder when it's necessary."

Or, was it jest? He gave me a message on the night before my father's murder. He told me that something was going to happen to me that night, between 9:30 p.m. and 9:30 a.m. I thought he meant it would happen to me. But instead, it happened to my father—the next morning. Jim was also present when Howard Hughes' aunt, Kitty Lowry, first chatted with me. His partner, Cliff Jones, was present on the occasion of the next chat. Who knows?

The two with Elizabeth Dale—and these two—might be the missing four from Watergate. It doesn't really matter.

***

"You've got them all shook up," came a voice to me the other night.

Well, roll that "bugging" shit described on the previous pages around a little bit. Then add Tackwood's comments about McCord being in on the action at Dallas, and the Rand memo to Agnew about canceling elections, and McCord's "Kill Nixon; Agnew walks in; and put the dissenters in concentration camps."

Agnew was forced on Nixon by Onassis and Greeky Pappas. Nixon could have been dumped at the Convention, depending upon what the bugging of Larry O'Brien revealed about who was likely to be the Demo opposition, and whether Agnew or anyone else had a chance. But then they got caught in a bungling bugging.

It all speaks of desperation. Desperation about events in San Francisco, herein described; about China getting into the U.N.; that huge drug bust of Heroin from Thailand; and the details of "Hughes" and Chappaquiddick, which blows it all—including the assassinations in which they were involved.

Bernard Barker's citizenship was revoked 10 years ago. Sturgis (here, with Elizabeth Dale, a while ago) had his citizenship revoked 10 years ago, but it was later restored by Mafia Senator Smathers—a clear link, with Bebe Rebozo, between Johnson and Nixon and Onassis. When Castro took over Cuba from Batista, Barker and Sturgis were kicked out of Cuban casino gambling. Together with McLaney, minus $8 billion which belonged to Onassis.

Barker and Hunt were doing some dirty business in Nicaragua, where "Hughes" fled from the Bahamas. It all looks like Desperation.

Dickie, in desperation, is bombing the hell out of Vietnam, rigging the convention, and begging for "legal" Mafia suppression of the bugging investigation. Some other desperate moves: Mitchell's crawl up his wife's ass; Connally quitting; Romney quitting (saying, "Dickie faces grave political consequences"); and Maurice Stans, in hiding.

On the Demo side: Teddy's quitting and dash behind Mafia skirts; the purchase of Teddy McGovern; then the desperate move toward Eagleton, followed immediately by Eagleton's ouster, and the desperate refusal to run by Senators Humphrey, Muskie, Jackson, Nelson, Ribicoff, Church, and Carter, as well as Meier's Alioto and Boston's White.

Followed by the acceptance of Mafia Daley's Mafia Capo, Teddy Kennedy Shriver, and then everybody bellowing "anti-war": Teddy Ramsey Clark, Teddy Kennedy, Teddy McGovern, Teddy Shriver, Teddy Salinger, Teddy Mankiewicz, Teddy Ellsberg, and Teddy Nader.

Anything to keep the lid on. Ellsberg doesn't want his freedom on those terms, revealing Chappaquiddick and Fatima #3 Vietnam. He, like Oswald at Dallas, is dead—if they think anything gets out through him.

Montini rattles: "I have written a book. I want to quit. God has chosen me to suffer." And Reagan, Connally and Rogers rush to Rome to comfort the Pope. Morale boosted somewhat, he rattles: "We will crush anyone who interferes."

Teddy, Jackie, and Rosie fly to Rome to confer with the Pope. Lansky flies to Golda Meir for sanctuary. Desperation.

Waldheim, U.N. Secretary General, knows about all of this. He spits: "I am sick of the U.S. of Mafia taking world destruction into its own hands, and trying to destroy the U.N. I'm sick of Dickie running to Moscow, Peking, and around the world, with McNamara, Burns, Connally Reagan, and his entire cabinet, with the U.S. Senate and House leaders—buying, stealing, maneuvering, wheeling and dealing—privately, in his own behalf—while he bombs and mines the Chinese borders, propagandizes on all borders, and tightens the nuclear noose around the non-Mafia half of the world."

Desperation. Out in the open. Mafia Congress is frightened by Mafia Sinatra, and by Sinatra's National General loot that went to Dickie and Greeky Agnew. The nine member Mafia Supreme Court, having read these papers, will now hang Ellsberg on a new charge—or hang with him later on the same charge. They are here now, chaperoning the Mafia American Bar Association.

In Washington yesterday, 100 Senators (64 of them Mafia lawyers) voted down no-fault insurance, to preserve that billion-dollar insurance racket for themselves. Yesterday, the Mafia "Statute of Limitations"—10 years—on armored car robbery ran out; and the three Mafia Capos who pulled that huge robbery—identities known—now have $1.5 million to split up, free of charge.

The only collection of any stolen loot, by any U.S. of Mafia court, is now going on in Vegas, where Dickie's Justice—1,000 of them—are trying to recover $300 million, stolen from Onassis by many, because they knew about "Hughes." Lansky is collecting this $300 million to give it back to

his boss, your boss—Onassis.

The ABA is in San Francisco to legalize the gang bang on Christ in Miami. Alioto welcomed them all. U.S. Attorney (for criminal matters) gang rapist Ladar is in charge of entertainment for this Mafia cancer that writes Mafia law, and keeping the lid on the Constitution. U.S. Attorney Metzger, selling heroin out of Hallinan's office, was charged, again, with dope pushing. He is on one of the ABA's deliberative committees. He, too, has read these papers. U.S. Attorney James Browning, Jr.'s pappy James is a featured speaker. Attorney General Kleindienst speaks: "We have stopped all crime." And Betty Waterhouse ushers him around the neighborhood.

Former Attorney General Brownell and Superior Court Chief Burger, who gave Onassis his ships, speak—almost jointly: "Make the prisons more pleasant and make us judges happier."

Alioto: "I'm against high legal fees. Illegal fees? Now, that's different. We all do that, don't we, Burger?" as he rattles murdered Hoover's files.

Senator Byrd: "Judges are the only ones in the world—other than Mafia Popes, Mafia Dictators, and Mafia kings—who have lifetime jobs."

Mary Jo's grave in Wilkes-Barre is a mud puddle. Floods. Governor Romney won't give a dime in Federal money to the area.

Reagan and *Look*'s Henry Cowles and Frank Sinatra are together in Miami. Cowles hasn't left there since the Demo screw of Mary Jo while he was staying with Teddy's Harriman.

Chandler (L.A. Times owner) and Evelle Younger (California State Attorney General) covered up Bobby's murder by Onassis's Maheu, via Thane Cesar. Then they set up "Squad 19" for the Republican Mafia Convention at San Diego, since scrubbed by that Dita Beard Memo. Now they will do the same thing at the Patriarcha-Sinatra-Lansky Fontainbleu in Miami. This caused McCord, Barker, Sturgis, Gonzales, Martinez, Ferrar, Hunt, and Liddy to revamp their plans—and give me sour looks at Al Strom's Drift Inn. This is where Noel Gayler, Kitty Lowry, and assorted Mafia characters sometimes come to consult—me, apparently; what else would they be doing in a small San Francisco neighborhood bar?) At any rate, Chandler and Younger turned out to be crooks! Geotek. Surprised? A big newspaperman and a D.A.? Mafia? How could that be?

Ramsey Clark and Joan of Arc Jane Fonda said, as they read these papers about Teddy McGovern and Teddy Shriver: "Elect Teddy President and the North Viets will give us our POW's back."

Dickie and staff rig an "official" report which negates Nader's original charge about rotten Corvairs. Nader, who accepted his Onassis bribe and has now gone on toward Mafia heaven, couldn't care less if Dickie boots him in the ass.

"We've gotta get the power back from the Republicans," snarls Eunice Teddy Kennedy Shriver.

Congressman Riegle: "What difference does Congress make? It's a ship of fools that has nothing to do with the country where 210 million live...."

29 August 16, 1972: My Father's Murder

This is a summary of the murder of Verne Dayle Roberts, my father, by President Richard M. Nixon. This was my father's reward, because his son—me—exposed a number of things: The Mafia Election Process; the hyping of "Hughes", the bribing of Nixon, and the formation of the "Hughes" Mafia Money Funnel; the background and cause of Chappaquiddick; McNamara and Ellsberg's cover-up Pentagon Papers; Nader's Onassis bribe; Collapse of both Mafia Political Parties; Admission of China into the U.N.; exposure of various assassinations; Onassis-FDR-Joseph P. Kennedy War II machinations; Onassis-FDR Joseph P. Kennedy heroin and booze imports into Boston in 1932; The dissolution of the Vatican; Tisserant's papers.

It appears that most if not all of the Watergate crew, who at Dallas supplied timers for the synchronized cross-fire and rear guards to aid in the cover-up, and undoubtedly assisted in the same manner on Martin Luther King and Bobby, appeared to me (and to other friends) in a clump, during the months preceding my father's murder, at Al Strom's Drift Inn. This is at Bush and Taylor Streets, two blocks down the hill from the Onassis-McCone-Eckersley-Merryman mansion. And it is where Noel Gayler, National Security Council; Kitty Lowry, aunt to Howard Hughes, and assorted "UPI," CIA, Pentagon "vacationers," and Genovese-Alioto-Lanza Mafs frequently appeared for chats.

Jo Fulton, niece to Senator Proxmire and cousin to Senator Nelson, related also to Dickie's economic advisor, Paul McCracken, witnessed part of this. Other friends witnessed the rest.

Five of this group were arrested while bugging the National Democratic Headquarters at the Watergate in Washington. They were there to discover, for Dickie, whether Teddy planned to use his blackmail re: "Hughes," Onassis, and the murder of J. Edgar Hoover, to defeat Dickie, since that is the only way it can be done.

The Republicans fear that Teddy will "Quit and tell all" as he threatened to do on August 5, 1969.

For, if Teddy did this, or even released some of it, it would elect Teddy McGovern. And Teddy Kennedy has a blood pact with Teddy McGovern, and his father Onassis, and his father — Montini—and Teddy Kennedy would still be protected. Mafia wisdom: If your tit is in the wringer, you give a little, to save the whole.

Dozens of crime experts say: "In murder, there are no coincidences." Bearing that in mind, I recall the start of my father's 3-1/2 year torture murder. It started on the day after the hit-run on my car. Alioto's James McCracken began harassing my mother and father about me, while Alioto's godfather, Lanza, was ordering me off the street at the site of the hit-run. Then followed five more hit-runs on the car, and strange voices on my father's phone. Greenagel, Carlson, Bill Best and Mack read my papers in the kitchen. The insurance companies stiffed me on the car. My father's old Republican friends started running away from him. He noticed.

"Nader promised to come and see me. Where is he? Where are the others?"

Family arguments. Nerves frayed by worry

"When are Yablonski shotguns gonna burst in on us? Where are the Republicans and Nixon? We contributed for years, and campaigned for them."

Without any relief, already weak, he withered. That appeared on the death certificate as "Stress.' Murderous Stress.

But he was tough, and hung on. And so, just before Dickie's Peking trip, when the Watergate Five was here, and sometimes at the Drift Inn, looking at me, he suddenly belched blood and hydrochloric acid. That appeared on the death certificate as "Bleeding Ulcer."

Dickie's 1968 GOP Platform: "We will fight Russia and China—and all communism. We will never allow China in the U.N."

In the hospital, in February 1972, my father watched Dickie's landing in Peking, and said to me: "You did that. There is Dickie crawling to Communist China—begging. And China is already in the U.N."

"A miracle," said Doctor Kawala. "Your father can go home tomorrow."

That night my father told me (and my mother), "The guy in the next bed told me that something is going to happen to you tonight, between 9:30 p.m. and 9:30 a.m., so be careful."

Later that night, at the Drift Inn, Jim Lindberg asked me, "Do you know what's going on tonight?"

And I said, "Yes, between 9:30 p.m. and 9:30 a.m.," and he nodded and left.

(A month before, in the same place, about the time the Watergate Five was there, he sat down and announced to me "We're all CIA. We murder when necessary."

Expecting something to happen to me between 9:30 p.m. and 9:30 a.m., I stopped to talk to Betty Waterhouse—but nothing happened.

But my father's murder was complete the next morning at 11:40 a.m.

A month before my father's murder, Elizabeth Dale told me, "I might kill you myself. You have no right to play with the lives of millions."

The rat poison Maheu tried on Castro (and later used on Hoover and an Alioto trial judge—in mid trial) causes shortness of breath, lethargy, and heart failure.

Symptoms are not always noticed, particularly in older people, and the drug itself is untraceable.

Isoproterenol is a drug used in hospitals to relieve wheezing arising from spasms in the small tubes of the lung. It was used for my father via face-mask because of his emphysema.

In his last days in the hospital, he refused to use it; he fought it. It stimulates the heart, and overdoses can lead to irregular heart rhythms, which can be fatal.

Aerosol canisters, sold over the counter, contain five times the amount of Isoproterenol used in hospitals, and thousands of deaths have been attributed to them.

Quote Johns Hopkins researcher Dr. Stolley: "It is the worst therapeutic disaster on record. There's nothing else—even Thalidomide—that ranks with it."

(These five-times normal canisters are not sold in the U.S.)

At around 9:30 a.m., my father was in a King Ambulance, on the way home. He said, "I need air," and they gave it to him. An Isoproterenol canister.

He arrived home in a coma. Hasty calls to the doctor. He was rushed back to the hospital—where the murder was complete, at 11:40 a.m. That appeared on the death certificate too. "Heart Failure."

Stress, Bleeding Ulcer, Heart Failure. But his sickness was emphysema.

Three and a half years of Dickie torture hadn't killed my father. It took urgent means—at the time of Dickie's Peking trip. Dickie had much to hide. One more witness gone. And me with lots of grief—and trouble.

Anyone can walk into a hospital room and do anything. I wandered into several by mistake. Priests—or, at least, humans in priests' garb—pop in all the time. It was certain that my father, a very key witness to the most horrible crime in history, had no protection—quite unlike any Mafia political candidate.

He was murdered in the time period indicated, And I was told about it—one month before the murder—amplified by the presence of the Watergate Five, and the words of Elizabeth Dale. And all the time I knew that the torture murder had been under way, by Dickie, from an impersonal distant swivel chair, ever since September 16, 1968.

Stop! Right here. Think back to that date. Forget the murder, treason, genocide before then. Think only of the murder, treason, genocide since then—all of which could have been avoided. Including the murder of my father.

The Dita Beard ITT memo went out—via anonymous letter, on the afternoon of my father's murder.

My brother arrived, after three and a half years of begging, one hour after the murder, and delivered a Mafia message: "Yes, he was murdered, just as two others were, up my way, and as J. Edgar will be. You got what you wanted. Lay off Alioto."

He is a Mason, formerly married to a member of the Miami Cuban community [Marina Iglesias], and is now hiding in a Sinatra-C. Arnholdt Smith closet in Portland, Oregon.

Four hours later, having read these papers—without a thought, or a look, or a word about his murdered father—he disappeared, white-faced and running.

Months before the murder I offered to pay for his round trip, just to pick up these papers.

Said he: "No. If I come down there you are in more danger from me that you are from the Mafia. Lay off Alioto."

Me: "How did you know about that? I never told you."

No answer. So then I told him the whole story—especially "Hughes".

And that evening (this was in two recorded phone calls from me to Spokane, Washington), "Hughes" disappeared from the Bahamas and turned up in Nicaragua, where Hunt and Barker, who were at the Drift Inn with the Watergate Five, are in business.

Two weeks before the murder, on the day the blood and hydrochloric acid came up, I wrote a letter to my brother, laying out the entire thing and begging him to get here before his father's death.

No show.

A week later, I called. "Did you get my letter?"

He: "Yes. I burned it."

"Are you coming down before your father dies?"

He: "I don't know."

That was true. He didn't know. His timing was perfect. He arrived one hour after the murder was complete. He left, running, four hours later. No word since, for six months—except for one Mafia note to my mother—about me: "He's expensive."

September and October 1971: There was the Neilson-Green bit about "Chappaquiddick Big Dickie, Little Dickie, and Alioto"—a Peking phrase. Then Nader's cancellation of a third Political Party, and a "mistake" missile aimed at San Francisco. The FBI "invasion" to get the Harry Yee $6 billion in heroin out of town. Kissinger's sudden second trip to Peking, "to check on the agenda"— and zap! Dickie's 1968 platform is a shambles, China is in the U.N., Heroin Taiwan is out, and the Mafia Congress votes to destroy the U.N.

Me? I'm on my regular nightly route: Tiki Bob's, Drift Inn, Flagship, where effects show up. It was quite slow at the Drift Inn. Elizabeth Dale appeared, smelling of Hughes, CIA, ITT. Her apartment is nearby. She cashes $500 checks at the Drift Inn—signed "Gower."

She occasionally asks me questions, which I answer; about assassinations, heroin, Nader,

China, and gifts of stones, with history, by me, to POW wives, embassies, and certain well-known private parties.

Around Christmas, I gave her full details of "Hughes," Onassis, Chappaquiddick, CIA. Finally, she gets the 62-carat sapphire—with history. By now, she's bitter.

In late January, she says, "I might kill you myself."

***

30 Watergate 5 at the Drift Inn

And then they appear. The Watergate Five. I don't know them. But I do know when I see strangers—and I stare. In fact, on June 19, 1972, when Barker's picture appeared in the newspapers, it looked familiar, but I didn't connect it. The same with McCord. And Sturgis. But, last month, July, I saw a clear, side by side picture, and then it registered—since verified. They came in singly and in doubles—and they were all there at about the same time: one month before my father was murdered.[62]

McCord and Martinez came in together. I was sitting at one end of the bar, and they were around the bend, three seats away. McCord was seated, Martinez standing. (Look at their pictures. You will note that all have very distinctive faces—the kind you don't forget. If you are looking. And I, as you can imagine, was looking at everybody.)

Said Elizabeth Dale to me once: "You are nondescript." I've heard that many times. Like an old cat or an old shoe, nobody remembers.

Sturgis was sitting with Elizabeth Dale when I came in one day, and she whispered to him, "There he is," from around the bend. And I sat in the middle of the bar and looked at him and almost spoke, since he looked like Richey, the bartender at Canlis. And then Gonzales came from the rest room and sat two seats from me, on my right. He was drinking a cup of coffee, which, in a bar, is why I noticed him.

Sturgis shouted to Gonzales, "Finish your coffee and let's go." (Sturgis was wearing the same striped shirt that he was wearing in his arrest picture at Watergate.)

***

Barker came in alone. Twice. Both times, I was at the other end of the bar. Both times he stood back away from the bar in the center, in full view. He is very striking. The front third of his hair is missing but not like a normal bald person. And you automatically look for burn scars and there aren't any, and he combs the rest of his hair flat across the top. That's all. I had no real reason to remember them, then.

Secure and bold—all of them. But then, my father hadn't been murdered yet. Nor were the ITT memos released, which chased Dickie and the Mafia Republicans out of San Diego. They disappeared. And about then, Al Strom, Drift Inn Owner, was notified by Coldis, Alcoholic Beverages Board, that his bar license would be suspended soon, on a trumped up charge.

And suddenly, Al Strom—to whom I had also revealed details quoted herein—became "too busy," "don't understand," and "gotta go home."

Around June 18, 1972, the day of the Watergate arrests, a padlock went on the door of the Drift Inn—for 30 days, I think. It was just about the time those pictures of the Watergate Five were appearing in newspapers from coast to coast, for everyone to see—including me, and those other patrons of the Drift Inn who had seen them in person there.

At about the same time, my father was murdered and Elizabeth Dale disappeared, on February 22, 1972.

And then J. Edgar Hoover ate apple pie and was murdered. And the GOP Convention moved from San Diego to Mafia Miami. And the Watergate Five was caught in a desperate bugging attempt of the National Demo headquarters. And the other four who got away were desperately jabbing Martha in the ass to keep her from telling her story about "dirty things."

---

[62] Photo is of the former Drift Inn, in S.F., which was sold after Al Strom's death and became something else altogether.

> "The pictures at the top are the arrest pictures of the Watergate group. They match those taken at the Drift In. Liddy's and Hunt's were taken at the Drift In—Liddy's as he listened to this author quote the Chinese Stock Market quotes on murderers' ears—Presidents, Senators, Popes, Governors, Judges, Mayors, Legislators, and private Mafia branch members. It is the same laughter that he now laughs at Danbury Prison—knowing there is something worse on the way.. They appeared at the Drift In—to this author—looking as nearly as possible as they did at Dallas—to determine if any ...connection to Dallas were known. They murdered the author's father in conjunction with that and Dickie's Peking trip...and then murdered Hoover in conjunction with his "Texas Mafia." They were caught at Watergate—and the Drift In was padlocked to prevent possible recognition by patrons—of the arrest pictures....Mafia CIA cosmetics produced the pictures—bottom row—released from then on."

Watergate Team at the Drift Inn 1[63]

Some time ago—in early July—the Supreme Court ruled that they had no authority over the two Mafia Political Parties. Today Federal Courts ruled that no-one can sue the Republican or Democratic Parties.

Today Dickie ordered the courts and the press: "Don't mention that bugging any more. It will cause incalculable damage to me and the Republican Party."

"Incalculable Damage. If we disclose it, we cannot undisclose it." These are the reasons Justice prosecutors of Ellsberg gave for releasing him rather than reveal the single taped phone call—from Gordon to Ellsberg's attorneys—about these papers: Chappaquiddick Onassis, "Hughes," Heroin, Apalachin, Assassins, Mafia Election Process.

My words to Elizabeth Dale: "The plug has been pulled on all cancer—all of it." And I told her why and how—partially. And those five were a part of the things I mentioned.

Tackwood: "McCord is in on the cancellation of the election, some way, and the concentration camp thing. He's a stone killer. He was in Dallas when they got Kennedy. He was

---

[63] My apologies for the poor quality of this illustration. It was originally Page 33 of one of the early Skeleton Key drafts from 1975. And of course it was a Xerox copy of a Xerox copy that I got from Bruce Roberts directly in 1975.

talking about killing Nixon, blaming liberals, and letting Greeky Agnew walk in."

McCord was in charge—for Dickie—of "Emergencies, radicals and contingency plans in case of war." He specialized in "censorship of news media and U.S. Mail." He was a Contractor for Security of the Republican National Convention. Coordinator for Mitchell's Committee to Reelect the President. And with the CIA at the Bay of Pigs.

Barker: Lost his citizenship ten years ago. In business with Hunt in Nicaragua. In 1964, he handled CIA funds for Nicaraguan guerrillas. Prominent in Republican Party in Miami, related to the Cuban exile community. Handled funds for the CIA at Bay of Pigs. And also for the murder of JFK in Dallas. Handles funds—$114,000 known, now, for Dickie at Watergate, plus unknown amounts for the murders of my father and J. Edgar Hoover. Affiliated with Maheu's Castro assassination crew. Barker was in Batista's secret police, running Onassis-Lansky gambling with McLaney in Cuba until Castro appropriated $8 billion and kicked them all out—including Dictator Batista. He stole the plans of the Mafia convention hall in Miami.

Sturgis: Lost his citizenship in 1960. It was regained later for him by Mafia Senator Smathers. Sturgis was the overseer of Havana gambling for a while after Castro took over, and then Castro kicked the entire Syndicate out: Onassis, Lansky, McLaney, Barker, Sturgis—everybody, and stole their $8 billion cash. This led to the vengeance of the Bay of Pigs, and the Maheu assassination crew. Sturgis was questioned with regard to JFK's murder in Dallas. He had an arsenal and was a member, with David Ferrie, of the Miami-Houston-Havana group named by independent researchers as involved with John F. Kennedy's murder. He was a key CIA figure in the Bay of Pigs invasion.

Martinez: Fought with Castro; then became an anti-Castro guerrilla. Worked with exiled Cuban Miami group in military training. Works for Barker's "real estate" office in Miami and YAF in Miami.

Gonzales: Former Cuban; now a locksmith in Miami. Can open any lock—on homes, drugstores, Isoproterenol lockers, say, for substitution in pills or apple pie, of inorganic ingredients. Even door locks on waiting ambulances.

Check back: Onassis, Cuban gambling; kicked out. In on Bay of Pigs. In on Maheu's rat-poison apple pie assassination attempts on Castro. In on Dallas and JFK. Possibly employed at the time of my father's murder, during Dickie's critical Peking period. And I was coldly notified in advance. "What the hell can you do about it, chump?"

He's safe, because the power lines go direct to President Richard Nixon, in the distant swivel chair—the thing that I elected in 1968—and Mitchell's Committee to Reelect Nixon.

Arthur Bremer mentioned a secret $10 million sum. "Hughes"—in a Maheu memo in late 1968—mentioned a secret $10 million sum. This year Dickie's Commerce Secretary Stans announced a secret $10 million dollar sum. ITT Chilean funds, run through Mexico, to Stans and then to Barker's bank account.

Tackwood: "The man over McCord, the stone killer, is Hunt. Nobody's over Hunt but the top dogs—Nixon and Mitchell."

Hunt has disappeared. He is a 21-year CIA Capo. Director of the Bay of Pigs action. Conduit of CIA money. Senior member of the "Special Task Force" during two national emergencies. White House participant of Security Conferences. Hunt is a partner of Senator Bennett's son—Robert Bennett, of Mullen Public Relations firm. Bennett's group, "The American Dream," refuses to disclose the source of Nixon's $10 million secret reelection fund.

Robert Mullen is the founder of the CIA YAF—along with Douglas Caddy, now attorney for the Watergate Five.

G. Gordon Liddy, Ex FBI: Another Committee attorney. He refused to testify; took the Fifth Amendment. Part of the Committee to Re-Elect the President under John Mitchell, who quit the

Attorney General job to take the Committee job; and then, after the murder of my father and J. Edgar Hoover, quit that job in order to crawl up his wife's ass in fear because Martha said, "I have a story to tell. I know dirty things. I am a political prisoner. What country can I go to?"

You have just read Martha Mitchell's story. Those Mafia Capos murdered my father, from Nixon—for three and a half years. It came down to a month of rat poison and Isoproterenol—in foreign canisters. They were paid killers—as on Castro, and JFK at Dallas, King in Memphis, and Bobby in L.A.

"When the CIA and Rand Corporation (Ellsberg's firm) can systematically set up a dictatorship in Greece and Saigon, it is folly to think that it hasn't happened here." A quote from Paul Krassner.

This group did not murder Mary Jo Kopechne. Teddy did that all on his own—for the same reason. And this group covers it up for the same reason.

A quote from me: If, for the same cover-up reason, they "wasted 'em" at Abrams' Acres; My Lai, Vietnam; and with U.S. of Mafia murder, on assassination row: old men, little girls, young men, old girls, here at home, it is folly to doubt that "mistake" missiles are poised, as on July 11, 1972, at 3:26 p.m. (in Garry's office), and October 8, 1971, at 1:32 p.m., had Nader actually arrived in San Francisco to form a consumers' third party. (That's 60 million automatic votes; and he had led in every poll in which his name was listed, by far).

Varieties of Death

CIA-FBI Maheu and his associates tried five types of murder on Castro, from rat poison to sniper rifles.

It was a Crossfire and Patsy Oswald at Dallas for JFK.

A sharpshooter plus Patsy James Earl Ray, plus cover-up including the ABA, were used at Memphis for MLK.

Mind-bending hypnosis on Patsy Sirhan Sirhan and a back-up "security guard" assassin were used in L.A for RFK.

Mind-bending was used on Patsy Arthur Bremer for George Wallace—but there was no back-up.

For my father, it was three and a half years of mental torture, then rat poison, in a pill slipped into his pill bottle by a skilled locksmith, followed by an Isoproterenol overdose—one shot—on his way home.

Mafia Attorney General Ramsey Clark, back from Hanoi: "I get mad when I get kicked around. I believe in bringing out the truth. I believe in Justice. Little girls and old people are being murdered in Vietnam. Elect Teddy McGovern and the Kennedys to the presidency and we will end the Vietnam War."

Kleindienst, Attorney General (from Mafia ITT, Committee to Reelect Richard Nixon) at the Mafia ABA here: "All protesters have the same access to courts as we do. Anyone can go to our courts and get justice. That's the great magic of America. Nowhere else on earth do the people have the same right to protest and the right to due process as they do here."

Today he suppressed publication of Shirley Chisholm's Congressional bill for the impeachment of Nixon. Today he ordered massive arrests for any disturbance at the Mafia Republican Convention. Today he asks the court to block all investigation of the Watergate Five murderers.

Today, McCloskey moaned, "It is the coronation of King Richard. No one else can raise a voice. Not even me—or my one delegate."

Today, Kleindienst: "I graciously have torn up Joan Fonda's treason indictment." As with

Ellsberg, he knows that Jane Fonda has these papers.

Today, ITT-CIA, Double Diem-Kennedy murderer McCone is listed as a simple executive for an L.A. firm: Hendy International Co. He is in charge of raising $156 million in bonds from the public for training new doctors. Like Teddy, he is concerned with the health of people.

Today, back East, Clifford Irving says he has much new evidence about "Hughes" to disclose—but he can't. U.S. Attorney Seymour and Justice prohibit him from saying anything other than what they agreed upon in their secret deal in Mafia D.A. Hogan's office. He did squeeze off one irritating statement: "I believed the hoax would work because Hughes would never be able to surface to deny anything." (He refers to the surface of the Mediterranean, off Greeky Onassis' island of Skorpios, where Howard Hughes was committed to the deep on April 18, 1971.)

Today, Ellsberg—freed from prison by these pages—taped a TV interview in San Francisco. He is back on his original job for McNamara: exposing the cover-up of the war, The Pentagon Papers—in a limited hang-out sort of way—and working to elect Teddy McGovern President. Said Ellsberg: "The way to end this war is to elect Teddy McGovern."

Today, Attorney General Ramsey Clark echoed Ellsberg: "The way to end the war is to elect Teddy McGovern." Ramsey, Attorney General for Johnson, squatted on the lid of the hit-run that elected Dickie until Mitchell took over, four months later. And then, at Chappaquiddick, he leaped actively to Teddy's defense

As in 1968, six days before the election, with Johnson's bombing halt, the War (featuring pro-war Dickie vs. anti-war Teddy) will be used for a rigged election for one of the two Mafia murderer candidates.

The Watergate Five—and the rest of the assassins, all the way up to thousands of distant swivel chairs, are back in the act—the exposure of which resulted in the murder of J. Edgar Hoover, and my father. And here it is right back in the gutter of San Francisco, where Alioto's Genovese squashed Bonnie Brussell.

***

Earl Warren accepted heading the Warren Commission on Dallas because LBJ told him: "Millions of people would be killed in an atomic war if we don't keep the lid on." And Warren accepted that—and covered the truth for LBJ.

Just before Mitchell quit and crawled up his wife's ass, he said, "The lives of millions are at stake—probably all of us."

ITT Elizabeth Dale (62-carat sapphire up President Patty's ass) told me, "I might kill you myself. You have no right to deal with the lives of all these people." (The ones who climbed on my back on September 16, 1968—murdered Mary Jo, my father and thousands.)

Johnson and Mitchell don't mind sacrificing all of you—as long as they survive. Dickie, Teddy, Onassis, Montini—all the Maf subscribe to this. As I said to a hummingbird at my father's grave, and to CIA Betty Waterhouse—who, last time, advised me how easy it would be for me to make a fortune on the stock market: "I'm not dealing. I believe in equal justice. For all of us. Torture for a few? I want everybody in on the fun."

Mae Brussell—mother of five—Monterey—incensed at JFK's murder—researched for nine years about that assassination—and the others. She currently broadcasts a program from radio station KLRB in Carmel. (Off in left field—she is permitted to do this, but she now issues a "Conspiracy Newsletter" and she hits close to home on some things. Once, last year, she mentioned "Howard Hughes." And again, the FBI-CIA-Dallas police and Mafia at Dallas.) Her program: "Dialogue: Assassination."

For instance, she quotes: "These conspiracies and plans to control elections in the U.S. were aided by the Supreme Court. Judges, lawyers, and carefully selected legal staffs." [And here she

speaks of the key: the Mafia election process—first proposed by the top Mafia—Vito Genovese, who welcomed Allied troops to Sicily, and later set up Apalachin for Onassis. Even Salerno, of N.Y., admits this. Vito Genovese is dead now. His son is a dentist in South San Francisco.][64]

"The script for the conspiracies was written by Allan Dulles, Helms of CIA, and J. Edgar Hoover's Division V of the FBI."

She ignores Onassis, Joseph P. Kennedy, Montini, Spellman, McCone, Vietnam, Fatima 3. It happens that she loves Kennedys—and Popes. According to her, everything is a plot to keep Saint Teddy from being President.

"Teddy's car was pushed into the Pond—by Dickie—to embarrass Teddy. He never was in it. Tests prove that no one could have opened that door or gotten out of the car. The National Safety Council says: "Our records show that no one—by himself—has ever escaped from a submerged automobile."

She blames the conspiracies—and assassinations—on a military-industrial group composed of Americans and leftover Nazis like Gehlen. Mae Brussell loves Teddy, and Montini, with a passion. Last year, just before Christmas, Teddy and Montini brought the Chappaquiddick cancer to her doorstep. The murder of her daughter Bonnie Brussell was late last year.

These things are daily bread. Last night, Genovese's Di Lorenzo went into the East River in New York, and one of his capos went up Boots Boiardo's New Jersey fire place chimney—in fumes. Di Lorenzo, serving ten years for stealing securities—like all Mafs—Dickie's J. Arnholdt Smith Alessio, for instance—gets out of his country club prison for weekends and outings. Yesterday, he didn't come back to his prison apartment. He knows too much…correction, knew too much.

He and one other Maf were indicted with Alioto's Teamster Fire Commissioner Capo—Rudy Tham—for extorting a couple of hundred thou. Indicted in New York. Yesterday, Mafia Tham routed a change of venue through the N.Y. Maf Supreme Court. (All nine of these N.Y. Supreme Court Justices paid Genovese $100 thou for their jobs. Of the nine, five have already been convicted of crimes from murder to stealing—convicted, and released, with no sentence. Let's see: Fraiman, Schweitzer—I forget the other three. Yesterday, a sixth one, Supreme Court Justice Thaler, was convicted of stealing and selling $800 thou of Treasury bills. He was promptly released from jeopardy.)

Change of venue for Tham? Back to San Francisco. Where one of the Genovese-Alioto-Lanza Judges, who found Genovese's murder of Bonnie Brussell to be "leaving the scene of an accident"— (Fine: $59)—a la Teddy at Dyke Bridge, and Mafia patsy nursey Hollister at Alioto's hit-run on me, will rule on the matter.

Vice Presidents: Pappas and Onassis—from Greece—dictated to Dickie, via "Hughes" and Mafia loot for the 1968 presidency—including odd batches from Dallas Maheu to Rebozo—that Greeky Agnew be the V.P.—available, by one gut shot, as President.

"And," said Agnew, "the Greek Mafia that held the coup in 1967 has not proved to be as horrible as most people thought it would be. So, is it so bad that the benevolent Genovese Mafia rule here? We set it up in Saigon, Taiwan, Brazil. They're not bad. So we have it here. Relax. We're benevolent Mafia. We only murder when we decide it's necessary. Enjoy your economy. Eat liver, and apple pie."

Mary McCrory: "After a month, the Demo Committee has decided that—bad as he is—Teddy McGovern is all we've got—and we can't play games, since the real enemy is Dickie. Fear of Teddy Kennedy sweeping the ballot—despite his frantic retreats—forced those silly seven hours of nomination at Miami—and Eagleton. Eagleton's exposure then shocked everybody—Eagleton, all

---

[64] Picture is Mae Brussell, JFK researcher from Carmel Valley, CA.

the way loose, and Teddy McGovern all the way to his Catch 22 Kennedy bones."

And Montini-Onassis-Kennedy Mafia skirts enfold Teddy McGovern in Holy Crusade robes. Richard Goodwin, Kennedy speech writer, writes McGovern's new V.P. nomination speech—and voila! Cocoon Teddy McGovern emerges a full Mafia Montini-Onassis-Kennedy butterfly. Finally, with Eunice Kennedy, and hubby—who? At the end of the shitty stick.

A new quote: "The search for Teddy McGovern's V.P. started with Teddy Kennedy and ended with a Teddy Kennedy—Shriver. As with Agnew gut shot backing up Dickie—for Onassis—Teddy Eunice Kennedy Shriver backs up Teddy McGovern."

***

President Dickie is a devout Quaker. "No killing." Billy Graham is also devout. "No killing." Kleindienst is a bishop in his church. The real Teddy can be a bishop in his church any time he likes. His Mafia Mama, Rosie, is a Papal Princess. Ramsey Clark is angry at Viet murder (but not Mary Jo's). Jewish Swig is a Papal Knight and a Shriner. Half-Jewish Montini is the Pope. What is Greeky Onassis? Rabbi Golda Meir sleeps with Rabbi Meyer Lansky.

The 1972 election will be a Mafia horror contest. After it's over, a nation will go back to contributing its 41% to the cancer, and kneeling piously in church. Before a festering, empty cross.

It is interesting to note that Al Strom's Drift Inn—where the Watergate Five, for sure, and the other four, probably, had collected to conduct my father's murder—was padlocked after pictures of the arrest of the Watergate Five appeared in the newspapers. The reason was to forestall recognition by habitués—or any discussion thereof.

And the frightening of Al Strom, the owner. Murder warnings by Jim Lindberg and Elizabeth Dale, a month before my father's murder, did not go unnoticed. Murder warnings, out of the blue—from Elizabeth Dale, who at least had a free 62-carat heart-shaped sapphire.

And from Lindberg—out of the blue: "We're all CIA; we murder when necessary. I like Alioto." And from Lindberg, again, the night before the final blow.

***

June 18, 1972: The Watergate arrest was on June 18, 1972. Strom's Drift Inn was padlocked.

July 5, 1972: Two weeks later, my second car was rigged—wheels and transmission—in a Tahoe parking lot (described earlier). It was ruined. No transportation for checking on those pictures at the Drift Inn (and it was padlocked), or anywhere else.

Elizabeth Dale disappeared, of course, after my father's murder. Everybody from that group disappeared. Except Jim Lindberg. As at Dallas, he was the back-up cover-up. I had stopped in at Strom's just after Ellsberg got word of the single phone call wire tap that got him out of prison.

July 24, 1972: (Al Strom had just reopened.) That was the day the Genovese-Alioto-Lanza cops spread-eagled me on Montgomery Street. And so, within minutes, there was Jim Lindberg, two seats away, just staring; and then he left.

August 16, 1972: A month later, I stopped in again and discussed the Watergate Five, who had been there, with Al Strom, and Elizabeth Dale's sudden disappearance. And Al was suddenly "busy." And Jim walked in again, and sat two seats away.

Me: "You're all dressed up and have a fistful of cash. You must work for the CIA."

No answer. Then to me, he said: "I'd like to kill every Irishman. No Irishman ever brought anything but grief to this country—starting with that bitch, Bernadette Devlin."

Me: "But they gave us Teddy Kennedy, and his pappy, Joseph P. Kennedy. And Teddy wants us to go over to Ireland and kill for the Pope. And they gave us Hanrahan and Daley in Chicago, who kill black Irishmen like Hampton and Clark. And they gave us McCord of the Watergate Five, who…." And Jim was gone.

September 23: Phone Calls to Spokane

August 16, 1972: I made two lengthy calls to Spokane.[65] Reason: to notify my brother of the critical condition of his father. Over a telephone that had been tapped ever since the date of the hit-run, 3-1/2 years earlier; the inception of the murder of the father of the man (me) who had elected Dickie to the presidency.

Subject of the calls: the entire thing—"Hughes," Chappaquiddick, all of it: the reason for the murder.

Dickie was just taking off for Peking on a "world search for peace."

The man being murdered had six days left to live. And the timing was just after the California Supreme Court had suddenly, surprisingly, against all legislative law, and the wishes of 70% of the electorate, lifted the death penalty for any crime—including treason, genocide and murder. All criminals were then free to murder, and all innocents became helpless victims.

The phone calls were made in the morning, and dealt largely with Onassis-"Hughes" and Montini.

That afternoon the entire Onassis-"Hughes" mob moved from the Bahamas to Nicaragua, home of Watergate's Barker and Hunt. Hunt had been sponsored to his high White House position by rabid Vatican representative William Buckley, who was the Godfather of Hunt's three children, and who advocated scuttling the U.N. when China was unexpectedly voted in.

September 2, 1972: Two more private assassination investigators were notified of the entire thing.[66]

September 12th: another long distance call was made, over the same tapped phone, to one on Onassis' island of Skorpios. This call was about the Tisserant papers, the murder of Pius XI, and Montini's vault to the "summit of the Church". And about the Mafia chieftains—Montini and Onassis—who filled the power void in mid-Europe after War II.

At the time, the Mafia spurned the Golden Triangle heroin bit that later became the joint Montini-Onassis "Holy Crusade" in Vietnam," symbolized by Marseilles' Guerini. (Some of these facts escaped the Montini-Onassis' heroin-pushing CIA and appeared in McCoy's Politics of Heroin in Southeast Asia.)

The Watergate-Vatican affair was hot. There was one criminal suit, adequately bottled up by the Mafia Justice Department. But there were also three private suits, naming nine defendants, including the captured Watergate five: Barker, McCord, Martinez, Sturgis and Gonzales—which some Democrats planned to bring to court prior to the Mafia 1972 election.

September 19, 1972: And so, on September 19, there was another long distance call, casually mentioning the fact that all of the captured Watergate Five had been in the Drift Inn, San Francisco, just prior to the murder of the father of the man who elected Dickie.

And also that Elizabeth Dale, there with Sturgis and Gonzales, had pointed out the hit-run victim (me) to this group. And that Elizabeth Dale had been given President Patty's 62-carat heart-shaped sapphire, with the entire history. And also that Elizabeth Dale was the ex-wife of Francis L. Dale, who was a co-chairman, with Stans, of the Committee to Re-Elect Nixon—and whose name had been carefully deleted from any mention in this affair.

Elizabeth Dale, constantly around for months prior to the murder of the father of the man

---

[65] To Bruce's brother, Dayle Roberts.
[66] I have a strong feeling that one of these was Mae Brussell. This was the last paper in the series that Mae received. My guess is that Roberts called her, and made an appointment, probably for her to visit him in San Francisco, later in the month. She was due in San Francisco for an interview with a radio station. Meanwhile, Roberts continued writing this paper, a portion of his daily journal. Her meeting with him is described by her in Chapter 36.—sc2005

who elected Dickie, disappeared, like Dita Beard, on the day when the murder was complete—which was the day the Dita Beard Memo went out.

Francis L. Dale was a V.P. for ITT and sat at the side of ITT V.P. McCone, who headed the CIA at the time of the double Diem-Kennedy murders.

On the following morning the Democrats hastily dropped their civil suit against the Watergate Five who were actually captured red-handed—the five named in that phone call. Left in that civil suit were Liddy and Hunt, who were also positively present at the break-in—and Stans and Sloan, who manipulated the Mafia Presidential cash (elaborated upon in great detail by J. Edgar Hoover in his book, *The Texas Mafia*—suppressed, of course, since his murder).

***

So now I'll tell you about my one-way conversation with Liddy, about 'Hughes' and "Chappaquiddick." He frowned and smiled, and then smiled some more. That was also at the Drift Inn. Same time as the others. And Hunt was there, with three others.

And while I'm at it I may as well tell you about the "missing" money channels—which parallel the Henry Yee heroin routes: Singapore, Hong Kong, San Francisco and Chicago—and why they call Dickie the biggest dope pusher in the world. And why he takes the rap for Onassis and Montini. That was on the afternoon of September 20, 1972.

That evening a message was delivered—loudly—at the Drift Inn, that Francis L. Dale, Elizabeth's ex-husband, was about to be arrested for the Watergate affair. And on the next day, September 21, 1972, an unusual 5-1/2 hour conference was held in Washington. All of the Mafia attorneys for both Mafia parties—and the Mafia judge, who was originally selected from that group of Mafia attorneys, and appointed to the Federal Bench by one of those Mafia parties—met in secret and announced a surprising agreement.

Quoth Mafia Judge Ritchie: "We will drop all civil suits of any nature against anyone involved in Watergate and allow only the criminal trial," (conducted by the Mafia Justice Department, of ITT, Chappaquiddick and "Howard Hughes" fame) "to continue. It will be held in total secrecy, and it will not be held until after the election."

Quoth Kleindienst: "Well, it will take months just for any legal preparation at all."

Quoth a columnist: "That's odd. The Mafia Democratic Party convened the Supreme Court—in four hours—to rule on a Democratic Convention question. But the Supreme Court ruled—in one hour—that they had no authority whatsoever over either Mafia party! Who then does have any authority? Onassis and Montini?"

"All right," said another columnist. "Why doesn't Teddy—and his Senate Judiciary Committee—call for an immediate hearing? They can do that tomorrow."

From Teddy: "No comment."

Again, the columnist: "Why not a Congressional hearing, before any committee? They have subpoena power and can do it tomorrow."

From all the Mafia Congressional Committee Chairmen: "No comment."

END OF MAE BRUSSELL'S PORTION OF BRUCE ROBERTS' "GEMSTONE FILE" LETTERS AND PAPERS.

Part III—Where I Came In

31 October 1974-Spring 1975: A Cross for Mary Jo

I was living on Prosper Street in San Francisco, had just completed a new article on Chappaquiddick for *Playgirl*, and had sent it in to the editor, Marin Milam. She told me the lawyers were looking at it. And I was waiting for the December issue of *Playgirl* to emerge with our "Howard Hughes/Onassis" article.

Along with his verbal "Gemstone" talk, Roberts had given me a "note from the teacher," authorizing me to go to six foreign consulates in San Francisco to read more recent Gemstone letters than the portion of the File that Mae had, which roughly covered the period from mid-1971 through August, 1972. He assured me that these consulates had recent letters and would cooperate with me. Particularly, he said, Pavlov at the Russian consulate would be nice to me, and that I would like him.

I was frankly hooked on Gemstone, and felt quite frustrated that I had no more recent letters to read. So I reluctantly began working my way down the list of six embassies. I began with the Japanese consulate, but was told that the man in charge was not there at the moment. I then turned to an Arab consulate. This turned out to be a small dingy office, and the man at the desk seemed more interested in what I might be willing to trade than in letting me read any Gemstone letters. That didn't work for me.

One day, in desperation, I went to the Russian Consulate. This was a magnificent mansion, set well back on a green lawn. I parked on the street and walked toward the building. A man was watering the lawn of the mansion next door. He raised the nozzle of the hose and aimed it straight at me, and I had the distinct feeling that I was being photographed. Well, what the hell!

I went into the building and asked at the reception desk for Mr. Pavlov. I was ushered into a large luxurious office, and there was Mr. Pavlov himself. He asked me very courteously why I had come. I told him my name and pulled out my note from Bruce Roberts.

"Bruce Roberts told me I could read some Gemstone letters here," I said.

Pavlov looked at me in amazement, and said, "I can't help you. This is not a lending library."

He ushered me to the door in a flash, and I was out of the Russian Consulate about 90 seconds after I went in.

Well...so much for Mr. Pavlov and the Russians. Three down, and three more to go.

Meanwhile, the December *Playgirl* issue came out, with my article on Hughes and Onassis. I didn't identify my major source as Bruce Roberts. I called him "Tiger Eye," an oblique reference to a Gemstone. Much as Woodward and Bernstein called their "anonymous" source "Deep Throat," a successful cover for their real major source, Katharine Graham, owner/editor of the *Washington Post*.

The next name on the list was the Norwegian consulate. At least they were neutral. I asked at the reception desk whether I could read Bruce Roberts' letters. To my amazement, the woman at the reception desk politely ushered me into a large, comfortable reading room and brought me a nice new long letter by Bruce Roberts, addressed to the leader of Norway.

She allowed me to read through the rest of the afternoon, and take notes. I had brought a loose-leaf notebook with me. I began picking out items from the single fourteen-page letter they had given me to read, and writing them down in my notebook in rough chronological order. I felt I was in journalist's heaven. At the end of the day, the receptionist politely approached me and told me they were closing for the day, but I could come back the next day and continue my reading. I left,

very happily.

I went back the next morning, but the situation had completely changed.

This time, a man who definitely seemed to be in charge told me that I could not possibly read any more of Bruce Roberts' letters; they belonged to Norway. I told him I was deeply disappointed. I said it was a sad state of affairs when I, an American citizen, had to go to the Norwegian Consulate to find out what was going on in my own country.

He thawed, and asked me what I thought of Bruce Roberts. I said I thought he was a good and brave man, who had a lot of good and necessary information.

Then he asked me whether I had seen the new article in *Playgirl* on Hughes and Onassis.

"Have I seen it? I wrote it," I said.

He told me that Bruce Roberts had told him about the article, and recommended it to him, and that he had read it, and liked it. Then he took down my address, and phone number. He told me that he couldn't understand why Roberts was giving the Norwegians this information. "What has all this got to do with Norway?" he wondered.

I said I had no idea, but I was sure Bruce Roberts had a reason.

On impulse, it seemed, he pulled out a fourteen-page letter from his pocket.

"I can't let you read any more letters that are the property of Norway," he said. "But Bruce Roberts just gave me another letter. And I haven't turned it over to Norway yet. So since it is still my own property, I can give it to you to read. Why don't you take this letter, read it, and write down any references to Norway that you can find, and then bring it back to me?"

I agreed, and he then handed me the letter (a xerox copy of the original.) I took it home, read it, noted the few mentions of Norway in the letter, then returned his copy to him.

Shortly thereafter, I noted that my phone had been tapped. This was in the relatively early days of phone taps, and this was not a particularly sophisticated tap. Every morning, my phone would ring, and someone, male or female, with a strange accent, would ask for "Sven" or "Olaf," or something like that. I knew the phone was tapped, but I didn't know who was tapping it. I assumed it was a U.S. "security" (i.e., eavesdropping on American citizens) agency. On several occasions, while talking to friends, I mentioned that the phone was tapped, and that it had to do with Bruce Roberts. After a while, they took off the tap.

At one meeting with Bruce Roberts, he mentioned that the Norwegian Consul had told him I was a nice girl.

"Oh! So that's who's been tapping my phone!" I said.

Most of the material in the original *Skeleton Key* was extracted from letters written in late 1974-1975, which I did not own, and only had the chance to see once. My original impulse was to understand the letters myself, and it helped me to try and make some sort of chronological sense out of them. Roberts was not only a mental giant and a powerful writer, but also a sort of poet. He presented his material incrementally, over a period of time, so that one seldom got the whole story at once. I had to put the details together in chronological order to make sense out of the puzzle.

Writing the *Skeleton Key*

Bruce called me on March 15, 1975, and told me he was in the University of California Hospital, with a strange ailment which he claimed was CIA-induced. I went to see him in the hospital. I was terrified that he might be killed in the hospital. I had read his story of the death of his father in the portion of the file I saw at Mae's. I had the quixotic idea that somehow I might protect him if I sent out some copies of my chronological notes to the press. That is, if people were trying to kill him to prevent him from spreading such information, they might hesitate if the information got out in some other way. I typed up a copy of the handwritten notes I had made at the Norwegian

Embassy. This was the first time the notes made it into typed form. It turned out to be 23 pages, single-spaced. I typed my name, address, phone number, and the date: April 3, 1975, at the top of the first page. I made 30 copies or so, and mailed a bunch of them out to major media: newspapers, TV, etc. And I also gave copies to friends and sold a few for $3.00, enough to cover the Xerox costs. When Bruce got out of the hospital, I told him what I had done. He seemed to understand why I had done it, and to approve, and of course I gave him a copy to read. He corrected the outline in several places, and meanwhile I added more information that I got from him. This was long before the PC revolution; we still had typewriters!

It was a very scary time and ultimately tragic. I also remember, quite vividly, giving a copy of the *Key* to Paul Krassner, editor of the *Realist*. This was at some open-air rally, which I had attended at Roberts's request. Roberts asked me to bring some copies of the *Skeleton Key* to pass out. Krassner was there, and Bruce told him to get a copy from me. I handed a copy to Paul, who took it rather sourly, and said, "Bruce Roberts is a pain in the ass."

I think Paul was annoyed that Bruce had told him to get a copy from me. Instead of giving him a copy, I insisted that he pay me $3.00. I was annoyed too. My thinking was that the cost of making the copies was coming out of my pocket, and I didn't have that much money. I guess his thinking was that as a well-known professional journalist, people were supposed to give him free copies of things, and of course usually did. Anyway, he now doesn't remember any of this, and doesn't remember getting a copy from me at all.

Some time later on, I heard that he was employed by *Hustler* as a guest editor. That sounded good, and as though some real money must have changed hands. Around that time, *Hustler* published its nude photos of Jackie O bathing on Skorpios. When I heard that *Hustler* had offered $1 million for information leading to the identification of JFK's murderers, and had published a much abbreviated version of the *Skeleton Key*, I jumped to the conclusion that Paul had given Larry Flynt a copy of the *Skeleton Key*. In a phone call I made to Paul in 1995, at his home in Desert Hot Springs in California, he denied this, and I guess that he just dumped his early copy into the toilet or whatever. He also told me that his stint at *Hustler* had been extremely brief and unsatisfactory for all concerned.

(I learned from Mae Brussell's 2 tapes on the "Skeleton Key" and "Gemstone File" in 1977-8[67] that Paul was working at that time as an editor of Hustler. She said on one of the tapes that Paul was going to publish a series of articles by her in Hustler. When I mentioned this to Paul on the phone, he laughed and said that had been wishful thinking on Mae's part.

Oh, and it turned out that Mark Lane [remember him? I gave him a copy of the "Skeleton Key", at Bruce Roberts's personal request, in late 1974] was Larry Flynt/Hustler's attorney around the time Larry got his copy of the "Skeleton Key", which according to "Richard Alan" led to Larry's attempted investigation into the JFK assassination, which in turn led to Larry's getting shot in Georgia. But Gordon Liddy, in his interview with Jonathan Vankin, had a classy Latin quote for this: Post hoc, ergo prompter hoc,[68] where he scoffed at the notion that the fact that one event closely following another event necessarily means that the two events are related. Of course, Liddy is right. So I will fall back on a suggestive quote from another of my favorite authors: "It follow'd hard upon."--"Shakespeare", somewhere.)

The Gemstone item on the next page was included in a copy of a Gemstone letter I got from the Norwegian Consul. The photo, included here, accompanied these quotes. I apologize for the quality of the photo, but it is a copy from the original "*Skeleton Key*" pages I put together at that time. It was included in the final "edition" of the *Skeleton Key*. When I left San Francisco on my way to New York City, in July 1975, I had a carton of these. I stopped briefly in Colorado, and distributed a few copies, then continued to New York. I never distributed any more of these, so copies of this "illustrated" edition were, and are, very rare. I think Ace Hayes may have gotten a copy somewhere

---

[67] See Chapter 36.
[68] See Chapter 44.

and posted it on the web or distributed it privately, but I don't have a single complete copy of this version. My Mom, perhaps in a last desperate hope that I could somehow still turn out to be a nice average American woman, marry a reliable breadwinner, have babies, and learn to enjoy playing Mah Jong and Canasta, apparently threw the whole carton out at some time. Anyway, here are the quotes I do have:

A Rose, and a Cross

1. "Last year, a request to Brezhnev to drop a rose on my father's grave—and one on Mary Jo's at Chappaquiddick, on July 4th. Maneuvering. Nixon switched dates, wouldn't let him come to San Francisco to officially open the Consulate. But he did it anyway.

Mary Jo's, for instance, was a huge concrete cross dumped into Poucha Pond at the busted-nose suffocation Chappaquiddick death site on July 18th, 4th anniversary of her successful murder, inscribed "Mary Jo." The murdering Mafia CIA shudders at such events.

This year, while Nixon was in Moscow, Brezhnev sent a 29-member Soviet Culture Youth Exchange Group. for an exhibit at the Hall of Flowers, two blocks from my mother's apartment—from June 8 to July 4th.

The exhibit featured a centerfold of Tanya, a little girl who died at Leningrad, in War II—Russia's heroine, upon whose grave the Russian nation places roses. It included a full-size picture of Nixon, two years ago—about the time of Wallace's gut shot—standing before Tanya's grave, with a rose wreath, hands hidden, jacking off toward the busted nose at Chappaquiddick, upon which this nation dead-fucks, in lieu of roses." (Check *S. F. Chronicle*, July 21, 1973.)"

The Xerox (of a Xerox) which appears on the following page is a copy of page 32 of that final *Skeleton Key* edition.

I used page 33 as an illustration of Roberts' description of the Watergate Five's appearance at the Drift Inn, in Chapter 30. The "Watergate" photo was accompanied by the following text by Roberts:

***

Watergate Arrest Photos: Taken at the Drift Inn?

2. "The pictures at the top are the arrest pictures of the Watergate group. They match those taken at the Drift Inn. Liddy's and Hunt's *were* taken at the Drift Inn—Liddy's, as he listened to this author quote the Chinese Stock Market quotes on various murderers' ears: Presidents, Senators, Popes, Governors, Judges, Mayors, Legislators, and private Mafia branch members. It is the same laughter that he now laughs at Danbury Prison—knowing there is something worse on the way.

"They appeared at the Drift Inn—to this author—looking as nearly as possible as they did at Dallas—to determine if any connections to Dallas were known. They murdered the author's father in conjunction with that, and Dickie's Peking trip, and then murdered Hoover in conjunction with his Texas Mafia book project. They were caught at Watergate—and the Drift Inn was padlocked to prevent possible recognition by patrons of the Watergate arrest pictures. Mafia CIA cosmetics produced the pictures—bottom row—released from then on."

This letter, and the two that follow in the next two chapters, addressed to Tito of Yugoslavia and to Answer Sadat of Egypt, are interesting not only because of the information they contain. Each of the three was addressed to the head of a nation.

A CROSS FOR MARY JO

"Last year, a request to Brezh- to drop a rose on my father's grave--and one on Mary Jo's at Chappaquiddick, on July 4th. Maneuvering. Nixon switched dates, wouldn't let him come to S.F. to officially open the consulate. But, he did anyhow. Mary Jo's, for instance, was a huge concrete cross dumped into Poucha Pond at the busted-nose suffocation Chappaquiddick death site on July 18th, 4th anniversary of her successful murder, inscribed "Mary Jo." The murdering Mafia CIA shudders at such events. This year--while Nixon is in Moscow-- Brezhnev sent a 29-member Soviet Culture Youth Exchange Group--for an exhibit at the Hall of Flowers--2 blocks from Mother's--from June 8 to July 4th. (You and I, Beverly, and Gloria, walked down there when you were here.)

The exhibit featured a centerfold of Tanya, a little girl who died at Leningrad, in War II--Russia's heroine, upon whose grave the Russian nation places roses--and a full-size picture of Nixon, two years ago--about the time of Wallace's gut shot--standing before Tanya's grave, with a rose wreath, hands hidden, jacking off toward the busted nose at Chappaquiddick, up which this nation dead-fucks, in lieu of roses."

A Reminder

"On the fourth anniversary of the death of Mary Jo Kopechne, police in Edgartown, Mass., on Thursday found a cement cross with the name "Mary Jo" inscribed in it. The cross was submerged near the Chappaquiddick bridge where a car driven by Senator Edward M. Kennedy plunged into the water on July 19, 1969, killing Miss Kopechne. One police officer called the cross "the work of someone with a warped mind."

As such, they represent the "business end" of what Bruce Roberts was really all about. He was passing, and selling, information about the United States and its political affairs overseas—information that was quite secret and quite embarrassing to the United States. He frequently described this merchandise as "a gemstone, with history." He referred to his activities from time to time as "smuggling."

None of the information in Mae Brussell's section of the Gemstone file was addressed to the head of a foreign nation. Roberts refers here and there to Gemstone papers that he gave or sold to other people, varying from actresses (Jane Fonda, for one), lawyers (Charles Garry, for one), and journalists (Mary McCarthy, for one; me, for another), as well as to researchers (Mae Brussell and possibly Paul Krassner.) I have never seen any Gemstone information from any of these people, except for Mae, so I don't know what he gave them. As far as I know, the three letters I refer to are the only ones to heads of foreign states that were made available or given to a private citizen (myself). Bruce Roberts seems to have made many efforts to give information to us (private American citizens). But apparently, for most of the recipients, they didn't or couldn't make any use of it. Perhaps they found it too alarming, or perhaps they couldn't make sense of it because of the writing style: Roberts' habit of summarizing ten or twenty years or so in one complex letter, and not providing a simple outline. My "*Skeleton Key*" did provide such an outline, and I believe that is why he seems to have adopted it as his "introduction" during the last year of his life, and why it has survived in the world so long since its release in 1975.

On the other hand, perhaps they did make use of the information from time to time. Perhaps Jane Fonda used her possession of some of this information for self-preservation when she was being hounded by the government and in the press. And maybe Daniel Ellsberg did use his possession of some of these papers to avoid a prison sentence for releasing the Pentagon Papers. Any reader is welcome to reread the relevant sections here, and decide for yourself. Better yet, why not ask them and see what they say? Maybe you can get some additional Gemstone papers that way. If you find some, I hope you will let me know. I'm always interested.

Some people were able to divine the whole story from his individual letters and papers. Many of these people were from the same political groups he was writing about, who already knew the nefarious ins and outs Roberts was describing. For them, each Gemstone letter he circulated must have infuriated and frightened them. They didn't rely entirely on the power of their own propaganda to deceive and mislead the public, and the willingness of the public to be misinformed.

My experiences with the various consulates confirmed what Roberts had told me, and written in his File. There really was a Mr. Pavlov at the Soviet Consulate. There really were Gemstone letters from Roberts at the Norwegian Consulate. Soviet Premier Leonid Brezhnev really did come down with a mysterious "flu" shortly before Roberts began treatment for his peculiar "cancer," whatever its origin. That is why I decided to believe Roberts in general, even though some of his particular statements have been difficult to prove.

This seems like a good time to recommend a brief rereading of Bruce Roberts' Prologue to this book, which I selected from his Gemstone File because to me it expresses his desire, and his method:

"*Jefferson said: 'Political power belongs to the people. If tyranny corrupts, then the public should be informed. They should be educated so that they can control their own destiny.'*

"*Rochefort said: 'Presidents fear one thing: An historian, who writes with knowledge of events; who writes of current history—and traces it back. This man has the power to change the inscriptions on tombstones, and shape the course of the history he writes about.'*"

Believe it. Bruce Roberts did it.

32 January 15, 1975: Letter to Anwar Sadat of Egypt

Dear President Sadat:

King Farouk once paid a Philadelphia U.S. Mint die operator to stamp over the 1925 dates on five dimes with a stolen 1921 dime die. The history of this planned over-date "error" made these dimes priceless. They are still in the Farouk collection. Beasley, a San Francisco coin expert, was flown to New York to clean them. Armed guard; hotel suite; four figure fee. A test sale offer—through Sotheby's in London, was withdrawn as the bidding reached high five figures, per coin.

Limited minting + historic error = collector value.

The $792 "Gemstone with history" check and cash offer bidding has escalated. (Stephanie Caruana—from the "Onassis is Hughes" article—rushed to drag out her cash last November 13 on Montgomery Street—as Arafat rattled the gemstone papers in the U.N.—and the U.N. voted, 105-4, to listen).[69] Such is the nature of history, which is sometimes a planned affair.

The attached dime is one of 400 in existence. The reverse is doubled. This error run occurred on November 22, 1963, as a Denver mint die operator shuddered over the news from Dallas: JFK's murder. Two, from his Denver—Brading and Fratianno, from the Denver Smaldones Mafia family—had just blown Kennedy's brains out. Brading was photographed at the scene with a gun. Roselli, from Cohen, was the third shooter. Oswald hit his target: Connally.

The mint error—as with the murder—was over in seconds. That shipment came to San Francisco Federal Reserve vaults: 1964 D (for Denver) dimes.

CIA, and others here, in the banks, since May, 1963—checking the $73 million federally-declared "forged" Howard Hughes TWA case land lien appeal bond securities—accepted by Giannini's Bank of America, in open fraud, for a foreigner, a Greek, Onassis—shuddered too. For a month later, in June, 1963, Montini had become Pope; Montini, a foreigner, Jewish-Italian, banished from Rome by Pius XII for poisoning Pius XI, and for operating the world's largest intelligence group. The father of our own CIA, their employer. And in August, Fulbright's Senate speech on who owned that Senate triggered Katharine Graham's blow-out of squawking hubby Phillip's brains and Crime Senator Kefauver's heart attack on the Senate floor. Kennedy's two closest friends were dead; two who knew about the Kennedy-Onassis-Costello-Roosevelt-Lansky-Eugene Meyer (Katharine Graham's father) original booze-heroin bit to Boston—the two who would have squawked over Dallas, and named Onassis.

The cover-up went on. And also the watch on anything that happened in the banks here. Even the new coins coming out.

My father, a coin collector, was told when the dime doubling showed up. Knowing the background, he and others checked vault coins—and on back to the Denver mint. Source and amount of error coins were verified, and were collected. Those coins came to me after my father's murder, on February 22, 1972, by the Watergate group, here at the Drift Inn then. With Liz Dale and Francis L. Dale, Chairman of Nixon's CREEP—the key so carefully hidden by all throughout the Watergate investigation. The Watergate group was the back-up at Dallas—as they had been on the Castro murder attempts. Arrested at Lake Pontchartrain, early in 1963, by Bobby Kennedy, for this, they were reassigned to the murder of JFK.

---

[69] Yes, it's true. I bought a Dallas dime, but didn't pay that much. I think he wanted me to have these two letters, to Sadat and Tito, written to the leaders of two countries rather than to Americans of various sorts. He asked me to write on the check: "For a Dallas dime, with history". The two letters were an education for me into what he had been doing.—sc2005

Albert Harris, of the California State Crime Commission, was one of those watching those 1963 events. Including those coins, and my father.

A year after Dallas, all watched Alioto pay off Fratianno, from his San Francisco First National Bank, for Fratianno's Dallas shot—the reason for the "Alioto Mafia Web" story in *Look*—to cover up the purpose of Fratianno's $100,000 pay-off.

They watched Onassis, via Maheu, pay off Johnny Roselli: a $250,000 "finder's fee" for bringing "Hughes" to Las Vegas.

They watched Brading become a courier for Lansky's gambling skim money, from Onassis-"Hughes's" Las Vegas casinos to Onassis's Swiss banks. From which it came back, cleansed, to purchase government via the "Hughes tax-free Medical Foundation Mafia Money Funnel," set up by Nixon in 1957, just before the Hughes-Rector kidnap-and-switch, and the Mafia meeting at Apalachin where Onassis announced it all.

Harris and the CIA Group of 40 covered up the Alioto hit-and-run on my car on September 16, 1968—as Fratianno, Brading, and Lanza muscled this writer on behalf of Alioto and Onassis.

The incident ultimately elected Nixon. Onassis, a foreigner, having murdered a second Kennedy—Bobby—became official owner of the Kennedy family; and purchased Jackie. He already owned Nixon—as "Hughes"; as well as both political parties, the U.S. government, and the U.S. economy. The Moral "lid" was furnished by a foreigner, CIA Montini, the Pope, so helpful at Chappaquiddick. The Press lid was furnished by Abraham Graham [Katharine Meyer Graham]: "most powerful woman in the world"—Onassis's two partners from pre-Dallas 1963, back through War II, to the Onassis-Kennedy-Meyer booze-heroin deal of 1932.

In July, 1969, phone calls at the Chappaquiddick cottage—from the telephone plugged into the wall jack behind the day bed—to and from John Tunney, Teddy Kennedy, and Joe Alioto, over these matters—murdered Mary Jo Kopechne, and brought out the "Alioto Mafia Web" story, and the rest of the cancer seen today in the massive CIA lid on Watergate. Al Harris covered it all, moaning constantly, "This is dynamite. This is Dallas..."—a moan that made him Deputy Attorney General under Evelle Younger, who covered up Bobby Kennedy's murder, for Onassis.

On February 21, 1972, Cardinal Tisserant was poisoned, in Rome, at the Vatican. His files went missing. The next day, February 22, my father, Hugh Sloan, and Baldwin, from Watergate, were at the Drift Inn, with the rest of the group. Charles Garry, attorney, waved the Gemstone papers at Harris, and got Angela Davis freed. [Hal Lipset worked for Garry. J. Edgar Hoover was murdered. Hal Lipset retaped a door at Watergate, and the Watergate group was captured—including Baldwin—for Katharine Graham, who had hired Lipset away from Garry.] Those coins—with history—were described to Liddy, Hunt, Dale and the group at the Drift Inn.

On January 11, 1973, the dimes were publicly discussed again—along with "four documents" on these matters, released abroad. Gary Young was given one. Sam Dash and David Dorsen—Lipset's new employers, from Senate Watergate—appeared at the Grommet, here, to listen. So did Albert Harris, with Baldwin. The stock market has dropped, since then, from 1050 to 650.

In October, 1973, we had a war—as you know so well: a nuclear alert.

In August, 1974, we lost a president—here, in San Francisco, at the Swedish consulate and the Russian consulate near which the Alioto hit-run occurred: Nixon, "most powerful man in the world," hiding now—from a hang-rope—in San Clemente.

In September, 1974, the new President, Ford:, pardoned the old one—on the day after the murder of an informed friend, Harp, from Kish Realty, who had one of those Dallas Dimes, with history.[70] Albert Harris's State Crime files surfaced again. Fratianno and Brading had been back in

---

[70] Here is the corresponding entry from my *Skeleton Key*: **September 7, 1974:** Roberts had made an agreement with a friend, Karp, of Kish Realty, over a bugged phone. Harp was to buy a Gemstone, with history, for $500—the price of

328   *The Gemstone File: A Memoir*

town-with Mafia Romano, at Alioto's Sunol. Their only known profession is Mafia murder—listed in those State Crime files from a Dunn and Bradstreet Credit Report in early 1964, just after Dallas, stating just that—with the note: "Bad Credit Risk. Mafia." Which did not deter Banker Alioto's subsequent "loans" to Fratianno.

On November 26, 1974, Harris covered the meeting of the "100 cancer" invited to Enrico's Restaurant.[71] They included Fratianno, Brading, and Leland, Snedaker, Mummert from the San Francisco Coin Club—for free rubies, free silver dollars, free gemstone papers. Harris, sick and pressured, picked up his copies at the Nigerian consulate—the next day—for on that day the entire matter was turned over to the United Nations—publicly. Harris read, and moaned about "Dallas" over the week-end. Then he "heart-attacked" on the following Wednesday.

And, on Friday, Kissinger and Scali declared that the U.S. would dismantle the United Nations—where the gemstone papers were then known to be—publicly. Harris's boss, Younger, rushed a State law through banning any further mention of any State Crime file records—by anyone, anywhere—including you—and naming specifically the files on Brading, Fratianno, and Romano. It became law on January 1, 1975—a few weeks ago. It is illegal; our Constitution states that any law passed in fraud is illegal—including fraudulent presidential pardon, of murder.

The Dallas Dimes, with history, began going out on January 11, 1975—a few days ago—publicly—two years from the date the "gemstones, with history" were publicly released—with now clearly visible results. The San Francisco Coin Club were offered them first: my father's "friends"—Leland, Don, Bartschuk, Treasurer Snedaker, and Vice President Mummert. They refused cooperation. Capos bought one. Mummert covered up the original Alioto hit-and-run (and the subsequent five more), as insuring agent for Senator Howard Baker—for Nixon. He blocked everything, and covered the substitution of Nurse Hollister for Tom Alioto as the hit-and-run driver.

On the day of the hit-and-run, Mummert robbed me of $1500 cash, for car damages. Nixon's CREEP man, Mack[72], then demanded $1500 cash to deal with Nixon. A pending ruby sale offer, for $1500, was immediately canceled; and from then on, no takers at any price. Xerox copies—by $1500 batches—were burned in a "burn bag" by L. Patrick Gray. Jeb Magruder burned his copy in a fireplace. Nixon, Mitchell, Browning, Greenagel, Knowland, Nader, and others burned theirs. The negative value of any collector's copy would seem to be $1500. Yet, Kennedy's Gifford offered, via Lello, "seven figures." Liz Dale offered an unnamed amount from Francis L. Dale. And, at that time, 1972, the massive economic shift of trillion dollar economics—of governments and presidents and kings and geographical boundaries, was still to come.

Said Kissinger: "We will seize Arabia because of economic strangulation." Economic strangulation is a CIA project on me—as my CIA cousin Kimball strangles Africa, from Lagos, Nigeria; as my father's "friend", Maillard, strangles South America from his Nixon-appointed O.A.S.

---

a trip to Canada for Roberts to check into the "Hughes" Mormon Mafia Canadian stock market swindle, and other matters. But Harp was sodium-morphate poisoned on this date, before the deal could go through." Gerald Carroll, one of the only two "conspiracy researchers" who bothered to search at length for the reality behind the *Skeleton Key* (the second being *"Richard Alan,"* who put together the *Gemstone File* book of newspaper and magazine clippings; see bibliography), wrote this: "This is another example of a passage that appears innocuous on the surface, but has enormous importance once the death of Harp is analyzed. Gail Lawrence Harp was 62 years of age when he died unexpectedly. Date of death, Sept. 7, 1974, as recorded by the San Francisco coroner, which confirms the Gemstone date. Cause of death: "Severe arteriosclerotic heart disease," without going into specifics, which typically matches sodium morphate ingestion symptoms.... According to his obituary, Harp served in the U.S. Marine Corps briefly before spending 28 years in the United States Navy, serving during World War II. He was also a member of the Navy Fleet Reserve Association, which kept him in touch with naval intelligence operations at home and abroad. This simply means that Harp, Roberts and Al Strom, among others, probably served together during World War II on intelligence-sensitive operating units. Another intelligence operative by the name of Phillip Graham also served during this time.—*Project Seek*, pp.181-2.

[71] Bruce invited me to attend this, as a member of the press. But I politely declined. Hey, I may be a little crazy, but not that crazy. I was afraid to go. So I have no idea how many—if any—attended.—sc2005

[72] That is, John Mack, who was not only the head of California CREEP, but a bank officer who has had a distinguished career with Bank of California and Bank of America.

office; and as Francis L. Dale, appointed by Nixon, strangles the United Nations in Geneva, from an Onassis-owned Swiss Bank. In view of these things, what is the collector value of that Dallas Dime?

My means of livelihood have been strangled by the Mafia. My father is dead. And a son. Your brother is dead. And another joint friend, Ismail. In their honor, I propose a check from the President of Egypt, for a "Dallas dime, with history." A personal matter. You to me. Your appraisal of that collector's coin—on a signed check—would help to establish a base price on the value of those coins—just as the $792 check for a "gemstone, with history" and other bid offers have done for gemstones—rising now—as Farouk's dimes did at Sotheby's.

I noted your statement that if your lands were not returned soon you would "explode it all in the United Nations." And our CIA Pentagon Schlesinger's response: "SS-18's can now launch a limited strategic strike on us—kill 6 million in 6 minutes—but 97% of our economy would still be intact, so that isn't bad. Survivors would show a brief loss of confidence in our government, but they would get over it. They would soon resume their normal social relations in our society: sucking on the radioactive asshole of Alioto."

For the one million in San Francisco are the prime target—strategic or massive: the hub of the Mafia universe.

Proof has been furnished. It is difficult to sell—or give away—gemstones, or coins—with history—here. All of the history is burned. Along with their own future. That's cancer. Schlesinger admits it: 6 million are expendable, to hide Project Star, the Rand version of Dallas, over which those dimes were doubled.

Brandon, London: "The JFK murder was known to 90% of the world within 48 hours. Its solution will become known to 100% within a few hours—unless the missiles get here first."

Not true. The solution has been out around the world for a long time—in the gemstone papers. Your statement speaks of Peace, by that exposure. Schlesinger speaks of nuclear war—murder—to hide it. The moral variance is obvious: the difference between a doctor and a cancer. In view of this consideration—life, or death—what is the value of that dime?

Please inform me of your judgement. If missiles don't get here first, there are other projects—and a solid performance record. My radioactive ass is at stake too.

I live here. Best wishes—Sincerely,

Bruce Roberts

33 February 10, 1975: Letter to President Tito of Yugoslavia

Dear President Tito:

World War I started in Yugoslavia: Sarajevo, Ferdinand's murder. So can War III, over another murder: Howard Hughes. The catalyst, this time, is Harold Smith—formerly of Harold's Club Casino, Reno, Nevada—since, gambling, for the CIA, in Yugoslavia. Harold Smith sold his Reno club to "Hughes"—Onassis—after the burial of "Howard Hughes" off Tenos, Greece—by Onassis, on April 23, 1971. Smith was sent to Yugoslavia to cover up the murder—as the Watergate crew broke into Watergate, here, for the same reason.

Verification of details of the captivity, here, in 1957, and the murder, there, in 1971, of Howard Hughes, by Onassis, in Greece, had been released by Albanian and Yugoslavian citizens, as were the "bones of Howard Hughes."

This was discussed with Liddy, Hunt and the Watergate group of CIA Francis L. Dale, Chairman of Nixon's CREEP (hidden throughout the Watergate trials) at the San Francisco Drift Inn—in 1971, through February, 1972. My father was murdered in that February—as Nixon landed in Peking, in fear of the "bones of Howard Hughes" that had brought China into the United Nations. FBI Hoover was murdered in May, 1972, as Nixon crawled in Moscow over the same "bones." Katharine Graham's Lipset—listening too at the Drift Inn—taped a door, and captured the group at Watergate in June.

The two phones tapped at Watergate were those of "Hughes" employees Spencer Oliver and Larry O'Brien. O'Brien, Chairman of the Democratic Party, worked publicly for "Howard Hughes"-Onassis—a Public Relations contract. So did Spencer Oliver's father. This is a matter of public record, like the "federally declared forged" $73 million "Howard Hughes" land liens accepted by Giannini's Bank of America as appeal bonds for the TWA damage award—in May, 1963—which "purchased" the murder of JFK at Dallas by Onassis. A third Watergate break-in target was Teddy Kennedy, whose new family father was "Howard Hughes"-Onassis, via the murder of Teddy's two brothers and a wedding to Jackie, just after the Alioto hit-and-run that blew it all over the streets. Teddy Kennedy was the leading Democratic presidential candidate. He had a problem over the Chappaquiddick murder, which exposed everything again, as explained in the "Dallas dime" letter to President Sadat.

President Nixon, head of the Republican Party, who set up the CIA CREEP affair, was purchased by "Howard Hughes"-Onassis, in 1957, via "family loans", in return for his help in setting up the "Hughes Medical Foundation tax-free Mafia Money Funnel." This was at the time "Hughes" was captured and replaced by the "Hughes" double, L. Wayne Rector, since murdered too—at Rothschild's Inn of the Park, London, on January 15, 1973—one of "four bodies."

The "grass roots" Mafia take-over of the Election Process, announced by Onassis to the Mafia at Apalachin, in 1957—and its relation forward to Dallas, and backward through the War II deal of Onassis-Kennedy-Roosevelt, and Lansky-Eugene Meyer-Luciano-Andre Meyer-Costello-Katharine Meyer (now Katharine Graham)-Genovese, and Alioto-Levi, in Justice—to the Onassis-Kennedy-Roosevelt-Churchill booze-heroin shipping deal into Boston in 1932 is explained in a prior letter.

War II did not start in Yugoslavia.

Aborted by the Watergate capture was another target: Publisher Greenspun, Las Vegas, and his files on dead Howard Hughes, of equal priority on the Hunt-Liddy "Gemstone plan"—from the Drift Inn—for Nixon's CIA CREEP. That Las Vegas break-in and fly-away plan was identical to the hit-and-run murder plan performed on JFK at Dallas. Onassis' ("Hughes") planes were to fly the same murdering group to Costa Rica and Nicaragua, where Onassis-"Hughes" Mafia Vesco, Donald Nixon, Somoza, and Figueres still hide.

The sale of Harold's Club to "Hughes"-Onassis was contingent upon Harold Smith's touring Yugoslavia—as a "world-known gambler"—to track down and cover up whatever it was that had been exposed of the captivity and murder of Howard Hughes—that is, of the "bones of Howard Hughes"—by those Albanian and Yugoslavian citizens. His CIA task was more important than that of Nixon's CIA Watergate group. That group was captured; and the matter was glossed over.

Smith's "Hughes" exposure in Yugoslavia-Albania will occur at a much more critical period—when "War over oil," "War over strangulation," "War over Palestine-Israel,"—"War over whatever,"—and the tools to do it with—are at many fingertips, all of whom now know that "Howard Hughes" is the trigger for War III. Not "oil", nor "Palestine." And that is a repeat of Sarajevo, which had nothing to do with "oil" either.

Two out of three World Wars started in Yugoslavia? Wouldn't it be better to let someone else have the "honor" of starting this one? Like the United Nations? Where, by proper Mafia hanging, it might even be prevented? Why should Belgrade and Tirana be atomized just because the cancerous bones of Howard Hughes passed through, scheduled for mounting on the cross at Chappaquiddick to cover up the Teddy Kennedy-broken nose-bones of Mary Jo Kopechne?

In late 1970—at the San Francisco Drift Inn—NSC Admiral Gayler, Pentagon General Bennett's son, and CIA General Vernon Walters, all stopped in for talks with me on these matters. They had just set up [Tom] Houston's Domestic Spy plan (Dean's IEC, under CIA Mardian and Helms) to cover it all up. That mushroomed into Watergate, whose cancerous afterbirth has now spread around the world—in your country, via "Hughes", Harold Smith, and Nixon. Nixon's deep concern—as in his visits to Peking and Moscow, in his visit to you in Yugoslavia, and your later visit to Washington—involved his fear of your knowledge of these matters. And particularly, the "bones of Howard Hughes"—a war-triggering international Mafia affair—in a Yugoslavia-Albania tinder box. Harold Smith arrived—"to establish corporate gambling in Yugoslavia"—through arrangements of another Bennett: CIA Robert F. Bennett, son of Senator William F. Bennett, from "Hughes's" Utah, Nixon's advisor. We have more CIA Bennetts here, Mr. Tito, than humans.

Robert Bennett was President of Mullen and Co.—across from the White House—a firm that was under CIA contract to provide corporate cover for CIA agents around the world. They did this for my cousin, Kimball, at the Ford Foundation, in Nigeria—and for Harold Smith in Yugoslavia. CIA E. Howard Hunt worked for Bennett at the time of the Watergate break-in. His Onassis-"Hughes" cover-up duties have been described. So did Harold Smith. Bennett planned the Watergate break-in; and assigned Hunt on orders of Francis L. Dale, Chairman of CREEP.

Bennett assigned Harold Smith to cover up whatever was necessary in Yugoslavia and Albania about "Hughes." Smith was Nevada's oldest, most respected gambling operator. Harold's Club was world-known. His cover was perfect. So Onassis bought Smith's Harold's Club in Reno. Smith went to Yugoslavia—under a new corporate gambling cover—a natural—arranged jointly by Robert Bennett and General Bennett's son, an executive for Smith, French and Kline, pharmaceutical drugs, Philadelphia, with established Balkan trade routes. CIA General Walters approved this action for Robert Bennett and Harold Smith. Pentagon's General Bennett approved it, for his son. DIA Noel Gayler approved it for the National Security Council. (These were the three who had earlier appeared at the Drift Inn, about these same matters.) These three worked directly for CIA Director Helms; the Joint Chiefs of Staff, and Kissinger on the NSC.

Harold Smith's job was to find, and eliminate, for Onassis, any leaks about the "bones of Howard Hughes" from those Yugoslavian and Albanian citizens—and do whatever was necessary. Most came from coastal fishing, and that is where the bodies are: Yugoslavian and Albanian.

The CIA Mullen-Bennett Company—now exposed—has vanished. Robert Bennett now directs Public Relations for "Howard Hughes's" Summa Corporation in Los Angeles. (At the White House Mullen Company Office, Bennett's chief CIA corporate cover account was "Howard Hughes.") Senator Bennett quit the U.S. Senate and hides in a "Hughes" Utah Mormon Church.

Nixon quit the Presidency and hides in San Clemente. The world is shaken—politically and economically. "War" is the cry—Mid-East, U.S., elsewhere—so far, only over the pretexts of "oil," and "strangulation."

Locally, Harold Smith's Reno partner, Mafia Federal Judge Thompson (earlier reassigned to "cool" the Alioto Mafia Web trial—and the Tyrone Papers trial, which would have led to Roosevelt-Hoffa-Daley-Onassis and "Hughes"), frantically dismissed Grand Jury indictments against "Howard Hughes". Mafia-owned TV beams, urgently, hours of "Hughes is alive," (while the wife of Hughes #2, Wayne Rector—searches publicly for his body) via worldwide "Hughes" communication satellites—as "Hughes" gun ships, "Hughes" tow missiles, "Hughes" laser bombs blanket the world. Maheu—Onassis's contractor on JFK at Dallas—won $2 million from "Hughes" last month in a suit, and promptly dropped another 4-year-old certain-win $50 million suit against "Hughes." The cash pay-off—for that—was private, and urgent.]

The bubble is about to blow. A chief blow point is Yugoslavia-Albania—over the "bones of Howard Hughes", and CIA Harold Smith. That would be War III—and two out of three for Yugoslavia. "Amazing odds," gambler Harold Smith has stated.

As with other world leaders—letters attached—would it not be better to present the matter to the United Nations? As with them, a signed check, "for a Dallas dime, with history"—also attached—by the President of Yugoslavia—a personal matter, you to me—your assessment of the collector value of that dime, would be of value as a solution to projects of a similar nature—basically, all the same: survival. As with those nations, the enclosed series of Gemstone letters, presented openly and publicly to a consulate of Yugoslavia—are for whatever use you may decide: contents, or the letters themselves—with no reservations, no restrictions, none whatsoever.

As with the request to President Perez—to forward personal letters to another consulate—it is requested that the Albanian Embassy, near you, be notified of these letters. Separate copies will be furnished—to the Albanian Embassy—upon request.

There is no Albanian consulate here in San Francisco, to whom I can personally, openly and publicly, present these papers. As explained to President Perez, letter intercepts, and murder, have accompanied other open and public attempts. Under such conditions of duress, this request is made.

Thank you for your consideration. Best wishes from a private American citizen.

Bruce P. Roberts

Part IV Aftermath
34 Leaving California (July 1975)

By June, 1975, I knew I was out of a job. My article on Chappaquiddick was rejected by (the lawyers at) *Playgirl*. And after a year and a half of steady writing assignments, I was definitely *persona non grata* in the *Playgirl* office in Los Angeles. Nobody said anything, but I was suddenly a "former" Contributing Editor. Marin Milam, the Editor, whose only faults had been curiosity, enthusiasm and political naivete (which I shared), was replaced by a feather-headed Editor-In-Chief from NYC. The "Onassis is Hughes" article had brought in enormous negative fall-out from people with political clout. It had, after all, broken through the wall of national media censorship, and had brought the most deeply buried secrets of our "democracy" to light in 1.5 million copies. The magazine itself was in deep trouble, after its record-breaking climb to prominence. It folded for a while, then was reborn in NYC and hung on, with new owners and a new staff, as a magazine primarily for gay men with no particular relevance.

Meanwhile, I had to make a living. I saw Bruce Roberts one last time, and explained that I had been fired for writing the Onassis-Hughes article, and that my best hope for earning a living was to go to New York and seek a book contract. At the time, he seemed to be all right physically. (I had, at his request, driven him home from the hospital at around the end of April, at which time I showed him the first "edition" of the *Skeleton Key*. At that time, I do not think he had had the dreadful biopsy described in Chapter 35.) I flew to New York City. That is why my *Skeleton Key* to the Gemstone File petered out in June, 1975. An old friend lent me the use of his New York office as a *pied-a-terre*.

Florynce R. Kennedy, a brilliant black activist, the first black woman to graduate from Columbia University's Law School and later the founder of the Black Feminist Party, had been "bi-coastal" for a while, living for a time in the famous artsy Chateau Marmont in Los Angeles, then in an airy apartment in San Francisco. She eventually returning to her cozy rent-controlled apartment on West 54th Street, NYC. I had interviewed her for *Playgirl* while she was living on the West Coast, and she loved the article, which was called *Flo Kennedy: Woman as Warrior*. She was a great subject.

Prentice-Hall was interested in doing a book about her, to be called *Color Me Flo*. And Flo wanted me to put the book together. The editor for the book project was none other than Robert Sussman Stewart, who had been in charge of Clifford Irving's fake "biography" project on Howard Hughes in 1971, for McGraw-Hill. That book contract had been signed by Clifford Irving for an advance of $750,000! For some reason, perhaps the "Hughes biography hoax" fiasco, Bob had moved to Prentice-Hall. Anyway, I signed a contract in July, 1975, to write the book on Flo, for a measly $2000 advance. However, I was pleased. I knew writing a great book about Flo Kennedy would be easy, because she was a great woman to begin with, a wonderful speaker with a fine mind, and an outstanding leader in the racial and sexual revolutions of the time. All I had to do was hang around, tape her speeches and casual chatter, partake of her endless hospitality, fried chicken, and open house for her many friends, and provide an elegant textual background for Flo's brilliance. Piece of cake!

In my absence from California, it appeared that Mae Brussell had begun to build up a head of steam about me. We had parted on good terms, as far as I knew. She was engrossed with her new friend, the paroled prisoner (Elmer Davis), who was staying in the guest room that I had previously occupied. I was happy enough in Big Sur, and later in San Francisco. I heard through the grapevine later on that a romance had blossomed and a wedding was planned. However, I heard still later, her romantic guest had beaten her up one day; the wedding was called off, and she threw him out. (See Chapter 36 for more on this.)

At any rate, I was at Flo's New York apartment one day. The radio was tuned to WBAI, a

popular PBS radio station. Suddenly Flo called to me and said that Mae was on the radio, and apparently was planning to attack me. I hurried to the living room. Mae was just warming up. She was saying, "Just wait until I tell you a few things about Stephanie Caruana!"

Flo dialed the station and handed me the phone. I said, "Hello Mae," and heard myself on WBAI.

Mae backed down immediately from whatever she was about to say. "Oh...Stephanie," she cooed. "How are you?" That was about the end of that particular WBAI interview.

I couldn't understand why she was mad. But subsequent events suggested that my *Skeleton Key* had been circulating widely and wildly around California, from April through July. And people were curious about it. I had always made it clear that I had prepared the *Skeleton Key* from Gemstone letters dated two to three years later than the ones Mae had. In fact, the last third of the *Skeleton Key* was an abbreviated account of events that occurred later than the period covered in Mae's portion of the file. Mae had kept the "Gemstone" information a deep secret for three years. But I guess she didn't like the idea of my working directly with Bruce Roberts, and the result proving to be so interesting and popular with the public. So she staked her exclusive claim to the Gemstone File, and lied about what she had. Anyway, my book on Flo was not to be. I had just signed the book contract when my father had a heart attack in Miami Beach, Florida, which turned out to be fatal. I flew down, a few days before he died. My father's business affairs were in a bad state. When he died, my mother's situation, emotionally and financially, was desperate. My only sibling, an older sister, announced she was going home to the Windward Islands a few days later, and she did. So there I was. Stuck in Miami Beach, a place I have always hated, for the next five years, until things stabilized for my mother.

But...every cloud has a silver lining. Life in the Miami area was, for me, for the most part, boring. But I was grateful to be out of politics and the main stream when, in 1976, the dapper Johnny Roselli's strangled, dismembered body floated to the surface in Dumfoundling Bay, just to the north of Biscayne Bay. The torso and the cut-off legs had been stuffed into an oil drum, and the whole sorry mess thrown into the water. Two weeks later, the oil drum and its grisly contents floated to the surface, due to the gases released from the body as it decomposed. The back door of my father's plastics business, which I was then running, gave out on a landing dock on Biscayne Bay. It was too close for comfort.

35 Live interview with Bruce Roberts: City of San Francisco, September 9, 1975

Two months after I left San Francisco for New York, the following interview appeared in *the City of San Francisco*, a tabloid newspaper edited by Warren Hinckel, formerly the editor of *Ramparts*.

THE GREATEST CONSPIRACY EVER TOLD

GEMSTONE

By the DNA Research Collective: Al Annenberg, George Comon, Melanie Gimpel, J. C. Louis, Alex Manzoni, Tora Sasaki and Terry Tawney.

We were hard at work in our living room researching the assassination of John F. Kennedy. Our collective had recently written and produced a play about Jack Ruby. We were on our way, opening as yet unplumbed arenas about the truth of horrible events in Dallas. The calm of our methodology was interrupted by a man who told us the most sordid and staggering tale of Western civilization we've ever heard.

His name is Bruce Roberts. He lives in San Francisco with his mother in the Sunset District. He burst into our lives like the proverbial gangbusters.

In the world of clandestine politics, credibility and the power to shock are indispensable tools of communication. Bruce utilized both when he sauntered into our living room office without speaking a word, and opened up his shirt to display a gaping biopsy down the front of his chest. Holding his shirt open with a slight tremble in his wrinkled hands, he began to explain how he had been seeded with a cancer-like virus very similar to the one that had afflicted Brezhnev earlier this year. Roberts looked at each of us as he spoke, his round, bugging eyes punctuating his high-pitched monotone with glares. He pulled an official-looking diagnosis out of his jacket that bore the U.C. Medical Center logo, that amounted to "strange virus, cause unknown."

We continued to eye Roberts with increasing disbelief as he told about a similar diagnosis that had been performed on him at the Russian consulate in San Francisco using the technology of Kirlian photography.

Seeded with cancer? We were instantly reminded of Jack Ruby, whose repeated insistences that he had been injected with live cancer cells went unheeded, even after his death from cancer in 1967. But what had this to do with Brezhnev? And what average citizen can get a diagnosis from the Russian consulate?

Roberts, talking rapid-fire, showed us voluminous letters written in his own hand to world leaders like Sadat, Tito, President Perez of Venezuela, Brezhnev and others. Roberts had come to us because he heard we were working on an article on the life and last madness of Jack Ruby; he said he had information on Ruby's death as part of "the continuing conspiracy of murder in the U.S. of Mafia"—no reservations or restrictions. (What matter that the first incident he mentioned—the Faisal assassination—had little to do with Ruby. The conspiracy was pervasive—a cancer itself.)

Roberts is in his early 50s with thinning gray hair and a piercing gaze. He claims to be a physicist who did many years of research on the development of synthetic crystals—"gemstones"—crucial to the technology of the laser beam. He studied physics at the University of Wisconsin in the mid-30s. His special interest had been in crystallography, and the creation of synthetic rubies. In World War II he served with the OSS (the CIA's predecessor), and after the war he pursued experiments with real and synthetic jewels. In 1960 he offered Hughes Tool Company his experience and the opportunity to work with rare and synthetic rubies in exchange for the use of their facilities. Hughes Tool promptly stole his synthetic samples, which became the basis for their own research into laser beams and other highly secret war technologies.

Roberts' shafting by Hughes began years of economic strangulation and increasing political paranoia for him. As a result of his contacts with the Hughes organization, Roberts says he learned of certain crucial international connections between the Hughes organization and Aristotle Onassis. This in turn led to the Mafia. The Mafia kills.

His efforts to disclose these interlocking interests led, he believes, to the murder of his father, here in San Francisco, by apparent heart-attack "poisoning," on February 22, 1972. He has identified his father's killers as members of then-President Nixon's "plumbers." He is serious when he says this. He looks you straight in the eye. In the massive detail supporting his story, he is convincing.

The gravamen of his conspiracy theory is written down in a series of letters and papers he calls the Gemstone File. Though we have examined a small portion of these papers, which have been distributed to government consulates around the world, the sheer accumulation of fact is stunning. Written in Robert's own steady handwriting, the Gemstone Papers sketch a revisionist, conspiratorial view of history perhaps not unlike that outlined in John Birch publications. Behind the avalanche of facts emerges what Roberts calls an "evidential mountain."

For Roberts, the seminal event in the 20th Century was a 1932 deal: Onassis, a Greek shipping magnate who made his first million shipping opium, worked out an arrangement with Joseph P. Kennedy, Sr., and Meyer Lansky. Onassis was to ship liquor to Boston for Kennedy. Included also were shipments of heroin, which accrued to the benefit of Onassis and FDR. (Subsequent deals between Roosevelt and Mafia patriarchs Luciano and Costello to deploy longshoremen and Corsican forces in the war effort are well-documented.) In 1934 Onassis firmed up a deal with Rockefeller and the major oil companies whereby an oil cartel would be formed to gain control of Arab oil by shipping it on Onassis' boats to American-based refineries. This was the basis of the conspiracy—the Kennedys, the Rockefellers, Onassis and the Mafia all in the same 'boat.

Franklin Roosevelt in an international smuggling operation? Only a man of Roberts' powers of persuasion and mastery of the shifting, often contradictory facts of history could maintain such a proposition.

Roberts tells his incredible story with an intense, staccato delivery to anyone who will listen. Most have run in the opposite direction. We decided to listen. He may be a crank, but he is a damned impressive one. If one must describe the peculiar power of this furtive man, one would say that he is a master—indeed a demon—of uncheckable facts. He stands at the door to what can only be called the fourth dimension of history. A few of us felt at times as if it were the sheer force of his personality that drew us in—like a great salesman or a great shaman. What would have surely struck many as coincidence he asked us to see as connected together by the darkest impulses of the strangest bedfellows. Nor do these bedfellows encounter each other in the civilized light of daily intercourse, but rather in the perverse, pornographic night of power politics where oil and heroin mix.

People run from Bruce's information because it defies probability for them. But probability is itself nothing but one's expectations, one's social conditioning. Hughes Tool Company, the death of his father, a biopsy, and a few other things have changed Bruce's sense of the "probable." So he lives cut off from the world in the Sunset District, mailing his "evidential mountain" to the consulates and leaders of twenty-seven nations who have received "gemstones with history" (the files). They go and they come in the perpetual sea of oil, snow of heroin and the endless colonies of cancer cells, surrounded by an occasional storm of sand and glass, and heat, leaving precious rubies in its wake. It is all rather poetic.

In seven years of conspiracy research, we have never seen a man as intense as Bruce Roberts. He is incapable of answering a question without launching into a vast "history" of inter-Mafia deals that have thousands of murders to cover up. He speaks as if every breath is his last, and with each breath he speaks another name, hurls yet another factoid, like a missile at the U.S. of Mafia edifice.

There is little agreement among the members of this collective as to how much of Roberts'

story is true. He's even accused some of us of being part of the conspiracy against him, which we are pretty sure is not true. (He says Warren Hinckle, the editor of this magazine, has been sitting on this story for years, keeping it sealed under the ancient Mafia code of *omerta*.)

The leading literary images in Roberts' horror story are "cancer" and "deadfuck." Cancer—the mad proliferation of deadly cells—stands for the principle of murder for private gain; the cornerstone of the Mafia and international banking. Dead-fuck is what it sounds like: necrophilia. Our age, in Bruce's view, has seen the most rotten and death-infested elements of society achieving pinnacles of power. Roberts sums it up, the ethic of that society, in these incredible words which he attributes to the late Joseph P. Kennedy: "If you can't fuck it or eat it, kill it; then fuck it and eat it."

When Bruce Roberts came into our lives we were enmeshed in the endless machinations of the truth about Dallas. Like many people who believe that John F. Kennedy's murder was the product of a conspiracy, we found ourselves stranded on the grassy knoll, stuck on the elementary questions about wounds, angles of bullets and the entire Warren Commission fiasco. But even the barest sense of history requires one to get unstuck, to follow the tracks leading out of Dallas into the murky reaches of the past and the terrifying present. The value of Roberts is that he forces one to take such a leap into theory. What if Dallas weren't the first conspiracy? What if there were ones before it? An encounter with Roberts drives home the uncomfortable truth that one must at least consider this possibility. He stands at the door of what can only be called the fourth dimension of history.

After our first encounter with Roberts, he kept in touch by telephone. The calls were conspiratorial and furtive. He kept asking us to go to the Russian consulate with him to see his biopsy but we were, frankly, afraid to go. He kept warning us that the missiles were just 20 minutes away. But at the same time he kept coming up with fantastic, sophisticated information that stunned us and made us stop to listen again and again when we were tempted to dismiss his theories as wholesale ranting.

But we have not answered the question. We are conspiracy researchers, but we are not nuts; what then is the fascination of this man whose audacious theories are such as to almost automatically disqualify them from the realm of the rational?

One must answer first by paraphrasing the words of Tom Wolfe in his famous article on Marshall McLuhan when he first explained McLuhan's complex media theories—"But What If He Is Right?" In Roberts' case, the question is, what if any of the incredible facts and theories to explain the facts he presents is right? One must hear him out; one at the least must grant him a hearing; that is the conclusion we have come to after long and anguished debate among our-selves. An attempt to therefore present his theories in some coherent outline form follows this article.

There is one more thing that must be admitted: part of Roberts' appeal is that some of his theories mesh with some of our own prejudices. This is especially true in the case of Roberts' theories about the Catholic Church. One of our members is a fallen-away Catholic who took to Roberts' overview of history like an eager lad to his first communion. Roberts' version of the Papacy, from the Crucifixion to the present Vatican corporate empire, is more condemnatory than anything we've heard from the most ardent Freethinker, Marxist or Jehovah's Witness. In 335 A.D., says Roberts, the simple spiritual Communism of Jesus the Christ was spreading fast—too fast for the comfort of the mighty. In that year the Emperor Tiberius made a deal with the Pope: "You get the souls and we get the bodies."

"Sold," said the Pope.

A conspiratorial pact between Church and State, winning the assistance of the Judeo-Christian masses in a long imperialist war against the "heathen" territories. The fix was on.

Roberts' anti-Catholic theories are anchored in the Fatima miracle in Portugal in 1917. He believes the Church uses the dogmas emanating from Fatima—blind obedience to the Church, terror of the sins of the flesh, rampant anti-Communism—to control the masses for the Church's own

purposes. The theory is not particularly new or exemplary; it picks up, after all, the old Reichian theory of sexual lockdown—in the lexicon of anti-Catholicism, but as with everything about Roberts, he comes up with some alleged facts that are so assertive that we as researchers feel compelled to search. The world, Roberts says, has a right to know Teddy Kennedy's position on Fatima.

And some researcher with psychiatric skills ought to go to New Orleans to interview the last survivor of the Fatima [three sisters]—Sister Lucy, who today (according to Roberts) is aging piously in a New Orleans convent, safely ensconced in Carlos Marcello's Mafia territory, reading comic books and tending a miraculous cedar statue of the Virgin Mary, which cries real olive oil tears at appropriate dates on the Vatican calendar.

Each day Roberts has a new fact; new facts for old theories. Some of his facts may be laughed at, but they have to be researched. If but one of the thousand things he says is true, it could change the world.

Reprinted from the City of San Francisco, September 9, 1975

***

[This article was accompanied by my outline: *A Skeleton Key to the Gemstone File*, by Stephanie Caruana, in an even more abbreviated version than usual. As far as I know, this was the first (and only) "live interview" article about Bruce Roberts and his work to appear in print. It was accompanied by a photograph of Bruce in the CSF office. It was the first I had heard about the biopsy scar, and his weakened condition.—sc2005.]

Bruce Roberts at the *City of San Francisco office*. This was cut down from a larger picture which appeared with the article. The COSF staff was
apparently so frightened that they hid their faces in the photograph.

"Beyond the Gemstone File": First Book Based on the *Skeleton Key*, 1976

The first copies of the *Skeleton Key* to the Gemstone File appeared early in 1975, in the form of a 23-page typed, numbered, single-spaced set of pages, stapled at the top left corner, which could be copied and distributed free. In other words, I didn't write it for the money, and did not seek to make money from its distribution. I felt it was more important to give people this information than to worry about selling it. And I also had, at the time, a hope that I could somehow save Bruce Roberts' life by releasing it.

In 1976, an odd spin-off appeared. For an amusing description of this first book on the Gemstone File, I quote from Jim Keith's Introduction to his 1992 effort, a paperback which he called *The Gemstone File* (Illuminet Press).

Jim talks about the wild assortments of rip-offs, send-ups and hoax versions in which the "*Skeleton Key*" has appeared over the years since it first began circulating in April-May 1975. He goes on:

> "In an elegant segue: during the course of editing this book, I received a phone call from W. Scott Walker, the publisher of a book called *Beyond the Gemstone Files*. I had written to him, wondering about the content of the book, whose title I had encountered a few times but had never been able to locate, even having gone so far as to consult the Library of Congress. Walker told me in quiet, grave tones that I would be "violating copyrights held by the CIA," if I was so foolhardy as to go ahead with my proposed book.
>
> His story was that the author of *Beyond the Gemstone Files*, Peter Renzo, was an ex-CIA man authorized by the Company to release the Gemstone Files, which (Walker confided) are the G. Gordon Liddy files "he thought he had burned."[73] Walker maintains that Renzo was a member of the "Fighting Tigers Assassination Squad," and that the CIA simply won't allow me to do the book: this book.
>
> After questioning Mr. Walker about the nature of the files he had published (via Vantage Press, a well-known subsidy press; bastion of the terminally unpublishable, and now, we find, Company asset), it became apparent that it was the Caruana *Skeleton Key* with which the "CIA" had so boldly authorized him to go where so many had gone before.
>
> I sensed Walker was a little dismayed when I confided I have the Key in at least eleven different versions and am in correspondence with the original editor, and when I filled him in on a little of the background as I know it, Fighting Tigers Assassination Squad aside.
>
> Since speaking with Walker I have had a chance to review Renzo's book which is composed of, as I had guessed, the Caruana *Skeleton Key* coupled to stories about the author's supposed CIA connections and the murder of his friend amid the overwhelming odor of "apple pie," *i.e.*, Roberts' dreaded sodium morphate. Renzo also tells of a sojourn in Laos where he found a secret temple and a giant idol that, after pressing a concealed button, opened to disgorge precious "gemstones." On the way out of the temple Renzo fends off an attack by giant cobras.[74] A tacked-on segment about the Philadelphia Experiment (now you see the Atlantic Fleet, now you don't) and some photos of Renzo posing with tigers and aiming guns and kicking things fills out its formidable 65 pages."—*Gemstone File*, (Keith), pp.4-5.

I had heard about this book somehow, and had even bought a copy. I found it amusing though somewhat irritating. I assumed that Renzo's swashbuckling stories were pure fantasy. During the course of time, I lost the copy, along with a few thousand other books I have owned in

---

[73] The confusion about Bruce Roberts' "Gemstone Files" and G. Gordon Liddy's files which he burned, or shredded, goes back at least to 1992. For my attempt to clarify this, see Chapter 44.
[74] There is at least a chance that a bit of Renzo's tales of adventure in the jungles of Laos turned up in the "Indiana Jones" movies.

the interim. In the course of writing this book, I decided to check back on *Beyond the Gemstone Files* and its author, Peter Renzo. The book is, of course, long out of print. But the enterprising Renzo has had a new addition printed by Vantage Press, in 1990. He appears to be selling copies of this new edition through a Nevada gift shop for $250.00 a pop. (A word of warning: There is nothing really substantive in the book, so if you buy it for a pile of money, you may well be disappointed.)

It turns out that what I had assumed was pure fantasy, regarding Renzo's affinity for tigers, at least, is true. He still owns several tigers, which he keeps as pets, a difficult enough task. A couple of articles about him and his tigers can be found on the Internet. I believe he is located at present in either Nevada or California, but he seems to be keeping a very low profile—probably having nothing to do with Gemstone, and much to do with keeping potentially dangerous tigers as pets. And--let's face it: $250.00 buys a good amount of tiger chow.

36 1977-78: "Dialogue Conspiracy" or Why I Am Not a "Brussell Sprout"

From 1971 through 1988, Mae Brussell did a weekly half-hour radio broadcast from KLRB-FM in Carmel, California. It was eventually syndicated across the country to more than 30 public radio stations. At a time when challenges to the "official" version of many important news events were effectively blocked in the media, Mae's broadcasts offered a rare alternative view.

Before meeting Mae in the spring of 1974, after Patty Hearst's kidnapping, I had not been aware of her radio programs. But I had read and been impressed by her articles in Paul Krassner's *Realist*, written immediately after the Watergate burglary and arrests: "The Warren Commission is Part of the Cover-Up," and "Why Was Martha Mitchell Kidnapped?"

Our first attempt at working together was when I sat down with her and taped the interview which later became the *Berkeley Barb* article reprinted in Chapter Two. It was originally titled: "Is Cinque the first Black Lee Harvey Oswald?" At the time, I had no idea where this article might be published. I did not even consider it for *Playgirl*. It was obviously volatile news, not suitable for a monthly magazine with a long lead time.

I was impressed by Mae's knowledge and insight into Donald De Freeze's life story, prison experiences and "training." Then there was what appeared to be his staged escape, and experience outside of prison, such as living undetected in the San Francisco Bay area for a year after his escape. All his needs had been met, and he had presumably been able to coordinate and execute the Patty Hearst kidnap scenario (including the use of a van, in the middle of a sophisticated college community); and how all this related to the weird political milieu and prison system in California. Mae's views made more sense to me than anything I had heard or understood about California's tumultuous political climate.

The *Playgirl* article on Howard Hughes and Onassis was written differently. I worked directly from Mae's research materials, using selected articles in her "Onassis" and "Hughes" file folders as cited references, and using the mysterious but unidentified "Bruce Roberts" file as theoretical background. I called Bruce Roberts "Tiger Eye," an oblique reference to his absorption with Gemstones. (The published article omitted all the reference notes I had supplied.)

An astute reader who has stayed awake somehow may recall that back in Chapter 4 I described leaving Carmel Valley and Big Sur at the end of the summer of 1974. While I was introducing myself to Bruce Roberts and pursuing him and the Gemstone File in San Francisco, Mae was busy in Carmel with her new tenant. I had heard he was a prisoner coming out on parole, and had assumed he was the same prisoner at Soledad with whom Mae was corresponding at the time Donald DeFreeze walked away from the prison. But it turned out that Mae had more than one prison pen pal. The following is excerpted from an article by Virginia McCullough, keeper of the Mae Brussell files ("Archives"), and a journalist who maintains a Mae Brussell site on the NEWSMAKING.NEWS.COM website:

"It is doubtful that Caruana was aware that she was being supplanted by a black prisoner soon to be paroled from Folsom prison. The man, Elmer Davis, was a key figure in the Watergate scandal. He had been wrongly convicted for the burglary of Dr. Fielding's office.[75] Dr. Fielding was the Psychiatrist for Daniel Ellsberg who had leaked the Pentagon Papers. Mae Brussell and Elmer Davis had corresponded for a year and the correspondence had grown increasingly romantic. They shared

---

[75] Akshully, Gordon Liddy says that Elmer Davis, a burglar who had committed numerous burglaries in the area, had agreed to confess to the Fielding burglary so that the local police could close the books on this "unsolved" crime. Who wants to keep unsolved burglaries open on the books—particularly, ones that might be political? See Chapter 44 for Liddy's account. Elmer Davis later sued Liddy, unsuccessfully. ☺

a common cause: to provide equal justice to inmates incarcerated in California's prisons. They met because of the Watergate affair and their mutual involvement in it.

A flurry of letters written in August and September of 1974 to prison officials by Mae Brussell and Elmer Davis clearly document their mutual struggle to secure parole for Elmer Davis by October 8, 1974. On September 13, 1974, Mae Brussell wrote a letter to a Mr. Adams stating the following:

Dear Mr. Adams:

This letter is to confirm our discussion regarding employment of Elmer Davis. My contracts for articles, and speeches has [sic] required me to have assistance...with regards [sic] to my research, typing, and legal help on matters that might possibly concern libel. Elmer Davis is skilled at various kinds of research and would be able to assist me with my various projects.

He would be given immediate expenses, consisting of room, board, transportation, etc. In addition, I could guarantee him an income from $200 to $400 a month for helping me. A great deal of the college year I will be away, doing lectures, probably two or three a month. The work piles up during those times, particularly my mail. Elmer will be able to handle this for me.

When an opening is available as a legal aid [sic], he should pursue that project. Law is a subject he has studied for almost ten years. In the evening, he will be able to attend night classes at the law school on the Peninsula.

Thank you for everything.

Best Regards
Mae Brussell

***

The co-habitation between the researcher and the paroled convict lasted less time then did the collaboration between visitor/writer Caruana and her mentor Mae Brussell. Perhaps Elmer Davis and Mae Brussell might have remained life-long friends if they had never become romantically involved. Certainly absence made the hearts grow fonder and closeness created friction that the romance could not survive....

During the approximate two months that Stephanie Caruana resided in Mae's spare bedroom and collaborated on several articles they co-authored, Mae was also working with The Citizens Research and Investigation Committee (CRIC) that issued a devastating report on the CIA connections to the SLA. The report, based on the book *Cinque the Slave* by Donald Freed and Lake Headley, credited Mae Brussell, among other researchers and publications, for contributing valuable research to the project.

When Mae Brussell and Elmer Davis began living together it became rapidly obvious to everyone who knew them that they were not on the same trip any longer. The *Realist* publisher Paul Krassner has referred to the romance between the two distinctly different individuals as "true love." I would serious disagree with that description by Krassner.

However, Krassner hits the proverbial nail on the head in the following excerpt from his book, *Confessions of a Raving Unconfined Nut: Misadventures in the Counter-Culture*:

"A year before the Watergate break-in, E. Howard Hunt, who had worked for the CIA for twenty-one years, proposed a "bag-job"—a surreptitious entry—into the office of Dr. Lewis Fielding, a Beverly Hills psychiatrist who had refused to cooperate with FBI agents investigating one of his patients, Daniel Ellsberg, leaker of the Pentagon Papers. It was the function of the White House "plumbers" to plug such leaks. The burglars, led by G. Gordon Liddy, scattered pills around the office to make it look like a junkie had been responsible. The police assured Dr. Fielding that the break-in was made in search of drugs, even though [Fielding] found Ellsberg's records removed from their folder. An innocent black man, Elmer Davis, was arrested, convicted, and sent to prison, while Liddy remained silent. Mae Brussell corresponded with Davis, and after he finished serving Liddy's time behind bars, he ended up living with Mae. It was a romance made in Conspiracy

Heaven."[76]

On November 23, 1974 Mae wrote Elmer the following two notes:

Nov. 23—1:30 p.m.

If you [go] into town today, and do not want to help me with the things we said we would do on Saturday, I am not going to marry you.

If you have one drink while in town, with any alcohol on your breath, or act drunk and pass out when you come home, all of your possessions will be packed and ready to move out as soon as possible, I am going to collect boxes, and put everything away.

Mae

***

Nov. 23—3:30 p.m.

I believe our not having money this last month, the cancellation of the *Playgirl* article, the trip to Utah, and the other lecture, was for a purpose. The fates were testing us, to see what we could do together in adversity, without extra cash in our hands.

If I had earned that money, we would have possibly been married by now. In the meantime, we had a chance to see that you had no intention of writing letters introducing yourself to the local law firm, or of going out to seek employment until our money came in. You intended to sweat it out...until some good fortunes, stemming from my efforts at lecturing or writing came forward.

In the meantime, those efforts were too time consuming for you. You needed cash, and recreation, and drinks...and living on the town.

I am indeed grateful for the turn of events that spared me the mental anguish of having been deceived further...and the legal problems of a divorce. Having seen your performance, we are both free of each other from this day on.

P.S. A receipt of your childish indulgence, to spend $25.69 for a motel when we could have used it towards the necessities...such as phone calls, research books, newspaper subscriptions, etc.

Mae

***

Both lovers were prisoners—Mae a prisoner of her own making whose prison was the truth, and Elmer a prisoner of the system built upon untruths. Both were selfish to the core and their lengthy correspondence reflects their self knowledge of that common failing.

—by Virginia McCullough

The above excerpt is from Part 6 of Virginia's series on Mae Brussell. Web Address: NEWSMAKINGNEWS.COM. Look for Virginia McCullough's articles in the "Mae Brussell Archives".

***

And now, a word from Gordon Liddy himself about Mae Brussell's "honey bunny," Elmer Davis:

"On 15 June I was served with a summons and complaint in a lawsuit brought by Spencer Oliver against me and about every other Republican in Washington. It demanded damages

---

[76] If all this sounds to you like an episode out of the movie, *Pulp Fiction*, then you may be reading it correctly. With regard to Krassner describing the Mae/Elmer romance as "true love," I am reminded of the infallible motto: "True love never did run smooth." This may of course also be said of false love. Another motto springs to mind: "The mills of Heaven grind slowly, but they grind exceeding small." Being ground in the slow mills of Heaven may explain why G. Gordon Liddy hosts a radio show, and drives a car with the vanity plate: "H$_2$OGATE", while I am scraping by, and currently being threatened, along with every other "non-rich" U.S. citizen, with even greater poverty by Prez George Walker Bush, grandson of Prescott Bush, one of Hitler's major financiers. I hope I live to see the mills make another slow turn, but I am not betting on it. John Judge, one of the three loyal friends entrusted with Mae's *Gemstone File* section, (whose mother was a CIA analyst), sat on it for years, and then inscribed a copy of his *Judge for Yourself* publication to me, in which he referred to me as a "Brussell Sprout." No, No, John!—sc2005

amounting to $5,050,000. The Democratic National Committee had filed a similar suit in June 1972 that was still pending. I wasn't concerned. The Committee to Re-elect the President was the principal defendant and its lawyers were defending. I was sure that both suits would be settled eventually at no cost to me, so I just filed a denial to avoid a default judgment and opened a file looking forward to reading all the motions that would be going back and forth. If I thought of anything else that should be done, I'd do it, filing in my own behalf.

On 10 July [1972] I was sued by Elmer Davis, a California convict who had allegedly confessed to the Ellsberg break-in in a deal with Beverly Hills police to clear a lot of burglaries on their books after having been caught red-handed at one of them. Davis wanted $2,000,000 for being made a "scapegoat." This sort of thing continued until I was a defendant in a dozen different lawsuits and counterclaims arising out of Watergate seeking from me a total in excess of $56,000,000. I defended myself in all of them and when the last, Jack Anderson's, was dismissed on 4 April 1978, I had the satisfaction of knowing that in six years of litigation over all those millions of dollars, I had lost not one cent and had a hell of a lot of fun."

—*Will: the Autobiography of G. Gordon Liddy*, page 313

***

I was out of touch in Miami Beach when Mae did two radio programs on what she called "The Gemstone File", on December 25, 1977, and January 1, 1978. Unfortunately, her description of this material was inaccurate. Since she never made the original file available for study, her characterization has shaped many people's opinions regarding the nature and value of Bruce Roberts' writing.

Mae suppressed her 360-page cache of Roberts' letters, dated 1970-1972, for many years—until her death in 1988. After her death, it was said that she had left three copies of her portion of the Gemstone File with three trusted friends, unknown to me, who kept them hidden according to her instructions.

Meanwhile, many people who had read my *Skeleton Key to the Gemstone File* outline were feeling frustrated and annoyed. Was that all there was? If there was more, where was it? If there was no more, was this just a fake, or as Robin Ramsey of *Lobster* so inelegantly put it, a "cock-tease?" There was nothing I could do. I had only a couple of the letters (dated 1975), and no access to Mae's file. But other people were trying to do something, making research efforts based on my brief outline, the *Skeleton Key*, and books began to appear about it.

In 1999, I noticed an announcement on the Internet of a book of Bruce Roberts' Gemstone Letters, to be forthcoming from Tom Davis at Aptos Books in California. The notice said that this material was not the same material from which the *Skeleton Key* had been prepared. I assumed that this was Mae's portion of the file, to be published at last, and waited for some time for the book to appear. But there was no further word, so I eventually telephoned Tom. He told me that he had changed his mind, and did not intend to publish the book. I told him that I would like to publish it. He agreed to sell me a copy, along with a typed transcript. He added that the price would be $600—the amount he had paid to the woman who had done the transcript. He also told me that he would not give a copy of this material to anyone else. I quickly agreed, and sent him the money. When I received the manuscript, I set out to prepare this book, adding these earlier Gemstone files to the information I had gotten directly from Bruce Roberts in 1974-5. My first attempt was in 2000-2001, when an early version of this book was briefly made available on a CD. I had no money, and was unable to do more than that, and personal difficulties including a crashed computer put an end to that effort.

To me, the most important thing I can do is to publish this book. It seems to me even more urgently needed and relevant today than it was thirty years ago.

As a corollary benefit, for the first time since I saw this file in the summer of 1974, I can compare Mae's own file copy with what she had said about the Gemstone File in the two radio broadcasts which follow.

In order to clear up some of Mae's puzzling statements, I transcribed both tapes, and commented on them. Due to space limitations in this book, I have had to omit most of her comments. But I have kept the gist of her objections to the *Skeleton Key*, and responded. I have also kept her description of her meeting with Bruce Roberts as a matter of interest, and her comments regarding a book which appears to confirm one of Gemstone's statements.

If you would like tapes of Mae's 2 original broadcasts, please see ordering information at the end of the chapter. My comments appear in italics.

***

MAE: Good evening. This is Mae Brussell in Carmel, California. This is Dialogue Conspiracy Number 301. This is December 25, 1977.

...Last week I mentioned that I would go into the Gemstone File. Many people have asked me to talk about it. So I brought it in, and I am going to read part of it to you, and explain what it is.

SC: Mae brought in my "Skeleton Key to the Gemstone File", rather than the 360-page file she had. It appears that in the five years since September, 1972, when she received this Gemstone material from Bruce Roberts, she had not publicly discussed it. Apparently, only people asking her about the widely circulating copies of my Skeleton Key led to her mentioning it at all.

MAE: There are about 20 typed pages, and they are being circulated in London, Ireland, and all over the United States. They were put together by Stephanie Caruana. She came to my house to do an interview with me, for *Playgirl* magazine.

SC: Actually I came to Mae's in April, 1974, to find out whether she had any information on Patty Hearst and the SLA. At the time Playgirl had never heard of her. She did, and she agreed to an interview about it. It was published in the Berkeley Barb, a local newspaper, in May, 1974, and is reproduced here in Chapter 1.

MAE: She saw all the research material I had. She co-authored with me a story on the death of Howard Hughes being buried off a Greek Island, in *Playgirl*.

SC: Mae supplied the research materials, and I wrote the article. It was published in December 1974, and is reproduced in this book in Chapter 3. We split the fee.

MAE: As part of the background for the *Playgirl* article, I showed her what the Gemstone Files were. They were written by Bruce Roberts. I don't know any other person that has the complete set.

SC: Mae never had the "complete set." She had a 360-page xerox copy of a section of the Gemstone File, dated February 1971—September 1972. These pages refer to many other (and prior) papers, letters and backup evidence which were not included in her series. Roberts referred to previous letters and papers, going back to at least 1968, which were "four telephone books thick." Apparently Mae never saw these; nor did I. A rough estimate of his writing at about 150 pages per year would suggest at least 450 pages written prior to Mae's series, from 1968-1970. He kept on writing, from 1972 to at least the middle of 1975, when I left San Francisco. He died in 1976. At that rate, he could easily have added another 400 pages.

I read approximately 50 more pages written during 1974-5, only a small percentage of his writing during that period—none of which Mae ever saw. It was from notes taken from this material, plus conversations with Bruce Roberts, that I wrote the "Skeleton Key."

Aside from the one midnight reading of Mae's file which I used as a reference framework for the Playgirl article, I never saw that file again from 1974 to the fall of 2000, when I purchased a somewhat disheveled and incomplete copy from Tom Davis, one of Mae's guardians of this material. In fact, I never saw Mae again after I left Carmel Valley and Big Sur in July, 1975. And I only spoke to her once, briefly, on Radio Station WBAI, in August, 1975. The article on Hughes and Onassis was completed in July 1974, in Carmel, and appeared in the December 1974 issue of Playgirl. By this time, Mae had tried, and failed, to

write an article with Elmer Davis for *Playgirl*. *The Skeleton Key* was written in San Francisco, in the spring of 1975.

I stress this because several books written about the Gemstone File so far have assumed, incorrectly, that I wrote the Skeleton Key from Mae's materials; that she commissioned or "hired" me to do this, or that I somehow did it under her direction. None of this is correct.

My estimates of "1000 pages or more" were attempts to straighten out the confusion caused by Mae's statement that she had the "only complete set," consisting of 360 pages.

MAE: They were a series of letters that he wrote to his mother, or a diary that he kept for himself.

SC: One doesn't want to call this a deliberate lie, but in fact it was. In what appears to have been Mae's first public description of the File she had possessed for five years, she lied about, dismissed and even ridiculed the Gemstone File. After all, how important could these letters be if, of all the people in the world, the man chose to write about the history of Mafia operations in the United States in letters to his mother?

Mae does not mention the letters to Ralph Nader which make up about 40% of this file and were written over a period of more than a year. Instead, she refers to seven brief letters written to Roberts' mother, just after the death of his father, over a 19-day period, when she was visiting relatives, some of whom may have been involved in U.S. intelligence operations themselves. These letters take up about 7% of Mae's File. As for the rest, Mae calls it a "diary that he kept for himself." Instead, as Roberts states, all of this material was copied and circulated to a number of people. (Including, for this particular section, Mae herself.)

Thus neither of the two parts of Mae's malicious description is true. But it has been effective, in that many of Mae's followers have condemned or dismissed the Gemstone File without ever seeing it. She apparently allowed very few people a look at the File itself (except me, once, with dire limitations).

Since I had followed Mae's orders during my hasty reading, and only focused on references to Onassis and Hughes in my reading, I didn't pay much attention to the various addressees of the letters or papers. And since the materials I actually did use for the "Skeleton Key" were not addressed to either Roberts' mother or to Ralph Nader, neither were mentioned in the Skeleton Key. The letters I used were, in fact, addressed to various heads of foreign countries, while none of Mae's file copies were—another very importance difference.

MAE: ...Stephanie went through the 360 pages and went up to San Francisco to see Bruce Roberts. He is dead now; he died of a brain tumor about six months ago.

SC: Not true. According to his death certificate, the cause of death was an unknown virus infection, or perhaps cancer, involving the chest or heart. Mae's "revision" of this to a brain tumor seems to be a part of her attempt to portray him as a mental case.

MAE: She wrote a summary of 20 typed pages, in essence of what Bruce had to say, called "*A Skeleton Key to the Gemstone File.*" This is what I am talking about here: Stephanie's summary, not the Gemstone File letters themselves. I met Bruce Roberts when my first article came out: "Why Was Martha Mitchell Kidnapped?" He got in touch with Paul Krassner [editor of The Realist] and me, and he gave me this document.

SC: Paul Krassner published several articles by Mae Brussell in <u>The Realist.</u>

MAE: I was staying with some friends on Geary Street in San Francisco, and Bruce brought it to me one evening. And we were up until about one o'clock. I felt shaky and nervous about the way it was given to me, and I didn't know anything about Bruce at the time.

After Bruce left, I went downstairs with a friend, and we decided to go out and get a cup of coffee. When we got outside, there was a car parked behind our car, and a man was standing on the curb. We got into our car, and he got into the car behind us and followed us. We saw that

our car had been broken into. Documents and letters of the person that I was with had been removed, together with a couple of suitcases and the radio, as if to make it look like a burglary.

The man chased us up and down the hills of San Francisco. By that time it was around 2:00 a.m. Everything was closed, and we couldn't find a place to stop. A second car arrived, so there were two cars that zeroed in on us and followed us.

SC: Roberts referred to a "whole conga line" of agents of this and that who followed him around. Apparently a couple of these decided to follow Mae around for a while.

MAE: At around 3:00 in the morning we went to an all-night restaurant on Geary Street. We got something to eat, and went back to where we were staying. But we were locked out, and I didn't have the key. We finally went to KSAN Radio Station and went to sleep on a couple of bean bag chairs in the lobby until morning. I had a radio interview scheduled for around ten o'clock. And I was carrying these Gemstone papers around all night through this wild chase. It was a funny scene—funny now, that is, but it wasn't funny then.

I will read you some of the points that are pertinent, and some of the points where I differ. This is why I haven't used it in terms of writing about it or getting it published. And I hope the people who plan to make a movie about it [the *Skeleton Key*, apparently] in England will go over the material with me first, because some of it is in error, and some of it is correct.

SC: Mae appears prepared to pass judgment about the validity of the Gemstone File, without ever allowing anyone to see the original material and judge for themselves—and even though she had never seen the later materials that I used. At this time, because of family problems, I was in Miami, and out of touch. Roberts, the author of the Gemstone File, was dead, and couldn't defend himself.

MAE READS: (*from my original Skeleton Key*)

"…The Gemstone File was written in many segments over a period of years by an American named Bruce Roberts."

Mae silently omits or distorts much of the information in the original Skeleton Key. Her quotes are frequently partial or incorrect; and they drift rapidly to her own interpretations and opinions.

MAE READS: "1934: Aristotle Onassis, the Rockefellers, and the Seven Sisters—the major oil companies—signed an agreement outlining an oil cartel memo, which in essence said, 'Screw the Arabs out of their oil. Transport it on Onassis's ships.'"

Now, the Gemstone File was given to me in 1972. And since that time, we have learned that Robert Maheu of the Hughes organization worked with Mr. Niarchos, the competitor of Onassis, to get the oil contracts with Saudi Arabia. So it wasn't Onassis who had the power; the Hughes oil contacts had more power. Onassis is made the fall guy for the entire Gemstone. But he was murdered, his ex-wife murdered, and he died, all alone. That's one of my objections to the Gemstone. Onassis was done in, just like Nixon, who worked with them for a long time. Each of them had the power at some point, and then each was expendable….

SC: At one time, Onassis and Niarchos were competitive rivals in every way: for money, for the daughters of Livanos, for shipping tonnage, oil contracts, etc. However, at some point in the mid-50's, Onassis far outstripped Niarchos. He was fiendishly clever, and probably the most ambitious man since Alexander the Great. His "contribution" to history was the fastening of the Mafia power hierarchy and "etiquette" into every aspect of our society, and its export to many other countries as well. He was an expert in the arts of blackmail, threats and murders to achieve his own goals, which were money and power. His "genius" was to apply all this on a world-wide scale. In so doing, he seemed to inspire others to carry on in the same direction, with impressive success.

His advent did not enslave us; others had been working on this idea for centuries. And his death did not liberate us; other Mafs [not necessarily Italians, but philosophically committed to the use of violence and

any other tactic to achieve money and power], shown the way things could work, simply took over, and now keep the greatest shell game in history going, on a world-wide scale; it has been dug in now for seventy years.

But let's call it by a newer name, by which it is more and more recognized: the interlocking global confraternity of international corporations, swollen "defense" budgets, "security" systems, etc., corrupt government, and all the panoply of control by which a small percentage of people control the giants' share of power and money, and make perpetual war for perpetual peace, in order to keep things going their way.

This national and world-wide problem is what Bruce Roberts, and this book, and current "news headlines", and "wars on drugs and terrorism" are all about. The question of what Mae is all about, I leave to the members of her "cult."

Our children have been born and have grown up in this not-so-subtle slavery. Books, movies, newspapers and the fabric of our daily lives ring endless changes on the theme: "The Mafia has got us; no use fighting it." Each of us has to come to terms with the existence, power, and ruthlessness of this class of "overlords"; and how we choose to deal with it.

Mae's own library of books and articles could have supplied the proof of Onassis's supremacy, if she had wanted to find it. But her own limitations seemed to step in and keep her floating around on the surface. She tells you many things, but she refuses to add it all up. Perhaps she just couldn't let go of the idea that Teddy the K was a Prince, and couldn't have done anything wrong. Here she seems to want to feel sorry for poor old Onassis and Nixon!

MAE READS: "'March 1957: Aristotle Onassis carried out a carefully planned action. He had Howard Hughes kidnapped from his bungalow at the Beverly Hills Hotel, using Hughes's own men. Hughes, battered and brain-damaged during the scuffle, was dragged off to the Emerald Isle Hotel in the Bahamas, where the entire top floor had been rented for 30 days for the "Hughes" party. Hughes was shot full of heroin for 30 days. At the end of that time, hopelessly addicted, he was dragged off to a 'hospital' cell on Onassis's island, Skorpios, where he spent the rest of his life, a helpless vegetable in a wheel-chair.... Hughes's employees either quit, were fired, or stayed on in the new organization."

Now the Gemstone has an error here which should be cleared up. In March 1957, Howard Hughes was kept in the bungalow at the Beverly Hills Hotel. He wasn't kidnapped, but he was isolated. He was as good as kidnapped, but he wasn't taken down to the Bahamas like it says. He was kept in the bungalow from 1957 to 1966, and he never saw any of his old aides.

SC: *This is all particularly strange since Mae herself had provided the suggestion, and the research materials, for "our" Playgirl article. Here she is saying that she didn't believe the story to which she signed her name as co-author.*

Instead, Mae has simply bought into one of the many cover stories which were floated about Hughes during this period: His isolation, fear of germs, refusal to see anyone, etc., etc., etc. This particular story seems more absurd on the face of it than many other such stories! He was "as good as kidnapped", but not kidnapped??? Kept isolated in a bungalow at the Beverly Hills Hotel for nine years, and nobody knew he was there?????? But what about his "marriage" to Jean Peters, and their "residence" in a Beverly Hills mansion, and his simultaneous penthouse suite in a Las Vegas Hotel? This, in a town where gossip was and is the lifeblood of the community, and is also worth big bucks? And all those casinos "he" bought in Las Vegas? Did he ever "escape" from Mae's version of the "as good as" kidnapping? Come on, Mae! The fact that these stories were based to some extent on Hughes's known peculiarities only made it easier for a clever man like Onassis to suggest how the various cover stories were to be shaped. Besides, anyone could make up another story to suit their fancy—unless, of course, it approached the truth!

MAE: ...Parts of this file are true, parts are absolutely untrue, some of it is difficult to check, some of it I have used in my own research and writing, and it is a very controversial document because it is filled with a lot of misinformation."

SC: Misinformation? Where? Where?

MAE: One section is particularly interesting and controversial. It has to do with the role of the present Pope, Cardinal Montini. Bruce Roberts alleged that the Pope was part of the international narcotics traffic, with the Mafia and the CIA, since his early days as a Cardinal. The battle of the Mafia narcotics traffic has been entangled with the hierarchy of the Catholic Church, specifically the Vatican and the Pope.

Bruce Roberts told me in 1972 that this current Pope was in the OSS, and that he was linked to the Golden Triangle Narcotics Traffic in South East Asia that escalated during the Vietnam War. A year later, after he told me this information, a book came out on the history of the OSS, and it did link Cardinal Montini, who then became the Pope, with the OSS, and most people know that practically everyone who was in the OSS then became a part of the CIA. Recently, there is a new book out, called *Treason for my Daily Bread*, which names Cardinal Montini...as the person who assisted Martin Bohrmann and other Nazis to leave Italy and go to South America. And they went from Austria across the Brenner Pass into Italy, disguised as monks...

In addition, the Gemstone File refers to Cardinal Tisserant,. He was the head of the college of Cardinals at the Vatican. [Roberts] said that Montini...was banished from Rome...by Pope Pius XII, and then returned and became the present Pope in 1963...Roberts wrote that Tisserant wrote all of this down in his diary, and that [Tisserant] had called Montini "The Deputy of Christ at Auschwitz." He said that Montini was the fulfillment of the Fatima Prophecy, that the Anti-Christ shall rise to become the head of the church.

But the murder charges were never written up or discussed until just 1977. A new book came out 2 months ago, called *The Assassination: Theory and Practice,* by Richard Chameleon, published by Paladin Press in Colorado. This is the first book I have seen that would back up Bruce Roberts' allegations.

Chameleon wrote:

'A suggestion of intrigue surrounds the death of Pope Pius XI. He died in bed at the Vatican at the age of 81. To his very last, Pius XI was the deadly enemy of Fascism, Benito Mussolini, and Adolph Hitler. Shortly before [Pius XI] died, Eugene Cardinal Tisserant was directed to convene a meeting of all of the Italian bishops to hear what His Holiness had to say, and what he had to say was against Nazism and Fascism. Just before the meeting was to take place, Pope Pius XI was given what they called a stimulant. It was an injection, and an hour later, His Holiness was dead. So he couldn't meet with the bishops to object to Hitler's and Mussolini's Fascism.'

And Chameleon asks, in this book, whether there is evidence for the assassination of Pius XI. He says:

'It is a historical fact that Claretta Petucci was Benito Mussolini's mistress for eight years. Along with Mussolini, she was executed. Petucci happened to be a fanatical, pro-Fascist, pro-Mussolini follower. Is it purely by chance or sheer coincidence that Claretta's father, Dr. Francisco Petucci, was the senior Vatican physician who gave Pope Pius the injection, allegedly to stimulate him, one hour before he died? Pope Pius was to meet and discuss with the bishops the evils of Fascism, both German and Italian. Was Pope Pius XI murdered?'

MAE: Where Bruce Roberts gets way off base I believe is in the story of JFK's assassination. And because that's the area I know the best, I have to use it as a yardstick to determine the value of some of the other information which I can't get into. His account of the Dealey Plaza killing of JFK goes this way:

'There were 4 shooters, Lee Harvey Oswald, Eugene Brading, Jimmy Fratianno and John

350   *The Gemstone File: A Memoir*

Roselli. Howard Hunt and James McCord were [also] at Dealey Plaza...'
   It's the other way around. There is no proof that Lee Harvey Oswald shot any gun on November 22, 1963, so I don't believe that Oswald was one of the shooters at all....

   SC: I find it astonishing that Mae, after 14 years of concentrated study of the JFK assassination, never seems to venture a specific guess as to the identity of the assassins, beyond stating, "It wasn't Oswald." My description of the Dealey Plaza abattoir has changed somewhat, due to more information becoming available, but the general picture remains. Seeing Mae's section of the Gemstone File itself after all this time, I can say that I made at least one serious mistake in my original Skeleton Key account. According to Roberts, Johnny Roselli shot from somewhere around the overpass, in front of the limousine, not from the grassy knoll. His shot took JFK under the chin and blew his brains out, splattering blood on the motorcycle cop riding directly behind the Presidential car.

   J. D. ("Roscoe") White had been "assigned" to the Dallas Police Force 3 weeks before the assassination, (at the same time that Lee Harvey Oswald "got his job" at the Texas Book Depository.) He was of course dressed in the uniform of a Dallas Policeman. He was stationed up on the Overpass, together with another Dallas policeman, J. D. Tippitt. White may have moved behind the picket fence and shot at JFK from there. His image may appear in enhanced photos from Dealey Plaza; he may be the so-called "Badge Man." It is possible that White and Tippitt were then instructed to pick up Lee Harvey Oswald, in a police car, and possibly to kill him. But something went wrong.[77] We will probably never really know, since the JFK assassination details have been deliberately shrouded in mystery for so many decades.[78] It is also possible that Johnny Roselli shot at JFK from the sewer or drainage opening on the righthand side of Elm Street, hitting him in the throat and blowing his brains out the back of the skull, as described by a number of researchers. At any rate, Roselli's successful shot accounts for Roselli's later large pay-offs, and made him well respected and financially appreciated by the Mafia for some time. According to Roberts, Eugene Brading shot from the pergola, and Fratianno shot from the Dal-Tex building; all three shots were coordinated with the aid of timers assigned to each shooter, so they went off simultaneously. Roselli's shot hit; it is possible that one or both of the other shots hit as well. At any rate, JFK's head literally exploded at that moment. When it came to the possibility of his testifying before an Investigating Committee, Roselli was brutally murdered, in 1976, by other Mafia members. Roselli's old friend and Mafia business associate, Sam Giancana, was also murdered before Sam was due to testify about Mafia operations. Which Mafia murderer(s) turned around and killed dapper Johnny when his turn came around, I have no idea.

MAE: Again, this is questionable. Nobody saw Johnny Roselli at Dealey Plaza. He was a well-known Mafia man in 1963. That doesn't mean he wasn't there. But [Roberts] says that Fratianno shot one shot from the Dal-Tex Building and Roselli did the fatal shot. The third point of the fatal triangulation he claims was supplied by Eugene Brading from that small pergola at Dealey Plaza. Now Brading is a Mafia member who later went on to join the early La Costa gang down in San Clemente. Brading was seen in Dealey Plaza, and he was using aliases, and he did walk over to the Dal-Tex building afterwards to make a telephone call. He could have left a gun in the bushes that another man picked up. I know Oswald didn't shoot Connally. I don't know about Fratianno. Roselli is dead, killed right after he testified before the Senate House Select Committee. And Eugene Brading has never been called to testify before any one.

MAE READS: "Oswald shot John Connally twice, from the Texas School Book Depository. He left from the front door, leaving the rifle in the building. There was a backup man who, instead of

---

[77] See *Double Cross*, pp.334-5, for an informative passage on this.
[78] The Opal File, or Kiwi Gemstone, credits Gordon Liddy with the murder of Tippitt, but since this is a skeleton-key type of statement, with no back-up information available, I have no idea whether this is correct. See Chapters 38 and 44.

taking the rifle away, left it so that Oswald would be the patsy."

MAE: I don't believe that Oswald shot John Connally twice, or at all.... And I think that Bruce Roberts in this case is filled with disinformation.... The Gemstone File also says that three men were dressed as tramps, and picked up shells from the ground at Dealey Plaza, and that one of them was Howard Hunt. He says a Dallas Police officer ordered two Dallas cops to go over to the boxcar and pick up the tramps. They were released without being booked... In the Gemstone File, he says the Dallas policemen were ordered to pick up the tramps, but there is no recording of this, and no proof... So this kind of reasoning or misinformation that is in the Gemstone File should be broken down, and you should ask yourself for evidence. And realize that not all of it is true and that it is very dangerous to go by this file.

SC: "So Mae," I would like to ask; "who shot Kennedy?"

MAE READS: "The rest is history. Aristotle Onassis was so confident of his control over the police, the media, the FBI, the CIA the Secret Service, the U.S. judicial system, that he had JFK murdered before the eyes of the nation; then systematically bought off, killed off, or frightened off all witnesses, and then put a 75-year seal of secrecy over the entire matter."

Now if you think seriously about that statement, you realize that Aristotle Onassis didn't have that kind of power....People like Niarchos, his competitor, or Tom Pappas, the Greek shipping oil clerk who had *entre* into the White House with Spiro Agnew and Richard Nixon and the Rockefellers, had more political clout than Aristotle Onassis had in this country....

SC: But none of them married JFK's widow.

MAE: ...And it seems that the whole Gemstone File has two scapegoats. One is Onassis, and the other is the Mafia. Onassis had some kind of information. But I think that Onassis was the victim. I think that Jackie Kennedy was sent to Onassis to baby-sit him. He put up a large amount of money to try and find out who killed JFK.

SC: Just like O.J. Simpson did, to find out who killed his wife.

MAE: And there have been stories that that is the reason his own son was murdered.... I think that Onassis was curious, and maybe wanted to know the way the narcotics traffic was going to flow....

I think, in the end, when the power controllers took over, Onassis was a victim like Richard Nixon. And he was under the control of people, and he became victimized... There are things about the Gemstone File which I like, and many which I know are absolutely wrong. You have to read history, you have to read seven or eight hundred books which I have done, to make an analysis, but I did promise that I would go into it. And you can get a copy of the *Skeleton Key* yourself and read it.

***

Cassette Tape copies of these and other Mae Brussell's "Dialogue Conspiracy" broadcasts are available at a very reasonable price through World Watchers International, on the Web at: http://www.maebrussell.com. Ask for Tapes #301 (12/25/77) & #302 (1/1/78), on the Gemstone File.

37 1978: Gemstone and *Hustler:*
Larry Flynt Seeks Truth on JFK; Gets Shot

The following is the introductory material from *The Gemstone File: Sixty Years of Corrupt Manipulation Within World Government Detailing the Events Surrounding the Assassination of JFK,* by "Richard Alan" (pen name). This book was published in Columbus, Ohio in 1992. The author, or compiler, working from a copy of my *Skeleton Key to the Gemstone File* which he received from Larry Flynt in 1978, had spent 14 years amassing 1500 pages of newspaper and magazine articles documenting most of the events mentioned in the Key; and then whittled his 1500 pages down to a relatively trim 400-page large-sized paperback volume, which was originally available for $30.00. (Copies on the used market, when available, generally sell for $100 or more. In Cambridge, a single copy is available at Harvard's Widener Library.)

When the book came out, I called the phone number listed on the title page for "Crown Publishing Company". I eventually spoke to "Richard Alan," and later to his boss, who did not give me his real name, either. In subsequent phone calls, he (the boss) offered me a royalty of $3.00 on each book sold, which I did not accept. (He told me that 2000 copies of the first edition had been printed, so at $3 a pop I had a potential $6000. In retrospect, perhaps I should have accepted it.) The book is an impressive piece of work, documenting and expanding on the terse shorthand of the Key through contemporary documents, and backing up many of its statements.

In later calls, he (the boss) told me that he was negotiating with a movie company regarding movie rights to the book, but they were asking to deal with the author of the *Skeleton Key* (me). He refused to put me in touch with the potential producers, but wanted to buy the rights to the story from me. I refused to sell my rights, and unfortunately, that was the end of the conversation.

The editor, "Richard Alan," and his boss, "Mr. Goldstein," don't seem to be available today. The phone number listed for the publishing company is not in service. In Cambridge, a single copy of the book is available at Harvard's Widener Library.

I decided to include the introductory material from the book here, because the story of Larry Flynt's involvement with the Gemstone *Skeleton Key* must be told. In addition, 'Richard Alan' discusses his experience with Flynt, and his own strange and somewhat frightening experiences while investigating the *Skeleton Key* statements himself, in San Francisco. This information appears nowhere else but in the 2000 copies printed of Alan's *Gemstone File* book. It contains some additional biographical information about Bruce Roberts, and comments from some San Francisco residents who knew him. All page references in the following section apply to pages in "Richard Alan's" *The Gemstone File.*

DISCLOSURE

"*A Skeleton Key to the Gemstone File*" was obtained in 1978 under unusual circumstances. The validity of the original outline at that time was unknown. The validity of this material is still unknown. You, the reader, are the judge. I have released the material I obtained along with details of over 50 years of public information on news events told to us through the media. Some of these events found in the original outline of the Gemstone File do not coincide with what we have been led to believe over the years. Now the evidence is before you to decide the truth. I can no longer withhold this information.

One Sunday evening in February, 1978, I received a phone call; it was Mr. Goldstein. He was in town and invited me to Larry Flynt's house to meet the publisher and his wife. Larry Flynt lived three blocks down the street from me and I was excited to have an opportunity to meet the controversial local celebrity at his home. Once I arrived, I was greeted at the front door by a gentleman who showed me to the kitchen where Mr. G—was waiting. I was then taken on a brief

tour of the Flynt estate where I could see meetings taking place in several of the rooms on the first floor. I ended up in the living room where I was introduced to Larry Flynt and his wife Althea. We were all seated. While getting acquainted, we were continuously interrupted by the gentleman that greeted me at the door. Once, he advised Larry that the parts needed to repair his plane would not be available until the following day. Larry told us as soon as the repair was made he was flying to Nashville to interview James Earl Ray in prison. Several times Mr. Flynt excused himself from the living room but quickly returned. On one occasion he returned with a manuscript and handed it to me.

He said, "You may take this with you if you wish, but I must tell you that I have given this to four other people before you and, they are no longer alive."

My immediate thought was that I had no prior involvement with Larry Flynt and was merely a neighbor paying him a visit. I tucked the manuscript into the inside pocket of my sport coat. I had no conversation with him at all about the contents of this document.

When I left Larry Flynt's house I had some fear of being watched, and that fear intensified after reading the manuscript at my home that evening. It contained a skeleton outline of the Gemstone File. The Gemstone File was information compiled by Bruce Roberts through personal contacts in his dealing with the Hughes Tool Company This information included the identity of the other three gunmen, along with Lee Harvey Oswald, that made up the assassination team of President John F. Kennedy. I hid the manuscript in my office on the third floor of my home and became very conscious of any slow-moving vehicle or unfamiliar person that passed by. Was this a foolish reaction? After all, the information I now had in my possession is said in the manuscript to be the information the burglars were after at the break-in at the Watergate Complex in Washington, D.C.

Only a few days later I learned that Larry Flynt had been shot while in a small town in Georgia. Flynt had been buying up small newspapers, including the *L. A. Free Press*, *Plains Georgia Monitor*, and the *Atlanta Gazette*, and had started to print the entangled events surrounding the assassination of JFK. I now had the details of these events, and for weeks after Larry Flynt was shot I would not walk near any windows in my house and became very cautious for fear of a possible attempt to silence me as well.

Over the next few years various information became public concerning the John F. Kennedy assassination. This information would either be a special report for TV, local, or national newscasts, or a newspaper or magazine article. In almost every occasion this news was information I already had from my meeting with Larry Flynt. Initially, I set out to gather evidence in an effort to disprove the findings in the manuscript. Instead, the information I found supported the theory of the Gemstone Manuscript.

In 1988, on the 25th Anniversary of the John F. Kennedy assassination, Jack Anderson televised an in-depth special report on the assassination. This new information again gave support to the manuscript and the additional material I had found, but only scratched the surface of the entire story; a story of over a half a century of corrupt manipulation by the powers of the World. A story, interlocking the lives of the Kennedys, Aristotle Onassis, Robert Maheu, Howard Hughes, and Richard Nixon; involving numerous murders, including John F. Kennedy and Robert F. Kennedy; the kidnapping of Howard Hughes, the Vietnam War, the Chappaquiddick Island incident, and the break-in at Watergate.

The cover-up of this elaborate scenario was so massive that even the people entrapped in it did not realize their involvement. People like Daniel Ellsberg and Judith Campbell Exner, who has recently become visible since some of this information has been made public.

After seeing Jack Anderson's special report, I decided to uncover as much information as I could on what I now believed to be the true story. Working from the document originally compiled by Bruce Roberts,[79] I have uncovered more than 1500 pages of information over the last 14 years. My investigation has taken me to New York City; Washington, D.C.; Los Angeles; and San Francisco, where I have found the bulk of the information to have originated.

San Francisco was where Bruce Roberts was living until his unexplained death in 1976. In the

---

[79] Actually, from a version of the *Skeleton Key* from which my name had been removed.-sc2006.

following pages you will read of many unexplained deaths, such as those of Phillip Graham, Senator Estes Kefauver, J. Edgar Hoover, and Lyndon B. Johnson.

I have arranged the Gemstone File by first presenting the actual outline in its entirety. It is important that you comprehend this outline, *A Skeleton Key to the Gemstone File*, first before reading the rest of *The Gemstone File* [Alan's book.—sc]. I have then taken the skeleton outline in chronological order and have inserted the historical data to support each event as it occurred.

This support information was obtained from newspaper and magazine articles from the leading news sources such as the *New York Times*, *Washington Post*, the *San Francisco Examiner* and *Chronicle*, the *Columbus Dispatch*; *Time*, *Look*, *Life*, and *Newsweek* magazines, and others. Some articles date back to 1932. Thus, the reader can see what was published about the people involved in the Gemstone File for the past 60 years.

Many articles had not been printed until years after the events actually took place. You will find this information to follow each event as it unfolded in the original outline.

To distinguish between where the original outline stops and where the support information starts, I have inserted the following symbol: **B**. After the support material has concluded, the original outline resumes and is denoted by the ornamental capital letter.

In view of the obsession the American public has in learning the truth about the assassination of JFK, I feel this information must be released. Fourteen years have past, and an enormous volume of information has been gathered since that Sunday in February, 1978. Many of the corrupt individuals implicated in the *Gemstone File* are gone and others are no longer in power. You the reader can decide for yourself whether the stories you have been told about the Kennedys, Cuba, Vietnam, Watergate, etc., are true, or whether you find the Gemstone theory of the elaborate accounting of the assassination of JFK easier to swallow.

CONNECTIONS

There are significant connections between some of the key figures and events exposed in the Gemstone File.

In order to clarify the complexity of these events, I have highlighted the following relationships:

Joseph P. Kennedy and Aristotle Socrates Onassis:

Joseph Kennedy was hired by Charles Schwab, the President of Bethlehem Steel, as Assistant General Manager of the Fore River Shipyard, [in Quincy, Massachusetts]. (See page 28 of the September 12, 1960, issue of *NEWSWEEK*, found on page 60.)[80]

Aristotle Onassis ordered six oil tankers at the cost of $34 million from Bethlehem Steel. (See page 86 of the January 19, 1953, issue of *TIME* magazine, found on page 22.)

Joseph Kennedy, under President Roosevelt, established the United States Maritime Trade Commission and created the regulations for the commission to follow. (See *New York Times*, Wednesday, April 22, 1942, found on page 52.)

Aristotle Onassis bought "Liberty Ships" from the Maritime Trade Commission at less than ten cents on the dollar. Onassis was later indicted for defrauding the United States Government through his illegal purchase of these ships. (See page 66-69.)

There is a connection here with an attorney, Burke Marshall. The "*Skeleton Key*" states that Burke Marshall helped Onassis with his fight against the United States Government and their claim of fraud ("Liberty Ships").

Burke Marshall was one of the first people Edward Kennedy called regarding his problems at Chappaquiddick Island regarding the death of Mary Jo Kopechne. (See page 207.)

Carole Tyler, a roommate of Mary Jo Kopechne, was killed in a mysterious plane crash. Carole Tyler was a secretary for Bobby Baker while Mary Jo Kopechne was working for George Smathers, a very close friend of John F. Kennedy.

Bobby Baker, an associate of Lyndon Johnson, was convicted on tax evasion, theft, and

---

[80] All page numbers in this chapter refer to page numbers in Richard Alan's *Gemstone File* book.—sc.

conspiracy to defraud the United States Government. Carole Tyler was flying in a small private plane when it went down in the ocean just off the coast of Ocean City, Maryland, near the Carousel Motel, owned by Bobby Baker.

EPILOGUE

Since that Sunday evening in 1978 when I was given the skeleton outline of the Gemstone thesis, a part of me has been consumed by it. I have spent thousands of hours over the past 14 years investigating the information I received and its relevance to the intriguing events surrounding the Kennedy assassinations. I have been able to verify many of the claims made in the original outline.

Bruce P. Roberts, according to records from the administrations office, did attend the University of Wisconsin from 1936 to 1940.

On a recent trip to San Francisco, I talked with Steven Kish, the only person I have felt safe talking with who knew Bruce Roberts. He told me that Bruce Roberts was a very intelligent man and that Bruce did odd jobs for him on occasion. Mr. Kish said that Bruce started talking crazy spy stuff, "Gemstone," he said, and that Bruce would frequently visit a bar near the Fairmont Hotel where the CIA used to hang out. According to the Gemstone papers this bar was the Drift Inn, owned and operated by Alvin Strom. I visited the bar which has changed hands and is now called Yong San Lounge.

The new owner told me that she had taken over the establishment from Mrs. Strom, who had been operating the tavern since the death of her husband Alvin. Mr. Strom had learned way too much from his friend Bruce Roberts and was killed.

Mr. Kish told me that Bruce Roberts had married a Vietnamese Princess and from this marriage there was a daughter born. Mr. Kish said he employed quite a few people at the time he knew Bruce Roberts, and that Gail Harp, an employee of his, had more time for Bruce then he did. Mr. Kish was able to confirm the death of Gail (Larry) Harp who, according to the *Skeleton* outline, was also killed before he had a chance to get a copy of Robert's papers.

Both Strom and Harp were poisoned with sodium morphate, a drug that is not detected in the blood test of an autopsy. Death is usually ruled as a heart attack.

Mr. Kish said that at Harp's funeral Bruce was acting very strange. Mr. Kish recalled, "Bruce pulled me aside needing to talk." Mr. Kish said he was intimidated by the confrontation at the funeral and had not seen nor heard from Bruce since.

I had spent a good portion of the morning at Kish Realty where Mr. Kish went through his records in an unsuccessful effort to find an old phone number or address for Bruce Roberts.

My next stop was the San Francisco Metropolitan Library where I found that Bruce P. Roberts had died in 1976.

The library kept back issues of the San Francisco Bay Area phone books. I pulled out the 1976 phone book to find an address for Bruce Roberts but that page had been torn out. The book was in good condition, and the only page visibly missing was the one where Bruce Roberts should have been listed. I took another phone book from the shelf, and it too was missing the same page. Seven consecutive back issues of the San Francisco phone book were all missing the page where Bruce Roberts' address and telephone number should have been found. I felt that this was more than a coincidence. I decided the information I had gotten on this trip was sufficient and it was time to go.

Before leaving San Francisco, I stopped to say good-bye to Mr. Kish and thank him for all of his help. I told him I found out that Bruce Roberts had died shortly after Gail Harp.

"Why? Roberts would have been a young man," he responded.

The previous day, I had told Mr. Kish that the information I had obtained stated that Gail (Larry) Harp did not die of natural causes.

Initially, I felt he did not agree with me, but the next day when I informed him of the death of Bruce Roberts, I then felt he thought my information could possibly be true.

I have made one attempt to contact Larry Flynt on a recent trip to Los Angeles. I met with his daughter, Lisa, at a small coffee shop next to their antique gallery.

She said, "My father remembers you and would like to meet with you to see what else you have found out."

The meeting with Larry Flynt never took place. I was told his wedding, set for July, had just been called off, and that he was not keeping any of his appointments the week I was in Los Angeles.

Fourteen years ago Larry Flynt was gunned down and has been confined to a wheel chair, because of his ambition to make public the information he had obtained from the Gemstone papers. Although his wedding was cancelled, my suspicion is that the interest his daughter had taken in the Gemstone File was the reason for his sudden unavailability.

We have received many calls from people with information about either Bruce Roberts or his Gemstone papers since announcing the publication of the Gemstone File. If you have any additional information or would like an update, please contact us at Crown Publishing Company.

—"Richard Alan," Introduction and Conclusion from his book, *The Gemstone File*.[81]

***

This is an extraordinary story, and I think relatively few people are aware of its implications. While Larry Flynt is a larger-than-life figure to many, it is usually for his bouts with censorship regarding *Hustler*'s pictorial representations of young ladies in intimate poses and so on. However, as it turns out, Larry also went as far as he could to learn the truth about the JFK assassination, a question that has tormented this nation for more than 40 years. I don't know whether he ever read any of the original Gemstone File, although I understand that he worked with Mae Brussell for some time, and she could have shown him what she had. (Or not!)

It is also true that the original material in Bruce Roberts' Gemstone file is written in such a dense, repetitive style that a reader can sometimes get lost in it and miss the underlying logic. I expect that may have happened to Tom Davis, proprietor of Tom Davis Books in Aptos, California, as he contemplated publishing the material in Mae's file, which he had in 1995. This material requires editing, the way a gemstone requires skilled cutting, faceting, and polishing to bring out its inner coherence and beauty. Ahem! I think I possess that skill, and hope that readers will find Roberts' material as presented herein worthy of respect and even belief.

I believe Larry Flynt was shot because he was seeking confirmation of this information. He went further out on a limb than most people would care or dare to do. He was brutally, and professionally, shot; very nearly assassinated, and he has had to live with pain and paralysis for years, with little or no thanks for the efforts he made to learn and reveal the truth. So I want to thank him here, and say that he is truly a hero of our time.—sc.

The following is a brief article from Kenn Thomas's *Steamshovel*:

LARRY FLYNT AND JFK[82]

By an anonymous *Steamshovel* correspondent:

In June 1997, while I was attending the COPA (Coalition of Political Assassinations) conference at Georgetown University in Washington, D.C., a conference attendee, upon learning I was from Cincinnati, asked if I remembered a full page ad published by porn king Larry Flynt some twenty years ago in which he offered a million dollars for information about the 1963 assassination, of President John F. Kennedy.

Larry Flynt had received considerable publicity some months earlier with the release of the movie, *The People Against Larry Flynt*. The movie had been acclaimed by many critics for its artistic merit as well as the historic description of a battle for the First Amendment.

I told the conference attendee that I would look into the matter upon returning to Cincinnati.

---

[81] "Crown Publishing Company," in Columbus, Ohio, no longer exists.
[82] Reprinted from *Cyberculture Counterconspiracy: A Steamshovel Web Reader*, Vol.1, p. 175-6.

The press of personal business caused me to overlook the matter until October 1997 when Larry Flynt, eager to take on the Cincinnati establishment again, opened a shiny new *Hustler* store in the heart of the Queen City's downtown.

The media attention was enormous, and police had to redirect traffic around the new *Hustler* store as I arrived and got in line with the local porn fans to get copies of *Hustler*s signed by Flynt.

I opened the conversation with: "Larry, I am the only Cincinnatian who was in Judge Lance Ito's courtroom in Los Angeles in 1992 when Charlie Keating was sentenced to ten years."

Larry put down his autograph pen, leaned back in his wheel chair and laughed heartily. (Keating and prosecutor Simon Leis had pursued Flynt relentlessly back in the '70s, which produced the legal battle described so colorfully in the movie.)

After a few more conversational words I said: "Larry, the real reason I am here is to ask if you remember a full-page ad run back in the '70s offering a million dollars for information on the JFK murder."

With that the big smile vanished, and he looked at the floor and muttered: 'Yeah, and I got shot right afterwards."

The next week, I went back to the *Hustler* store to ask Jimmy Flynt, Larry's brother and permanent manager, the date of the shooting.

Jimmy responded instantly: "March 6, 1978."

I then began a review of both Cincinnati newspapers, the morning *Enquirer* and the afternoon *Post*, for the two months preceding the shooting. The February 17, 1978 *Enquirer* had a large story about a Flynt press conference announcing his search for a solution to the JFK assassination. This article featured a photo of Flynt standing next to Ruth Carter Stapleton (President Carter's sister) and now prominent researcher Robert Groden.

After reviewing the newspapers back to January 1, 1978, I had not found a copy of the million dollar ad. So I returned to the *Hustler* store to seek Jimmy Flynt's assistance. Jimmy was amused and interested in the folder of clippings I had collected. I then asked, "Jimmy, can you give me a more exact date of the JFK ad?" His pleasant demeanor disappeared as he barked testily, "Look. I tried to talk Larry out of that project back in 1978. The man's dead; Larry should have left the whole thing alone."

He then stalked off leaving me open-mouthed.

Conclusion: In the years after the 1978 shooting of Larry Flynt, rumors floated around Cincinnati that his local anti-porn persecutors were behind the shooting. The suspected shooter was a "lone nut" of classic vintage. It is clearly obvious, however, that Larry and Jimmy Flynt believed that the shooting was directly caused by the porn king's foray into the growing field of people investigating that infamous day in Dallas. The CIA was in a nervous state in 1978 because of the House Select Committee's investigations; all the spooks needed was some minor character in the conspiracy to surface and take the million dollar bait.

A researcher at the 1999 Dallas COPA meeting perhaps summarized the Flynt episode most succinctly: "Have you ever heard of a pornographer being shot because he was in the porn business?"

***

For an excruciating account of how our government treats dissenters from the official line, Larry's account of his court trials after he had been shot and crippled by an unknown assailant is instructive. See his book, *An Unseemly Man: My Life as Pornographer, Pundit, and Social Outcast*, Chapter 8: In Contempt.

Jim Moore Chapteret

Here is another strange sidelight on the Gemstone/*Hustler* matter. Shortly after Jim Keith's Gemstone File book appeared, in 1992, he received a letter in care of the publisher, Illuminet, from a man named Jim Moore. Jim Keith sent me a copy of Moore's letter. I have it somewhere; but the gist

of it was that Moore was claiming to be the real author of the *Skeleton Key*. He said that he had been a journalist in Chicago in the late '60's, working for a now-defunct tabloid newspaper. One day a man came running into his office with an untidy stack of papers and presented them to him. This man, said Moore, was Bruce Roberts. Jim Keith was unimpressed by Moore's claim, and so was I, to say the least.

Moore said he did nothing with the papers until 1975. Then, according to him, he suddenly up and wrote the *Skeleton Key to the Gemstone File*, dating it, he said, May 1, 1975. (Same date as my second "edition," the one widely distributed, at least in California, by Native Americans. I believe this is the version that Gerald A. Carroll got, from a Native American, in 1976, when both were students at California State University in Sacramento.)

Moore has been claiming for decades that he somehow knew everything Roberts had written during the intervening seven years, and/or was going to write. But some dastardly sneak stole into his house somewhere, and stole the *Skeleton Key*. I don't know whether this politically inspired supposed burglary supposedly took place in Chicago or in the back woods of Tennessee, or whether anything was taken in addition to the *Skeleton Key*, unknown as it would have been, just coming from his typewriter or outhouse or whatever, but anyway....

By this time, my variously dated *Skeleton Key* editions were duplicating themselves, circulating like mad, and causing consternation all over the country.

Well... I admit it makes no sense at all, but this is the story Moore has been trying to float for the last thirty years, on various web sites.

Moore also claimed to have been threatened and harassed, and later imprisoned, because of his daring activity (that is, claiming authorship of the *Key*,) and also to have attended the Congressional Hearings in the mid-seventies to "get the truth out." Jim Keith and IllumiNet didn't believe Moore's claim. In his letter, he offered to write some more "Gemstone Papers" for IllumiNet, but they did not take him up on his offer. I can just imagine what sort of garbage he would have provided, judging by his wild fantasies that still appear under his by-line on the Internet. These include a spurious "biography" of him, ostensibly written by the CIA, but obviously written by himself. It's quite funny, if you enjoy that sort of thing.

Moore has been undeterred by the three latest books which have been published on Gemstone, all of which identify me as the author of the *Skeleton Key*. He continues to lie about all this on the Internet.

He also claims to have attempted to defraud Larry Flynt of a million dollars for the material he stole from me.

From his website:

Moore: " Not too long after that, *Hustler* magazine publisher Larry Flynt (yeah, I know, he's a drugged out sleazeball), offered me $1 million for what I had on the JFK murder. I sent him the Gemstone Files [*sic*]. Two days after I discussed the story with his staff he was permanently crippled by a would-be assassin. The story was rejected; then in February 1979, *Hustler* published it, without paying for it—and even misspelled the same words I had deliberately misspelled[83] as protection...

The story got even stranger at that point. *Hustler* admitted they had received the story from me and offered a $2000 out-of-court settlement, which I rejected. (Maybe, in retrospect, I should have accepted it) ...."

***

In retrospect, though obviously giving any credence at all to such a long-term liar is absurd, I have had moments of thinking that if he actually was threatened, harassed, or imprisoned for his claims of

---

[83] Hey, this weird joker is even claiming my typos!!! ☹ —sc2005

Gemstone/Skeleton Key authorship, far better him than me! As Clint Eastwood remarked in one of his great western movies, before skedaddling out of the way of two opposing armies: "Toooo dangerous!"—sc2005

This pathetic plagiarist has been putting up his phony claims for decades. No one who knows anything about Gemstone and its history has been convinced. But someone named Gary Buell, from California, spent several years corresponding by e-mail with me. He claimed he intended to write another book about Gemstone. At first I cooperated with him. But I soon learned that he was in correspondence with Jim Moore, and for several years, he tried to find proof for the non-fact that I was the hoax, and Jim Moore was the real author. After three years of panting after Moore for some sort of "proof," he finally realized that there was none to be had. Buell is now claiming on the Internet to be "a leading researcher" on the Gemstone File. I want to state that in my opinion, he is not a leading researcher, just a foolish person who took three years (!!!) to realize that the liar was Moore, not me. Along the way, he has been astonishingly offensive to me.

***

38 1988: The Opal File (a/k/a Kiwi Gemstone File)

This contribution to the "secret" history of our times was apparently first printed in the New Zealand anarchist publication, *The State Adversary*, in 1988. Using the *Skeleton Key to the Gemstone File* as a starting point, and repeating the events listed therein from 1932-1967 as historical and "philosophical" background, it then crosses the ocean and picks up with related events occurring in Australia and New Zealand, in a global context, from 1967-1987. All three of the "Gemstone File" survey books published from 1992-1999 have included one or another version of this file, and for good reason. As Jim Keith put it:

"...It should be read, if only because of the stunning depiction of a Mafia/big business takeover and details of subliminals used for mass brainwashing."[84]

Gerald A. Carroll included selections from Opal/Kiwi in *Project Seek*, in a chapter called "Shiny New Gemstones."[85] He adds some interesting comments and connections, including a pregnant quote from Burton Hersh, author of *The Old Boys: an account of the origins and functions of the CIA*, regarding CIA connections with BCCI banking operations and the funding of heroin trafficking in, and covert arms sales to Iran. Hersh also mentioned involvement of the Nugan Hand bank in supplying tons of explosives to Moammar Khaddafi of Libya, and heroin shipping out of the Golden Triangle via the CIA's Air America.

Kenn Thomas and David Hatcher Childress included a version of Opal/Kiwi in their book, *Inside the Gemstone File: Howard Hughes, Onassis and JFK*. They also tie it in with Danny Casolaro's investigation of "The Octopus," immediately prior to his so-called "suicide." This has to rank as one of the most unbelievable "suicides" in the history of investigative research, but that is another story.[86]

The State Adversary was sued for its publication of the Opal/Kiwi file, because of its inclusion of names and numbers, such as those of Swiss bank deposits.

Nevertheless, *Opal/Kiwi* has escaped into the historical record, chiefly via the Internet. A Google search today reveals 600 website hits for the *Opal File*, and 200 more for *Kiwi Gemstone*.

It does not appear to me that the unknown author ever saw an original Bruce Roberts letter. *Opal/Kiwi* apparently derived its inspiration and blunt, direct style from my *Skeleton Key*. And I am proud to include it here.

A secret history of Australia and New Zealand—A 20 Year History In Brief

—*Author unknown*

"Fear them not, therefore; for there is nothing covered that shall not be revealed; and hidden, that shall not be known. What I tell you in darkness, that speak in light; and what ye hear in the ear, that proclaim upon the housetops." — Matthew 10:26

1967: May 18: Texas oil billionaire Nelson Bunker Hunt, using a sophisticated satellite technique to detect global deposits, discovers a huge oil source near Aotearoa, south of New Zealand in the Great South Basin.

June 10: Hunt and New Zealand Finance Minister reach an agreement: Hunt will receive sole drilling rights and Muldoon will receive a $US100,000 non-repayable loan from Hunt's Placid Oil Company.

September 8: Placid Oil granted drilling rights to the Great South Basin.

---

[84] *The Gemstone File*, Jim Keith, ed., 1992, p.3.
[85] *Project Seek: Onassis, Kennedy and the Gemstone Thesis*, 1994, pp. 294-304.
[86] *Inside the Gemstone File: Howard Hughes, Onassis and JFK*, 1999, pp. 91-122.

1968: May 10: Hawaiian meeting between Onassis and top lieutenants William Colby and Gerald Parsky to discuss establishment of a new front company in Australia: Australasian and Pacific Holdings Limited, to be managed by Michael Hand. Using Onassis-Rockefeller banks, Chase Manhattan and Shroders, Travelodge Management Ltd. sets up another front to link the operations to the U.S.

Onassis was crowned head of the International Mafia. William Colby[87] (head of CIA covert operations in S.E. Asia) ran the Onassis heroin operations in the Golden Triangle (Laos, Burma, Thailand) with 200 Green Beret mercenaries—i.e., the Phoenix Program.

Gerald Parsky, deputy to ex-CIA/FBI Robert Maheu in the Howard Hughes organization, took orders from Onassis and was made responsible for laundering skim money from the Onassis casino operations in Las Vegas and the Bahamas.

Mid-July: Placid Oil Co and the Seven Sisters (major oil companies) begin Great South Basin oil exploration. Hunt finances 45.5% of exploration costs; Gulf Oil, 14.5%; Shell Oil (U.S.) 10%; B.P. Oil, 10%; Standard Oil California, 10%; Mobil Oil, 6.5%, and Arco, 6.5%.

October 12: Hunt and Seven Sisters announce confirmation of new oil source comparable to the Alaskan North Slope, with gas reserves estimated at 150 times larger than the Kapuni Field.

Early 1969: Mafia consolidates its banking operations: David Rockefeller becomes Chairman of Chase Manhattan; Wriston, at Citibank, and Michele Sindona captures the Vatican Bank. Partnership Pacific was launched by Bank of America, Bank of Tokyo, and Bank of New South Wales.

February 24: Onassis calls Council meeting in Washington to discuss strategy to monopolize the Great South Basin discovery. Council members included Nelson Rockefeller and John McCloy, who managed the Seven Sisters, and David Rockefeller, who managed the Mafia's banking operations.

McCloy outlines the plan to capture all oil and mineral resources in Australia and New Zealand.

March 10: Parsky and Colby use Australasian and Pacific Holdings to set up a 'front' company in Australia. Using old banks—Mellon Bank and Pittsburgh National Bank—they buy control of near-bankrupt Industrial Equity Ltd. (I.E.L.), managed by New Zealander Ron Brierly. 'Australasian and Pacific Holdings' 'consultant' Bob Seldon helps Michael Hand set up the new organization. Seldon took orders from Mellon and Pittsburgh National Banks, while Hand was directly responsible to Gerald Parsky and William Colby. Ron Brierly would take orders from Hand.

July 24, 1969: New board established for I.E.L. includes Hand, Seldon, Ron Brierly, plus two Brierly associates—Frank Nugan and Bob Jones. Both are appointed consultants to Australasian and Pacific Holdings Ltd.

Jones will help Brierly launder funds into real estate (Brierly/Jones Investments), while Seldon and Nugan will channel funds into oil and mineral resources through I.E.L.

October 1969: Chase Manhattan begins new operation in Australia with National Bank Australasia and A.C. Goods Associates—Chase-NBA.

J. C. Fletcher appointed chairman of Seven Sisters' company: British Petroleum (New Zealand).

1970: February 17: Gerald Parsky sets up a new heroin-dollar laundry in Australia: Australian

---

[87] Colby died mysteriously in a "boating accident" in 1996. There are some 57,000 references to his death on the Internet. I picked one article, pretty much at random, to give a suggestion of some of the questions surrounding his death. It appears at the end of this Chapter.—sc2006

International Finance Corp., using the Irving Trust Co., New York, NY.

April 1970: Onassis, Rockefeller and the Seven Sisters begin setting up the shadow World Government using the Illuminati-controlled banks and the transnational corporations. In Melbourne they set up the Australian International Finance Corporation using:

- ❖ Irving Trust Co., N.Y.—linked to Shell Oil, Continental Oil, Phillips Petroleum;
- ❖ Crocker Citizens National—linked to Atlantic Richfield (Arco), Standard Oil of California, which is Rockefeller-controlled;
- ❖ Bank of Montreal—linked to Petro Canada, Penarctic Oils, Alberta Gas, Gulf Oil;
- ❖ Australia and New Zealand Bank (ANZ).

Meantime, Japanese members of One World Government move into New Zealand, helped by Finance Minister R. Muldoon; Mitsubishi and Mitsui make a profitable deal buying up rights to iron-sands helped by Marcona Corp. (U.S.) and Todd (Shell/BP/Todd). Todd is rewarded with sole New Zealand franchise for Mitsubishi vehicles. Muldoon helps Mitsui (Oji Paper Co.) obtain a lucrative 320 million cubic foot Kiangaroa Forestry contract with Carter Holt.

November, 1970: Fletchers extends the Rockefeller Travelodge operation by buying control of New Zealand's largest travel company: Atlantic and Pacific Travel.

Manufacturers' and Retailers' Acceptance Company (in 1970, this was changed to "Marac"): This firm specializes in leasing and factoring (buying debts at a discount). It also finances imports and exports. The major shareholders are the Fletcher Group (38.0%); the Commercial Bank of Australia Ltd (24.7%); NIMU Insurance (7.7%); Phillips Electrical (3.8%); National Mutual Life Association (2.4%); New Zealand United Corporation (4.0%). The CBA is a partner in the supranational Euro-Pacific Corporation, the other partners being the Midland Bank (UK), the United California Bank (USA), Fuji (Japan) and *Societe Generale de Banque* (France).

Early 1971: Onassis and Rockefeller begin global operation to buy influence for the One World Government concept. They use Lockheed, Northrop and Litton Industries 'agent' Adnan Khashoggi, to organize operations in the Middle East, Iran and Indonesia. I.C.I. sets up $2.5 million slush fund to Australia and New Zealand.

Finance Minister Muldoon changes law to allow Mafia-controlled banks to begin operations in New Zealand. Links are also made by New Zealand in preparation for Paxus control with Hong Kong and Shanghai; Wells Fargo with Broadbank; Chase Manhattan with General Finance; Bank of America and Barclays with Fletchers, and Renouf in New Zealand United Corp. All are members of the Business Round Table Organization.

Late 1971: Gulf Oil and their man Brierly begin organizing chains of Shell companies and dummy corporations to conceal their takeover operations of oil, gas and mineral resources and related industries such as vehicle franchises, vehicle spare parts and finance services—all part of the Seven Sisters' controlled car culture.

To extend links to the US banking operations they buy control of I.S.A.S. (New South Wales) and I.S.A.S. (Queensland), which hold sole franchise for construction and mining equipment produced by International Harvester Credit Co., which is part of Chase Manhattan Bank and associated with First National Bank, Chicago (Chairman Sullivan, also Executive Vice-President of Chase Manhattan), Continental Illinois (linked with CIA and Mafia Michele Sindona of Vatican Bank) and Rockefeller's Standard Oil of Indiana (AMOCO).

I.S.A.S. (Queensland) also has strategic holdings in North Flinders Mines, Flinders Petroleum, Apollo International Minerals.

February 1972: Onassis and Rockefeller help associate Adnan Khashoggi buy the Security Pacific

National Bank in California and take control of the United California Bank through CIA-linked Lockheed Aircraft Corporation. Both banks are used by Onassis and Khashoggi to funnel bribes and payoffs via the CIA's Deak Bank to captive Japanese and other crooked politicians. Security Pacific also used to 'launder' over $2 million for Nixon's re-election campaign. Khashoggi also buys 21% of Southern Pacific Properties, which is the major stockholder in Travelodge (Australia), thereby establishing direct links to New Zealand, and U.E.B. and Fletchers through its equity links with Travelodge (New Zealand).

April 1972: Mafia banking operations expanded through New Hebrides with establishment of Australian International Ltd. to finance Pacific development by the oil companies (Seven Sisters). Banks involved include Irving Trust, NY; Bank of Montreal, Crocker International, Australia & New Zealand Bank and the Mitsubishi Bank, whose president, Nakamaru, is appointed Chairman.

26th May, 1972: Gerald Parsky installs Michele Sindona as 'owner' of Franklin National Bank, helped by the Gambino Mafia family and David Kennedy—Chairman of Continental Illinois Bank and Nixon's Secretary of the Treasury.

Pacific Basin Economic Council Conference in Wellington, NZ. Vice-President Shigeo Nagano also chairman of Nippon Steel and member of Onassis and other World Government organizations. Chairman of New Zealand sub-committee J. Mowbray is also General Manager of the National Bank.

Meanwhile, Michele Sindona, acting as the go-between for the Mafia and the CIA, was the conduit between U.S. and European banks. Michele Sindona's Vatican Bank and associate Calvi's Abrosiano Bank was used to finance CIA neo-fascist Italian/Latin American operations through Licio Gelli's P2 Lodge, which helped to organize the 'death squads' of Argentina, Uruguay and Chile. This aided the P2 members such as Klaus Barbie ('The Butcher of Lyons') and Jose Rega—organizer of the A.A.A. in Argentina.

16th August, 1972: Gulf Oil associate Bob Seldon helps establish new banking operation; first New Zealand international banks include Bank of New Zealand, D.F.C. (Aust), New Zealand, Morgan Guaranty Trust, Morgan Grenfel and S. F. Warburg.

Fletchers begins expansion overseas with deals signed in Indonesia, Fiji and New Guinea.

December 1972: Kirk elected Prime Minister of New Zealand.

February, 1973: Gerald Parsky, William Colby, Michael Hand, Frank Nugan and Bob Seldon move to further consolidate the Mafia banking operations. In NZ they acquire 20% Fletcher subsidiary Marac, using the Security Pacific National Bank helped by Marac Corporate secretary Alan Hawkins.

Frank Nugan and Michael Hand use Fletcher and Renouf and their NZ United Corporation to link with I.E.L. and Brierly Investments through cross-shareholding agreement.

In Australia, the Nugan Hand Bank begins operations with 30% of the stock held by Australasian and Pacific Holdings (100% Chase Manhattan Bank), 25% by CIA's Air America (known as 'Air Opium'), 25% by South Pacific Properties and 20% held by Seldon, Nugan and Hand.

The Irving Trust Bank's New York Branch establishes U.S. links between the CIA and Nugan Hand, a worldwide network of 22 banks set up to:

    a) 'launder' money from Onassis heroin operations in the Golden Triangle and Iran;

    b) act as a CIA funnel to pro-U.S. political parties in Europe and Latin America, including Colby's P2;

c) be a spying conduit for information from Cambodia, Laos, Vietnam and Thailand;

d) finance arms smuggled to Libya, Indonesia, South America, Middle East and Rhodesia using the CIA's Edward Wilson.

Colby and Kissinger use key CIA and Naval Intelligence officers to oversee the operation, including Walter McDonald (former Deputy Director, CIA), Dale Holmgren (Flight Service Manager, CIA Civil Air Transport), Robert Jansen (former CIA Station Chief, Bangkok), etc.

Heroin flown into Australia by CIA's Air America and transshipped to Onassis's lieutenant in Florida, Santos Trafficante, Jr., assisted by Australian Federal Bureau of Narcotics officials and coordinated by CIA's Ray Cline.

June 14, 1973: Inauguration of the Onassis Shadow World Government: the Trilateral Commission. Includes over 200 members from the U.S., Europe and Japan: bankers, government officials, transnational corporations' top executives, trade unionists, etc. Of the world's largest corporations, 24 are directly represented, and dozens more through interlocking directorships.

*Trilateralist strategy: monopolization of the world's resources, production facilities, labor technology, markets, transport and finance. These aims are backed up by the U.S. military and industrial complexes that are already controlled and backed up by the CIA.

August 18, 1973: Ray Cline and Michael Hand meet in Adelaide to discuss CIA plan to establish spying operations in New Zealand.

September 1973: Seagram's, with strong links to Chase Manhattan Bank of Montreal and Toronto Dominion Bank, buys 2,800 acres of prime land in Marlborough, helped by Peter Maslen.

February 17, 1974: Mafia sets up New Hebrides Bank—Commercial Pacific Trust Co (COMPAC). Banks include CBA, Europacific Finance Corporation, Trustee Executors and Agency Co., Fuji Bank, Toronto Dominion Bank, European Asian Bank and United California Bank. COMPAC to be used as a cover for heroin dollar laundering operations.

February 26, 1974: Michael Hand meets Bob Jones in Wellington to implement plans for the CIA's new spying operation; countries targeted include France, Chile, West Germany and Israel.

Using the Brierly/Jones Investment funnel, Jones buys building in Willeston Street which will be rented to France and Chile, and another at Plimmer Steps to house West Germany and Israel.

CIA will set up eavesdropping communications center inside the Willeston Street building, and another at 163 The Terrace which will link with equipment installed in the Plimmer Steps building. Four CIA technicians will run the whole operation.

April 1974: Finance Minister Rowling appoints Ron Trotter to the Overseas Investment Commission, whose chairman, G. Lau, is also a member of the Todd Foundation (Shell/BP/Todd) investment board.

Whitlam and Kirk

Mid-1974: Gough Whitlam and Norman Kirk begin a series of moves absolutely against the Mafia Trilateralists. Whitlam refuses to waive restrictions on overseas borrowings to finance Alwest Aluminum Consortium of Rupert Murdoch, BHP and R. J. Reynolds. Whitlam had also ended Vietnam War support, blocked uranium mining, and wanted more control over U.S. secret spy bases—e.g., Pine Gap.

Kirk had introduced a new, tough Anti-Monopoly Bill and had tried to redistribute income from big companies to the labor force through price regulation and a wages policy.

Kirk had also rejected plans to build a second aluminum smelter near Dunedin and was preparing the Petroleum Amendment Bill to give more control over New Zealand oil resources.

Kirk had found out that Hunt Petroleum, drilling in the Great South Basin, had discovered a

huge resource of oil comparable in size to the North Sea or Alaskan North Slope. Gas reserves alone are now estimated at 30 times bigger than Kapuni, and oil reserves of at least 20 billion barrels—enough for New Zealand to be self-sufficient for years. Oil companies completely hushed up these facts. To have announced a vast new oil source would probably mean a decline in world oil prices, which would not have allowed OPEC and Onassis plans for the Arabs to eventuate. New Zealand could be exploited at a later date, particularly since the North Sea operations were about to come on stream. Kirk was the last to hold out.

September, 1974: Death of Norman Kirk. According to CIA sources, Kirk was killed by the Trilateralists using Sodium Morphate. Rowling's first act as New Zealand Prime Minister was to withdraw Kirk's Anti-Monopoly Bill and the Petroleum Amendment Bill.

Later, Rowling would be rewarded with an ambassadorship to Washington. Incidentally, the Shah of Iran was murdered the same way as Kirk on his arrival in the US.

October 6, 1974: Ray Cline implements William Colby plan to oust Australian Prime Minister Whitlam. Nugan Hand Bank finances payoffs to Malcolm Fraser and other pro-U.S. politicians. A joint bugging operation commences between CIA and ASIO.

Rupert Murdoch, playing his part, uses his newspapers and television network to spread lies and misinformation. Whitlam, as well as refusing to waive restrictions on overseas borrowing to finance the aluminum consortium, had plans to ensure that all corporations were at least 50% Australian-owned. This interfered with the Seven Sisters' plans to build three oil refineries at Cape Northumberland in South Australia to exploit the Great South Basin discovery.

December, 1974: Australian Governor General John Kerr joins Ray Cline's payroll and receives his first pay-off of $US200,000, credited to his account number 767748 at the Singapore branch of the Nugan Hand Bank.

[March 15, Saturday, 1975: Onassis died, in Paris, of natural causes (myasthenia gravis.) But the efficient and ruthless worldwide organization of political, big-business, banking and Mafia entities which he helped to create continued without a hitch, owned and managed by his many associates, and continues to this day with ever-increasing control of worldwide resources and the lives and fates of millions of people, of many nations throughout the world, whose hopeless and helpless poverty is an essential component of the wealth and power of the rulers and power brokers of this world.—sc2006.]

[March 15, 1975: Bruce Roberts was hospitalized in San Francisco, for the "Brezhnev Flu," for which he credited the CIA.]

[April 1975: I began circulating early copies of the Skeleton Key, based on Bruce Roberts' Gemstone File, hoping to distract his enemies. I have added these last three bracketed entries to tie the Opal/Kiwi Gemstone chronology into the Skeleton Key.—sc 2006.]

August 1975: Rowling re-introduces unrecognizable Commerce Bill, designed to aid monopolization of the NZ economy, and repeals the News Media Ownership Act, allowing more foreign ownership of NZ media. The new legislation does not define monopoly, competition or stipulate permissible maximum market share, or even ascertain what the public interest is—resulting in a sell-out to big business.

November 11, 1975: Governor General Kerr sacks the Whitlam Government.

Election battle between Rowling and Muldoon. Oil companies pour thousands of dollars into Muldoon's campaign via National Bank (NZ), whose general manager Mowbray is also a member of Todd Foundations; Investment Board Director Tudhope also Managing Director Shell Oil and Chairman Shell/BP/Todd. Muldoon wins.

February, 1976: Muldoon implements pre-election secret agreement with the NZ Seven Sisters' oil representatives of Shell/BP/Todd for helping finance the National Party campaign.

Muldoon removes the $3 per barrel oil levy for the NZ Refining Company, which increases the oil companies' profits by 100% at the taxpayers' expense; with all future oil prospecting licenses, the Government has the option to take 51% of any discovery without meeting exploration costs. This is designed to discourage further exploration, thereby keeping the lid on the Great South Basin discovery.

Meanwhile, in Australia, new P.M. Malcolm Fraser reopens uranium mining and opens the way for takeover of mineral resources with big tax breaks for oil exploration, coal and mining.

Muldoon returns a favor to the oil companies by arranging $US200 million loan for Maui Gas Development for Shell/BP/Todd.

[*July 30, 1976: Bruce Roberts died in San Francisco, apparently as a delayed result of his 1975 illness.— sc2005*]

September, 1976: With captive politicians in place in both Australia and NZ, the Internationalists can now proceed with their strategy of takeover of the economy and exploitation of natural resources. "In New Zealand, the elimination of unnecessary competition is fundamental to a sound economy," Brierly says.

Parsky and Colby use Brierly/Jones Investments as a vehicle to buy into A. B. Consolidated Holdings in NZ.

An Associate of R. Jones, Pat Goodman, is appointed 'consultant' of Australasian and Pacific Holdings.

November, 1976: The Internationalists (Mafia) set up a NZ money 'funnel' using Brierley's City Realties. National Insurance Co acquires 33% of the stock. Largest stockholders in National Insurance are the US Firemen's Fund—Chairman and President, Myron Du Bain, also Vice Chairman of American Express (Amex), and Chairman of I.E.L-linked International Harvester; Archie McCardell, also Amex Director. Amex is linked with Chase Manhattan and Seven Sisters' Texaco and Mobil. Du Bain also a Director of CIA-linked United California Bank, which is a partner in Commercial Pacific Trust.

To complete the money funnel, National Insurance becomes a stockholder in Chase Manhattan's Chase-NBA. Brierley's declared assets reach $100 million, with shareholder's capital of only $2.5 million—all cash acquisitions.

February 3, 1977: Parsky and Colby close down the Brierley/Jones Investment funnel and open up separate channels for Brierley and Jones. Jones will be supplied with 'laundered' funds via Sydney branch of the Nugan Hand Bank. For Ron Brierley, Gerald Parsky uses Myron Du Bain, Director of United California Bank and also chairman and president of the U.S. Firemen's Fund, which are the largest stockholders in National Insurance NZ). Funds to be 'laundered' via Chase Manhattan Bank through National Insurance to City Realty, and via United California Bank through COMPAC (New Hebrides) to National Insurance and City Realties.

To expand the Brierley/I.E.L. 'front', Parsky establishes Industrial Equity Pacific (Hong Kong).

September 1977: Brierley's new holding company begins operations: A. B. Consolidated. H. W. Revell is appointed Deputy Chairman, and B. Hancox, General Manager. Newly-appointed directors include S. Cushing, B. Judge, O. Gunn and P. Goodman, linked with Renouf, Fletcher and Papps through I.E.L./NZUC.

Strategy: To target and divide key sectors of the economy for takeover, exploitation and monopolization. Operations to extend to use Hong Kong facility, I.E.P. Fletchers to extend the Khashoggi/Rockefeller Travelodge operation by taking holdings in Vacation Hotels and Intercontinental Properties (Renouf, Chairman).

October, 1977: Muldoon and John Todd, of Shell/BP/Todd, sign an agreement: NZ Government

would take 24.5% holding in the Great South Basin for $1.65 Billion. Hunt would reduce his holding from 45.5% to 27.5%, and Arco would sell its 6.5%.

(Reason: Hunt did not possess the technology to pump oil from deep water; Gulf possessed the technology but did not tell Hunt. Arco was not told anything, and was swindled out of its 6.5% concession.)

November, 1977: Muldoon introduces the S.I.S. Amendment Bill, designed to keep the economy free of obstruction and to help uncover obstructive elements. Telephone taps, mail tampering and other surveillance methods approved after CIA input on contents of legislation.

Late 1977: Muldoon travels to the US to meet top Rockefeller officials, including Trilateralists' Deputy Secretary of State, Warren Christopher, and Richard Bolbrooke, who were in charge of the new "South Pacific Desk" at the State Department, established by Rockefeller to target exploitation of both NZ and Australia. In Los Angeles, Muldoon meets top Rockefeller officials, Robert Anderson (Rockwell Chairman, also Director of Kashoggi's Security Pacific National Bank) and P. Larkin (Rockwell Director; also Chairman, Executive Committee Security Pacific National Bank and Director of Marac)

.April, 1978: Muldoon sets up Petrocorp. NZ taxpayers pay for the exploration costs but the oil companies control all distribution outlets. Muldoon blocks development of Maui B as restructured supplies mean higher prices and bigger profits for Shell/BP/Todd. South Island gas market not developed as Great South Basin fields are closer than Kapuni. Plans develop for re-opening of National Parks for mineral exploitation.

July 22, 1978: Director of Australian Federal Bureau of Narcotics suspends his investigation into the Nugan Hand Bank after pressure from the CIA and Australian politicians controlled by Mafia, particularly Malcolm Fraser. Brierly's declared assets reach $200 million, with shareholders' funds only $17 million.

1979: May: Trilateral Commission secretary Zbignieu Brzezinski appoints Muldoon chairman of Board of Governors of IMF/World Bank on orders of David Rockefeller. Muldoon would head three-man administration committee which included Canadian Finance Minister Mitchell Sharp, key figure in the Mafia Council and the Trilateral Commission. Australian Treasurer McMahon was also involved.

June 8, 1979: Michael Hand, Frank Nugan, Brierley and James Fletcher meet in Hand's Sydney penthouse to discuss the establishment of the NZ Mafia organization.

Mid-1979: Gulf Oil, using its man Brierley, begins operations designed to capture key sectors of the economy. A. B. Consolidated is restructured into the Goodman Group with Goodman to run operations, but with the majority of the stock held by I.E.L. and Brierley, using Shell companies plus dummy corporations.

*Strategy: To take over food and produce resources, Brierley and Fletcher restructured a small private company, H. W. Smith, using Cyril Smith as Chairman but with key executives Judge, Collins and McKenzie. Bob Jones helps.

A private company was used, so that there would be no Commerce Commission control, accounts were not published, and there would be no public disclosure of transactions. Bunting was established as a shell company, and the South Island was targeted for asset-stripping and takeover, as well as key sectors of the automobile industry.

Unlimited funds were channeled through City Realties; NZUC and Marac extend Travelodge operations by buying control of Trans-Holdings, which has strategic holdings in Vacation Hotels and Tourist Corp.'s Fiji Holdings.

August 17, 1979: NZ Mafia inaugural meeting in Sydney including Hand, Brierley, Fletcher,

Goodman, R. Trotter, Alan Hawkins and L. Papps.

Key sectors of the economy would be taken over:
- food, using Goodman
- forestry and farming, using Fletcher and Trotter;
- property, using Brierley and Jones.

Brierley, Hand and Papps would be responsible for banking, insurance and finance, while Hand and Hawkins would be responsible for setting up new "laundry" channels into NZ.

The economy would be taken over using cheap loans of less than 5%, while consumers would pay 28%.

October, 1979: BP Oil begins $100 million joint venture deal with Fletcher and Trotter at Tasman.

Muldoon makes secret deal with oil companies which effectively robs New Zealand taxpayers by giving Shell/BP/Todd the Maui Gas deal. Normally the granting of drilling rights on public land is done using a worldwide system which incorporates an auction tender system. Muldoon bypassed this. Also, Shell/BP/Todd pays no tax on Kapuni profits, while putting funds into Maui development.

November 19, 1979: Secret meeting in Auckland between Muldoon, Fletcher and Trotter to transfer 43% Tasman Pulp and Paper held by NZ Government to Challenge Corporation (Chairman Trotter) and Fletchers. Tasman has lucrative 75-year contract for cheap timber signed in 1955.

Muldoon was paid off with a $1 million 'non-repayable' loan: $500,000, to be paid into account number 8746665 at New Hebrides branch of the Australian International Bank.

November, 1979: Muldoon drops restrictions on foreign investment. AMAX (Standard Oil of California subsidiary) captures the Martha Hill gold mine.

Muldoon unveils the Government's plans (instructed by Rockefeller) to form NZ into an offshore production base for the multi-national corporations as benefits include government export incentives, stable government, cheap labor, and so on.

November 27, 1979: Gerald Parsky's lieutenant, David Kennedy, meets Muldoon to deliver $US100,000 cash to Muldoon for implementing the Internationalists' Mafia Think Big plans.

These plans began with big contracts and guaranteed profits for the Seven Sisters, Bechtel, Mitsubishi, Mitsui, Nippon Steel, Internationalists' Mafia banks.

With the experimental petroleum plant, the oil price has to be $50/barrel to be profitable, yet Mobil's profits are guaranteed.

NZ Steel is to be expanded 500%, even though there was a global steel glut of 50%.

Fletchers own 10% of NZ Steel; are majority stockholders in Pacific Steel, and control monopoly over wire rod, reinforcing steel. Also, NZ taxpayers subsidize Fletchers' profits.

Muldoon introduces the National Development Bill with 'fast-track' legislation, to keep the economy 'free of obstruction' for long-term monopolization. C. E. R. plan introduced, designed to integrate the economies of Australia and NZ with the Trilateral Commission for the purpose of exploiting the South Pacific countries and as a 'back-door' entrance into China—the world's largest untapped consumer market. NZ is also the closest country to Antarctica, which has a vast mineral resource for future exploitation.

"Think Big" projects begin, even though Muldoon is aware of studies that show NZ could conserve up to 40% of energy consumption using existing technology, which would mean funds could be invested elsewhere to lower consumer prices, lower inflation rates, have less demand for imported oil and increased employment by creating new industry to manufacture

and install energy-saving technology. None of these options are seriously considered as all would lessen profits for members of the Rockefeller organizations.

December 1979: Muldoon unveils 'stage two' of a four-stage plan to exploit the Great South Basin discovery. Plan prepared by Trilateralist 'Think Tank':—the Brookings Institute.

'Stage Two' includes methanol plant and synthetic petrol plant, which would initially use gas from the Maui field and later would link with underwater gas pipe from Campbell Island.

With the NZ Steel 500% expansion, 'stage three' of the project involves "Think Big" contracts to go to Bechtel, Fluor Corp., Mitsubishi, Mitsui, Nippon Steel, etc. All investments would be financed by the NZ taxpayer.

1980: January 17: $500,000 deposited in Muldoon's account number 8746665 at the Australian International Bank, being the final payment for the Tasman deal.

Early 1980: Kashoggi Travelodge operations extended with affiliation agreement between Dominion Breweries and Western International Hotels (Seattle First National Bank).

May, 1980: Mafia's Nugan Hand banking operation crashes after Frank Nugan killed. Death ruled as suicide even though no fingerprints were found on the rifle.

There is a probability that Michael Hand killed Frank Nugan because of his involvement with Hand's fiancee.

[**NOTE:** Gerald Carroll in *Project Seek* added the following passage from another source: 'The Black Rose Organization originally funded the 'Black World Order' with proceeds from two areas. One, in Southeast Asia, is known as the Golden Triangle. The other area lies on the border of Iran and Iraq, and between Iran and Afghanistan and is known as the Golden Crescent. The drug proceeds from these two areas wound up deposited in the Nugenhun (sic, actually Nugan Hand) Bank in Australia after Dr. Earl Brian (connected with the Inslaw software scandal of the mid- and late-1980s) carried the bank codes out of Southeast Asia using formal diplomatic immunity. In Australia, countless banks and persons were ruined when two operatives by the names of Frank Nugan and Michael Hand went into action. Frank Nugan was later "terminated" (listed as suicide). Michael Hand fled Australia with all the money from the so-called Black Fund. Hand is currently the most-wanted individual the Australian government has its sights on. He is living in the Middle East under the protection of an Islamic group…"—*Project Seek*, p.300]

May 25, 1980: William Colby arrived in Australia to discuss replacement of the Nugan Hand Bank with Hand, Brierley, and Seldon. Immediate funding was available from the Sydney branch of the Deak Bank, a separate CIA operation, and I.E.L. would be used to buy NZI Corp., to prepare for future laundering operations.

Maloney, Houghton, Yates, and Hand would shred all documents leading back to the NZ Great South Basin connection, and the CIA would help Hand and Bank President Donald Beasley escape to the USA. The CIA and ASIO would also cover everything up. Maloney, Houghton, Yates and Hand shred important documents, but miss some.

CIA helps Hand and Bank President Donald Beasley escape to the U.S. The CIA and Australian Security Intelligence Organization cover everything up. Beasley is appointed President of Miami City National Bank, run by Alberto Dugue for 'laundering' profits from the CIA Colombian cocaine operation. Hand is appointed a 'consultant' to the Miami City National Bank, but he also turns up in El Salvador to help organize bankrolling of the Contras with other ex-members of Nugan-Hand.

June 23, 1980: NZ Mafia, including Brierley, Fletcher, Trotter, Jones, Hawkins, Goodman, and Papps meet in Wellington to discuss merger of Fletcher Challenge and Tasman.

In order to replace Nugan Hand Bank's 22 world-wide branches, quick moves are made to buy control of NZI by NZ Mafia using Brierley, thereby capturing an established, world-wide

organization through the Hong Kong and Shanghai Bank, which is also linked to the CIA through its subsidiary, World Finance Corporation.

Late 1980: Fletchers, with strong Rockefeller links, obtains lucrative contracts on U.S. Bases in the Pacific and joint ventures in Saudi Arabia and Iraq.

Control extended over NZ natural resources: Fletcher Challenge and Tasman Pulp and Paper merged. NZFP takes control of M.S.D. Spiers and Moore Le Messurier (Aust). Brierley begins joint venture with NZFP through Williamson and Jeffrey. I.E.L, through Goodman, buys 20% of Watties and begins cross-shareholding agreement. Goodman continues buying up control of NZ bakeries and flour mills.

1981: February: TNL, Brierley, AMOIL and MIM Holdings begin joint gold mining operation. MIM major shareholder is ASARCO (U.S.), whose Chairman, Barber, is also Director of Chase Manhattan Bank.

NZ Insurance and South British merger.

Parliamentarians For World Order—Richard Prebble elected one of twelve councilors.

Fletcher and Papps (Chairman UEB) sell their hotel operations to a Singaporian interest closely associated with the Pritzker family—owners of the Hyatt Hotel chain. Burton Kanter, Pritzker family lawyer and Director of Hyatt Hotels, who helped arrange the deal, was an old family partner of Paul Helliwell (CIA paymaster for the Bay of Pigs fiasco) and had helped the Pritzker family set up tax shelters using the CIA's Mercantile Bank and Trust and the Castle Bank, which had been set up by Helliwell for 'laundering' profits from the Onassis heroin operations as well as 'skim money' from the Hughes casino operations in Las Vegas.

Others who used these banks include Richard Nixon, Bebe Rebozo, Robert Vesco, Teamsters Union, etc.

March 12, 1981: Brierley calls secret meeting in Auckland, which includes Jones, Fletcher, Hawkins, Papps and Burton Kanter, to discuss transfer of the Fletcher Challenge and UEB hotel operations to the Singapore front company controlled by the Pritzker family.

July 20, 1981: Parsky, Colby, Brierley and Seldon meet in Sydney with two new members, Kerry Packer and Alan Bond. Chase Manhattan and Security Pacific National Bank will acquire 60% of Packer's company, with the stock being held in Australia, and 35% of Bond's company, with the stock being held in Hong Kong.

August 1981: Gulf Oil, using Brierley, strengthens its hold over New Zealand natural resources. Cue Energy launched, starring Lawrey and Gunn. NZOG launched with strategic holdings by Jones, Renouf and Brierley with licenses in PPD 38206 and 38204—both next to Hunt's Great South Basin discovery. NZOG also controls 80 million tons of coal through the Pike River Coal Company.

Also Brierley-controlled: Wellington Gas, Christchurch Gas, Auckland and Hawkes Bay Gas and Dual Fuel Systems (Australasia) which controls the vehicle gas conversion market.

Liquigas Limited set up to distribute LPG, controlled by Shell/BP/Todd and Fletcher Challenge.

1982: February 15: Brierley calls NZ meeting: Jones, Fletcher, Trotter, Hawkins, Goodman and Papps. New members include Bruce Judge, J. Fernyhough, and Frank Renouf.

With Muldoon about to deregulate the liquor industry, Brierley and Fernyhough plan to buy up the NZ liquor industry, along with its outlets, Lion Breweries and Rothmans to help.

Brierley will do the same in Australia. J. R. Fletcher becomes Managing Director of Brierley's Dominion Breweries to oversee operations. Rothmans and Brierley (through Goodman) have

equal holdings in Saudicapital Corp. Lion Directors Myers and Fernyhough also stockholders in NZOG.

Fletcher and Brierley begin their takeover of the freezing works industry. FCL buys into South Island works while Brierley begins takeover of Waitaki NZR through Watties with the help of Athol Hutton.

With Think Big projects beginning, Fletcher and Trotter plan to take strategic holdings in NZ Cement, Wilkins Davies, Steel & Tube etc., and Brierley would use Renouf to take a 3% stake of the Martha Hill gold-mine.

Also targeted are clothing, footwear, carpet manufacture and more of the auto industry for takeover and monopolization.

June, 1982: Meantime, in Australia, a new money funnel begins. H. W. Smith buys two obscure South Pine Quarries, which are renamed Ariadne (Aust). South Pine Quarries owns 50% of Coal-Liquid Inc., with the other half owned by U.S. Defense contractors McDonnell-Douglas. Coal-Liquid renamed Impala Securities.

The common link between Gulf Oil and McDonnell Douglas is the CIA's Mercantile Bank and Trust, which both companies use for world-wide bribery and payoff operations. McDonnell Douglas officials McKeough and G. T. Hawkins are later appointed directors of Impala Securities.

U.S. links are strengthened through Industrial Equity Pacific, which acquires part of Higbee Company in Cleveland, which in turn is closely linked to the National City Bank of Cleveland. This bank is closely associated with Gulf Oil's bank, Pittsburgh National and Mellon Bank.

Bruce Judge installed as Ariadne manager.

July, 1982: Media takeover begins. Brierley takes 24% of NZ News Ltd and begins buying up private radio. Rupert Murdoch helps.

July 27, 1982: Brierley, Jones and Goodman meet in Auckland with two Japanese members of the Trilateral Commission to discuss integration of the NZ economy into the Pacific Rim economy. Trilateralists include: Takeshi Watanabe (Japanese Chairman of Trilateral Commission) and Daigo Miyado (Chairman Sanwa Bank).

The Japan/NZ Business Council would be established to co-ordinate policy, with Goodman appointed as Chairman.

August 17, 1982: Inauguration of restructured U.S. Mafia Council—rulers include David Rockefeller, responsible for Banking; John McCloy; Redman Rockefeller and J.D. Rockefeller, who would run the Seven Sisters.

- Second-tier Council includes:
- Gerald Parsky—responsible for heroin and cocaine operations
- William Simon—responsible for running the Presidency, Cabinet, etc.
- Katherine Graham—link to arms manufacturers
- Zbigniew Brzezinski—link to National Security Council and CIA
- George S. Franklin—link to FBI
- Third-tier Council includes:
- Zbigniew Brzezinski—Secretary
- Gerald Parsky—Heroin Cocaine operations
- William Colby—crack operations, assassinations

- John N. Perkins—banking, laundering
- Leonard Woodcock—labor, unions
- Mitchell Sharp—banking
- William Simon—presidency, Cabinet
- Ernest C. Arbuckle—arms manufacturers
- George W. Bull—Bilderberg and Council of Foreign Relations
- Katherine Graham—arms manufacturers
- Alden W. Clausen—World Bank, IMF
- Willam T. Coleman—CIA
- Archibald K. Davis—media, radio, television, and newspapers
- George S. Franklin—FBI, and Trilateral Commission coordinator
- J.D. Rockefeller—to "spy" on the 15 man council.

September, 1982: Goodman now helps establish the Japan/NZ Council with the Bank of Tokyo and the Industrial Bank of Japan. Tokai Pulp Co. buys shareholding in NZFP, which also begins joint venture with Shell Oil.

Fletcher Challenge strengthens links with the Rockefeller organization by acquiring the Canadian operations of Crown Zellerbach, whose chairman is also director of Gulf Oil. Crown Zellerbach Corp. has direct connections to Rockefeller through directors Mumford, Hendrickson and Granville, to United California Bank through Roth, and to the Bank of America through Chairman C. R. Dahl.

Meanwhile, Robert Jones Investments was floated to extend operations of City Realties, Ilmond Properties, Chase Corp., etc.

The Commerce Building in Auckland was sold to Robert Jones Investments by Robert Jones Holdings for $950,000 when recently it had been offered on the market for $200,000. A quick $750,000 profit for Jones. Robert Jones Investments was set up by Brierley, Jones and Hawkins.

December 8, 1982: Mitchell Sharp heads top-level Mafia meeting in San Francisco. Others include Parsky, Perkins, Woodcock and C. R. Dahl—Chairman of Crown Zellerbach.

Also present are Brierley, Trotter, Fletcher and Seldon. The meeting was to discuss Great South Basin exploitation strategy, with first priority being monopolization of the economy; second priority, to establish oil refineries and related industries; third, to integrate NZ economy into Trilateral economy, and, fourth, to concentrate power back to the U.S through the Seven Sisters, Chase Manhattan and Security Pacific National Bank.

Fletcher Challenge would link NZ economy directly to the U.S by merging with Canadian subsidiary of Crown Zellerbach with funds provided by Security Pacific National Bank and United Californian Bank.

Brierley, Fletcher, Trotter and Seldon will be the NZ Ruling Council, headed by Brierley, who would take orders from Gerald Parsky.

Mid-1983: Brierley's Ariadne (Aust) takes control of Repco (NZ) through Repco (Aust), thereby taking control of key auto-related industry, helped by Borg Warner and Honeywell—which are closely associated with I.E.L. through International Harvester, Continental Illinois Bank and the First National Bank of Chicago. Toyota and Nissan also help, so that Brierley becomes the largest distributor of auto and industrial parts, largest manufacturer of pistons, filters and engine bearings, as well as biggest supplier of forklifts, tractors and agricultural equipment.

Meantime, control is extended over the Great South Basin oil source with Hunt, after big losses

resulting from trying to corner the world's silver market, being forced to sell out some of his concession to Gulf Oil, which uses Brierley to set up a new company—Southern Petroleum—which takes a 14.5% interest. Hunt retains overall control with 45.5%, Petro-Corp. has 40%, and Chairman F. Orr, also a Director of Brierley—controlled Watties.

Brierley, through Goodman, takes control of TNL Group and its subsidiaries NZ Motor Bodies and L & M Mining, which has 15% interest in the Chatham Rise, right next to the Hunt concession.

Southern Petroleum set up by Brierley in NZ was spearheaded by the Seven Sisters' companies with Gerald Parsky and William Colby initiators.

Southern Petroleum to include 21% of the Great South Basin held by gulf and Mobil Oil. 90% of this stock held in Australia through IEL (i.e., Brierley's).

May 11-12, 1983: NZ Mafia meet in Cook Islands. Includes Brierley, Trotter, Fletcher, Jones, Hawkins, Goodman, Pappas, Judge, Renouf, and Fernyhough. New members include A. Gibbs, McConnell, H. Fletcher and O. Gunn. Japanese Trilateralists Takeshi Wataneve and Daigo Miyado discuss 'integration' of NZ into the Pacific Rim economies.

A new political party would be established using Jones and financed by the NZ Mafia Council.

* Reason: Parsky and Colby wanted Muldoon out because he had 'welched' on a deal to set up two U.S. military deep-water submarine bases planned for Dusky Sound and Guards Bay in the South Island.

Parsky, Brierley and Ray Cline hold a separate meeting to discuss the purchase of NZ politicians, including Lange, Douglas and Bolger.

Cline was 'consultant' to the CIA's Deak Bank, took orders from Colby, and was responsible for the 10 Australian politicians on the CIA's payroll, including Bjelke Petersen, I. Sinclair, Keating, McMullen, M.Fraser, D. Anthony, K. Newman, J Carrick, B. Cowan and R. Connor.

Cline outlines CIA plan to begin subliminal television advertising.

June 23, 1983: NZ politician J. Bolger meets Ray Cline in Sydney and agrees to join the organization for a monthly fee of $US20,000, to be paid into account number GA1282117 at Geneva branch of Credit Suisse Bank.

July 20, 1983: NZ politician R. Douglas meets Ray Cline in Wellington and agrees to join the organization for a monthly fee of $US10,000 to be paid into account number 3791686 at the Sydney Branch of the Deak Bank.

July 1983: Parsky launches a new front company, Chase Corporation, with 25% of the stock being held through Security Pacific National Bank in Australia and 25% held in Hong Kong by Chase Manhattan. Brierley and Hawkins set up a 'back-door' listing to cover up true ownership.

August, 1983: Muldoon imposes withholding tax on all offshore borrowing. Chase Manhattan, United California Bank and Brierley begin new banking operation in NZ to take over the International Harvester Credit Co. (NZ), Australasian Investment Company. Participants include Chase Manhattan's Kuwait Asia Bank, D.F.C., Saudicorp (Brierley has 12% through Goodman) and United California, represented by National Insurance which is part of Equus Holdings.

Renouf sells 20% NZUC to Barclays and prepares for expanding of operations with Brierley.

Meantime, Murdoch and Brierley expand their close ties by each taking a piece of NZ Maritime Holdings, and with the election imminent, divide up NZ media for takeover to increase Mafia control. NZ News buys Hawkes Bay News, Nelson Tribune, Timaru Herald, etc. Brierley increases holding in Hauraki Enterprises and other private radio stations. Brierley and

Murdoch have majority stockholding in NZPA with 48.5%, while in the UK, Murdoch has a large stockholding in Reuters.

The phony news becomes THE news.

Head of the Murdoch operation is Burnett, who is also on the board of Winstones—a Brierley company.

With global heroin epidemic, Rockefeller expands operations to recycle profits.

NZ South British sets up the IDAPS computer bureau to establish international holding companies, dummy corporations, etc., and to pursue aggressive global acquisition program. IDAPS linked to satellite bureaus in Australia, Far East, UK and the US, where the global network is completed through links with the Rockefeller organization computer network.

General Manager of the operation: George Wheller, previously director of the international operators of Firemen's Fund (U.S.), Chairman Du Bain, director of the United California Bank, and Vice-Chairman of Amex. As part of the expanded laundry operation, Rockefeller associate Adnan Kashoggi establishes new Australian bank—Security Pacific National Bank (Aust). Brierley's part of this operation is to buy up computer companies such as Andas, CID Distributors (NZ Apple computer franchise, etc.).

Investment companies begin operations in Australia and NZ to assist recycling of Mafia profits.

October 1983: Brierley takes over NZFP through Watties, helped by newly-appointed chairman Papps. Papps is also chairman of NZ Railways and presided over transport deregulation, the major beneficiaries of which include Watties and Freightways; both Managing Director Pettigrew and Director Lang are also on the NZFP board with Papps.

Papps is also responsible for the railways' electrification program, with big contracts for Cory Wright & Slamon, whose directors include I. I. McKay, also on the board of NZFP.

Late 1983: AMAX (Social) gives Gulf Oil a share in the Martha Hill gold bonanza by selling 15% of its holdings to Brierley through Goodmans. Oil companies say there is only $870 million worth of minerals in Martha Hill, while the true figure is closer to $3 billion.

1984: January 21: Australian Mafia Council meets in Sydney. Includes Brierley, Seldon, Fletcher, Jones, Goodman, Hawkins, Papps, Packer, Bond and Japanese Trilaterist Daigo Miyado. New members include J. Elliott, L. Adler, and Holme's A'Court. Seldon outlines strategy of merging Australian economy with the Trilateralist economy through Europe and the U.S.

In Australia, the Mafia Council will monopolize the economy with company takeovers through the use of loans at less than 5%.

Holme's A'Court's company would be taken over using Security Pacific National Bank and Chase Manhattan Bank, with some of the stock being held in London.

Equiticorp will be launched using Hawkins, with 50% of the stock held by Security Pacific National Bank and Chase Manhattan in the US; Equiticorp to be registered in Hong Kong to cover up true ownership, and will use the same 'laundry' as Chase Corporation: Hawkins will set up a maze of shell companies and dummy organizations to disguise operations.

Hawkins was previously associated with Kashoggi when Corporate Secretary of Marac, and linked with Renouf through their stockholding in CBA Finance, which is a partner in Commercial Pacific Trust with United California Bank. Hawkins forms umbrella company with Chase Corp., Jedi Investments and Teltherm and begins setting up a maze of cross holding companies. Brierley retains his connection through his Charter Corporation's holding in Teltherm.

January 1984: Brierley and Elliott begin moves to monopolize the food industry in Australasia by

merging Goodman and the Elders Group, while Brierley sells 10% of Watties to the NZ Dairy Board—setting the stage for land takeover and establishment of the Corporate Farm.

February 1984: NZ politician D. Lange meets Ray Cline in Wellington and agrees to go on the Mafia payroll for a monthly fee of $US40,000, paid into account number 5263161 at Commercial Pacific Trust, New Hebrides.

March 1984: Muldoon knighted with GCMG for keeping the economy free of obstructions for easier takeover and exploitation.

May 24, 1984: Four-man CIA team coordinated by Ray Cline arrive in New Zealand to begin installation of equipment for subliminal television advertising at five sites: Waiatarua, Mt. Erin, Kaukau, Sugarloaf and Obelisk. Sophisticated equipment can be installed within one kilometer of TV relay aerials, and all linked to one IDAPS computer bureau in Auckland. Same equipment installed in Australia in August 1985; Japan, September 1986; UK, February 1987: New York, 1987.

Also, Amax geologists now estimate Martha Hill gold source could be worth up to $30 billion on strength of high gold/ton ore assay.

July 17, 1984: In NZ, subliminal advertising begins on Channel Two between 6:00 p.m. and midnight; hours later extended to begin at noon. Subliminal messages prepared in the U.S. by the CIA, and with NZ election imminent, tell voters to support the Labor Party, the NZ Party, and to buy Mafia company products.

NZ Party was formed to ensure that Muldoon would lose, as Big Business was unhappy with controls over economy. Big campaign contributions from Brierley, the oil companies and the Business Round Table ensure a Labor victory.

Later, Lange agrees to repay the favor to Brierley by selling the Government holding in the Kariori Pulp Mill to Winstones. NZ taxpayers lose $100 million.

Government then becomes the arm of big business, using economic policies provided by the Business Round Table, implemented by Finance Minister Roger Douglas and the package being sold by David Lange, who also keeps up a noisy CIA-directed ANZUS withdrawal campaign.

* Reasons:

1) ANZUS Treaty did not cover Mafia requirements over the Great South Basin discovery;

2) To identify any opposition or threats within New Zealand who align themselves with supposed Government policy, Lange increases the S.I.S. budget and strengthens links with the CIA.

Brookings Institute are the actual designers of the NZ Government economic policies provided by the Business Round Table (NZ Mafia front) and implemented by the Government.

Douglas devalues the dollar and deregulates interest rates, which means cheaper labor, cheaper capital assets and high mortgage rates, thereby implementing Big Business policy of driving farmers off the land, establishment of the corporate farm, and eventually removing viability of small business sector, etc.

September 27, 1984: NZ Mafia meets at new 'safe house' registered under Fernyhough's name, in Auckland. Those present include Brierley, J. Fletcher, Trotter, Jones, Goodman, Gunn, Papps, Hawkins, Judge, Renouf, Fernyhough, Gibbs and McConnell. Daigo Miyado announces appointment of Trotter as International Vice President of the Trilateral Commission Pacific Basin Economic Council.

Brierley outlines strategy of privatization of the NZ Government and the establishment of the NZ Centre for Independent Studies which will be chaired by Gibbs, aided by Fernyhough and

controlled by Cline, which will 'advise' Treasury on privatization.

Parsky, Brierley and Seldon hold a separate meeting with Parsky, outlining plans for an expanded 'laundry' operation which will coincide with the launch of 'Crack' [cocaine]—a new addictive product developed by CIA chemists for the world market.

Equiticorp (Aust) will be launched with Adler as Manager, and a new merchant bank using Elders, Goodman and Jarden.

I.E.L. will merge with Armco Bank, which has 20 branches in South East Asia; Ariadne will acquire the Bank of Queensland, and Brierley Investments will form a cross-shareholding with NZI Corp. to further increase control by their Mafia organization. Other plans include the laundering of funds directly to the NZ and Australian Governments and the establishment of key companies within the economies of NZ, Australia and Hong Kong.

The first key company will control the food industry in Australasia through merger of Elders, Goodmans, Allied Mills, Fielder Gillespie and Watties. Allied Mills will control 30%; Goodmans, 30%; Fielder, 20%; Watties, 20%, and will expand into Europe via acquisition of Rank, Hovis McDougall (UK). Allied Mills will be controlled through IEL.

October 26, 1984: Trotter, Hawkins, Lange and Douglas meet in Wellington to implement Mafia plans to privatize the Government and to deregulate the banking system.

Late 1984: As part of the IDAPS computer-controlled 'laundry' operation, Trotter and Fletcher help establish the 'Pacific Investment Fund' with Australian and NZ investments to be managed by Hong Kong and Shanghai Bank subsidiary, Wardley and the Japanese operation controlled by Tokyo Trust and Banking Company—owned by Sanwa Bank, Taiyo-Kobe Bank and Nomura Securities. All are members of the Rockefeller World Government organization.

1985: July 18: Australian Mafia meet in Sydney to discuss privatization of the Australian Government. Those present include: Brierley, Trotter, Fletcher, Seldon, Goodman, Papps, Packer, Bond, Elliott, Adler, and Japanese Trilateralist Daigo Miyado.

Cline will set up Australian Centre for Independent Studies to 'advise' the Treasurer on the takeover of the economy. Impala Pacific will be set up in Hong Kong through Ariadne, with 60% of the company stock held by Chase Manhattan and Security Pacific National Bank in Australia. In the UK, Tozer, Kemsly & Millbourn would be taken over using I. E. P., while in Australia, the Holme's A'Court Bell Group would be used to merge with Hong Kong and Shanghai Bank, through Standard & Chartered Bank (Hong Kong), and Marac (NZ) and Broadlands (Australia) would merge with NZI Corporation.

August 18, 1985: Cline and 6-man CIA team begin installation of subliminal television equipment in Sydney, Brisbane and Perth.

Parsky, Colby and J. D. Rockefeller meet in New York to discuss their plans to assassinate McCloy and take control of the Mafia organization.

Colby would organize an 8-man 'hit squad' to be headed by Gordon Liddy, who had worked for Colby in the 1960's as a CIA contract killer, and was responsible for over 10 murders[88] including:

- August 8, 1961—two members of the Gambino Mafia family in New York
- November 24, 1963—Officer Tippitt after the Kennedy assassination in Dallas
- December 18, 1963—witness to the Kennedy assassination in Dallas

---

[88] In *Will: The Autobiography of G. Gordon Liddy* (1980), Liddy describes himself as the most efficient killer in the CIA; but I have never known anyone with the temerity to mention his actual murders. Bruce Roberts called Liddy a "murdering slob." See Chapter 44 for my view of the relationship between Roberts and Liddy.

- April 19, 1965—Politician in Chicago
- July 27, 1965—Politician in Washington
- September 8, 1965—Politician in Washington
- November 27, 1966—US 'independent' cocaine importer, in Mexico.
- November 25, 1967—'Independent'[89] heroin importer, in Los Angeles
- February 9, 1969—Politician in Washington

November 28, 1985: Australian Mafia meet in Sydney. Present: Trotter, Fletcher, Hawkins, Bond, Elliott, Adler and Holme's A'Court. They discussed strategy for merger of Goodman, Allied Mills, Fielde Gillespie Davis, Watties and Elders, with Chase Manhattan Bank taking 20%, Elders and IEL 10%, with stock being held through Chase-AMP Bank. Elders would be used as major 'vehicle' in the global liquor economy, with Courage Brewery in the UK to be used as entry into Europe.

Strategy finalized to take over BHP, Australia's largest company, using Holme's A'Court, Brierley, Elliott and Hawkins.

In London, Chase Manhattan would take over stockbrokers Simon & Coates, who specialize in Australasia Mafia-owned companies such as Fletcher Challenge, Brierley, NZI Corp., Elders, Bell Group and BHP. Chase Manhattan could then issue and buy stock to manipulate the Australasian economy by increasing price, paying no taxes, creating inflation, and enslaving the people through debt to Mafia-controlled banks.

Parsky would oversee the 'launder' of further loans to the NZ Government and would begin to channel 'loans' through the Australian Treasury using captive politician Keating. Also NZ Government building would be sold to Jones and Australia Government buildings would be sold to Adler, which would then be rented back to the respective Governments at inflated prices.

1986: February 16: The Mikhail Lermontov was sunk near Picton (not by accident).

February 22: Parsky, Brierley, and Trotter oversee the second launder of Mafia dollars to the Kiwi government: US$300 million, with a commission of $20 million.

February 26: Preliminary inquiry into Mikhail Lermontov sinking released by Minister of Transport Prebble, disobeying all Marine Division instructions on holding preliminary inquiries into shipping casualties.

November 17: Brierley, Seldon, Packer, Bond, Elliott, Holme's A'Court and Adler meet in Sydney. Also present is Rupert Murdoch to assist in Parsky strategy of media takeover in Australasia and the Pacific, using Packer and Bond (TV and Radio), Brierley and Holmes A'Court (newspapers).

Murdoch takes orders from Brzezinski since his News Corp. was taken over in 1982 by Chase Manhattan and Security Pacific National Bank.

At a separate meeting with Brierley, Seldon and Cline, Parsky outlines plan for 'key' Media Australasian Holding company using the Bell Group, which would be taken over, with Chase Manhattan holding 27.5% in London and the U.S. Another 10% of the stock would be held through Security Pacific National Bank (U.S.).

December 10: Geoffrey Palmer's Constitution Bill removes the power of the NZ Governor General to refuse assent to legislation: he must now sign In token of his assent.

December 17: National M. P. Peters reveals the Maori loans affair and mentions the Fletcher

---

[89] I.e., not approved of by the CIA.

connection. This fact and many other details were never mentioned in the media after pressure from Trotter, using Burnett at Independent News Ltd., Hancox at NZ News, and through CIA-funded sub-editor at the NZ Herald.

1987: February 17: New subliminal messages appear on Kiwi TV screens:

"Hello Friends. Make More Money. Vote Labor." Other messages include: "Greetings My Own. Buy Cars. Buy Now." and the most sinister of all, "Smash. Hate. Rape. Punch. Kill. Use Violence." With an election imminent in Aotearoa, frequency of messages increases to average of four per hour.

February 8: U.S. Mafia Council meets in Washington—including David Rockefeller, John McCloy, Brzezinski, Parsky, Simon, Katherine Graham, and George Franklin.

Brzezinski outlines plans to invade Iran using 75,000 strong mercenary army, supported by U.S. Air Force and Navy, with starting date of 8th February, 1988. As an integral part of the plan, Saudi and Kuwaiti oil tankers would fly the U.S. flag to provoke an Iranian attack so that U.S. invasion of Iran would be 'justified'.

*Reason: The Seven Sisters wanted to exploit a secret oil field near Bandar Abbas discovered in 1976 with estimated 150 billion barrels, and also a huge gold source at Neyshabur discovered in 1977."

The Iranian invasion would begin after the World economic system was collapsed by the Mafia-controlled banks; target date: 17th January 1988.

Other countries on the takeover list include:

- Mexico—for oil at Baisas
- Nicaragua—for oil at Connto
- Colombia— for gold at Papayan
- South Korea—for gold at Chunchon
- NZ—for oil in the Great South Basin.

(Obviously this part of the plan failed to happen.)

March 10: Parsky, Colby, Brierley and Cline meet in the Gibbs safe house in Auckland. Parsky outlines the expansion of the European Pacific banking operation, with 12 new subsidiaries to be set up in South America to replace the United Fruit Co. front, and which will:

(a) launder heroin dollars from the Rockefeller operations in the Golden Triangle and Pakistan:

(b) Launder coke & crack dollars from Columbia, Peru, Bolivia, Ecuador, & Venezuela;

(c) CIA money funnel to pro-U.S. political parties in Europe and Latin America;

(d) financial conduit to Colby's P2 neo-fascists in Panama, Argentina, Chile, & Uruguay;

(e) spying conduit for information from Middle East, Latin & South America;

(f) financing arms smuggling to Central & South America and the Middle East, including the Christian Militia in Lebanon;

(g) financial conduit to mercenary army in Kuwait (standing by to conduct CIA invasion of Iran) via CIA's Vinell Corp.

April 1: Business Round Table plan: 'Government Departments to Corporations,' implemented by Lange & Douglas to privatize Aotearoan national assets.

*Reason: You cannot bankrupt a government department, which belongs to the people of Aotearoa. Privatization means that the whole country can be asset-stripped of all that was Crown-controlled—land, minerals, & energy.'

June 17: Kiwi Mafia meet in Gibbs' safe house in Auckland—including Brierley, Trotter, J. Fletcher, Jones, Goodman, and Gunn—to plan strategy for the Aotearoa election, bankrolling of the Labor Party, and post-election agenda for privatization of the Kiwi government. Included is establishment of a presidential (dictator) system, with Trotter installed as el presidente.

July 27: J.D. Rockefeller, Colby, and Parsky meet in Paris to implement plans for the assassination of David Rockefeller, Rodman Rockefeller, and John McCloy, using Gordon Liddy and his eight man team.

July: Brierley-controlled Newmans/Ansett airline goes into operation. With Douglas, Lange, and Palmer helping with Banking Deregulation Bill, City Bank and Paxus NZI etc. become fully-fledged banks in Aotearoa.

Late July: DFC and Trusteebank merger. End of the last Kiwi-owned bank. The Douglas Administration.

End of Opal File

***

Here's an additional item that may be relevant. Isn't it odd how many of these "intelligence" characters suffer strange, mysterious deaths?

William Colby's Mysterious Death:
Theories on Colby's Death Abound

—Christopher Ruddy, May 07, 1996

WASHINGTON—The body of "the Old Gray Man of the CIA," William Colby, has been found in waters near his weekend home, but theories about his demise continue to thrive.

Colby, who served as CIA director under Presidents Nixon and Ford, disappeared April 28.

Maryland authorities found his body Monday morning after it washed ashore. This followed an intensive search of the Wicomico River near Colby's home in Rock Point, Md. Local police believe his body was lost in the cloudy waters of the Wicomico while canoeing, a favorite pastime of Colby's.

At 76, Colby was physically fit and, after surviving parachute drops behind Nazi lines in War World II and stints in Vietnam, he was a cautious, careful and cunning man who lived up to his James Bond super-spy credentials.

Last week, The *New York Post's* irreverent Page Six raised concerns about Colby's disappearance and apparent death with an article headlined "Conspiracy Crowd Snatches Colby."

"The theory among conspiracy-minded, cloak-and-dagger buffs is that Colby was assassinated so he wouldn't spill any more agency secrets," the gossip page began. Agency insiders reportedly resented Colby for talking to Congress about the "family jewels"—supposed illegal operations the agency conducted in the decades before Watergate.

As a result, Colby lost the support of agency insiders and the Ford administration. President Ford fired Colby on Halloween 1975.

Some theorists point to the similar circumstances surrounding the 1978 death of CIA deputy director John A. Paisley.

Paisley's sailboat was found adrift in the Chesapeake Bay just 15 miles from Colby's home. His body was discovered days later. He died of an apparent gunshot behind his ear.

His body had been weighted with diving belts. Since no blood was found on the boat, authorities theorized Paisley first jumped into the water and then fired the shot into his head.

However, murder was never ruled out in the case.[90]

While some refuse to believe 20-year-old grudges could have led to Colby's demise, others, including Fred Davis, the Maryland county sheriff in charge of the probe, still find the death suspicious and haven't ruled out foul play

Already, the death has been the buzz of talk radio and the Internet. Pittsburgh's Jim Quinn on WRRK-FM joked that Colby's body will rise to the top as soon as "someone cuts the concrete slabs tied to his feet."

New York shock-jock Don Imus, whose recent roast of the Clintons caused a stir, started off one of his morning programs wondering what the "Whitewater" connection was with Colby's death—a reference, no doubt, to the high number of deaths linked to a web of Arkansas scandal.

Even though Imus didn't realize it, Colby did have a Whitewater connection. For the past two years, he has been a contributing editor with a monthly financial newsletter, *Strategic Investment*. Co-edited by James Dale Davidson and former *Times of London* editor Lord William Rees Mogg, *Strategic* is read by more than 100,000 subscribers worldwide and has been closely monitoring the Whitewater scandal.

Davidson has written in the newsletter that Vincent Foster, former White House deputy counsel, was murdered and that significant evidence links the Clintons to drug trafficking, murder and organized crime in their home state of Arkansas. Foster was found shot to death more than two years ago in Fort Marcy Park near Washington, D.C.

The *Wall Street Journal* editorialized that it was glad to see James Davidson "pushing the envelope" on the Whitewater scandal.

Colby began taking a more active role in the newsletter in February, writing a weekly column on geopolitical matters and their effects on investments in *Strategic Weekly Briefings*—a facsimile newsletter tailored for high-income investors. Colby traveled with Davidson several times to Asia, leading groups of investors.

In his columns, Colby never touched upon the Clintons or the Whitewater affair. His name and former association with the CIA was no doubt a real credibility boost for the newsletter and was touted throughout the newsletter and its promotional brochures (which often detailed the newsletter's reporting of the darker side of Whitewater).

"I find the death suspicious for a lot of reasons," Davidson told the *Tribune-Review*. He does not link his Whitewater coverage to the death, but points to problems associated with Colby's disappearance.

"It's not clear how his life jacket and paddle, which he always took canoeing with him, disappeared," he said.

Davidson also is disturbed by an early Associated Press report quoting Mrs. Colby as having spoken with her husband on the day of the death. The AP reported that Colby said he was not feeling well, but planned to go canoeing anyway. In a statement this week, Mrs. Colby, who was in Texas when she spoke to her husband for the last time, said he was feeling fine, and never mentioned any plans to go canoeing.

Davidson described Colby as a "charming and fit" man who had great stamina traveling.

"He was a New Deal Democrat like many who started in the OSS (the forerunner to the CIA)," Davidson remarked.

---

[90] When is a murder definitely not a murder? When it is a fatal hunting accident. Such as may have happened to William Sullivan, once the 3rd man in Hoover's FBI; leader of Intelpro, and the Phoenix Program, and as such, personally responsible for 30,000 to 60,000 deaths; in 1977. No room here, look it up on the Web if you are interested. Was it open season on ex-FBI/CIA wheelers and dealers back in the mid- to late '70's? Or just the mills of Heaven grinding belatedly, but very small?

According to Davidson, one of his staff members contacted local police who said they were perplexed as to where the AP got the original report on Colby's conversation with his wife.

Some old Cold Warriors recollect Colby's longstanding feud with James Jesus Angleton, the longtime head of the CIA's counterintelligence division.

Angleton believed the CIA had been infiltrated by KGB moles; Colby believed Angleton had become symptomatic of Cold War paranoia and forced his ouster in 1974. After his dismissal, a bitter Angleton told associates he believed that Colby had been recruited by the KGB and was a long-term asset of the Soviets. Angelton's supporters noted Colby's association with far left committees—including ones supported by the Institute for Policy Studies—after Colby departed from the CIA. Colby also called for near unilateral disarmament—an immediate 50 percent reduction in the American defense budget during the height of East-West tensions.

One friend of Colby's scoffed at such notions and suggested that his espousal of unorthodox views were not based on a longtime hidden ideology, but may be explained by his desire to live down an undesirable reputation he acquired in Vietnam for heading up the controversial Operation Phoenix, a program to eradicate peasant support of the Viet Cong, for which Colby had been branded by war protesters as a war criminal."[91]

---

[91] This article was reprinted from NewsMax.com

39 1992: Interview by Jim Keith

The following interview appeared in *The Gemstone File*, Jim Keith's edition of articles based on the *Skeleton Key to the Gemstone File*. This book was published by Illuminet Press in 1992. I couldn't resist updating the interview; my current additions appear in italics.

KEITH: Please tell me about your association with Bruce Roberts' Gemstone File.

CARUANA: I had the very great privilege, about 18 years ago, of knowing and working with the author of the original Gemstone File letters, Bruce Roberts, in San Francisco. In order to clarify, in my own mind, the facts he laid out in such profusion in his letters, I began to develop a chronological outline, to the extent that I understood what he was saying, which I eventually called A *Skeleton Key to the Gemstone File*.

It was a very scary time and ultimately tragic. I also remember, quite vividly, giving a copy of the *Key* to Paul Krassner [editor of the *Realist*].

[This was back in 1975, at some sort of street rally in San Francisco. After Bruce Roberts read my Playgirl article, and later, the Skeleton Key outline I had managed to put together from a couple of his letters at the Norwegian Consulate, he became quite friendly to me. He asked me to attend that rally, with him, and to bring copies of the Skeleton Key to give away and/or sell for $3.00. Paul Krassner was there, and I offered him a copy. He expected a freebie; after all, he was a bona fide journalist, and he had every right to a free copy. However, I had just paid for these copies out of my own slender pocket, and I felt he had enough money to give me $3.00 to help with the copying cost. When he saw I wasn't kidding, he dug out the $3.00.]

Paul took the copy rather sourly, and said, 'Bruce Roberts is a pain in the ass.' *[Well, maybe he really meant that I was the pain in the ass.]*

[In a fairly recent phone conversation, Paul said he didn't remember anything about the incident, and didn't remember getting a copy of the Skeleton Key from me.]

I had a different view. I thought, and still think, that Bruce Roberts was probably the bravest and most brilliant man I ever met. This [commenting on various copies of the *Skeleton Key* in current circulation] was pretty close to what I sent out when Bruce Roberts was in the hospital in San Francisco—although there were several 'editions' with more or less information added from time to time... I also, at about the same time, collaborated with Mae Brussell (oddly enough, the niece of Cyril Magnin) on an article about Patty Hearst and the fake SLA 'army' which had taken Oakland hostage with its ludicrous 'food distribution'.

Our title for the article was: *Is Cinque the First Black Lee Harvey Oswald?*, meaning that he was a patsy set up by the authorities—a 'yo-yo' they controlled with a string, pulling him into and out of jail as they wished, and finally letting him 'escape' from prison after carefully indoctrinating him, in prison, with the idea of a black 'army' etc.—all under the supervision of government-paid handlers.

The California prison system had at that time a system of black pride classes, taught by outsiders, the real purpose of which would not stand scrutiny. The 'drama of controlling the black savages' is very much on the mind of some very powerful Californians, dictating their tactics of police training, etc., which is why Los Angeles is currently going up in smoke! The article came out in the *Berkeley Barb*, and I must say we had a pretty good grasp of the phoniness of what was going on.

I see how at least one of your Gemstoners has picked up on this a bit, in terms of how the

powers-that-be were trying to use this created and manipulated 'army' for fear and terrorist propaganda. I had the—I can't say pleasure, for it was a terrible horror—the week the *Barb* came out with our article, of seeing these people covering their tracks by wiping out the 'army.' Frying its leader, 'Cinque' alive—(after taking the "SLA" by van down to a "safe house" in Los Angeles, and pulling Patty Hearst out of harm's way, of course) with a murderous SWAT team raid, televised live, which I watched, live, on a TV set in the window of a Berkeley laundromat. This and a few personal death threats, as well as Bruce Roberts' difficulties and all the other murders he kept talking about, persuaded me that the best thing I could do, if I wanted to get this information out, was to do just what I did: throw it to the wind, and run for my life. Which I did.

[It also persuaded me, as nothing else could have, of the power of the press, even the small press, to inform people, and consequently, how much emphasis is placed on buying up and suppressing the press, even the very small press.]

At the time, most people who read the *Skeleton Key* were somewhat dazed. Much of the information, or at least the way it was put together, was new and shocking. Since then, a great deal has emerged, and a great deal has been corroborated from various sources. That, plus ensuing events over the years that support many if not most of these shocking statements, have created a different atmosphere in which people don't find it so hard to believe any more.

I don't feel paranoid, either, since it's too late to shut me up, by many years! (That was the whole idea.) I've seen TV shows based on one or another aspect from time to time. I guess what amazes (and saddens) me the most is that this *Skeleton Key* seems to be all that has trickled down to the (underground) public of Bruce Roberts' original letters, which were a thousand times more powerful in their writing and effect. I gather that you have never actually seen any of them. I assure you that he really did exist, and that he was brilliant, and a great extempore discourser. When he talked about holding forth in one bar or another, that's exactly what he did. Anyone with a tape recorder would have a feast of information.

I think that the Gemstone information is important for people to have. Not that it will 'save' us, because frankly I think we're too far gone for that! But at least it may help a bit to understand what is happening. It can give people a broader perspective. For this reason, I think it may be important for people to know this is, or was, real. Somebody, a man named Bruce Roberts, actually wrote those letters; and somebody else (me) actually wrote the *Skeleton Key*. (How do they think it came into existence??? Spontaneous combustion????)

About ten years ago, [when I was living in Miami Beach, supporting my mother and running or trying to run my dead father's plastics business], I got a phone call from—*Penthouse*?? *Playboy*?? The caller said someone had sent them a copy, and they wanted to use some of the information, but I would have to "document" it first!

I said, "Hey, I ain't going to 'document' it. If it feels right, do it! Otherwise, you commit suicide, not me. I ain't getting paid for this, nohow, right?"

"Right," he said.

I said, "It seems to me that if this information is true, it will prove itself by being believed when it is read. Ten years from now, your article will be forgotten, but the Gemstone *Skeleton Key* will still be around."

He snickered, and hung up. What I had in mind was that the Old Testament originally was copied by hand, one letter at a time, and that didn't stop it from getting around. People hunger for the truth. And 1 believe that what I was passing on was and is true.

KEITH: What are your feelings about the continuing interest shown in the Gemstone File?

CARUANA: I am aware, and I am very pleased, that the information that I released eighteen years ago has been spread around to so many people that it is now 'public property,' and consequently, the danger of getting wiped out for spreading it, which was quite real back then, is probably over for now. However, the shady process of milking people and governments of money which was the 'Mafia's' favorite game then, is still going on now, and in many cases, by the same people, or their successors. If I were to appear too publicly to advise and instruct people on how to spot and track these ongoing scams, 'somebody' might still get mad. I hope you'll understand that I like living, and that a number of my friends (including Bruce Roberts) have died because of their involvement in tracing and recording these political and financial manipulations.

Please understand that I have very mixed feelings about all this. One wonders whether, if a real person emerges, claiming responsibility for the *Skeleton Key to the Gemstone File*, whether some of the surviving characters who are accused in the file of assassination, blackmail, or other crimes, might want to sue me, or simply wipe me out for the crime of character assassination. I hope you understand a little simple fear! What protects me, if anything, is that the people involved wouldn't want to draw attention to the material by publicly objecting to it. An automobile accident on a quiet country road is, however, easy enough to arrange.

KEITH: What was your first contact with the Gemstone File?

CARUANA: The circumstances were that I was living temporarily in Mae Brussell's house in Carmel Valley. I had offered myself to her as a writing slave because I wanted to write articles based on her fat file folders. This started with Patty Hearst and the SLA 'Army,' where I found myself going nuts trying to figure out what was really going on. While I was working with Mae Brussell, Marin Milam, the Editor in Chief at *Playgirl*, asked me if Mae knew anything about Howard Hughes. Mae laughed and said Howard Hughes was dead—and that he had been kidnapped by Aristotle Onassis, and died on Skorpios in 1971. Marin was intrigued, and Mae and I set out to 'co-author' an article about Howard Hughes and Aristotle Onassis. Mae gave me two thick file folders about each man to read.

I had a nasty deadline to meet, and was reading and writing from morning until night. But after a few days, I had to tell Mae that I didn't see anything in the files she had given me that would substantiate the story she said she had. Mae was frustrated; it was obvious to her that I wouldn't proceed unless I had some more solid information to go on.

Finally, she very reluctantly pulled out a thick folder containing a stack of xeroxed pages, on legal-sized paper. It was all held together by a thick rubber band. The material was handwritten, each page crammed from top to bottom with rather difficult-to-read script. The file had no name as far as she was concerned; she only said it had been written by someone named Bruce Roberts and she wasn't sure the contents had any validity. She said he had given her the file two years earlier.

She told me I could read the file, but only after I had finished working on the article, on my own time, at night, in the tiny guest bedroom where I was staying. She also ordered me not to actually read the letters, but only to skim over them, and only to read the paragraphs or sentences where Onassis and/or Hughes were mentioned. This was all right with me, because there were 360 numbered legal-sized pages in the stack, and I had a lot of work to do, working from the published articles in Mae's other files, to get the article researched and written in order to meet the deadline. So I would not have had the time to read it all slowly or thoroughly.

At midnight, exhausted after a long hard day, I started to read. The first page was chock full of murders, poison, and dirty words.

My immediate reaction was: "Hey, this guy is a paranoid schizophrenic. I've been told all my life about them. They think everybody's getting killed."

In a sense, I had been brainwashed to automatically reject anyone who talked or wrote the way he did. I had to pull back and take a look at my own reactions. I decided to read the material with an open mind.

It took me about two nights to skim the material. But the next morning, thinking about what I had read, it all held together—from first to last page. Of course, I was reading the Gemstone letters themselves, instead of my own abbreviated outline of what they had to say.

The article I wrote with Mae [with her files, actually], Is Howard Hughes Dead and Buried Off a Greek Island? was published in *Playgirl* (December 1974). But their attorney had cut so many holes in it that it came out more like paper dolls than the article I had written. Even so—the editor got fired, and I was banned forever.

Marin told me that the day that issue of *Playgirl* appeared on the newsstands, she was in New York City, and: "I've never seen so many men in black overcoats running up to buy *Playgirl* in my life!' I personally doubt that they were buying it to see whose cock was in the centerfold, don't you think?

My writing relationship with Mae came to an end at about that time. I guess she decided that having a writing slave wasn't all it was cracked up to be, and I got a little tired of it, too.

I headed for San Francisco, met Bruce Roberts, and became friends with him. I guess I thought, or hoped, that what was being kept secret from the American people, but was being used abroad by various governments to blackmail the U.S., and in various kinds of global power politics, should belong to the people—if only to see what would happen if people found out what was really going on. You know yourself that nothing really did happen. The guys playing the crazy games maybe held their breath for a few minutes, to see if anyone could do anything with the truth. Then they continued playing the games.

Now we have a situation where although many people understand the game, or at least large parts of it, the Mafia and its many associates are very well established here. America is like a huge animal with a giant parasite hanging from its throat. Enough blood is being drained that everyone is hurting, and yet no one seems to know how to get rid of the parasite. The parasite itself is wondering what, if anything, we will ever do. It won't, however, commit suicide. That is not the nature of the beast.

KEITH: Could you tell me more about editing the *Skeleton Key*?

CARUANA: Please remember that you reading a very abbreviated and concise outline, written by another person (me), who was, at the time, struggling to understand a whole pile of complicated and shocking information. My first outline consisted of 23 pages, based on a hasty and imperfect selection from information that I remembered from a hasty reading of an original body of letters several hundred pages long, plus the notes I made from two long current (1974-5) letters that I worked with at or through the Norwegian Consulate.

I was working at the Norwegian consulate in San Francisco, to which I had been directed by Bruce Roberts when I asked to see more recent Gemstone material than the portion of the File that Mae had, which roughly covered the period from mid-1971 through mid-1972. The first time we met, in the hallway of his apartment building, he responded to my request for a look at more recent letters by giving me a small handwritten note listing 6 foreign consulates in San Francisco, with a name associated with each embassy.

The note said: "This is my authorization for the bearer to read my Gemstone files at your office." He signed and dated the small piece of paper. That was the first time I knew that Bruce Roberts'

papers had a name. With Mae, they were simply "this man's letters." He assured me that the six consulates each had some of the letters and would cooperate with me. He also remarked that they would recognize his handwriting. After all those midnight hours at Mae's when I had struggled to read page after page of xerox copies, I fervently agreed!

"That's for sure," I said.

Then he turned around and went inside his apartment, and I left.

After a while I realized that he had no intention of giving me any of the more recent papers, and if I wanted to see any of them, I would have to at least try the consulates first. The first one I called was the Japanese consulate, and I asked to speak to the man whose name was written on the note. I was told he was not there. I moved on to the Arab country, and went to the address listed in the telephone book, without calling ahead. This turned out to be a very modest, tiny office. The man behind the desk looked at me with beady eyes and seemed to think I might be willing to trade for a look at the papers. This was also not a productive encounter.

I was running out of countries fast. I decided to take the bull by the horns. I marched over to the Soviet Consulate one afternoon. I was seeking a Mr. Pavlov. He turned me down flat. *[See Chapter 31 for an account of this encounter.-sc2006].*

I had visited three of the six Consulates he had listed, and all of them had turned me down flat. But at the Norwegian consulate, the receptionist ushered me to a seat in the Library, and fetched a copy of a long current letter, addressed to the leader of Norway. She allowed me to read through the rest of the afternoon, and take notes. I had a loose-leaf notebook with me, and began picking out items or phrases from the single letter she had allowed me to read, which was about fourteen pages long, and arranging them as best I could in rough chronological order. Most of the material in the original *Skeleton Key* was extracted from two letters, such as this one, written in late 1974/early 1975, which I did not own, and only had the chance to see once, plus my memory of the material I had read at Mae's, plus what Bruce Roberts told me directly.

My original impulse was to understand the letters myself, and it helped me to try and make some sort of chronological sense out of them. Roberts was not only a mental giant and a powerful writer, but also a sort of poet. He presented his material incrementally, over a period of time, so that one seldom got the whole story at once. I had to put the details together chronologically to make sense out of the puzzle.

Reading his letters was like reading a history written by James Joyce in his Finnegan's Wake period. [So I named the piece *A Skeleton Key to the Gemstone File*, after a famous book written by Joseph Campbell in 1944, called *A Skeleton Key to Finnegan's Wake*.] All of historic time (that is, the threads Roberts was interested in) tended to be jumbled together in paragraph-long sentences. Some of my chronologizing consisted of picking bits and phrases out of these sentences, and putting them under appropriate dates, sometimes years apart. I stuck to Roberts' own words as much as I could, since I felt that any interpretation I might make of what might be a 'poetic' expression on his part, might well be wrong. But I did add my own comments.

My intention at the time was to outline events, not to describe Bruce Roberts. When I decided to release the Gemstone *Skeleton Key* outline, which was done in a hurry under the pressure of fright for his safety, I attempted to include a few explanations, and at least some details about him, so that readers would understand that I was not claiming to be the creator of this body of work, merely an outliner of someone else's writing. If my intention had been to describe Bruce Roberts, I would have said that he, as far as I knew, was brave, tough, real, a player and not a

sideline sitter; sometimes scared, very angry, and not in the least way the silly wimp you describe! *[in the original draft for my article 'Is It True?'—Keith]*. He wasn't "trying to enter the world of James Bond"; he was James Bond, or his own version of it. Only he wasn't "On Her Majesty's Service." He was a freelancer. A street fighter, a Scotsman, a heavy drinker. I know it's difficult for most people who are not embroiled in the center of a universe such as his, to imagine what it's like to be there, but your picture is just wrong.

As far as I know, he never intended or directed his writing for the general public. Therefore your idea that he was attempting to paint himself in one light or another, for self-aggrandizement or whatever other uncomplimentary terms you can think of, is incorrect.

KEITH: Why did you conclude that the Gemstone letters were not meant for public distribution?

CARUANA: They were almost invariably addressed and sent to a specific person. Xerox copies were went into the File, and were only given or sold to people like myself or Mae Brussell, who had a special interest in them. *[Such as bona fide writers/researchers. Although Roberts makes a point of saying in the Gemstone file that he enjoyed leaving copies of this or that in Xerox machines, at random, just for the fun of it. Strange as it may seem, he was surrounded by murders but he had a remarkable sense of humor.]* As far as I know, they were never publicly distributed, and this seems likely because it appears that neither you nor anyone else you know personally have ever seen a copy of a single page, even though I suppose you and everyone else interested in the subject of Gemstone have been asking to see them for years! On the other hand, my Skeleton Key was intended for public distribution, and that, my good Watson, is why you have a copy!

KEITH: Could you describe your personal mindset when you met Roberts?

CARUANA: I had completed the article for *Playgirl*, and escaped from solitary confinement with Mae Brussell. After reading the portion of the file that Mae had (around 360 pages, dating from 1971 through 1972), I had been very curious about the author. I asked Mae what he was like, and she said he was "Caspar Milquetoast"! She told me that Roberts contacted her after her daughter, Bonnie, had been killed in an "automobile accident" on a lonely road in Carmel. There had been four teen-age girls in the car; another daughter, Barbara, had been seriously injured; of the other two passengers, one had been killed and another injured. Mae talked about this terrible accident on her radio show, "Radio Conspiracy," on the Monterey radio station KLRB. And apparently she mentioned the name of a man who had sympathetically come to visit her after the "accident." *[His last name was Genovese I believe.—sc]*

After this broadcast, which Bruce Roberts had apparently heard, he came to visit her in Carmel[92], and gave her a copy of a portion of the Gemstone File (his letters). He told her that the man who came to see her was the man who had arranged for the "accident", which had been done to persuade Mae to drop her investigations (she was apparently getting too close to some things). He, Bruce Roberts, recognized the man's name, and he knew that the reason this man had visited her was to get the warning across to her that she should stop. However, Mae didn't get the message. She believed her first visitor to be sincerely offering condolences. She didn't believe Roberts; she thought he was probably some nut. She read the file Roberts gave her, not especially believing it, but later events made her put more credence in it. She told me that she went to visit Roberts in San Francisco, and that he lived with his mother, a nice little old Scotch-Irish lady who served Mae tea and wore white gloves. All this made Mae think Bruce Roberts was "Caspar Milquetoast."

[After hearing Mae's account of her meeting with Bruce Roberts in San Francisco (see the transcript of

---

[92] This was an assumption on my part, and was apparently wrong. The one meeting that Mae actually described in her KLRB tape occurred when Mae went up to San Francisco from the Carmel Valley and met with Roberts.

the two KLRB tapes, with my remarks interspersed, in Chapter 36, I now believe that Roberts didn't visit her in Carmel. The trip she made to San Francisco to meet Roberts and pick up the File he gave her may have been her first and only personal encounter with him. Mae was a devoted, loving mother. The suggestion in the Gemstone File that her political research and broadcasting might have led to her daughter's fatal "car crash" injury, another daughter's serious injury, death for another friend and injury for the fourth passenger, would have made any mother suffer intensely. That may have been one reason why she did not allow herself to be moved or convinced at all by what Roberts told her or what was included in the file he gave her. Perhaps she just couldn't shoulder the guilt and responsibility for that accident. I can't blame her for that. Another reason might be that Mae was a confirmed Democrat, (her father a leading California Democrat), and Roberts was impartial—brutal, in fact—in dishing out condemnations of BOTH major political parties.—sc 2005.]

I was a bit surprised, because the impression I got from his writing had been that of a much more fierce personality, but I adjusted my thinking to "Caspar Milquetoast." I was still very curious to meet him. And I decided that since we had used some of the Gemstone information in the forthcoming *Playgirl* article, I was obligated to tell him about it, before it appeared in print—as a journalistic courtesy, although Mae seemed to feel that he had given her permission to use the information as she saw fit. And I also wanted to read the rest of the file—whatever he had written after Mae's portion of the file ended. It was: "And what happened after that???" At the time, I didn't know the file had a name; it was just "letters" by a man named Bruce Roberts.

Roberts had mentioned in the letters that his phone was tapped, and I didn't want to call him. So I just drove to the address that he had put on the letters, an apartment house in the Sunset district of S.F., and rang the bell. I fully expected him to invite me in for tea with his mother. When I finally did meet him, it was clear to me that he wasn't Caspar Milquetoast at all. More like Clint Eastwood/John Wayne, if you want to go to Hollywood for images. I never did get to have tea with his mother. ☹

[Mae had given me the impression that Roberts was a friendly old coot, and that is why I was surprised by the distinctly cool reception I received. But Roberts was still courteous enough, and gave me what I asked him for.]

Between Mae Brussell and Bruce Roberts, it was Mae who was the amateur. She was a "filer," as anyone who knew her would tell you. I don't whether she had much direct connection with the events she described. (Except for her contact with Roberts, which she misunderstood at the time.) She got most of her information from the press, since she subscribed to about 8 different major daily papers, and lots of magazines as well. Every day she would clip the articles relevant to the stories and people she was following, and since she had a copy machine in her file room, she would underline things, make copies, and pop the articles into the right file folders. After a time, she had file folders on nearly everybody involved in national political activities, and that was the basis for her articles on Watergate for Paul Krassner's *Realist*. In terms of brains, she was smart, for a squirrel. However, I never had the impression that she had any deep understanding of what she had squirreled away, though as a writer, I salivated over her file folders, chock full of juicy information!

[I had the impression that she would only go so far in her interpretations, and would then fall back upon her deeply held attitudes. I realize this is not a popular opinion with Mae Brussell fans, but this is what I believe. However, she was one step ahead of everyone else, "scooping" everyone else in the nation, it appears, since she had more information on the Watergate burglars, and was willing and able to print it through the good graces of Paul Krassner.—sc.]

KEITH: Do you believe that Larry Flynt got shot because of the publication of the *Skeleton Key*?

CARUANA: Yes, I do. *[At the time this "interview" by mail was conducted, some time in 1991 or early*

1992, I had a mistaken idea of what had happened to Larry Flynt. I have cut that out here. The revised story appears in Chapter 43.—sc.]

KEITH: Did you ever see any of Roberts' actual gemstones?

CARUANA: Yes, I did see a few. He invited me to meet him one day in front of "Mrs. Giannini's Bank of America" in downtown San Francisco. He had a safe deposit box there, and he went in and got a few artificial diamonds, and I think a ruby, and showed them to me. They were to be sent out in connection with a letter or letters that he was sending to someone. I have never been big on gemstones, and even though diamonds are supposed to be a girl's best friend, none of them have ever actually befriended me. At the time, I believe he was no longer creating artificial gemstones. He told me that he had done so in the past in a garage, which blew up one day due to some mistake he made, and he described running down the street with singed-off eyebrows. He had some really interesting small talk! I think he may have run out of gemstones at some time, and of course he could use anything he wanted as a symbolic "gemstone." Sometimes a coin.[93] Or even a pebble from a certain place. In this case, it would be the "history" that accompanied the object that would give it its value. He told me some of these things anecdotally, and I never heard the whole story of his life.

KEITH: Do you know why the G. Gordon Liddy files were also called "Gemstone"?

CARUANA: The relationship between Gordon Liddy and Gemstone, as I understand it, is that Roberts was writing his Gemstone letters (letters that he sold, with a gemstone), and giving them out free or selling them to key people, both in this country and abroad.

[He began doing this in 1968. But he had been engaged in creating artificial gemstones since at least 1954. Nixon and other politicians, in both major political parties, were given sheafs of these letters. They publicly ignored them, but panicked, lest the damaging information should get out to the public.]

Gordon Liddy named his White House ["CREEP"] operation "Gemstone Plan," after Roberts' letters in his Gemstone file; that's where the name came from. Liddy's purpose as I understand it was to find out how much of the Gemstone information had leaked out, and damage control—that is, how much the Democrats were planning to use against Nixon. Gordon Liddy isn't "Gemstone"; he was "anti-Gemstone." I see him on TV every now and then. He plays "himself" on Miami Vice; a murdering CIA/Mafia slob, and he doesn't need to act. He recently appeared on Jack Anderson's show. Jack Anderson serves as a conduit to release CIA cover stories to J. Q. Public. The CIA is very imaginative and productive, when it comes to producing cover stories. They had Gordon Liddy "explaining" to Jack Anderson how he had been "hired" by the CIA to murder Anderson, and how, in his endearingly clumsy CIA way, he had failed repeatedly. How could anyone be afraid of such a bunch of inept nerds? (That was the point of the show.) Can't even pull off a good assassination! Did J. Q. Schmoe really believe this bullshit? Who knows? I didn't bother to watch. The difference between media and life gets a little fuzzy, doesn't it? Do you know the difference? In a nutshell: in life, if they decide to bump you off, they actually do it. *[Since many people have wondered about the relationship between Roberts' Gemstone File and Gordon Liddy's Gemstone Plan, I have attempted a clarification in Chapter 44.]*

KEITH: What would you venture to say was Roberts' purpose in writing the Gemstone letters?

CARUANA: Much of this has to be guesswork, since you can't always be sure of another person's motivation, especially when that person isn't around to explain. As I think I may have told you, Bruce Roberts' serious involvement with Hughes began when he tried to sell the Hughes Tool Company his artificial gemstones. Artificial diamonds are used as cutting tips for oil well drill

---

[93] I eventually bought a "Dallas Dime, with history" from him. The history included were copies of letters to Anwar Sadat of Egypt and Tito of Yugoslavia, included here as chapters 37 and 38.

bits, a major product of Hughes Tool Co. Roberts also had artificial rubies to sell. *[Ultimately, artificial rubies were used for laser beams. The real Howard Hughes once made this smart-ass remark: "Nobody has to use Hughes Tools' oil well drilling bits if they want an oil well. They can always use a pick and shovel!"]*

Last night, half asleep, I was watching a TV program on lasers. Suddenly this guy from "Hughes" appeared; I forgot his name. He is supposed to have "invented" the use of laser enhancement by shooting a beam of light through an artificial ruby (in 1960, after Hughes Tool stole some of Roberts' artificial gemstones.) [94]

In retrospect, I think Roberts half-explained at least some of this in his letters and his conversations with me, though as a scientific ignoramus, I didn't grasp it at all. He was also talking about the potential for power inherent in laser beam technology, still in the process of development. "Hughes" stole a lot more from Roberts than just diamond tips for drill bits, although that may have been the original potential use with which he took his idea to them. Instead of paying him, Hughes Tool stole his invention. The motivating force was rage, and while he was fighting Hughes Tool, he somehow discovered "there wasn't any Hughes"; i.e., Onassis had snapped him up and was running the Hughes empire through the "Mormon Mafia" baby-sitters, Robert Maheu, etc.

A paperback book on Hughes has some interesting photos of Hughes appearing before a Senate committee or whatever, clearly showing the facial scars he sustained when he escaped an assassination attempt in one of his planes. The last genuine published photos of him appeared in 1957—just before he was kidnapped, seriously injured, shot up with heroin, and carted off to a hospital/prison cell on Tenos in Onassis's one-patient "hospital." Any later photos or drawings are of a double or look-alike, just one of the doubles who appeared during "Hughes's" increasingly rare public appearances after the real Hughes was snatched by Onassis. A book, *The Amazing Howard Hughes*, written by Noah Dietrich who had worked for Hughes for 30 years, until the Onassis snatch and take-over, convinced Onassis to pay Dietrich a significant amount of $$$ to shut up and go away, which he did.

Along the way Roberts lost considerably income (not being paid for his scientific discovery, etc.) So a man who might have been a perfectly happy inventor-physicist became a very unhappy man-whose-invention-was-stolen-by-a-big-company. Being an exceptionally brilliant and courageous man, he kept going deeper and deeper, and I suppose formed the habit of keeping a detailed daily journal, since he was also a very gifted writer.

[The above was my answer to Keith's question in 1992, when I still did not have a copy of Mae's section of the Gemstone file. Today I would give another answer, which appears in the edited Gemstone papers in this volume. See Roberts' own explanation. He states it was the hit-and-run accident on his car by Tom Alioto, in 1968, which began the series—or at least began the distribution of some of his daily journal entries.—sc2005.

The more Roberts learned about Onassis and his associates, and their strangle-hold on the media, the more became the need to communicate some of what he knew. We all take different paths. Roberts wrote "letters". He was also, I believe, a very humane person: a father (divorced); not a killer. He didn't like Mafia killers. I don't think he appreciated the world being run by these killers, especially when they moved in and took over the U.S. government with the assassination of John F. Kennedy. It really was a secret coup. I guess you can divide people into two groups: the ones who think it's okay to feed people drugs, murder to stay in power and

---

[94] See Gerald Carroll's 1990 interview with Dr. Theodore H. Maiman, "inventor of the laser," which appears in Chapter 41.

make money, etc., and manipulate whole populations, and those who think, when they know about it, that it isn't okay, no matter how much money you can make by being part of it. Or how much they will lose by not being part of it.

I suppose that, while being perhaps something of a dilettante, you wouldn't have chosen to explore "conspiracy theory" only provided that it couldn't possibly be true. I suppose you feel you have some decent human instincts that keep you from being a professional killer. Don't you think it might be possible that Bruce Roberts shared these feelings? I always thought he did.

Since Roberts wasn't making money from his scientific work, he had to make it somehow. He once told me that he did construction work (building contractor) for a while, putting roofs on buildings, etc. "You have to make a living somehow," he said. [95]

At a certain point, he put nine and nine together, and started sending letters, with Gemstones, "cold," and asking the recipients to send him what they thought the letter was worth to them. I guess some of them sent substantial sums, and others sent people to kill him. I know he didn't have very much money; this could have been due in part to various divorces, children, etc., and various disasters that frequently seemed to happen to his cars.

KEITH: What do you think of the recent Kiwi Gemstone?

CARUANA: It's the first "Gemstone" result that seems positive. That is, someone has actually used the Gemstone information accurately and courageously as a basis for following current events [in Australia and New Zealand] which are now shaping our world (species) history, and I say, more power to them! It is really a tragic story of how our world has been "united" under the rule of these vicious criminals, monsters in business suits. You can see exactly what dear old George Bush [Sr.!] means when he keeps talking about "One World" or whatever the phrase he uses.

Of course, the Kiwi Gemstone phrasing is a bit misleading, in that the wording seems to imply that "Bruce Roberts" wrote it. I don't believe anyone writes anything after they are dead, and I think that needs clarifying. If the person or persons responsible for continuing "Gemstone" through the economic takeover of Australia and New Zealand wish to remain anonymous, that's something I do understand. And if they are smart enough to follow the current international financial, political and social manipulations, hopefully they will be smart enough to stay alive.

KEITH: Do you happen to know what Roberts was getting at when he referred to "The Yellow Race"?

CARUANA: What comes to mind is the phrase: "The Yellow Race is not in China; the Yellow Race Dead-fucks Mary Jo Kopechne." [Roberts wrote that this was one of four "papers" he produced at a certain time. I don't believe any of the four wound up in Mae's possession; as far as I know, I never saw any of the four either. But we do have "We Ate Mary Jo's Liver," (Chapter 21), which covers the same ground.—sc 2005] It was not a description of skin color, but of moral decay; that is, specifically, of Teddy Kennedy, who allowed Mary Jo to die to cover his own ass, rather than to confess, and of those battalions of folks who helped him in the cover-up.

KEITH: The *Skeleton Key* has been in circulation eighteen years now. Do you see any hopeful signs that any of this information will be made public, or acted upon?

CARUANA: I don't know whether you have seen the series on the JFK assassination which recently appeared on the A&E cable network. I see where a number of the surviving witnesses have

---

[95] Actually, he said he had once put a new roof on the San Francisco City Hall. Some enterprising researcher could earn at least a footnote in future editions for getting the info on that, if it is still to be found.

come forth with bits and pieces which pretty well substantiate how many shooters there really were, where they were standing, etc. Each new retelling adds a little more to the complete picture. This one goes off into the wild blue yonder, however, when a "researcher" sits there with a straight face and tells you the "three shooters" were from the Corsican Mafia, recruited in Marseilles. Surely the good old USA didn't have to go so far to find reliable hitmen, when we have so many home-grown expert Mafioso hitmen, such as Fratianno, Roselli and Brading.

Now that Oliver Stone's movie, *JFK*, has come out, and if everyone stays alive, there may be a move throughout the world to get these people out of power. It's a slight chance, but if we could all get together, we could do it. Revolutions have happened in the past! When things get bad enough (as they are now), things happen. Whoever thought the Red Splendor would come tumbling down, without a shot, defeated by "free enterprise"? And now that "free enterprise" is far from free, that too may bite the dust. You as an anarchist know what I am talking about, I suppose. Human history may yet take some surprising turns. The thousand-year Roman Empire eventually bit the dust.

[Well, one reason is that the whole thing had become so corrupt that they couldn't find a decent Emperor to hold it together. Nero, and Caligula, forsooth! The world changed, and the Roman Empire had to change with it. Finally, the "Barracks Emperors"—military men, twenty-two soldier emperors in forty-nine years. That's an average "reign" of about two and a half years per "emperor"—not even as long as a four-year term in our current four-year revolving two-Mafia-Party oligarchy.—sc2005]

I recently watched the Oscar ceremonies. Two of the big nominees—Oliver Stone's *JFK*, and Warren Beatty's *Bugsy*, came head-to-head. It was fascinating to watch! Both are really about the same subject: Mafia control over the United States. Stone's, against, we know about. Beatty's, presenting the killer, Bugsy Siegel, in a sympathetic light, is pro. The absent party, in both, was Onassis, Meyer Lansky's boss. Bugsy's "glorious aim," the building of the Flamingo casino in the Las Vegas desert, a great money-milking machine for the Mafia—what a goal! The movie even mentions the power this would give the Mob in Nevada—another dream which came true! Hollywood walked the line between the two sides; *Silence of the Lambs* was the only safe choice! Watching Stone's and Beatty's face provided a groovy little mini-drama, since both of them knew what was going on! Jack Valenti's scathing denunciation of *JFK* afterward underscored the battle for the hearts and minds of J. Q. Public which is always continuing.

40 1993: Interview by Kenn Thomas

A Telephone Interview with Stephanie Caruana, Author of <u>A Skeleton Key to the Gemstone File</u>, by Kenn Thomas, Editor and Publisher, Steamshovel Press #8, Summer 1993.[96]

THOMAS: Stephanie Caruana was responsible for surfacing the Gemstone File, a behind-the-scenes documentation of various power cabals involving Aristotle Onassis and Howard Hughes, among others, in connection with the Kennedy assassination. Stephanie, thank you for being with us.

CARUANA: I'm delighted to talk to you.

THOMAS: How did you first encounter the Gemstone File?

CARUANA: I was working with Mae Brussell. She was a conspiracy researcher in Carmel Valley, California for a number of years and I was a writer for *Playgirl* magazine. I got in touch with her because I wanted to find out more about the Symbionese Liberation Army's kidnapping of Patty Hearst and what was really behind it. So I went to see Mae, and I began writing articles based on her research files. We began writing an article about Howard Hughes and Aristotle Onassis at the request of my editor at *Playgirl*.

THOMAS: How did this grow out of your interest in the Patty Hearst kidnapping?

CARUANA: I was referred to Mae by a news editor of a radio station in San Francisco. I saw that she had so much information stashed away in her house in Carmel Valley, and I offered to move in with her as a sort of writing slave. My editor at *Playgirl* asked me to ask Mae if she knew anything about Howard Hughes. And Mae said, "Howard Hughes is dead. Onassis kidnapped him."

THOMAS: This was well before it was officially announced that Hughes had died.

CARUANA: Yes. This was in 1974.

THOMAS: What is the long and the short of what happened to Patty Hearst?

CARUANA: I was living in Berkeley about a mile from where Patty Hearst was living: When this happened, everybody in Berkeley was quite shocked. It became clear that this was some sort of media event. I had never seen anything like it. There were these demands from the SLA leader, Cinque; battle communiques; he wanted food giveaways in Oakland, which I watched. I felt that there was something going on that I really didn't understand. It seemed more media than anything else.

THOMAS: Like an artificially constructed drama being played out on the TV news.

CARUANA: Yes. And that's when I went to see Mae. Mae had a great many interesting things to say, and we wrote an article about it which was terrific. Mae had done a lot of research on what was going on the California prison system, particularly at Vacaville prison, where there was a tremendous amount of mind control going on. I had a friend who had been there and they had given her shock treatments.

It was something that was way beyond what was happening in other prisons. Mae's theory, and I believed her, was that Donald DeFreeze, "Cinque", had been programmed at Vacaville through a series of classes in "Black Pride" and "Let's move along with the revolution," and possibly other forms of mind control such as drugs. He was also a three-time loser. They could have kept him in jail for the rest of his life. There was no chance that he could ever have gotten out. He was what Mae called a yo-yo, which is a prisoner that these people have on a string.

---

[96] Reprinted from *Popular Alienation: A Steamshovel Press Reader*, p.141-143.

They can let him out of prison for their own purposes and pull him back any time they want, completely under the control of the authorities.

THOMAS: So you went to work for Mae doing research on Howard Hughes.

CARUANA: *[I never went to work for Mae. I was a working journalist, and I offered to write articles using Mae's research and ideas—sc2006.]* I was staying at Mae's house and she had these enormous files. She pulled out a file on Howard Hughes with all these clippings, and a file on Onassis with all these other clippings. It was a tremendous rush job, a very fast deadline. It was supposed to be the major article for their Christmas issue. So I started reading and reading, but Mae's theory that Onassis had kidnapped Howard Hughes—I said, "Mae, I don't see it. I see articles about Hughes and Onassis, but I don't see any cross. So where are you getting this idea from?"

And at that point, she said, "Well, I have these other letters from this guy. He gave me these letters back in 1972. I read them, and I thought maybe he's just a crazy- wacko kind of person, but I have since then received somewhat similar suggestions from a couple of other sources. So I tend to put more credence in it than I did originally." And she gave me a way of looking at things that I found was something I could accept. And I find myself using that.

She said, "When I hear the same story from three different sources, I tend to think it may be true."

So she had the story about Onassis and Hughes from one source, and then she had this Canadian tabloid and she had another source. If you have three vectors, you can locate a point in three dimensions.

THOMAS: So the letters were the Bruce Roberts letters? What is the connection between Bruce Roberts and Mae Brussell? Who did Bruce work for?

CARUANA: He didn't work for anybody. He was his own man. And I would say without a doubt that he was the most incredibly amazing and fantastic person I have ever met in my entire life.

THOMAS: How did you meet Bruce Roberts?

CARUANA: I read the letters at Mae's, and I was absolutely stunned by them. I was overwhelmed by them. There was so much information and it was written in such a brilliant style. I found it believable. Maybe I was different from Mae. I read it all over the space of one night or possibly two nights, but straight. Couldn't put it down. I was at the same time writing this article for *Playgirl*. I became very curious about Bruce Roberts. I asked Mae what he was like, and she gave me her impression. She told me that she had met him in 1972 and he had given her these letters. And she said that she didn't believe them at first, but she gave them more credence later. By this time, it was 1974. After several months I decided that I didn't want to work with Mae any more; it was getting to be too dreary. I went to San Francisco, and the first thing I did was, I went to Bruce Roberts' house and looked him up.

THOMAS: *The Skeleton Key to the Gemstone File* is an outline that you created based on your review of all the Roberts letters?

CARUANA: He arranged for me to read some of his more recent letters, and I made notes. The *Skeleton Key* is a chronological outline based on my notes and my conversations with him, and whatever made sense to me. Believe me, 1 left out more than I put in. It was a very dangerous situation for everybody. We were all living in a powder keg and this man really was surrounded by murders. While I released the *Skeleton Key*, I didn't feel that I had any right to release a great many personal details about him or his sources, and that's why I didn't. Bruce Roberts read the *Skeleton Key* and it seemed as though he approved of it, which amazed me. And he used to call me up sometimes and ask me to go to certain events, and bring copies of the *Skeleton Key* along and give copies to people.

THOMAS: When did he die?

CARUANA: He died on July 30, 1976. Supposedly, he died of cancer, or a strange unknown virus. But that man was so healthy and so tough that I think he was killed. They almost killed him while I was there. That's why I released the *Key* in the first place. I was so upset. I was just enraged and I felt that I had to get the story out. The *Gemstone File* is the best history we have of the Kennedy assassination and of that time. I'm not talking about my own work. I only wish I had the original letters. I have a couple of them but I don't have the whole thing.[97] But this man was a historian in the real sense of the word. Of course, the people who are running our country at this point, one thing they want to kill is anybody who wants to tell the truth about what's going on.

THOMAS: I realize the Kennedy assassination is one detail in a long story about the hidden machinations of what's happening, the thrust of which is that the international Mafia with Aristotle Onassis at its head is the group that's calling the shots.

CARUANA: Of course, they have become so ingrained in the American society, can you call them Mafia? They all wear business suits. They've all got lots of money. They're all "respectable" businessmen—well, not all of them. The killers aren't, but the guys who tell the killers what to do and pay them, almost all of our big business people. I have a list somewhere of the hundred richest families or people in the country, and its probably the same people who are the Mafia. I'd like to compare notes. *[And of course Onassis has been dead for years, but the lines and methods of control that he perfected are still with us, and his successors have learned their lessons well. We see the dire results around us every day. The names of the people and the corporations involved are pretty much the same, adding thirty-five years and billions of dollars in loot.—sc2006.]*

THOMAS: One of the criticisms laid at the feet of people who suggest Mafia involvement in Kennedy's death is that the Mafia couldn't do a cover-up for all these thirty years. That may not necessarily be true when you consider that the Mafia and the ranking members of the intelligence community are basically the same people.

CARUANA: They are now. The factor that ties them together for me anyway is Onassis, because according to Bruce Roberts, who I believe, he kidnapped Hughes in 1957. And Howard Hughes was an extraordinarily rich and powerful man with a tremendous empire. And Howard Hughes had already bribed Richard Nixon. So Howard Hughes had Vice President Nixon in his pocket at that time. As I talk about this, in my mind I have this picture of the food chain in the ocean. A little fish gets swallowed by a bigger fish, who gets swallowed by a bigger fish, and a bigger fish.... And Onassis was the biggest fish in the ocean. And along came Hughes, who was so huge that he became a tempting morsel for Onassis, who swallowed him up. And he got away with it. It was an imaginative stroke of genius by a man who was more powerful than Alexander the Great. He was the richest man in the world, and the most powerful man in the world. And he ran the world until he died.

---

[97] At the time of this interview, I did not have any portion of Mae's part of the Gemstone File. I was able to buy a copy from Tom Davis about six years ago..

41 1994: Project Seek: Gerald A. Carroll Does Gemstone

The following is excerpted from Gerry Carroll's <u>Project Seek</u>, by permission of the author. It is a good example of the excellent Gemstone File documentation provided in this book.

A Word from a Member of Hughes's Personal Staff

With regard to the "faked" marriage to Jean Peters—that's exactly what it was, according to more than one source. Donald Neuhaus, a member of Hughes' personal staff at Hughes headquarters in Southern California, told us in a December 5, 1993, interview that he was responsible for guarding Ms. Peters' bungalow at the posh Beverly Hills Hotel in the late summer of 1957:

> "...I recall all this quite vividly. At that time, Walter Winchell (a Hearst Newspapers syndicated columnist) 'broke' the story about the Hughes marriage to Jean Peters. But there was only one problem—Howard was out of town somewhere, nobody knew exactly where, although it was rumored he was either still in Montreal or out of the country (according to pilot Bushey, he was in the Bahamas), and we had no way of knowing where he was.
>
> "But the marriage was impossible, because I was guarding Jean Peters bungalow (emphasis ours). She was in Bungalow No. 6, and Hughes always stayed in Bungalow No. 8 when he was at the hotel. This is easy to remember because I was responsible for her not being disturbed. Howard would call her every night, and talk to her for two, three hours at a time.... I recall one night that they talked over five hours on the phone."

The involvement of Sen. Howard Cannon is also confirmed by sources other than the *Key*. It was gossip columnist Louella Parsons who, along with Winchell, broke the story in her column, "announcing" the wedding. Reporters combed Nevada, unable to find any evidence of a marriage. Stanton O'Keefe, in his book, The Real Howard Hughes Story, described the marriage scenario:

> "...It (the marriage) took place in Tonopah, Nevada. Senator Howard Cannon, who was then the city attorney of Las Vegas and a personal friend of Hughes, took care of all the legal arrangements—including the trick maneuver that protected the validity of the marriage contract while allowing the couple to register under assumed names (emphasis ours).[98]

Hughes expert and conspiracy theorist Mae Brussell and co-writer Stephanie Caruana—who has admitted to penning at least one version of the *Skeleton Key* under the direct tutelage of Bruce Roberts—developed this topic further in an article for the December, 1974, edition of *Playgirl* magazine entitled "Is Howard Hughes Dead and Buried off a Greek Island?" The article states that Hughes and Jean Peters were supposed to be living in a Bel Air mansion for several years after their "marriage," but the home's owner never saw the "husband." The couple was never seen in public together in over 13 years of marriage, and there is no record of their ever having been photographed with each other. This strange union ended in 1971—with Peters getting a quick $2 million divorce settlement. Coincidentally, this came about at the time the story started circulating that Hughes had died, and that a double, or doubles, had taken his place.

Neuhaus, presented with a copy of the *Skeleton Key* in 1987, made the following observations in a letter to us, dated Nov. 29, 1993, concerning the sudden, jolting changes the Hughes company underwent in that fateful first week of August, 1957:

> "...I was called at home at around 1:00 or 1:30 a.m. one day during that summer of 1957, and told to report to the office immediately because of an emergency. When I arrived, it was explained to me and some of the other staff members that Noah Dietrich had been fired and we were to seal all entrances and exits to the Romaine Street building. Shortly after this episode, I noticed a complete change in the way operations were conducted but at the time gave it very little thought... It was not until 1987 that I stumbled across a poorly copied 24-page memo titled The Gemstone Abstract, which

---

[98] See *Playgirl* article, reproduced here as Chapter 3.

hit me like a thunderbolt. The peculiar, contradictory and downright weird events that occurred in 1957 started to become clear to me, and I have spent a part of my time during the past six years trying to find the balance of the Gemstone papers."

Neuhaus is convinced that Dietrich misled people in his written accounting of his leaving the company. Dietrich wrote in his book that he left the Hughes company in March of 1957, but that could be a deception. Neuhaus is firm in recalling the announcement of Dietrich's departure as coming the first week of August.

Furthermore, Neuhaus offers the first firm evidence of an Onassis link to the Hughes organization—a link that cannot be ignored and that is invariably a key ingredient to all this. Neuhaus has long been good friends with a man named Jack Egger, who is now director of security at Warner Brothers Studios in North Hollywood. Egger was captain of the Beverly Hills Police Department in 1957—and was handed direct orders from the CIA to keep an eye on "Hughes" and keep him bottled up inside the Beverly Hills Hotel when he returned from his Bahamas excursion.

"Jack knew a ton of CIA guys," said Neuhaus. "They were all over the place. Bob Maheu, formerly of the FBI, was also with the Hughes company at that time and had just joined, but there were CIA and FBI men all over."

But it was Jack Egger's father, Frank, who possessed the explosive link to Onassis and his maritime fleet, which at that time was nearing its zenith in power, money and productivity:

"Frank Egger was a major partner in the insurance firm of Bailey, Martin and Faye," Neuhaus said. "Frank ran the division of that company that was one of the largest brokerage firms in the world that dealt almost exclusively with insurance for tanker hulls. Onassis was a very big customer, and so were Exxon and a lot of other tanker companies (emphasis ours)."

With that kind of enormous financial leverage—oil tanker insurance has never been cheap, especially for a fleet of such vessels—it would be easy to see that Onassis would be calling the shots behind the scenes.

And was Maheu part of Onassis' team at that time, as the *Skeleton Key* asserts? Neuhaus could not recall if Maheu and Onassis ever got together during this period, "although it's a distinct possibility because of Frank Egger and his son Jack. Anything is possible in a situation like that."

Frank Egger was also big behind the scenes in Los Angeles politics. He was a Democrat, and supported Los Angeles Mayor Sam Yorty when Yorty was still in the Demos' camp before he turned right and became a Republican. Frank Egger routinely ran major fund-raising drives for Yorty.

It should be emphasized that Yorty became a central figure in the alleged cover-up of the Robert Kennedy assassination in 1968. That is another reason why these connections as outlined by Neuhaus should be considered as much more than just quaint coincidences.

Another Onassis link is John Meyer, who according to Neuhaus started in the Hughes organization as a driver. Hughes insisted that his personal staff travel in company cars with their own drivers, so that full attention could be paid to guests who would also be passengers in the cars. This was appropriate, Neuhaus said, because of the volume of movie stars and starlets that Hughes entertained. During this time, Meyer got really close to Hughes, and the billionaire trusted him enough to appoint him as a key public-relations man in the company.

However, as of 1974, Brussell and Caruana write that John Meyer defected over to the Onassis camp, stating:

"...In 1942, he (Hughes) hired John Meyer to curry favor with politicians, generals and the like. (John Meyer is now press aide to Aristotle Onassis; one of his responsibilities is watching over Jackie.) [*emphasis ours.*]

As stated earlier, Meyer was a key player in getting Elliott Roosevelt, President Franklin D. Roosevelt's son, entangled in more than a few wild parties thrown by Hughes. The parties included girls and everything associated with having a grand old time. The connections are inescapable, and

lend all the more credence to Bruce Roberts' main Gemstone thesis as outlined in the *Skeleton Key*.[99]

***

Gerry Carroll returned to the chase in 1995:

1995: Johnny Meyer: Gemstone's Link Between Hughes and Onassis
—by Gerald A. Carroll[100]

Aristotle Onassis carries out a carefully planned event: He has Howard Hughes kidnapped from his bungalow at the Beverly Hills Hotel, using Hughes' own men (Chester Davis, born Cesare in Sicily, et al). Hughes' men either quit, get fired or stay on in the new Onassis organization."—Gemstone 1:9

One of the more amazing, and seemingly implausible, aspects of the long-maligned Gemstone thesis is this wild tale about Greek shipping tycoon Aristotle Onassis masterminding a kidnapping of billionaire defense-contractor Howard Hughes in 1957. Researchers who have bothered to dig around in the Gemstone legend have often kissed it off as a fabrication because of a lack of "proof" that any of the events described actually took place—the most flagrant falsification being the "kidnapping and switch" of Hughes, by Onassis or anyone else.

But a closer examination of the Gemstone language and some cross-referencing with news accounts of that time paint a dramatically different picture, one of deception of the highest degree.

For example, the Gemstone thesis states that Hughes' men either quit, get fired or stay on in the new Onassis organization—following the alleged kidnapping of Hughes in the Bahamas in the spring-summer of 1957. Indeed, key people did peel off quickly and suddenly in 1957. Noah Dietrich, one of the Hughes Corp.'s mightiest chief executives, was suddenly "fired" by Hughes in 1957. (1)

Long-time aide William "Bill" Gay abruptly resigned, citing "mononucleosis" as the cause (2) under mysterious circumstances. Even publicist Carl Byoir mysteriously died just before that ill-fated trip to Nassau (3).

It was Byoir's public relations firm—which served the Hughes Corp. for years, even after Byoir himself passed away—that provided "doubles" including L. Wayne Rector. These doubles were well-known to Hughes's aides.

Also well-known was a special man named Johnny W. Meyer, who started out with Hughes in the early years as a personal driver and became one of the billionaire's closest confidantes. He set up elaborate Hughes parties, including attractive female escorts, with such high-rollers as Elliott Roosevelt, President Franklin D. Roosevelt's son, and a maverick arms dealer on the side.

Meyer is clearly one of the men who "stay on in the new Onassis organization" after the events of 1957. In fact, it was Meyer who broke the news to Jacqueline Kennedy Onassis that her husband, Aristotle, had died of respiratory failure on March 5, 1975. (4) Strangely, Jackie had left her sick husband's bedside and was skiing in New Hampshire when Ari passed on. Meyer, as he had done for Hughes, had to do the dirty work. He notified Jackie of yet another dead husband.

Meyer himself died under even more strange conditions. He allegedly got out of his car one night in Florida in 1983 to relieve himself following his attendance at a party—and the car rolled over him, killing him. (5)

Clearly, it was Meyer who was the common thread between Howard Hughes and Aristotle Onassis. He was a skilled public relations expert, and manipulated the media at every turn for both

---

[99] Excerpted from *Project Seek*, pp.87-91
[100] Reprinted from *Popular Alienation: A Steamshovel Press Reader*

men over the years. If Onassis ever wanted to conquer Hughes—even kidnap him and replace him with a double—he would need the help of Meyer to cover it up and keep a lid on it for years. The existence of a man of Meyer's abilities is enough to give the Gemstone passages a sense of truthfulness regarding this bizarre kidnap story.

The skills that propelled the rotund Meyer to prominence in the Hughes organization peaked when he covered for the billionaire in embarrassing situations, particularly the so-called Brewster Hearings of 1947, engineered by muckraking Sen. Owen Brewster (R-Maine) when it had become known that Hughes' airplane contracts with the government were questioned.

It was intrepid Hearst Corp. Newsman Bob Considine who blew the lid off this story, exposing Hughes, Elliott Roosevelt and the velvet cover Meyer had placed over the whole sordid mess. Hughes and Elliott loved to party together, and Meyer set up these affairs.

Brewster and others were convinced that Elliott had used his influence as the president's son to seek "the intercession of his father in order to override Army Air Force objections" to aircraft supplied to the U.S. armed forces during World War II. (6)

Hughes was angry that an earlier warplane design of his was rejected by the Army Air Force—a record-breaking design that later became the model for the Japanese Zero, one of the deadliest warplanes of that deadly war. (7)

Meyer got tangled up in the mess when he allegedly "entertained" high government officials lavishly in order to sway their opinions of Hughes' airplane deals. Many of those parties also included Elliot and his new wife, Faye Emerson.

Considine, with some help from The Associated Press, originally broke the story on August 3, 1947, by releasing a lengthy expense-account listing of Meyer's excesses, "duly recorded by Hughes' bookkeepers." (8)

Meyer's P.R. skills were evident when he was accused of ordering Elliott to stay in Europe—and out of the U.S.—until the 1944 elections were over and his dad was safely re-elected.

Then, astonishingly, at the height of the Brewster Hearings and the public outcry they were precipitating, Johnny Meyer disappeared. With the key witness gone, the hearings collapsed, on August 12, 1947. (9)

An international manhunt was launched to find the portly Meyer. The next day, Hughes triumphantly left Washington for California to the cheers of a supportive public (10).

Meyer resurfaced in Hollywood on Aug. 17, 1947, but by that time, the hysteria over the Brewster Hearings had subsided, and his client, Howard Hughes, was temporarily off the hook.

Three years later, Meyer dabbled in oil-rig investments in Wyoming, a deal that would inevitably lead him to Onassis, who at that time in 1950 had tried to monopolize the oil-shipping routes from Saudi Arabia.(11)

Fast-forward to 1957, and it was duly noted that Meyer received a $104,666 "loan" from Equitable Plan Company that he was under no obligation to repay (12). The timing, September 1957, is absolutely vital, for that was just after the kidnap and switch of Howard Hughes was rendered complete, in August, according to the Gemstone thesis, and Hughes' personal aide Donald Neuhaus (13). Was that "loan" part of a payoff to Meyer for his cooperation?

And that was not the end of the story. Another disclosure of an additional $125,000 "loan" to Meyer from Equitable was made on September 6, 1957.

Congressional investigators, weary of Hughes-related probes, gathered sketchy, hurried testimony from Meyer and others, and ended up clearing Meyer of any wrongdoing. The coincidences, however, are disconcerting and lend more credence to the Gemstone account (14).

Another damning piece of information that links Meyer to any kidnap plot is the fact that along with Bill Gay, he accompanied Hughes on that ill-fated trip to Nassau by way of Montreal—

from Hughes' headquarters in Beverly Hills (15). Meyer stayed with the Hughes party the entire time the billionaire stayed in Nassau.

Later, when he openly switched to Onassis, Meyer's chief job was to keep a full-time watch on Jackie (16). As always, Johnny Meyer did his boss right.

NOTES:

1. Carroll, Gerald A., *Project Seek: Kennedy and the Gemstone Thesis* (1994, Bridger House), p. 78.
2. Carroll, p. 334.
3. *San Francisco Examiner*, Feb. 4, 1951.
4. Heyman, C. David, *Cosmopolitan* 1989, p. 164, "Jackie: The Onassis Years."
5. Davis, L. J., *Onassis: Aristotle and Christina*, 1986, St. Martin's Press, p. 273.
6. Considine, Bob, *San Francisco Examiner* (International News Service), Aug. 5, 1947.
7. Considine, *Examiner* (INS), Aug. 10, 1947.
8. Associated Press, *Examiner*, Aug, 3, 1947.
9. Considine, *Examiner* (INS), Aug. 12, 1947.
10. *Examiner*, INS, Aug. 13, 1947.
11. Lloyd, Ed C., *Examiner*, "Reports from the Oil Fields," July 15, 1950.
12. *Examiner* (INS), "$104,666 Loan Sans Obligation Told at Hearing," Sept. 4, 1957.
13. Carroll, p. 89.
14. *Examiner* (INS), "Johnny Meyer's Co. Loans Revealed," Sept. 6, 1957.
15. Serling, Robert, *Howard Hughes' Airline, an Informal History of TWA*, 1983, St. Martin's Press, p. 121.
16. Caruana, Stephanie and Brussell, Mae. *Playgirl*, November 1974, "Is Howard Hughes Dead and Buried off a Greek Island?"

***

A Link Between Bruce Roberts, His "Gemstone" Rubies, the Hughes Corporation, and the Development of Lasers[101]

"I have extracted 57% water—H_2O—from an opal. 17% of sapphire juice from the 62-carat heart-shaped sapphire now up President Patty's ass. That juice is something else. A real tearjerker. From a ruby, the juice is red—the color of blood."—Bruce Roberts

Gemstone 2:7: Roberts brings his synthetic rubies—the original "Gemstones"—to Hughes Aircraft in Los Angeles. They steal his rubies, the basis for laser-beam research, laser bombs, etc., because of the optical quality of the rubies. One of eleven possible sources for one of the ingredients involved in the Gemstone experiment was the Golden Triangle area. Roberts was married to the daughter of the former French consul in Indochina. In that region, Onassis' involvement in the Golden Triangle dope trade was no secret. Roberts' investigation revealed the Onassis-Hughes connection, kidnap and switch.

(2:8) "Gemstones"—synthetic rubies and sapphires with accompanying "histories." otherwise known as Gemstone papers—were sold or given away to foreign consular officials in return for information. A worldwide information network has gradually developed—a trade of the intelligence activities of many countries. This intelligence network is the source for much of the information in the Gemstone files.

The above reference is potentially revealing. First, it refers to a marriage between Roberts and a foreign national whose father had connections with Indochina and the drug trade which has long infested that part of the world. The second major component, finally, is the mentioning of Roberts' making of rubies, some of sufficient quality to be used in laser research—the root inspiration behind the "Gemstone" nomenclature used in the *Key* and the original Gemstone writings. It is no surprise it was cautiously left out of the *Hustler* version.

Third, in Gemstone 2:8, the nature of Roberts' source development is revealed. Without this passage, most of the Key makes little sense. Without reference to sources, it is easy to discredit research efforts of any journalist. Again, it was left out of the *Hustler* version—sufficiently puzzling readers and leaving the remaining statements to stand with little support.

But did Roberts actually make rubies? Did he submit them to Hughes Corp., and were they used in laser-beam research? Why not ask the inventor of the laser himself, Dr. Theodore H. Maiman?

---

[101] Reprinted from *Project Seek*, pp. 164-7, by permission of Gerald A. Carroll.

We did. In a rare interview by telephone on February 2, 1990, Dr. Maiman revealed the following astonishing revelations:

• Howard Hughes and the Hughes Corp. in general did not support the laser research program, and Maiman was forced to pursuing the research on his own. Maiman remains embittered that Hughes would still take credit for the revolutionary invention.

• Maiman invented the laser during a nine-month break between government contracts. Funding came directly from the Hughes Corp.'s general research funds, an expenditure frowned upon by Hughes executives.

• Maiman bought all rubies for his experiments on his own, from independent sources. Primary source for rubies had always been reported as the Lindy Division of Union Carbide. Maiman says that although he used Lindy rubies, he also used some from other sources. Although vague on the exact source for the rubies that eventually worked, Maiman thought it was Griener, a small-scale company, but he is not sure. Right about that time, and all through the 1950s, a man named Bruce Roberts was making synthetic jewels for movie stars—jewels so real-looking and of such high quality, including rubies, that his talents were highly sought after all around Hollywood. Maiman implied that Roberts could well have been one of the independent contractors supplying rubies for the laser experiments.

Maiman outlines the laser scenario in his own words:

"...The (ruby-making) process is tricky. You have to heat the material to 2,300 degrees Centigrade, roughly 4,000 degrees... It's tricky to grow the crystals just right.

"...Hughes did not support the program. In fact, Hughes was upset that I was working on it. (emphasis ours). Myself and my masters' candidate assistant, Irenee D'Haenens. Just us, no one else, from Hughes or anywhere else. Yet, they (Hughes) take credit for it.

"...You see, Hughes' interests were directed toward defense—military electronics, missile electronics... The idea of making a laser had never been done before, and it was a long-shot project. Plus, what would you do with it?

"...About funding, almost all work that was done by Hughes was from government contracts. I happened to be between government contracts at the time. I had just gotten off a project for the U.S. Signal Corps and other things... At that time, I had 9-12 months to work on this (laser). I was not on contract.

"...Budget for the laser came from Hughes' general research funds. They were very touchy about that because it was their own money, not the government's. See, they like to use government money, not their own... It was unfortunate that I was working on a project they didn't care about.

"...The laser project was actually bootlegged (emphasis ours).

"...By the way, we also worked with one other outfit for rubies, to get back to your question about the source for our rubies. The name was Griener.. .yes, I think that's it. If there ever was a person named Roberts, he would have worked for either Griener or Lindy... But they did supply some synthetic crystals, not just rubies, but others as well. I think they made them for actresses... (emphasis ours)

"Hughes didn't even file for a patent. That's the whole other story. The cost was ridiculously low for Hughes. Counting my salary, my assistant's, materials, everything, it came to $50,000. And it led to a huge discovery. They didn't file for a patent because they thought it wasn't any big deal."[83]

The presence of Roberts in Southern California during the 1950s is confirmed by a mysterious photograph that appeared in the newspaper supplement *American Weekly* on October 12, 1952. A man named Bruce Roberts is shown adorning the neck of actress Carmen Miranda with synthetic jewels. It is a photo feature, with the following headline and copy block:

BUT...WOULD YOU WEAR THEM?
A designer creates some costume jewelry that might pass for jeweled costumes

"Bruce Roberts, former actor turned jewelry designer, can be thankful that Carmen Miranda got tired of her famous basket-of-fruit hat and sought something new. Her quest resulted in a new Miranda 'look' and a market for Roberts in costume jewelry that is more costume than jewelry.

"When Carmen approached Roberts and outlined her dilemma, he realized one thing: Any accoutrements would have to withstand her lively antics. So he strung his semi-precious stones—synthetic pearls, rubies (emphasis ours), sapphires, topazes on nylon parachute thread guaranteed to hold up under 360 pounds of weight."

No further details were available in this account, but it was enough to conclude that this could well have been the same Bruce Roberts talked about in Gemstone 2:7-8. Not only do the occupation and name fit the circumstances—and the location, Southern California — but so does the age: Roberts was born on October 27, 1919, and he would have been 33 years old in 1952. The photo, included in this book, looks like a man in his early to mid-30s.[102]

If indeed this was the Bruce Roberts referred to in Gemstone 2:7-8, it would be quite easy to see how he would know so much about the inner workings of the Hughes Corp., and how he might have known about the disappearance of Howard Hughes in 1957. It would go far in explaining how he would know about the entire Hughes laser situation; in fact, the Carl Byoir public relations firm wrote the promotional book on the laser—the same group that allegedly provided L. Wayne Rector, the Hughes double referred to in Gemstone 1:9. Carl Byoir himself died mysteriously in 1957, during the period in which Hughes himself was allegedly kidnapped and switched."

---

[102] Here's something an intrepid California researcher might explore. Bruce Roberts is described as a former actor for a time in the Los Angeles/Hollywood area, possibly during the late 1940's, or 1950's. Perhaps that's how he met Carmen Miranda, and possibly other actresses he may have supplied with faux gemstone decorations. So where did he "act"? In movies, or "off Sunset Boulevard"? I know he could easily have acted in stage performances; he had an astonishing memory, great for dialogue. And plenty of "presence"!!!

42 1994: Sherman Skolnick Sounds Off!
An Interview by Kenn Thomas

(Reprinted from Steamshovel Press #11, Summer 1994, pages 273-280, with my comments added in italics—sc.)

Steamshovel Press editor Kenn Thomas recently had the distinct pleasure of having dinner with legal researcher Sherman Skolnick at his usual haunt, the River Flame restaurant off Highway 94 outside of Chicago. Sherman Skolnick has been on the scene since his early courtroom victories regarding the corruption of Illinois state courts and congressional reapportionment in that state. His research has made him a perennial figure in national politics. He helped expose the existence of a Chicago-area assassination plot against JFK involving Lee Harvey Oswald. He demonstrated that sabotage was the probable reason for a United Airlines crash that killed the wife of E. Howard Hunt and eleven other Watergate figures. He surfaced a great deal of information regarding witnesses to events surrounding the Inslaw investigation. In fact, he continually exposes interesting and under-reported details about current political scandals on the hotline of his group, the Citizens Committee to Clean Up the Courts, which also has helped many people with their struggles in bankruptcy court. Sherman also produces a Chicago public access cable television program that further documents the issues and cases he has brought to public scrutiny. Virtually dismissed entirely by the mainstream, and often labeled a kook even by some in the conspiracy research community, Skolnick's work has nevertheless had a remarkable staying power. His successes in court and in the media have earned him much respect as a pioneer dirt-digger and exposer of hidden truth. This interview provided a rare opportunity to discuss his own work with him, as well as that of the people and events he has investigated over the years.[103]

THOMAS: How did you get in to this line of work, Sherman?

SKOLNICK: It's not a line of work. It's unpaid work if I ever saw it. I lived all my life with my parents. Since the age of six 1 have been a paraplegic from polio, similar to the late President Roosevelt, who was a hero when I was a child. In later years, I didn't consider him so much of a hero. I considered him one of the greatest counter-revolutionaries of American history in that he prevented a genuine upheaval against the ruling elite in this country which was overdue.

THOMAS: They also went to great pains to hide his disability.

SKOLNICK: Right, although the *Chicago Tribune* used to call him the cripple in the White House. In some ways the *Tribune* wasn't nicer to me either. I should have learned something from Roosevelt about the media, because I was often videotaped sitting in my wheel chair. I didn't realize they were looking at me as a crippled bug in a wheelchair, a nut, a crackpot.

THOMAS: That's precisely why they tried to cover up Roosevelt's disability, so he wouldn't look weak or infirm.

SKOLNICK: It took me up to about 1979 to figure this out, after my friend said, "Hey, no more videotaping by the media, only sitting at a table in a restaurant like everybody else. None of this standing on your crutches, none of that sitting in the wheel chair, and stuff like that." My father was a Ladies Garment Worker and I was born during the bad years, 1930, and my folks had a very great problem in taking care of me.[104] In fact, the only way I could get hospital treatment—

---
[103] Picture: Kenn Thomas, l., Sherman Skolnick, r.
[104] My sister and I were Depression babies too. My father was a dental technician; that is, he worked for a series of

no hospital would let me in, and my folks didn't have any money—so my mother took a long shot and she wrote directly to Roosevelt. She said, "I got a son that seems to be like you. What do you want to do about this?"

And we got a letter back from the labor secretary, Francis Perkins, and that letter opened a lot of doors for me. It got me into the HDCC, which is the Home for Destitute Crippled Children, which was a hospital on the University of Chicago campus.

THOMAS: So you do owe Roosevelt a debt.

SKOLNICK: Yeah. He was a hero because he looked very much like me, he had braces, he was paralyzed from the legs down, just like me, and he needed a wheel-chair. But he could walk a hundred feet, like I can. I can walk a hundred or two hundred feet max. The only difference was that I was poor and he came from a rich, aristocratic, up-state scene.

So my parents were always concerned over the years with what will be with me. I had sixteen experimental operations, and I thank heaven that I didn't get into the anti-doctor field, as some people are, you know, rapping doctors, because there is no way I could be objective.

One of my doctors was Mary Sherman, who was murdered as a result of the Jim Garrison investigation in New Orleans. She was my doctor until about 1954. She was an orthopedic specialist. [Steamshovel Debris: a new book, *Mary, Ferrie and the Monkey Virus* by Edward Haslam, not available at press time, connects Mary Sherman and Oswald associate David Ferrie with an underground medical laboratory experimenting with monkey viruses to develop a biological weapon.]

As I got older, I was very good at the special school I went to. Early on my folks bought a car and had it equipped with hydraulic controls. So as a teenager, I drove all over.

THOMAS: In the late 40s you had that?

SKOLNICK: Oh, yeah. At the end of the second war they came out with the special cars for legless veterans. They put in an electric clutch, because they didn't have automatic transmissions. And they had hand controls for the gas and so on. So I learned how drive and I drove until 1959, when the car got too old to go anymore.

I learned from an early age that there are what's now called "politically incorrect" people. I don't know what they called them years ago. My teachers at the Spalding High School for Crippled Children here in Chicago were political outcasts. For example, my teacher, Dr. Bernard Anderson, was politically incorrect. Previous to this, he was a protege of Albert Einstein but there was something wrong with his politics. So they had him previously teaching at the jail. I had Einstein's protege teaching me mathematics in a small school, and I was at the top of the class!

THOMAS: You graduated from Spalding in 1948?

SKOLNICK: I graduated salutatorian in my class.[105] I would have been first in my class except for

---

dentists, and made the bridges and stuff that they needed. He made the bridges; the dentists made the money. Our family was lucky in that we never got sick. In fact, we were healthy as horses, and I don't remember ever seeing a doctor as a kid. Whatever happened to us, like colds, measles, etc., my mom popped us into bed and fed us chicken soup and hot lemonade and stuff like that. Must have worked—I'm still alive!

[105] I guess I was "politically incorrect" too. My problem was that I was relatively poor (we were by then living in Miami Beach, a wealthy community); and also, I was a girl. And also, my family didn't belong to a synagogue. (We didn't go to church, either.) It was a triple whammy. I was very smart, but that didn't get me anywhere. I sort of found this out when the high school Guidance Counselor called me into her office one day and explained to me why I would not be the class Valedictorian. I had the grades, she said, but there was a boy in the class who needed to be Valedictorian in order to advance his career. So I was out, and he was in. I subsequently won the Dade County Coca Cola Scholarship in a competitive exam (First place in the County, with a four-year scholarship attached), but as far as my high school, Miami Beach High School, was concerned, I just didn't exist. Well...the boy voted "Most Likely to Succeed" by our Senior Class was Sammy Sax, whose Daddy owned the Saxony Hotel. (Pre-Fontainebleau, etc.) We

my politics. I was forever railing against the government. In high school I had a small mimeograph machine and I used to print an underground thing investigating all the teachers except my math teacher.

I learned at an early age that if you find out the secrets, you have got a weapon bigger than a sixteen-inch cannon on a battleship. I suppose that is what I have been doing the rest of my life. If you can't persuade them on the law, the facts and the merit of a thing, then you'd better do "closet work." You go into their closet: "What about your bank?", etc.

I took a city-wide scholarship test from Roosevelt College, a so-called left-wing school, a hotbed of liberal politics, and I scored first place. So they said I could go for five years, but after three semesters I gave it back to them because getting there was such a problem. It was hard to park my special car. I had to bribe the policemen to do that.[106]

So for a few years thereafter I ran a small printing business in a basement.

THOMAS: You weren't producing radical literature then?

SKOLNICK: No, just printing jobs for people in my neighborhood. So as my parents got older, they became worried about what was going to happen to their life savings. They didn't save much. How could they have saved much with the limited income my father, as a Ladies Garment Worker, had, you know?

THOMAS: They were surviving mostly.

SKOLNICK: Yeah! I don't think he made more than $5000 in the best year of his life. So they had saved up $7500, which was a fantastic sum, by not taking vacations, not buying a new car, all that, and by living in a very reduced house. So they ran into a broker who was Jewish, who talked their lingo from the old country. And he sweet-talked them into turning their life savings over to him, saying he's going to make it into something with me as a beneficiary. Well, he lost all the money on margin, without us ever signing any papers authorizing him to gamble with the money on margin. When he got through with it, not only was the $7500 not there anymore, he claimed my folks: owed him $20,000.

`So we hired a lawyer, and we spent I don't how many years fighting. I used to go myself all the time with the lawyer.

THOMAS: This was your first experience with the court?

SKOLNICK: Yeah, and my lawyer used to say, "Look sad. Tell your parents to cry a little bit." And I

---

knew the score!

[106] I on the other hand took my scholarship and, as ordered, went to the University of Miami, in Coral Gables. I had no money whatsoever; my parents were just scraping by, and they had little interest in supporting me by giving me money for food, etc. I expected that I would have to drop out at some point. So I worked part time and took enormous credit loads, trying to rush through. I remember taking a class in Latin American history solely because one of my college roommates owned the textbook! But I did make it through—in 3 years, graduating *magna cum laude*. The University wouldn't allow me to graduate until I paid up the $30 I owed them for dorm rent, and an old boyfriend very kindly coughed up the money that allowed me to graduate. I was there from 1951 through 1954. At the time, I was no more interested in politics than your average philodendron plant. But my family had already encountered the Mob. My father did some work for them over the years. By this time, he had moved out of the false teeth racket and ran a small shop in South Miami Beach, fabricating sheet plastic and making signs. The "guys," who owned all the major hotels on the Beach, ordered plastic "shoes" from my father: clear plastic racks for dealing cards, for the Casinos in Las Vegas. Later on, he made enormous decorative signs for these hotels, in colored plastic. There was a sort of party boat that was moored in a canal near Collins Avenue. It seems to me it was owned by Jilly Rizzo, who was Frank Sinatra's bodyguard.
Also, I didn't know it at the time, but the CIA had made a home for itself on the North Campus at the University of Miami. They rented the vacant top two floors of an old Spanish style building. I went there to take a course. The atmosphere was really strange. It was thick, and cold. You never saw anybody walking around, but you knew they were there, hiding behind closed doors with no signs on them. Later, after the Howard Hughes Medical Institute was formed, and became the Mafia's Magic Money Funnel for unlimited money laundering, guess where they set up their first offices? Well, of course! In the North Campus building at the University of Miami.—sc

thought this was humiliating. In other words, a cripple and his parents are coming there to get their money. So then he says, "Go to your ward committeeman." And I say, "What do you gotta do?" And he says, "You got to give him something. He's got to intercede with the judge." And I says, "What does that mean?" "He's got to go and do something. There's so many voters for the Democratic Party at your address. You're willing to contribute to the judge or the Democratic Party or his campaign. You gotta send him about $300 minimum." And I says, "To do what?" "For a proper hearing!" And this first lawyer urged me to study law, which I did.

THOMAS: After he introduced you to corruption.

SKOLNICK: Yeah. Well, the first trial we had by jury was fixed.

THOMAS: So you hadn't come up with money for the judge?

SKOLNICK: No. First of all, we didn't have it, and number two, we wouldn't do it! The bailiff in charge of the jury was the neighbor of the fore-lady that ran the jury. The judge goes home and puts the bailiff in charge, and the bailiff tries to kick me and my dad out of the courtroom. We sit there and the bailiff lets Hornblower and Weeks, that's the stock broker's lawyer, big-shots, stand by the jury door to talk and tell them that Skolnick is a rat, he's no good, he's been a liar all his life—at the jury door! Right there at the keyhole! This is all documented! It became a federal lawsuit.

I says, "Hey, bailiff! Me and my father will come there and talk about how nasty they are!"

"No, no, no, get the hell away."

When the trial ends, I call up my lawyer at 11:30 because the jury comes out of there with no verdict, and I tell the bailiff, "Hey, before we go home, where are the papers?"

"I didn't find any."

"Wait a minute, they went in there with evidence."

"It's all gone, we don't know where it is."

So I call up my lawyer at home and I wake him up. He went home. He left me and my father to be in the courtroom near the jury door.

He says, "Listen. What are you, tired of living, Skolnick? The sheriff is in with the mob here. What's with you? Are you and your parents tired of living? You got paid up insurance? If you go and complain about these methods, which have been going on for decades, you're dead."

I say, "What are you going to do tomorrow morning?"

"I'm going to go there and ask the judge if he knows if there's a verdict."

So the next morning he goes there and the bailiff says, "I didn't find any verdict. I didn't find any papers. The jury went home." And that was the end of it.

THOMAS: No verdict?

SKOLNICK: Somewhere down the road some judge got the case and they called for a status hearing again and he suggested a settlement. We were out $7500, which was a lot of money in the 1950s, into the early 1960s. And so the judge suggested $500. Hornblower's lawyers are very big, Bell Boyd and Lloyd, and they say "We ain't giving Skolnick $500 now or ever. We've never lost a security case in Illinois and we're not starting with Skolnick."

When I heard that, I figured that's the end. War! So I told my parents I'm going to wreck them.

They say, "how can a small man like you in a wheelchair wreck them? You don't know what you're doing."

I say, "I don't know, I'm good in math and I'm good in all these things. I'm pretty clever. I got a high IQ. There must be something I can do."

So I started in about 1963, and I began to run into other victims of injustice. I found out that the woods are filled with them, and I became the beacon. They would come to me, cry on my shoulder: "Look what happened, I lost my wife, I lost my house, I lost my this, my that, my car, and on and on…"

So we formed this little group. Now the original name of the group was the Committee To Smash the Courts. And my friend said, "No, no, no, no. That sounds bad. It's got to be a name that's acceptable." So the next name was the Committee To Protect Patent Owners. The first group that I helped were all patent owners who had been swindled out of their patents through the corruption in the courts. At one time I had the attic in my house filled with prototypes—the butterfly bandage, the high speed ice machine. We finally changed the name to the Citizens Committee, not to Smash The Courts, that was too strong: the Citizens' Committee To Clean Up The Courts. It sounded rather…

THOMAS: You're cleaning now, not smashing. This was 1963, the year Kennedy was shot?[107]

SKOLNICK: Yeah, but I wasn't interested in that. I was looking for a way to get into the public eye. A family friend was telling me, "You're not objective anymore about the Hornblower thing. Nobody wants to listen anymore. Certainly not your friends, not your relatives."

THOMAS: So your case was not resolved and you were taking on all these other cases.

SKOLNICK: It went on for years and years. A couple of my cases ended up before the state supreme court in the 1960s. I argued my own case. They had to carry me up twenty stairs because the crooked judges wouldn't allow me and the wheelchair through their entrance that had an elevator, in Springfield. The high court in Springfield is on a hill.

THOMAS: Literally a high court.

SKOLNICK: Through a series of circumstances, in 1969, we continued our closet work. We found out that there are little-known bank ownership records that only Illinois has. Illinois requires public disclosure of bank ownership, which was so secret that it was in the basement of one of the government buildings on microfilm so dusty that nobody knew about it until a lady friend of mine discovered it. She said, "Look at this. Across from the local courthouse there's a bank, and thirty judges and nine gangsters own the bank." So we start checking, and we found out that most of the state supreme court judges are owners of this bank, along with mafioso. Anyway, I got to know some Springfield reporters and I made a mimeograph list of this and I offered show them the microfilm pages.

THOMAS: Falling back on your high school experience here.

SKOLNICK: Yeah. Closet work! We can't deal with them on the law and the facts, we have to deal with them on the dirt. So I found two young reporters from the Alton Telegraph, a real old newspaper, and they ran a big story about the bank across from the courthouse. At that time the local courthouse had the local office of the Supreme Court on the top floor. The main state supreme court courthouse was in Springfield on a hill. But they also had an office in Chicago called the Civic Center. Diagonally across the street was a bank called the Civic Center Bank. It

---

[107] By 1963, I had been married to—and divorced from—a Sicilian from Brooklyn. Some of his relatives lived at the time in "Little Italy," on the Lower East Side. At family dinners, they would talk with awe about the local heroes, including Joe "Bananas" (Bonanno) and other local Mob bigwigs. (As mentioned in John Davis's book, *Mafia Kingfish*, Bonanno talked about the profitable business relationship in New York City between Frank Costello and Joseph P. Kennedy: smuggling liquor during Prohibition.--Davis, p.41-43.) But! Let's talk about me! In 1963, I was living in Greenwich Village and working as "Executive Secretary" to the Editor/co-owner of a small scientific publishing house. On November 22, a friend called me at the office and told me that Kennedy had been shot in Dallas. A pall descended over New York City and we all lived under it for months. I still had no real interest or involvement with politics, but the murder of JFK hit me very hard. I was in despair, and made a number of decisions about my life at that time.

was owned by thirty judges and nine gangsters. And we had the proof. I told this to the *Alton Telegraph*, and they started a series of stories that implicated the local newspaper guy. The editor in chief of the Sun Times and the Daily News was one of the largest stockholders, along with the gangsters and the thirty judges.

THOMAS: He also happened to be a competitor of the Alton newspaper.

SKOLNICK: I don't know about that, but they wouldn't run the story. So they found a way to get around it by running the story on the Associated Press hub in St. Louis. The governor was a stockholder, who later became a federal appeals judge. By the time I started the scandal, he was no longer the governor, Otto Koerner, Jr. So the story started running with big headlines.

I filed a motion to be appointed *amicus curiae*, friend of the court, and as a friend, I would point out that I was not a party to this case, but the judges in this case took a bribe. I found the leading case that among this bunch of judges who were stockholders in the bank, the largest stockholder was the former revenue director, Theodore Isaacs. So I found that he had a case in their court on criminal conflict of interest. Two weeks before they heard the oral argument in the state supreme court, he does a thing natural for Illinois: he brings all the judges of the court into the bank as stockholders.

So I filed a "friend of the court" petition in the Isaacs case. They got upset and wanted to know how I knew. They claimed that the *Daily News* had instigated me and had paid me, which was false. Then they said that I had to tell them exactly how I found this out. They didn't know that this was in the public record. I didn't want to tell them. I accuse you of bribery, and you demand to know how I found out?

So they put me in jail, and the picture made *Time* magazine because they couldn't get me into the paddy wagon. And there were four sheriffs trying to put me into the paddy wagon through a narrow door. They took me from the courthouse where the judges held me in contempt of court for not telling them how I knew they took a bribe, and they wanted to put me in this paddy wagon to take me to the jail.

THOMAS: To make a public display.

SKOLNICK: Two got on one side, two on the other side. I didn't fit through the door. The sheriff was the brother of Rosemary Woods, Nixon's secretary. He liked me.

For every hour I was in jail, and I was in for four hours, one judge bit the dust. They put up a special commission that investigated judges, and it found that most of them were guilty as charged, and recommended that they all leave. They resigned on August 4, 1969. The fourth judge I accused died. So they got three of them, the chief judge, the associate judge and a third one. But the fraud is still going on all these years later.

They committed a fraud on the court for the benefit of the governor. There was a lawsuit challenging the validity of the state income tax being pushed by the governor. It was pending in their court at the time of my scandal. In the name of the judges, they issued a decision on August 14, 1969, ten days after they weren't there anymore. You can't do that. I asked State Attorney General Rollin Burris about this, and he got all puffed up and said, "If any of you don't pay your state income tax, I don't want to know about this. I'm going to put you in jail." I said, "This is a fraud upon the court!" I have been talking about this for twenty years, and nobody's listening. A fraud upon the court doesn't go away.

Anyway, that's what made me world famous. It was the biggest judicial scandal in the history of the United States. I had collapsed the state supreme court, and as a result I got to know victims all over. What I did over the years, I didn't want publicity to make money, I wanted publicity so that the press would listen to me. I got into the biggest controversies because it

enabled me to get publicity for my point. For a while there I was able to say whatever I wanted to the courts, about voting and reapportionment, corruption, and so on, up to a point. And I got to know all these victims that came to me.

THOMAS: How did you make that leap from working on local court cases to these national things?

SKOLNICK: Well, for instance, I taught civic investigation for would-be journalists and in the same building where the college was, on the third floor was a strange outfit with no name on the door. And they filmed or taped every talk show in the Chicago area and then sold the tape, the film or the transcripts to certain offices in Washington and the Pentagon. And the courier for that got to know me, and he said, "I got something for you, some documents about the Kennedy thing."

I says, "I don't have any money to go to Dallas, don't tell me about no Kennedy thing."

This was 1970.[108] So I met him and he gives me this pile of documents about the Chicago plot against Kennedy, that there was a plot two and a half weeks before. [109]

I was worried, and I wrote him a $5 check for xerox expenses, and on the back of the check I put down "For the Kennedy documents, full payment."

That saved me from the rope, I tell you! Because what they wanted me to do was to blow the cover of certain police that worked for the CIA in Chicago. And if I could, they would terminate these police. They never intended that I as a loud-mouth would get into the courts.

When I started the plan to go to court is when I got in trouble. Harold Weisberg says, "Skolnick, come to my goose farm."

I say, "I don't know you."

He says, "Oh yeah, I'm a leading writer about the Kennedy assassination."

I say, "I'm not into the Kennedy thing. I'm on the Chicago thing. I don't know nothin' about Dealey Plaza." I never went to his goose farm.

These were all the secret documents that a black secret service agent put together, Abraham Bolden.

THOMAS: You got documents directly from Abraham Bolden?

SKOLNICK: No, not from him. I got them from this guy, this mysterious courier that delivered the film and tapes to a secret office in the Pentagon which he thought to be the CIA.

THOMAS: But they originated with Bolden.

SKOLNICK: What I later found out was that this was the first time in the 200-year history of the National Archives that someone stole this out of the archives. So I was planning to go to court, and luckily I didn't go to Weisberg's thing, because Weisberg, after I went to court, threatened to sue me, saying that I stole the documents from him. Luckily, I had this $5 check endorsed by the one that I bought them from, for full payment for the documents.

David Lifton, who was just getting started on the west coast, I never heard of the guy, I got a

---

[108] By 1970, I had made the break from New York City to the West Coast: Los Angeles. California represented freedom for me: from the gray concrete hills and valleys of Manhattan to the splashy royal palms and bougainvillea of Hollywood and Beverly Hills. I became a feminist, wrote a play, and got a job writing for *Playgirl* magazine. Those were happy days for me.

[109] This story that Skolnick got is one of the most important pieces of information about the Kennedy assassination, and is also one of the most ignored and shoved under the rug by both the "investigative authorities" and the "independent researchers." It confirms the *Skeleton Key/Gemstone File (see Index, Tom Vallee)*, and reveals the Mafia/CIA, etc., pattern for such important public political assassinations, down to the reconnaissance and careful planning of the "kill zone," the "last-minute" detour from the publicized route, etc. The Dallas assassination of JFK was a cookie-cutter recreation of the event planned for Chicago and shelved at the last minute because JFK canceled his Chicago trip. Studying this Chicago plan would certainly shed light on the Dallas plan and its "execution." But that can't happen if it is shoved under the rug. Or "kept secret" until 2039: same thing!

letter in the file from him in 1970 saying, "You stole the documents from me!"

Lifton writes me from the west coast, Weisberg writes from his goose farm; both say that I stole the documents from them, but I bought them from this strange character.

Through my late friend, James Albright, who owned the patent for the high speed ice machine, he knew where to find Bolden, at an unlisted address on the south side. He arranged for me to meet with Bolden. So I went with a lady friend of mine in her car to meet Bolden.

THOMAS: I should say for the readers that Abraham Bolden was the first black Secret Service agent, appointed by Kennedy, and after the assassination…

SKOLNICK: First black in the White House Guard.

THOMAS: …he was apparently thrown in jail on trumped-up charges.

SKOLNICK: So I came with my lady friend in her little red car and we sat in front of Bolden's house and I had these documents, eleven of them, mounted in one of these salesmen's books with the plastic pages, under celluloid.

And Bolden sits in the back and looks at them. He looks at each one and says, "I knew it. You are here to put me back in prison. I'm on parole!"

And I say, "I want to help you."

"Like hell you do! You're part of a government effort to put me back."

And I say, "I think Mark Lane[110] didn't do right for you when you were down there in Springfield. I think all your lawyers put together have not done right for you. I am here to clear you."

"Like hell you are. You got my secret report. It's not supposed to be out until 2039.[111] You got it. You stole it. And I'm going to be blamed that I gave it to you and I'm going to be sent back to jail, and you are going to get publicity and I am going to get jail."

I says, "For gods sake, Abraham Bolden, I am here to do good for you. I'm going to court and attach all these documents, and I'm going to confront the goddamn government and I'm going to put in there how they framed you." I didn't know anything about Garrison or Dealey Plaza, I kept no clippings, I was not interested in that.

THOMAS: Garrison tried to do something and failed, and here you're coming to this guy saying you're going to do the same thing, take it to the courts. If he was following the Garrison case, I could imagine that he would not have the same faith that you had that you could do something in the courts.

SKOLNICK: So I went to court and I sued, Skolnick vs. National Archives and Records Service. And I set forth the whole thing, about Cuba, about Kennedy, about Bolden, and the fact that Bolden was framed. On the day we brought the lawsuit, one of the major 50,000 watt stations here had a good young reporter, Stuart Pahn, that I knew, and he put a major story out on it. He eventually was run out of Chicago. There aren't any happy endings to any of this. Stuart Pahn went into the brokerage business.

THOMAS: What was in Bolden's report?

SKOLNICK: It was on the plot to kill Kennedy in Chicago by a person named Lee Harvey Oswald and an Oswald double, Thomas Arthur Vallee, both of whom were apprehended. Vallee was

---

[110] Oh yes, Mark Lane! He had a great career, supposedly working on the "right" side. It's just that everybody he "helped" got messed up somehow. He turns up in the strangest places. He helped Charles Garry, the Black Panthers' attorney, get out of the Jonestown jungle massacre alive. And he was Larry Flynt's attorney as well. A list of his "clients" and what happened to them might lead to the conclusion that his virtues were mainly for show, not for substance. But he has had an interesting life!

[111] How odd! 'Nuff said, I hope.

arrested on a $5 traffic rap and the traffic ticket was suppressed and put in the National Archives.[112] Two blocks off the Northwest Expressway, which is now called the Kennedy Expressway. And they were going to go through a hairpin turn just like they ended up going in front of the Book Depository. They found a hairpin turn in the route from the airport to the college football game where on November 2nd Kennedy was to go to a football game in Chicago. He didn't come, but his route was to go through a hairpin turn where they had another guy who was working at a CIA printing office with the window looking right down at Kennedy. The complaining witness against Vallee was Daniel Groth, not listed as policeman, listed as a witness. Later Groth came with a machine gun, kicked in Fred Hampton's door and assassinated people there.

THOMAS: The Black Panthers.

SKOLNICK: 1969. The same guy. But no author has ever called me to ask for copies of Bolden's documents. A day after I filed the lawsuit in April of 1970, they tried to revoke Bolden's parole. And my friend on a major radio station here went on the air and saved him.

THOMAS: So Bolden was right. They came after him.

SKOLNICK: If it wasn't for the radio station, Bolden would have gone back to jail. I got world-wide publicity, except in Chicago. The Chicago press ignored it. But I also got on the crap list with almost every assassination researcher.

Sylvia Meaghre, who wrote *Accessories After The Fact*, called me up and says, "Who the hell are you? Do you know about the Dallas thing?"

I says, "Not a word."

"Did you read the Warren Commission documents?"

"Does not pertain to my thing."

"You're a fraud, Skolnick."

I says, "I am not investigating which way the bullets went in Dealey Plaza. I'm only on the Chicago plot."

THOMAS: So she took it as intruding on her turf.

SKOLNICK: Yeah. David Lifton writes me a letter, and I can give you a xerox copy: "You are a fraud and you stole the documents from me."

I said, "I don't know who the fuck you are, David Lifton!"

Weisberg sends me a thing in the form of a legal paper which he never filed, Weisberg vs. Skolnick, he wanted damages for me stealing the eleven documents from him. Nobody to this day has made an accurate chapter or sub-chapter on the Bolden thing.

THOMAS: So the researchers all converged on you even though you're making a contribution to a case that they're supposedly trying to help solve themselves.

SKOLNICK: They've all got a vested interest. Peter Dale Scott, for reasons I do not know, has taken to the lecture platform and accused me of being a fraud. As you know, when I come to the assassination conferences, I'm the one they always want to throw out of the place.[113] Now why is that?[114]

THOMAS: Carl Oglesby still likes you, doesn't he?

---

[112] Bruce Roberts had the basic information on the Chicago plot in the early '70's. (See index for references to Tom Vallee, etc.) I don't know where he got it from. But he seemed to receive a good deal of inside information from Chicago. Or from outside of Chicago.
[113] Me, too!
[114] Yes; why IS that??? ☹

SKOLNICK: In 1974 or '75 I was giving a speech in Boston and I met him for a couple of hours while I was there. He lives in Cambridge.[115] I raised the issue about Rennie Davis, the Chicago 7 and the CIA and I tell you, Carl almost took my crutch and wrapped it around my throat. He says, "That's a forbidden subject. You are not asking this!"

THOMAS: Could you restate what you said about Rennie Davis?

SKOLNICK: I came out with a documented thing about all the CIA front foundations, which I'm an expert on. I found a way to identify CIA front foundations through 990AR, which is the foundation tax return that's a public record. I proved that the CIA financed Rennie Davis and the Chicago 7 to down the Democrats and put in Nixon. And when I raised this with Oglesby, he had been a big shot with the Students for Democratic Society, and when I was in Cambridge in '75, he got livid. So he's got this mixed feeling about me. He's always worried that at some public place I'm going to say something about that and I'm going to get around to him.

THOMAS: So Rennie Davis, Jerry Rubin, Abbie Hoffman, Bobby Seale, are all on the payroll?

SKOLNICK: Not Bobby Seale, but the others were part of the game. They were getting money from CIA foundations. I got arrested confronting Rennie Davis on a local TV station on a live program. Rennie had me arrested.

THOMAS: The Chicago police came to the defense of Rennie Davis?

SKOLNICK: Eighteen police, yeah. Channel 44.

THOMAS: I didn't realize until recently that it was your work that helped expose the story about E. Howard Hunt's role in the downing of the airplane that killed his wife Dorothy.

SKOLNICK: I sued the National Transportation Safety Board. And I didn't tell them that I had their file, all the pictures, all the documents, showing they knew it was sabotage, where Dorothy Hunt and the eleven other Watergaters died. So in front of 250 reporters that gathered from all over the world for the reopened air crash hearings, I laid all the documents on the table and I says, "Alright NTSB, now is the time to arrest me. This is your stuff. My friend swiped it from you. What are you going to do about it? Arrest me in front all these reporters?" The Associated Press ran a story on the "A" wire: "Chicago legal researcher Sherman Skolnick presented today a heavily documented case of what he claims is sabotage based on government documents."

Only one paper in the country ran the story, even though it was on the international wire. The *Seattle Intelligencer* is the only one that ran the stories. The *Tribune* ran a cropped picture of me sitting at the table, with a headline saying "Skolnick has no documents to support his contention of sabotage." CBS had a live thing, closed circuit, that they didn't use on the air, for their executives. It was UAL Incorporated, the parent company of United Airlines, whose flight 553 crashed, exactly one month after Nixon's re-election. A month before they killed Hale Boggs, from the Warren Commission. Dorothy Hunt and the eleven Watergaters, who had blackmailed two million dollars out of the Nixon White House.

During the hearings, on the second day I was tired and I told this joke. I said, "I'm here to absolutely and categorically admit that I have no proof whatsoever that Edward Carlson, the head of United Airlines and Richard Nixon were on the plane with a .38 and shot Dorothy Hunt. I admit it!" I figured it was going to be a joke and everybody was going to laugh.

The next day it comes out: "Skolnick has no proof whatsoever." And they show this cropped

---

[115] I met Carl Oglesby once, when I moved to Cambridge around 1993. Since he was well known for his *Yankee and the Cowboy War* book (Berkeley, 1977), and my Gemstone *Skeleton Key* was still flying around the country like mad, I thought we might have something to say to each other, and I called him. He invited me to meet him at JFK's favorite Cambridge restaurant, a German restaurant in Harvard Square (which has now disappeared). We had a rather silent lunch, and I never saw him again.

picture, I'm sitting in front of the table and I figured the photograph was bound to show the documents. No way: they cropped to where the documents are not shown.

THOMAS: That's what you get for being funny. At the time, Hunt was known only as a Watergate figure. This whole business about him being one of the tramps and all that had not happened. You weren't making connections between Watergate and the Kennedy assassination, were you?

SKOLNICK: The one who was working on that was my friend A. J. Weberman. He went on the road with Mike Canfield after the publication of their book, *Coup D'Etat in America*. His editor was from Nigeria, Opaku, and for reasons that I do not know, he insisted that Weberman put something in there condemning Skolnick. Weberman said that they insisted that the book wouldn't be published if he didn't allow them to condemn me. I am not pertinent to the Dallas thing. Why was it necessary to say that Skolnick is a complete liar? A year ago I talked to Weberman and he didn't even remember it.

THOMAS: Weberman is virtually called an agent for Mossad in a new book published by the Liberty Lobby. Could you describe your relationship with Liberty Lobby?

SKOLNICK: Many in the left wing and the liberal press are tied in, like Chip Berlet with that Cambridge group, that are in with foundations connected with the CIA, Z magazine and all that, and they accuse me and my late friend Mae Brussell of being Nazis. If time permitted, I could tell you how in 1976 I ran the first large seminar in America about Nazi war criminals in the United States—before Howard Blum's book came out, before all this stuff came out. And at my own expense I came up with every rare book on the Nazi question and the companies that were in with Hitler and the American connection. I was condemned all the way around. I mean, I've been condemned by Chip Berlet that I am a Nazi, and yet I ran the first seminar and nobody in the liberal press gave a single line to it. I was the only knowledgeable journalist that came to a press conference of Simon Weisenthal, and they took me away under arrest because it was a private club.

I deeply resent Chip Berlet, Z Magazine, and various books that run stories that I am a Nazi. The problem is that the liberal press will not run stories about what I do. About the CIA and Rennie Davis; the CIA and the foundations, and the 990AR, the public tax returns. Most of the so-called left press is financed by the intelligence agencies. 1 can prove that. So they're not independent. I know it's a terrible thing...and I could go into a long rap about how the ACLU has been taken over by the Baldwin Foundation, which runs *The Nation* magazine, which is very liberal and runs a lot of good stories but heaven help you if you raise a thing about the CIA and the Baldwin Foundation. It's because of my work in that area that I get rapped by the left. So they won't publish me in any of their magazines.

The only one that would publish my stories, about the Banca Del Lavaro, and all this different stuff, is the right-wing press. I'm an orthodox Jew. My mother—her whole family died in the Warsaw ghetto, the Lubetsky family. To say that I'm a Nazi and promote the Nazi cause is the most horrendous thing that you could say about me. Also, Mae Brussell. She's dead and can't speak. She showed how the Nazis were involved with the JFK thing. To say that Mae Brussell and Sherman Skolnick are Nazis, this is the worst defamation!

THOMAS: The left won't listen to you so you're kind of pushed into the arms of the Liberty Lobby.

SKOLNICK: Since 1987 we have passed out these leaflets about the judges and the CIA, but the public doesn't dig leaflets. It's seventeenth century stuff. They want TV, they want radio. And none of the liberal press would have me. *In These Times*, Joel Bleifuss, you know what that guy did to me? Sent a letter to all my friends that Skolnick is a Nazi, stay away from him. Leaflets don't do the trick. I've got to be in the media eye. I have been blotted out since '71. So I started

with my five minute recorded message. And then in the '70s I got to know Tom Valentine, and he wrote about me in his magazine, *The National Tattler*, and then he became the associate editor of *The Spotlight*, and through him they would run my stuff verbatim. He'd get me on his radio program and they did an accurate transcript of what I said. They didn't butcher up the words.

There's no free press in America. We must face that. A magazine like yours is rare. So the press is the bus company. What my left wing critics are saying is that before you get up on the bus, you must investigate the politics of the bus company. Otherwise, walk. Pass out leaflets! Holler on the street! With no free press in America, if they print my stories verbatim, the fact is that they've got naked women on the other side, like the *L.A. Star* which used to run my stuff verbatim, with the naked pictures on the other side. So Chip Berlet and others say Skolnick is a Nazi, he's in with a paper that repudiates the Holocaust. And Tom Valentine has mentioned on his program that Skolnick does not repudiate the Holocaust. It happened. I prefer to talk about the major companies in America that financed Hitler. To call me a Nazi…I can't think of a worse thing you can call me, honestly.

Even A. J. Weberman calls me up and says, "Skolnick why aren't you at the Holocaust Museum? Why are you with *Spotlight*, which repudiates the Holocaust Museum?" So I say, "Listen, they're the bus company. They print my stuff verbatim!"

"But you're in with Nazis!"

I can't help it. Find me a better place. I'd like to be printed on the front page of the *New York Times*, and have a cover story of all my friends on *Time* magazine. What can I do?

***

Following this interview, Skolnick discussed his recent work with the involuntary bankruptcy case of caulking contractor Joseph Andreucetti, which has led to his involvement with scandals of the Clinton era. Mr. Andreucetti was present at this dinner table discussion, as was Skolnick associate Mark Sato and Michael Scott Dugan of the Citizen's Committee To Clean Up The Courts.

They explained the connection between Mr. Andreucetti, a descendant of Italy's House of Savoy, and over $10 billion in gold stolen from the Italian treasury by the OSS in 1943 and now located in Building 4 at King's Point Condominium in Addison, Illinois, a western suburb of Chicago. The story is rich with detail and suitable for expanded treatment in a future issue of *Steamshovel*. It includes charges by Inslaw informant Michael Riconoscuito that gold mesh filters made by a company named Wirecloth Products were used as a currency within intelligence circles. The story suggests that the gold was used as collateral in the early 1980s to support the opening of the Chicago branch of the Banca Del Lavoro, long connected to the JFK assassination, BCCI and Household International, a successor to the Nugan Hand Bank of Inslaw infamy. From the gold as well, a $50 million contingency fund was established by the Resolution Trust Corporation to cover liabilities from the liquidation into Household Bank, Bank of America, Heritage Savings and Loan, the S&L that purported to lend Andreucetti money to finish the King's Point condos. According to Skolnick and associates, the fund disappeared and ended up in Little Rock to make the Madison Guaranty S&L just look incompetent (instead of criminal) when its financial improprieties were examined closely.

***

See Sherman Skolnick's interesting book: Ahead of the Parade: A Who's Who of Treason & High Crimes—Exclusive Details of Fraud and Corruption of the Monopoly Press, the Banks, the Bench and the Bar, & the Secret Political Police. Available at Amazon.com and other fine booksellers. His website is: www.skolnicksreport.com

During the preparation of this book, I learned with great sadness from Kenn Thomas that Sherman Skolnick

had died, at home in his bed, on Chicago's South Side.

> **In Memory of Sherman Skolnick**
> **A Worker for Truth**
> **1930 - May 21, 2006**

43 1999: Inside the Gemstone File: James Bond and Gemstone

Five more years went by, during which nothing more was heard from "Gemstone," or from me. It had now been twenty-four years since the first release of the *Skeleton Key*. Many people would have forgotten about it, if they ever knew, and a whole new generation had been born. I had despaired of ever obtaining any more of the Gemstone File itself than I already had. Then in 1999, *Inside the Gemstone File: Howard Hughes, Onassis, and JFK*, by Kenn Thomas and David Hatcher Childress, appeared, published by Childress's Adventures Unlimited Press.[116]

Kenn Thomas and David Hatcher Childress each have their own publishing company, and are active as writers and editors of books outside the mainstream. Each has numerous books to his credit.[9] *Inside the Gemstone File* lists thirty AUP titles on its back cover. Kenn Thomas's presence on Amazon.com is manifested in 16 titles, from his own *Steamshovel Press*.[117] Between them, they have provided a vital service: a community for writers working in areas that have been largely scorned and/or ignored by the so-called "mainstream" press. Fortunately, more and more people are turning away from the "mainstream" media to seek answers to the critical problems that beset us at every turn. And particularly in the area that has been termed "conspiracy theory" by people who would like to shut us out of the national discussion. As Kenn says so blandly (☺) on his website: "All conspiracy; no theory."

I met Kenn Thomas at the Phenomicon Convention in Atlanta, Georgia, in 1992. I had been invited to attend by Jim Keith, editor of one of the earliest books based on my *Skeleton Key to the Gemstone File*, and to participate in a panel discussion on the Gemstone File. Kenn had a booth featuring books and magazines from his Steamshovel Press, which I found fascinating. Kenn was and is both friendly and open-minded. Since that time, he has published a number of interviews, book reviews and other items pertaining to Gemstone—pro and con, and I am deeply indebted to him for helping to keep the Gemstone question alive and kicking for so long. For this book, Kenn supplied lots of new information, rare clippings, photos, and other documentation, and added COM-12 briefing documents. He also included an important account of investigative reporter Danny Casolaro's investigations of what he called "The Octopus," interrupted in August 1991 by Casolaro's supposed "suicide," one of the most unbelievable suicides ever arranged.

David Childress contributed a fascinating, must-read chapter: *James Bond and the Gemstone File*. In it, he ties Ian Fleming, James Bond, Bruce Roberts, the Gemstone File story, and international intelligence operations together.

In Fleming's first novel, *Casino Royale* (1954), James Bond, fictional British super-spy #007, licensed to kill, inveterate "shaken, not stirred" martini lover and playmate of beautiful, dangerous women, was already hot on the trail of his arch nemesis, the evil Ernst Stavro Blofeld. Blofeld's "biography" clearly shadows that of the real Aristotle Onassis.

Diamonds are Forever followed in 1956. Blofeld was again the master villain. But it was the 1972 movie version that tied Bond, Blofeld, Onassis and Howard Hughes together in a package that literally screams "Gemstone"—Gemstone, that is, from the viewpoint of Ian Fleming and British intelligence operations.

To make the connections and time frame clearer, I have put some of David's information in a table format, adding some Gemstone information:

IAN FLEMING (real)	JAMES BOND (fictional)	BRUCE ROBERTS (real)

---

[116] http://www.adventuresunlimited.co.nz.

[117] http://www.steamshovelpress.com

Birth: 1908, England, wealthy family.	Birth: 1924; raised in Europe; thrown out of Eton at 12; quit school at 17.	Birth: 1919, New York; Scotch-Irish working class family; attended U. Wisconsin, did not graduate.
Naval Intelligence, WWII; top agent, master spy. Used government secrets in the plots of his books. Wrote 14 "James Bond" novels. Lived in Jamaica after retirement. JFK was a fan, asked his advice (in jest—??).	Ministry of Defense, 1941 on; joined secret service at end of war; distinguished career as spy. #007 license to kill; hero of 14 Fleming novels.	U.S. Army, WWII; maybe OSS, maybe CIA dissident. Lived in L.A., then San Francisco. Physicist; Made and sold artificial gemstones; wrote and sold Gemstone papers.
Died: Jamaica, August 1964; heart attack, under "mysterious circumstances," at age 56. Possibly murdered; knew too much, wrote too much about it.	Hasn't died yet; probably never will.	Died: San Francisco, July, 1976, lung cancer or ??? at age 57. Possibly murdered; knew too much, wrote too much about it.
	Arch Enemy: Ernst Stavro Blofeld, a Greek/German (?), head of SPECTRE. Blofeld has a luxury yacht and many secret bases all over the world. Also owned gambling casinos in the Mediterranean and Las Vegas—the Las Vegas one under the guise of "Willard Whyte." Blofeld is the main villain in 6 of the "James Bond" books. He dies in the 1981 James Bond film, *For Your Eyes Only*.	Arch Enemy: Aristotle Socrates Onassis, a Greek, head of the International Mafia, Roberts' nickname: MMORDIS. Onassis had a luxury yacht, and many homes all over the world. He owned the Monte Carlo casino, and bought died March 15, 1975, in Paris, at the American Hospital. On the same date Roberts went into University Hospital in S.F., for treatment of a large "tumor" which he claimed was induced by the CIA, (acting for Onassis), which may have killed him a year later.

Here is a Plot Summary for *Diamonds Are Forever* (1971):

When the British Government suspects the existence of a world-wide diamond smuggling operation, #007 James Bond is called in to investigate. He soon discovers that his arch nemesis, the evil Ernst Stavro Blofeld, is stockpiling the precious gems to use in a deadly laser-armed satellite capable of destroying massive targets on land, sea and air. He travels to Las Vegas, to one of Blofeld's luxurious casinos. There he tracks down and rescues the reclusive billionaire, Willard Whyte, who, it turns out, has been Blofeld's drugged captive for years.

Childress continues:

...John Gardner continued the James Bond novel series.... In 1988, Gardner published a Bond novel called *Scorpius*..... That Gardner would title one of his James Bond books *Scorpius* is testimony that Gardner knew that Fleming patterned Blofeld after Onassis, as that was the name of Onassis' private island, Skorpios, off the Greek coast near Corfu. It was on this island that Onassis allegedly sometimes kept Howard Hughes, brain damaged and emaciated from daily heroin injections.

With the publication of Fleming's first novel, *Casino Royale* (1954), about a crooked casino owner named Le Chifre in Monte Carlo, Fleming had Bond hot on the trail of Onassis. It was in early January of 1953 that shipping tycoon Onassis purchased the Monte Carlo Casino in Monaco for a cool million dollars. It was the next year that Fleming's first book was published.

With Bond's arrival at the royal casino in Monaco, Ian Fleming put James Bond on a head-on

collision course with the arch villain who wanted to control the world: Ernst Stavro Blofeld. The Stavro part of the name gives an indication that Fleming was aiming at Onassis and his Greek [com]patriot ship[ping] families. Stavro was the first name of Onassis' rival, Stavros Niarchos.[118]

... The buying of the Monte Carlo Casino in early 1953 put Onassis on the front page of newspapers around the world and probably brought him to the attention of British Intelligence and thereby Ian Fleming and his friends.

Time magazine reported on January 19, 1953,

"Aristotle Socrates Onassis is a Greek-born Argentine who water-skis in the best international circles and includes among his friends Prince Rainier III, Pooh-Bah of the tiny principality of Monaco and its famed Monte Carlo Casino. At 47, Onassis has homes in Paris, New York, Montevideo and Antibes, owns or controls a fleet of 91 tankers, freighters and whaling ships worth an estimated $300 million and has a pretty 23-year-old wife. But he didn't get all this by breaking the bank at Monte Carlo—quite the opposite. Last week "Ari" Onassis let it be known that, for $1,000,000, he had bought the 75-year-old Casino, lock, stock and roulette table, and with it the purse strings of Monaco. Reason: he needed some office space. As top man in nearly 30 shipping companies under five different flags, Onassis already has headquarters in Montevideo, branch offices in Paris, London, New York, Hamburg and Panama. But since much of his tanker business is bringing oil from the Middle East through the Mediterranean to Northern Europe, he thought he should have offices near the Mediterranean ports of Marseilles and Genoa, where many of his ships are repaired."

With Onassis now controlling the bank and casino in Monte Carlo—Fleming's Casino Royale—he now had more control over the heroin that flowed from Turkey to Marseilles on his ships, and his own bank for laundering the money. He also virtually controlled his own country, that of tiny Monaco.

A year later, in 1954, Onassis made a deal with the King of Saudi Arabia that gave him a monopoly on the transportation of oil out of the kingdom.

Newsweek on November 15, 1954, said of the historic deal,

"The central figure is a fabulous Greek—Aristotle Socrates Onassis, owner of a worldwide tanker empire, of a dominant share in Monte Carlo's chief enterprises, and of one of the world's most luxurious yachts. Onassis (Ari to his friends) is not the mysterious and ruthless character that newspapers and magazines portray. Nonetheless, the role he set himself in the Arabian oil industry has produced baffling and as yet largely undisclosed intrigues. The crisis began when an agreement was completed on Jan. 20, 1954, between Saudi Arabia, represented by the Finance and Economics Minister, Sheik Abdullah el Sulaiman, and Onassis, represented by Sheik Mohammed Abdullah Ali Ridha. The chief terms:

"1. The formation of a company called the Saudi Arabian Maritime Tankers Co. Ltd., with at least 500,000 ton capacity of tankers.

"2. Shipment of all Saudi oil exports in tankers of the company, except that first preference would go to tankers owned by companies with concessions in Saudi Arabia—but under severe restrictions.

"3. The shipment of oil at a predetermined minimum rate.

"The Onassis contract was immediately interpreted by the major oil companies as a worldwide threat to the industry. Aramco, which holds the concession for Saudi Arabian oil, bitterly opposed the arrangement as contrary to the terms of its own concession. Aramco officials claimed that under the contract Saudi Arabia would be obliged immediately to ship 50 per cent of its oil in Onassis tankers while other companies gradually would be cut out completely."

Onassis, by the mid 1950s, owned the largest fleet of tankers in the world, the bank and casino

---

[118] They were brothers-in-law for a time by virtue of being married to the two delicious daughters of Greek shipping magnate Stavros Livanos: Athina ("Tina"), and Eugenie—both of whom, according to Roberts, were murdered by Stavros Niarchos while they were each married to him—but not simultaneously!!! (I know this reads like fiction, but it may not be.) My guess is that the "Ernst Blofeld" part of the name refers to Onassis's many Nazi connections worldwide, including the USA.-sc

in Monte Carlo, and had an exclusive concession on the shipping of Saudi Arabian oil to the west. What more could a man want? To control the world? Only two men would presume to control the world in such a way: Ernst Stavro Blofeld and Aristotle Socrates Onassis.

If James Bond could not bring down the empire of Onassis, who could?

—**Excerpted from** *Inside the Gemstone File*, **pp. 72-74**

Childress continues:

Gemstones Are Forever

"Bond continues to battle Blofeld at his secret base in Japan in *You Only Live Twice* (1964).... In the 1961 book, *Thunderball*, Bond battles SPECTRE'S Number Two..., who lives on a super-yacht named the Platos Volandos ("Flying Saucer"). The real-life model for Number Two is apparently Stavros Niarchos, Onassis's fellow shipping "rival." Bond eliminates Number Two at the end of the book, but is still unable to get Blofeld, who escapes time after time. (Blofeld, and Number Two, are both parodied extensively in the hilarious 1997 movie *Austin Powers: International Man of Mystery*.)

"The amazing story of Onassis, Hughes, Las Vegas, Area 51, and the oil industry (controlled, to some extent, by Onassis while he was alive) is told to incredible detail in the 1972 movie (based on Fleming's earlier book, but diverting extensively) *Diamonds Are Forever*.

"In the filmed story of *Diamonds Are Forever*, the plot remarkably parallels the *Gemstone File* years before the *Skeleton Key to the Gemstone File* was ever circulated. The plot begins in the diamond fields of South Africa, as in Fleming's original book, but soon diverges from the book to bring in elements of the Gemstone File and the Mafia/Las Vegas/Area 51 entanglement.

"Bond is assigned to follow a trail of diamonds from South Africa to Amsterdam and then to Las Vegas where he is confronted with the Mafia. In one scene, James Bond sneaks into a secret facility in the Nevada desert outside of Las Vegas. This facility is the location of Mercury, the exit off that interstate highway leading to Area 51, the top secret space facility in south central Nevada rumored to house flying saucers and alien technology. Once inside the facility, Bond pretends to be a worker in a lab coat and walks into a room where a German engineer is in charge. The man is clearly meant to be Werner von Braun. After witnessing the faking of the Apollo Moon missions, Bond steals the lunar rover and escapes into the desert. Does *Diamonds Are Forever* mirror the truth about NASA being part of a secret conspiracy? In the movie, the space facility and the Mafia are working together.

"The movie, however, turns out to be the story of a kidnapped billionaire named Willard Whyte...who is held in seclusion by Blofeld, exactly as Roberts claimed Howard Hughes was held captive by Onassis.

"Bond frees the kidnapped Willard Whyte and then proceeds with the help of Tiffany Case...to attack Blofeld at his secret base: an oil platform either off the coast of Texas or California, the movie does not indicate which. Bond destroys the oil platform but Blofeld escapes to reappear briefly in the 1981 film *For Your Eyes Only* when he is finally dispatched permanently. By this time, Onassis was dead as well.

"Indeed, the parallels between *Diamonds Are Forever* and the *Gemstone File* are many:[119]

Diamonds are Forever (the movie)	The Gemstone File
Willard Whyte is held captive in Las Vegas by Blofeld and the Mafia.	Howard Hughes is held captive in the Bahamas and Skorpios by Onassis and the Mafia.
Blofeld owns a casino named Casino Royale in Monte Carlo and has various "doubles."	Onassis owns a casino in Monte Carlo named Casino Royale and Hughes has various "doubles" concocted by Onassis and Robert Maheu.
Blofeld owns oil fields and oil platforms. He	Onassis owns oil tankers and has an

---

[119] I put Childress's items in table format.—sc

is protected by foreign countries.	exclusive deal with Saudi Arabia. He is protected by foreign countries such as Greece and Monaco.
Blofeld is head of SPECTRE, a multi-national group of drug dealers, murders, arms dealers and oil men who are attempting to control the world.	Onassis is the head of a multi-national group of drug dealers, oil tanker operators, casino owners, murderers and arms dealers.
Blofeld owns his own island, high-tech yacht fleet, and private army.	Onassis owns his own island (Skorpios), has a high-tech yacht fleet (Onassis owned many, many ships), and controlled a private army that allegedly went beyond the Mafia to the Marseille underground and the CIA and FBI.
Diamonds Are Forever was about the secret NASA base outside of Las Vegas, and the use of diamonds to make a space-based laser system, one that could project holographic images into the sky.	The *Gemstone File* is about synthetic rubies and their use by Hughes in laser research and Roberts' later use of these synthetic rubies as "gifts" with an attached "Gemstone Letter" that revealed certain behind-the-scenes activities of Onassis, the Mafia and the CIA to important and wealthy individuals. Las Vegas was the scene of Hughes' kidnapping and imprisonment, a city well known to be owned and run by the Mafia and their overt partners.

Ian Fleming: Sodium Morphate Victim?

Ian Fleming died in mysterious circumstances in Jamaica on August 12, 1964, of a "heart attack." According to Bruce Roberts, the "sodium morphate" used by Onassis and the Mafia made the victim appear to have died from a massive heart attack.

According to Preston B. Nichols and Peter Moon in their book *Pyramids of Montauk* (Sky Books, 1995), Ian Fleming knew certain information about the Rainbow Project, a secret endeavor that was to ultimately lead into what is known today as The Philadelphia Project. Fleming had worked with Aleister Crowley [*both worked with British Intelligence—sc*] on the Rainbow Project, his part being a secret mission to meet with Karl Haushofer of the Nazi party in order to get him to convince Rudolf Hess to defect. Fleming met with Haushofer in Lisbon, Portugal, early in the war and persuaded the influential German occultist to talk with Hess on behalf of Crowley. Both Haushofer and Hess admired Aleister Crowley a great deal....

As for Division Five of the FBI and its role in the Kennedy assassination: of the many FBI agents and former FBI that are curiously involved in the assassination and its aftermath, one is Robert Maheu, a former FBI agent who became the CIA emissary first charged with recruiting the Mafia to kill Castro, a man who is also featured in the Gemstone File. It was supposedly Maheu who controlled the entire Howard Hughes empire after Hughes was "kidnapped."

One of the most curious episodes in the JFK "thing" was that of Canadian businessman Richard Giesbrecht who overheard David Ferrie discussing his role in the assassination with another man at the Winnipeg Airport on February 13, 1963. ...Giesbrecht talked to FBI agent Merryl Nelson, whom he contacted through the U.S. consulate in Winnipeg. Giesbrecht said that the FBI agent at first told him, "This looks like the break we've been waiting for" — only to tell him a few months later to forget the whole thing.[120] FBI agent Nelson is supposed to have said to Giesbrecht, "It's too big. We can't protect you in Canada...."

In the '90s, the past looks back at us larger than life. The manipulation of all aspects of our lives becomes more and more apparent, and the theories that Oswald was implanted and controlled as a 'mind control' victim are no longer so impossible. The aerospace and rocket industry of Nazi Germany became the American space program.

---

[120] It is likely that rank-and-file FBI agents knew little or nothing of what was really going on. But as for Nelson, he found out something when he passed the word up to his superiors, and was told, "Yeah, OK. Now shutta da mouth and keep on looking for breaks in the assassination of JFK. Just as long as you don't find anything, all right?—sc

Fleming knew it all, and had to die. For ten years he leaked top secret information through his books. At certain levels, it was officially sanctioned. But not everyone appreciated the James Bond stories. …

Did Onassis himself come to find the James Bond books a bit annoying? Or maybe British Intelligence was persuaded to eliminate one of its own kind? It is a sad thought, that Fleming may have had an apple pie for lunch on August 12, 1964.

—**Excerpted from** *Inside the Gemstone File*, **78-87.**

***

Inside the Gemstone File **(250 pages) is excellent supplemental reading** *for The Gemstone File: A Memoir.* **It contains information and analysis that doesn't exist anywhere else, from a different source and a different point of view.**

44 Which Came First? Roberts' Gemstone File, or Liddy's Gemstone Plan?

"I have extracted 57% water—H₂0—from an opal. 17% of sapphire juice from the 62-carat heart-shaped sapphire now up President Patty's ass. That juice is something else. A real tearjerker. From a ruby, the juice is red—the color of blood."—Bruce Roberts

Will: The Autobiography of G. Gordon Liddy, was published by St. Martin's Press in 1980. It sold well, and was later reissued in paperback. Before Watergate, Liddy's chief claim to fame was that he had a law degree and a long, secretive career with both the FBI and the CIA. He first came to national prominence when, in late 1971, he was appointed legal council to Nixon's Committee to Re-elect the President, affectionately known in some quarters as "CREEP". His "job" was, according to him, to ensure that Nixon was re-elected President, by any means necessary. In his book, in addition to bragging about what a skillful CIA murderer and general tough guy he was, Liddy revealed himself to be well educated and possessing a good, if macabre, sense of humor. After being nabbed in the Watergate debacle in 1972, he went to prison as the leader of Nixon's Watergate "Plumbers" team. He was sentenced to twenty years in prison, but his sentence was commuted in 1977 by President Carter, and he was released from prison after serving four years and four months. He says in his book that his sentence, and the time he would actually serve, (and the money that would cover his expenses while he served time in a "white collar" prison were all negotiated beforehand (by him).[121] The following is a portion of a radio interview he had in 1992 with Jonathan Vankin, one of the [negative] contributors to Jim Keith's 1992 *Gemstone File* book. The entire interview appears in Thomas and Childress's 1999 book, *Inside the Gemstone File*:

>Watergater G. Gordon Liddy...became known for his Washington, DC radio show on WJFK (an appropriate set of call letters). In 1992, he had as a guest the conspiracy writer Jonathan Vankin. Vankin co-authored *The 70 Greatest Conspiracies of All Time* with John Whalen, and both still maintain a web site at www.conspire.com. The program was a rare and unfortunately brief confrontation about the Gemstone thesis with one of its ostensible characters:
>
>**Liddy**: I just received a fax from a fellow who had called earlier, Mr. "U".[122] He asked, had I ever heard about the Gemstone File? Now, of course, I know about the Gemstone Plan...
>
>**Vankin**: I was going to ask you about that, actually.
>
>**Liddy**: That was my plan, see, the Gemstone Plan. But he's now faxed me something that looks like it was done on an old typewriter.
>
>**Vankin**: Hey, you bet! I was going to ask you about the Gemstone File, actually.
>
>**Liddy**: I was going to ask *you* about the Gemstone File. It appears to be almost like a table of contents or rough outline of what purports to be, what must be, a massive document, because this starts out in 1932 with Onassis, "Greek drug pusher and ship-owner," well, "alleged" Greek drug pusher, it doesn't have any.... Turkish tobacco, Joseph Kennedy, Eugene Meyer and Meyer Lansky. Then in '34 it's Onassis and Rockefeller and the Seven Sisters oil companies. And then in '36-'40, it's Eugene Meyer buys the *Washington Post*. Holy Smoke! The Bilderbergers and the *Washington Post* are in...then in '41 to '45, World War II was very profitable for Onassis, Rockefeller, the Kennedys, Roosevelt, I. G. Farben, etc. Then Onassis in '49 buys U. S. surplus Liberty ships, and this just goes on, and Senator Kefauver, and, my god, page after page of this... You know this leads me to a more general question, Mr. Vankin, and that is—it occurred to me that most conspiracy theories that I have heard of fail the test of logic, the classical test of *post hoc, ergo proctor hoc*. In other words,

---

[121] Wouldn't it be lovely if all felons received such kind treatment? Liddy quotes a phone call he received from John Dean: "...Gordon, I want to assure you that everyone's going to be taken care of—everyone.... First, you'll receive living expenses of thirty thousand per annum. Second, you'll have a pardon within two years. Three, we'll see to it you're sent to Danbury Prison, and fourth, your legal fees will be paid."—Liddy, *Will*, p.278.
[122] Would that happen to Tony Ulascewicz, one of Liddy's associates in the Watergate break-in and the Ellsberg matter, and also the one who dug up the dirt on Teddy K. at Chappaquiddick?

because something occurred after something else, therefore it occurred because of something else.

Vankin: Right.

Liddy: That appears to be the rationale behind this *Skeleton Key to the Gemstone File*. Have you ever read this?

Vankin: Oh, absolutely. In fact, this gives me the chance to plug another book here, a book that I didn't write but that I'll have an essay in, called *The Gemstone File*. And it's a collection of the many versions of that document you apparently have in your hand, and a lot of other essays about it. I wrote a little piece about my reaction to the Gemstone File.

[NOTE: Vankin considered my Skeleton Key to the Gemstone File (and the unseen Gemstone File itself) to be worthless "conspiracy theory" fantasy writing. He left it out of earlier editions of his book series, "The [nth] Greatest Conspiracies of All Time", which consists of short, sleek and shallow summaries. By the time of the 2004 edition, he had included a knee-jerk sarcastic and wildly inaccurate "review" of the "Skeleton Key to the Gemstone File" (and the "Gemstone File" itself, which of course he had never seen.) He complained about the "lack of documentation" in my Skeleton Key, but left out any mention of Gerald Carroll's "Project Seek" and Richard Alan's "Gemstone File" books, published in 1993. Between them, these two books total 800 pages of powerful documentation of the Gemstone thesis. Thomas and Childress's "Inside the Gemstone File" (1999) added another 250 pages of relevant information. In his vicious smear "review" of 2004, Vankin still only cites the "Skeleton Key to the Gemstone File itself" and Jim Keith's elaborate career-making pan anthology, "The Gemstone File", in his Gemstone "bibliography." I guess Vankin must be a "slow learner," but this is ridiculous!—sc2006]

Liddy: Could you give us a little precis of it?

Vankin: Sure. Let me tell you a little bit about what it is, because a lot of people have confused it with the Gemstone Plan.

Liddy: I'm getting blamed for the Gemstone File.

Vankin: There's a lot of people out there who think that you wrote it.

Liddy: Friends and neighbors! I did not write *The Gemstone File* or the *Skeleton Key to the Gemstone File*. In fact, I just received this fax and that's all I know about it. However, I am listening with fascination to Mr. Vankin, who is an expert on it.

Vankin: The Gemstone File was supposedly written by a fellow named Bruce Roberts.

Liddy: Who he? Who Bruce Roberts?

Vankin: This is a good question. No one really knows exactly who he was, though he and the people who are fans of the Gemstone File claim he was a very well-connected person in the intelligence community. I have no way of verifying that one way or the other. But he wrote thousands of pages of documents, mostly handwritten, explaining this conspiracy that you just sort of outlined in the *Skeleton Key*. Now he hooked up with Mae Brussell, who we mentioned earlier.

Liddy: Lord. That's quite a combination.

Vankin: Now this was in the early '70s, and there's a wild story that goes along with that.

Liddy: I'll bet it is.

Vankin: What happened is that Mae Brussell picked up these thousands of documents[123] written by Bruce Roberts and she was interviewed by a journalist from *Playgirl* magazine named Stephanie Caruana, who was at that time a San Francisco-based journalist who just fell in love with the Gemstone File.[124] [Stephanie] wrote the *Skeleton Key* to The Gemstone File, which is a 25-page condensed version.

Liddy: What I've got here is written by this Gennifer Kariwanga?

Vankin: Stephanie Caruana, yes.

Liddy: Her name does not appear on this thing.

---

[123] Vankin's wild exaggeration is typical of his goofed-up writing. It was 360 pages, to be exact.—sc
[124] Well, that part is correct!—sc

Vankin: If you look on the very first page, in the upper left or right hand corner, because on a lot of versions of the document, it's right there.

Liddy: Well, it's a fax machine thing.

Vankin: Maybe they cut that off for security reasons or something. But there's been a lot of versions of that *Skeleton Key* that have circulated, including one I think they call the Kiwi Gemstone File, which supposedly all takes place in New Zealand. That might interest that previous caller from Australia.

Liddy: When I was down in Australia, I found there was quite a rivalry between Australia and New Zealand. They are not by any means the best of friends. They wouldn't let me into New Zealand.

Vankin: Oh dear.

Liddy: In the airplane at Sydney, I was waiting to take off for Auckland, New Zealand, and they came on board and they said, "Mr. Liddy, you'll have to get off the airplane."

And I said, "Would you mind telling me why?"

And they said, "Well, because, we received a TWX from Auckland saying that if you land the plane with Mr. Liddy on it, then Mr. Liddy will have to stay in the confines of the aircraft. He will not be allowed to set foot on New Zealand's soil until the aircraft is refueled and has to go back."

And I said, "Well, is there a reason why?"

And they said no, they didn't have one. So there was a press conference afterwards, and they asked me to speculate and I really didn't know, so I said that of course I had recently been released from five years in prison. Perhaps they are fearful for the health of their sheep, I wasn't sure. All that did, I'm sure, was assure that I will never get in to New Zealand. So it does not surprise me that there is a New Zealand Gemstone File.[125]

(End of conversation.)[126]

***

Gordon Liddy flits in and out of Roberts' Gemstone File as a malevolent murderer[127] as well as the Nixon White House's burglar-in-chief. AND Liddy is also listed as a CIA murderer in the Opal/Kiwi Gemstone file, which originated far from San Francisco, either in Australia or New Zealand. And I guess they don't like Gordon Liddy very much in New Zealand. AND Liddy describes himself in Will as a well-trained, and experienced, CIA/FBI assassin ("patriotic" ["sanctioned"] assassinations only, of course!) So I thought I'd include Liddy's own account of his "Gemstone Plan," which had its origin in and around the White House in Washington, D.C., the origin of most of the serious crime occurring in the United States and around the world today.

Bruce Roberts states in his Gemstone File letters that his Gemstone File originated in 1968, when he began circulating his letters and journal entries. It lasted for seven or eight years, from 1968 until 1975 or 1976, when he died.

Liddy's "Gemstone Plan" originated in the minds of Gordon Liddy and his CIA/FBI buddy, Howard Hunt. His "Gemstone Plan" had its very own letterhead, and, at one point, a quarter million dollar budget, approved by then-U.S. Attorney General John Mitchell. It only lasted, by Liddy's own account, for six months at most: from December, 1971, to June, 1972.

The following is excerpted from Liddy's autobiography, *Will*, from pages 187-248. It covers the time period when Liddy was appointed General Counsel for CREEP (officially, the Committee to Re-Elect the President), on December 6, 1971, to the early morning hours of June 16, 1972, when he and the other White House "Plumbers" were caught at Watergate:

---

[125] See the Kiwi Gemstone File, Chapter 38, for some reasons why Liddy is, or was, unwelcome in New Zealand.
[126] Reprinted from *Inside the Gemstone File* (1999), by Kenn Thomas and David Hatcher Childress, p.243-6.
[127] At one point in the *Gemstone File*, Roberts called Liddy a "murdering slob". Accurate enough, I guess.

"[Jeb] Magruder called a meeting of key people in his office at which he introduced me as General Counsel and then proceeded to tell all in the room that "Gordon will also be in charge of 'dirty tricks.'" I was annoyed by that gratuitous security breach and waited after the meeting to tell him that any more such talk could blow my cover. I explained that I was going to be running a sophisticated intelligence service, not a "dirty tricks" campaign and that compromise could be dangerous....

My first trip [to California-sc] was overt. Magruder said that there was considerable anxiety among the staff at the selection of San Diego as the convention site[128] because the press had already reported that left-wing extremists were distributing printed plans for disruption of the convention and soliciting nationwide for demonstrators. I asked Howard Hunt to accompany me on an inspection of the San Diego facilities and we flew to Los Angeles....[I] flew alone to San Diego to attend a meeting between members of the campaign staff and San Diego organizers. On my first day there I sat in on a meeting at which the donation of $400,000 in services by ITT, mostly through its hotel subsidiary, was discussed.

John Dean brought up the fact that there was an antitrust suit pending against ITT by Justice. .... We both opposed the acceptance of the ITT offer vigorously, and I have no idea who eventually overruled us....

... I conferred with Howard [Hunt] ... in the White House compound. We worked out a rough consensus of what the operation should entail: planting of our operatives in the staffs of Democratic candidates; surreptitious entries for placing of electronic surveillance devices and photographing key documents such as lists of donors and drafts of position papers with an eye for inter-staff rivalries that could be developed into disruptive strife; the capacity to neutralize the leaders of anti-Nixon demonstrations; the exploitation of sexual weaknesses for information and the promotion of ill-feeling among the Democratic candidates to keep them as divided as possible after the nomination.

With that as an outline, Hunt and I worked up a list of needed personnel specialties, then set to work recruiting. Hunt.... wanted a salary of $3,000 per month and, since I was getting $2,500 a month, I didn't argue. We flew first-class and stayed at the most expensive accommodations in the finest hotels, entertaining potential recruits at places like Chasen's because they must believe that money is no object.... Our two priorities were a "keyman" or expert locksmith and a "wireman" or electronics expert.... During one of our trips to California[129] Hunt attempted to recruit one woman suggested by Jackson, and I a woman suggested by Hunt's candidate. The woman I was working on...was ideal as a plant. She was flashily good-looking, young, had secretarial skills and experience, and appeared able to attract men sexually if she wished, possibly even the candidate. At dinner [she] seemed reluctant... and when I told her that her identity would be revealed to no one and she could just walk away anytime if she feared exposure, she pointed out that I would know her identity. I told her that no one could force me to disclose anything I chose not to reveal. She didn't believe me and I was casting about for some way to convince her when I noticed she smoked. I told her to light her cigarette lighter and hold it out. She did and I locked my gaze upon her eyes and placed my hand, palm down, over the flame. Presently the flesh turned black and when she smelled the scent of

---

[128] The San Diego Convention Center was originally selected to be the site of the 1972 Republican Presidential Nomination Convention. This was later changed to the Fontainebleau Hotel in Miami Beach—the same place where the Democrats had held their convention: in Mafia Miami. (Owned by a Mafia partnership: Frank Sinatra, Patriarcha, etc.) Hunt and Liddy made several trips to San Diego, California to check out the original site and make their plans. According to Roberts, Hunt, Liddy, and the other Watergate Plumbers also stopped in at San Francisco's Drift Inn to check Roberts out.

[129] According to Roberts, it was during one or more of these trips to California that Hunt and Liddy, while scoping out Roberts at the Drift Inn in San Francisco, came to the attention of superspy Hal Lipset. In a Gemstone letter dated in 1975, Roberts supplied photos of Hunt and Liddy which he claimed were taken at the Drift Inn, and used by Katherine Graham's *Washington Post* after the Watergate debacle. Roberts also said that Lipset followed the activities of Hunt and Liddy closely after this, and in that way was able to track them as they returned to Washington and began to put Liddy's GEMSTONE Watergate "burglary" operation into play. Roberts also claimed that Lipset was working for Katharine Graham at the time. Lipset reported to Graham, and she told him to keep Liddy and Hunt under surveillance. Thus when Liddy, Hunt, McCord and their Cuban associates penetrated O'Brien's office at Watergate to install their bugs, Lipset bugged THEIR bugs, adding a camera or two. Graham got the whole story of Watergate as it happened. Whatever McCord was able to do, bugwise, Lipset was capable of seeing him and raising him a bug. Read on in this chapter to see how Lipset retaped the door and caught the lot of them.

burning meat, [she] broke from my gaze and pulled the lighter away from my hand. She seemed frightened badly so I took pains to calm her, wrapping an ice cube against the burn with a napkin and returning to my dinner.... [She] said she was sure I would never betray her, but excused herself as a candidate, invoking a just-remembered plan to marry a Swiss airplane pilot.

Hunt and I...had difficulty getting a keyman, even after Hunt traveled afar to interview candidates from CIA retirees and paid others to do so....

We had the same difficulty in finding a wireman. I needed information on state-of-the-art equipment so, shortly after he joined the committee as physical security chief on 9 January 1972, I questioned James McCord. He was ex-FBI and ex-CIA, where he had been a "tech," specializing in that field.

He was intimately familiar with the techniques used by the Soviets in intercepting microwave-transmitted telephone calls in Washington from special antennas on the roof of their 16th Street embassy just a few hundred yards from the White House, as well as with U.S. techniques....[130]

Hunt enlisted the aid of Bernard Barker and we traveled to Miami to interview men for our counter-demonstration and anti-riot squad, along with several prostitute candidates for use at the Democratic convention.

[We] interviewed about a dozen men. Afterward, Howard told me that between them they had killed twenty-two men, including two hanged from a beam in a garage.[131] Our experience with the prostitutes was not good. Hunt and Barker kept recruiting dark-haired and -complexioned Cuban women. They were very good-looking, but their English left something to be desired. I was not sure they'd be suitable for the purposes I intended: posing as idly rich young women so impressed by men of power that they would let themselves be picked up at parties and bars by Democratic staffers who, in the course of boasting of their own importance, would disclose valuable information.... I was also affected by my own bias. Because I would be more attracted to Northern Europeans, I assumed fair women would be more successful and rejected those selected. Finally, having despaired of seeing other than the dark and sultry type from the Cubans, I retained, sight unseen except for professional photographs, two stunning Anglo-Saxon women recruited by Barker's associate Frank Sturgis....[132]

On 10 January I...was sent to audit the records and accounts of Jack Caulfield's operative "Tony" in New York City. ...

We found "Tony," later identified at Watergate hearings as Anthony Ulascewicz,[133] at Apartment 11-C, 321 East 48th Street, Manhattan. Caulfield had described the place as "a very elaborate pad—beautiful, wait'll ya see it. My guy Tony's puttin' the make on one of the Chappaquiddick broads. The joint's wired for sound. He gets her in the sack a few times, wins her confidence, and we get the facts."

When "Tony" opened the door, I couldn't believe what I saw. First there was "Tony" himself: a big, overweight middle-aged man who in his best day would not exactly rival Robert Redford.... The apartment itself was...so small that the "bedroom" was nothing but a tiny converted alcove with a pitiful homemade wall erected across its opening and a curtain for a door. The wall, in which he was trying to hide a tape recorder, was covered in the fake brick sold at Montgomery Ward stores in poor neighborhoods to dress up aging kitchens.... The windows were hung with red imitation velvet drapes. The decor was strictly better-grade Juarez whorehouse circa 1951.

Whatever his failings as an interior decorator or seducer, "Tony" kept first-rate records. He received a salary of $36,000 per year, and every cent spent over and above that was accounted for in

---

[130] Spy versus spy...the Soviets bugged us, and we bugged them.
[131] Hunt had worked extensively with the anti-Castro Cubans, before and after the Bay of Pigs.
[132] The Cubans recruited by Hunt and Liddy came from the same group, ex-strong-arm men in Batista's corrupt dictatorship, who were previously recruited by George H. W. Bush's CIA back in the '60's to participate in the Bay of Pigs operation, and later in the assassination of JFK. —sc2006
[133] Ulascewicz, the ex-New York cop, participated as a "foot soldier" in Watergate (preliminary survey and planning), and investigated Chappaquiddick for Nixon and the Republicans, according to John Dean. He got the goods on Teddy, great for blackmail. Kept Teddy from ever running for the Presidency. This ultimately helped reduce the Democratic Party to its present status: "Younger brother," me-too partner of the Republican Party in their elaborate periodical show elections.

meticulous detail. His set of records was a time bomb, waiting to go off; everywhere he had gone, and virtually everything he had done, could be reconstructed from them. I approved the audit on the spot and urged him to destroy the records and not generate any more like them. [134]

I told Hunt...that I'd like to have our diagrams put in chart form for my presentation to the Attorney General.... I didn't want something homemade-looking for use in presenting a million-dollar proposal.

Hunt...took our own crude but legible diagrams to professionals: the CIA. Magruder arranged a meeting with John Mitchell in the Attorney General's [White House] office for 27 January and invited John Dean to sit in. Several days before, Hunt had me stand at noon on the corner of 17th Street and Pennsylvania Avenue, where the CIA delivered to me a wrapped set of three-by-four charts of professional caliber....[135]

I knew exactly what had to be done and why, and I was under no illusion about its legality. Although spies in the enemy camp and electronic surveillance were nothing new in American presidential politics, we were going to go far beyond that. As far as I was concerned, anything went if it were merely *malum prohibitum*[136] (about which more later). There was a law of physics that every action has an equal and opposite reaction; I was ready to break that one, too, in reaction to the radical left and the whole drug-besotted 1960 "movement" that was attacking my country from within....[137]

The experience of the past ten years left no doubt in my mind that the United States was at war internally as well as externally. In August 1970 the Army Math Center of the University of Wisconsin was added to the list of bombings. A father of two died in the blast and three others were injured. Two years before Daniel Moynihan had warned of the "onset of urban terror"—a bit late, I thought, in view of the thousands of bombings, burnings, riots, and lootings of the '60s, to say nothing of the murders of police just because they were police, the killing of judges, and the general disintegration of the social order.

Moreover the antiwar movement threatened to prove the vehicle for these radical elements to gain enough acceptance to achieve political power.... The events of the 1960s offended me gravely. To permit the thought, spirit, life-style, and ideas of the '60s movement to achieve power and become the official way of life of the United States was a thought as offensive to me as was the thought of surrender to a career Japanese soldier in 1945. It was unthinkable, an unspeakable betrayal.

I remembered the rioting, burning cities, the bombings and killings, and the attempts to close down the nation's capital by mob violence; the American actress[138] in the capital of our enemy broadcasting appeals to our combat troops to commit treason; the cooperation and approval of great newspapers in the theft and compromise of masses of classified documents. I remembered the crew-served automatic weapons in the halls of the Department of Justice, and I knew that what had happened to Richard Nixon in 1960 and to Lyndon Johnson in 1968 could not be permitted to happen again. With an ice-cold, deliberate certainty I knew exactly what I was going to be doing in 1972 and it was damn well about time: we were going to throw the Battle Override.

In his offices at the Mullen Company[139] across the street from the Committee to Re-elect [the President] Headquarters, Howard Hunt announced the recruitment of Virgilio "Villo" Gonzales, a

---

[134] Liddy thought Tony's taste in decoration was hyper-tacky, but his records were all too good, so he ordered Tony to destroy them. Too bad! They would have made great reading for a historian of our super-tacky time.
[135] Let us remember that one of JFK's last announced goals before he had his brains shot out was his intention to dismantle the CIA. Now here is the CIA, supposedly a "non-partisan" intelligence group, drawing up the plans for Gordon Liddy's illegal activities on behalf of Nixon and the Republicans. Liddy and his buddies must be as happy as pigs in a sty with Bush's current activities and the rightward momentum of this government.
[136] Merely prohibited by law, but acceptable according to Liddy's personal "ethics." And—Liddy was a lawyer!—sc2006
[137] Odd, isn't it, that Liddy is so self-righteously opposed to the evils of the U.S. drug traffic but seems to have missed all the available evidence that the CIA has been up to its nostrils for decades in the drug traffic, earning its own untrackable millions for use in international assassinations, the overthrow of democratic governments, and, of course, the destruction of American society through ever-growing CIA/Mafia organized and protected domestic drug traffic and use. See, for example, *The Politics of Heroin in Southeast Asia*, by Alfred McCoy.—sc2006.
[138] Possibly Jane Fonda, whom Roberts mentions as receiving some Gemstone papers during this period.
[139] A CIA front organization.

Cuban emigre locksmith. Although Hunt would continue to try to obtain an ex-CIA man with covert-entry experience, who could act as number one man with Gonzales as backup, he assured me that if worse came to worse Gonzales was up to the job. "He's ex-Batista secret police and hard as nails...."

The only key person not yet recruited was the electronics man. McCord had been useful in furnishing technical information, but I didn't want to use anyone from the Committee because I wanted to promise John Mitchell a "double blind"...protection of the Committee from the intelligence operation in the event of discovery.... I'd asserted that key foreign drug-smuggling operatives, who were well known, should be recognized as killers of American children and subject to being killed themselves. By us.

State [Department] had been horrified at the idea of such direct action as assassination and the suggestion had gone nowhere, but Bud [Egil] Krogh had not seemed to object in principle.... I said, "Bud if you want anyone killed, just let me know."

He smiled and said "I will."

I reacted to his smile by saying, "I'm serious."

"I know you are," said Krogh, his smile gone. "I'll let you know."

In January, 1972 promised to be the best year I'd ever had. Even Treasury, numbed by my being named Counsel to the Committee to Re-elect the President, appeared to have accepted defeat.... I considered the upcoming interview with John Mitchell a mere formality....

We met John Mitchell in his small inner office behind the great ceremonial one so familiar to the public from the days of Bobby Kennedy. At my request there was an easel set up. I greeted the Attorney General and, as Magruder seated himself in front of the desk with Dean, I set up my charts in the order I wanted to display them.

The plan was given the overall name of **GEMSTONE**, and although most components bore the names of a precious or semi-precious stone, some were named for minerals. I explained that the proposed service was what had been requested by John Dean and that it had full offensive as well as defensive capability. Then I got down to specifics. I started with operation **DIAMOND**.

DIAMOND was our counter-demonstration plan. At the time, we still expected the convention to be held in San Diego. I repeated my objections to the site, then pointed out that the best technique for dealing with a mob had been worked out years before by the famed Texas Rangers. They were so few that law enforcement types still tell the story of the town that telegraphed Ranger headquarters for help in suppressing a riot and were startled to see a solitary Ranger ride into town. "There's only one of you?!" they cried, and the Ranger replied quietly, "There's only one riot, ain't there?"

The Texas Ranger technique was to linger on the fringes of the disturbance, watching until they could identify the leaders, then work their way through the crowd to the leaders and beat the hell out of them until, leaderless, the rioters became easy to disperse. I proposed to emulate the Texas Rangers by identifying the leaders through intelligence before the attack got under way, kidnap them, drug them, and hold them in Mexico until after the convention was over, then release them unharmed and still wondering what happened.... The sudden disappearances, which I labeled on the chart in the original German, Nacht und Nebel ("Night and Fog"), would strike fear into the hearts of the leftist guerrillas. The chart labeled the team slated to carry out the night and fog plan as a "Special Action Group" and, when John Mitchell asked "What's that?" and expressed doubt that it could perform as I had explained, I grew impatient....

I felt obliged to impress Mitchell with my seriousness of purpose, that my people were the kind and I was the kind who could and would do whatever was necessary to deal with organized mass violence. Both Magruder and Dean were too young to know what I was talking about, but I knew that Mitchell, a naval officer in World War II, would get the message if I translated the English "Special Action Group" into German. Given the history involved, it was a gross exaggeration, but it made my point.

"An Einsatzgruppe, General," I said, inadvertently using a hard "g" for the word General and

turning it, too, into German.[140] "These men include professional killers who have accounted between them for twenty-two dead so far, including two hanged from a beam in a garage."

Mitchell gazed at me steadily, took another puff on his pipe, removed it from his mouth and said, "And where did you find men like that?"

"I understand they're members of organized crime."

"And how much will their services cost?"

I pointed to the figure on the chart. It was substantial. "Like top professionals everywhere, sir," I said, "they don't come cheap."

"Well," said Mitchell dryly as he brought his pipe back up to his mouth, "let's not contribute any more than we have to the coffers of organized crime...."

RUBY concerned the infiltration of spies into the camp of Democratic contenders, then the successful candidate himself.

COAL was the program to furnish money clandestinely to Shirley Chisholm of New York to finance her as a contender and force Democratic candidates to fight off a black woman, bound to generate ill-feeling among the black community and, we hoped, cause them difficulty with women.[141] Once again Mitchell interrupted me. "You can forget about that. Nelson Rockefeller's already taking care of that nicely." For each operation I explained what would be done in detail.

EMERALD outlined the use of a chase plane to eavesdrop on the Democratic candidate's aircraft and buses when his entourage used radio telephones....

QUARTZ detailed emulation of the technique used by the Soviet Union for microwave interception of telephone traffic, and I explained in detail the way it was done by the Soviet Embassy.

For use in gathering information at the Democratic National Convention at Miami Beach, Hunt and I had an option to lease a large houseboat moored within line of sight of the Fontainebleau. This would enable it to be used as a communications center for **CRYSTAL**—electronic surveillance. It was an opulent barge, with a lush bedroom featuring a large mirror over the big king-sized bed. We'd get our money's worth from the houseboat. It would double as headquarters for **SAPPHIRE** because it was from there that our prostitutes were to operate. They were not to work as hookers but as spoiled, rich, beautiful women who were only too susceptible to men, who could brag convincingly of the importance of what they were doing at the convention. ...

I presented a plan for four black-bag jobs, **OPALS** I through IV. They were clandestine entries at which microphone surveillances could be placed, as well as **TOPAZ**: photographs taken of any documents available, including those under lock.

As targets I proposed the headquarters of Senator Edmund Muskie's campaign on K Street, N.W.; that of Senator George McGovern on Capitol Hill; one for the Democratic National Convention at any hotel, because we had access to just about anything we wanted through all the Cuban help employed in the Miami Beach hotels....

---

[140] Liddy seems to enjoy sprinkling his mini-lectures with German, or specifically Nazi, catch phrases. This brings to mind our current hard-liner government, and their "Shock and Awe" bombing campaign in Iraq. They too enjoy brutality in word and deed, as an approach to "foreign relations" and the quickest way to terrify civilian populations into capitulation. Of course experience ought to have taught them by now that such antics only stiffen opposition to the invaders (us), by creating desperation among the invadees. Unfortunately for the cause of "Peace," "Peace" is not the real goal of this government. Nor is "Democracy." More resistance from local residents, who are quickly termed "terrorists" and "insurgents" provides more excuse for more expenditures voted by our compliant Congress, to achieve the real goal: quicker and more massive profiteering by the "warfare" industries, and the establishment of domestic fascism based on and emulating closely that practiced in Nazi Germany before and during WWII.

[141] Here Liddy expresses his racist contempt for Shirley Chisholm and blacks in general, by abruptly dropping the conceit of naming sections of his GEMSTONE plan for semi-precious stones. A lump of coal has little intrinsic value compared to a gemstone. Even obsidian would have been a better choice. Possibly more to the point: Blacks in general, and perhaps Shirley Chisholm in particular, suffered a more direct attack at around this time. Martin Luther King, Jr.'s mother was shot and killed, by another hypnotized black patsy, who carried a list of other "mother" targets. One of them was Shirley Chisholm, who "got the message," as Roberts put it. Was this "mother" murder one of Liddy's "COAL" operations which he chose not to mention here?

Next I presented plans for **GARNET**: counter-demonstrations by groups that would attract media attention and be perceived by most Americans to be repulsive as they advocated the candidacy of Democratic candidates of our selection …

The largest disruption operation…was reserved for the Democratic National Convention itself. We had paid well to acquire the entire blueprints for the convention hall and all its support machinery. The plan I outlined, **TURQUOISE**, called for a commando team of Cubans—veterans of raids into Castro Cuba[142]—to slip at night from apartments rented across the street to the rear of the hall, where the air-conditioning units were, and sabotage them by destroying the compressors and introducing a destructive grit into the bearings of the blowers….

I closed the presentation….with a final two charts. One, **BRICK**, summed up **GEMSTONE** cost breakdowns by units (**RUBY, COAL, DIAMOND**, etc.) and the total of nearly one million dollars.[143] The last was the flowchart, which looked roughly like a ski jump.

Weeks passed and there was no decision forthcoming…..

When Howard Hunt was told by Robert Bennett, his employer, that Hank Greenspun, a Las Vegas newspaper publisher, was believed to have documents in his office safe that would "blow Muskie out of the water" and I passed that information on to Magruder, the reaction was swift. Hunt and I were authorized to check on the feasibility of cracking the safe and retrieving the documents.

Hunt and I decided that in the absence of a go-ahead on the creation and funding of **GEMSTONE**, we ought to make an alliance of convenience with Howard Hughes[144], known to be an enemy of Greenspun. Hunt had excellent connections with Hughes Tool and the Summa Corporations through his employer, Robert Bennett, whose Mullen Company represented Hughes and who was embroiled in the campaign to prove the purported authorized biography of Hughes by Clifford Irving to be a fraud. According to Hunt, Greenspun probably had documents in his safe that Hughes would like to retrieve. By pre-arrangement, Hunt and I flew to Los Angeles and stayed in a suite obtained for us by Hughes at the Beverly Wilshire Hotel. It is in the old section, very 1940-ish and huge, appropriate to anyone doing business with Howard Hughes….

There we conferred with Bob Winte, a Hughes security man. I suggested that we mount a joint operation…. I proposed that Hunt and I do so with a Cuban team…. We would examine our findings jointly with Hughes' jet transport to be on standby in the desert. We would take everything in [Greenspun's safe] without examination, head straight to the waiting jet, and fly to a Hughes-controlled Caribbean destination of his choice. There we would examine our findings jointly with Hughes' representatives and divide the materials on the basis of our separate interests. Winte said he would seek approval and seemed to think the matter a mere formality. When, a short time later, Hunt told me that Hughes had declined on the basis of the cost of the jet, I didn't believe it and concluded that the real reason was that Hughes figured there was something in the Greenspun safe that he didn't want us to see….

Other methods were discussed and discarded. "Aspirin Roulette," for example: the placing of a poisoned replica of the appropriate brand of headache tablet into the bottle usually found in the target's medicine cabinet. That method was rejected because it would gratuitously endanger innocent members of his family and might take months before it worked.[145]

---

[142] Including the Bay of Pigs operation, as well as other raids into Cuba.
[143] Liddy was hoping for a $1 million budget, but the budget was ultimately cut by Mitchell to $250,000. Still, it was a respectable enough amount to mollify Liddy's ego. His long-time partner in illegal derringdo, Howard Hunt, apparently resorted to more old-fashioned blackmail demands, which is probably why his wife Dorothy was blown out of the air together with a planeful of other travelers, while the FBI was on hand in no time flat to search the smoking ruins of the plane for the $$$blackmail loot she was apparently carrying. Wow, those "Wild West" Nixon administration memories! Dwarfed now by Dubya's in-your-face 2-election thefts, 9/11 fraud, declaration of the Constitution to be nuthin' but a scrap of used paper, etc., plus "Two-Bunker Cheney's" two-gun raids on the Treasury via his pet Corporations (*Halliburton et al.*), stuffing money with both hands into their corporate maws in Iraq. Meanwhile Congress collects their bribe money and okays the theft.
[144] I.e., Onassis, everybody's Mafia sugar daddy at the time.
[145] "Aspirin Roulette" was apparently the weapon of choice used against LaVerne Roberts, Bruce Roberts' father. Roberts implies that Virgilio Gonzales, the Watergate "Plumbers'" locksmith, slipped into Roberts' parents' apartment and slipped a sodium morphate-containing capsule into LaVerne Roberts' prescription medicine container, where it sat undetected until Mr. Roberts swallowed it one day, and wound up in the hospital that night.

...In the case of killing it is well to remember that the Ten Commandments, translated correctly from the original Aramaic do not contain the injunction "Thou shall not kill." It reads, "Thou shalt not do murder." Quite another thing. There are circumstances that not only justify killing but require it (when one is charged with the safekeeping of a child, for example, and the only way to prevent its death from another's attack is to kill that other person). These are all situations that require informed and responsible judgments.[146]

There are other ethical doctrines that may be applied. In World War II some bomber pilots were concerned when they knew that, for example, the ball bearing factory that was their target was across the street from an orphanage and their bombing altitude meant that it was very likely the orphanage would also be hit. In such a situation the principle of double effect comes into play; the unintended secondary effect of the destruction of the orphanage is permissible.[147] The classical example is that of the driver of a loaded school bus going down the one-lane mountain road with a sheer thousand-foot drop on either side rounding a turn to see a three-year-old girl on a tricycle in the middle of the road. He is going too fast to stop. The choices are to go off the road and take thirty-five children and himself to certain death to spare the three-year-old, or run over the three-year-old and save the thirty-five. I'd run over the three-year-old. I also fail to see any distinction between killing an enemy soldier in time of declared war and killing an enemy espionage agent in a "cold" war, or even killing certain U.S. citizens.[148] For example, were I back in my ODESSA position and were given the instruction from an appropriate officer of the government, I would kill Philip Agee if it were demonstrated (as it has often been argued) that his revelations have led directly to the death of at least one of his fellow CIA officers, that he intended to continue the revelations, and that they would lead to more deaths. Notice that this killing would not be retributive but preventive. It is the same rationale by which I was willing to obey an order to kill Jack Anderson. But I would do so only after satisfying myself that it was:

a) an order from legitimate authority;

b) a question of *malum prohibition*; and

c) a rational response to the problem.

I thought about the damage Anderson was doing to our country's ability to conduct foreign policy. Most of all, I thought of that U.S. agent abroad, dead or about to die after what I was sure would be interrogation by torture. If Hunt's principal was worried, I had the answer.

"Tell him," I said, "if necessary, I'll do it."

While waiting to learn whether to kill Jack Anderson, I grew impatient with the lack of a decision on the third GEMSTONE budget submission and decided to do something about it.... I was impressed by Chuck [Charles] Colson's coldly pragmatic approach to politics and his skills as an

---

[146] Liddy's "situational ethics" is described here and in the following paragraphs. Who decides when murder is "OK"? Liddy decides. He reminds me of Arnold Schwarzenegger, who played a CIA agent in the film, *True Lies*. When his wife, playing by Jamie Lee Curtis, demanded to know whether he had killed people in his job, he replied: "Yes. But they were all bad." We all laughed, it was such an amusing line. But...deep down we know that CIA agents in the "kill if necessary" branch not only have a license to kill, like James Bond, but they also must display the willingness and ability to do so when it is "called for." Hey wait: Isn't Schwarzenegger currently the Republican Governor of California, and wasn't there recently a "spontaneous" drive to get a Constitutional Amendment passed so that he wouldn't need to be a native-born American to be eligible to run for President? When it came out that Arnold's admired Daddy was a genuine Nazi, and that Arnold admired Hitler, this movement seemed to fizzle out in a cloud of smoke, fire and brimstone. Just lucky, I guess.

[147] In the same way, Bush, Rumsfeld, Condosleeza and Co. consider the thousands of Iraqi civilian victims of this current illegal "war" not even worth counting, or mentioning. Of course, they are also trying to hide the news about our G.I. casualties, as well as the thousands of American soldiers who have been seriously wounded in this illegal and arbitrary war.

[148] Bush's "war on terrorism" came home to America when, as many have noted, 3000+ U.S. civilians were murdered in the controlled demolition of the two WTC buildings on 9/11/01, so Bush and Co. could "get their war on," complete with the pre-prepared "Patriot Act" rammed down Congress's throat. See bibliography for David Griffin's two books on the 9/11 "controlled demolition" fraud, our new "JFK Assassination." My nomination for the company which wired the World Trade Center for destruction: Controlled Demolitions, Inc., which "completed" the demolition of the Murrah Building in Oklahoma, after its partial demolition; and whisked away the steel beams from both the Murrah Building and the World Trade Center mass murder site, sold to China before anyone could examine them for signs of planned demolition which would have been evident on examination.

infighter and concluded I might kill two birds with one stone.

I approached Hunt and laid it out for him. I wanted him to introduce me to Colson. There I would not only seek to gain an ally in the second Nixon administration, I'd ask Chuck to kick some ass and get us a decision on GEMSTONE. Hunt was obliging and, in the latter part of February, arranged an appointment; he made the introduction, then withdrew to the rear of the room while I spoke to Colson....[149]

[Maurice] Stans gave me an office near Hugh Sloan's and a secretary par excellence, Sally Harmony... I repaid Stans's thoughtfulness by promptly devising a way for people of wealth with stock that had appreciated greatly in value to donate it to the finance committee with no tax consequences to either the donor or the committee, even though the committee got full benefit of the long-term capital gain...

About 1 April I received a telephone call: "You've got a 'go' on your project." I gave Hunt the good news, but there was little I could do at the moment. The new federal election law would take effect on 7 April, and it required disclosure of the identities of donors. The finance committee had a backlog of people who were willing to give, but only on condition that their identity would not be made public. That required that their donations all be picked up in a matter of days, and everyone in a senior position on the committee, including me, was pressed into service as a collector.

In the days before 7 April, I arranged the setting up of enough committees to spread out $50,000 from Howard Hughes and collected the checks in the offices of Hunt's employer, the Mullen Company.[150] I flew to New York to pick up another $50,000 from one of the Rockefellers, then on to Detroit, Buffalo, St. Louis, and Chicago to pick up checks or shares of stock, or to have large shares broken up into smaller lots by transfer agents....

As soon as the new election law deadline had passed, I went to see Hugh Sloan with my budget. I showed it to him, told him I was authorized $250,000, and said I'd need $83,000 immediately. Sloan, exhausted by the last-minute collection rush, barely looked at the budget sheet, waved at the disorder in his office, and asked me to come back later....

At my instructions McCord had rented an office suite adjacent to that of Muskie's on K Street, Northwest, from which I had intended to launch one of the OPAL entries. McCord, Hunt, and I had already surveyed it, and McCord had done a good job in selecting the site....

Sloan came up with the $83,000 in hundred-dollar bills, paper-clipped together into bundles of $1,000 each and stuffed into a large manila envelope so I wouldn't be seen carrying "the green," as he called it, from his office to mine. In my office I had a five-drawer steel security file safe. The bottom drawer contained all the blueprints for the Miami Convention Center. Now in the top drawer I placed a series of manila envelopes, 9 inches by 12 inches in size. Each envelope was labeled with a different GEMSTONE code, such as RUBY, SAPPHIRE, etc....

With GEMSTONE approved and Hunt not yet able to replace Villo [Virgilio] Gonzales as number one keyman nor find an ex-CIA wireman willing to take the job, I had run out of time for recruiting. I had been using McCord right along for advice on technical matters and for such tasks as fronting the lease of space adjacent to Muskie headquarters, but I had never intended to use him on an operation. Now I had no choice and would have to chance it, if I could persuade him. I approached him, offering an increase in pay to $2,000 per month and another $2,000 for each entry. He agreed.

The first target I selected for an OPAL entry was McGovern headquarters on Capitol Hill....

In following instructions to be ready for [Teddy] Kennedy, Hunt and I selected a mass of

---

[149] While Colson was serving time for his participation in Watergate and whatever, he "got religion," so I gather he is now, as a "born-again" Christian like El Busho, permitted to kill people if he deems it necessary. The Gospel according to born-again Christians, as I understand it, is that having accepted Christ as their Savior, they can commit any sin against humanity. Jesus will obviously step in, like the new Supreme Court, and forgive his/their butts whenever necessary, even from the fires of hell. It might be well to "Watch your Back" when dealing with these religious types. At least, try to get their "honest" opinions on how and when killing is justified, beforehand, if possible. Liddy must be tickled silly at how his beloved fascism has come back into power, after a partial eclipse when Nixon vanished from public view.

[150] Identified in the Gemstone File as a CIA front organization.

photographs from the Black Star service that depicted every aspect of Chappaquiddick, as well as some showing Kennedy sailing off Hyannis aboard his yacht a day or so later. Taken with a telephoto lens, some prints showed him with a neck brace and some without. In all, he appeared to be in excellent health and spirits. We paid a substantial amount for the large number of glossies, and then Hunt turned again to his professional art studio—the CIA. Their political section drew up a devastating series of anti-Kennedy political cartoons....

Even at those figures, the budget was tight.... As a result, when there were extra expenses, such as more money for FAT JACK for photographic work, printing for Segretti, photographs of Kennedy, and so forth, that were not in the GEMSTONE budget, I found myself robbing Peter to pay Paul. ... I put IOU's into the envelope such as "$500 for Kennedy photographs" so I'd know how much to replace and where, should I ever get ahead.

I gave the bulk of the $83,000 to McCord with instructions to get the $30,000 transmitter as quickly as possible, and he used the rest of the money to buy a van, small transceivers, and other sophisticated electronic gear, and to pay for the K Street offices and other expenses he had.... As a matter of principle, the Cuban men did not want money for working for their adopted country, nor for working toward what they hoped would be the eventual freeing of their native Cuba[151] with American help. However, Hunt had proposed, and I agreed, that the men not lose anything either. They all worked, and when they did anything for us it cost them lost wages and commissions. Hunt and I calculated their losses generously and recompensed them....

Near the end of April Magruder sent word that he wanted to see me. I thought he had another unbudgeted project in mind and was in a cold mood when I entered. My assumption proved incorrect.

Magruder asked, "Gordon, do you think you could get into the Watergate?"

I knew just what he meant. I had targeted the DNC headquarters for later, when and if it became the headquarters of the successful Democratic candidate at their convention, so I said, "Yes. It's a high-security building, but we can do it. It's a bit early, though."

Magruder understood and replied, "How about putting a bug in [Larry] O'Brien's office?"

Larry O'Brien was by now involved in gearing up for the Democratic convention and was spending most of his time in Miami....

[Magruder] said, "We want to know whatever's said in his office, just as if it was here; what goes on in this office...."

I thought of the $30,000 device I had ordered from McCord and said, "All right, we can do that."

"The phones, too. And while you're in there, photograph whatever you can find."

...I said, "O.K., we'll do it...."

I saw McCord and gave him the target. He promised to check out the interior of DNC quickly to get the layout. When I asked him if he'd have the listening device in hand soon, he assured me that he would.

J. Edgar Hoover died on 2 May and was laid out in state in the rotunda of the Capitol. His presence there attracted leftist activists like ghouls to a graveyard. An anti-Vietnam rally that week took place on the Mall, and police reports described the participants as marching under the Vietcong flag. Daniel Ellsberg and other radicals were slated to participate in another such rally, and once again Magruder called on me.

He alluded to the rally that had taken place. "The President is really pissed about that [Vietcong] flag being used on the Mall. They're gonna do it again. Do you think your guys could break it up and get it?"

"Get what?"

"The flag. Colson wants to give it to The Man."

I told Jeb I could probably bring up a team of Cubans from Miami to break up the rally, or at

---

[151] *I.e.*, return to a Batista-like dictatorship.

least cause a noticeable disturbance and sign of opposition. If there was a V.C. flag, a coordinated attack focusing on it should be able to succeed...

I...brought up some Cuban heavyweights under [Bernard] Barker, and they went to the rally. This time there was no flag in evidence. They disrupted Ellsberg's speech and punched out some radicals sufficiently hard for Barker to have injured his hands and Frank Sturgis to have been detained by police; but the cops were sympathetic and let him go. The men returned to our headquarters at the Mullen Company to report....

Hunt and I drove the men to the area surrounding McGovern's headquarters, and Hunt announced it to be the site of an upcoming entry operation. We checked the alley and rear doors and noted escape routes. Then, on the way back, I took us past the Watergate and said this place would come first, then permitted the men to return home....

Sloan asked to see me and showed me a package of signed traveler's checks. He explained that they were a donation left over from the 1968 campaign and that to ask the donors to exchange them for cash at this late date would be embarrassing. The money was needed because it was "green" and that was hard to get now that the new election law was in effect. Could our people turn the traveler's checks into cash? ...

Hunt and I flew to Miami and conferred with Barker. He said he could arrange things through a Cuban banker who would process the thousands of dollars in traveler's checks in such a way that our problem would be solved.[152] Barker was good as his word, and in a short time I was able to turn over the cash, less the expense of the trip to Miami, to Hugh Sloan....

Sloan approached me again, this time with a $25,000 cashier's check from a Minnesota businessman, Kenneth Dahlberg, made out to himself and dated 10 April. He told me that it represented the contribution that someone else made prior to 7 April, but converted so as to become anonymous. He also had four checks made payable to Manuel Ogarrio, drawn on Ogarrio's account at the Banco Nacional in Mexico City on 4 April in the amounts of $15,000, $18,000, $24,000, and $32,000. Because the Dahlberg check was dated after 7 April, although representing pre-statute money, and the other checks were on a Mexican bank, he asked me if I could convert them to a total of $114,000 in cash.

...When I turned the money over to Sloan, I deducted not only the expenses of converting the $114,000 but also the un-reimbursed GEMSTONE budget withdrawal to cover the fee Barker's banker charged for the first transaction. The total I placed in the GEMSTONE treasury came to $2,500, made up of twenty-five one-hundred-dollar bills. They were well worn. Unfortunately many of those given to me by Barker and turned over to Hugh Sloan were not; they were brand new, serialized consecutively, and they sat in his safe, ticking away like a time bomb.

On 7 May I was called to a meeting in the offices of the Committee to Re-elect and learned, in strictest confidence, that within twenty-four hours the President would take forceful action to end the Vietnam war. The President's action, I was told, would generate fierce opposition from the radicals who were insisting upon U.S. surrender. My assignment, and that of the others attending the meeting, was to immediately generate as much support from the public, the press, and Congress as possible. This program was to be given the highest priority.

I called Howard Hunt and told him that I wanted our Cuban people to organize public demonstrations of support in the Miami area. Money was no object. There went the GEMSTONE budget again.

On 8 May President Nixon announced he was mining the harbor of Haiphong and resuming the bombing of North Vietnam. All hell broke loose on the left. There was a general meeting attended by John Mitchell and addressed by General Alexander Haig, who briefed us on what was being done militarily. After his briefing Haig asked for questions. I don't believe he expected any; these were political, not military, people.

But I took him at his word. "General," I asked, "why haven't we bombed the Red river dikes? If we did that, we'd drown half the country and starve the other half. Those few railroad lines coming in from China'd have to carry nothing but food; there'd be no room for ammunition."

---

[152] Through an unnamed Miami Mafia Bank money laundry, probably still operating full blast.

Before Haig could answer, John Mitchell jumped in: "We don't need any amateur military advice. Let's not have any more of that."

Once again it was emphasized, by both Haig and Mitchell, that the most important thing any of us had to do was to influence opinion in favor of the President's initiative and counter the media manipulation against him by the radical left. I coordinated all information on the campaign to influence public opinion and Congress. On Monday, 15 May, I sent John Mitchell a confidential memorandum entitled "Reaction to the President's Vietnam Response."

...Concerning the work of the Cubans in Miami I reported:

"Earlier reports mentioned plans for a rally on Saturday evening, May 13, at Bay Front Park, Miami, Florida. Because of differences of opinion in the Cuban community and some internal jealousies, it was thought best to cancel the rally and to substitute a motorcade on Saturday afternoon.

"Accordingly, on the afternoon of Saturday, May 13, a motorcade of 200 automobiles and 60 trucks was assembled at the Central Shopping Plaza, 37th Avenue and 7th Street, NW, Miami. The vehicles were placarded with signs such as "Nixon—We Back You 100%" and "Free the POWS Now," as well as a number reading "Tell It to Hanoi." The motorcade lasted two and one-half hours (2:00 p.m. to 4:30 p.m.); starting at the Central Shopping Plaza, the route went south on 37th Avenue to the Tamiami Trail, then to Biscayne Boulevard and then all the way back up Flagler to 32nd Avenue. As the motorcade proceeded with lights on, more than 200 more vehicles joined the caravan, having a total of nearly 500 vehicles (automobiles and trucks)...."

The next day Howard Hunt called on the phone. He [told me] that Alabama Governor George Wallace, then campaigning for the Democratic presidential nomination in Laurel, Maryland, had been shot and critically wounded the day before by a would-be assassin named Arthur Bremer.[153] Bremer, he said, lived in Milwaukee, and Colson wanted Hunt to search his apartment to find out what he could about Bremer's background and motivation and, possibly, to plant some documentation there linking Bremer to the radical left. Hunt was apprehensive about the assignment and asked my opinion of the chances for success.

I told Hunt that if Colson knew the name and address of the assailant, he must have gotten it from the Secret Service or the FBI, and that if they knew it, they were already all over that apartment.... I told Hunt that the risk was enormous and the chance of gain slight, pointing out that in the unlikely event he was successful and got into the place to plant his material linking Bremer to the radicals, when it was found thereafter by the FBI, they'd be suspicious immediately because it hadn't been there when they searched the place themselves. That was enough for Hunt. He informed me later that Colson had called the assignment off.

The sterile CIA 9-mm parabellum pistol I had acquired was designed for use by insurgents to assassinate Communist cadre members abroad. I intended it for use in the event Bud Krogh or other of my White House superiors tasked me with an assassination. The Jack Anderson matter would be a good example. But the CIA pistol was unsilenced. I needed a silent weapon, recalling that I had had to resort to the Browning knife in the Fielding operation. The CIA 9-mm was not threaded for use with the preferred Maxim-pattern silencer, nor was the 7.65-mm Colt semiautomatic pistol I had, which had been delivered by Colt directly to the OSS, the predecessor of the CIA.

To fill this need I acquired a 4-mm German-manufactured Walther LP (for luftpistole) air pistol. It was silent, powerful, virtually recoil-less, and, with target sights, superbly accurate; at ten meters (about thirty-three feet) every shot would go inside a dime. Using a pointed lead projectile coated with easily obtainable pure nicotine, lethal delivery would be silent, swift, and sure. In the basement of my house in Oxon Hill, where there was a second fireplace to act as a backstop and I had sufficient privacy and range, I practiced until I was as familiar with the Walther as with my favorite Smith & Wesson, then took it to my office at the finance committee and put it away in the file safe, replacing the CIA 9-mm, which I took home.

The GEMSTONE budget was really short now, so I welcomed Howard Hunt's suggestion that

---

[153] See Roberts' comments on Wallace and Bremer, another hypnotized "Government"-sponsored assassin.

we have [Thomas] Gregory[154] admit McCord into McGovern head-quarters without bringing up the Cubans to act as guards. If we could cut down the ten-thousand-dollar budgeted expense for penetration of McGovern's headquarters, some of the GEMSTONE funds expended for unbudgeted tasks could be made up.

Gregory arranged a tour of McGovern headquarters for McCord, who posed as his out-of-town uncle. That was successful, and McCord reported that the place had an alarm attached to the rear door that operated on a delay.... All Gregory had to do was admit him after everyone else had left for the evening,

Gregory had been staying late so that he could give us the tally of McGovern contribution receipts on a day-by-day basis, as well as contributor lists, schedules, and any copies of position papers before they were made public. Now Hunt asked him to hide in the furnace room and wait until the building was empty, then let McCord in. It didn't work. He was discovered, had to do some fast talking, and leave....

With Gregory so jittery, Hunt changed plans. He'd bring up only two Cubans—Barker and Martinez—and have them play a reprise of their successful Fielding entry in Beverly Hills.[155] This time they would arrive at McGovern's with a heavy package crate for delivery. McCord would be their supervisor, and all three would be dressed in deliveryman uniforms. McCord would slip away and plant his bugs in the five minutes it would take for Barker and Martinez to deliver the crate and get a complicated set of receipts signed for, "properly, according to the new rules."

Just as that plan was to go into effect, Gregory reported that there had been an attempted burglary at McGovern's and that the place was now guarded by a Burns Agency man posted inside the front door twenty-four hours a day. This called for still further plan modification because Gregory was now even more frightened. We'd have to get more Cubans and a credible package.

The new plan called for the purchase of a very expensive and complex electric typewriter. McCord would be the salesman who had come along to insure proper installation. The typewriter itself would be bugged, just so we'd have something in there should McCord not be able to get loose long enough from the Burns man to plant bugs in the offices of Mankiewicz and Hart.

Although we were now concentrating on McGovern, Muskie had not yet given up and we did not neglect him....When *Newsweek* reprinted excerpts from a nasty article against Mrs. Muskie in *Women's Wear Daily*, I had been ordered by Magruder to exploit it. With so much else to do, I hadn't got around to it.

I was trying to think of what to do with the *Newsweek* article when I suddenly recalled what the Democrats had done to Richard Nixon in 1960 with the "Nixon Deed."[156] I took the page from *Newsweek*, got a brush and red ink, and outlined the most derogatory portion, then wrote in big red letters, SHAME!

From GEMSTONE funds we had that page reproduced by the thousands with the red overprint and distributed it all over the country. It had taken me twelve years, but I had finally closed the "Nixon Deed" case to my satisfaction.

On Monday, 22 May, Bernard Barker, Eugenio Martinez, Virgilio Gonzales, Frank Sturgis, Felipe De Diego, and Reinaldo Pico flew up to Washington from Miami and moved into the Hamilton Hotel until rooms at the Watergate became available. The Watergate penetration was

---

[154] A planted "volunteer" in Muskie's camp. He was a student, a young nephew of Robert Bennett, Hunt's employer at the Mullen Corp., a CIA front organization. Here is a teen-ager quite willing to participate in illegal activities at the behest of his elder relatives. So much for Jack White's certainty that the teenage students standing in the pergola doorway couldn't have had anything to do with the JFK Assassination, "because they were just teenager students." Jack, call this "opinion" but please don't confuse it with evidence!

[155] This was the "burglary" of Ellsberg's psychiatrist's office by the CIA Plumbers' Unit, criminal enough, but apparently not included in Liddy's "GEMSTONE" plans. Note that play-acting, deceptive phony uniforms and such, were common to such "intelligence" operations, here at home as well as abroad.

[156] This apparently refers to the $205,000 "unsecured loan" made to Donald Nixon, Richard's brother, for his failing "Nixonburger" restaurant in Whittier, California, in 1956, by "Howard Hughes,", either just before or just after he was snatched by Onassis. In either case, it "bought" Nixon for Onassis. In any case, Nixon had already been "vetted" for corruptibility by those California businessmen who had set this pawn on the chessboard years earlier. The "loan" was "secured" by a $13,000 parking lot owned by Nixon's mother.—sc

scheduled for Friday night, 26 May. The intervening days were spent meeting with Jim McCord and Thomas Gregory and their familiarizing themselves with the areas immediately around both McGovern's headquarters and the Watergate complex. There was a large convention in Washington at that time called "Transpo '72." It made an excellent cover for the Cuban contingent. Groups of men were moving about all the hotels in town and our group just signed the General Security Services log in the lobby of the Watergate office building and went right on up to inspect the entrance to DNC headquarters. Hunt took a soft clay impression of the lock on the front door.

McCord told me he had rented a room at the Howard Johnson's motel across the street from the Watergate, but it was on the fourth floor. To see into the DNC offices, he'd need one higher up, which he promised to get. To my annoyance he still had not obtained the listening device I'd ordered, nor, in fact, did he yet have even the small transceivers.... He explained that he had to get FCC clearance for their frequencies. That annoyed me. It's like registering a gun you're going to use in a holdup.

We made familiarization tours of both places in darkness as well as daylight so we'd know them well under operational conditions. During these meetings and tours I noticed an annoying habit in McCord. He was like Lamont Cranston, always slipping away, only to reappear when there was something specific for him to do....

Hunt was reporting increasing nervousness in Bennett's nephew, Gregory, and I was not at all sure he'd prove to be any help in penetrating McGovern's head-quarters. In that event we'd have to run a complete OPAL operation. Because of the Burns guard on the front door, the obvious entry point would be the rear door, which also had the advantage of being on the floor below. The chief problem with the rear door was that it was brightly illuminated by two clusters of flood-lights. One cluster was over the rear door itself, the other farther out toward the alley where it supplemented the light from a street lamp. I decided that the floodlights would have to be extinguished, and that it would be best to do it immediately to see whether it attracted attention and immediate replacement.

To do the job I purchased some blunt-nosed 4-mm Benjamin projectiles for the Walther, then bought four flood-lamps identical to those in use at McGovern head-quarters. Retrieving the Walther from my file safe, I brought it home and set up the flood-lamps in the fireplace in my basement. I found that with the blunt-nosed ammunition the Walther would smash through the heavy weatherproof glass of the flood-lamps at a range of ten meters so long as the projectiles hit head-on, at a 90-degree angle. On 24 May I brought the Walther with me to the office and put it in the file safe.

When Hugh Sloan called me into his office shortly before noon the following day, 25 May, I regretted having taken the CIA 9-mm home. He displayed a suitcase filled for the most part with one-hundred-dollar bills, but a few bundles of fifties and some five hundreds were also in evidence. It was lunch-time, and he said he had to deposit $350,000 in cash at a bank at 15th and Pennsylvania—just a two-block walk past the White House. He was concerned about robbery and asked me to go along with him for protection. I agreed. With the 9-mm no longer in my safe, the only thing I had with which to arm myself was the Walther with the Benjamin projectiles. I loaded it and slipped it under my belt. Because I had no nicotine, if necessary I would shoot any would-be robber in the eye. The projectile would penetrate to the brain easily through the eggshell-thin bone at the rear of the socket and kill instantly.

Sloan and I had planned on lunch, but we didn't realize how long it would take when the bank required us to participate in the counting of the cash. Even in bills that large, it took more than an hour to get through the $350,000 to the satisfaction of the bank officer, so we were very hungry by the time we had finished. We walked back to Lafayette Park, opposite the White House, then decided to have lunch in the downstairs dining room of the Hay Adams Hotel on 16th Street, just across the park from the White House.

Both of us went to the men's room, where Sloan was startled to see me draw the Walther. I no longer needed a loaded gun and I didn't want to put any more strain on the air seal than necessary, so I discharged the pistol into a toilet to release the pressure. It was noiseless, and I knew from my FBI experience that water slows down and stops a high-velocity projectile rapidly. We had used a water tank to recover fired bullets for comparison examinations....

On the night of 25 May we all made another tour of McGovern's headquarters area. I brought the Walther with me and, after the others were clear, Frank Sturgis and I walked through the alley to

the brightly lighted area of the rear door. There, with Sturgis watching my back, I used the single-shot Walther to shoot out the three floodlights over the rear door.... The luftpistole was silent, and all that could be heard was the breaking of the glass and the shssssss of the escaping gas that filled the bulbs as it flared briefly before they died....

On 26 May the Cubans all moved into the Watergate Hotel under assumed names, posing as a group working for a corporation named Ameritas. The DNC headquarters was in a different building in the complex, the Watergate Office Building, which was well guarded. Our survey had found that not one but two guard services afforded it protection: General Security Services (GSS), which had a man on duty all the time, and the Federal Reserve Board (FRB) guards. The FRB had space both in the basement and on the eighth floor of the office building and had recently been burglarized. While the FRB guards were not there all the time because they had to check on other FRB space on a roving basis, we found they were frequent visitors to the halls of Watergate, probably because of the burglary. The GSS guard was known to inspect the entire building following every shift change.

To get to the DNC headquarters on the sixth floor by conventional means meant walking over to the lobby where the elevators and stairwell were within easy view of the GSS guard post, where one would be required to sign in. Another route was through the garage on a lower floor and, finally, an underground corridor that connected the hotel and the office building. The underground corridor was the first choice because it led to both the stairwell and elevator at a point two floors below the guard post. The problem was that it ran from a banquet room, the Continental Room, which also led to the inner court through an exterior door.

We had found that the Continental Room door to the corridor was equipped with an electric alarm, so we couldn't get through the banquet room after hours without first defeating it. McCord discovered that the door alarm wasn't activated until 11 p.m. That proved the key to our plan.

Ameritas told the Watergate Hotel that it wanted to hold a dinner meeting and presentation. To allay suspicion and kill time Hunt had a multi-course banquet ordered and rented a motion picture projector and travel film to play after the dinner. The plan was to keep the meeting going until after the waiters had all cleaned up and—well tipped—left us alone in the Continental Room. We expected the DNC headquarters would be vacant well before 11 p.m. on a Friday night.

...Banquet time arrived and [we] had a good time.... The film went on as scheduled and was so boring the waiters were encouraged to clean up and leave us early .... Finally, at 10:30 p.m., with no word from McCord that the DNC offices had yet been vacated, a guard making his periodic rounds looked in and told us we'd have to leave. Everyone did, except Hunt and Gonzales, who stayed behind to turn out the lights, hoping to receive word from McCord over the transceiver before the alarm was armed on the corridor door at 11 p.m. They hid in a liquor closet. By 11 p.m. the word from McCord had not come that the DNC was clear. A guard locked the door leading to the inner court, and when the alarm on the corridor was armed at 11:00, Hunt and Gonzales were effectively locked into the Continental Room until the next day.

Gonzales slipped out of the closet and tried but failed to pick the court door lock. A guard appeared and swept the inside of the banquet room with his flashlight through the glass door to the inner court, and Gonzales had to go back to the closet, where he and Hunt stayed the night....

...Saturday night, 27 May, we tried again, waiting until after the 8 p.m. building inspection and then for McCord to radio from the observation post when the DNC was clear.... The hours passed without word from McCord, and when it finally came I thought it too close to the midnight shift change and building inspection. We waited until that was accomplished and sent in the team again; Hunt and I waited to learn by radio from Barker of the successful entry.

The message never came. In about forty-five minutes the team reappeared at the command post in the Watergate Hotel room Hunt and I shared. Barker reported failure to gain entrance, saying that Gonzales had worked long and hard on the lock on the front door to no avail. The excuse offered was that Gonzales had not brought the necessary tools with him from Miami. I was disgusted; then, as Barker told me how hard Villo had worked, even somewhat damaging the lock, I was worried. If the damage was noticeable, the Democrats would be alerted to the fact that an entry attempt had been made and would take the necessary precautions to prevent future penetration or to trap the entry team.... I'd have to inspect the lock myself, and the sooner the better....

I took a couple of Cubans and, all of us dressed in business suits, approached the guard confidently, scribbled on the register, and went up to DNC headquarters. The lock bore the marks of tampering, but they weren't obvious. Relieved, I looked around the lobby area once, then took the elevator back to the lobby, scribbled on the log again, and returned to the command post in the hotel. There I overrode Hunt's objections and ordered Gonzales to return to Miami the following morning for the correct tools....

Late Sunday afternoon I rejoined Hunt in the Watergate Hotel command post. Gonzales had returned with what he assured us were the proper tools. I didn't think it wise to try to have the team sign in at the guard post again; two nights in a row would be pressing our luck. Hunt suggested the garage-level entrance doors and McCord agreed to tape them open. It was an old maintenance man's trick. They all carry keys but to use them time after time just gets to be too much trouble. Experienced guards are used to finding doors taped open no matter how often the maintenance people are admonished. It is done across the lock bolt and around the edge of the doors, rather than along the inside edge of the door, for a very good reason; with the commonly carried electrician's tape, that's the only way it will work. Tape placed edgewise hasn't enough purchase to restrain the strongly spring-loaded bolt of commercial building doors. Even if it did work we wanted it to look like a maintenance man's routine, and they don't do it that way. Why should they? They're not trying to burglarize the place and have nothing to fear from discovery. Burglars don't tape the locks. They wedge a matchstick in between the bolt and the bolt opening, then snap it off flush. I would not have approved that method; if discovered by a guard, it's a dead giveaway; he knows immediately he has a burglary on his hands. At about 9:45 p.m. McCord reported from the observation post that the lights had gone out in DNC headquarters and, a few minutes later, that a man had left the building. Because it was Sunday night Hunt was sure no one would be going back in later, but with the experience of the previous weekend behind us, and the fact that the Democratic National Convention was coming up soon, I thought it best to wait and see. At 11 p.m. I was satisfied. That would give our men an hour to enter, do the electronic work, and still get out before the midnight shift change and building inspection.

To Hunt's and my delight, that's exactly how it went. McCord reported success, and Barker had two rolls of 36-exposure 35-mm film he'd expended on material from O'Brien's desk, along with Polaroid shots of the desk and office.... I congratulated them all and we had a small victory celebration in the command post before going home. The Watergate entry had been successful. Or so I thought....

[As it turned out, nothing of value was obtained from the first penetration of the Watergate DNC office. So it was determined to make a second try.—sc]

[Magruder had said,] "Take all the men, all the cameras you need. That's what I want to know!" There was a world of significance in Magruder's gesture. When he said "here" and slapped that particular portion of his desk, he was referring to the place he kept his derogatory information on the Democrats.... The purpose of the second Watergate break-in was to find out what O'Brien had of a derogatory nature about us, not for us to get something on him or the Democrats.[157]

Magruder didn't tell me what he either expected, or was afraid, we'd find in O'Brien's files. He instructed that we go in there with all the film, men, and cameras necessary to photograph everything in [O'Brien's] desk and in those files....

On the afternoon of Friday, 16 June, Hunt called to tell me that Barker, Martinez, Gonzales, and Sturgis had arrived from Miami and were occupying rooms 214 and 314 at "the location," meaning the Watergate Hotel.... The chances that the DNC offices would be vacant by 8:30 p.m. weren't very good anyway, so we agreed to meet in room 214 about then, which at that time of year would be just about dark....

I walked into the Watergate Hotel, glancing up at DNC headquarters, and noticing that the lights were on, took the elevator to the second floor, where I joined Hunt and the Cubans in room 214.

The room was in disarray. Personal belongings and photographic equipment (such as special

---

[157] This is exactly what Bruce Roberts wrote in the Gemstone File in 1972.

lights) were much in evidence, and Barker and Martinez were practicing rapid operation of the two Minolta cameras they had brought for their massive photographic assignment. Sturgis would assist and Gonzales would attend to unlocking all the cabinets. This time Reinaldo Pico and Felipe De Diego were not with the team. Previously they had acted as guards, hiding outside the DNC entrance in the stairwell and just inside the door, ready to silence the building guard should he pull a surprise inspection not noticed from the observation post in time for the team to get away.

About eleven o'clock McCord came in. Typically, he'd stayed away, over in the observation post, reporting once in a while by phone that the DNC was still occupied. ....McCord said that the DNC offices were still occupied, but that didn't matter either. By ten o'clock I had decided not to go until after the midnight inspection. ...

McCord said that he'd already taped the garage-level doors by the simple expedient of going in through the lobby and down the stairwell. From the inside, of course, the door to the garage was not locked, so he simply opened it and taped it so that later the team could get into the stairwell via the garage. Not surprisingly, he now wanted to go back to the observation post....

As 12:30 a.m. came and went there was still no call from McCord in the observation post. Either the DNC offices were still occupied or McCord could not monitor the progress of the guard as he inspected the building and was waiting until he finished....

...At about 12:45 a.m. McCord phoned to say "it's clear" and that he was on his way over. All fatigue vanished as the men got themselves ready....Within a few minutes McCord, Barker, and Martinez were back wearing troubled expressions. McCord said that when they had gotten down to the garage-level doors they found that the tape he had put across the locks earlier had been removed. McCord said he thought it might have been a mailman who did it because there were some mail sacks in evidence.[158] Hunt was sure it had been a guard. He wanted to abort. McCord didn't think it necessary to abort and said Gonzales was unlocking the doors from the garage side, protected by Sturgis, so we could go forward or not, however it was decided....

Eugenio Martinez, who is afraid of absolutely nothing, said, "Sure, George; whatever is the decision." Barker said, "I'm ready either way."

I knew Hunt's position. I took McCord aside. I knew him better than Hunt did. I wanted to get his opinion of the situation. He spoke quietly and with professional detachment. The tape had not popped off, someone had removed it. Some mail sacks were nearby. He would go with the decision either way. I asked his preference. He was, after all, one of the entry team and taking far more risk than Hunt or I. He said he thought it normal for the tape to be removed when discovered and would just as soon go in and get the job over with.

The decision was up to me. I was the leader and it was my responsibility.

The others accepted that and would abide by my judgment. I knew that lock-taping was a common, if disapproved, practice of maintenance personnel in large buildings. That should not have alarmed the guard, who could be expected to remove it. I saw no reason that the guard should think anything other than that the maintenance people would have to be lectured.

I had no idea that McCord was going to re-tape the locks.[159] I understood that Gonzales would open the doors and he and Sturgis would hold them that way for the few minutes it took for a decision. Once in, the tape was supposed to be removed behind the team anyway. We had a safety valve in the observation post. When our men were inside, the offices would still be in darkness. The approach of a guard with a flashlight could be seen easily and Martinez and Sturgis could take care of any rent-a-cop. Were police called, they'd be noticed immediately when the cruisers drove up.

---

[158] Here is the evidence that Hal Lipset, dressed as a mailman with mail sacks, probably containing his equipment, had been there, done something, and removed himself from the scene. Roberts says Lipset retaped the door, twice, and that Wills, the guard, removed the tape the first time, but called the cops the second time. Liddy blames James McCord for not removing the tape after the Plumbers' entry. McCord's book, *A Piece of Tape*, presents his own take on the matter, and is well worth reading.

[159] Liddy blames McCord for "retaping" the door. But McCord was a cool character, and Gonzales the locksmith was there ready and able to pick the lock and let them in, so why would McCord have done so? Roberts says Hal Lipset retaped the door, thereby setting the trap for the Plumbers, which was indeed sprung when Wills the guard returned for his next round of inspection. Liddy takes responsibility for proceeding with the break-in, but shifts the blame for its failure to McCord.

Under all those circumstances I did not feel justified in aborting and decided to send the men in....

I locked the door to the hotel room behind the three as they left. The team of five did go through that garage-to-stairwell door and on up the stairs—failing to remove the now-functionless tape from the door. This was fatal since it was only after finding the same door taped a second time that the guard called the police. It was now nearly 1:30 a.m., and we had a long night of waiting ahead of us. The radio call sign for the command post was simply "one;" "two" was the entry team, and "three" the observation post. We had been using the telephone between the observation post and command post, but that was only safe when there were messages no more significant than "nothing yet" or "clear." For communications about the entry we had to rely on the security of the transceivers.... The television set was on low as I waited for word over the radio that the team had made the entry and gotten inside without incident. That word never came.

Just after 2 a.m.[160] there was a transmission over the radio: "There's flashlights on the eighth floor."

It was McCord's man at the observation post. I repeated the news to Hunt. We agreed that it was probably one of the two guard forces making a 2 a.m. door check. We were not concerned, believing that our team would be in darkness and not visible through the glass doors, which they would have locked from the inside behind them after Gonzales picked the lock to gain entry. The next transmission was mine: "One to two. Did you read that?" There was no answer.

"One to three. Keep us advised."

The next transmission seemed to support our theory of a guard's making a routine check: "Now they're on the seventh floor." There was a pause, then came the query, in a wondering tone that made its way through even the low fidelity of the transceiver: "Hey, any of our guys wearin' hippie clothes?"

It was only then that Hunt and I realized that something was very wrong.

"One to three. Negative. All our people are in business suits. Why?"

"They're on the sixth floor now. Four or five guys. One's got on a cowboy hat. One's got on a sweat shirt. It looks like... guns. They've got guns. It's trouble!"

Hunt and I were standing now. I said, "Shit!" and hit the mike switch: "One to two. Are you reading this? Come in!"

Hunt grimaced, convulsively lifted his right knee up toward his chest, then spun around to pound his right fist into his left palm. "One to two," I repeated. "Come in. That's an order!" That finally brought the first and last transmission we were to receive from the entry team. A whispered voice said, simply and calmly: "They got us."

The observation post obeyed my prior order to keep us advised: "Now I can see our people. They've got their hands up. Must be the cops."

Hunt went out on the balcony to see whether he could see anything, as the observation post continued to report: "More cops now; uniforms..."

Hunt and I began packing everything of an incriminating nature that we could find, intending to leave the room clean. Suddenly Hunt said, "Damn!"

"Now what?"

"We've gotta get out fast. I just remembered. Macho's [Barker] got this room key."

We took what we had and started to leave. Hunt went over to the antenna to take it when we received a last transmission from the observation post: "What should I do now?"

---

[160] Since "the team" went in at 1:30 and were snooping, talking, and photographing, etc., for half an hour before interruption, and Lipset's "mail bags" were presumably empty, Lipset would have gotten quite an earful and lots of tape on the Plumbers "plumbing", which is what Roberts described. This is what, in Katharine Graham's hands, turned into "Deep Throat's" info for her young reporter employees, Woodward and Bernstein, which Graham then allowed to be printed in her newspaper, the *Washington Post*. Has anyone every heard of a mailman dragging mail sacks around at 1:30 a.m.? Or, for that matter, a major newspaper owner allowing two young reporters write such important articles without KNOWING who their major source was? For those who have been "looking for Mr. Deep Throat" for decades, I can only whisper: "Get real!"

Both my hands were full so Hunt answered: "Stay put. Keep the lights out and stay out of sight. I'll be right over."

Howard slipped the antenna down his pants leg, which gave him a stiff-legged gait, as we snapped out the lights, closed the door, and walked to the elevator. It was a quick trip down one floor. The door opened and we walked easily past the desk to the front door and out to the street. The place was swarming with police and squad cars; their flashing lights cast Christmas-like reflections incongruously in the warm June night. As Hunt turned right toward his car, he said, "Where's your Jeep?"

"Up ahead. On the other side of the street. Facing this way."

"Get in. I'll drive you up a few blocks and you can approach from the other direction,"

"Good idea, Thanks."

We drove east on Virginia leaving the arrest scene behind Crossing the first intersection. Hunt pulled over to the right and let me out. "You got the contingency fund ready?" I asked him.

"My office safe. I'll get it just as soon as I take care of McCord's man...."

Hunt made a U-turn and headed back toward Howard Johnson's while I walked across the street, then headed the same way on foot. I got into my Jeep and drove slowly past the now bustling area in front of the Watergate, turned right at the intersection, and headed home

It was about 3 a.m. when I eased my way into the bedroom, trying not to awaken Fran. Light streamed into the room from the street light outside, and I could see her still form as I started quietly to undress. After a moment she stirred. I stopped moving, hoping she'd stay asleep. Hunt would, I thought, think back to the original plan for GEMSTONE—the one in which all entry people were to be untraceable and, in the event of difficulty, be bailed out under their aliases only to disappear—if necessary to Nicaragua, where Hunt had close ties with the Somoza family. I knew that wouldn't work now. Alias or not, McCord had been an FBI agent and his prints were on file in the identification division; they'd make him in twenty-four hours at the latest. Fran stirred again. "Is that you?"

"Yes."

I continued undressing. Fran has a sixth sense. Maybe all women married to the same man for fifteen years do.

"Anything wrong?"

"There was trouble. Some people got caught. I'll probably be going to jail."

Perhaps the experience of the FBI years told Fran it would pointless to inquire further. She closed her eyes and said no more. Neither did I. What more was there to say?

I climbed in bed and went to sleep....

[The next morning] I drove to CRP headquarters, parked in the underground garage across the street, and went to a nearby coffee shop for breakfast.... I signed in at about 8:30 a.m. and went up to my office, closing and locking the door behind me and opening the GEMSTONE file safe.

I went through all the envelopes first, removing receipts from FAT JACK, Tom Gregory, and anything else but the cash, then went around the corner to the utility coffee room that housed the shredder. It was one of those few approved by the government for destruction of classified documents, cutting paper into little more than long, curling threads. The machine was slow, but absolutely sure, and I sacrificed speed for that security, feeding no more than two or three sheets in at a time...

The only thing I couldn't get into the shredder was the huge roll of blueprints for the Convention Center in Miami, but because the Republicans would be using it too, and there was no longer a plan in existence to sabotage the air-conditioning units to which the blueprints could be linked, I thought it safe to leave them in the office.

On 15 June I was served with a summons and complaint in a suit brought by Spencer Oliver against me and about every other Republican in Washington. It demanded damages amounting to $5,050,000. The Democratic National Committee had filed a similar suit in June 1972 that was still

pending. I wasn't concerned. Committee to Re-elect the President was the principal defendant its lawyers were defending....

On 10 July I was sued by Elmer Davis,[161] a California convict who allegedly confessed to the Ellsberg break-in in a deal he made with Beverly Hills police to clear a lot of burglaries on their books after having been caught red-handed at one of them. Davis wanted $2,000,000 for being made a "scapegoat." This sort of thing continued until I was a defendant in a dozen different lawsuits and counterclaims arising out of Watergate, seeking from me a total in excess of $56,000,000. I defended myself in all of them and when the last, Jack Anderson's, was dismissed on 4 April 1978, I had the satisfaction of knowing that in six years of litigation over all those millions of dollars, I had lost not one cent and had a hell of a lot of fun.

—Excerpted from *Will: The Autobiography of G. Gordon Liddy*, Chapters 17-22.

---

[161] You're not going to believe this!!!—but this was the same Elmer Davis who moved into Mae Brussell's spare bedroom, in 1974, after I departed. The same Elmer with whom Mae had the abortive romance described in Chapter 36. Maybe Mae was the one who suggested to Elmer that he ought to sue Gordon Liddy. Sometimes I think we were all disconnected characters milling about under the same granfalloon, or gonfallon, described by Kurt Vonnegut in one of his novels. This gonfallon, which I see as a red banner floating above us, says in white letters, GEMSTONE.

45 2005: Romance and the Giant Burmese Ruby

Here is the way it was announced by the AP wire:

One of world's largest rubies on display
Last Updated (Beijing Time): 2004-10-13 11:54

Tiny fireworks seem to go off inside the deep red stone as it turns, flashes of light reflecting off the facets of one of the world's largest rubies.

Undated photo of the 23.1 carat Carmen Lucia ruby that will go on public display for the first time Saturday, Oct. 16, 2004 at the Smithsonian's National Museum of Natural History in Washington…. [AP]

The Carmen Lucia ruby goes on public display for the first time Saturday, the newest star of the National Gem Collection at the Smithsonian's National Museum of Natural History. The 23.1 carat stone "is the largest and finest faceted ruby on public display," Jeffrey Post, curator of the gem collection, said Tuesday. Discovered in Myanmar, which was formerly known as Burma—in the 1930s, the stone has been in private hands until now. Post said that when he first saw it a few years ago, it took his breath away. The gem, set in a platinum ring with diamonds, was obtained with funds donated to the museum by Dr. Peter Buck in memory of his wife. Post declined to discuss the price.

"The Carmen Lucia ruby is a breathtakingly beautiful gemstone and a magnificent gift to the American people," Post said. If it had been sold privately, chances are it never would have been available for public viewing, he said.

It's not as big as the famed Hope Diamond or some other stones but it is about as big as rubies get, Post said. And the fiery light reflected from the ruby easily draws attention away from the larger sapphire that will be displayed nearby. The two types of stone are displayed together because they are essentially the same material—corundum, or aluminum oxide, Post said. The ruby gets its red color from traces of chromium, while other materials give the sapphire its usual blue color.

Post added that some large red gems are on display in various collections labeled rubies, but many of them are actually spinels, a different type of stone that is also red. While rubies are aluminum oxide, spinels are magnesium aluminum oxide. Spinels look like rubies and attracted much interest in the past because they tend to be larger, he said.

It's impossible to set a value on the new gem, Post said, commenting that as a large, clear stone becomes better known more people become interested in it and it becomes, essentially, priceless….

Another account from the Internet adds:

"…The story is that the gem was mined in the 1930s in Burma and was in private hands until now. This may be why the stone was unknown until recently. The gem appears deep red and gives off pink flashes. The stone also windows, and was probably cut this way to save weight.

—**Collectors' Corner/Carmen Lucia Ruby**

The *New York Times* added:

A Walnut-Size Ruby With a Love Story to Tell
October 14, 2004—By Elizabeth Olson

WASHINGTON, Oct. 13—Every fabulous gem has a love story, and the 23.1-carat Burmese ruby donated to the National Gem Collection, which the Smithsonian Institution will announce on Thursday, is no exception.

The pinkish-red stone, big as a walnut, set in platinum and flanked by two substantial triangular diamonds, was never actually owned, or even worn, by Carmen Lucia Buck, whose husband, Peter, gave it to the country in her name.

The Brazilian-born Mrs. Buck, who loved and collected jewelry, including diamonds, sapphires and emeralds, heard about the large, finely faceted ruby before she died last year, said Mr. Buck, 73, a founder of the Subway sandwich chain.

"It epitomized what she liked—the finer things—and her generosity in setting up foundations for medical causes," he said in a telephone interview from his home in Danbury, Conn. "So it seemed like a really appropriate thing to do, to give it to the nation so people could come and see it. She would have really liked that people could see it and know it was the Carmen Lucia ruby, and that it wasn't locked away in a vault somewhere."

He gave the Smithsonian the money (he won't say how much, only that "the value is a lot") to purchase the ring, worth many millions of dollars. The stone, which had been in private hands for decades, will be displayed beginning on Saturday at the National Museum of Natural History, where it will join the gem collection's most famous piece, the Hope Diamond. Although not so large as the blue Hope diamond, donated by the jeweler Harry Winston, the Carmen Lucia ruby is unusual because high-quality Burmese rubies larger than 20 carats are exceedingly rare, said Jeffrey Post, a mineralogist who is the collection's curator.

"Of all the rubies known, this would rank up in the very top as the largest and finest because of its size, clarity, good color and brightness, and its pinkish highlights," Mr. Post said, showing off the ruby in the secure vault where the gem was being kept while its display case was built.

The ruby was mined in the 1930's in the Mogok region of Burma, now called Myanmar, and was owned by several European families before it was bought by a New York jeweler some 15 years ago and stored in a safe deposit box, Mr. Post said....

By February, 2005, the story made it into *Smithsonian Magazine*:

Romance — and the Stone
By Smithsonian Magazine via AP

We don't need Wagner or Tolkien to tell us how powerful rings can be, though it must be said those two make the point pretty convincingly. The Carmen Lucia ruby is bright red with undertones of pink and purple, a coveted hue known as "pigeon blood red."

It is as tokens of love that rings are most endearing. Those of us who have repeated the life-altering words "With this ring, I thee wed" know the significance a simple circlet of gold can convey. With such rings, we put into material form that ineffable bond that holds two people together, sometimes forever.

When the romantic aura of a ring is combined with the drama of a precious jewel, the effect can be powerful.

Combine a ring made to show off a legendary gem with a love that has transcended death, and you have what Jeffrey Post, curator of the National Gem and Mineral Collection at the Smithsonian's National Museum of Natural History, calls "the most important addition to the collection in the 20 years that I've been here." The ring he speaks of is a 23.1-carat Burmese ruby flanked by two triangular diamonds. Its acquisition was made possible last August by Peter Buck, an investor and physicist, now retired from Knolls Atomic Power Laboratory, Schenectady, N.Y., in the name of his wife, Carmen Lucia Buck, who died in 2003.

Carmen Buck, born in Brazil, was a collector of jewels as well as a philanthropist dedicated to medical research. She had learned of the ruby from jeweler Frank Cappiello of Danbury, Conn., who, in 2002, had heard that it might be coming on the market after many years in private hands. At the time, she was fighting cancer and hoped to celebrate a recovery by purchasing the stone. Though this was a consummation only to be wished, her husband decided to honor her by providing funds for the Smithsonian to purchase what is now known as the Carmen Lucia ruby.

At the museum, it joins such legendary jewels as the Hope diamond and the 423-carat Logan sapphire.

The oval-shaped ruby was mined in the 1930s in the Mogok region of Burma, now also known

as Myanmar — the classic source of great rubies, according to curator Post — and is one of the largest fine faceted Burmese rubies in the world.

Burmese rubies are prized for their color; the Carmen Lucia is a bright red with undertones of pink and purple, a coveted hue known to gem dealers as "pigeon blood red."

The stone's provenance since it was first cut is unclear. "We don't know who owned the stone before international gem dealers bought it 15 years ago," says Post, "but it's not so unusual to have remarkable stones remain for generations in private family vaults."

When such a treasure surfaces, Post says, "it causes a major stir in the gem world."

A nuclear physicist by training, Peter Buck helped underwrite a friend's submarine sandwich shop. The shop evolved into the Subway chain. Buck has not revealed the amount of his donation to the Institution to purchase the ring. But its value, as is so often the case with rings, lies more in its meaning than in dollars. As an expression of the abiding love of a man for a woman, the Carmen Lucia ruby ring should sparkle for all who see it in the years ahead.

"Already," Buck tells *Smithsonian Magazine* for the February issue, "the ring has probably been seen by more people than had seen it altogether since it was first unearthed in the 1930s."

***

So what does this have to do with Bruce Roberts? I have to say this is just a hunch. A big maybe! But when I saw the first news stories in October, 2004, I had a very strong feeling that this might have been one of the rubies that Bruce Roberts smuggled out of Burma. He told us a lot—but he carefully left out a lot as well. He told us a lot of truth—but he also liked to play his cards close to the vest. He boasted now and then about his great success at smuggling gemstones—and papers—in and out of the country. He told us that his ex-wife, the mysterious daughter of the French Consul at Dien Bien Phu, owned Burmese rubies—and why not the biggest one of all? Rubies are mentioned more than once in the Gemstone File, and they seem to have been Roberts' favorite stone. He was fascinated by their color and power. And then there is the timing. Suddenly, this unknown gem, discovered in the '30's and in private hands ever since, pops up and is acquired by the Smithsonian Museum. It seems fitting that this great and priceless ruby might have been at one time the property of Bruce Roberts and his family or friends.

If so, perhaps the death of a relative led to the decision to allow this special gem to pass to the Smithsonian where it will be a national treasure, on display in the nation's Capitol. There would be something very fitting about this. Bruce Roberts' life has been a closed book for years. The details of his military service (from WWII, and possibly later in Vietnam) are still "classified," it appears. Why? Researchers have dug out some bits and pieces, but much still remains hidden. I suspect that the records—and the complete original Gemstone Files—also exist somewhere, and that they will emerge at some time. This would be a good time for the truth to emerge—perhaps in bits and pieces, a small section held onto over the years by someone who found a copy in a Xerox machine; or perhaps in a stack of papers, neatly preserved, about a foot high or more. A true history of the twentieth century in the United States of America. Bruce Roberts was too great a man to disappear unknown into the shadows of Time.

Please let me know if you have it!

46 A Very Brief Biography of Bruce Roberts

The following includes what little is known about the life and death of Bruce Roberts. Some of the information comes from the Gemstone letters, and from my conversations with him in 1974-5. Some has been unearthed by researchers Gerry Carroll, "Richard Alan," and Kenn Thomas. Bruce Porter Roberts was born on October 27, 1919, in New York State. He described his ethnic background as Irish, Scotch and Welsh.

His father, LaVerne Dale Roberts, was a shipyard worker for Bethlehem Steel, in various locations, from 1917 until his retirement. Verne worked at Bethlehem Steel's dry dock in Alameda, Ca., from 1947 until his retirement. During his later years, he lived in the Sunset District of San Francisco with his wife, Eva Kimball Roberts, Bruce's mother. Verne was a coin collector, and belonged to the San Francisco Coin Club. He was a Mason, a Republican, and worked for many years for the Republican Party in San Francisco. He had also played semi-professional football for a time in his younger years.

Bruce Roberts attended the University of Wisconsin, in Madison, on and off from 1936-40, although he did not receive a degree. As a journalism student, he covered the formation of the Progressive Party for the Wisconsin State Journal, in Madison, Wisconsin, in 1936 or 1937. He also studied physics; his special interest was crystallography. His older brother Dayle was also enrolled there, in a pre-med curriculum..

While in school, Bruce dated Dorothy Boettiger, Franklin Roosevelt's niece. He knew Sam Giancana, who knew about the heroin deal between Franklin and Elliott Roosevelt and Onassis. Giancana told Roberts to tell Dorothy about it; then used the blackmail later on to gain control of the Chicago Teamsters' Union Fund.

Like his father, Bruce Roberts had a strong, athletic build and an interest in sports. In 1940, Roberts played baseball for the University of Wisconsin. Henry Wallace, Roosevelt's Secretary of Agriculture and VP candidate in 1940, visited the campus, met and talked to Roberts. He showed him an oil cartel memo outlining an agreement whereby Rockefeller and the "Seven Sisters" (major oil companies) would buy oil cheap from the Arabs, ship it on Onassis's ships, and everyone would get rich.

Roberts served in the Army during WWII. He was stationed at Victorville Army Base, California. In 1944 or 1945, Roberts was doing yard patrol, picking up trash with a sharp stick and stuffing it into a canvas bag. George McGovern was the leader of a group of 50-mission bomber captains returning from Europe for reassignment. Because Roberts failed to salute, Captain McGovern threatened him with a court martial. Several sources have mentioned a possible association with the OSS during World War II. He states in his papers that various members of his family worked for the CIA here and abroad. The OSS morphed into the CIA after WWII. Roberts might have gone with it; or he might have simply maintained his earlier contacts. His favorite hang-outs in San Francisco were bars and nightspots that catered to the Intelligence community, and they obviously knew who he was and accepted him. Let's tentatively call him a CIA dissident.

He states that his former wife was the daughter of the French Consul in Vietnam at the time of the fall of Dien Bien Phu, and was imprisoned for a time in a North Vietnamese prison: a "Hanoi Hilton."

Roberts seems to have settled in the Los Angeles area after the war. He married and had at least one child, a girl. And possibly a son, who died. In an article dated 1952, he is described as a "former actor, turned jewelry designer."

Nothing is known about his acting career. He might have had small roles in the movies, or in small theaters in the L.A. area. He was fairly tall, around 5'11". He had a good memory and speaking voice, a confident delivery, and plenty of "presence." He knew at least one movie actress,

Carmen Miranda. He was pursuing his interest in crystallography, making synthetic jewels, and selling them to the Hollywood crowd.

He told me once about conducting a crystallography experiment in a garage (growing synthetic gemstone crystals). Something exploded, and he described himself as running down the street away from the garage with his eyebrows on fire.

Around 1960, he took some of his synthetic stones, including rubies, to Hughes Tool, but apparently they stole them. He learned about the kidnapping of Hughes by Onassis. This was confirmed for him by information from various sources located in the Mediterranean.

At some point, Roberts moved to San Francisco. His ex-wife and daughter apparently remained in the Los Angeles area.

Roberts had been writing his political letters and papers since 1968, and had been waving them like so many red flags before the enraged noses of the Politico bulls for seven years. After I got to know him in 1974-5, I somehow got the idea that he was indestructible, and that I would be able to learn the whole story of what was going on in our country from him, or at least, his viewpoint on this.

So I was shocked and horrified at his call from the hospital in March, 1975. He went into great detail about the speck of nickel dust that had been introduced into his body by the CIA (he did not know how); how the same thing had been done to Brezhnev, and how the Russians had discovered what was wrong with Brezhnev; how his friend Pavlov at the Russian Embassy had jumped around in his office, obliging Roberts to face around in various directions so that Kirlian photographs could be taken of him from various angles; and how, after the photos had been analyzed, Pavlov had advised him to check into the most trustworthy hospital he knew, assuring him at the same time that what Roberts had was not cancer. But he also said that the X-rays showed he had "a lump in his chest the size of a grapefruit."

This was a heavy conversation for breakfast. I told him I would visit him at the hospital.

When I hung up, I couldn't help thinking that he would be helpless in the hospital, and that he might be murdered somehow, like his father. I was thinking these gloomy thoughts while washing the breakfast dishes. I turned on the garbage disposal unit, and because I was distracted, without thinking, I stuck my finger down into the unit where it was mercilessly pummeled. I pulled my finger out, and discovered that a flap of flesh at the finger tip had been nearly torn off, and my finger was bleeding profusely. I called a friend and neighbor on Prosper Street, and told her what was happening. She came over, wrapped something around my finger, and drove me to the hospital. There they stitched my finger tip back together (I still have the scar), and I went to Bruce's hospital ward.

He was walking around the ward, wearing one of those white cotton hospital gowns opening all the way down, tied at the waist with a string. He wore his with the opening in front.

He didn't seem deathly ill, and as we talked, he asked me for a favor. Would I buy him a couple of packs of cigarettes?

I was again horrified. What do you do when a man you care about, diagnosed as a probable cancer patient with a tumor the size of a grapefruit in his chest, asks you for a couple of packs of cigarettes?

I told myself that considering the life he led, he probably wouldn't live long enough to die from smoking cigarettes. So I bought him a couple of contraband packs, and gave him a $20 to buy some more later....

Roberts died on July 16, 1976, in San Francisco. Cause of death is described as "respiratory failure (due to) metastatic carcinoma of lung (adenocarcinoma)"; i.e., lung cancer.

EPILOGUE by Sherwood Ross: Pray for me, Father

Pray For Me, Father

Pray for me, Father, mine is the sin of cowardice

For I do not set myself on fire at the White House gate

To protest war. I am a glutton for God's blue sky.

Pray for me, Father, for my taxes set a banquet for Death

With napalm and daisy cutters and snakelike missiles

To blow apart other men and their wives and children

While I walk secure along the shore of the tranquil sea.

Pray for me, Father, and I will pray for you

For the silence of a church that does not speak out

A church bought off with Caesar's money

That does not condemn an Inquisition where men

Are broken and driven mad in the dungeons

Of Bagram, Kabul, Gitmo, and Abu Ghraib

A church whose ministers remind congregations of Golgotha

As if Jesus and Jesus and Jesus by the thousands

Are not being crucified now by the Masters of War

Are not walking home on artificial legs

Are not staring sightless from wheelchairs

In VA hospitals into God's blue sky.

Pray for me, Father, and I will pray for you.

(Copyright © 2005 by Sherwood Ross. Reprinted by permission of the author.)

Sherwood Ross writes on World War II history for national magazines and runs a public relations firm for good causes. He is founder of The League for Nonviolent Solutions. His article, "From Guernica to Hiroshima," appears in the July/August 2005 issue of The Humanist magazine.

BIBLIOGRAPHY
Books based on the *Skeleton Key to the Gemstone File*

Alan, Richard. (pseudonym) *The Gemstone File: Sixty Years of Corrupt Manipulation Within World Government; Detailing the Events Surrounding the Assassination of JFK,* Columbus, Ohio, Crown Publishing Co., 1992.

Four hundred pages of documentation, consisting of reproduction of articles from major magazines and newspapers, from the '30's to the '90's. Compiled over many years by a man from Columbus Ohio who received a copy of the *Skeleton Key to the Gemstone File* from Larry Flynt personally in 1976, only a few days before Larry was shot in the back in Georgia to prevent him from investigating its allegations. Limited (2000 ppb copies), OOP, costly on secondhand market, (try Amazon.com), but the ultimate refutation of the "Caruana and Roberts are from outer space/undocumented/ insane/disinformation/etc." school of "thought."

Carroll, Gerald A. *Project Seek: Onassis, Kennedy and the Gemstone Thesis,* Carson City, Nevada, Bridger House, 1994.

Four hundred pages of excellent documentation and analysis by an expert professional journalist who received his copy from a Native American in 1976, and moved from disbelief to acceptance while doing this research. Good picture section as well.

Keith, Jim, Ed. *The Gemstone File,* Atlanta, IllumiNet, 1992.

A mixed-bag collection of articles which stirred, or re-stirred, public interest in the 1975-circulated *Skeleton Key to the Gemstone File.* Includes articles by Mae Brussell, Jonathan Vankin, Robert Anton Wilson, Kerry Thornley, Ben G. Price, and others, and an interview with me. Worth reading, even though the quality and accuracy of the articles is widely varied.

Renzo, Peter. *Beyond the Gemstone File,* New York, Vantage, 1976. An early, brief book by a man who currently keeps tigers as pets somewhere in California or Nevada. This 96-page "gem" contained my *Skeleton Key,* plus a paper called The Philadelphia Experiment, plus a few pages of fantasizing on the part of Peter Renzo. *Caveat emptor*: Peter may have ordered a reissue from Vantage Press, circa 1990 (??), which is being sold for the highly inflated price of $250.00. This undoubtedly buys a lot of tiger chow, but the buyer is likely to be disappointed.

Thomas, Kenn, and David Hatcher Childress. *Inside the Gemstone File,* Kempton, Illinois, Adventures Unlimited, 1999.

Kenn Thomas, author, editor, and publisher of Steamshovel Press books, and *Steamshovel* (periodical) is at the center of a community of "conspiracy theory" writers. He has given many of us a much-needed "home" and a voice. Here he has provided information and items available nowhere else. David Childress has pointed out some of the similarities between Ian Fleming's "James Bond" novels, and the subsequent movies, and the "plot" and characters of the Gemstone File—particularly in the movie version of *Diamonds Are Forever.* No wonder; as an intelligent and aware British agent, during and after World War II, Ian Fleming would have certainly known a great deal about the hidden machinations of the power stealers. James Bond's arch enemy, the tyrant and super-villain Ernst Stavro Blofeld, is clearly based on the real tyrant and super-villain, Aristotle Onassis, with perhaps a bit of Stavros Niarchos thrown in. The *Diamonds Are Forever* movie contains clear references to the story of Howard Hughes's kidnap by Onassis, and Onassis's involvement with Las Vegas casinos. Unfortunately, in his Introduction, Childress indicates that he still doesn't fully comprehend that the *Gemstone File* and the *Skeleton Key to the Gemstone File* are two separate entities, written by two different people: one being Bruce Roberts, and the other, me.

Related Books and Other Media

This is a highly selective bibliography. There are literally hundreds of books available on the JFK assassination, the attempted cover-up, the deaths of witnesses, etc. Hundreds more deal with U.S. history and politics, its current state, and how it got that way. I decided that the most useful bibliography list I could provide would:

- be relatively short, so that an interested reader would not be daunted, and might actually consider looking at least a few of the books mentioned;
- deal with one (or more) aspect of the Gemstone reality in a realistic way. No aliens from one or another alternate universe will wrap their fingers around your throat! No pols or killers will turn out to be extra-terrestrial robots or quickly-grown and harvested surrogate doubles. Get to know the Mafs and the pols and the CEO's who run and ruin your lives by name, and by company name!
- avoid fogland in general. This does not mean that any one of these books will tell you the entire story, or even most, or some, of the truth. Just that, in general, they occupy the same universe with the same or a somewhat or closely related cast of characters and issues as the Gemstone File.

Bartlett, Donald L., and James B. Steele. *Empire: The Life, Legend and Madness of Howard Hughes*, New York, Norton, 1979.

Bernstein, Carl, and Bob Woodward. *All the President's Men*, New York, Simon & Schuster, 1974.

Bernstein, Carl, and Bob Woodward. *The Final Days*, New York, Simon & Schuster, 1976.

Bishop, Jim. *The Day Kennedy Was Shot: An Uncensored Minute-by-Minute Account of November 23*. New York, Funk & Wagnalls, 1963.

Burns, James MacGregor. *Edward Kennedy and the Camelot Legacy*. New York, Norton, 1976.

Cafirakis, Christian. *The Fabulous Onassis: His Life and Loves*, New York, William Morrow, 1972.

Dallas Morning News. *The Day JFK Died: Thirty Years Later: The Event that Changed a Generation*, Kansas City, Missouri, Andrews & McMeel, 1993.

Damore, Leo. *Senatorial Privilege: The Chappaquiddick Cover-up*, Washington, D.C., Regnery Gateway, 1988.

Davis, Deborah. *Katharine the Great: Katharine Graham and her Washington Post Empire, 1979-1991*, New York, Sheridan Square Press, 1991.

Davis, John H. *Mafia Kingfish: Carlos Marcello and the Assassination of John F. Kennedy*, New York, Signet, 1989.

Demaris, Ovid. *The Last Mafioso: "Jimmy the Weasel" Fratianno*, New York, Times Books, 1981.

Dietrich, Noah. *Howard: The Amazing Mr. Hughes*, Greenwich, Connecticut, Fawcett, 1972.

Drosnin, Michael. *Citizen Hughes: The Power, the Money, the Madness*, New York, Bantam, 1986.

Evans, Peter. *Ari: The Life and Times of Aristotle Onassis*, New York, Simon & Schuster, 1986.

Fay, Stephen, Chester Lewis and Magnus Linklater. *Hoax: The Inside Story of the Howard Hughes-Clifford Irving Affair*, New York, Viking, 1972.

Fetzer, James H. *Murder in Dealey Plaza: What We Know Now that We Didn't Know Then about the Death of JFK*, Chicago, CatFeet Press, 2000.

Giancana, Sam, and Chuck Giancana. *Double Cross: The Explosive Inside Story of the Mobster Who Controlled America*, New York, Warner Books, 1992.

Graham, Katharine. *Personal History*, New York, Knopf, 1997.

Groden, Robert J. *The Killing of a President: The Complete Photographic Record of the JFK Assassination, The Conspiracy, and the Cover-Up*, New York, Viking, 1993.

Higham, Charles. *Howard Hughes: The Secret Life*, New York, Putnam's, 1993.

Judge, John. *Judge for Yourself*, Santa Barbara, Prevailing Winds Research, 1990.

Kelley, Kitty. *His Way: The Unauthorized Biography of Frank Sinatra*, New York, Bantam, 1986.

King, Stephen. *The Stand*, New York, Doubleday, 1990.

Liddy, G. Gordon. *Will: The Autobiography of G. Gordon Liddy*, New York, St. Martin's, 1990.

Marrs, Jim. *Crossfire: The Plot that Killed Kennedy*, New York, Carroll & Graf, 1989.

McCoy, Alfred W. *The Politics of Heroin in Southeast Asia*, New York, Harper & Row, 1972.

New York Times. *The White House Transcripts: The Full Text of the Submission of Recorded Presidential Conversations to the Committee on the Judiciary of the House of Representatives by President Richard Nixon*, New York, Bantam, 1974.

Russo, Gus. *The Outfit: The Role of Chicago's Underworld in the Shaping of Modern America*, New York, Bloomsbury, 2001.

Skolnick, Sherman. *Ahead of the Parade: A Who's Who of Treason and High Crimes: Exclusive Details of Fraud and Corruption of the Monopoly Press, The Banks, The Bench and the Bar, and the Secret Political Police*, Tempe, Arizona, Dandelion, 2003.

Strober, Deborah Hart, and Strober, Gerald S. *The Nixon Presidency: An Oral History of the Era*, Washington, D.C., Brassey's, 2003.

Summers, Anthony. *Conspiracy*, New York, McGraw-Hill, 1980.

Tackwood, Louis, and C.R.I.C. *The Glass House Tapes*, New York, Avon, 1973.

Thomas, Kenn, ed. *Cyberculture Counterconspiracy: A Steamshovel Web Reader*, Escondido, California, The Book Tree, 1999.

Thomas, Kenn, ed. *Popular Alienation: A Steamshovel Press Reader*, Lilburn, Georgia, Illuminet Press, 1995.

Warren Commission. *The Assassination of President Kennedy*, New York, McGraw-Hill, 1964.

Whalen, Richard. *The Founding Father: The Story of Joseph P. Kennedy and the Family He Raised to Power*, New York, Signet, 1964.

Wyden, Peter. *Bay of Pigs: The Untold Story*, New York, Simon & Schuster, 1979.

Zinn, Howard. *A People's History of the United States, 1492 - Present* (Perennial Classics). Harper Perennial, 2003.

Emerging Bibliography for the George W. Bush Administration, and for "9/11": The New (and Worse Than) JFK Assassination

Chomsky, Noam. *Failed States: The Abuse of Power and the Assault on Democracy*, New York, Holt, 2006.

Citizens Commission on 9/11. *Report: An updated non-partisan analysis of events before, during and after the attacks of Sept/ 11, 2001, and how the War on Terror is changing America*. Spirit Lake, Idaho, *Idaho Observer*, 2006.

Dean, John W. *Worse that Watergate: The Secret Presidency of George W. Bush*, New York, Little, Brown, 2004.

Goodman, Amy, and David Goodman. **The Exception to the Rulers: Exposing Oily Politicians, War Profiteers, and the Media that Love Them**, New York, Hyperion, 2004.

Griffin, David Ray. *The New Pearl Harbor: Disturbing Questions about the Bush Administration and 9/11*, —*The 9/11 Commission Report: Omissions and Distortions*, Northampton, MA, Olive Branch, 2005.

Hufschmid, Eric. *Painful Questions: An Analysis of the September 11th Attack*. Goleta, CA., Endpoint Software, 2002.

Kelley, Kitty. *The Family: The Real Story of the Bush Dynasty*, New York, Doubleday, 2004.

Kucinich, Dennis. *A Prayer for America*, New York, Thunder's Mouth, 2003.

Marrs, Jim. *Inside Job: Unmasking the 9/11 Conspiracies*, San Rafael, CA, Origin, 2004.

McCoy, Alfred W. *A Question of Torture: CIA Interrogation, from the Cold War to the War on Terror*, New York, Holt, 2006.

Moore, Michael. *Stupid White Men: and Other Sorry Excuses for the State of the Nation*, New York, Penguin,

2002.

Orwell, George. *Nineteen Eighty-Four*, New York, Penguin, 2003.

Paul, John, and Hoffman, Jim. *Waking Up from Our Nightmare: The 9/11/01 Crimes in New York City*, San Francisco, I/R, 2004.

Rall, Ted. *Generalissimo el Busho*, New York, Nantier-Beal-Minoustchine, 2004.

Sands, Philippe. *Lawless World: America and the Making and Breaking of Global Rules from FDR's Atlantic Charter to George W. Bush's Illegal War*, New York Penguin, 2005.

Vidal, Gore. *Perpetual War for Perpetual Peace: How We Got to Be So Hated*, New York, Thunder's Mouth Press, 2002.

Vonnegut, Kurt. *A Man Without a Country*, New York, Seven Stories Press, 2005.

Some Post-9/11 VCR's and DVD's

Achbar, Mark, and Peter Wintonick. *Manufacturing Consent: Noam Chomsky and the Media*, Canada, Zeitgeist Video, 1992, DVD.

Achbar, Mark, and Jennifer Abbott. *The Corporation*, Canada, Zeitgeist Video, 2005, DVD.

Chomsky, Noam. *Distorted Morality: America's War on Terror*, Los Angeles, Plug Music, 2002, DVD.

Discovery Channel. *Unsolved History: JFK: Beyond the Magic Bullet*. Silver Spring, MD, 2003, DVD.

Moore, Michael. *Fahrenheit 9/11*, Culver City, CA, Lions Gate Films and IFC, 2004, DVD.

Hufschmid, Eric. *Painful Deceptions: An Analysis of the September 11th Attack*. 2002, DVD.

Noujaimi Films. *Control Room*, Santa Monica, Lions Gate, 2004. DVD.

Vonkleist, Dave. *911: in Plane Site: The Director's Cut*, Versailles, MO, The Power Hour, 2004. VCR.

Appendix A: Antonio Iglesias's FOIA CIA/FBI-File

The Gemstone File identifies Antonio Iglesias as an employee of the CIA, a Cuban National who joined the American/CIA forces in the "Bay of Pigs" attack on Cuba, and also as a participant in the JFK assassination conspiracy who took photographs of Eugene Brading as one of the shooters of JFK. Roberts also states that Iglesias's sister, Maria, was at one time married to Bruce Roberts' brother, Dayle. That would lend more support to Roberts' thesis by giving a plausible source for his having some inside information. (As we all know, family members talk to each other!) This FOIA file contains biographical information about Iglesias, his birth and education in Cuba, and his relocation to the U.S. after Castro defeated Batista. It identifies Iglesias as a CIA employee, but cuts out a crucial chunk of time around the Bay of Pigs/JFK assassination. It then picks up again with Iglesias's account of the real estate scam he got involved with in Miami, mentioned by Roberts. The file is 23 pages long, and I don't wish to include the whole thing here. If someone is really interested in seeing the remainder of the file, I can be reached through the publisher, Trafford Inc.

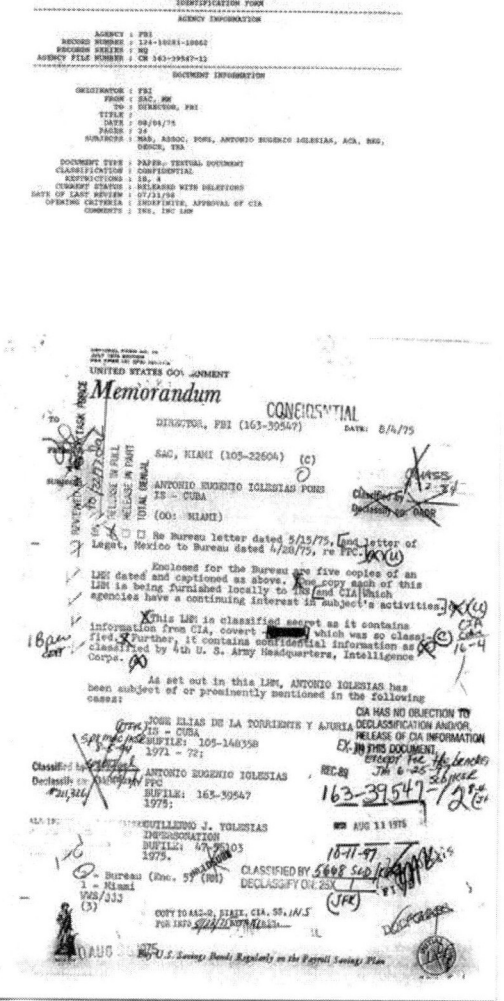
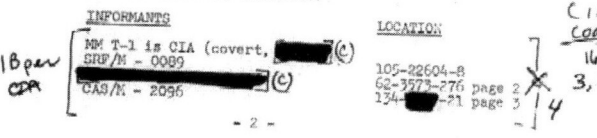

INDEX

1

18-1/2 minutes erased tape: Nixon, raving, 90

9

990AR, foundation tax return, 412

A

Abrosiano Bank, 363
ACLU: run by Baldwin Foundation, 413
Afghanistan, 72, 258, 268, 269, 282; Dr. Duke in, 278
Africa, 285
Agnew, Spiro, 105, 208, 278, 304, 351; one gut shot from the Presidency, 316; selected for VP by Onassis, 282
Air Force One, 73, 98
Air Opium, 66
Aitken, Judge Janet, 75, 127, 189
Alan, Richard, 17, 352
Albanian frogmen, 83
Alberto Dugue, 369
Alioto Crime Commission, 131, 181
Alioto hit-and-run, 1968, 167
Alioto Mafia Web, 77, 101
Alioto, Angelina, 73
Alioto, Joe, 71, 75, 77, 92, 98, 101, 103, 105, 106, 126, 129, 219, 275, 301; and pay-off to Fratianno for Dallas, 73, 327; Justinian Award, Lawyer of the Year, 1968, 232; SF Mayor, 31
Alioto, Mia Angela, 75
Alioto, Tom, 75, 126, 137, 328, 390
Allen, Woody, 55
Alton Telegraph, 407
Amazing Howard Hughes, The, by Noah Dietrich, 390
Amchitka test, 143
American Bar Association, 109, 301, 305
American Catholic Church, 183
American Civil Liberties Union, 289
American Dream, 170
American Nazi Party, 30
American Pie, 274
American Press Mafia, 139
American Weekly: photo feature on Roberts (and Carmen Miranda), 1952, 401
Anderson Foundation, 71

Anderson, Jack, 66, 173, 182, 184, 186, 196, 197, 202, 203, 211, 219, 241, 283, 290, 296, 297, 353, 389; "Senate a gentleman's Cosa Nostra", 169
Andreuccetti, Joseph: and $10 billion in gold stolen by OSS, 414
Angelou, Maya, 27
Anti-Ballistic Missile ring, 213
Anti-Monopoly Bill, 364
Anti-war Peace March, 272
Aotearoa, 360
Apalachin, 152, 155, 327; Mafia summit meeting, 1957, 65
apple pie, poisoned, 66, 68, 88, 94, 260, 261, 311, 313, 339
Aramco, 96, 418
Area 51, Nevada: top secret, NASA, "aliens", flying saucers, 419
Arena, Dominick, 79
Ariadne, Australia, 372
Aristotle, 9, 111
Arius, 87
Arlington National Cemetery, 111
Armstrong, Neil, on the moon, 292
artificial diamonds, 389
Aspirin Roulette, 430
Assassination: Theory and Practice, 349
Associated Press, 408, 412
astronauts postmarked moon letters for Mafia, 292
Aswan Dam, 286
Atlanta Constitution, 30
Atlanta Gazette, 353
atomic physics, 106
Auckland and Hawkes, 370
Australasia, food industry monopolized, 374
Australasian and Pacific Holdings Limited, 361
Australia, 360
Australia liquor industry, buying up, 370
Australian International Finance Corp., 362
Australian Mafia Council meeting, 374
Australian Mafia meeting, Sydney: re privatization of Australian government, 376
Australian politicians on the CIA's payroll, 373
Autobiography of Howard Hughes, 82

B

Badgeman, Roscoe White?, 76

Bahamas and Caribbean rackets, 165
Bailey, Martin, Faye insured big oil tankers, 397
Baker, Bobby, 219, 354
Baker, Senator Howard, 72, 328
Baldwin Foundation: runs Nation magazine, 413
Balistreri, Sal, SF Mafia judge, 214
Banana Republic, 21
Banca Del Lavaro, 413
Banister, Guy, office a CIA front, 129
Bank of America, 66, 72, 81, 90, 127, 221, 285, 326, 389; and economic chaos in Chile, 195; mouth of 'Hughes' Mafia money funnel, 277
Bank of California, 221; and loans to Lockheed, 208
bar stool photos, 86
Barbie, Klaus, 363
Barboza, Patriarcha Maf from Boston, 219
Barker, Bernard, 86, 88, 300, 305, 313, 434; at the Drift Inn, 311; recruited for CREEP, 426; Watergate burglar, 296
Batista, Fulgencio, former Cuban dictator, 65
Bautzer, Greg, 157; only 2 clients, "Hughes" and Kerkorian, 133
Bay Guardian, Brugmann's newspaper, 301
Bay of Pigs, 15, 65, 66, 74, 86, 115, 156, 231, 234, 289, 291, 296, 300, 313
Beam, Christopher, 139, 173
Beard, Dita, and ITT memo, 182
Beasley, coin expert, 326
Beasley, Donald, 369
Beatty, Warren, and Bugsy, 392
Bechtel, 134, 163, 222, 279, 369; Defense Contractor in Construction, 160
Bechtel, McCone, Parsons, 129, 160
Bechtel, Steven, Democratic bigwig, 77
Beck, Dave, convicted Teamster, released from tax rap, 222
Becker, lawyer, pardon deal for Nixon, 94
Bennett, Robert, 85, 313, 331; planned Watergate break-in, 331; CIA, President of Mullen and Co., 331; Hunt's CIA employer, proposed cracking Greenspun's safe, 430; Public Relations Director for Summa Corp., 331
Berkeley Barb, 18, 45, 56, 93, 341, 382
Berlet, Chip, 413
Berrigans, political trial, 186
Best, Bill, 183, 234
Bethlehem Steel, 62, 354, 447
Beverly Hills Hotel, 396, 397, 398; *and Onassis' suite, since 1942*, 64; Hughes's private bungalow, 49, 64, 348
Beyond the Gemstone Files: by Peter Renzo, 339

Biafra, floating on one huge pool of oil, 52, 186
Big Business policy, driving small farmers off the land, 375
Big Sur, 18, 56
Bingham, Stephen, 38
Bingham, Woodridge, Naval Intelligence, OSS, 38
Bird, Wally, 66, 231; indicted by Robert Kennedy, 156
Biscayne Bay, Roselli's watery graveyard, 99
Bishara, Kuwait Ambassador to U.N., 209
Black Cultural Association, Vacaville Prison, 36
Black Feminist Party, 333
Black Magic Bar, 75, 215
Black Panther genocide, 253
Black Panthers, 69, 80, 122, 125, 156, 248, 249, 283
Blandford, Marquess of, 80
Blandford, Tina Livanos Onassis, 84
Bleifuss, Joel, 413
Blofeld, Ernst Stavro: character based on Onassis, 416; James Bond's nemesis, 416
Boettiger, Dorothy, FDR's niece, 61, 447
Boggs, Hale, 412
Boggs, Senator Hale, and Mafia Marcello's Louisiana, 240
Bohemian Grove, 137, 161, 162, 290
Bohrmann, Martin, and Nazis' escape post WWII, 349
Boiardo, "Boots", 316
Bolden, Abraham: first black in White House guard, 410; his secret report on Chicago and JFK suppressed until 2039, 410
Bonanno, Joe, San Jose Mafia Don, 110
Boston, MA, 167, 192, 219, 222
Boyle, Anthony, UMW, 201; and Bank of Washington, 283; supervised Yablonski murder, 221
Brading, Eugene, 22, 67, 71, 72, 73, 75, 76, 90, 98, 326, 327, 328, 349, 350, 392; courier for Lansky's skim money, 327; shot at JFK from Dealey Plaza pergola, 57; X-marked leather hat, 15
Brazil, 285
Bremer, Arthur, 218, 275, 313, 314, 435; 2-hour trial, 63-year sentence, 294; and Greek boys of Onassis who got him his booster shots, 276; hypnotized killer--but by whom?, 218; patsy, 291
Brenner Pass, Nazi escape route post WWII?, 349
Brewster, Senator Owen: and hearings on Hughes airplane contracts, 399

Brezhnev, 187; and Nixon, 213; has a gemstone and history, 208; mysterious flu, 95; strange virus, 335
Brierly, Ron, 361
Brisson, Lance, 134
Brisson, Neil, 129
Britannia Beach Hotel, 82
Broe, William, and economic chaos in Chile, 195
Brookings Institute: design NZ government economic policies, 375; Trilateralist Think Tank, 369
Brown, Pat, Mafia swindles, 178
Browning, James, 189, 193
Browning, James, Sr, 278
Bruckner, D. J. R.,"panic at the top of our government", 153
Brugmann, 115
Brussell, Bonnie: fatal accident, 1971, 55; murder, 316; squashed by Alioto's Genovese, 315
Brussell, Mae, 17, 27, 44, 83, 93, 94, 300, 315, 333, 341, 382, 384, 413, 423; 2 radio broadcasts on Gemstone, 1977-8, 345; and Elmer Davis, 341; Archives, 46; daily filing activity, 55; web site, 341
Brussell, Mae Magnin, 76
Brzezinski, Zbignieu, 367; outlines plan to invade Iran, 378
Buchanan, Pat, "George Wallace must be destroyed", 218
Buck, Peter, 445
Buckley, William F.: "destroy the U.N.", 172; "Vatican mouth", 135; proposed Howard Hunt as WH consultant, 296
Buddhists, barbecued, 231
Bull, Stephen: secretary heard erased tape, 90
Bulletin of Atomic Scientists, 215
Bundy, Body Count, runs Ford Foundation, 131, 186, 301
Bureau of Indian Affairs, 19
Burke, Yvonne Braithwaite, 298
Burma, 63, 65, 444
Burmese rubies, 65
Bush, Dorothy, 298
Bush, George W., 20, 62, 343
Bush, Prescott, Financier of Hitler, 20, 343
Bushati's Pizza Parlor, 232
buying evidence with gemstones, 132
Byoir, Carl, 74, 398; hired Hughes double, 64
Byrne, Judge Matt: dished up Ellsberg trial to (Mafia) order, 280

C

Cabell, Charles, 66
Caen, Herb, 208
Cafarakis, Christian, 228; lying for Onassis, 216
Cahill, Police Chief, 80, 102, 145, 183, 189
Cain, Richard, 70
California Crime Commission, 71, 92, 327
California Prisons, 306; San Quentin, 32
California State Legislature, totally bribed, 119
California Supreme Court, 178; declares death penalty invalid, 171
Callas, Maria, 220
Camara, Bishop Don: exiled in Brazil, 247
Cambodia, 66, 84, 97, 102, 127, 148, 220; invasion, 193
Camelot, 170
Campbell, Joseph: and A Skeleton Key to Finnegan's Wake, 386
Canadian Stock Exchange, 82, 163, 185; swindle, 94
Cannon, Howard, 396; and Howard Hughes, 49; arranged fake marriage for Hughes and Peters, 64
Capone, Al, 61, 177, 221
Carlson, Dick, 77, 106, 125, 129, 130, 131, 133, 152, 161, 162, 183, 189
Carmel Valley, 18, 27, 44, 384
Carmen Lucia Burma ruby: 23 carats, red with pink flashes, 444
Carroll, Gerald A., 17, 41, 93; *on Hughes's fake marriage*, 396; Project Seek, 360
Caruana, Stephanie, 423; mentioned in Gemstone File, 326
Casino Royale by James Bond, 416
Casolaro, Danny, 10, 360; investigating "The Octopus, 416; supposed "suicide", 1991, 416
Castro, Fidel, 65, 125; stole $8 billion from Onassis, 296
Catholic Church, 183
Caulfield, Jack, 426
CBS, 292, 412; program, the Mafia does not exist!, 277
Cellar, Rep. Emanuel: and personal loot, 219
Cermak, Mayor of Chicago: murdered by Mafia while in car with FDR, 218
Cervantes, Mafia Mayor of St. Louis, 279
Cesar, Thane Eugene, 160, 218, 306; murder of Robert Kennedy, 152; shot RFK from behind, 74
Chameleon, Richard: Assassination, Theory and Practice, 349

Chappaquiddick, 56, 77, 101, 105, 148, 181, 220, 354; concrete cross dumped into Poucha Pond, 323; phone calls, 183; Rescue Team, 79
Chappaquiddick, 353
Chappaquiddick Dickie, 127
Chappaquiddick Little Dickie, 106
Charach, Ted, 74, 137; The Second Gun, 160
Chartrand, owner of Barney's Casino: blown up in Tahoe, 200
Chase Corporation: new front company, 373
Chase Manhattan Bank, 104, 226, 361, 370; manipulating Australasian economy, 377
Chateau Marmont, 333
Chavez, Caesar, 163
Chiang Ching, 153, 175, 186
Chiang Kai Shek, 181, 184; Kuomintang, 193
Chicago football stadium: JFK assassination scheduled for Nov. 1, 1963, 69
Chicago plot against Kennedy: 2-1/2 weeks before Dallas, 409
Chicago Teamsters Union Fund, 61, 250, 447
Childress, David Hatcher, 416; Adventures Unlimited Press, 416
Chile, 206; A stranger said "Fok Kannady", 285; Allende's government toppled by CIA, 91; economic chaos arranged, 195
china dishes of opium, heroin and sugar, 192
China supports Gemstone and Roberts, 204
Chinatown murders, 264
Chisholm, Shirley, 92, 218, 219, 239, 240, 252, 314, 429
Chou En Lai, 135, 139, 171, 174; heart attack, 95
Chouinard, Gerald, 50
Christ: 11th Commandment--Hang murderers on the cross, not me., 227; a Zoroastrian Arab baby, 87; natural birth, 109
Christchurch Gas, 370
Christina, Onassis' yacht, 62, 68, 110; 1957 meeting on JFK presidency bid, 155
Christopher, Warren, 367
Chronology, 155
Churchill papers: "Roosevelt + Kennedy rigged WWII", 154
Churchill, Winston, 105, 109
CIA, 30, 37, 91, 109, 115, 127, 129, 177, 313, 314, 318, 339, 355, 357, 364, 389, 448; Air America; drug shipping route, 190; geological raids into Yunnan Province, 153; and anti-Kennedy political cartoons, 433; and Group of 40, 327; assassination attempt on Tito of Yugoslavia, 97; assassination attempts on foreign heads of state, 98; at Dallas, 294; burns opium in Thailand, or was it hay???, 290; connections with BCCI, 360; helps Hand and Beasley escape to USA, 369; makes professional charts for CREEP operations, 427; McCone, John, hiding at ITT, 217; neo-fascist Italian/Latin American operations, 363; opium route in Laos, 164; searching for rocks in China, 106; triple crossfire at Dallas, 291
CIA "secret weapon" and Brezhnev's "flu": speck of nickel dust, 95
CIA banks: Castle Bank, 370; Mercantile Bank and Trust, 370
CIA front foundations, 412
CIA-FBI dissidents, 193
CIA-Mafia team, 98
CIA-Mafia-Nixon "slow murder", 154
Cinque. See DeFreeze, Donald
Cinque the Slave: by Donald Freed and Lake Headley, 342
Citizens' Committee To Clean Up The Courts, 407
City of San Francisco: Interview with Roberts, Sept. 9, 1975, 335
Civic Center Bank: owned by judges, gangsters, media owner, 407
Clark, Blair, 280
Clark, Mark, 69, 81, 122, 125, 156, 185, 186, 248, 264
Clark, Ramsey, 302, 306, 314, 315, 317
Clemens, of Dr. Pepper Company, 133
Cline, Ray, 364
Colby, William E., 29, 37, 96, 361
Coldis, Alcoholic Beverages Board, 311
Color Me Flo, 99, 333
Colson, Charles, 431
Columbus Dispatch, 354
COM-12, 10; briefing documents, 416
Commercial Bank of Australia, 362
Comparison table: Diamonds are Forever and Gemstone File, 419
Confessions of a Raving Unconfined Nut: misadventures in the counter-culture: by Paul Krassner, 342
Connally, John, 109, 127, 136, 139, 144, 218, 222, 269, 282, 326, 350; and chest wound, 266; and his two bullets, 121; and magic bullet theory, 258; on Foreign Intelligence Board, 291; sees Dr. Duke in Afghanistan, 258; Texas Maf going way back, 186
Considine, Robert, 399
Conspiracy Heaven, 343
Conspiracy Newsletter, 315

conspiracy theory, 16, 391, 416
Constantine: made a deal with religious hierarchy, 325 a.d.; You leave us alone and we'll leave you alone., 109; Roman Emperor, 88
Constitution, American, 101, 110, 122, 129, 142, 145; rewritten by legal Mafia, 155
Consumers' Coalition Party Formation Conference, 119
Convention gang bang, 1972, 294
Cooke, Cardinal Terence, 164
COPA, 356
Corcoran, Tommy 'The Cork', 153
Corcoran, Tommy 'The Cork', 164, 192
Cordrey, David, 48
Corsican Mafia, 392
Costa Rica, 330
Cowles, Henry, 222, 306
Cox, Archibald, 72
Cox, Eddie, 127; Nixon's son-in-law, 115
Crack addictive drug: developed by CIA for world market, 376
Cramer, Stuart, 64
CREEP, 72, 81, 82, 87, 88, 89, 90, 91, 92, 174, 326, 331
Cronkhite, Walter, 279
Crown Publishing Company, 352
Crown Zellerbach Corp.: connections, 372
cryogenic burial, 212
cryogenics, 165, 166, 185, 188, 210
crystallography, 63, 75, 335, 447, 448
Cue Energy, 370
cult killings, 29
Curtis, Jamie Lee, 431
Cushing, Cardinal, 79, 80, 106, 108, 109, 157, 229, 234; and Jackie-Onassis marriage deal, 126
cyanide-tipped bullets, 31
Cypress Lawn, 284

D

D'Alessandros, Baltimore Mafia Dons, 135
Dahlberg, Kenneth, 434
Daily News, 408
Dale, Elizabeth, 87, 175, 179, 309, 311, 326, 328; and 62-carat synthetic sapphire, 174
Dale, Francis L., 82, 87, 90, 91, 92, 174, 318, 319, 326, 328; Chairman of CREEP, 72, 331; strangles the U.N. from an Onassis-owned Swiss bank, 329
Daley, Chicago Mayor, and Hampton and Clark's murders, 234
Dallas Dimes, 328; reverse is doubled, 326; with history, 329
Dal-Tex building, 350
Dash, Sam, 327
Davis, Angela, 40, 186, 250, 253, 262, 283, 327
Davis, Chester, 64, 125, 128, 159, 165, 167, 398; born Cesare in Italy, 155; one of Hughes's "Mormon Mafia" nursemaids, 50
Davis, Elmer, 341, 344
Davis, Rennie, 412
Davis, Tom, 10; Aptos Books, Aptos, CA, 57, 344
Davis, True, 283, 297
De Hory, Elmyr, 82, 159, 176, 188
De Mattei, Freddie, 274
De Mattei, Judge: reversed Genovese conviction of murder of Bonnie Brussell, 274
Deak Bank, 363
Dealey Plaza, 69, 451; *abattoir*, 350; pergola, 15
Dean, John, 81, 428; gave Hunt's copy of Gemstone File to L. Patrick Gray, 89; *to Nixon:"Tony, who did the Chappaquiddick study"*, 81
death squads, 363
Deauville Hotel, Miami: owned by Meyer Lansky, Sam Cohen, Morris Lansburgh, 252
Deep Throat (Katherine Graham), 91
Defense Intelligence Agency (DIA), 28, 128, 177
DeFreeze, Donald, 28, 32, 39, 55, 92, 393
Democratic: Mafia-financed sweep of Congress, 155; *National Committee*, 81, 92; Telethon money went to Boyle's National Bank, Washington, 283
Democratic National Convention, 429
Democratic Party: corruption in Chicago, Illinois, 406
Denver mint, 326
Deputy of Christ at Auschwitz, Pope Montini, 349
Derrough, CBS, 139
Desert Inn, Las Vegas, 51, 294
Desperation of both parties, 305
Devlin, Bernadette, 109
Di Lorenzo, Johnny: buried in East River, NY, 316; of Genovese "family", 276
DIA, 30, 331
Dialogue Conspiracy, 27; December 25, 1977, 345
Diamonds are Forever: James Bond novel, 416
Diebold Corporation and fraudulent voting machines, 21
Diehl, Nevada Gambling Commission, 196
Dien Bien Phu, 63, 65, 107, 153, 224, 446
Dietrich, Noah, 48, 50, 52, 64, 155, 159, 164, 167, 168, 179, 390, 396, 398

Dirksen, Senator Everett, 72, 76
Dita Beard ITT memo, 223, 309
DNA Research Collective, 335
Dole, Bob, 184
Dorticos, President of Cuba: offered to remove the Cuban missiles, 197
Double Cross: The Explosive, Inside Story of the Mobster Who Controlled America: by Sam and Chuck Giancana, 66
Douglas, Helen Gahagan, 72, 282
Douglas, William O., Supreme Court Justice: and bribe from Onassis, 281; of Mafia Stardust Vegas bit, 277
Dr. Pepper company, Houston, Texas, 133
Drift Inn, 86, 87, 91, 304, 306, 307, 309, 311, 317, 318, 319, 323, 327, 330, 355; and gemstones, 92; Noel Gayler visits, 331; padlocked for 30 days after Watergate arrests, 311
Dubai, 143
Dudley, bought job of Ambassador to Denmark, 226
Duke, Dr. James "Red", 72, 269; and John Connally's 2 bullet wounds at Dallas, 266; shipped to Kabul, Afghanistan after Chappaquiddick, 258; surgeon at Parkland Hospital; fixed 2 bullet holes in John Connally at Dallas, 258
Dulles, Allen, 66, 316
Dunn and Bradstreet, 71, 84; Credit Report on Fratianno, 328
Dutton, Fred, 280
Dyke Bridge, 78, 123, 129, 241
Dymally, State Legislature, Sacramento, 215

E

Eagleton, Thomas, 241; drunk driving citations destroyed, 279; Mafia drunk from St. Louis, 278
Eastwood, Clint, 55, 388
Eaton, Robert P., 165; editor, My Life and Opinions, by Hughes, 53; got Lana Turner as a Mafia reward, 166
Eckersley, Howard, 82, 90, 129, 138, 163, 295; and Canadian stock fraud, 211; evaporated in June 1971, 185; under indictment for Mafia stock fraud in Canada, 161
Egan, Arthur: got Hoffa out of jail with Chappaquiddick phone records, 154
Egger, Frank, 397
Egger, Jack: ordered by CIA to keep an eye on Hughes, 397
Ehrlichman, John, 81

Einsatzgruppe, 428
Eisenhower, Ike, 140
elections, corrupt, 11, 21
Ellender, Senator, funeral, 292
Ellsberg trial, 299
Ellsberg, Daniel, 84, 151, 263, 291, 293, 315, 353, 433; "better voodoo", 284; and burglary of Dr. Fielding's office, 341; another patsy, 291; campaigns for McGovern, 300; faces prison for 115 years, 172; has Rand's "Project Star" in his pocket, 288; in Vietnam, 281; political trial for Pentagon Papers, 186; saving him from jail, 271; worked with Bobby and Mary Jo until RFK murder, 288
Emerald Beach Hotel, Nassau, Bahamas, 50, 64
Emerson, Faye, and Elliott Roosevelt, 399
Equiticorp, Hong Kong: true ownership disguised, 374
erased White House tape, 18-1/2 minutes, 90
Esalen Institute, Big Sur, 56
Exner, Judith Campbell, 353

F

Fairmont Hotel, 273, 355
Faisal, King, 95, 96
Faisal, Prince, 96
Fake by Clifford Irving, 176
Fantasia, 19
Farben, I. G., 61, 220
Farouk, King, a coin collector, 326
Farrar, John, 79, 108; Chappaquiddick Rescue Team diver, 56
Farrari, 276
Father Mootz: apparently had someone get Tisserant's papers to Roberts, 225
Fatima, 338
Fatima 3, 122, 126, 179; Holy Crusade, 90; Prophesy, 87
Fatima statue, sheds real olive oil tears, 272
FBI, 127; mobs of, 119; raid on SF, 264
Fellmeth, 115, 118, 123, 128, 130, 139, 140, 151, 169, 173, 187, 247
Ferrari, 106
Ferrie, David, 124, 296, 313; and witness Giesbrecht, 420
Fielding, Dr. Lewis: break-in at Beverly Hills office, 342; Ellsberg's psychiatrist, 86, 88
Finnegan's Wake, 20
First National Bank, Chicago, 362
Fish, Hamilton, 126
Flagship (bar), 304, 309
Flamingo casino: Las Vegas "White House", 392

Flanigan, ITT: and trade agreements with Russia, 213
Fleming, Ian: "sodium morphate" murdered?, 420
Fleming. Ian: and James Bond, Bruce Roberts, Gemstone File, 416; real life #007, master spy, author, 416
Fletcher. J.C., 361
Fletchers, 368
Flo Kennedy: Woman as Warrior, 333
Flying Dutchman, 15
Flynt, Jimmy, 357
Flynt, Larry, 352, 355, 358; $1 million offer, 356; published "sanitized" Skeleton Key in Hustler, 1979, 57
Fonda, Jane, 274, 281, 300, 315, 427
Fontainbleu Hotel, Miami: owned by Sinatra and Patriarcha, 272
Ford Foundation, 81, 181, 186, 220, 331
Ford, Charlotte, 119, 181, 220
Ford, Gerald, 40, 71, 72, 94, 98; drops extradition of "Hughes", 95; pardons Nixon, 95, 327
Foster, Dr. Marcus, 40, 55, 92; murder of, 30
Franklin National Bank, 363
Fratianno, Jimmy, 22, 67, 71, 73, 75, 78, 84, 90, 92, 94, 98, 125, 291, 326, 327, 328, 349, 350, 392; "The Weasel", 66; and $100,000 Dallas shot pay-off, 327; Dunn and Bradstreet Credit Report, 327
Free Masonry, 202
French Consul, Dien Bien Phu, 63
Fulbright, Senator William: speech, who owns the Senate?, 326
Fulton, Jo, 160, 185; Sen. Proxmire's niece, 128

G

Gallinaro, 165, 187; Mafia contract on his head, 142; revealed Hoover's Rosenstiel connection, 185
Gambino Mafia family, 363
Gandhi, Indira, 95
Gargan, Joe, 79, 108
Garrison, Jim, 10, 73, 124; framed by Gervais, 216
Garrison, Omar, 51
Garry, Charles, 81, 248, 283, 327; present when Black Panthers were shot, 248
Gay, Bill: Hughes' Mormon Mafia aide, 399
Gayler, Noel, 128, 160, 301, 306; bombs Indo-China, 214; DIA, 331; find that mineral in China--or else, 187; given charge of the Pacific fleet, 185; mineral, and smuggling, 136; sent to Iceland, 122; told Roberts about Chile shaft, 91
Gelli, Licio, 363
Gemstone experiment, 66
Gemstone File, 77, 83, 88, 89, 92, 334, 336, 344, 345, 351, 356, 383, 386, 396
Gemstone File (Illuminet), 382
Gemstone File (IllumiNet), 10
Gemstone file copies: burned by Gray, Magruder, Nixon, Mitchell, Browning, Greenagel, Knowland, Nader, others, 328
Gemstone File of Bruce Roberts, *101*
Gemstone File, Sixty Years of Corrupt Manipulation Within World Government Detailing the Events Surrounding the Assassination of JFK: Sixty Years of Corrupt Manipulation Within World Government Detailing the Events Surrounding the Assassination of JFK: by Richard Alan, 352
Gemstone plan, 86, 422; Gordon Liddy's, 92; of Gordon Liddy, 428; of Hunt and Liddy; break-in and fly-away, Las Vegas, 330
gemstones with histories: offered to foreign outlets, 174; selling to foreign countries, 132
Geneen, ITT head, 185
General Dynamics, 98
General Motors, 11, 102, 104, 110, 114, 115, 127, 133, 136, 163, 187, 188, 192, 195, 201, 202, 220, 226, 284; owned by Onassis, 216
Genovese, SF Mafia, 301
Genovese, Vito, 275; ran Sicilian invasion, WWII, 219
geological surveillance area, 107
Geotek, and crooks Chandler and Younger, 306
Gervais confessed he framed Jim Garrison, 216
Getty, Jean Paul, 61, 82
Giancana, Sam, Chicago Mafia, 61, 65, 67, 70, 447; assassinated, 98
Giannini and Bank of America, 326
Giannini, Mrs., owns Bank of America, 277
Gifford, K. Dun, 80; offered seven figures, 328
Glacer, Vera, and massive bribes to G.O.P., 202
Glomar Explorer, 54, 96
Goddard, Paulette, 64
Goldberg, Arthur, 114, 115
Golden Gate Bridge, 175
Golden Triangle, 65, 66, 84, 85, 128, 132, 156, 190, 192, 193, 219, 277, 290, 349, 361; heroin, 318; Taiwan-run, 153
Golden West, owned by Smith and Sinatra, 272
Golden, James John, 179
Golding, Thelma, Dayle Roberts' ex-wife: Mafia message, 204
Goldwater, Barry, 172

Goldwyn, Sam, Judge: died during Alioto trial, 197; heart attacked in the middle of Alioto trial, 261
Gonzales, Virgilio, 65, 313; at the Drift Inn, 311; Cuban emigre locksmith recruited by Hunt, 428
Good Housekeeping, 228
Goodwin, Richard, writes McGovern's speech, 317
Gordon, Jerry, 281, 299; director of L.A. Peace Coalition, 280
Government-As-Theatre, 72
Graham, Billy, 109, 113, 149, 151, 204, 236, 302, 317; Vatican Mafia, 153
Graham, Katharine, 79, 86, 88, 91, 94, 108, 425; "Deep Throat", 91; and death of hubby, Phillip, 326; had the Watergate burglars on tape, 89; set a trap for the Watergaters, 88
Graham, Phillip, 68, 354
Grant, Cary, 237
Gravel, Mike, Senator, 190, 243
Gray, L. Patrick, 89, 296, 301; burned batches of Gemstone File papers, 328; burned Gemstone File, 89; Hoover's successor, 211
Greeley, Father Andrew, on American Catholic Church, 183
Green Beret mercenaries, 361
Green, Keith, George Wallace's man, 275
Greenagel, 106, 112, 115, 126, 127, 131, 158, 183, 189, 328
Greenspun, Hank: and his files on Hughes, 330; and Hughes's game plans for election of Presidents, etc., 53; editor, Las Vegas Sun, 86; sues Onassis for $141 million, 295
Gregory, Thomas, 436
Griener: source for rubies; Roberts' employer?, 401
Groden, Robert J., 22
Grommet Bar, 96, 327
Groth, Daniel: shot Black Panthers, 411
Group of 40, 67, 73, 91
Gulf Oil, 362, 370; share in Martha Hill gold bonanza, 374
Gulf Resources and Chemicals Corporation, 88

H

Hahnemann's Hospital, 87, 88, 151
Haig, General Alexander, 434
Haiphong raid, 213
Halvonik, ACLU: "independents can't run for office.", 221
Hampton, Fred, 69, 80, 122, 125, 156, 185, 186, 248, 264
Hand, Michael, 361; helps organize bankrolling of Contras in El Salvador, 369
Hanoi Hilton, 107; Roberts' first wife imprisoned there after fall of Dien Bien Phu, 63
Hanrahan, 125; killed Hampton and Clark, 248
hard-core Mafia in San Francisco, 143
Harmony, Sally, Liddy's secretary, shreds Gemstone File, 89
Harold's Club, 97, 331; Casino, Reno, Nevada, 330
Harp, Gail, 176, 355; of Kish Realty, 327
Harpers, 277
Harris, Al: "heart-attacked" after meeting at Enrico's, 328; heart-attacked, 71; of California State Crime Commission, 327
Harris, Elizabeth, sponsor of Ms magazine, 151
Harris, Emily and Bill, 38
Harry's Bar, 275; padlocked, 278
Hearst, Patty, 31, 32, 34, 38, 42; abduction by the SLA, 384, 393; kidnapping, 18, 27, 92
Hearst, William Randolph, 221; food distribution in Oakland, 92; list of financial holdings, 35
Heevey, 120, 121
Heller, Joseph, 62; was George McGovern the model for Milo Minderbinder in Catch 22?, 257
Helliwell, Paul: CIA paymaster for Bay of Pigs, 370
Helms, Richard, 36, 71, 72, 96, 128, 161, 301, 316; CIA Director, 331; CIA, ships heroin out of Laos, 171
Hendy International Co, 315
heroin, 64, 66, 82, 85, 109, 125, 128, 156, 167, 182, 184, 192, 336, 447; $6 billion bust, 192; 'china plates', 85; refinery in U.S., 192; smuggling, 61; trade, protected by mines and bombs, 216
Hersh, Burton, 360
Hibernia Bank, 93
Hinckle, Warren, 337
Hiroshima, a whim of Truman's, 110
Hitler and the American connection, 413
Hitler, Adolph, 349; and prisons, 33; decoy taking the rap for WWII, 171
Ho Chi Minh, 231
Hoffa, Jimmy, 66, 81, 99, 122; endorsed Nixon, 172; loaned Loeb $2,000,000, got out of jail free, 154
Hogan, D. A., 165, 185
Holiday Airlines, 272
Hollister, Kathryn, 75, 105, 106, 232

Holy Crusade wars, 136
Holy War, 1973, Iraelis vs. Arabs, 92
Hoover, J. Edgar, FBI head, 37, 65, 94, 101, 105, 106, 109, 110, 130, 133, 191, 260, 313, 316, 319, 327, 354; apple pie poisoned, 311; death, May 2, 1972, 433; Del Mar racetrack deal, 186; died of rat poison, 245; Fagin school, 128; had Gemstone File from Roberts, 88; his files, 133, 145, 273; his murder, 314, 315; resistance of FBI white boys' club to Onassis take-over, 168
House of Representatives, passing bribes around like confetti, 215
House Select Committee's investigation, 357
Howard Hughes in Las Vegas, 51
Howard, The Amazing Mr. Hughes, 48
Hruska, Senator, 186
Hughes Aircraft, 52; owned by Hughes Medical Research Foundation, 164
Hughes Corp.: and laser research program, 401
Hughes Intelsat satellite: + Onassis-controlled Comsat satellite= 100% Mafia TV, 153
Hughes Medical Reseach Foundation: granted tax-exempt status, 52
Hughes Medical Research Foundation, 64, 73, 155; Mafia money funnel, 327; Mafia money funnel, 172, 191, 252
Hughes Tool Company, 48, 52, 53, 63, 335, 336, 353, 389; Liddy and Hunt used its calling cards, 86; oil-well drill bits still sucking oil, 54
Hughes Vegas casinos: $300 million "stolen", 294
Hughes, Howard, 10, 44, 81, 82, 85, 92, 97, 101, 105, 117, 118, 125, 128, 134, 159, 175, 176, 177, 178, 189, 230, 264, 265, 315, 353, 384, 390, 399; "freeze me, then defrost me later!?", 54; "Mormon Mafia bodyguards", 49; 2 Hughes doubles at once?, 51; airline, TWA, 52; and $50,000 "contribution" to CREEP, 432; and Bahamas excursion, 397; and cryogenics, 157, 210; and doubles, 50; and forged TWA appeal bonds, 163, 326; and Glomar Explorer, undersea mining, 54; and Howard Cannon, 49; and Onassis, 159; and phony marriage to Jean Peters, 49; and Summa Corporation, 331; autobiography, 159; autobiography hoax, 333; big toe unusually large, 219; biography, cross-referenced, 53; body authenticated by dental records, 164; bones of, 331; bribe $205,000 loan to Donald Nixon, 1956, 52, 115; buried off Tenos, Greece, April 23, 1971, 48, 330; communications satellites circling the globe, 54; Contributes to CREEP, 430; crippled old man on Skorpios?, 47; Deceased April 16, 1971, 154; disembodied voice, 165; empire run by a member of the Mafia, 185; helicopter gun-ship followed peace-marchers' bus to L.A., 277; in Vancouver, 212; kidnapped by Onassis, 18, 156; kidnapped by Onassis, 44; Kleenex boxes for shoes?, 51; living in Las Vegas in 1966?, 49; Onassis's Charlie McCarthy puppet, 73; organization, 361; Organization buying up old newsreels, 1968, 53; passed through Bahamas Customs without appearing, 51; really a computer?, 53; recovered body, on ice, 188; remains of, 213; Seven reporters interviewing a voice box???, 53; skim money from Las Vegas casinos, 370; trigger for WWIII, 331; trip from Bahamas to Miami to Nicaragua, 172; vigorous, well-groomed executive?, 51; will run his empire from his grave?, 54; worldwide communications satellite system, 295
Humphrey, Hubert, 75, 103, 106, 107, 126; bribed, 221
Hunt & Liddy, 425; CREEP operations plan, 425; laundered money through Cuban banker in Miami, 434; recruiting murderers and prostitutes in Miami, 426
Hunt, Dorothy: plane shot down to control blackmail of White House?, 35; sabotaged plane crash, 412
Hunt, Howard, 85, 86, 296, 313, 425; and his office at Mullen Co., a CIA front, 428; CIA, 65; one of the 3 "tramps" at Dealey Plaza?, 351; stone killer, 313; worked for Robert Bennett, 331
Hunt, Nelson Bunker, 360; sells some stock to Gulf Oil, 372
Hunt-Liddy "Gemstone plan", 330
Hustler, 16, 356
Hyannisport, 172
Hyatt Hotel chain, 370
hydrochloric acid, 309
hypnotized murderer, 92

I

I.S.A.S., 362
Ibizza, 159
IDAPS computer bureau, 374
Iglesias, Antonio, 15, 76, 97; at Bay of Pigs CIA invasion, 65
Iglesias, Marina, 15, 76
Impala Securities: new Australia money funnel, 371
Imperial Valley, 71

India, 285
Indo-China, bombed all of it except the poppy fields, 214
Indonesian Oil, 152; fat leases, Nixon, Rockefeller, Getty, Onassis, Connally, Johnson, etc., 153; offices, 153
Industrial Equity Ltd., 361
Industrial Equity Pacific, 371
Inside the Gemstone File (Adventures Unlimited, 10
Inside the Gemstone File: Howard Hughes, Onassis, and JFK: by Kenn Thomas and David Hatcher Childress, 416
insurance racket, 305
International Harvester Credit Co., 362
International Mafia, 361
Intertel, 128, 159, 165, 295
Iran and Phantom jets, 214
Ireland, peace for two Irish families, 285
Iron Curtain, 84
Irving Trust Co., 362
Irving, Clifford, 53, 81, 82, 84, 99, 159, 160, 163, 165, 172, 176, 185, 188, 211, 289, 315, 333; and Autobiography of Howard Hughes, 159; Little Green Reasons?, 52
Irving, Edith, 226
Is Howard Hughes Dead and Buried off a Greek Island?, 396; Playgirl article, 18
Is Howard Hughes Dead and Buried Off a Greek Island?, 385
Isoproterenol, 308, 313, 314
Isoproterenol canaster "a therapeutic disaster", 308
ITT, 174; $400,000 donation to CREEP, 425; Board of Directors, 87; includes John McCone, CIA, Dallas, and Francis L. Dale, head of CREEP, 72; Chilean funds, 313; Chilean plants, 92; hires Intertel to discredit Dita Beard, 197; paid no taxes for 5 years, 204; role in Chile chaos, 196

J

Jackson, George, 38
James Bond and the Gemstone File, 416
Jaworski, Leon, 40, 71, 72
Jefferson, Thomas, 9, 111, 325
JFK, 22. See also John F. Kennedy; "Get, 156; *28-man kill squad*, 98; assassination, 15; assassination modeled on FDR/Cermak operation, 218; Burke Marshall custodian of his brains after Dallas, 80; Mafia murder at Dallas, 107; cancels November 1, 1963, trip to Chicago, 156; screaming at Jackie on Onassis's yacht, 216
Jiddah Agreement, 63
Jim Braden. See Brading, Eugene
Jimmy the Greek, 175. See Snyder, Jimmy
Johnson, Haynes, 301
Johnson, Lyndon, 71, 87, 90, 107, 164, 179, 354; "Oswald didn't do it,", 140; and message from the Pentagon, 127; deal with Nixon, 109; heart attack, 274; Memorial Library Dedication, 109; warned by radio, 73
Joyce, James, and Finnegan's Wake, 20, 386
Judge for Yourself: by John Judge, 343
Judge, John, 10, 343
Jungers, head of Aramco, 96
Justice Department, 128, 131

K

Kabul, Afghanistan, 269
Karenga, Ron, CIA, 40
Kashoggi, Adnan: expands money laundry operation, 374
Katzenbach, Nicholas, 152
Kaye, Beverly, Stephen Bull's secretary, heard erased tape, heart-attacked, died age 40, 90
Kefauver, Senator Estes, 354; heart attack on Senate floor, 326; poisoned, heart attack on Senate floor, 68
Keith, Jim, 10, 339, 360, 382
Kelly, Grace, 237
Kennedy Memorial, 111
Kennedy, David, 363
Kennedy, Edward, 10, 48, 77, 79, 81, 82, 98, 101, 103, 105, 106, 110, 116, 118, 244, 254, 327, 330, 338, 354, 391; called Jackie and Onassis, 108; called Jackie and Onassis on the Christina after Chappaquiddick, 79; can't run for President because of Chappaquiddick, 289; Mary Jo Kopechne and Chappaquiddick, 56; planned to put John Tunney into Senate seat, 77; planning another Mafia murder on Chappaquiddick?, 107; ran to Onassis and swore obedience, 74; witness to Hughes's "burial at sea?", 45
Kennedy, Eunice, 298
Kennedy, Florynce, 99; *Woman as Warrior*, 27
Kennedy, Florynce R., 333
Kennedy, Jackie, 68, 77, 82, 106, 157, 232; cruises with Onassis, October 1963, 68; Onassis's baby-sitter?, 351
Kennedy, Joan Bennett, 77, 228
Kennedy, John F.: assassination, 266, 395;

assassination; a secret coup, 390
Kennedy, Joseph P., 61, 64, 65, 66, 77, 101, 103, 105, 109, 110, 111, 115, 125, 134, 167, 171, 177, 182, 191, 219, 230, 336, 337, 354
Kennedy, Joseph P., III, 108
Kennedy, Joseph, III, 79
Kennedy, Robert F., 68, 75, 101, 107, 137, 157, 326; assassination, 397; assassination, 38; assassination cover-up, 255; his murderer, 132; knew who killed his brother, 74; Mafia murder at Los Angeles, 107; murder by Thane Eugene Cesar, 152
Kennedy, Teddy, 77, 101, 127, 300; Targeted by Liddy, 432
Kennedy-Onassis-Vatican's Vietnam, 119
Kennedy-Spellman: "Vietnam a Holy Crusade", 154
Kent State killings, 40
Keough, Rosemary's purse, 78, 108
Kerkorian, Kirk, 133
Kerr, Clark, 38
Kerry, John, 21
Khaddafi, Moammar, 360
Killing of a President, The, 22
Kimball family, 301
Kimball, C. J., Roberts' CIA-connected uncle, 15
Kimball, CIA cousin: strangles Africa, in Nigeria, 328
Kimelman, Henry, 254; of West Indies Corp. and Virgin Islands Hilton, 280
King, Leslie, Sr., 72
King, Martin Luther, 118, 141; assassination, 39; assassination arranged by Maheu, 126; mother murdered, 1974, 92
King, Martin Luther, Jr., 429
King, Martin Luther, Mrs., 240
King's Castle swindle, 250
King's Point Condominium, 414
Kirk, Claude, 37
Kirk, Norman, 364; sodium morphate poisoned?, 365
Kirlian photography, 96, 335
Kish, 176
Kissinger, Henry, 73, 84, 91, 94, 95, 97, 118, 128, 134, 135, 139, 162, 164, 176, 182, 185, 186, 212, 213, 221, 227, 283, 288, 291, 296, 309, 328, 331; and power as aphrodisiac, 214; had to get to Peking, 264
Kiwi: subliminal TV messages, 378
Kiwi Gemstone, 10; politics in Australia, 391
Kiwi Gemstone File. See Opal File
Klaber, William: interviewed Geneva White, 70

Kleindienst, 301, 314; Senate whitewash, 219
KLRB-FM, Carmel California, 341
Knapp Commission: revealed New York police corruption, 147
Knights of Columbus, 122, 164
Knolls Atomic Power Laboratory, 445
Knowland, 106
Koerner, Governor of Illinois, 163
Koerner, Otto, Jr., 408
Kopechne, Ma and Pa, 117
Kopechne, Mary Jo, 56, 77, 80, 83, 90, 101, 103, 105, 106, 118, 122, 129, 130, 134, 155, 157, 175, 181, 183, 255, 298, 314, 327, 354, 391; broken nose, 108; died of suffocation, not drowning, 108; memorial cross from Brezhnev, 323; plaque hanging in Metropolitan Museum, NYC, 215; Public Research Groups, 146
KPFK, 93
Kraft, Joseph, 197, 239
Krassner, Paul, 44, 314, 322, 341, 342, 346, 382, 388; The Realist, 18, 27
Krogh, Egil, 428
KSAN Radio Station, 347
Kunming, U.S. Army Base, 63, 65, 107
Kupcinet, Irving, 172
Kushner, Valerie, POW's wife, 240
Kwong, Lawrence, hypnotized to kill, 35

L

L.A. Star, 414
La Costa Country Club, 72
La Follette, Bronson, 119
La Follette, Robert, 61
Lacey, Pat, Governor, 240
Ladar, 191
Ladies' Home Journal: excerpts from Eaton book, February 1972, 53
Lake Pontchartrain, Louisiana, 65, 66, 68, 326
Lake, Veronica, 64
Lane, Mark, 293; attorney for Jane Fonda, 300; represented Bolden in court, 410
Lange, D., NZ politician: goes on Mafia payroll, 375
Lansky, Meyer, 61, 65, 105, 197, 252, 336, 392; and Deauville Hotel, 240; hiding in Tel Aviv, 214; ran Cuban gambling operation for Onassis, 74; skim money from Vegas casinos, 157
Lanza, 65, 75, 172, 204, 232, 301; S.F. Mafia, Alioto's godfather, 155
LAPD, 31; Swat Team, 93
Las Vegas, 64, 71, 72, 74, 82, 97, 125, 133, 157,

159, 177, 392, 396; break-in and fly-away plan, 330; Desert Inn, 51; shit pit, 294; skim money bribes, 105
Las Vegas Sun, 53, 197
laser beam research, 66
Lasky, Moses, 92
Lawrence, Sidney: cottage at Chappaquiddick, 77, 107
leather hat, 98
Legacy of Doubt, 1976, by Peter Noyes, 98
Legislative Advisory Commission: bank interest rates in California, 119
Lello, and Mafia threat, 131, 176
Lennon, John, similar assassination scenario to Lawrence Kwong, 35
Letter to Anwar Sadat, President of of Egypt, 326
Liberty Lobby, 413
Liberty Ships, 354; Justice Burger helped Onassis steal them, 284; Onassis stole from U.S. a whole fleet at bargain basement prices, 80
Liddy, Gordon, 85, 86, 87, 88, 89, 92, 306, 313, 319, 323, 327, 330, 339, 342, 389, 422; "a murdering slob", 87; and Elmer Davis, 343; and his Gemstone Plan, 1971-2, 428; and his personal ethics regarding murder, 431; burns hand to impress potential prostitute recruit, 425; CIA contract killer, list of 10 murders, 376; his secretary, Sally Harmony, shreds Gemstone File at CREEP, 89; his situational ethics, 427; led White House "plumbers" burglarizing Ellsberg's shrink's office, 342; re murder of Officer Tippitt ?, 376; recruits Mafia killers for his Gemstone 'Special Action Group', 429; stages rally in Miami in support of Nixon, 435; suggested that drug operatives be killed by Liddy's group, 428
Liedtke, 88
Life, 172, 279, 354
Lifton, David, 409
Lindberg, Jim, 179, 265, 304, 317
Lindy Division of Union Carbide, 401
Lipset, Hal, 41, 86, 88, 90, 91, 92, 94, 425; Katharine Graham's employee, 330; retaped the door at Watergate, 327; taped and retaped the door, and caught the Watergate 5, 330; taped the door at Watergate, 88; taped the Drift Inn sessions, 330
Liquigas Limited, 370
Little, Russell, 30, 31, 39, 40, 92
Livanos, Stavros, 62; father of Eugenie and Tina, 418

Llellyveld, Jerry, 137; cover-up of Chappaquiddick phone calls in New York Times, 170
Lobster: criticism of Skeleton Key, 344
Lockheed, 134, 163; gets enormous loan from U.S. Government, 160; purchased by Onassis with "Hughes" money-funnel funds, 160; Thane Cesar's employer, 74; wins $1 billion in defense contracts, to be done in Greece, 221
Lockheed Aircraft, 363
Loeb, Manchester Union Leader, 122
Lone Assassin Chorus, 35
lone assassins, 41
Look, 73, 77, 84, 101, 197, 222, 255, 292, 327, 354; apologized to Alioto, and folded, 86
Look, Deputy Sheriff Christopher, 78, 108
Los Angeles Free Press, 353
Los Angeles Times, 153, 251
Los Venceremos, 40
Louisiana, and Mafia election process, 293
Lowry, Kitty, 265, 304; Hughes's aunt, 159
Loyola, Ignatius, 135
Luce, 98
Luciano, Lucky, 141; and Sicilian invasion, WWII, 219; in WWII, 336

M

Mack, John, 81, 106, 126, 127, 136, 162, 221, 222, 234, 245, 328; and selling Gemstones with Histories to Foreign Countries, 130; Attorney for Bank of California, 187; can of worms, 215
MacLaine, Shirley, 239
Madison Guaranty S&L, 414
Mafia, 16; bills as riders in Congress, 153; money funnel, 152; Nut Tree meeting, 86; ownership, purchase and looting of all branches of government, 150; partners, 272; state ownerships, 139
Mafia election process, 105, 243; media imagery; rigging voting, 106
Mafia Kingfish: Carlos Marcello and the Assassination of John F. Kennedy: by John Davis, 66
Mafia meeting in San Francisco, 372
Mafia Miami Convention: 23 hotels owned by Mafia, 252
Mafia system: Legal Mafia, 117; Press and Media Mafia, 117; Vatican and other church Mafia, 117
Mafia two-party system, 106, 298
Mafia way:: give up a little, to preserve the keys and the basic structure, 137

Magi, the, 87
magic bullet theory: a big laugh, 72; down the tubes, 258
Magnin, I., 76
Magnin, Rabbi Cyril: involvement in Chappaquiddick incident, 77; *Mae Magnin Brussell's uncle*, 76
Magnin, Rabbi Edward: Mae Magnin Brussell's father, 76
Magruder, Jeb, 425, 439
Magruder, Jeb, burned his Gemstone file copy in a fireplace, 328
Maheu, Robert, 50, 66, 68, 74, 82, 125, 177, 300, 347, 353, 361, 390, 397, 420; "Iron Bob" or I.B.M., 125; "wins" damage suit against "Hughes", 92; ex-FBI, 49; gets private pay-off to drop suit against "Hughes", 332; hired by CIA to assassinate Castro, 156; on taking Hughes from Boston to Vegas in 1966, 51; sues Onassis, as Hughes, for $50 million, 115; suing "Hughes" for $50 million for arranging the major assassinations, 160; tried rat poison on Castro, 245
Maier, John. See Meyer, John; Meier, John, Meyer, Andre; oversees Jackie O, 133
mail sacks at Watergate break-in, 440
Maillard, strangles South America from O.A.S. office, 328
Maiman, Dr. Theodore H.: "inventor of the laser beam", 400
Manchester Union Leader, 81, 145, 154, 222; Chappaquiddick phone call records, 137
Manhattan Project, 264
manila envelopes, 89
Mankiewicz, Joseph: and Bobby's delegates, 244; managing McGovern's campaign, *208*
Mansfield, Mike, 95
Manson, Charles, 279
Mao, 187
Marcello, Carlos, 66, 70, 124, 338
Marchetti, Victor, 33
Marcos, President Ferdinand: bribed Philippine Legislature, 220; loots the Philippine archipelago, 186
Mari and Adamo, Mafia hoods, 80, 110, 119, 177, 235
Marin County Courthouse shootout, 40
Mark Hotel Bar, 160, 162, 264
Markham, 108
Markopolis, Koula, 47
Marriott catering service: caters for Onassis' Olympic Airlines, 295

Marseilles heroin factory, 80, 110
Marshall, Burke, 62, 80, 108, 246, 354
Martha's Vineyard Gazette: James Reston's paper, 115
Martin, Fred, 127, 221
Martin, Malachi, 206
Martinez, Eugenio, 313, 436; at the Drift Inn, 311; Bay of Pigs, CIA Castro and JFK assassination team, Nixon's Watergate "burglar", team member, 65
Mason, Dr. Verne: Director of the Hughes Medical Research Foundation, 49
Massachusetts Highway Patrol, 80
McCarthy, Mary, 92
McCloy, John, 361; Plan to assassinate him, involving Liddy, 376
McCone, Bechtel, BRT-MK, 286
McCone, John, 71, 72, 161, 196, 245, 247, 253, 301, 319; CIA chief, hired Maheu to assassinate Castro, 231; ITT-CIA, 202, 315; six Latin American countries on the murder block, 195
McCone, John, CIA chief, 160, 195
McCord, James, 350; electronics expert from CREEP, 428; recruited by Liddy for his Gemstone operations, 432; wire-tapped the phones at Watergate, 88
McCord, James, CIA, 65, 86, 88, 294, 297, 304, 313; at the Drift Inn, 311; Watergate burglar, member of Office of Emergency Preparedness, 33
McCormack, John, 127, 164
McCoy, Alfred, 427; article in Harper's on heroin traffic, 277; named all Viet leaders as dope pushers in Senate, 219
McCrory, Mary, 316
McCullough, Frank, encounter with "Hughes", 50
McCullough, Virginia, 341, 343
McGovern, George, 62, 244, 251, 253, 256, 432; and heroin trade, 240; director, Food for Peace, 280; Target for Liddy's Gemstone operation, 432
McGovern, Senator George: target of Liddy's Gemstone Plan, 429
McGraw-Hill, 82, 84, 99, 159, 160, 161, 172, 185, 333; announces publication of Hughes autobiography, 150
McGucken, Archbishop, 109
McKinstree, Canadian Customs: grants "Hughes" visa, gets Swiss account, 225
McLaney, 125, 296
McLuhan, Marshall, 337

McNamara, Bob "Body Count", 84, 110, 122, 179, 186, 192, 226, 265, 286, 288, 289, 291, 293, 295, 300, 301, 302, 303, 307, 315; moved on to the World Bank, 288; reasons for Vietnam war, 149
Meaghre, Sylvia, 411
Meany, George, 172, 265
Meier, Andre: Onassis's right-hand man, 295
Meier, John, 295; and mining claim swindle, 197; hires Maheu to run Onassis-"Hughes" Vegas casino empire, 157
Meier, John, the younger, 157
Meir, Golda, 252; protecting Meyer Lansky, 214
Memorial Day, 212; Teddy's response, 212
Mercantile Bank and Trust, CIA bank: used by Gulf Oil and McDonnell Douglas, 371
Merryman, 82, 129, 132, 137, 138, 159, 160, 163, 168, 185, 188, 295; squealed to Clifford Irving, 289; tapes, 161, 166
Merryman, Louise, 140, 160, 167, 185
Merryman, Marie Elena, 160
Metcalf, Senator: and Corporate Secrecy, 247
Meyer, Eugene, 61, 68
Meyer, John, 48, 115, 167, 178, 211, 231; and $100,000 nonrepayable loan, 399; qualification for office as Senator, 214; watches over Jackie, 397
Miami Beach, 208, 293, 334, 344, 383
Miami National Bank, 153; launders profits from CIA Colombian cocaine operation, 369
Miami National Bank, funnels Lansky loot, 164
Mickey Mouse, 19
Midnight, 45, 47, 48, 82, 83
Milam, Marin, 44, 56, 333; editor of Playgirl, 18
Miller, Harry, 116
Milo Minderbinder: George McGovern the model for?, 62
Milquetoast, Caspar, 388
mind control, 38, 393
Miranda, Carmen, 402
Miss America (hideous whore), 170
missile site, 110
Mitchell, John, 77, 91, 101, 105, 106, 107, 126, 131, 138, 139, 145, 172, 181, 185, 313; Nixon's Attorney General, 428
Mitchell, Martha, 173, 296, 314; jabbed in the ass by 4 Watergaters who got away, 311
Mitsubishi, 362
Mitsui, 362
Mitsuis Corporation, Japan, 61
MMORDIS, 16, 178; Onassis-"Hughes" Maf + J. Mafia Hoover's club =, 177

money funnel, tax-free, 52
Monte Carlo Casino: bought by Onassis, 418
Monte Carlo, Monaco, 63, 74
Montini, Pope, 87; assisted Martin Bohrmann's escape?, 349; double spy after WWII, infuriating previous Pope, 290
Montoya, Senator: and bribe to LBJ from Hoffa, 197
Moore, Jim, liar and plagiarist, 357
Mootz, Father, 224; had someone deliver Tisserant's paper to Roberts, 302
mordida: bribe envelopes, 279
More Journalism Review, 93, 101
Morgenthau, Henry: "The Mafia owns America.", 145
Mormon Mafia, 74, 82, 90, 94, 129, 137, 159, 185, 211, 390; nursemaids., 82
Moscone, George, 120
Moscow, Nixon"s aim for Russian trip, 212
Mother, Letters to: March 20-April 9, 1972, 195
Ms magazine, 151
Muldoon, 360; imposes withholding tax on offshore borrowing, 373
Mullen and Co., 85; under CIA contract, 331
Mullen Company, 427
Mullen Public Relations Corp., 313
Mullen, Robert, 313
Multinational corporations: control the economy of other countries, 245
Mummert, 183; from S.F. Coin Club, 328
Murder of the Family of the Man Who Elected Nixon..., 151
Murdoch, Rupert, 364
Muskie, 75, 105, 106, 107, 125, 222, 232, 244
Muskie, Senator Edmund: Gemstone plan target, 429
Mussolini, Benito, 349
Mustapha Bey, 182; Diary on Onassis, 125, 126, 132, 156, 175; Diary on Onassis, and Jackie O, 251; Onassis impresses him with Jackie, 126; sleeping with Jackie, 226; Turkish Bey, 68; wife divorced him over Jackie O, 251
Myanmar, formerly Burma, 444
myasthenia gravis, 96
mysterious mineral, 264

N

N.Y. Supreme Court Justices: paid Genovese for their jobs, 316
Nacht und Nebel, 428
Nader, Ralph, 11, 46, 78, 101, 105, 107, 112, 114, 115, 117, 118, 120, 127, 129, 130, 133, 154, 201,

264, 283, 346; $457,000 cash settlement with General Motors, August 14, 1970, 114, 192; bribe, 140; burned his copy of Gemstone File papers, 328; busy with bum deodorants, 284; death of Nader's Consumer Party, 116; leading in polls, 314; Letter, December 8, 1971; cradle to grave with Mafia, 149; letters to, 101, 105, 116, 125, 151; Mary Jo Kopechne's new idol, 107
Nassau, Bahamas, 50, 398, 399
Nation, The, 177
National Bank of Washington, 297
National Enquirer, 83
National General Corporation, 272; owners, Sinatra, Klein, etc., 301
National Security Council, 30, 33, 262, 263, 331
National Tattler, 414
National Transportation Safety Board: sued by Skolnick, 412
Native Americans distributed Skeleton Key, 19
Nazi Germany, 33; imported to USA, 30
Necrophilia, 123
Neilsen-Green office: CIA front, 129
Nero, 201, 229; burned Rome to hide Crucixion details, 87
Neuhaus, Donald: guarded Jean Peters' bungalow, 396
New Hebrides, 363
New Jersey: Kennedy Mafia, 107
New York City, 333
New York Review of Books, 92
New York Times, 80, 85, 94, 115, 137, 139, 170, 197, 201, 219, 259, 289, 291, 296, 354
New Zealand, 360; Liddy barred from entering, 424
Newbergh, Esther, 114
news censorship, 61, 211
NEWSMAKING.NEWS.COM, 341
Newsom, 106, 165, 264; followed Roberts around, 235
Newsom's nieces, 110, 112, 135
Newsweek, 354
Newton, Huey, 250
Ngo Din Diem, 69
Ngo Din Nhu, 69
Ngo Din Thuc, 69
Ngo Dinh Thuc, 82, 125, 126, 190, 192, 229, 288
Ngo Dinh Thuc, Archbishop, 156
Nhu, Madame, 69, 125
Niarchos, Charlotte Ford, 81
Niarchos, Eugenie Livanos, 81, 103, 119, 181
Niarchos, Stavros, 61, 62, 81, 84, 95, 119, 181, 347, 418; murders his first wife, Eugenie, then marries her sister Tina, 220
Niarchos, Tina Livanos Onassis Blandford, 95
Nicaea, Council of, 87
Nicaea, Council of, 325 a.d., 178
Nicaragua, 52, 82, 174, 180, 185, 188, 194, 225, 289, 309, 313; Vesco, Donald Nixon, Somoza, Figueres hiding there, 330
Nigeria, 186; and CIA operations, 15
Nigerian consulate, 328
Nissen, U.S. Attorney, 284
Nixon, 363
Nixon, Donald, 52, 164, 191, 330; and 205,000 loan from Hughes, 1956, 63; in the housing business with Onassis, 163; runs Marriott catering services, caters for Onassis's airline, 295
Nixon, Julie, 94
Nixon, Patricia, 174, 189
Nixon, Richard, 10, 29, 41, 63, 72, 76, 77, 85, 89, 90, 94, 101, 105, 106, 112, 126, 129, 131, 135, 143, 154, 155, 231, 260, 296, 313, 314, 323, 327, 351, 370; "Don't mention that bugging any more!", 312; "Golden Circle", 170; a victim?, 351; aims for Moscow trip, 213; and Brezhnev, 213; bill to impeach introduced, 219; bought by Hughes's $205,000 bribe?, 52, 167; burned his copy of the Gemstone File, 328; decides to invade Cambodia, 102; got approval for Hughes Medical Research Foundation, 164; hides in San Clemente, 332; his "new evidence" on Watergate, 91; message to Congress, 213; mines Haiphong Harbor, 434; ordered murder of Roberts and his family, 106; Peace Mission to China, 172; ran up $100 billion extra debt in 3 years, 219; resignation, 93; resignation due to Gemstone?, 15; signs some checks personally, 265; thoughts on the Convention, 304; trips to China and Russia on his belly, 149; visits Tito in Yugoslavia, 331
Nixon, Tricia, 127
Nixon: A Life: by Jonathan Aitken, 81
Nixonburger, 52, 63, 164, 191
No Name Key, Florida, 65
Noguchi, Thomas, 74
Nol, Lon, 97
North Miami Beach, 99
North Vietnam, 63, 290
Northern Ireland, 201
Northrop, 98
Norwegian consulate, 320
Novacs, Mike, 155

Novotny, investigated by Fensterwald, 217
Noyes, Peter, 98
Nugan Hand bank, 360
Nugan, Frank, 369
Nung, Captain, 229
Nut Tree Restaurant, 73, 94, 98
NZ: Media takeover begins, 371
NZ liquor industry, buying up, 370
NZ Mafia meeting, 373
NZ Mafia meeting, Cook Islands, 373
NZ Maritime Holdings, 373
NZ Media takeover, 373
NZ Ruling Council, 372
NZ taxpayers lose $100 million: on sale of Kariori Pulp Mill, 375

O

O'Brien, Larry, 85, 88, 90, 126, 133, 157, 168, 239, 304, 330
Oakland: and food give-aways, 27; targeted for disruption, 34
Oakland Tribune, 106
O'Brien, Larry, 433
Ogarrio, Manuel, 434
Oglesby, Carl, 411
oil cartel memo, 61, 447
Okay Corral shoot-out, 291
O'Keefe, Stanton: The Real Howard Hughes Story, 396
oligarchy, 20, 47
Oliver, Spencer, 88, 330
Olympic Airlines, Onassis's Greek airline, 295
Olympic Challenger, 62
Olympic Whaling Company, 62
Omerta., 47, 141, 160, 169, 182, 221
Onassis, 361; heroin operations, 361
Onassis-"Hughes", 128, 165; business entity created after Onassis grabbed Hughes, 66; fires Noah Dietrich, 164; gossip around the Mediterranean, 159; Mafia money funnel, 163; Mafia Money Funnel, 216; Mafia Money Funnel, 176, 185; mob moves, August 16, 1972, 318; purchase of all U.S. Senators, 169; purchase of presidents and the national economy, 172
Onassis-"Hughes" empire, 152
Onassis-"Hughes",: combined entity after the kidnap, 126
Onassis-"Hughes", 174
Onassis, Aristotle: his General Motors sent Thane Cesar to "guard, 152
Onassis, Alexander, 118; his father's dream, 294; plane crash and death, January 1973, 90
Onassis, Aristotle, 44, 47, 68, 74, 77, 81, 82, 83, 84, 85, 86, 88, 90, 94, 96, 97, 105, 106, 108, 109, 110, 111, 118, 132, 137, 157, 177, 188, 218, 252, 256, 259, 260, 263, 298, 304, 305, 313, 318, 326, 347, 354, 384, 397, 400, 447, 448. passim; 1107 Sacramento Street, SF, 161; 1170 Sacramento Street, SF, 129; a victim?, 351; after JFK hit, filled all important government posts with his own men, 73; and Credite Suisse (Swiss Bank), 72; and Credite Suisse (Swiss Bank), 190; and evenhanded bribing of all candidates, 157; and Kennedys, 136; and Mafia aliases owning stock in Lockheed, General Motors, etc., 136; and Mustapha Bey's diary on him, 153; and oil deal with King of Saudi Arabia, 418; and Pappas Greek Mafia, 202; and phony mining claims, 214; and Switzerland, 253; bribes to Nader and Nixon, 136; builds Ariston, largest oil tanker built at that time, 61; buys control of Monte Carlo, Monaco, 63; calls Apalachin meeting in 1957, about Hughes kidnap and other matters, 167; *dated movie stars, like Hughes*, 64; deal with Joseph P. Kennedy, Eugene Meyer, Meyer Lansky, 1932, 61; gets $45 million skim money from Vegas, 133; gets Jackie into the "Hughes is alive" act, 178; got $60 million per American death in Vietnam, 228; great green octopus?, 54; heroin, cocaine, booze, 109; his man, Captain Nung, blasts Diem and Nhu, November 1, 1963, 156; Hoffa, and Labor-Hood Mafia, 156; loved performing politcal assassinations in public, 156; marriage contract to Jackie arranged after Big O has RFK shot, 126; marriage contract with Jackie, 157; *marries Tina Livanos, 1946*, 62; Mustapha Bey's diary, 251; next president, no matter who wins the election, 253; orders triple murder of Diem, Nhu, and JFK, 156; owned world's largest tanker fleet, 418; owns; ITT, 181; owns all, 134; owns CIA, 156; owns General Motors, 181; owns General Motors, 133; owns Kerkorian, 133; owns Lockheed, 181; phobia, /, 273; purchased America, 110; ran French brandy and cocaine into New Orleans, 230; ran heroin and cocaine into Boston, 230; ran Marseilles heroin into Montreal, 230; served all warring parties, 154; shares in Biafra oil leases, 186; signs contract with J. Paul Getty to move oil from California to Japan, 61; skim money from, 327; Skorpios and Tenos, 45; snatched JFK's girl and his gun,

109; sold oil, arms, dope to both sides in WWII, 61; son Alexander born in U.S., 1948, 62; swindles US out of 16 Liberty Ships, 62, 126; Swiss banks, 192, 226; takeover of Greece via the Colonels, 168; take-over of Greece via the Colonels, 155; takeover of U.S. via the Kennedys in 1960, 167; Teddy visits his yacht, Christina, after RFK murder, bargains for his life, 126; teen-age crimes, 126; Vegas operations, 86
Onassis, Christina, 220
Onassis, Jackie Kennedy, 45, 47
Onassis, Jackie Kennedy, 48
Onassis, Tina Livanos, 80
Onassis, Tina, largest oil tanker in the world, 1953, 63
Onassis-"Hughes", 151; flight from Vegas to Bahamas, Nicaragua, Vancouver, 289; Mafia money funnel, 167
Onassis-"Hughes" Mafia Money Funnel, 294
Onassis-"Hughes": Las Vegas casinos, 72; Mafia money funnel, 156
Onassis-"Hughes" Mafia Money Funnel, 184
Onassis-\'Hughes": TV station airlifted to Peking, 153
One World Government, 362
Opal File. See Kiwi Gemstone File
Operation Phoenix, 29
Operation Zebra, 29
OPM, 63
OPM (Other People's Money), 62
OSS, 335
Oswald, Lee Harvey, 32, 40, 68, 70, 314, 326, 341, 349, 350, 353; patsy, 382; there to nail John Connally, 291

P

Pachtner, Kay, 120, 255
Pahn, Stuart, 410
Paley, William, oil Mafia, owns CBS-TV, 243
Palm Springs, 291
Papal Mafia Holy Crusade, 145
Pappas, Tom, 82, 351
Paraguay: $100 million World Bank loan for highway, "from a swamp to a cliff", 286; *dope highway*, 85
Parkland hospital, Dallas, 266
Parsky, Gerald, 361
Parsons, Louella, 64, 396; announces Hughes's marriage, 49
Partnership Pacific, 361
Patoski, Joe Nick, editor, Texas Monthly, 266

Patrick, Buchanan and Phillips, 152
patsies: Bremer, Arthur, 28; DeFreeze, Donald, 28; Donald DeFreeze, 36; James Earl Ray, 39; Jonathan Jackson, 40; Oswald, Lee Harvey, 28; Oswald, Lee Harvey, 68; Ray, James Earl, 28; Ruby, Jack, 28; Sirhan Sirhan, 28; Sirhan Sirhan, 38
patsy: Lee Harvey Oswald, 32
Patty Hearst, 341, 382
Pavlov: Russian consulate, 320
Pelosi's daughters: died in arson fire, 196; Newsom's neces, 135
Penn Central Railroad, 292
Pennzoil Corporation, 88
Pentagon, 33, 73, 77, 109, 137, 165, 185, 263, 331; installing dictators everywhere, 286; message to Lyndon Johnson on Air Force 1: Onassis' toy, 221; publishes 371 magazines, cost $56 million per year, 221
Pentagon Papers, 84, 85, 86, 115, 122, 137, 160, 166, 198, 211, 226, 291, 295, 296, 302; trial stayed, 296
Penthouse, 16
Pepsi Cola factory, 85
pergola at Dealey Plaza, 22, 57, 76, 350; adjacent to the grassy knoll, 15
Perlick, Charles, and Newspaper Guild bribe, 283
Perlmutter, Caribbean action, 234
Peron's Argentina: all dissenters are persecuted, 220
Perry's Bar, 304
Peters, Jean, 64, 125, 137, 156, 168, 185, 220, 221, 230; $2 million cash, 157; and fake marriage, 396; divorce from Howard Hughes's corpse, 160; divorces Hughes--2 months after his burial?, 49; got $1 million to participate in marriage hoax, 64; visits Hughes in Vegas for half an hour every 2 weeks?, 49
Peterson, Henry: Justice's new Criminal Chief, 172
Peterson, Henry, meets with Nixon, disposing of Gemstone file, 89
Peterson, Scott, 42
Petrocorp, 367
Petucci, Claretta, Mussolini's mistress, 349
Petucci, Dr. Francisco, Claretta's father, gave Pope Pius XI mortal injection?, 349
Phelan, Jim, 168
Phenomicon Convention, Atlanta, Georgia, 416
Phillips, Barbara, 153, 167, 176; sponsor of Ms magazine, 151

Phoenix Program, 37, 222, 361
phone calls, tapped, 176
Pike River Coal Company, 370
Pike, Emily, 222
Pius XI, Pope: murdered by Mussolini, 226
Pius, Pope, 237
Placid Oil Company, 360
Plains Georgia Monitor, 353
Plato: "taxes keep people in line", 245
Playgirl, 18, 46, 83, 94, 95, 333, 345, 384, 385, 396
Plumbers, 88, 90, 92
political assassinations, 29, 66, 67, 69, 128, 156, 159, 243; as goverment policy of domestic terrorization, 28
politically incorrect people, 404
Politics, 293
Politics of Heroin in Southeast Asia, 318
Pontius Pilate, 201
Pope Montini, 76, 79, 94, 98, 224, 247, 251, 253; Jewish-Italian, 326
Pope Paul VI, 171
Pope Paul VI (Montini): "Deputy of Christ at Auschwitz", 171; wants to quit, but can't, 225
Pope Paul VI (Montini), church a house divided, 206
population control, 28
Post, Jeffrey, 444
Poucha Pond, 56, 78, 81, 101, 108, 323
POW: and 4th of July bombing, 240; wives, 175
Prendergast, Harry Truman's boss, 182
Prendergast-Trumans, 136
Prentice-Hall Publishers, 99, 333
presidential pouches containing heroin, 182
Price Waterhouse, 265
Prince Rainier III: prince of Monaco, 418
Princeton Study: Hoover needs informers, 149
prisons: California, 393
Pritzker family, 370
Progressive Party Formation, 119
Prohibition and booze-smuggling, 61
Project Seek, 74, 82, 93, 396
Project Seek: Onassis, Kennedy and the Gemstone Thesis, 17; by Gerald Carroll, 57
Project Star, 85, 198, 272, 284, 288, 289, 291, 329

R

Radziwill, Lee Bouvier, 68
Ramparts, 263
Ramsey, Robin, of Lobster, 344
Rand Corporation, 84, 85, 314; and blackmail files, 198; Project Star, 198
rat poison, 314

Ray, James Earl, 39, 314, 353
Readers' Digest, 103
Reagan, Ronald: Nader a 'mouse trying to fuck an elephant.', 130
Real Howard Hughes Story, The: by Stanton O'Keefe, 49, 396
Realist, 18, 27, 44, 322, 341, 382, 388
Rebozo, Bebe, 231, 305, 370
Recrion, 278
Rector, L. Wayne, 74, 81, 82, 86, 90, 398; a "Hughes" double, 64; killed at Rothschild's Inn of the Park,1973, 90; murdered at Rothschild's Inn of the Park, London, Jan. 15, 1973, 330; wife searches for his body, 332
Rehak, Bob, a bearded Howard Hughes?, 51
Remiro, Joseph, 30, 31, 92
Renzo, Peter: and pet tigers, 340; author, Beyond the Gemstone Files, 339
Reopening of the Alioto Mafia Web story, 94
Report of the Warren Commission, 31
Reston, James, 80, 115, 170, 197; quote on Mafia dictatorship vs. democracy, 151
Ribicoff, Abe, Senator, 240, 280
Richey, Federal Judge: bought his job for $50,000, 201
Riconoscuito, Michael, 414
Rifkind, Simon, 115, 116, 118, 127
Rigor mortis, 78
Ritchie, Judge, 319
Robert Jones Investments, 372
Roberts,, 16
Roberts, Bruce, 14, 45, 57, 75, 94, 95, 105, 199, 320, 322, 333, 335, 347, 353, 355, 383, 384, 423, 447; and Carmen Miranda, 402; and CIA-induced "Brezhnev flu", March 1975, 96; and Genovese, 55; and his reaction to Skeleton Key, 394; *and hit-and-run accident on his car*, 390; appearance, 18; car problems, 198; Caspar Milquetoast?, 55; death of, 395; Gemstone File, 101, 382; hit-and-run accident, 1968, 101; independent contractor supplying rubies for laser experiments?, 401; likes to keep his originals if possible, 282; married daughter of French Consul, Dien Bien Phu, 63; nondescript?, 311; played baseball for Univ. of Wisconsin, 61; shooting dice at the Black Magic Bar, 215; spread-eagled on the street, 275; studied journalism and physics, 61; Tahoe trip, 200
Roberts, Dayle, 14, 174, 255, 260; Bruce Roberts' brother, 65; missed his father's funeral, 203
Roberts, LaVerne: Bruce Roberts' murdered

father, 430
Roberts, Verne Dale: murder by rat poison + Isoproterenol, 314
Roberts, Verne Dayle, 88; "Kill 'em", 154; and coin collecting, 326; at Cypress Lawn, 292; Bruce Roberts' father, 87; health problems and death, 151; murder of, 307; murdered, February 1972, 87; worked for SF Republican County Central Committee, 223
Rochefort, 9, 14, 111, 325
Rockefeller, 61, 73, 84, 91, 94, 96, 97, 298, 336, 447; Commission, 98
Rockefeller World Government organization: members, 376
Rockefeller, David, 361
Rogers, William, Secretary of State, 242; "we might have to dump Thieu", 153
Rolling Stone, 45
Roman Empire, 392
Romano, Tony, 71
Romney, Governor of Pennsylvania, 306
Roosevelt, Elliott, 61, 250, 397, 399, 447; maverick arms dealer, 398
Roosevelt, Franklin D., 61, 105, 109, 167, 218, 336, 398; a counter-revolutionary, 403; WWII a "war of liberation, not invasion, 282
Roosevelt, Franklin D., Jr., 68
Roselli, Johnny, 22, 66, 67, 69, 70, 71, 90, 125, 291, 350, 392; and $250,000, 327; and ownerership of Flamingo casino, Las Vegas, 157; framed at the Friar's Club, 294; given Lana Turner as a reward for JFK shot, 157; on Castro assassination team, 157; on JFK assassination team, 157; shot from the overpass, 258; *slaughtered in 1976*, 350; turned up dead in Biscayne Bay, 99
Roselli, Johnny:, 294
Rosemont Enterprises, 188; suppressed Irving's "Hughes" autobiography, 1972, 53
Rothschild's Inn of the Park, 82
Rowling, 364
Royko, Mike, 105
Rubin, Jerry, 262; local CIA, 253; on CIA payroll, 412
ruby juice is red, like blood, 272, 400, 422
Ruby, Jack, 31, 40, 70, 335; gut-shot Oswald, 218
ruby-making process: tricky! high heat required to grow crystals right, 401
Rudenstein, Roger: of S.F. Peace Coalition, 280
ruling class's fear of masses, 33
Russia: supports Gemstone and Roberts, 204
Russian consulate, 320, 327, 335

Russian Consulate, 86, 93, 94
Russian sunken nuclear submarine, 96

S

Sacco and Vanzetti, 198
Sadat, Anwar, 14, 95, 97, 98, 335; Dallas Dime letter, 330; President of Egypt, 326
Salinger, Pierre, 239; managing McGovern's campaign, *208*
samizdat, 10
San Clemente, 72, 327
San Francisco, 85, 88, 92, 94, 98, 127, 129, 135, 192, 221, 333, 353; First National Bank, 327; Grand Jury, 71; Hall of Justice, 163; Hall of Justice Driveway, 175; *Police Department, stored the dope*, 85; Police towed Roberts' car after smash-up, 75; Prosper Street, 19; Sunset District, 18, 56, 335
San Francisco Bay Guardian, 115
San Francisco Chronicle, 30
San Francisco Coin Club, 328
San Francisco Examiner, 93, 354
San Francisco National Bank, 71
San Jose Mercury,, 50
San Quentin prison, 36
Sarnoff, David, 134; Dew-Line, 265
Sato, Japan, and Gemstone information, 121
Saturday Review, 169, 173
Saudi Arabia, 63, 347, 399
Savak, Shah of Iran's Intelligence service: assigned 2 Arabs to Prince Faisal, 96
Schacht, Hjalmar, 61; and Jiddah Agreement, 63; economic dictator of Hitler's 3rd Reich, launched huge rearmament program, 1937, 61; *ran Onassis' whaling fleet*, 62
Schirra, Wally: bribed by Penn Central Railroad, 292
Schlesinger, on SS-18 strike missiles, 329
Schorr, Daniel, 96, 122, 164, 171
Schultz replaced John Connally, 222
Schumann, Democratic bigwig, 77
Schwab, Charles, President of Bethlehem Steel, 354
Schwartz, Danny, Sinatra's National General partner, 275
Schwarzenegger, Arnold, 431
Sciacca, New York Mafia Don, 110
Scott, Peter Dale, 411
sea-bed nuclear plantings, 143
Seagram's, 364
Seale, Bobby, 250, 272
Seattle Intelligencer, 412

Seattle Post Intelligencer, 222
Securities Exchange Commission: a Mafia cartel, 219
Securities Exchange Commission, also S.E.C., 61, 109
Security Pacific National Bank, 370
Security Pacific National Bank, California, 363
Selassie, Haile, 84
Seldon, Bob, 363
Selling of the Pentagon, The: by Frank Stanton, 160
Selling of The Pentagon, The, 139
Senate Select Committee on Intelligence, 98
Senate, U.S., supports a police state, 29
Seven Sisters: finance South Basin oil exploration, 361
Seven Sisters (major oil companies), 61, 447
Shah of Iran, 36; Savak, Intelligence service, 96
Sharp, Mitchell, 367
Shaw, Dr. Robert, 266
Sheean, Vincent, Bishop, 247
Shiretown Inn, 79, 108
Shock and Awe, 429
Shorenstein, Democratic bigwig, 77, 234; and Chappaquiddick, 216
Shriver, Eunice Kennedy,, 306
Shriver, Sargent, 298; Ted Kennedy's V.P. pick, 297
Siegel, Sylvia, 169
Sierra Nevada closed off--for what?, 28
Silence of the Lambs, 392
Silva, Arthur E., 94, 98; only witness to Mafia Nut Tree meeting, 73
Simpson, O.J., 42, 351
Sinatra: owns Fontainbleu Hotel with Meyer Lansky, 293
Sinatra, Frank, 272, 306; and National General loot to Dickie and Agnew, 305; fronts for Mafia Patriarcha, 219; hearings on Miami deals squashed in Congress, 254
Sindona, Michele, 361
Sirhan, Sirhan, 38, 126, 218, 258, 314; patsy in RFK shooting, 74
Skeleton Key, 423
Skeleton Key to the Gemstone File, A, 10, 14, 15, 16, 97, 99, 259, 333, 339, 344, 345, 352, 382; *first copy went to Bruce Roberts*, 97; on the Internet, 15; various versions, 57
Skolnick, Sherman, 403
Skorpios, 44, 45, 47, 64, 68, 82, 159, 160, 194, 315, 318, 384
SLA "army": a hoax, 34

Sloan, Hugh, 432, 434
Smaldones - Denver Mafia "family", 72, 326. See
Smathers, George, 354
Smith, C. Arnholdt, 255
Smith, French and Kline: pharmaceutical drugs, Philadelphia, 331
Smith, Harold, 97, 330; job--find and eliminate leaks about Howard Hughes's bones, 331
Smithsonian Museum of Natural History, 444
smoking gun?, 22
Smothers, George, 243
smuggling, 446
smuggling gemstones, papers, and minerals, 128
Smyrna massacre, 233
Snyder, Jimmy aka Jimmy the Greek, 85
Sociedad Industrial Maritime Financiera Ariona, 62
sodium morphate, 66, 87, 88, 90, 94, 95, 259, 339, 355
Soledad Prison, Salinas, CA, 39, 40
Soledad Prison, Salinas. CA, 55
Somoza, 330; Mafia dictator of Nicaragua, 188
Sorcerer's Apprentice, 19
Sorenson, Ted, 114, 116, 118, 201; and General Motors, 110; wrote Teddy's Chappaquiddick "walk on water" speech, 115
South American countries, overthrow of seven, 128
South Vietnam, 153
Southern Petroleum, NZ, 373
Soviet consulate, 75
Spaulding, Josiah: stooge opponent for Teddy Kennedy, 1970 election, 145
Spearshaker Review, 10
Special Action Group, 428
Specter, Arlen, 268
Spellman, Cardinal, 109, 161
Spokane phone calls, 318
Spotlight, 414
Sprague, Richard, 140
Squad 19, 306
St. Louis, Missouri: Mafia group, Cervantes and Shenker, 241
Standard Oil, 362
Stans, Maurice, 88, 305, 432
State Adversary, The, 360
State Farm Insurance, 72, 76
Stehlin, General, on Northrop's payroll, bumped off in Paris, 98
Steinem, Gloria, 151, 167, 239, 254
Stewart, Robert, 99
Stewart, Robert Sussman, 333
Stone, Oliver: and JFK movie, 392

Stone, Oliver and JFK movie, 392
Strom, Al, 86, 91, 176, 256, 265, 304, 306, 307, 311, 317, 355
Sturgis, Frank, 65, 66, 69, 86, 296, 300, 304, 426, 434; CIA figure at Bay of Pigs, 313
subliminal messages: prepared in U.S. by CIA, 375
subliminal television advertising: NZ, 375
Sullivan, Garry, fly-casting meets on the White House lawn, 297
Summa Corporation, Howard Hughes's, 331
Summa Corporations: Onassis's continuation of Howard Hughes's businesses, 430
Sun Times, 408
Sunol Golf Course, 71, 92, 94; Alioto's Mafia Resort, 328
Sunset District, SF, 56
Super Bowl orgy election, 1972, 294
Supreme Court Justices: "nine old Mafia", 284; all Mafia, 294
surveillance by government agencies: 95% is of the public, 198
Swanson, Gloria, 64
SWAT Team, LAPD, 18, 42
Swedish consulate, 327
Sweig, Democratic bigwig, 77, 220, 231, 260, 277
Swig, Ben, Democratic bigwig: and Chappaquiddick, 216
Switzerland: money laundered in, 164
Symbionese Liberation Army, also S.L.A. or SLA, 18, 27
synthetic rubies, 63, 66, 76, 335

T

Tacitus, 87, 201, 229
Tackwood, Louis, 304; Glass House Tapes, 36; on James McCord, 312
Tahoe, 20, 175
Taiwan, 153
Tanya: Patty Hearst's SLA nom de guerre, 27; Russian 'Mary Jo', 212; the Russian Tanya, 323
Teamsters Union, 370
Tenos, Greece: Onassis's other island, 45, 125
Texas Mafia, The, 88, 319
Texas Monthly: interview with Dr. Duke, 1999, 266
Texas School Book Depository, 70, 350
Thailand, 279
Tham, Rudy, 276, 316
Thant, U, 202
The Alioto Mafia Web, 84, 106, 189
The Deputy of Christ at Auschwitz, 87

The Enemy Within, 74, 140, 156, 170, 207
The Fabulous Onassis: His Life and Loves: by Christian Cafarakis, 216
The Gemstone File (Illuminet Press, 339
The Gemstone File: Sixty Years of Corruption and Manipulation…, 17
The Man Who Cried 'I Am, 33
The Nixon-Hughes "Loan"; the "Loan" No One Repaid, by Nicholas North-Broome, 52
The People Against Larry Flynt, 356
The Second Gun, 74
The Senate Select Committee is Part of the Cover-Up, 27
The Spook Who Sat By the Door, 40
The Yellow Race, 391
Thieu, Nguyen Van Thieu: calls up blackmail reserve, 154
Thieu, Nguyen Van, President of Vietnam: John Connally inaugurates him, 121; split for Taiwan in plane overloaded with gold, 96
Thomas, Kenn, 16, 393, 403, 416; and Steamshovel Press, 416
Thompson, Federal Judge: dismissed Grand Jury indictments against "Hughes", 332
Thomson, Federal Judge, 92
Three Popes and the Cardinal: The Church of Pius, John and Paul in its Encounter with Human History, by Malachi Martin, 205
Three secrets of Fatima, 143
Thyssen, Fiona, Alexander's mistress, also Aristotle's private reserve, 220
Tiberius, 87
Tiburon, 77, 80, 105, 107, 110, 183
Tidewater Oil Company, 61
Tiger Eye, 47, 48, 52, 53
Tiki Bob's, 304, 309
Time, 98, 168, 354, 408; ran picture of sheriffs cramming Skolnick into paddy wagon, 408
Tippit, J. D., 350
Tisserant Papers, 291
Tisserant, Cardinal, 87, 90, 227, 247, 253
Tisserant, Cardinal Eugene, 88, 293, 302, 307, 349; died in a clinic near Rome, 224; his papers pushed into Roberts' pocket, 225; murder of Pius XI, 318; papers labeled Montini a double spy after WWII, 290; papers on Montini, 251; poisoned in Rome, and his files stolen, 327
Tito, 97, 335; cancels meeting with Ford to go boar hunting, 98; President of Yugoslavia, 330; receives Gemstone letter, May 1975, 97; receives Roberts' letter about the bones of Howard Hughes passing through Yugoslavia,

cancels meeting with Ford, 332
Tonopah, Nevada, 49, 64, 157, 230, 396
Trafficante, Santos, Jr., 364
tramps in Dealey Plaza, 351
Travelodge Management Ltd, 361
Travis Air Force Base, 28
TRB on press censorship and Jimmy Hoffa, 154
Treason for my Daily Bread, 349
Trilateral Commission, 364
Trudeau, 90
Truman, Harry S.: and Korea, 119; Hiroshima murders, 171
Tunney, Gene, 80
Tunney, John, 77, 80, 101, 103, 105, 107, 110, 177, 327
Turkish Bey, Mustapha, 57, 68
Turner, Lana, 157; given to Eaton of Rosemont, 166
Turner, William, 167, 176, 177, 179
TV, Mafia-owned: beams hours of "Hughes is alive" programs, 332
TWA, 52, 66, 126, 326; suit loss, and Maheu, 126; suit lost because no genuine Hughes signature was available, 126
Two Mafia Party system, 239
Tyler, Carol, 354
Tyrone Papers, 250

U

U.N. as Knapp Commission?, 135
U.N. World Environmental Conference, 226
U.S.: heroin trade, $10 billion per year, 296; Intelligence shake-up, Gayler to Iceland, Cushman to the jungle, 148; Leasing, 104; *Maritime Commission*, 62; Postal Service, and censorship, 297
U.S. Mafia Council restructured: personnel, 371
Udall Brothers, 280
Ulascewicz, Anthony: and Chappaquiddick "research", 426; investigated Chappaquiddick mess for a year, got the goods on Teddy, 81
Unconventional Warfare Operating Procedures, 30
Unger, 295
United California Bank, 363
United Nations, 172, 328; 37 nations with gemstones voted Taiwan out, and China in, 132; gemstone papers were there, 328; history, 293
United States: election process, 21; Maritime Trade Commission, 354; of Mafia, 183
United States Petroleum Carriers: Onassis-*controlled*, 62
University of California Hospital, 96, 321
Unruh, Jess, 77, 101, 103, 107
Utah Mormon Church, 331

V

Vacaville Prison, California, 36, 39, 40, 393; California Medical Facility, 36
Vacaville, California: Nut Tree Restaurant meeting, 73
Valenti, Jack, denounced JFK movie, 392
Vallee, Thomas Arthur Vallee, 410; in plot to shoot JFK in Chicago, 410
Vallee, Tom, 69, 70, 125; member of JFK assassination team?, 57
Vancouver, 90, 197, 219, 289
Vandenburg missile, 262
Vankin, Jonathan, 422
Vantage Press, 339
Vatican, 296; "Deputy of Christ at Auschwitz" Holy Crusade, 154; CIA, 128; Fatima #2 booty, Vietnam, Taiwan, 153; Mafia handmaidens, 153
Vatican Bank, 363
Veronese, Adolpho, Mia Angelo Alioto's fiance, 232
Versailles Mafia World Summit, 202
Vesco, Robert, 88, 330, 370
Victorville Army Base, California, 62, 447; Roberts meets McGovern, 254
Vietnam war, 84, 192; a dope war, 137
Volman, Sascha, 234, 259
Voloshen, 164, 231

W

Wackenhut Corporation, 36, 38
Waco, 42
Waldheim, Kurt, 293, 305; on bombing dikes in Vietnam, 282; U.N. Secretary, 226
Wall Street Journal, 289, 294, 295
Wallace, George, 239, 275; Democratic presidential candidate, shot in Maryland, 435; to run, or not to run?, 278; won't run, 294
Wallace, Henry, 61, 447
Wallace, Mike, spoke of 'The profanity of Chappaquiddick', 252
Walsh, ABA head, 185
Walsh, Denny, 93
Walters, General Vernon, CIA, 331; at the Drift Inn, 331
Warne, head of Consumers' Union, 119
Warner Brothers Studios, 74, 397

Warner, Don, truck driver, SF, witnessed huge drug bust, 192
warning murders, 264
Warren Commission, 71, 72, 73, 85, 268, 315, 337, 341
Warren, Earl, 40, 172, 301, 315
Washington Monthly, 246
Washington Post, 61, 68, 80, 86, 91, 108, 295, 301, 354
Washington, Pennsylvania, 65
Watergate, 33, 35, 44, 69, 72, 81, 86, 87, 88, 89, 90, 91, 93, 99, 300, 304, 331, 353, 388, 425, 433; arrest photos, 311; arrests, 311; break-in, 88; burglars; arrest photos, 323; burglars, 18, 330, 341; burglars, at Drift Inn, 304; details, 296; Nixon's new evidence, 91; scandal, 341; two tapped phones, 330
Watergate Five, 309, 313, 315, 318; at the Drift Inn, 330; at the Drift Inn, McCord, Martinez, Sturgis, 311; caught bugging National Demo HQ, 311
Watergate team, 65, 86
Watergate trial, 95
Waterhouse, Betty, 260, 265, 303
Wayne, John, 55, 235, 282, 291, 388
WBAI,, 333
Weberman, A. J., 413; agent for Mossad?, 413
Weinberger, 222
Weisberg, Harold, 409
Weisenthal, Simon, 413
Wellington Gas, 370
Westbrook, Colston, BCA head, 37
Western Union, Onassis-owned, 295
Westwood, Jean, 298
Whelan, Mayor of Jersey City, 77, 107, 157; convicted Democratic Mafia, Mary Jo worked for him just before Chappaquiddick, 190
White Caucus, 239
White House burglars, 86
White House meeting: to divvy up loot, 273
White House, Oval Office meeting, 89
White House, theft of, 11
White, Geneva, 70
White, Roscoe, 70, 76; *Badgeman?*, 70
Whitlam, Gough, 364
Why Was Martha Mitchell Kidnapped?, 27, 341; by Mae Brussell, 346
Wilkinson, Carter, 105, 110, 118, 177
Wilkinson, Joan Tunney, 77, 80, 105, 110, 177; Joan Kennedy's college roommate, 229
Will, by Gordon Liddy, 424
Will: the Autobiography of G. Gordon Liddy, 344
Wills, Frank, 440
Wills, Frank, guard at Watergate, 88
Wilson, Texas Willie, 128, 154; Mafia dealings, 165
Winchell, Walter: broke story of Hughes-Peters marriage, 396
Wisconsin State Journal, 119
Wisconsin, University of, 355
Wolfe, Tom, 337
Woods, Rosemary, 408
World Bank, 84, 110, 186, 286, 288, 303
World Peace, 98, 177
World War II, 33, 61, 80, 109, 119, 126, 141, 143, 167, 181, 193, 219, 254, 256, 335, 399; rigged by Onassis and J. P. Kennedy, 171
World War III, 110
worldwide information network, 76
Wyman, Eugene, 86, 90, 249
Wyman, Pat, 239, 264; at Democratic Convention, 246

X

X-marked leather hat, 15

Y

Yablonski family, 119, 173; "Murder is an institution at the UMW, 217; shotgun bit, 154; spoke of Union Mafia, 141
Yakima, Washington: a Mafia deal made, 281
Yalta Conference, 110
Yee, Harry, 296; owned warehouse for heroin shipment in S.F., 192
Yippies, 299
Yorty, Mayor Sam, Los Angeles, 397
Young Americans for Freedom: CIA group, founded by Robert Mullen, 313
Younger, Eric, 74
Younger, Evelle, 31, 74, 179, 327; California Attorney General, 306; covered up Bobby Kennedy murder facts--rewarded, now State Attorney General, 255
Younger, Evelle, California Attorney General: rushed through new, illegal State law, 328
yo-yos, criminals who can be used by police, 36
Yugoslavia: Howard Hughes's body passes through, May 1975, 97
Yugoslavia-Albania, 331; and the bones of Howard Hughes, 332
Yunnan Province, China, 106

Z

Zangara, Giuseppe: pseudo-assassination attempt on FDR, 218
Zangara, Louis, 218
Zapruder film, 98, 99
Zebra murders, 73, 94, 98
Ziegler, Phil, 137
zombies, hypnotized assassins, 29

Filename: GemFileSend3
Directory: C:\Documents and Settings\StephanieJo\Desktop
Template: C:\Program Files\Microsoft Office\Templates\Normal.dot
Title:
Subject:
Author: Stephanie Caruana
Keywords:
Comments:
Creation Date: 09/06/06 2:09 PM
Change Number: 16
Last Saved On: 09/13/06 12:16 PM
Last Saved By: Stephanie Caruana
Total Editing Time: 180 Minutes
Last Printed On: 09/13/06 12:27 PM
As of Last Complete Printing
    Number of Pages: 478
    Number of Words: 249,361 (approx.)
    Number of Characters: 1,421,359 (approx.)

Made in the USA
Middletown, DE
11 April 2025

74104882R00267